Successful Writing at Work

Successful Writing at Work

SECOND EDITION

Philip C. Kolin
University of Southern Mississippi

D. C. Heath and Company
Lexington, Massachusetts • Toronto

To
Eric, Kristin, and Janeen
Julie and Loretta
and
MARY

Preface

Successful Writing at Work is a comprehensive introductory text designed for use in technical, business, professional, and occupational writing courses. Like the first edition, the approach in this second edition is practical, emphasizing that communication skills are essential for career advancement and that writing is a vital part of many jobs. Throughout, students are given detailed guidelines for creating clear, well-organized, and readable writing.

Teachers will find the following features of the second edition especially useful:

- A wide range of writing models taken from such varied sources as student papers and reports, business correspondence and proposals, and magazine and journal articles.
- Two complete, fully documented student research papers following the new MLA format for parenthetical documentation.
- Emphasis on audience analysis: memos, letters, proposals, questionnaires, and reports are analyzed from the point of view of the intended audience, that is, personnel directors, employers, coworkers, customers, and so forth.
- New emphasis on the writing process: the stages of planning, drafting, revising, and proofreading are considered throughout.
- Numerous detailed exercises, allowing instructors to test student mastery of every major concept.
- Topics introduced sequentially, moving from the fundamentals of writing (paragraphing, sentence structure, word choice) to shorter assignments (letters and memos) to more complex forms of business writing (instructions, questionnaires, proposals, reports).
- The student/reader is regarded as a professional seeking advancement at different phases of a business career; as a job candidate looking for a position (Chapter 6); as an employee who must meet the needs of em-

ployers and customers (Chapter 7); as a business person who must write a persuasive proposal to win a contract (Chapter 14).

- Practical applications useful both to readers who have no on-the-job experience and to those with years of experience.
- An *Instructor's Guide* with answers to exercises, which include model letters and memos.

The second edition has been improved to make it a more effective tool for the instructor and a more comprehensive and helpful resource for the student. Three new chapters (on paragraphs, documentation, and proposals) are included, and two other chapters (on sentences and long reports) have been extensively revised and expanded. To reflect more closely the steps taken in the actual process of writing, the early chapters have been rearranged: students are now asked to consider larger structural units (such as paragraphs) before turning to smaller stylistic choices of sentences and words. The new examples and exercises added to every chapter make the discussion of occupational writing more useful and current. Much more information on computers, for example, can be found throughout this second edition.

An Overview of the Chapters

A brief overview of the second edition will show how these new materials have been integrated. Section I deals with the overall writing process. Chapter 1, setting the stage for all occupational writing, identifies the basic concepts of audience analysis, purpose, message, style, and tone, and relates these concepts to on-the-job writing.

Chapters 2, 3, and 4 form an important unit on the basic elements of effective writing. Chapter 2 explains in detail how to construct effective paragraphs, with special emphasis on the needs of readers in business and industry. Chapter 3, on sentences, gives guidelines on how to create clear and economical sentences. Chapter 4, on words, prepares students to make appropriate choices for their message.

Section II deals with business correspondence. Chapter 5 introduces the nuts and bolts of letter writing and focuses on selecting the appropriate format, language, and tone. Chapter 6, covering the job search, takes students through the process of preparing a placement file, writing a résumé and a letter of application, anticipating interviewers' questions, and accepting or declining a job. For greater teaching flexibility, I have included three different letters of application and résumés from applicants with varying degrees of experience—to help new and veteran job seekers alike. Chapter 7 examines the rhetorical strategies writers must employ to produce a variety of business correspondence—complaint, adjustment, order, sales, and collection letters.

Section III provides techniques for gathering and summarizing information. Chapter 8 takes students on a guided tour of the library, shows them how to locate printed and audiovisual materials and how to profit from a computer search, and provides them with an annotated appendix of useful reference works. A new Chapter 9 is devoted to several styles of documentation—and particularly to the new MLA parenthetical method. A sample student research paper, "Stress and the Computer Programmer," illustrates this method of documentation. In Chapter 10 students will learn how to write clear and concise summaries and abstracts. Chapter 11, on questionnaires, shows students how to construct reliable questions, select informants, organize responses, and write a questionnaire survey report. Chapter 12 supplies practical advice on designing visuals, includes a new section on the tools and materials needed to create these visuals, and explains how to coordinate visuals with written commentary. A new section on computer graphics concludes this chapter.

In Section IV students are asked to apply the skills they learned in Section III to more complex writing assignments. Chapter 13 covers writing accurate instructions and selecting appropriate language and visuals. Chapter 14 focuses on three common types of proposals—an internal proposal for an employer, sales proposals (solicited and unsolicited) for customers, and a research proposal written for a teacher. Chapter 15 outlines the principles common to all short reports and then discusses specific types, with expanded coverage of test and laboratory reports. Instructors will also find the discussion of unusual-occurrence reports especially detailed. Finally, students are cautioned about the legal implications of what they write and told how to avoid legal pitfalls.

To make it more accessible to students, Chapter 16 on long reports has been completely revised for this second edition. In this chapter students are encouraged to see a long report as the culmination of all their work in the course or on a major project at work. The individual parts of such a report are discussed in detail, with a new student-written model report, "The Positive Effects of Robots in American Industry," used as an illustration.

Chapter 17, on the importance of audience analysis in oral communication, offers common-sense advice on handling briefings and on constructing and delivering formal speeches.

Acknowledgments

I am grateful to the many friends who gave me the benefit of their suggestions as I prepared the second edition of *Successful Writing at Work*. At the University of Southern Mississippi, they include Linda Goff, David Goff, Mittlee McCall, Harry McCraw, Mackie Odom, Michael Stuprich, David Roberts, Joycelyn Trigg, and David Wheeler. I also thank Ovid Vickers, East Central Junior College; Colby Kullman, University of Mississippi; Laura Weaver, University of Evansville; Kristine Stutliff, Southwest Missouri State University; and Mark Winchell at Clemson University.

I am deeply indebted to the following instructors who offered many valuable suggestions as they reviewed the second edition of *Successful Writing at*

Work: Stephen A. Bernhardt, Southern Illinois University; David Brooks, Jefferson Community College; Joseph B. Harris, Parkland College; Del McGinnis, Delgado Community College; Joan R. Sherman, Rutgers University; Arthur Wagner, Macomb Community College; and Darlene Zulauf, Moraine Park Technical Institute.

My thanks go to my editors at D. C. Heath for their assistance, encouragement, and friendship—Paul Smith, Judith Leet, Holt Johnson, and Ed Catania. I am again indebted to Ann Sykes, who typed several drafts of this edition with exceptional dedication.

Finally, I thank my wife, Janeen L. Kolin, for patiently reading and evaluating every word I wrote and rewrote.

Contents

3 Writing: Sentences   55

4 Writing: Words   77

Section II

Correspondence

5 Letter Writing: Some Basics

6 How to Get a Job: Résumés, Letters, Applications, Interviews, and Evaluations

Section III

Gathering and Summarizing Information   229

10 Summarizing Material 295

11 Preparing a Questionnaire and Reporting the Results 325

12 Designing Visuals

Section IV

13 Writing Clear Instructions

16 Long Reports

17 Oral Reports

Section I

Backgrounds

1

Getting Started: Writing and Your Career

What skills have you learned in school or on the job this year? Perhaps you have learned techniques of health care in order to become a nurse, respiratory therapist, or dental hygienist. Maybe you have received training in law enforcement to prepare yourself for work with a crime-detection unit or a traffic-control department. Possibly you have studied or worked in industrial technology, agriculture, computer science, hotel and restaurant management, or forestry. Or maybe you have improved skills needed to be an executive secretary, salesperson, office manager, computer programmer, or accountant. Whatever your area of accomplishment, the facts and practical know-how you have acquired are essential for your career.

You need an additional skill, however, to ensure a successful career—that is, you must be able to write clearly about the facts, procedures, and problems of your job. Writing is a part of every job. In fact, prior to securing a job, your first contact with an employer is through your letter of application, which determines a company's first impression of you. And the higher you advance in an organization, the greater the amount of writing you will be doing.

Offices and other workplaces contain numerous reminders of the importance of writing—"in" and "out" boxes, file cabinets, typewriters, word processors, and printers. Why? Writing keeps business moving. It allows individuals working for a company to communicate with one another and with the customers and clients they must serve if the company is to stay in business. These written communications take the form of memos, letters, order forms, instructions, questionnaires, proposals, and reports. This book will show you, step by step, how to write these and other job-related communications easily and well.

Chapter 1 presents questions you can use to make the writing process easier and more effective. This chapter also describes the basic functions of on-the-job writing.

☞ Four Keys to Effective Writing

Effective writing on the job is carefully planned, thoroughly researched, and clearly presented. Whether you send a routine memo to a coworker or a special report to the president of the company, your writing will be more effective if you ask yourself four questions.

1. *Who* will read what I write? (Identify your *audience*.)
2. *Why* should they read what I write? (Establish your *purpose*.)
3. *What* do I have to say to them? (Formulate your *message*.)
4. *How* can I best communicate? (Select your *style* and *tone*.)

The questions *who? why? what?* and *how?* do not function independently; they are all related. You write (1) for a specific audience (2) with a clearly defined purpose in mind (3) about a topic your readers need to understand (4) in language appropriate for the occasion. Once you answer the first question, you are off to a good start toward answering the other three. Now let us examine each of the four questions in detail.

Identifying Your Audience

Knowing *who* makes up your audience is one of your most important responsibilities as a writer. Look for a minute at the American Heart Association posters reproduced in Figures 1.1, 1.2, and 1.3. The main purpose of all three posters is the same: to discourage individuals from smoking. The essential message in each poster—smoking is dangerous to your health—is also the same. But note how the different details—words, photographs, situations—have been selected in order to appeal to three different audiences effectively.

The poster in Figure 1.1 emphasizes smoking problems that are especially troublesome to a teenager: red eyes, bad breath, discolored teeth, and unattractive hair. The smiling teen pictured without a cigarette appears to have avoided these problems. The message at the top of the poster plays on two meanings of the word *heart*: (1) smoking can harm the heart and (2) smoking can interfere with romance. Teenagers are particularly sensitive to the second meaning.

The poster in Figure 1.2 is aimed at an audience of pregnant women and appropriately shows a woman with a lit cigarette. The words at the top and bottom of the poster appeal to a mother's sense of responsibility as the reason to stop smoking, a reason pregnant women would be especially likely to respond to.

Figure 1.3 is directed toward fathers and appropriately shows a small child seated on his father's lap. The situation depicted appeals to a father's wish for happiness for his child. The words in the poster warn that a father who smokes may die prematurely and make his child's life unhappy.

The copywriters for the American Heart Association have chosen appropriate details—words, pictures, et cetera—to convince each audience not to

Fig. 1.1   No-smoking poster aimed at teenagers.

© Reprinted with permission of the American Heart Association.

smoke. With their careful choices, they successfully answered the question, "How can we best communicate with each audience?" As an indication of their skill, note that details relevant for one audience (teenagers, for example) could not be as effectively used for another audience (fathers).

These three posters illustrate some fundamental points you need to keep in mind when writing for an audience:

- Members of each audience differ in backgrounds, experiences, needs, opinions.

Fig. 1.2   No-smoking poster directed at pregnant women.

© Reprinted with permission of the American Heart Association.

Fig. 1.3   No-smoking poster appealing to fathers.

© Reprinted with permission of the American Heart Association.

- How you picture your audience will determine what you say to them.
- Viewing something from the audience's perspective will help you to select the most relevant details for that audience.

Some Questions to Ask About Your Audience

You can form a fairly accurate picture of your audience by asking yourself some questions *before* you write. For each audience for whom you write, consider the following questions.

1. *Who is my audience?* What position does the reader hold? There's a big difference between writing to a vice-president for industrial relations and writing to a coworker. What specific duties does my audience have to perform? What kind of education, social background, and interests does my audience have?

2. *How many people will make up my audience?* Is it just one individual (the nurse on the next shift, the desk sergeant) or many (all the users of a product manufactured by my company)? If I write a letter to a customer, will my boss also want to see and approve it? As a general rule, the more diverse your audience, the less technical must be your discussion.

3. *How much does my audience already know about what I am writing about?* Are you writing to people who are familiar with all the technical procedures you know? Or are you addressing an employer or customer who, however intelligent, is not an expert in your field and cannot be expected to know technical details and language? Will your reader know as much about a problem or an issue as you do? Most often you will be writing to people who do not know as much about a job as you do. Such readers need more background information, more definitions of terms, and more explanatory visuals than a technically trained audience would. You may have to provide easy-to-understand comparisons and nontechnical summaries for these readers.

4. *What is my audience's reason for reading my work?* Is it a part of my readers' routine duties—such as a progress report? Are they looking for answers to special problems? Do they want to find a list of benefits from me that another writer or company cannot offer? Will they want to have complete details or do they prefer a summary of the main points?

5. *What is my audience's attitude toward me and my work?* Am I writing to readers who are friendly and eager to receive my work—for example, my memo to my boss saying that sales are up? Will my reader be skeptical—for example, a customer whose business I want to attract by selling him or her a new piece of equipment or service? Is my reader antagonistic—for example, a disappointed customer whose request I must refuse? What are the reasons the reader is skeptical or antagonistic? Such readers will want more detailed or more logical explanations than sympathetic readers. It is important to address directly the reasons for their disbelief or complaints.

6. *What do I want my audience to do after reading my work?* Should they store it for future reference, review it and send it to another office or individual, or act on it at once? Do I want the reader to use my work to purchase something from me or my company, approve my plan for a change within our company, agree with a decision I have made, or gather additional information for me? Have I made clear what I expect next from my reader?

As your answers to these questions will show, you may have to communicate with many different audiences on your job. If you work for a large organization that has numerous departments, you may have to write to such diverse readers as accountants, office managers, personnel directors, engineers, public relations specialists, marketing specialists, computer programmers, and individuals who install, operate, and maintain equipment. In addition, you will need to communicate effectively with customers about your company's prod-

"The 475C model with
TURBO TRANSMISSION is
the state of the art in loaders.
It's an investment that pays
out in productivity. Less
upkeep, too."

"I can really do a day's work in
this cab. It's insulated,
pressurized, and mounted
to keep noise, dirt, and
vibration out."

"This machine's a money-
maker. Its boom size matches
our 85-ton trucks, and keeps
them hustling."

"All the lube points are right
here. There's even a test port
for the hydraulics. That makes
my life easy."

Courtesy of the Clark Company. Reprinted with permission.

ucts and services. Each group of readers will have different expectations; and you need to understand these differences if you want to supply relevant information.

The advertisement in Figure 1.4 concisely illustrates how the writer for a manufacturer of heavy-duty equipment identified the priorities of five different audiences and selected appropriate information to communicate with them. For the owner or principal executive, the writer appropriately stresses financial benefits: the machine is a "money maker" and is compatible with other equipment so additional equipment purchases are unnecessary. A production engineer is more interested in other information. For this reader, the writer

**Fig. 1.4   "Everything You Asked For,"
an ad by the Clark Company.**

*"I've never seen a machine
this size that can move
so much material as fast and
as easy as this one."*

emphasizes "state-of-the-art" transmissions, productivity, and upkeep. To appeal to operators, the writer focuses on how easy it is to run the machine—the pressurized cab keeps out environmental problems that interfere with the job. A maintenance worker is concerned about such things as "lube points" and "test ports," not costs or operational comforts. The writer has selected appropriate information about making this worker's job easier and quicker. For the production supervisor, the writer has emphasized the speed and efficiency the machine offers. The lesson of this ad is clear: give each reader the details that he or she needs to accomplish a given job.

In some cases, you may not be able to identify all the members of your potential audience. Then, assume that you have a general audience and keep your message as simple as possible.

Establishing Your Purpose

By knowing *why* you are writing, you will communicate better and writing itself will be an easier process. The reader's needs and your goal in communicating with them will help you to formulate your purpose. It will help you to determine exactly what you can and must say. With your purpose clearly identified, you are on the right track. As you start to write, state for yourself your goal in communicating. Don't worry about the way it sounds. It is more important at this stage to work on ideas.

> I want people to know how to log on to the computer.

Think over what you have written. Try to rewrite your purpose more precisely.

> I want to teach new employees the security code for logging on to the company computer.

Since your purpose controls the amount and order of information you include, state it clearly at the beginning of every letter, memo, or report. Such an overview will help the reader to follow and act on your communication:

> This memo is to acquaint new employees with the security measures they must take when logging on to the company computer.

> The following report will give you a detailed account of my progress to date on completing my research study this semester.

The general goal of job-related writing is often to inform (through letters, instructions, reports) or to gather information (through memos, or questionnaires). But job-related writing can also persuade. A letter of application for a job, a sales letter, a memo with a list of recommendations for your boss, or a proposal are examples of persuasive, job-related writing. Here is an example of an opening statement from a memo where the writer's purpose is to inform:

> As you requested at last month's organizational meeting, I have conducted a study of our policies for renting our safe deposit boxes. This report describes, but does not evaluate, our current procedures.

If the writer's purpose were to persuade, he or she would state it differently:

> As you requested at last month's organizational meeting, I have conducted a study of our policies for renting our safe deposit boxes. This report compares our current procedures with industry standards and recommends changes that would make our policies competitive and up to date.

The following preface to a pamphlet on architectural casework details contains a model statement of purpose suited to a particular audience:

> This publication has been prepared by the Architectural Woodwork Institute to provide a source book of conventional details and uniform detail terminology. For this purpose a series of casework detail drawings, . . . representative of the best industry-wide practice, has been prepared and is presented here. By supplying both architect and woodwork manufacturer with a common authoritative reference, this work will enable architects and woodworkers to communicate in a common technical language. . . . It is hoped that besides serving as a basic reference for architects and architectural drafters, it will be an effective training tool for the beginning drafter-architect-in-training. It should also be a valuable aid to the project manager in coordinating the work of many drafters on large projects.[1]

After reading the preface, readers will have a clear sense of why they should use the casebook and what to do with the material they find in it.

Formulating Your Message

Your message is the sum of *what* facts, responses, and recommendations you put into writing. A message includes the *scope* and *details* of your communication. The details are those key points you think readers need to know to perform their jobs. Scope refers to how much information you give readers about those key details. Some messages will consist of one or two sentences: "Do not touch; wet paint." "Order #756 was sent this afternoon by Federal Express. It should arrive at your office by March 21." At the other extreme, messages may extend over twenty or thirty pages. Messages may carry good news or bad news. They may deal with routine matters, or they may handle changes in policy, special situations, or problems.

Keep in mind that you will adapt your message to fit your audience. For technical audiences such as engineers or technicians, you may have to supply a complete report with every detail noted or contained in an appendix. For other readers—busy executives, for example—you would be wrong to include such technical details. A short discussion or summary of the financial or managerial significance of these details is what this group of readers would want to have.

Consider the message of the following excerpt from a section on "Tips on Communication," included in a metropolitan telephone book. The message provides factual information about a change in mailing policy, informing the general public about acceptable and unacceptable sizes of first-class and third-class mail.

---

[1] Reprinted by permission of Architectural Woodwork Institute.

New Size Standards for Domestic Mail

Nonstandard Mail

The following material is considered nonstandard mail. First-class mail weighing one ounce or less and single piece third-class mail weighing two ounces or less which

1. Exceeds any of the following:
   (a) Height—6⅛ inches
   (b) Length—11½ inches
   (c) Thickness—¼ inch
2. Has a height to length ratio which does not fall between 1:13 and 1:25 inclusive.

In the near future, a surcharge will be assessed on each piece of nonstandard mail in addition to the applicable postage and fees.

New Minimum Sizes

Effective November 30, 1978, all mail must be at least .007 of an inch thick and mail which is ¼ inch or less in thickness must be

1. At least 3½ inches in height and at least 5 inches long.
2. Rectangular.

The preceding message is appropriate for a general audience, readers who are given neither less nor more information than is required. However, employees of the U.S. Postal Service or individuals working in the mail rooms of large companies or in mail-order houses need more detailed instructions. Because of their specialized work, these individuals would consult the more technical and elaborate *Postal Service Manual.*

Selecting Your Style and Tone

Style is *how* something is written rather than what is written. Style helps to determine how well you communicate with an audience, how well it understands and receives your message. It involves the choices you make about the construction of your paragraphs, the length and patterns of your sentences, and the choice of your words. (Chapters 2, 3, and 4 discuss each of these elements of style in detail.) For now keep in mind that you will have to adapt your style to take into account different messages and different purposes and different audiences. Your words, for example, will certainly vary with your audience. If all your readers are specialists in your field, you may safely use the technical language and symbols of your profession. Your audience will be familiar with such terminology and expect you to use it. Nonspecialists, however, will be confused and annoyed if you write to them in the same way.

The average consumer, for example, will not know what a *pitometer* is; but by writing "volume control on a radio" you will be using words that the general public can understand.

Tone in writing, like tone of voice, expresses your attitude toward a topic and toward your audience. In general, your tone can be formal and impersonal (a scientific report) or informal and personal (a letter to a friend or a how-to article for a consumer). Tone, like style, is indicated in part by the words you choose. For example, saying that someone is "interested in details" conveys a more positive tone than saying the individual is a "nitpicker." The word *economical* is more positive than *stingy* or *cheap*. The tone of your writing is especially important in occupational writing, for it determines how readers will respond to you, your work, and your company. The wrong tone in a letter or proposal might cost you a customer.

The following two descriptions of *heparin*, a drug used to prevent blood clots, illustrate two different styles, and two different tones. The first description appears in a reference work for physicians and is written in a highly technical style with an impersonal tone.

HEPARIN SODIUM INJECTION, USP ℞

Description: Heparin Sodium Injection, USP is a sterile solution of heparin sodium derived from porcine intestines, standardized for use as an anticoagulant, in water for injection with sodium chloride, if needed for isotonicity, and may contain 1% benzyl alcohol as a preservative.

Actions: Heparin inhibits reactions which lead to the clotting of blood and the formation of fibrin clots both in vitro and in vivo. Heparin acts at multiple sites in the normal coagulation system. Small amounts of heparin in combination with antithrombin III (heparin co-factor) can prevent the development of a hypercoagulable state by inactivating activated Factor X, preventing the conversion of prothrombin to thrombin.

Dosage and administration: Heparin sodium is not effective by oral administration and should be given by deep subcutaneous (intrafat, i.e., above iliac crest or into the abdominal fat layer) injection, by intermittent intravenous injection, or intravenous infusion. The intramuscular route of administration should be avoided because of the frequent occurrence of hematoma at the injection site.[2]

The writer has made the appropriate stylistic choices for the audience, the purpose, and the message. Physicians reading the description will understand and need the technical vocabulary the writer uses; these physicians will also require the sophisticated and lengthy explanations in order to prescribe heparin correctly. The author's authoritative, impersonal tone is coldly clinical, which, of course, is also appropriate because the purpose is to convey the accurate, complete scientific facts about this drug, not the writer's or reader's opinions or beliefs.

---

[2] Copyright © 1979 *Physicians' Desk Reference*, published by Medical Economics Company, Inc., at Oradell, New Jersey 07649.

The second description of heparin below, on the other hand, is written in a nontechnical style and with an informal, caring tone. This description is similar to those found on information cards given to patients about the drugs they are receiving in a hospital.

> Your doctor has prescribed for you a drug called *heparin*. This drug will prevent any new blood clots from forming in your body. Since heparin cannot be absorbed from your stomach or intestines, you will not receive it in a capsule or tablet. Instead, it will be given into a vein or the fatty tissue of your abdomen. After several days, when the danger of clotting is past, your dosage of heparin will be gradually reduced. Then another medication you can take by mouth will be started.

The writer of this description also made the appropriate choices for the purpose and for the readers. Familiar words rather than technical ones are suitable for nonspecialists such as patients. Note also that this audience does not need elaborate descriptions about the origin and composition of the drug. The tone is both personal and straightforward because the purpose is to win the patient's confidence and to explain the essential functions of the drug, a simpler message than the one for physicians.

The trend today in occupational writing is to make letters, reports, proposals more natural and personal and less impersonal, formal, or stuffy. But adopting a personal tone does not mean that you address the reader in a chummy, even disrespectful way. Quite the contrary, a business letter or report needs to be personal and professional at the same time.

☞ Functions of Job-Related Writing

Job-related writing characteristically serves five basic functions: (1) to provide practical information; (2) to give facts rather than impressions; (3) to provide visuals to clarify and condense information; (4) to give accurate measurements; and (5) to state responsibilities precisely.

These five functions tell you what kind of writing you will produce after you successfully answer the *who? why? what?* and *how?* just discussed.

Providing Practical Information

On-the-job writing requires a practical here's-what-you-need-to-do-or-to-know approach. One such practical approach is *action oriented*. In this kind of writing, you instruct the reader to do something—assemble a ceiling fan, test for bacteria, perform an audit, or take an inventory. Another practical approach of job-related writing is to have someone understand something—why a procedure was changed, what caused a problem or solved it, how much progress occurred on a job site, or why a new piece of equipment should be purchased.

Examples of such practical writing are a letter sent from a manufacturer to customers to explain a product recall or a memo sent to employees telling them about changes in their group health insurance policy.

The following description of Energy Efficiency Ratio combines both the action-oriented and knowledge-oriented approaches of practical writing:

> Whether you are buying window air-conditioning units or a central air-conditioning system, consider the performance factors and efficiency of the various units on the market. Before you buy, determine the Energy Efficiency Ratio (EER) of the units under consideration. The EER is found by dividing the BTUs (units of heat) that the unit removes from the area to be cooled by the watts (amount of electricity) the unit consumes. The result is usually a number between 5 and 12. The higher the number, the more efficiently the unit will use electricity. You'll note that EER will vary considerably from unit to unit of a given manufacturer, and from brand to brand. As efficiency is increased, you may find the purchase price is higher; however, operating costs will be lower. Remember, a good rule to follow is to choose the equipment with the highest EER. That way you'll get efficient equipment and enjoy operating economy.[3]

Giving Facts, Not Impressions

Writing on the job is concerned largely with those sensory things that can be seen, heard, felt, tasted, or smelled. The writer uses *concrete language* and specific details (discussed on pages 83–85). The emphasis is on facts rather than the writer's feelings or guesses. The following discussion by a group of scientists about the sources of oil spills and their impact on the environment is an example of writing with objectivity. It describes events and causes without emotions—anger or tears. Imagine how much emotion could have been packed into this topic by the residents of the coastal states who have watched such spills come ashore.

> The most critical impact results from the escapement of oil into the ecosystem, both crude oil and refined fuel oils, the latter coming from sources such as marine traffic. Major oil spills occur as a result of accidents such as blowout, pipeline breakage, etc. Technological advances coupled with stringent regulations have helped to reduce the chances of such major spills; however, there is a chronic low-level discharge of oil associated with normal drilling and production operations. Waste oils discharged through the river systems and practices associated with tanker transport dump more significant quantities of oils into the ocean, compared to what is introduced by the offshore oil industry. All of this contributes to the chronic low-level discharge of oil into world oceans. The long-range cumulative effect of these discharges is possibly the most significant threat to the ecosystem.[4]

---

[3] Reprinted by permission of New Orleans Public Service, Inc.

[4] *The Offshore Ecology Investigation* (Galveston: Gulf Universities Research Consortium, 1975) 4.

Fig. 1.5   Use of visual to convey information.

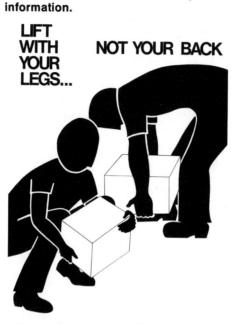

© National Safety Council, Chicago.

Providing Visuals to Clarify and Condense Information

Visuals are indispensable partners of your words in conveying information to your readers. On-the-job writing makes frequent use of visuals such as tables, charts, photographs, diagrams, and drawings to clarify and condense information. The construction and use of these and other visuals are discussed in detail in Chapter 12. Visuals play an important role in the workplace. As a poster or as an illustration in an employee handbook, Figure 1.5 helpfully reminds readers about correct lifting procedures and thereby prevents injuries.

Visuals are extremely useful in making detailed relationships clear to readers. A great deal of information about the growth and diversity of commercial TV stations is condensed in Table 1.1. Consider how many words a writer would need in order to supply the data contained in the table. Note, too, how easily the numbers can be read when they are arranged in columns. It would be far more difficult to decipher them if they were printed like this: Commercial TV stations in operation: 1965, Total 586, VHF 487, UHF 99; 1966, Total 598, VHF 491, UHF 107, and so forth.

In addition to the visuals already mentioned, use the following graphic devices within your letters and reports to make your writing easier to understand:

- Headings (such as Four Keys to Effective Writing or Functions of Job-Related Writing)

Table 1.1 Commercial TV stations in operation, 1965–1985

Year	Total	VHF	UHF
1965	586	487	99
1966	598	491	107
1967	620	497	123
1968	648	504	144
1969	675	506	169
1970	690	508	182
1971	696	511	185
1972	699	510	189
1973	700	511	189
1974	705	513	192
1975	711	513	198
1976	710	513	197
1977	728	517	211
1978	727	516	211
1979	732	516	216
1980	746	517	229
1981	752	519	233
1982	772	524	248
1983	802	526	276
1984	870	536	334
1985	904	539	365

Source: Reprinted, with permission, from the *1985 Broadcasting/Cablecasting Yearbook.*
Note: The number of stations is as of Jan. 1 of the year noted.

- Subheadings to divide major sections into parts, such as:
    1. Providing Practical Information
    2. Giving Facts, Not Impressions
- Numbers within a paragraph, or even a line, such as (1) this, (2) this, and (3) also this
- Different types of s p a c i n g
- CAPITALIZATION
- *Italics* (indicated in typed copy by underscoring)
- Asterisks * to * separate * items * or to *note key items
- Lists with *bullets* (raised periods like those before each entry in this list)

Keep in mind that such visual devices must be used carefully and with moderation. They should never be used just for decoration or to dress up a letter or report. Used properly, they can, however, help you to organize, arrange, and emphasize your material. They make your work easier to read and recall for an audience. For example, headings make your organization visible to readers and help them preview your ideas. Use bullets or numbers when you have many related points: by setting your points in a list, you make it easier for readers to follow and compare them.

Giving Accurate Measurements

Much of your work will depend on measurements—acres, bytes, calories, centimeters, degrees, dollars and cents, grams, percentages, pounds, square feet, units. Readers will look carefully at these measurements. Numbers are clear and convincing. An architect depends on specifications to accomplish a job; a nurse must record precise dosages of medications; a sales representative keeps track of the number of customers visited; and an electronics technologist has to monitor antennae patterns and systems. The following discussion of mixing colored cement for a basement floor would be useless to readers if it did not supply accurate quantities.

> The inclusion of permanent color in a basement floor is a good selling point. One way of doing this is by incorporating commercially pure mineral pigments in a topping mixture placed to a 1-inch depth over a normal base slab. The topping mix should range in volume between 1 part portland cement, 1¼ parts sand, and 1¼ parts gravel or crushed stone and 1 part portland cement, 2 parts sand and 2 parts gravel or crushed stone. Maximum size gravel or crushed stone should be ⅜ inch. Mixing of cement and pigment is done before aggregate and water are added and must be very thorough to secure uniform dispersion and the full color value of the pigment. The proportion varies from 5 to 10 percent of pigment by weight of cement, depending on the shade desired. If carbon black is used as a pigment to obtain grays or black, a proportion of from ½ to 1 percent will be adequate. Manufacturers' instructions should be followed closely and care in cleanliness, placing, and finishing must be regarded as essential. Colored topping mixes are available from some suppliers of ready mixed concrete.[5]

Stating Responsibilities Precisely

Job-related writing, since it is directed to a specific audience, must make absolutely clear what it expects of, or can do for, that audience. Misunderstandings waste time and cost money. Directions on order forms, for example, should indicate how and where information is to be listed and how it is to be routed and acted on. The following directions are taken from different job-related communications, showing readers how to perform different tasks.

- Include agency code numbers in the upper-right corner.

- Items 1 through 16 of this form should be completed by the injured employee or by someone acting on his or her behalf, whenever an injury is sustained in the performance of duty. The term *injury* includes occu-

---

[5] Reprinted by permission from *Concrete Construction Magazine*, World of Concrete Center, 426 South Westgate, Addison, Illinois 60101.

pational disease caused by the employment. The form should be given to the employee's official superior within 48 hours following the injury. The official superior is that individual having responsible supervision over the employee.

- The Journal Tape from each cash register is to be removed on a daily basis. Record the register number and date on the exterior of the Journal Tape as it is removed. Place each day's Journal Tapes, along with the corresponding day's Cashier's Balance Sheets and bank deposit records, in a small bag, i.e., 10 lb. bag. Record the date on the face of this bag and staple it closed.[6]

Other kinds of job-related writing deal with the writer's responsibilities rather than the reader's. For example, "Tomorrow I will have a meeting with the district sales manager to discuss (1) July's sales, (2) the possibility of expanding our Madison home market, and (3) next fall's production schedule. I will send you a report of our discussion by August 3, 1986." In a letter of application for a job, writers should conclude by asking for an interview and clearly inform a prospective employer when they are available for an interview—weekday mornings, only on Monday and Tuesday afternoons, or any time after February 15.

☞ The Writing Process

Writing is a *process*, a series of changes. To write effectively, you have to see your writing through several stages. You cannot start off with the final draft of an important memo, letter, or report. You have to plan what you are going to say before you say it to your readers. That planning involves discovering the most appropriate ideas for your readers and then conveying those ideas in your writing—by each paragraph, sentence, and word. It involves reading your work with a critical eye and revising it until it says what you want in a way that is appropriate for your readers. Writers who don't plan their work start out and end up frustrated. They wonder where and how to begin as they stare with panic at a blank sheet of paper that seems to shout "Fill me, or else." And they often end with an incomplete or irrelevant piece of writing that is not well received by the intended reader.

The duration and number of steps in the writing process depend on the type of writing you have to do. A brief memo to a coworker about a routine matter may require only a few moments of planning—to sketch out your ideas—before writing the memo. But a longer, more detailed and delicate memo, letter, or report will demand considerably more planning. The most recent research shows that writers discover what they want to say while in the process of writing.

---

[6] Reprinted by permission from *A&P Store Management Manual*, NCR 2125.

Five different stages in the writing process can be identified: (1) brainstorming, (2) outlining, (3) writing the rough draft(s), (4) revising, and (5) preparing the final copy. Let's briefly examine each of these steps.

When given an assignment, the first thing to do is to use the technique of brainstorming. *Brainstorming* is listing any information that comes to mind about the topic—in any order and as quickly as possible. It's like thinking out loud except that you are recording your comments on paper. The result will be a series of jottings so don't worry about neatness or organizing at this stage. The purpose of brainstorming in the writing process is to get something—anything—on paper as a start. Not all of your ideas from brainstorming will appear in the final version of your paper. As you study your list, you will see that some ideas are irrelevant, some very incomplete, and some just right. Revise the list by eliminating the irrelevant thoughts and rearranging and completing the relevant ones. Those ideas that do survive from your list will not usually be in the same order on your revised list as they were on your earlier list.

The next step in the writing process is to make an *outline* based upon your revised brainstorming list. For a short assignment, your outline can be brief and informal—for no one's eyes but yours. It might be written in short phrases, incomplete sentences, legible only to you. Don't worry about correct outline style—roman or arabic numerals, or subdivisions. For longer projects (proposals, long reports), however, you may have to prepare a formal outline to obtain your employer's approval of your work. In either case, outlines are valuable tools. They visually depict the order and relationship of your ideas; and it is always easier to evaluate something you can see. Another benefit of an outline is that it is flexible. As you read and reread it, you can shift items around until you believe they are in the most effective order for your purpose and for your audience. Thanks to an outline, you can add, drop, expand, substitute, subordinate, or coordinate ideas.

From your outline, move to the *rough draft* stage. During the rough draft stage you take information from your outline and put it into sentences and paragraphs. As its name implies, the rough draft is not the polished or final copy of the work you send to your readers. It is an early version of that final memo, letter, or report. You may write one or many rough drafts depending on the time you have and the complexity of your written work. The rough draft was made to tinker with, and the more tinkering you do, the better your final draft will be.

Some writers, however, find it helpful to start a rough draft *before* outlining; they then outline from their rough draft to make sure that their paragraphs are carefully organized and that the reader can see the order in which the paragraphs have been arranged. Other writers combine drafting and outlining, doing a little of both as they work through their rough draft. You may want to experiment and see which method works best for you.

After the rough draft stage, you will *revise* and *edit*. Look at your rough draft. Start with large issues. First pay attention to see if you have included *all the relevant information* readers need and that this information is *in the most effective order.* You may still add or delete information or switch it around at this stage. But double-check to see that your information is complete and accurate. Once you are sure about the content and order of your information, then check your rough draft for style. Make sure your writing is clear and easy to read. Rework your sentences. You may have to shorten some, expand others. You may have to move them around within or between paragraphs. Check to make sure they are punctuated properly. Examine your words to ensure they are precise and appropriate for your audience. Have you said things in language readers will understand and expect? Don't forget to see if your words are spelled correctly.

If time permits—and keep in mind that often you will be writing to meet a deadline—let your rough draft sit for a few hours or even a day or two. When you return to it you will be a far more objective and knowledgeable critic. You will be amazed at the mistakes you will spot and how easy it will be to change or correct your work. Pretend you are the intended audience, reading your ideas for the first time.

The last stage of the writing process is having the *final copy* prepared from your last, revised rough draft. Don't assume that once that final version is prepared it is ready to go sight unseen to your reader. Make sure that you have time to proofread it. (You will find some helpful procedures on proofreading a final copy on page 103.) Double-check that final copy to ensure that all the parts are included and in the right order. A missing part of a report or letter can spell disaster on the job and perhaps mar all your good, hard work.

☞ How This Book Will Work for You

This book is based on the belief that writing substantially influences your career. Effective writing can help you to obtain a job, to perform your duties more successfully, and to be promoted for your efforts. Guidelines and examples found in this book emphasize the progress you can make in your career by acquiring effective writing skills. Specifically, *Successful Writing at Work* will

1. describe the function and format of a variety of job-related communications
2. show you how to write each type of communication
3. teach you how to supply an audience with the information it must have

The book is organized to coincide with your own progress in writing. Chapters 2, 3 and 4 present the basics of writing you must master if you are to advance in your profession. From the basics, the book discusses how you should write a business letter (Chapter 5) and a letter of application and résumé for a job (Chapter 6) and then turns to the letters most frequently written on a job (Chapter 7). In your job you will be responsible for gathering, documenting and summarizing information (Chapters 8–11). And most important, you will have to report your findings both in writing (Chapters 12–16) and orally (Chapter 17). In your writing course this term, you can evaluate step by step your progress toward fulfilling professional goals.

Another useful feature of this book is that it frequently represents the view of the audience (prospective employer, customer, supervisor, questionnaire respondent, proposal evaluator) receiving the work you write. Each type of communication is discussed in terms of what readers will be looking for. In Chapter 6, for example, a letter of application and comments appropriate at an interview are discussed in the light of what personnel directors seek when they recruit new employees. In Chapter 7 your readers are customers or agencies from whom you are ordering merchandise or to whom you have supplied merchandise or services. In Chapter 10, which deals with summaries, your reader is a busy executive who does not have the time to read a twenty-page report and will rely on your two-hundred-word summary of it instead. Each of these readers represents a different challenge. The insights you will gain from this book about readers' needs should prove extremely useful. With these insights, you will be able to prepare yourself better psychologically for writing assignments in business and industry. You will also learn how to manage your own writing resources to your best advantage.

☞ Exercises

1. What is your chosen career field? Make a list of the kinds of writing you think you will encounter or have already encountered in this career.

2. Make a list of the kinds of writing you have done in a history or English class or for a laboratory or shop course.

3. Compare your lists for exercises 1 and 2. How do the two types of writing differ?

4. Bring to class a set of printed instructions, a memo, a sales letter, or a brochure. Comment on how well the printed material answers the following questions:
   (a) Who is the audience?
   (b) Why was the material written?
   (c) What is the message?
   (d) Are the language and ideas appropriate for the audience, the purpose, and the message?

5. Cut out a newspaper ad that contains a drawing or photograph. Bring it to class together with a paragraph (75–100 words) of your own describing how the message of the ad is directed to a particular audience and commenting on why the illustration was selected for that audience.

6. Pick one of the following topics and write two descriptions of it. In the first description use technical vocabulary. In the second use language suitable for the general public.

(a) spark plug	(l) word processor
(b) blood pressure cuff	(m) bread
(c) carburetor	(n) money
(d) drill press	(o) fishing reel
(e) camera	(p) car's ignition system
(f) legal contracts	(q) calculator
(g) electric sander	(r) PAC MAN game
(h) cement	(s) can opener
(i) muscle	(t) thermostat
(j) protein	(u) trees
(k) stereo	(v) food processor

7. Select one article from a daily newspaper and one article from either a professional journal in your major field or one of the following journals: *Advertising Age, American Journal of Nursing, Business Marketing, Business Week, Computer, Computer Design, Construction Equipment, Criminal Justice Review, Food Service Marketing, Journal of Forestry, Journal of Soil and Water Conservation, National Safety News, Nutrition Action, Office Machines, Park Maintenance, Scientific American, Today's Secretary.* State how the two articles you selected differ in terms of audience, purpose, message, style, and tone.

8. Compose a letter to a local business asking for a contribution of goods, services, or funds for a worthwhile cause. Be persuasive.

9. Read the following article and identify its audience (technical or general), purpose, message, style, and tone.

Microwaves

Much of the world around us is in motion. A wave-like motion. Some waves are big like tidal waves and some are small like the almost unseen footprints of a waterspider on a quiet pond. Other waves can't be seen at all, such as an idling truck sending out vibrations our bodies can feel. Among these are electromagnetic waves. They range from very low frequency sound waves to very high frequency X-rays, gamma rays, and even cosmic rays.

Energy behaves differently as its frequency changes. The start of audible sound—somewhere around 20 cycles per second—covers a segment at the low end of the electromagnetic spectrum. Household electricity operates at 60 hertz (cycles per second). At a somewhat higher frequency we have radio, ranging from shortwave and marine beacons, through the familiar AM broadcast band that lies between 500 and

---

Raytheon Magazine (Winter 1981): 22–23. Reprinted by permission.

1600 kilohertz, then to citizen's band, FM, television, and up to the higher frequency police and aviation bands.

Even higher up the scale lies visible light with its array of colors best seen when light is scattered by raindrops to create a rainbow.

Lying between radio waves and visible light is the microwave region—from roughly one gigahertz (a billion cycles per second) up to 3000 gigahertz. In this region the electromagnetic energy behaves in special ways.

Microwaves travel in straight lines, so they can be aimed in a given direction. They can be *reflected* by dense objects so that they send back echoes—this is the basis for radar. They can be *absorbed,* with their energy being converted into heat—the principle behind microwave ovens. Or they can *pass through* some substances that are transparent to the energy—this enables food to be cooked on a paper plate in a microwave oven.

Microwaves for Radar

World War II provided the impetus to harness microwave energy as a means of detecting enemy planes. Early radars were mounted on the Cliffs of Dover to bounce their microwave signals off Nazi bombers that threatened England. The word radar itself is an acronym for *RAdio Detection And Ranging.*

Radars grew more sophisticated. Special-purpose systems were developed to detect airplanes, to scan the horizon for enemy ships, to paint finely detailed electronic pictures of harbors to guide ships, and to measure the speeds of targets. These were installed on land and aboard warships. Radar—especially shipboard radar—was surely one of the most significant technological achievements to tip the scales toward an Allied victory in World War II.

Today, few mariners can recall what it was like before radar. It is such an important aid that it was embraced universally as soon as hostilities ended. Now, virtually every commercial vessel in the world has one, and most larger vessels have two radars: one for use on the open sea and one, operating at a higher frequency to "paint" a more finely detailed picture, for use near shore.

Microwaves are also beamed across the skies to fix the positions of aircraft in flight, obviously an essential aid to controlling the movement of aircraft from city to city across the nation. These radars have also been linked to computers to tell air traffic controllers the altitude of planes in the area and to label them on their screens.

A new kind of radar, phased array, is now being used to search the skies thousands of miles out over the Atlantic and Pacific oceans. Although these advanced radars use microwave energy just as ordinary radars do, they do not depend upon a rotating antenna. Instead, a fixed antenna array, comprising thousands of elements like those of a fly's eye, looks everywhere. It has been said that these radars roll their eyes instead of turning their heads.

High-Speed Cooking

During World War II Raytheon had been selected to work with M.I.T. and British scientists to accelerate the production of magnetrons, the electron tubes that generate microwave energy, in order to speed up the production of radars. While testing some new, higher-powered tubes in a laboratory at Raytheon's Waltham, Massachusetts plant, Percy L. Spencer and several of his staff engineers observed an interesting phenomenon. If you placed your hand in a beam of microwave energy, your hand would grow pleasantly warm. It was not like putting your hand in a heated oven that might sear the skin. The warmth was deep-heating and uniform.

Spencer and his engineers sent out for some popcorn and some food, then piped the energy into a metal wastebasket. The microwave oven was born.

From these discoveries, some 35 years ago, a new industry was born. In millions of homes around the world, meals are prepared in minutes using microwave ovens. In many processing industries, microwaves are being used to perform difficult heating or drying jobs. Even printing presses use microwaves to speed the drying of ink on paper.

In hospitals, doctors' offices, and athletic training rooms, that deep heat that Percy Spencer noticed is now used in diathermy equipment to ease the discomfort of muscle aches and pains.

Telephones without Cable

The third characteristic of microwaves—that they pass undistorted through the air—makes them good messengers to carry telephone conversations as well as live television signals—without telephone poles or cables—across town or across the country. The microwave signals are beamed via satellite or by dish reflectors mounted atop buildings and mountaintop towers.

Microwaves take their name from the Greek *mikro* meaning very small. While the waves themselves may be very small, they play an important role in our world today: in defense; in communications; in air, sea, and highway safety; in industrial processing; and in cooking. At Raytheon the applications expand every day.

10. Explain how the advertisement on page 26 (Fig. 1.6) illustrates the techniques of occupational writing described in this chapter. Specifically, comment on how the ad reveals that the copywriter successfully analyzed the intended audience. Pay attention to advertising copy (words), the photograph (visuals), and the situation depicted. Also explain how the ad illustrates five characteristics of on-the-job writing.

Fig. 1.6   An advertisement meeting the specific needs of an audience.

LOOK AT HOW MUCH MORE YOU GET
WHEN THE NAME ON THE BOX IS TRANS-LUX.

Valerie Hynes
Customer Care
Service

Joe Boyd
Maintenance Service

Eric Matthews
Relocation Service

Lynn Carpenito
Product Coordinating
Service

Ed Lyons
Consultation Service

George Tanaka
Installation Service

Gail Stevens
Instruction Service

Face it. You have better things to do than worry about your communications terminal. That's why Trans-Lux doesn't just supply equipment. We offer a full line of special support services to make certain you get the most for your dollar—now, and in the years ahead. From the selection of your Trans-Lux terminal, through installation, training and ongoing use, we stand ready to serve you in every way.

We pay as much attention to you *after* you lease or buy a Trans-Lux teleprinter as we do before. All of the valuable services shown above are yours with any teleprinter you choose.

When it comes to teleprinters, you can rely on Trans-Lux—whether your office's communications are domestic or international; whether you use the Telex, TWX (Telex II), DDD or Easy-Link networks; whether you require one terminal or twenty. You'll receive high performance equipment that's designed, engineered and manufactured by Trans-Lux—and backed by our full line of valuable support services.

FREE CONSULTATION

Without charge or obligation, we'll evaluate your needs to make sure you're getting the most out of your current teleprinter. Call TOLL-FREE now:

1 800 243-5544, EXT. 105
IN CONNECTICUT, CALL 203 853-4321
IN CANADA, CALL 416 624-2311

TRANS-LUX
C O R P O R A T I O N

110 Richards Avenue • Norwalk, Connecticut 06854
Telex 965863 • TWX 710-468-0241

Canadian Trans-Lux Corporation, Ltd.
5446 Gorvan Drive, Mississauga, Ontario L4W 3E8
Telex 06-961375 • TWX 962-9103

Courtesy of Trans-Lux Corporation, Norwalk, Conn. Reprinted with permission.

2

Writing: Paragraphs

This chapter will show you how to construct and organize your paragraphs. A paragraph is the basic building block for letters, reports, instructional manuals, or any piece of writing. If you master the art of writing paragraphs, you should be able to handle any kind of business or technical writing. A *paragraph* is (a) a group of related sentences (b) arranged in a logical order (c) supplying readers with detailed information (d) on a single important topic. Each of these points is discussed in detail in this chapter.

☞ The Importance of Paragraphs

Paragraphs give readers the necessary navigational clues to understand your work. The following three functions of paragraphs are equally important.

1. Paragraphs divide your message into segments. They break complex messages into smaller, more understandable segments for readers. Imagine what a piece of writing would look like without indentations or white spaces to divide it into paragraphs. Without the paragraph breaks, readers would not know where to find key statements and would wonder where one part of a message began and another stopped. Furthermore, an unbroken piece of writing is intimidating to readers; paragraph breaks provide pauses to help refresh your reader, if only momentarily.

2. Paragraphs group related details for readers' benefit. Think of a paragraph as an information block. Each block (or paragraph) treats only one main idea at a time; that is, it usually contains a general statement and sufficient details to explain that statement. Within each information block you provide readers with only the relevant details they will need to understand clearly that portion of your message. By collecting all related details in one paragraph, you make it easier for readers to understand them in terms of the main idea.

3. Paragraphs link ideas to make your work easy to understand. Paragraphs are not written in isolation. Each paragraph should flow smoothly and logically into the next, linking the different information blocks that comprise your message. Transitions (discussed on pages 35–39), especially at the beginning and end of your paragraphs, hook one part of your message to another. In this way, paragraphs show how the different parts of your message are connected and related to each other, how one part "fits" into the next. Paragraphs also help readers to link ideas by saying to them: you have finished one part of the message; now stop to consider what you have read before starting a new part.

☞ Four Types of Paragraphs

Paragraphs are not all alike. Generally speaking, you will use four types of paragraphs—supporting, introductory, transitional, and concluding. Each of these differs in length, purpose, and position in your work. Each meets your readers' needs in a specific way. The following section describes each type of paragraph, explains how to write it, and provides examples.

Supporting Paragraphs

Supporting paragraphs are the workhorses of letters and reports. They carry the information that supports the purpose and message of your writing. They are also called *middle* or *body paragraphs* because they appear between the introduction and conclusion of your work to provide explanations, directions, descriptions, or commentary. More of them will be found in your writing than any other type of paragraph.

A supporting paragraph expresses one central idea, and its sentences contribute to the overall meaning of that idea. The supporting paragraph does this by giving readers a *topic sentence*, which states the central idea, and *supporting information*, which explains the topic sentence.

The topic sentence is the most important part of the paragraph for readers. It tells readers what your paragraph is about. More specifically, a topic sentence:

- summarizes the content of a paragraph
- forecasts the kinds of information readers can expect to find in the paragraph
- explains why you included or excluded certain details

Your topic sentence is a pledge to readers that every other sentence in the paragraph will support it. You will learn more about writing topic sentences on pages 32–34.

Supporting information includes data to convince readers that what you say about the central idea is accurate and complete. These data can include a range of statistical information—facts about costs, dates, employees, changes in policies—or your interpretation of such facts.

The following paragraph is an example of a carefully constructed supporting paragraph. It contains a clear topic sentence (highlighted in italics) as well as adequate and relevant supporting details.

> *Fat is an important part of everyone's diet.* It is nutritionally present in the basic food groups we eat—meat and poultry, dairy products, and oils—to aid growth or development. The fats and fatty acids present in these foods ensure proper metabolism, thus helping to turn what we eat into the energy we need. These same fats and fatty acids also act as carriers for important vitamins like A, D, E, and K. Another important role of fat is that it keeps us from feeling hungry by delaying digestion. Fat also enhances the flavor of the food we eat, making it more enjoyable.

This paragraph contains only one central idea—fat is an important part of everyone's diet. The paragraph does not stray from this central topic; every statement refers to the role of fat in the diet. The topic sentence both summarizes and forecasts what readers can expect to see in the paragraph. And the rest of the paragraph uses relevant information (fats are nutritional, ensure proper metabolism, carry vitamins, delay digestion, flavor food) to support the topic sentence.

To picture the structure of a well-made supporting paragraph, visualize a capital T as in Fig. 2.1. The topic sentence is like the crossbar (or top) of the capital T; the individual sentences supporting the topic sentence are like the column of the T.

Note how the paragraph about fat in the diet can be visually redesigned to reveal its T shape.

Fat is an important part of everyone's diet.

provides nutrition

ensures metabolism

carries vitamins

delays hunger

flavors food

The T-shape is just one of many structural shapes paragraphs may take. In other patterns, the topic sentence may come halfway through or at the end of the paragraph or be implied instead of stated. But in business or technical writing, it is customary and desirable to have the topic sentence come first. On pages 32–33 you will learn more about why topic sentences should be placed first.

Fig. 2.1   A T-shaped paragraph.

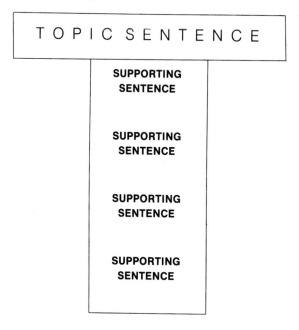

Introductory Paragraph

An introductory paragraph gives readers a preview of your work—telling them what they can expect to find in your letter or report. The introductory paragraph to a memo, a letter, or a short report is generally brief—one to three sentences.

In your introductory paragraph, come to the point at once. Note how the following introductory paragraph previews what the report will cover. The paragraph also makes a helpful connection for the reader by referring to her previous request.

> Our sales department has compiled the data you recently requested on third-quarter sales. The following brief report provides you with the specific information you need on (1) retail, (2) wholesale, and (3) foreign sales.

A number of introductory paragraphs might be used in a long report. Note how, in the following example, the first paragraph establishes the topic and the second describes what readers can expect to learn about that topic.

> The U.S. government is the world's largest buyer of goods and services. One of the major responsibilities of the Small Business Administration (SBA) is to see that small businesses obtain a fair share of this vast government market.
>
> This manual explains how the government buys goods and services, how most businesses sell to the government, and how the SBA helps small business owners sell to federal purchasing agencies and their prime contractors.

Transitional Paragraphs

Transitions move the reader from one idea to another. You can provide transitions through individual words (see pages 36–37) or through sentences at the beginning or end of a paragraph. Another way is to write transitional paragraphs to take readers from one section of a letter, memo, or report to another. (They are also called *linking paragraphs* because of this function.) Think of a transitional paragraph as a bridge across which readers can see where they have been and where they are going. As the following examples show, transitional paragraphs are generally very brief—one or two sentences.

Up to this point we have considered the engineering advantages of the Rudex system. Now we will turn to the financial benefits it offers us.

The above process will so saturate materials with solution that they may be too wet to use properly. The following instructions will show you how to dry and recomb the materials.

The same kind of popularity generated by the earlier subdivision can be found at the new construction site. Here are some examples.

Concluding Paragraphs

Like introductory paragraphs, concluding ones can be brief—usually only a few sentences. Concluding paragraphs can perform one or all of the following three functions.

1. They can summarize the main points by recapping the key points of your message without giving any new information.

In summary, the main features of the plan ask the city to reroute traffic on Clinton Avenue, to install a traffic signal on the corner of Adams and Fourth Streets, and to change Concord Place into a one-way thoroughfare.

2. They can draw conclusions by interpreting or emphasizing the significance of the information you have presented.

In conclusion, then, the soundest investment opportunities for our firm lie in Continental Driftwood securities. They offer the lowest rate of capital, supply the highest interest yield, and have the most stable financial history.

3. They can make recommendations by calling for a specific action.

After studying the responses of customers to our recent survey, I recommend that we do the following by the last week in May:

a. extend our store hours on Friday night from 8:00 P.M. to 9:00 P.M.
b. open on Saturday morning at 8:30 A.M. instead of 9:30 A.M.
c. close at 6:00 P.M. rather than 7:00 P.M. on Monday, Tuesday, Wednesday, and Thursday nights.

Remember that you need a concluding paragraph to avoid ending a letter or report abruptly. Concluding paragraphs give readers a sense of completion, of having stopped officially and in a satisfying manner. You can give readers this sense of completion by using such phrases or words as *finally, in conclusion, last of all* in the concluding paragraph.

☞ Writing Topic Sentences

The topic sentence is the pilot of each paragraph. Carefully worded and restricted, it helps readers to grasp your main idea; and it helps you to control the kinds of information included in that paragraph.

How can you create an effective topic sentence? As with other types of writing, you work in stages. Usually you will start with brainstorming to collect ideas and facts; and then you will draft a topic sentence to explain or summarize these details. You may have to discard some ideas or facts and revise the topic sentence several times. In other words, you will work back and forth, adjusting the content of the paragraph, then the topic sentence, then the content again, and so on.

Keep in mind this idea of writing as a process, that is, your paper evolves from rough early stages and drafts (that only you see) to a completed paper (for your reader). As you work, pay close attention to the following three guidelines, which will help you produce an effective paragraph.

1. Make sure you provide a topic sentence. In their rush to supply readers with the facts—measurements, working principles, descriptions—some writers forget to include a topic sentence to explain what all the details mean. As it stands, the following paragraph lacks a topic sentence and thus deprives readers of the writer's reason for discussing the mechanics of a wind turbine.

> Sensors found on each machine detect wind speed and direction and other important details such as ice loading and potential metal fatigue. The information is fed into a small computer (microprocessor) in the nacelle (or engine housing). The microprocessor automatically keeps the blades turned into the wind, starts and stops the machine, and changes the pitch of the tips of the blades to increase power under varying wind conditions. Should any part of the wind turbine suffer damage or malfunction, the microprocessor will immediately shut the machine down.

With the addition of a suitable topic sentence—"The MOD-2 wind turbine is designed to be operated completely by computer"—readers can more clearly identify the central topic and understand what the details have in common. To make sure you include a topic sentence for every paragraph, ask yourself if the first sentence in the paragraph explains or clarifies everything else in that paragraph. If it does, chances are you have an effective topic sentence.

2. Put your topic sentence first. Place your topic sentence at the beginning—not the middle or end—of your paragraph. Because the beginning sentence occupies an emphatic place, readers are sure to give it their attention. In some business and technical writing, the topic sentence at the beginning of each paragraph is even underscored to help busy readers grasp main points quickly. By seeing that main point up front, readers are not kept in doubt or suspense. Burying the key idea in the middle or near the end of the paragraph makes it harder for readers to act upon your information, as illustrated by the following poorly written paragraph.

> In the last two years the cost of insurance on the trucks has increased almost 17 percent. We are now paying $2300.00 to the Rawlins Agency whereas in March of 1985 we had a bill of $1935.00. Although it will be impossible to predict the price of gasoline for even one season, let alone a single year, certainly it will go up, too. Also, we have been receiving many orders from customers who live outside a 40-mile radius of Bloomington which makes our policy of providing free delivery even more costly. Whenever one of the delivery trucks is in the shop for repair, we can expect a bill of at least $150.00, if this year's rates continue. Another major expense is the cost of drivers' overtime. Two of them have logged more than 35 hours of overtime in the last month, amounting to $450.00.

Eager to assemble all the facts about the firm's delivery trucks, the writer did not consider the reader's need to have the reason for these facts in the first sentence of the paragraph. The writer's main reason for compiling the facts is buried in the fourth sentence of the paragraph—the company's present policy of supplying free delivery to customers is costly and should be changed. If the writer began with that fact, the reader would then have been better prepared to follow and interpret the figures about the costs of operating the trucks.

3. Make sure your topic sentence is restricted. If restricted, a topic sentence identifies only one central idea. A broad or unrestricted topic sentence does not zero in on a single idea. Instead, it encourages the writer to stray from one central topic into the territory of numerous, other topics. The result is a paragraph that lacks direction and focus. Here are two examples of broad topic sentences.

> Computers have changed the ways we do business.

> Working conditions are important.

These two sentences, if used as topic sentences, would fail to give readers a clear understanding of the central idea the paragraph will develop. In the first sentence the writer goes astray by using the vague word *ways,* which can apply to almost any computer application in business—producing copy, making graphics, scanning records, storing information. Revised, this sentence focuses on a more precise use of the computer and in a particular business context.

> The new Aldridge 200 has improved the way we now bill our customers.

As a topic sentence, the second sentence is even more misleading than the first. The phrase "working conditions" suggests many different topics (legal, physical, social, psychological, and environmental conditions) and does not specify for whom or why such conditions are important. An appropriate revision might be:

> The rate of overtime pay will boost our employees' morale.

A broad topic sentence leads to a shaky paragraph for two reasons. On the one hand, the paragraph will not contain enough information to support the topic sentence. On the other hand, a broad topic sentence will not be able to summarize or forecast accurately the information available in the paragraph.

It is important to remember that broad topic sentences are part of the process of writing a restricted topic sentence. The first time you write—or any writer writes—a topic sentence, it is likely to be too broad. The next step is to revise and rework the sentence until it is restricted. A broad topic sentence is one starting point for a restricted topic sentence.

☞ Three Characteristics of an Effective Paragraph

Effective paragraphs have unity, coherence, and completeness. In the following pages, each of these characteristics is described, together with techniques you can follow to achieve these characteristics in your paragraphs.

Unity

A unified paragraph sticks to one topic without wandering from it. Every sentence, every detail in the paragraph supports, explains, or proves the central idea stated in the topic sentence. A unified paragraph includes only relevant information and excludes unnecessary or irrelevant comments. However, a unified paragraph offers readers more than just pertinent details. It assures them that the appropriate information they need is included in that paragraph and not lodged elsewhere. For example, in a progress report a paragraph on the work you have already completed should not include details about work you hope to accomplish during the next report period.

Let's say you are writing a report for an insurance company about the increasing popularity of recreational vehicles (RV's). You might include sections (and paragraphs) about the variety of RV's, their costs, the training and licensing of dealers, and the amount of taxes RV owners pay. You might want to include a section on the convenience and advantages of RV's to show why they are popular. In fact, one of your supporting paragraphs in such a section might have the following topic sentence: RV's offer owners the comforts of a home on wheels. Which of the following points would support that central idea?

1. RV's can come equipped with showers.
2. Ad valorem taxes on RV's have increased 13 percent in the last three years.

3. Some RV's come equipped with microwave ovens.
4. RV's get fairly decent mileage on the highway—around 16 miles per gallon.
5. Dealers can customize any van to suit an owner's taste.
6. The number of RV dealerships in the state has doubled over the last six years.
7. RV's often have large swivel chairs—captain's chairs—comparable to recliners.
8. Financing is an important part of the dealer's job.
9. RV's carry their own air-conditioning units equipped with thermostat control for steady-state cooling.
10. Some RV's offer built-in desks.
11. RV's come in many forms—vans, motor homes, trailers, slide-in pickup trucks.
12. RV's can be small and compact (sometimes even crowded) or large and spacious.

Only points 1, 3, 7, 9, and 10 would be relevant for a paragraph whose central idea was on the comforts of home that RV's offered buyers. The other points would destroy the unity of that paragraph.

Point 2 raises a comparison between homes and RV's—they both require the owner to pay taxes—but information on a tax increase would hardly support the idea of home comfort in an RV. Point 4 expresses an advantage but not a relevant one. A house does not travel by gasoline. Points 5, 6, and 8 would belong in a paragraph on RV dealers. Point 5 appears to be relevant, but note that the emphasis in it is on the dealer's ability, not on the RV's comparison with a home. Point 11 belongs in a separate paragraph because it does not support the topic. And as it is currently worded, point 12 contradicts the idea expressed in the topic sentence. The writer needs to stress the comforts an RV offers; saying that some RV's are crowded does not support that idea.

Coherence

A paragraph is coherent when all its sentences flow smoothly and logically to and from each other. Sentences in a paragraph need to stick together; they are like links of a chain. By showing the connections, you will help readers understand the precise relationship a sentence has with the one preceding it. By making clear the relationships that exist between your sentences, you help to make clear the relationship that exists between your ideas. Clear thinking equals clear writing.

Four Ways to Achieve Coherence

You can clarify relationships between your sentences (and paragraphs) by using transitional words and phrases, by repeating key words and ideas, by using pronouns and demonstrative adjectives, and by using parallel grammatical structures.

1. Use transitional words and phrases. One of the easiest ways to achieve coherence in a paragraph is to use transitional words and short phrases like those included in Table 2.1. Note how these words are arranged according to the types of relationships they signal to readers. For example, when readers see words like *also, furthermore, in addition,* the message the writer conveys is, "Go ahead; you are on the right track." Words used to contrast ideas—*however, on the other hand, in contrast*—prepare readers for this message: "Go in the opposite direction from the one you have been following." And transitional words and phrases signaling that your work is coming to an end—*finally, in short, to summarize*—tell readers "Prepare to stop; here comes a wrap-up." Be careful how you use these transitional devices. They should not be employed arbitrarily. Transitions should be logical and natural.

A paragraph without such transitional words and phrases lacks coherence as the following example demonstrates.

> Advertising a product on the radio has some advantages over using television. Radio rates are much cheaper. A one-time 60-second spot on television can cost $540. Advertisers can purchase nine 30-second spots on the radio. The production costs are low on radio. Advertisers can pay extra for models and voice-overs. Radio offers advertisers immediate scheduling. Ads appear the same week a contract is signed. Television stations are booked up months in advance. Radio gives advertisers a greater opportunity to reach potential buyers. Radio follows listeners everywhere—in their homes, at work, and in their cars. Television is popular. Television cannot do that.

Now read a version of the same paragraph with effective transitional words and phrases added in italics.

> Advertising a product on the radio has *many* advantages over using television. Radio rates are much cheaper. *For example,* a one-time 60 second spot on local T.V. can cost $540.00. *For that money,* advertisers can purchase nine 30-second spots on radio. *Equally attractive* are the low production costs for radio advertising. *In contrast,* television advertising often includes extra costs for models and voice-overs. *Another* advantage radio offers advertisers is immediate scheduling. *Often* the ad appears during the same week a contract is signed. *Because* television stations are *frequently* booked up months in advance, it may be a long time *before* an ad appears. *Furthermore,* radio gives advertisers a greater opportunity to reach their potential buyers. *After all,* radio follows listeners everywhere—in their homes, at work, and in their cars. *Although* it is very popular, television cannot do that.

2. Repeat key words or ideas. Repeating key words or ideas in a paragraph provides continuity for readers by keeping important ideas constantly before them. Key words link different parts of the paragraph for readers and show how the paragraph is put together. The following paragraph effectively repeats the key words *fringe benefits* or *benefits* for readers.

Table 2.1 Transitional words and phrases

Addition	also	in addition
	and	many
	besides	moreover
	furthermore	next
	first, . . . second, . . . third, . . .	too
Cause/Effect	and so	hence
	accordingly	if
	as a result	on account of
	because of	since
	consequently	therefore
	due to	thus
Comparison/Contrast	in the same way	in contrast
	equally	in spite of
	likewise	nevertheless
	similarly	on the contrary
	but	on the other hand
	conversely	still
	however	yet
Condition	although	if
	even though	provided that
	of course	to be sure
	granted that	unless
Conclusion	finally	in short
	at last	in summary
	in conclusion	to conclude
Emphasis	as a matter of fact	of course
	after all	obviously
	above all	again
	in fact	to repeat
	indeed	unquestionably
Illustration	for example	specifically
	for instance	in particular
	in effect	that is
	in other words	to illustrate
Place	alongside of	behind
	at this point	there
	below	next to
	here	where
	in front of	wherever
Time	afterwards	now
	at times	presently
	at the same time	next
	beforehand	once
	currently	soon
	during	subsequently
	earlier	then
	from now on	until
	later	when
	meanwhile	while

Fringe benefits are an important part of recruiting and retaining qualified employees. In a highly competitive job market, such *benefits* rather than salary may determine if a talented professional accepts or declines a job. Traditionally, *fringe benefits* were limited to basic hospital and surgical insurance and to pension plans. But today they extend to dental and optical riders on company insurance policies. Other more lucrative *fringe benefits* include the financial rewards companies offer loyal employees—profit-sharing options to buy stock at reduced rates and generous bonuses for diligent sales activities.

Notice how the writer's lively use of transitional words (*but, also, for example*) prevents the four references to *fringe benefits* from becoming dull or redundant. The reader is made aware of the controlling sense of fringe benefits in the paragraph without being overwhelmed by the repetition of the phrase.

3. Use pronouns and demonstrative adjectives. The use of personal pronouns (*he, she, him, her, they,* and so on) also contributes to the coherence of a paragraph. When readers connect the pronoun with its antecedent (the noun to which it refers), they tie sentences and ideas together. Demonstrative adjectives (*this, that, these, those*) also help readers to link related pieces of information. As their name implies, these adjectives emphasize and distinguish specific objects or features for readers. In the paragraph that follows, the connections that pronouns and demonstrative adjectives make between sentences are graphically emphasized through boxes and lines.

Traffic studies are an important tool for store owners looking for a new location. These studies are relatively inexpensive and highly accurate. They can tell owners how much traffic passes by a particular location at a particular time and why. Moreover, they can help owners to determine what particular characteristics these individuals have in common. Because of their helpfulness, these studies can save owners time and money and possibly prevent financial ruin. They should be done before any contemplated move.

4. Use parallel grammatical structures. Writers can provide a great deal of coherence by using parallel grammatical structures. When readers see how ideas are related grammatically, they can more easily see how they are related logically. (See pages 62–64 for a discussion of parallel grammatical structures.) Note the use of parallelism in the following paragraph.

Orientation sessions accomplish four useful goals for trainees. First, they introduce trainees to key personnel in accounting, data processing, maintenance, and security. Second, they give trainees experience logging into the DataBase system, selecting an appropriate menu, editing core documents, and getting off the system. Third, they explain to trainees the company policies affecting the way supplies are ordered, used, and stored. Fourth, they help trainees understand their responsibilities in such sensitive areas as computer security and use.

In this paragraph parallelism is at work on a number of levels. The four sentences about the four goals start in the same way grammatically to help readers categorize the information. Within individual sentences, the repetition of *present participles* (log*ging,* select*ing,* edit*ing,* get*ting*) and of *past participles* (order*ed,* us*ed,* stor*ed*) helps the writer to summarize information and to see the related nature of the activities being explained. Note that the transitional words *first, second, third, fourth* convey a sense of parallelism as well as of sequence.

Completeness

Completeness means that your paragraph provides a well-developed and satisfying information block for your reader. In a complete paragraph you provide readers with a restricted topic sentence and sufficient information to clarify, analyze, support, defend, or prove the central idea expressed in your topic sentence.

A complete, carefully developed paragraph is an information block—containing the following types of supporting information for readers:

- names of specific individuals
- dates
- examples of a term, plan, situation
- measurements—size, shape, designs, temperatures, etc.
- costs and other figures
- descriptions of locations
- statistical details

Individually, these facts might not mean much to readers. But when linked in your paragraph, they provide the support readers need. Readers need these specific supporting details to understand a concept, perform a task, or evaluate a plan you are proposing. Without such supporting details, your paragraph will be underdeveloped, undernourished, incomplete.

One sure sign of an incomplete paragraph is that it leaves readers with questions, not answers. "Have I missed something?" "Is that the whole story?" "How did the writer arrive at that conclusion?" "Why is X better than Y?"

How will you know if your paragraph is complete? Chances are that a series of skimpy shoestring paragraphs lack necessary supporting data. Such paragraphs in most cases lack substance; they need to be beefed up. But measuring length alone is not the only way to determine if a paragraph is developed sufficiently. Even a paragraph of four or five sentences can be incomplete if it contains a series of generalities and does not provide factual details. A paragraph is complete when it leaves no confusion in the reader's mind about what you intended, about how the reader is supposed to respond, and about why such a response is both necessary and appropriate.

The following paragraph is incomplete because it lacks the specific details necessary to explain and prove the assertion made in the topic sentence:

> Farmers can turn their crops and farm wastes into useful, cost-effective fuels. Much grown on the farm can be converted to energy. This energy can have many uses and save farmers a lot of money in operating expenses.

This paragraph desperately needs more information. It raises the following questions: "What specific materials lend themselves to energy use?" "How can crops and farm wastes be turned into energy?" "What are some specific uses of this new energy?"

In the revised version that follows, the answers to these questions are given through specific examples and explanations.

> Farm crops and wastes can be turned into fuels to save farmers money on their operating costs. Alcohol can be distilled from grain, sugar beets, potatoes—even from blighted crops. Converted to gasohol (90 percent gasoline, 10 percent alcohol), this alcohol can be used to run such farm equipment as irrigation pumps, feed grinders, and tractors. Similarly, through a biomass digestion system, farmers can produce methane from animal or crop wastes. This methane can be an important source of the natural gas used for heating and cooking. Finally, cellulose pellets, derived from plant materials, are an important solid fuel that can save farmers money in heating barns.

Examples of energy-rich fuels (alcohol, methane, cellulose), and specific farm uses of these fuels make this a complete paragraph.

☞ The Appearance of Paragraphs

The way your paragraphs look can influence how easily readers will understand the information they contain. The following guidelines on the appearance of paragraphs will help you make them readable and aid you in evaluating them for completeness.

1. Avoid excessively long paragraphs. Long paragraphs are hard for readers to follow. A paragraph of the right length contains only the details readers need to understand the main point of that paragraph. Anything else would make the paragraph too long. Long paragraphs tend to contain deadwood, to repeat the same idea (though in slightly different words), or to include information that belongs in another paragraph. You can shorten these paragraphs by cutting out deadwood or repetition. Another cause of excessively long paragraphs may be broad topic sentences. By more narrowly limiting your topic sentence, you will be able to shorten the paragraph.

2. Avoid stringing together a series of short paragraphs. An entire letter or report made up of one- and two-line paragraphs does not make the reader's job easier. On the contrary, making each sentence or two into a new paragraph may frustrate a reader. Such shoestring paragraphs suggest to the reader that there aren't enough details to support the main point. They also say that the information is not organized into meaningful blocks or that the writer is not distinguishing between central ideas and supporting information. If your paragraphs are too short because of a lack of supporting details, include more relevant facts for readers (see earlier section on paragraph completeness, pages 39–40). A string of short paragraphs may also be the sign the topic sentence is missing. Look at the short paragraphs to see whether they can be combined into one paragraph under one central idea.

3. Use visual clues to show emphasis and organization. Headings prepare readers for the information found in a group of related paragraphs and make organization visible. Headings also emphasize the major ideas of a memo or report. Within paragraphs, italics, boldface type, bullets, and numbering can emphasize points as well as break them down into smaller, easier-to-understand units. Figure 2.2 gives examples of these visual clues.

4. Make your paragraphs visually attractive. Don't squeeze a paragraph onto the page. Readability is enhanced when you use relatively neat segments of prose for your paragraphs with plenty of white space surrounding them. Compact paragraphs (40 to 60 spaces per line; 8 to 10 lines per paragraph) are easiest to read. White space on the page makes readers feel comfortable and shows that you have not crowded ideas together. Thanks to word processors in today's automated offices, you may be able to experiment with the most pleasing format for readers of your paragraphs. More specific guidelines on spacing will be found in Chapter 5 (pages 102–103; 111).

☞ Patterns of Paragraph Organization

As you have seen, information in a paragraph should be unified, coherent, and complete. That information must also be presented in a logical and orderly sequence. Without organization each paragraph would be simply a list of unrelated ideas, which would not explain how the ideas are related. To explain the relationship of the ideas within a paragraph, you will have to choose an appropriate pattern of organization. The ones you select will depend on three things about the writing assignment: (a) the nature of your message, (b) the purpose of your work, and (c) the needs of your audience. In a short letter or memo, you may be able to develop your ideas using only one or two patterns for all the paragraphs. However, in a longer report you may use many patterns, and you may also combine patterns.

In the following pages, examine how paragraphs can be organized by means of these commonly used patterns: examples, description, time, space, comparison and contrast, definition, classification, and cause and effect.

Fig. 2.2   Use of visual clues to show emphasis and organization.

Audio Interference and Remedies

INTERFERENCE TO AUDIO DE-VICES (TELEPHONE, STEREOS, AM/FM RADIOS)

Telephones, electronic organs, stereo/hi-fi equipment, or AM/FM radios can be susceptible to interference. The source of interference will determine the effect on your audio device. For instance, if the equipment is picking up a nearby radio transmitter, you may hear the voice of the operator. When electrical interference is present, you may hear a sizzling or popping sound.

If you are receiving interference from a nearby radio transmitter, you should contact the operator and provide the Radio Operator Guidelines section of this handbook.

1. Generally, internal modification of your equipment must be made to eliminate the interference.
2. For **safety** reasons, it is recommended that any modification be made by a qualified service representative. The service representative should make the modifications in the home while the interference is occurring, in order to locate the point at which the interfering signal is entering the equipment.

Telephone Interference

Transmissions from a nearby radio transmitter can be picked up by your telephone system. The interference could enter the system at the following points:

1. drop wire leading to the house
2. telephone wiring inside the house
3. in the telephone instrument itself

Customer Owned Telephones

If you own your telephone and interference is occurring, the dealer or manufacturer should be contacted to assist you with modifications that will eliminate the interference.

Note: All telephone equipment must meet FCC registration standards and any internal filtering or modifications must be made by the manufacturer of the equipment or by other companies authorized by the FCC to do so.

Some states permit a telephone company to charge customers for service visits when they determine that the equipment is customer-owned.

Federal Communications Commission, *How to Identify and Resolve TV Interference Problems,* 2nd ed. (Washington, D.C.: U.S. Government Printing Office, 1982).

Examples Pattern

To use the examples pattern, begin with a statement (your restricted topic sentence) and then offer examples proving or explaining that statement. In the following paragraph, the author wants to prove that owning and operating an automobile is an escalating expense. To do that, the author selects examples of the costs a driver will encounter over the life of the car.

The cost of owning and operating a motor vehicle is of major significance as Americans experience increasing demands on their incomes. It costs more than $14,300 to purchase a large-size American car. If the car is driven 120,000 miles over a period of 12 years, the total cost to the owner will be $35,853 as the following expenses show. During the 12 years it will cost about $8,604 (excluding taxes) for some 7,059 gallons of gasoline. To maintain and repair the car, the owner can expect to pay another $6,232. Insurance will run about $3,991. Expenses for parking and tolls will be about $939. And, finally, the driver can expect to pay $1,787 in taxes.[1]

Description Pattern

Use the description pattern to explain what something—a tool, a site, any object—looks like. Start your paragraph with a topic sentence that identifies what you will describe. Then provide a part-by-part practical description giving readers precise details about size, shape, color, function, or other relevant information. Your description may also emphasize any special features. The following paragraph describes the appearance and function of a golf ball.

A golf ball has three interrelated parts that make it function effectively—the center, the threads, and the cover. The center of the golf ball, a liquid of clay, glycerine, and water, gives the ball its bounce. This small but compact center is like a ball within a ball. Wound around the center of the golf ball are hundreds of tiny rubber threads. When the ball is hit by a golf club these threads at first contract and then expand to give the ball its velocity. The cover, two hemispherical shells made of thermoplastic, contains indentations, or dimples, that affect the way the ball spins in flight. Without them, the ball would not travel as far or as fast.

Time Pattern

A paragraph organized by a temporal pattern discusses events in the order in which they occurred. This pattern is very versatile. You might use a chronological sequence in a paragraph summarizing events for a progress report or in a paragraph analyzing how a certain problem developed. You might use this pattern to outline the steps in a physical process such as continental drift or radiation. Or you might employ the temporal pattern in giving instructions on how to do something. Note how the following paragraph arranges information about women's participation in the U.S. labor force chronologically.

Over the last 30 years, the number of women in the U.S. labor force has steadily increased. In fact, since the end of World War II, women have accounted for about 60 percent of the net growth of the American labor force. According to the Bureau of Labor Statistics, in 1950 slightly less than 34 percent of all American women were employed outside the home. By 1960 that number was 38 percent. In

---

[1] U.S. Department of Transportation, *Cost of Owning and Operating Automobiles and Vans.*

1970 the percentage of women in the labor market had increased to 43.4 percent. And by 1980 one woman out of two, or 51.6 percent, was participating in the U.S. labor force. It is estimated that by the year 2000 as many as 80 percent of all American women will be in the U.S. labor force.

A chronological pattern is also essential when readers have to follow instructions in a strict order. To point out that sequence, label each step.

> To clean a storage tank, follow these steps exactly. First, ventilate the tank to release noxious fumes. Second, wash out the tank with water to dispel flammable vapors and to further reduce the chances of an explosion. Third, remove any sludge or deposits with Anixyl 345 or Metathine 45XT. Finally, allow the tank to air for at least 36 hours.

Space Pattern

A paragraph with a spatial pattern of development arranges information according to a particular view of an object or its location. Consider the many perspectives or views possible—from top to bottom, from bottom to top, from inside to outside, from outside to inside, from front to back, from back to front, from left to right, or from right to left. Choose a view that is most appropriate for your topic and your reader. In the paragraph below, the writer arranges the types of protective clothing worn by industrial workers from helmets to shoes, or from top to bottom. This head-to-toe order helps readers follow the information in a familiar sequence; the writer does not jump from goggles to overalls to helmets.

> Protective clothing is available for every part of the industrial worker's body. Hard hats protect the worker's head from the impact of falling objects when the individual is handling stock. Caps and hair nets keep the worker's hair from catching in machinery. Face shields, safety goggles, glasses, and similar kinds of clothing guard the worker's eyes from splashing chemicals or flying debris. Protective vests, jackets, aprons, and overalls shield the worker's body from cuts or bruises from heavy or rough-edged stock. The worker's hands are protected from the same kinds of injuries with special gloves. Finally, safety shoes and boots shield the worker's feet from being injured by falling stock.[2]

Comparison/Contrast Pattern

This pattern for organizing the ideas can show readers the similarities (comparisons) and the differences (contrasts) between objects, plans, locations, or the like. In a single paragraph you show either similarities or differences or both. You can also use this pattern to explain an unfamiliar concept or object by comparing it to one known to readers. When you use this pattern, always identify in the topic sentence the points or objects you are comparing or con-

---

[2] U.S. Department of Labor, *Concepts and Techniques of Machine Safeguarding* (1980): 10.

trasting. The following paragraph both *compares* and *contrasts* two types of home mortgages.

> Before making a loan application, prospective home buyers need to know the two most popular types of mortgage—the conventional mortgage and the adjustable-rate mortgage (ARM). The conventional mortgage gives buyers a fixed rate of interest over the life of the loan, for example, 13½ percent for 25 years. The ARM, however, has interest rates that vary as the rate of interest paid on Treasury Bills varies. For example, an ARM may begin at 11 percent but in a year or two either escalate or decrease by 2 percent or more. With a conventional loan, monthly mortgage payments are fixed. With an ARM, on the other hand, they can change each year, depending on the financial market. A conventional loan may be more expensive for home buyers to obtain than would be an ARM. Lending institutions generally demand higher discount points (costs to rent the money) for fixed-rate mortgages than for ARM's. Therefore, home buyers will have to decide between the stable but initially higher rate of a conventional mortgage and the fluctuating, initially lower rate of an ARM.

Or you can use a separate paragraph for each subject of the comparison and contrast.

> The traditional office exists in a one-to-one environment: each manager has a secretary. Each secretary has nonspecialized functions—typing, filing, copying, scheduling, answering telephones, and doing correspondence with an electric typewriter and a copier, resulting in much retyping and duplication of effort. The manager waits for the secretary, and the secretary waits for the manager. The situation always generates more paperwork. The traditional solution is to hire more people, use more overtime, or miss more deadlines.
>
> The automated office, however, is no longer a one-to-one arrangement. One secretary supports several managers and oversees several people, each with a different specific function. Managers use automation (telephone, dictation equipment) to create or implement ideas. The secretary, using automated equipment such as information processors or transcription equipment, distributes information largely through electronic means (terminals). In this modern type of office, the skills of existing personnel, particularly those performing secretarial functions, are used most effectively.[3]

Definition Pattern

When you organize a paragraph by definition, you set boundaries around what a term or concept means. Definition is especially useful in on-the-job writing because of the many technical words you may have to explain to customers or to professionals outside your field. Some of the "boundaries" that may belong in a definition paragraph, depending on the situation, include: (a) what the term means; (b) where and when the term originated; (c) what its applications or characteristics are; and (d) what examples or illustrations of the term will

---

[3] *USAF Medical Service Digest* (Nov.–Dec. 1982): 15–16.

help readers to understand it. Note how the following paragraph on flexitime uses many of these techniques.

> Flexitime refers to a policy of replacing the traditional fixed work hours with a more flexible schedule set by employees within certain prescribed limits. These limits typically include a *core time* and *flexible time*. During core time, such as 9:30 a.m. to 3:00 p.m., all employees are required to be at work. Flexible time is a period before or after core time when employees can exercise their option to start or leave work. [Flexible time] is usually between 7:00 a.m. and 9:30 a.m., and 3:00 p.m. and 6:00 p.m.[4]

Classification Pattern

To classify is to sort *related* objects (types of wrenches or types of microcomputers) into mutually exclusive groups according to a consistent principle. In libraries, the Dewey decimal system classifies all books into one of ten large branches of knowledge, hence its name "decimal system." The same objects can usually be classified according to several different principles as long as the classification is done systematically and logically. For example, items on a shopping list can be arranged in one of several ways; in one classification, you may list items according to how essential they are to you: essential—items that are needed immediately (milk, bread), less essential—items needed at some time in the future (more soap, dog food), and luxuries—items you can live without (snack foods, extra cookies). Or using a different classification, you may list items on your shopping list according to how many calories they contain: high calorie (chocolates), medium calorie (bread, milk), and low calorie (lettuce). Or yet another shopper may classify items according to their location in the supermarket—to avoid retracing steps.

A writer, for instance, might want to classify sound systems into stereo, tape, and digital systems, or alternately choose to classify only stereo systems, classifying them according to good, medium, or poor sound quality. Whichever system is chosen, the writer should use it consistently.

For on-the-job writing, the classification pattern is especially helpful when you have to identify or evaluate different products, sites, or plans for an employer. The following paragraph classifies for a store manager different types of burglar alarms.

> An appropriate burglar alarm system can help protect the merchant. Basically the merchant can choose from two types of alarms. The central alarm alerts a security or police agency but does not warn the burglar. The local alarm, usually a siren or bell, goes off at the site of the break-in. Whether the alarm is central or local, the merchant has a wide choice of alarm-sensing devices. Among them are radar motion detectors, invisible photo beams, detectors that work on ultrasonic sound, and vibration detectors. Also, there is supplemental equipment such as an

---

[4] *Supervisory Management* (Feb. 1984): 38.

automatic phone dialer. This device phones the police and the store owner to give them verbal warning when an alarm is breached.[5]

Cause-to-Effect Pattern

In a cause-to-effect pattern, the paragraph starts with why something occurred (the cause) and then tells readers what resulted (the effect). This pattern is useful as the structure for a letter of complaint, an investigative report or a proposal. In writing a proposal you try to convince readers that if your plan (the cause) is adopted, certain good things will follow (the effects). With this pattern you can describe any problem or decision, and then trace its effects. In the following paragraph the writer begins with the causes of the employees' problems (the improperly positioned video display terminals, or VDT's) and then lists some of the effects of that action (glare, backache, decreased productivity).

> When new VDT's were put in a month ago, they were installed incorrectly. They were placed too low, at the wrong angle, and in the wrong lighting conditions. As a result, our employees have experienced a number of problems. They have complained of an annoying glare from the reflection of room lighting on the screen. In addition to experiencing eyestrain, employees have had low backaches because they have to slump in their chairs to focus on the screens, which were not tilted up and not placed high enough on the desks. Consequently, our employees' efficiency dropped 15–20 percent during the last month.

Effect-to-Cause Pattern

To use an effect-to-cause pattern, begin the paragraph with the effect—the result or outcome of something—and then identify its causes. This pattern is especially useful when substantiating why something happened. Make sure that you document the relationship between effects and their causes with specific, relevant information. In the following paragraph, the writer links increased tourism (the effect) to its multiple causes.

> Over the last eighteen months tourism has continued to increase in Hillview. A major reason for this increase is the opening of the Rocky Mountain Theme Park. Attendance at this park has grown each year since its opening in 1983. The completion of the Dodge County Metro Center in March of last year also contributed to increased tourism. Residents from nearby states frequently attend rock concerts at the center and often spend an extra day or two in Hillview to shop or to sightsee. Three new hotels have also increased tourism. In the past year five conventions were held in Hillview, two more than last year.

---

[5] Small Business Administration, "Preventing Burglary and Robbery Loss" (1965).

☞ The Paragraph—An Overview

Paragraphs are essential to the success of your written work. They can introduce, support, provide transitions between, and conclude your ideas. A key part of your paragraph is the topic sentence, which should be suitably restricted and placed first in the paragraph to help readers grasp your central idea quickly. One simple model to follow is the T-shape, particularly useful for supporting paragraphs.

In their final form, your paragraphs should be coherent, complete, unified, and the appropriate length for your message. Depending on that message, you may organize your paragraphs according to any of the patterns explained on pages 41–47. A long piece of writing will contain paragraphs following many or all of these patterns. Once you can construct a paragraph as a unified information block, you will have mastered one of the basics of writing.

☞ Exercises

1. The following sentences would be poor choices for topic sentences because they are too broad. They do not help a reader focus on a single, unified topic. Revise these sentences to make them suitable topic sentences by restricting the topic. The first one has been done for you.
   (a) Highway safety saves lives. (Traffic engineers have found that artificial lighting can reduce night accidents.)
   (b) Cable stations offer many benefits to subscribers throughout America.
   (c) Our company would be interested if conditions were right.
   (d) The Social Security System is under attack.
   (e) Auto mechanics (or welding, or any field) is an exciting profession.
   (f) A job applicant's qualifications mean a lot.
   (g) Banks play a significant role in the economy.
   (h) Medical science can perform wonders.
   (i) Knowledge of chemistry will help all students.
   (j) This is a big year for our school.
   (k) Vacations can be taken anywhere and at anytime.

2. Write a complete, unified, and coherent paragraph on one of the topic sentences you revised for exercise 1.

3. The following paragraphs lack a topic sentence. Supply an appropriate topic sentence for each of these paragraphs and explain how your topic sentence will help readers follow the paragraph better.
   (a) Certainly customers in wheelchairs would most directly benefit from this change. Individuals who wear braces, who use a cane or a walker, or who need other types of assistance find it difficult to walk up a flight of stairs. Individuals with asthma or other breathing problems often find stairs a menace. In addition to these individuals, parents with

small children in carts or strollers would find the ramp convenient. Older citizens, too, would benefit from this small but significant alteration in the front of the building.

(b) Maryville Power Association (MPA) now has more than 12,600 circuit-miles of high-voltage lines and 339 substations. Of its existing lines, about 70 percent of the circuit miles are 230,000 volts or higher. The grid is connected at more than 100 locations with 17 other transmission systems. Besides scheduling and dispatching power from the federal dams, MPA exchanges over its grid about 8 million kilowatts of power for non-federal utilities. In total, MPA supplies about 50 percent of the power generated in the region and transmits about 80 percent of the region's power.

(c) In a 1978 study carried out by the National Institute for Occupational Safety and Health (NIOSH), the medical technologist ranked seventh in work-related stress out of 130 professions. By 1980 the medical technologist had moved up to the number four spot. The study concluded that this stressful environment results from the demands of the medical technologist's job. These demands include making life-and-death decisions, communicating with a variety of highly trained health-care professionals, and working long hours, including nights and weekends. Having to prepare reports in very short times under trying conditions was also a contributing factor.

4. The topic sentence is buried in each of the following paragraphs. Find it and rewrite it if necessary and then put it first in the paragraph. If necessary, revise the other sentences in the paragraph to account for the change.

(a) For a noise barrier to work, it must be high and long enough to block the view of a road. Noise barriers do very little good for homes on a hillside overlooking a road or for buildings that rise above the barrier. Noise barriers can have functional limitations. Openings in the noise barrier for driveway connections or intersecting streets destroy its effectiveness, too. In some areas, homes are scattered too far apart to permit noise barriers to be built at a reasonable cost.

(b) Sometimes shoplifters have special hooks or belts on the insides of their coats; or they wear tricky aprons and undergarments, which are designed to hold innumerable articles. Some sleight-of-hand thieves slip merchandise into packages or into boxes that have a hinged top, bottom, or end. Salesclerks should know how to spot devices used by shoplifters. Employees should also be suspicious of and watch shoppers who carry bulky packages, knitting bags, shopping bags, and umbrellas. These are handy receptacles for items that a shoplifter purposely knocks off counters.

5. The following paragraphs lack unity. Rewrite them to eliminate unnecessary or irrelevant information.

(a) The Hanks Company has decided to construct its new lighting store in

Burton Hills to attract more customers. This location will serve a busy market of 200,000 customers from Pasco, Downers Grove, and Middletown. Customers in these areas will no longer have to make an hour-long drive to Omaha for special lighting. The new lighting center offers them 23,000 sq. ft. of display space and gives the Hanks Company one of the largest stores in the region. This new location will also attract customers from the Portersville community, who must frequently drive to Omaha. The financing of the lighting center will be done by Perry and Associates of Fort Worth.

(b) A person does not need extensive training to operate the new microcomputer effectively. In many ways, it is no more difficult to operate than a typewriter. Our employees did object, however, to giving up their typewriters; some of these machines have been in the company for 10 years. The microcomputer uses a very simple language called BASIC. This language was developed about 15 years ago and has worked well in other offices like ours. Written in English, BASIC can be taught to our operators in less than a day. Storage capacity and speed will make the microcomputer a valuable addition in the office for our operators.

6. The following paragraphs lack coherence. Rewrite them using the four techniques discussed in this chapter: transitional words and phrases, repetition of key words, the use of personal pronouns and demonstrative adjectives, and grammatical parallelism.

(a) High-altitude photography has many uses. Land forms are measured and mapped. Accuracy is important for the measurement of water and other resources. Foresters find out the volume of trees, and foresters will be interested in knowing whether the trees are infested. Wildlife can be measured. Future highways and pipelines are always sketched out on the drawing board. Aerial photography helps city planners and geologists. Applications include shoreline changes. Geologists can measure the damage caused by floods. Changes in the landscape come from storms and hurricanes. Aerial photography records important data.

(b) Our company prefers the Lodex word processors. The other models are expensive. About $300.00 separates the price of a Lodex from the prices charged by other vendors. The service contract provides us with good terms. Repairs are made free of charge for the first 90 days. A discount on parts is available at 30 percent. Flexible software will help our efficiency. Other vendors have limited means. Lodex provides 12 hours of free instruction for our staff.

7. For each of the following topic sentences, explain which pattern(s) of paragraph organization would be most appropriate and why.

(a) Computer time-sharing offers the small business many financial advantages over buying its own hardware.

(b) Installing three ceiling fans saved the office more than $200.00 on our electric bill last month.

(c) Vandalism is behavior that defaces or destroys property.

(d) Over the last seven years video games have become more sophisticated.

(e) Enzymes in our mouth help us to digest the food we eat.

(f) The living room was redecorated from floor to ceiling.

(g) Today a nurse must be a budget director as well as a care giver.

(h) Computer graphics offers a business many advantages over traditional, manual graphics.

(i) Ergonomics is the applied science of designing equipment to meet the needs of workers.

(j) The mailroom has changed from sorting mail manually to sorting it by electronic scanning.

(k) After inspecting the property on November 30, I found that the major deterioration had begun in the basement and spread upstairs.

(l) For many workers coffee is a necessary evil.

(m) The new credit policy was primarily designed to help customers buy larger quantities of goods.

(n) A door lock has a number of important, interconnected parts.

(o) For all practical purposes, ours is a paperless office.

(p) A large oak tree looks like a multicolored umbrella.

(q) The U.S. Postal Service instituted the nine-digit zip code to speed the delivery of mail.

(r) Over-the-counter drugs are packaged to protect consumers from poisoning.

(s) The gears on a ten-speed bicycle are part of a complex network.

(t) Music videos are mini-musicals.

(u) If not used properly, pesticides are poisonous to people and pets.

(v) Because the park was not carefully kept up, patron use dropped 18 percent in the last six months.

(w) Based on their prices, houses in our town fall into one of four categories.

(x) A roof includes more than just shingles.

8. From the topic sentences in exercise 7, select three which follow different patterns of organization and write an appropriate paragraph for each of these.

9. Analyze the paragraphs included in the following article, "Emergency Preparedness Via Cable TV." Classify them according to the four types, and according to pattern(s) of organization. List the transitional words or phrases used to link paragraphs.

Emergency Preparedness Via Cable TV

By William Rushton

(1) In any kind of emergency, most Americans turn first to their television sets. Because 98 percent of U.S. homes have TV sets, television is the most immediate and available communications resource we have. Proper understanding of emerging communications technologies and some advance planning on the local level would enable us to enhance significantly the usefulness of this resource for emergency purposes.

(2) Chief among these new technologies is cable television, which currently is capable of bringing 50 or more channels by wire into homes. In the past these houses could at best receive only a dozen or so channels "over the air." Cable is the highway of the new telecommunications environment, distributing programs from broadcast stations, satellites, microwave feeds, and local nonbroadcast origination studios ("access centers"). These cable services offer a wide variety of traditional entertainment and a new world of nonentertainment services. By the end of this decade, the vast majority of Americans will have access to cable services.

(3) Cable's multiplicity of channels gives rise to "narrowcasting," the targeting of a small segment of an audience and programming its specific needs. Access channels, particularly government access channels, can be used for programs that discuss very narrow and specific issues, with phone-in discussion by the target audience involved. Cable's initial role, therefore, might be in planning for energy emergency preparedness. Phone-in cable shows, for example, offer a mechanism by which the government can *interact* with its citizens.

(4) Another major advantage in using cable in emergency situations is its localism. In most states, cable utilities are franchised by local municipalities, offering access channels (similar to a local community TV "station") to communities that might not have a local broadcast station. During the blizzard of 1978, for example, the town of Danbury, Connecticut (which has no broadcast television station) effectively used its cable system as a 24-hour emergency information center.

(5) Many cable systems have specific emergency facilities built in, such as an emergency command station or a direct feed from such a facility. Moreover, the centralized nature of cable distribution (from a processing center called a "head end") allows a cable operator to run an electronic message (or "crawl") along the bottom of the screen on all channels simultaneously, announcing an emergency and calling public attention to a specific channel for relevant emergency details. In the case of a derailed tank car of hazardous chemicals, for example, or a zone downwind from a nuclear power plant accident, it might be easier to reach the affected area by phone calls or electronic messages directly to a cable system or two than to try to reach all the broadcast stations, running the risk of panic in nonaffected areas. Instructions to one zone might be vastly different from instructions to another. Moreover, new devices are on the market now that

U.S. Department of Energy, *The Energy Consumer* (Dec. 1980–Jan. 1981): 24.

would allow your cable to signal you even if the television set is off, a service no broadcast outlet can offer.

(6) Another advantage of cable TV is that in the event of a severe long-term emergency—such as disruptions of imported oil supplies, with resulting restriction on private auto use—cable television offers what may be our only long-term solution for certain public information-dissemination and service-delivery tasks. "Teleconferences," "telecourses," and "telemedicine" (preventive medical care and social work activities) can be offered over cable *without the need of the viewer to travel.* Not all information or social service activities can be conveyed on cable, of course, but enough of them can be so that any medium-to-long-range energy crisis could be made more manageable. In the long term, cable might be our only choice to curtailing or eliminating such services altogether in an emergency.

(7) In conclusion, cable television can provide many emergency services for the public good. The technology is here, and its applications are proven and helpful.

3

Writing: Sentences

A successful paragraph depends on successful sentences. If you develop confidence in your ability to construct sentences and link them together so that your message is clear, you will make good progress toward writing clearly and persuasively.

The way in which you construct sentences can determine whether you succeed or fail in writing. Sentences will tell readers how well, or poorly, you combine words to express thoughts. If your sentences are clear, varied, and concise, readers will find your messages easier to understand and act on. Moreover, they will thank you for not having to reread your work in order to understand your message. On the other hand, if your sentences are unclear, immature, crowded with excess baggage, or illogical, readers will question your powers of reasoning and action. Employers will certainly not reward writers who embarrass them or cost the company money because of unclear or misleading sentences.

Chapter 3 supplies you with the fundamental information you need to write effective sentences. The chapter begins with some basics in sentence structure and punctuation and then turns to ways of writing clear and lean sentences. By studying this chapter carefully you will learn to

1. Construct and punctuate sentences correctly
2. Use the appropriate voice—active or passive
3. Use parallelism
4. Write sentences that say what you mean
5. Write sentences that are economical and easy to read

☞ Constructing and Punctuating Sentences

A sentence is a complete thought that is expressed by a subject and a verb and that makes sense and can stand alone. The first step toward success in writing sentences is learning to recognize the differences between phrases and clauses.

The Difference Between Phrases and Clauses

A *phrase* is a group of words that does not contain a subject and a verb; phrases cannot stand alone to make sense. Phrases cannot be sentences.

in the park	*No subject:*	Who is in the park?
	No verb:	What was done in the park?
for every patient in intensive care	*No subject:*	Who did something for every patient?
	No verb:	What was done for the patients?

A *clause* does contain a subject and a verb, but—*and this is important*—not every clause is a sentence. Only independent clauses can stand alone as sentences. Here is an example of an independent clause that is a complete sentence.

> *subject*   *verb*   *object*
> The president closed the college.

A dependent (or subordinate) clause also contains a subject and a verb, but does not make complete sense and cannot stand alone. Why? A dependent clause contains a subordinating conjunction—*after, although, as, because, before, even though, if, since, unless, when, where, whereas, while*—at the beginning of the clause. Such conjunctions subordinate the clause in which they appear and make the clause dependent for meaning and completion on an independent (or main) clause.

> After
> Before
> Because $\left.\right\}$ the president closed the college
> Even though
> Unless

"After the president closed the college" is not a complete thought. This dependent clause leaves us in suspense. It needs to be completed with an independent clause telling us what happened "after."

> *dependent clause*   *independent clause*
>   *subject   verb   phrase*
> After the president closed the college,   we   played   in the snow.

Sentence Fragments

Complete sentences do not leave the reader hanging in mid-air, wondering who did something, how it was done, or under what conditions it was done. An incomplete sentence is called a *fragment*. Fragments are phrases or dependent clauses. They either lack a verb or a subject or have broken away from an independent (main) clause. A fragment is isolated; it needs an overhaul to supply missing parts to turn it into an independent clause or to glue it back to the independent clause from which it became separated.

You can avoid writing sentence fragments by following a few rules. In the next few pages, incorrect examples are preceded by a minus sign; corrected versions, by a plus sign.

1. *Every sentence must have a subject telling the reader who does the action.*

   − Being extra careful not to spill the water. (Who?)
   + The aide was extra careful not to spill the water.

2. *Every sentence must have a complete verb.* Watch especially for verbs ending in *-ing*. They need another verb (some form of *to be* or *have*) to make them complete.

   − The woman in the blue uniform. (What did she do?)
   + The woman in the blue uniform directed traffic.
   − The machine running in the computer department. (Did what?)

   You can change the last fragment into a sentence by supplying the correct form of the verb.

   + The machine *is* running in the computer department.
   + The machine *runs* in the computer department.

   Or you can revise the entire sentence, adding a new thought.

   + The machine running in the computer department handles all new accounts.

3. *Do not detach prepositional phrases* (beginning with *at, by, for, from, in, to, with,* and so forth) *from independent clauses.* Such phrases are not complete thoughts and cannot stand alone. Correct the error by leaving the phrases attached to the sentence to which they belong.

   − By three o'clock the next day. (What was to happen?)
   + The supervisor wanted our reports by three o'clock the next day.
   − For every patient in intensive care. (What was done?)
   + Nurses kept hourly reports for every patient in intensive care.

4. *Do not use a subordinate clause as a sentence.* To avoid this kind of sentence fragment, simply join the two clauses (the independent clause and the dependent clause containing a subordinating conjunction) with a comma— *not* a period or semicolon.

   − Unless we agreed to the plan. (What would happen?)
   − Unless we agreed to the plan; the project manager would discontinue the operation. (A semicolon cannot set off the subordinate clause.)
   + Unless we agreed to the plan, the project manager would discontinue the operation.

− Because safety precautions were taken. (What happened?)
+ Because safety precautions were taken, ten construction workers escaped injury.

Sometimes subordinate clauses appear at the end of a sentence. They may be introduced by a subordinate conjunction, an adverb, or a relative pronoun (*that, which, who*). Do not separate these clauses from the preceding independent clause with a period, thus turning them into fragments.

− Some of the new employees selected the high-risk option in their policy. While others did not.
+ Some of the new employees selected the high-risk option in their policy while others did not. (The *while* subordinates the clause, and therefore that clause cannot stand alone.)
− An all-volunteer fire department posed some problems. Especially for residents in the southern part of town.
+ An all-volunteer fire department posed some problems, especially for residents in the southern part of town.

(The word *especially* qualifies *problems,* referred to in the independent clause.)

The Comma Splice

Writing fragments involves using only bits and pieces of complete sentences. Another common error that some writers commit involves just the reverse kind of action. They weakly and wrongly join two complete sentences (independent clauses) with a comma as if those two sentences were really only one sentence. This error is called a *comma splice.* Here is an example:

− Gasoline prices have risen by 10 percent in the last month, we will drive the car less often.

Two independent clauses (complete sentences) exist:

Gasoline prices have risen by 10 percent in the last month.
We will drive the car less often.

A comma alone lacks the power to separate independent clauses. As the preceding example shows, many pronouns are used as the subjects of independent clauses—*I, he, she, it, we, they.* A comma splice will result if you place only a comma between two independent clauses where the second clause opens with a pronoun:

− Mary approved the plan, she liked its cost-effective approach.
+ Mary approved the plan; she liked its cost-effective approach.

However, relative pronouns (*who, whom, which, that*) are not preceded by a period or semicolon unless they introduce a question:

- − She approved the plan. Which had the cost-effective approach.
- + She approved the plan, which had the cost-effective approach.
- + Which plan had the cost effective approach?

Four Ways to Correct Comma Splices

1. *Remove the comma separating two independent clauses and replace it with a period.* Then capitalize the first letter of the first word of the newly reinstated sentence.

   + Gasoline prices have risen by 10 percent in the last month. We will drive the car less often.

2. *Delete the comma and insert a semicolon.*

   + Gasoline prices have risen by 10 percent in the last month; we will drive the car less often.

   The semicolon is an effective and forceful punctuation mark when the two independent clauses are closely related—that is, when they announce contrasting or parallel views, as the two following examples reveal:

   + The union favored the new legislation; the company opposed it. (contrasting views)
   + Night classes help the college and the community; more students can take more credit hours. (parallel views)

3. *Insert a coordinating conjunction* (and, but, or, nor, for, yet) *after the comma.* Together, the conjunction and the comma properly separate the two independent clauses.

   + Gasoline prices have risen by 10 percent in the last month, and we will drive the car less often.

4. *Rewrite the sentence* (if it makes sense to do so). Turn the first independent clause into a dependent clause by adding a subordinate conjunction; insert a comma and add the second independent clause.

   + Because gasoline prices have risen by 10 percent in the last month, we will drive the car less often.

(Of the four ways to correct the comma splice, the last example is the most suitable for the sample sentence, because the price of gasoline affects how much a car is driven.)

How Not to Correct Comma Splices

Some writers mistakenly try to correct comma splices by inserting a conjunctive adverb (*also, consequently, furthermore, however, moreover, nevertheless, then, therefore*) after the comma.

> – Gasoline prices have risen by 10 percent in the last month, consequently we will drive the car less often.

But because the conjunctive adverb (*consequently*) is not as powerful as the coordinating conjunction (*and, but, for*), the error is not eliminated. If you use a conjunctive adverb—*consequently, however, nevertheless*—insert a semicolon or a period before it, as the following examples show:

> + Gasoline prices have risen by 10 percent in the last month; consequently, we will drive the car less often.
> + Gasoline prices have risen by 10 percent in the last month. Consequently, we will drive the car less often.

☞ Using the Appropriate Voice: Active or Passive

"Voice" refers to whether the subject of a sentence performs the action or receives it. In the active voice a subject performs the action and so appears in the first (and subject) part of the sentence. In the passive voice the subject becomes the recipient of the action and no longer occupies the first part of the sentence, but now appears in the last part or is even omitted.

Active voice: The recruiting staff made three visits.

Passive voice: Three visits were made by the recruiting staff.

Passive voice: Three visits were made.

In sentence 1 the writer stresses the actions of the staff. In sentence 2 and especially in 3 the writer is more interested in the number of visits than in who made them.

When to Use the Active Voice

The active voice is usually more forceful and direct than is the passive voice. It generally requires fewer words than the passive voice. Sentence 2 contains two more words than are in sentence 1: "were" and "by." These extra words show how passives are formed. Verbs in the passive voice are constructed with some form of the verb *to be* followed by a *past participle* (here *made*); often a prepositional phrase with *by* indicates the presence of a passive verb ("by the recruiting staff"). You can often change the passive into the active voice by making the subject of the sentence what is included in the *by* phrase: "The recruiting staff made three visits."

Since both the active and the passive voices have advantages, use both in your work. The active voice, however, offers writers these benefits:

1. The active voice gives instructions authority and clarity.

   Active: Remove the hex nut.

   Passive: The hex nut should be removed.

   Active: Wear protective eyeglasses.

   Passive: Protective eyeglasses should be worn.

2. The active voice can eliminate awkwardness.

   Active: I completed two years of technical training.

   Passive: Two years of technical training were completed by me.

   Active: Ms. Rodgers spoke about the new design.

   Passive: The new design was spoken about by Ms. Rodgers.

3. The active voice lets readers know that another person, not a machine, is writing to them in letters and reports.

   Active: The tour director arranged the plans for your travel.

   Passive: Plans have been arranged for your travel.

   Active: I can make an appointment for you.

   Passive: An appointment can be made for you.

You will find that using sentences in the active voice will make your letters and reports easier to read and to follow. The active voice shows exactly who is in charge and who has accomplished certain tasks.

When to Use the Passive Voice

Scientists often use the passive voice in order to emphasize the experiment or the procedure rather than the individual performing it. They believe that references to "I" detract from the objectivity of the work. Many scientists would prefer the second of the following two sentences:

Active: The biologist performed the experiment three times in forty-eight hours.

Passive: The experiment was performed three times in forty-eight hours.

Clearly, some contexts call for the "I" and the active voice in reporting scientific data. But the passive voice does have its advantages when you are writing about a process—changing hydrogen and oxygen into water, for example—when the emphasis is not on the human actor, but on the changes brought about through scientific law.

The passive voice also serves the following useful functions:

1. The passive voice can be used when the actor is unknown.

   The car was stolen at noon. (The thief's identity is not known.)

   The practice was started in 1955. (Who started it is not known.)

   Monthly house payments are scaled down during the first five years of the mortgage. (By whom?)

2. The passive voice can be used when the object is more important for the reader than is the actor.

   The injection of insulin was given at 6:30 A.M.

   Pieces of the bullet were found in the dining room wall.

   The generator was periodically inspected.

3. The passive voice can be used as a business strategy when anonymity is necessary or when emphasis on the subject has unfavorable moral implications. Compare these two sentences:

   Mr. Jones fired the mechanic.

   The mechanic was fired.

   The first sentence emphasizes the fact that it was Mr. Jones who dismissed the mechanic; the second sentence does not even mention Mr. Jones. Sometimes for legal reasons a person's identity must be kept secret:

   The juvenile was arraigned in court.

   The suspect's identity was not revealed by the police.

   The pilot's license was suspended by the Board.

☞ Using Parallelism

Parallelism expresses the similarity of ideas by placing them in the same grammatical form. Parallel forms may use the same part of speech or the same type of phrase or clause. Using parallel grammatical units for parallel ideas enables you to group related points, to clarify relationships, and to emphasize your message for readers. Readers seeing repeated grammatical forms will find it easier to read your work and to understand the comparisons you are making. To use parallelism effectively, make sure that the grammatical forms are the same and that the ideas actually are equal and related. The following examples show parallelism in grammatical forms:

Present participle:	listening	reading	writing	speaking
Infinitive:	to listen	to read	to write	to speak
Noun:	listener	reader	writer	speaker
Lack of parallelism:	to listen	reading	writing	to speak

The writer's duties specified in the following list are parallel because they have equal importance and because they are expressed with the same grammatical form (all start with present participles):

The specific duties of a proposal writer involve

- defining the problem for readers
- describing the solution
- establishing a schedule
- planning a budget
- assigning personnel
- writing progress reports

Note how parallelism is violated in the next example in which each duty is expressed in a different grammatical form:

The specific duties of a proposal writer involve

- defining the problem for readers
- the need to describe the solution
- establishment of a schedule
- is responsible for budget plans
- has assigned personnel
- writes progress reports

Note how the writer of the following sentence calls attention to the report's characteristics through the series of adjectives.

The report was clear, concise, and informative.

Compare the following faulty sentences (in which words are not parallel) with the corrected versions.

Faulty: The student was enthusiastic, cooperative, and she knew the material very well. (After two parallel adjectives, the writer introduces an independent clause and thus destroys the parallelism.)

Correct: The student was enthusiastic, cooperative, and knowledgeable. (all adjectives)

When you list a group of parallel words in a series, be sure that you are consistent in using *the, a, in,* or *that* with them. Use the article, preposition, or pronoun either before each element or before only the first element.

Faulty: We have stores in Cleveland, Detroit, Kokomo, and in Chicago.

Correct: We have stores in Cleveland, in Detroit, in Kokomo, and in Chicago.

Correct: We have stores in Cleveland, Detroit, Kokomo, and Chicago.

Parallelism is used with prepositional phrases to group related information.

Faulty: The new lights were installed within the hallways, on the roof, and they were included in the parking lot, too.

Correct: The new lights were installed within the hallways, on the roof, and in the parking lot.

Parallelism of clauses works well as long as you warn readers by beginning each clause in exactly the same way:

Faulty: Hiring qualified employees is a matter of screening applicants carefully, interviewing them diplomatically, and then to run a reference check.

Correct: Hiring qualified employees is a matter of screening applicants carefully, interviewing them diplomatically, and running a reference check.

Establishing proper parallelism can be especially tricky in sentences that use the following *correlative conjunctions—either/or, neither/nor,* and *both/and.* Keep in mind that the information on either side of these correlatives has to be grammatically identical. Study the following faulty examples and their revisions.

Faulty: He told the operator to either repair the equipment or to replace it. (*Either* is *in the middle of* one infinitive and its counterpart *or* is *in front of* the other infinitive.)

Correct: He told the operator either to repair the equipment or to replace it. (Both *either* and *or* have the same position—before the infinitive.)

Faulty: All employees are entitled to both fifteen vacation days and to eight holidays. (This is confusing; do the employees receive two fifteen-day vacation periods?)

Correct: All employees are entitled both to fifteen vacation days and to eight holidays.

☞ Writing Sentences That Say What You Mean

Your sentences should say exactly what you mean—without double-talk, misplaced humor, or nonsense. Sentences are composed of words and word groups that influence each other. Like molecules, they bump and rub into each other, exerting a strong reciprocal influence. The kinds of errors discussed in this section can be eliminated if you remind yourself to read your sentences to see how one group of words fits into and relates to another.

Logical Sentences

Sentences should not contradict themselves or make outlandish claims. The following examples contain such errors; note how easily the suggested revisions handle the problem.

Illogical: The manager's order establishes a new precedent for our time. (A precedent is something that has already been established; hence it cannot be new.)

Revision: The manager's order will establish a precedent.

Illogical: Steel roll-away shutters make it possible for the sun to be shaded in the summer and to have it shine in the winter. (The sun is far too large to shade; the writer meant that a room or a house, much smaller than the sun, could be shaded with the shutters.)

Revision: Steel roll-away shutters make it possible for owners to shade their living rooms in the summer and to admit sunshine during the winter.

Sentences Using Contextually Appropriate Words

Sentences should use the combination of words most appropriate for the subject matter you are writing about. Here are some illustrations of sentences containing inappropriate words, together with suggested revisions:

Inappropriate: The building materials need to be explained in small, concrete steps. (The writer was thinking of "concrete" in terms of teaching; the context, though, encourages the reader to picture cement stairs.)

Revision: The building materials need to be explained separately and carefully.

Inappropriate: The members of the Nuclear Regulatory Commission saw fear radiated on the faces of the residents. (The word "radiated" is obviously ill-advised; use a neutral term.)

Revision: The members of the Nuclear Regulatory Commission saw fear reflected on the faces of the residents.

Inappropriate: The game warden is shooting for an increase in the number of nonresident licenses this year.

Revision: The game warden hopes to increase the number of nonresident licenses this year.

Sentences with Well-Placed Modifiers

A *modifier* is a word, phrase, or clause that describes, limits, or qualifies the meaning of another word or word group. A modifier can consist of one word (a *green* car), a prepositional phrase (the man *in the telephone booth*), a relative clause (the woman *who won the marathon*), or an *-ing* or *-ed* phrase (*walking three miles a day,* the man was in good shape; *seated in the first row,* we saw everything on stage). You will learn more about modifiers and readability on page 71.

A *dangling modifier* is one that cannot logically modify any word in the sentence.

– When answering the question, his notebook fell off the table.

To correct the error, insert the right subject after the *-ing* phrase.

+ When answering the question, he knocked his notebook off the table.

You can also turn the phrase into a subordinate clause:

+ When he answered the question, his notebook fell off the table.
+ His notebook fell off the table as he answered the question.

A *misplaced modifier* illogically modifies the wrong word or words in the sentence. The result is often comical.

− Hiding in the corner, growling and snarling, our guide caught the frightened cub. (Is our guide growling and snarling in the corner?)
− All travel requests must be submitted by employees in green ink. (Are the employees covered in green ink?)

The problem with both of the examples above is word order. The modifiers are misplaced because they are attached to the wrong words in the sentence. Correct the error by moving the modifier where it belongs.

+ Hiding in the corner, growling and snarling, the frightened cub was caught by our guide.
+ All travel requests by employees must be submitted in green ink.

Misplaced modifiers may also be corrected by recasting the sentence.

+ While the frightened cub was hiding in the corner, growling and snarling, our guide caught it.
+ Our guide caught the growling and snarling, frightened cub, which was hiding in the corner.

Note that each "correct" version has a slightly different emphasis; the choice depends on the aspect of the situation you wish to stress.

Misplacing a relative clause (introduced by such relative pronouns as *who, whom, that, which*) can also lead to problems with modification.

− Our firm decided not to move to the office in Salem that needs remodeling. (It is the office, not the town, that needs to be remodeled.)
+ Our firm decided not to move to the office that needs remodeling in Salem.
− The salesperson recorded the merchandise for the customer that the store had discounted. (The merchandise was discounted, not the customer.)
+ The salesperson recorded the merchandise that the store had discounted for the customer.

To avoid problem sentences like those above, always place the relative clause immediately after the word it modifies.

Correct Use of Pronoun References in Sentences

Sentences will be vague if they contain a faulty use of pronouns. When you use a pronoun whose *antecedent* (the person, place, or object the pronoun is referring to) is unclear, you risk confusing your reader. Here are some examples of unclear pronoun references, with revisions following:

Unclear:	After the plants are clean, we separate the stems from the roots and place them in the sun to dry. (Is it the stems or the roots that lie in the sun?)
Revision:	After the plants are clean, we separate the stems from the roots and place the stems in the sun to dry.
Unclear:	The park ranger was pleased to see the workers planting new trees and installing new benches. This will attract more tourists. (The trees or the benches?)
Revision:	The park ranger was pleased to see the workers planting new trees and installing new benches, for the new trees will attract more tourists.
Unclear:	When Bill talked with his boss, he became angry. (Who became angry, Bill or his boss?)
Revision:	When he talked with his boss, Bill became angry.

You can correct faulty pronoun references by replacing the unclear pronoun with the noun it stands for as in the last example where the vague *he* in the independent clause is replaced by the clear and specific *Bill*. The reader will then know exactly which word is the subject or object of the sentence. Another way to correct misleading pronouns is to rewrite the sentence.

☞ Seven Guidelines for Writing Readable Sentences

As you have seen, sentences need to be grammatically correct and punctuated properly. But if you want to write successfully, your sentences must also be easy to read. In fact, one of the biggest complaints in the business world is that something is hard to read. The problem almost always lies in the writer's poor sentences. Because the writer did not consider the reader's needs, such sentences are often long, unclear, and in the passive voice. When you write unclear sentences, you force the reader to reread and puzzle over your work. This confusion wastes time and causes the reader frustration. Write to be understood the first time. Write to inform, not mystify, your readers.

This section will give you seven specific guidelines to follow to help you write easy-to-read—lean and clean—sentences. As you study these guidelines, keep in mind that readability depends on the following:

- the length of your sentences
- the order in which you list information in your sentences
- the way in which you signal the relationships of your sentences

1. *Write sentences that tell who does what to whom or what.*
   The clearest sentence pattern in English is the subject-verb-object (*s-v-o*) pattern.

     s   *v*   *o*
   Sue mowed the grass.

            s   *v*   *o*
   Today's newspaper contains a special supplement on our school.

This pattern tells who does what to whom. Readers find this pattern easiest to read and understand because it provides direct and specific information about the action. Hard-to-read sentences obscure or scramble information about the subject, the verb, or the object. Poor writers, for example, bury the subject in prepositional phrases in the middle or the end of the sentence or smother the verb in phrases, or allow an object to act like a subject.

Not all clear sentences, however, follow the subject-verb-object pattern. You might use a subordinate clause in addition to the subject, verb, and object in the independent clause. Regardless of your sentence pattern, you owe readers clear information on who performs what action to whom.

To write sentences that tell readers clearly what's going on, follow these steps. First, identify the subject—the person, place, or concept that controls the main action. (Avoid using vague words such as *factors, conditions, processes,* or *elements* for subjects; these words will lead to trouble.) Next, select an action-packed verb that shows what the subject does. Then point out the object that is acted upon by the real subject through the verb.

In the following unclear sentences, subjects are hidden in the middle of their sentences. Revised, these sentences clearly tell what has happened.

Unclear: The preparation of the patient for surgery was done correctly by the nurse. (Who did what to whom?)

Clear: The nurse prepared the patient correctly for surgery.

Unclear: An assessment of the market helped our company design its new food blender. (The main action is designing. Who did it?)

Clear: Our company designed its new food blender by assessing the market.

Unclear: The fact that delivery schedules were changed hurt our business. (Who is the subject—*the fact that?* delivery schedules? What actually hurt business?)

Clear: Changes in delivery schedules hurt our business.

Unclear: The control of the ceiling limits of glycidyl ethers on the part of the employers for the optimum safety of workers in the workplace is necessary. (Who is responsible for taking action? What action did they take? For whom was that action taken?)

Clear: Employers must control the ceiling limits of glycidyl ethers for the safety of workers.

Start your sentence with its real subject. Don't delay the subject by putting unimportant or unnecessary words ahead of it. For example, you give readers a false and slow start by beginning with a dummy subject such as *there is/there are, it appears that, it seems that.* These impersonal constructions push the real subject back and make it harder to read the sentence. The result is a wordy and less emphatic sentence as the following examples show.

Dummy subject: There is only one option that is feasible.

Real subject: Only one option is feasible.

Dummy subject: There were many times during the trial when the defense attorney asked for a recess.

Real subject: The defense attorney asked for a recess many times during the trial.

Dummy subject: It is essential to realize that each quarter the manager needs accurate figures to prepare the budget.

Real subject: The manager needs accurate figures each quarter to prepare the budget.

2. *Arrange information logically within your sentences.*

The order in which you list information within a sentence can help or hinder a reader in understanding your message. You cannot list details in just any order. Construct your sentences to make sure readers receive information in the most logical, helpful way. The pattern you use will, of course, depend on your topic. The content of the sentence will help you to choose the more logical pattern: chronological, cause to effect, action to reaction, and the like.

Poor: They shut the computer off once they finish with their program.

More logical: Once they finish their program, they shut the computer off. (Since finishing the program precedes shutting the computer off, give readers the information in this order.)

Poor: My strengths are in neurological and geriatric nursing to give you some background about my work experiences.

More logical: To give you some background about my work experiences, my strengths are in neurological and geriatric nursing. (Tell readers why you are giving them the details first, so that they know what the details mean.)

3. *Avoid needlessly complex or lengthy sentences.*

How long should your sentence be? The answers to this question vary, depending on the educational level of your audience and the subject you are writing about. Be guided by one rule, however: write so that it is easy for your reader to understand you. Generally, the longer the sentence, the more difficult it is to understand; therefore, do not pile one clause on another. Most readers have very little trouble with sentences ranging from eight to fifteen words. On the other hand, readers find sentences over twenty to twenty-three words much more difficult. As a general rule, keep your sentences under twenty words in order to reach most readers; yet write like a mature and professional individual. The following sentence is too long for readers to understand, even the second time through. The revision is much easier to read.

Too long: The planning committee decided that the awards banquet should be held on May 15 at 6:30, since the other two dates (May 7 and May 22) suggested by the hospitality committee conflict with local sports events, even though one of those events could be changed to fit our needs.

Easier to read: The planning committee has decided to hold the awards banquet on May 15 at 6:30. The other dates suggested by the hospitality committee—May 7 and May 22—conflict with two local sports events. Although the date of one of those sports events could be changed, the planning committee still believes that May 15 is our best choice.

4. *Combine a series of short, choppy sentences.*
Avoiding long, complex sentences only to write short, simplistic ones will not make your reader's job easier. In fact, a memo, letter, or report written exclusively in short, staccato sentences makes for boring reading. They may adversely affect your reader's view of your message because such sentences sound immature. To avoid this error, vary your sentences both in length and structure. The most effective on-the-job writing blends short sentences with long ones to achieve variety and to reflect different logical relationships. For example, a sentence containing a subordinate clause followed by an independent clause may signal a cause-to-effect relationship to readers. A sentence with a series of parallel independent clauses points to the equality of the ideas spelled out in these clauses. A short sentence at the end of a paragraph can emphatically summarize a main idea. When you find yourself writing a series of short, choppy sentences, such as in the following example, combine them where possible and use connective words similar to those italicized in the revision.

Choppy: Secretaries have many responsibilities. Their responsibilities are important. They must answer telephones. They must take dictation. Sometimes the speaker talks very fast. Then the secretary must be quick to transcribe what is heard. Words could be missed. Secretaries must also type letters. This will take a great deal of time and concentration. These letters are copied and filed properly for reference.

Smoother: Secretaries have many important responsibilities. *These* include answering the telephones and taking dictation. *When* a speaker talks rapidly, the secretary will have to transcribe quickly *so* that no words are omitted. *Among the most demanding* of their duties are typing letters accurately *and then* making copies of them and filing those copies properly for future reference.

5. *Use active verbs rather than verb phrases where verbs are disguised as nouns.*
   To sound important many writers avoid using simple, graphic verbs (see page 85). Instead these bureaucratic writers add a suffix (*-ation, -ance, -ment, -ence*) to a direct verb (*determine*) to make a noun (*determination*) and then couple the new noun with *make, provide,* or *work* to produce a weak verb phrase (for example, *made a determination of, provide maintenance of, work in cooperation with*). A verb phrase imprisons the active verb inside a noun. The following weak sentences with verb phrases are rewritten to make them more readable and emphatic.

Weak: The officer made an assessment of the damages the storm had caused.

Strong: The officer assessed the damage the storm had caused.

Weak: The investigators made an entrance into the wilderness site at dusk.

Strong: The investigators entered the wilderness site at dusk.

Weak: The city provided the employment of two work crews to assist the strengthening of the dam.

Strong: The city employed two work crews to strengthen the dam.

6. *Avoid piling up modifiers in front of a noun.*
   It's hard for readers to grasp your message when you string a series of modifiers in front of a noun. Modifiers are subordinate units that should clarify and qualify the noun to which they refer. When you put too many of them in the reader's path to the noun, you confuse the reader who does not know how one modifier relates to another modifier or to the noun. To avoid this problem, rephrase the sentence by placing some of the modifiers in prepositional phrases after as well as before the nouns they modify.

Crowded: The ordinance contract number vehicle identification plate had to be checked against inventory numbers.

Spaced: The ordinance contract number on the vehicle identification plate had to be checked against the inventory numbers.

Crowded: The vibration noise control heat pump condenser quieter can make your customer happier.

Spaced: The quieter on the condenser for the heat pump will make your customer happier by controlling noise and vibrations.

7. *Avoid unnecessary* that/which *clauses.*
   Wordiness can be the writer's greatest weakness and the reader's most common complaint. (Chapter 4 will help you find the words and phrases you need for a more concise, direct style.) *That/which* clauses using some form of the verb *to be* (*is, are, were, was*) are infamous for adding words but

not meaning. They are popular with bureaucratic writers, who like to draw an idea out beyond the number of words it needs. The information contained in that/which clauses can often be adequately represented by an adjective as the following wordy sentences and their revisions show:

Wordy: The pain medication that was prescribed by the doctor was very helpful to her father.

Concise: The pain medication prescribed by the doctor helped her father. (Note how the revision reduces "was helpful to" to "helped" and thus saved words and time.)

Wordy: I think the news magazine, which appears bi-monthly, will be one which keeps employees up to date on current events at Balko Industries.

Concise: I think a bi-monthly magazine will keep employees informed about current events at Balko Industries.

Wordy: The organizational plan that was approved last week contains a number of points which are considered to be especially important for new employees.

Concise: The organizational plan approved last week contains important points for new employees.

☞ Writing Effective Sentences: A Brief Summary

Writing clear, readable sentences is easy if you remember the reader's needs. A reader wants to be able to get through a sentence and understand its message on the first attempt. To help readers do this, make sure that you punctuate sentences correctly, select verbs in the appropriate (usually active) voice, identify all pronoun references accurately, and follow the seven guidelines found on pages 68–72.

☞ Exercises

1. Punctuate the following sentences correctly.
    (a) Cooking can kill many bacteria in food, it cannot kill them all.
    (b) Bass fishing attracts many tourists to the lake. Not just during the summer but also during the fall.
    (c) No new accounts will be opened today, therefore the credit office is closed.
    (d) The charges for our service are reasonable, they come to barely $35.00.

(e) Ms. Jones-Fairley likes our contract, she will sign it and mail it tomorrow.

(f) The Land Rover is popular with sports enthusiasts partly because it is economical. And partly because it is so rugged.

(g) The patient received an injection for pain, however, he said that it did not help.

(h) Because real estate values soared; many buyers were unable to own their own homes. Which angered them.

(i) The college is offering five sections of Business English this term, many of them are in the late afternoon and night.

(j) The sales manager had to prepare her report by that afternoon. Because the buyer wanted to review it before the conference tomorrow.

(k) The buses left for Dayton punctually. On the hour and on the half.

2. The following sentences contain an awkward use of the passive voice. Rewrite them using the active voice to make them less awkward and easier to read.

(a) Little attention has been paid by your office to our request for additional information.

(b) The enclosed forms should be completed by you no later than August 15.

(c) The dinner was planned by her staff to celebrate her thirtieth birthday.

(d) A comet was seen by those citizens who stayed up late last evening.

(e) Discretion should be exercised by employees when answering complaint letters.

(f) Faster ways of notifying customers have been found by one of our employees.

(g) Appropriate uniforms were to be worn by all police officers attending the ceremony.

(h) The blocking of the canal had been planned by the Corps of Engineers for two years.

(i) It was determined by management not to approve a new employees' health center.

3. The following sentences contain errors in parallelism. Correct these sentences to make the grammatical units in them parallel.

(a) Willard likes swimming, hiking, and to fish.

(b) Silver is used in aerial photography, microfilming, for medical and industrial x-rays, and printers use it, too, to make photographic plates.

(c) Please return overshipments promptly and also I want you to reimburse any amounts paid over charges.

(d) You either must repair the circuit or it has to be replaced.

(e) Use a visual to emphasize key points, as a way of arousing interest, and when you want to summarize a lot of statistical data.

(f) The agency did not know who was responsible, where the individual lived, or the time the individual would return.

(g) In the saddle stitch method, printed material is bound using metal staples or cloth stitches are inserted.

(h) Once a conference is on our schedule, the personnel director is responsible for sending out announcements, the seating arrangements, what type of menu to serve, and also has to provide information on housing.

(i) The new Challenger word processor offers four advantages for our firm:

- it includes 15 software packages
- the warranty extends to 160 days
- provides a full-scale training program
- state-of-the-art features are included.

(j) During their orientation employees learn about company products and policies, how to prepare appropriate reports, and are introduced to the heads of the various departments.

(k) We received questions from customers on how long it takes to complete the process, the cost required for additional safety features used in the process, and whether marketing advantages associated with the process were present.

(l) The shipment neither was on time nor could it have been accurate.

(m) The local television station either had to change its programming or it would be in trouble with the FCC.

4. The following sentences are contradictory or contain words that are inappropriate for the context. Rewrite these sentences to correct the errors.

(a) In metric terms, our new olympic swimming pool is twenty-five feet long.

(b) His report discusses the differences in jogging between the United States and Great Britain.

(c) The operator fed the load onto the truck using a hydraulic fork.

(d) Sampling all of the residents of Cherry Hill, we found that 25 percent wanted the zoning laws to remain the same, 40 percent wanted them modified to include multiple family housing, and the other 45 percent wanted changes in housing and transportation.

(e) The watch commander was happy to report that convictions exceeded arrests.

(f) The local committee threw its spirited support behind the opposition to the new liquor laws.

(g) The nonsoluble retaining wall will let in only a small amount of water.

(h) New drilling techniques make it possible to create oil faster.

(i) The applicant did not plan ahead and was, therefore, ready for the interviewer's questions.

(j) Health food stores take a great interest in nuts.

5. Rewrite the following sentences to correct dangling and misplaced modifiers.

(a) When preparing school papers, your dictionary will be a great aid.
(b) Using the Heimlich maneuver, a bolus of food will be forced out of a person's airway.
(c) We purchased a new model from the salesclerk with adjustable arms.
(d) Topped with a tasty hollandaise sauce, the waiter brought us a delicious salad.
(e) Allowing for a 3 percent margin for error, the specifications arrived on the builder's desk this morning.
(f) Before turning the patient, intravenous solutions are given.
(g) The bank almost closed before we got there.
(h) Fastened securely, the officer left the compound.
(i) The teacher gave the test to the new student that covered the first third of the textbook.
(j) The plumber repaired the sink in our office that was stopped up since last week.
(k) The show dog ran away from the trainer with a leash around his neck.
(l) All travel requests must be submitted by employees in triplicate.
(m) The meal is prepared by the chef delicately seasoned with oregano.
(n) Almost maintenance-free, the housekeeper liked the new electric broom.
(o) Before placing the specimen under the microscope, proper care has to be taken.
(p) About the size of a quarter, most Americans did not like the Susan B. Anthony dollar.
(q) My neighbor went to see the dentist with a huge cavity.
(r) Turning the machine counterclockwise, the springs were loosened.
(s) The tax collector sent a bill to every property owner in Madison County that was due by April 1.

6. Rewrite the following sentences to correct faulty pronoun references.
   (a) The head nurse ordered the aide and the technician to help the patient in Room 334. She came at once.
   (b) The boss sent four different memos to the maintenance department about the problems with refuse on the weekends. They really made an impact on the department.
   (c) As Barbara saw Mary, she shouted with joy.
   (d) The filter was placed over the vent, but it was too small.
   (e) The machine had to be primed and oiled regularly, which insured a quick start.
   (f) An all-purpose battery would be better in this car than an expensive one.
   (g) The white mice were placed in the new cages, and they were to be cleaned daily.
   (h) Mr. Martin told Mr. Jones that he had found his glasses.
   (i) A check-up is important for good health. That is something you want to have.

    (j) Fourteen recruits joined the force in the months of July, August, and September. They will not be forgotten.

7. Rewrite the following sentences to make them easier to read. They contain one or more of the errors discussed on pages 67–72 of this chapter.

    (a) There are a number of businesses that have succumbed to failure recently due to the fact of their being mismanaged.

    (b) The work activities classification internal quarterly notification report is due at the end of this week.

    (c) Long open conveyor belts, which are used for the transportation of coal particles, can be considered to be a significant source of pollution.

    (d) It is, therefore, expensive to secure the importation of food from abroad because so much of it is shipped by costly carriers.

    (e) When mud guards have been allowed to drop down, damage may result to the side racks.

    (f) It seems apparent that there are a number of inconsistencies between the reports from Baxterville and New Platz.

    (g) The continuation of the fluoridation of the city water supply is advocated strenuously by the residents of West Allentown.

    (h) Since such material, which is normally considered to be confidential, would require the approval of several departments within the organization, it is unfortunate to note that the chances for public dissemination are currently negative.

    (i) Evasive action roadblock techniques diminish the promotion of terrorist activities.

    (j) Flowing from hot to cold substances, heat is a form of energy.

    (k) The power is supplied by a six-cylinder, in-line, liquid-cooled, standard-regulation, gasoline-powered engine located in the front of the truck.

    (l) To rotate the auger at a slower speed with more power, place the transmission in first gear.

    (m) Relative to emissions from the iron and steel processes, inspection techniques have certain fundamental characteristics regarding costs which are the same for every technique so used.

    (n) The recent purchase of a Multi-Writer can lead to the improvement of routine office data-processing functions, which will save the company many hours of time and dollars in costs provided that effective training programs accompany the acquisition of the Multi-Writer and that it does not become dated and that it is compatible with our existing data-processing equipment, which resulted in a large expenditure for the firm last year.

    (o) If it has the appearance of being spoiled or gives an emission of an odor, the destruction of the food shipment is imperative.

    (p) There are a number of precautions that it is believed by the Department of Public Safety must be put into effect within the next year.

4

Writing: Words

Words are the most basic units of writing. They are like bricks out of which you construct larger structures. If your words are correct, precise, and appropriate, then so too will be the letters, forms, and reports you fashion from those words. Chapter 4 discusses some of the most common problems writers face with words and offers some suggestions on how to avoid or repair ineffective word use. Specifically, after reading this chapter, you will learn to

1. Spell words correctly
2. Match the right word with the right meaning
3. Select precise words
4. Cut unnecessary words
5. Eliminate sexist language
6. Avoid jargon and slang

☞ Spelling Words Correctly

Your written work will be judged on how well you spell. A misspelled word may seem like a small matter, but on an employment application, incident report, or letter, it stands out to your discredit. Readers will inevitably wonder about your other skills if your spelling is incorrect.

Your professional work places a double duty on you as a speller. You must learn to spell correctly the technical terms of your field as well as the common words of the English language. The following suggestions can help to improve your spelling:

1. Keep a college-level dictionary at your desk (not on a shelf where you have to reach for it) and use it. Better yet, buy a small pocket dictionary and carry it with you.

2. Also keep on your desk a specialized dictionary or manual that lists technical vocabulary you use on your job.
3. Make a list of the words you have the most trouble spelling. Write them down in a small spiral notebook for easy reference. You can also place in this notebook any new and difficult words you encounter.
4. Double-check your spelling before submitting your work.

The chances are that many of the words you have trouble spelling are the same words that cause others difficulty. Alerting you to the following five danger areas may help you to spot words that are tricky to spell.

1. *Silent letters.*

a*c*quaint	fas*c*inate	le*i*sure
ai*s*le	for*e*arm	man*e*uver
as*c*end	ga*u*ge	min*i*ature
*c*holesterol	hemorr*h*age	mor*t*gage
code*i*ne	hyg*i*ene	n*e*utral
colum*n*	*k*napsack	vacu*u*m
diaphra*g*m	lik*e*ly	We*d*nesday

2. *Use of* ei *and* ie. *In general,* i *before* e, *except after* c.

ie	*ei*	*exceptions*
believe	ceiling	ancient
cashier	conceive	conscience
chief	deceive	deficient
experience	perceive	financier
yield	receive	society

3. *Double consonants.* Many words double a consonant when a verb changes from present to past tense (prefer / preferred) or when the root form changes from verb to noun (occur / occurrence).

   admit / admitted / admittance
   commit / committed / *but* commitment
   omit / omitted
   plan / planning
   repel / repelling / repellent
   write / written / *but* writing
   profit / *but* profited

4. *Prefixes and suffixes.* When adding a prefix (*un-, il-, mis-*), do not change the spelling of the word to which it is attached.

   *il*logical
   *mis*spell
   *un*necessary

Watch out for the following suffixes:

-able	*-iable*	*-ible*
acceptable	appreciable	audible
dependable	justifiable	combustible
noticeable	negotiable	edible
profitable	reliable	eligible
serviceable	variable	visible

5. *Plurals.*
   (a) When a word ends in *y*, drop the *y* and add *-ies* if the *y* follows a consonant: apology / apologies; army / armies; history / histories; library / libraries; party / parties. If the word ends in *y* and the *y* follows a vowel, just add *s*: bay / bays; toy / toys; turkey /turkeys.
   (b) Words that end in *f* or *fe sometimes* change these letters to *v* before adding *-es:* calf / calves; half /halves; knife / knives; life / lives; leaf / leaves; self / selves; shelf / shelves; wife / wives.
   (c) Nouns ending in *o* after a vowel form their plurals by adding *s*: patio / patios; stereo / stereos; studio / studios; zoo / zoos. When the *o* follows a consonant, add *-es* to form the plural: echo / echoes; hero / heroes; potato / potatoes; tomato / tomatoes. *Exceptions:* lasso / lassos; piano / pianos; tobacco / tobaccos.
   (d) Some nouns do not form their plural by adding *-s* or *-es*. Instead, they use an older kind of plural (ox / oxen; child / children), or they indicate a change in number in the middle of a word rather than at the end (foot / feet; tooth / teeth), or they use a foreign plural (criterion / criteria; curriculum / curricula; phenomenon / phenomena; syllabus / syllabi). Some nouns for animals are the same for both singular and plural: fish, deer, sheep, snipe. Finally, some words are "false" plurals; they end in *s*, leading you to think that they are plural. These nouns, however, are always singular in meaning and are never spelled without the final *s*: economics, measles, pediatrics, scissors.

6. *Apostrophes.*
   (a) To form a contraction, the apostrophe takes the place of the missing letter or letters: I've = I have; doesn't = does not; he's = he is; it's = it is. *Its* is a possessive pronoun (the dog and its bone), not a contraction. There is no such form as *its'*.
   (b) To form a possessive, follow these rules.
      (1) If a singular or plural noun does not end in an *-s*, add *'s* to show possession:

Mary's locker	the woman's jacket
the truck's battery	the women's jackets
San Francisco's streets	anybody's time
children's books	the company's policy

(2) If a plural noun ends in *-s*, add just the ' to indicate possession.

employees' benefits	computers' speed
lawyers' fees	police officers' training
horses' auction	the boss's schedule (singular noun)

(3) If a proper name has just one syllable and ends in *-s*, use *'s* to form the possessive.

Jones's account	Keats's poetry
Charles's desk	James's word

If the name has more than one syllable and ends in *-s*, add just the '.

Williams' house	Jenkins' chart

(4) If it is a compound noun, add an ' or an *'s* to the end of the word.

brother-in-law's business	Ms. Allison Jones-Wyatt's order

(5) If you wish to indicate shared possession, add just *'s* to the last name.

Warner and Kline's Computer Shop	Sue and Anne's major

If you want to indicate separate possession, add an *'s* to each name.

John's and Mary's transcripts	Shakespeare's and Byron's poetry

(c) To form the plural of numbers, letters, and words used as words, generally add *'s* to avoid confusion.

seven 10's (less confusing than 7 *10*'s)	your report contains too many *if*'s
the 4's are too light on my copy	the manager's *must*'s need to be car-
cross your t's and dot your i's	ried out at once
the H.T.C.'s are on our stationery	1980's (sometimes 1980s)

☞ Matching the Right Word with the Right Meaning

The English language contains many common words that are frequently mistaken for each other because they are pronounced alike but spelled differently. These words are called homonyms. *Meat* (food) and *meet* (to greet) are examples. When a dispatcher orders employees to keep overtime to a "bear minimum," no reference to a grizzly is intended; rather, *bear* has been confused with *bare*. Similarly, the mechanic who writes on a work order to "idol" down a car has confused *idol* (religious image) with *idle* (a verb meaning to slow down).

The words in the following list frequently are mistaken for one another.

By studying the correct spelling, part of speech, and meaning of each, you will save yourself time and embarrassment.

accept (to receive); *except* (to omit, to *ex*clude)

adept (skillful—adjective); *adopt* (to take into one's family legally—verb); *adapt* (to change—verb)

advice (a recommendation—noun); *advise* (to counsel—verb)

affect (to change, to influence—verb); *effect* (a result—noun; to bring about—verb)

ascend (to climb); *assent* (to agree to, to concur)

beside (next to—The book is beside the bed.); *besides* (in addition to— Besides Joan and Jack, who will go?)

brake (to stop—verb; a mechanism to halt a vehicle—noun); *break* (to split, to fracture)

breath (air inhaled—noun); *breathe* (to inhale air—verb)

bullion (gold bars); *bouillon* (broth)

canvas (cloth—noun); *canvass* (to take a poll—verb)

capital (major, chief—adjective—That was a capital idea; wealth in money or property—noun—The capital we invested was very large; the leading city—noun—Concord is the capital of New Hampshire.); *capitol* (the building where a legislature meets—noun)

cent (one penny); *scent* (a smell); *sent* (past tense of the verb *to send,* cause to go)

cite (to document—verb); *site* (place, building location—noun); *sight* (vision, something seen—noun)

coarse (rough—adjective); *course* (class, plan—course of action—noun, or agreement, as in *of course*—adverb)

complement (something that completes—noun; to add to—verb—The green rug complements your curtains.); *compliment* (to praise, to flatter—verb—I compliment you on your sense of color.)

continual (happening frequently—adjective—The business executive receives continual phone calls.); *continuous* (unbroken, never stopping—adjective—The flow of blood through our bodies is continuous.)

discreet (showing respect, being tactful—adjective—The manager was discreet in answering the complaint letter.); *discrete* (separate, distinct—adjective—Put those figures into discrete categories for processing.)

dual (double—adjective); *duel* (fight, battle—noun)

elicit (to gather information—verb); *illicit* (illegal—adjective)

fair (just or attractive—adjective; exhibition, carnival—noun); *fare* (food on a menu, price charged to travel—noun)

hare (rabbit); *hair* (covering on the scalp)

hear (to listen—verb); *here* (in this place—adverb)

imply (to suggest); *infer* (to draw a conclusion)

it's (contraction of *it* + *is*—the apostrophe replaces the *i* of *is* in it + is—
It's not time for dinner.); *its* (possessive pronoun—The ship lost its
anchor.)

lay (to put something down); *lie* (to recline, to sleep)

Present	*Past*	*Past participle*
lay	laid	laid
lie	lay	lain

(The man laid the package down; he then lay down on the couch.)

lose (to misplace something—verb); *loose* (not tight—adjective)

may be (two-word verb phrase—I may be at home tonight if I do not have
to be at the office.); *maybe* (one-word adverb meaning perhaps—
Maybe it will snow tomorrow.)

pair (two, a couple—noun); *pare* (to cut with a knife—verb); *pear* (a fruit—
noun)

peace (calm, no war—noun); *piece* (a portion)

personal (private—adjective); *personnel* (staff of people working for a company—noun)

perspective (a sight the eye beholds—noun); *prospective* (expectant, waiting
for something to happen—adjective—Prospective employees
must furnish employers with references.)

plain (simple, not fancy—adjective; an open field—noun); *plane* (air-
plane—noun; to make smooth and level—verb; a flat surface in ge-
ometry—noun)

prescribe (to order medications); *proscribe* (to prohibit)

precede (to go ahead—An arrest precedes a conviction.); *proceed* (to carry
on with something, to continue—The laboratory technician proceeded with the test after the coffee break.)

principal (main, chief—adjective; head of a school—noun); *principle* (a policy or belief—noun—The principal reason for the democratic
principles in the Constitution is to protect human rights.)

respectful (showing esteem for—adjective—respectful of the rights of citizens); *respective* (pointing to certain individual(s) or ideas—
adjective—those respective three dealers)

right (correct—adjective; the opposite direction of left—noun); *rite* (religious ceremony—noun—the rite of marriage); *write* (to form letters,
to compose—verb)

stationary (not moving—adjective); *stationery* (memos, letters, envelopes—
noun—The *-er* in *stationery* could remind you of the *-er* in *paper*.)

straight (not bent or crooked—adjective); *strait* (a narrow body of water—
noun—Strait of Magellan—*or* something confining—strait-
jacket—adjective)

than (a conjunction used in comparisons—It's bigger than both of us.); *then* (an adverb of time—Then we went home.)

their (a plural possessive pronoun—Where is their house?); *there* (that place—adverb—Go over there.); *they're* (a contraction of *they* and *are*—They're happy in their new jobs.)

two (the number); *to* (toward—preposition); *too* (also—conjunction; excessive—adverb—There is too much slack in the lines.)

ware (goods for sale—noun); *wear* (to dress—verb); *where* (place—pronoun)

weather (state of the atmosphere—noun); *whether* (if—conjunction—I don't know whether she plans to attend.)

week (seven days in a row—noun); *weak* (not strong, infirm—adjective)

who's (contraction of *who* + *is*—Who's next for promotion?—apostrophe is the place holder for the *i* of *is*); *whose* (possessive pronoun—Whose book is this?)

you're (contraction of *you* + *are*); *your* (possessive pronoun—You're going to like their decision; they agree with your ideas.)

Selecting Precise Words

Clear writing can save an employer time and money; and it can save you the frustration of additional explanations over the phone or in rewriting your work. Precise writing gets the job done right the first time. You can be precise, though, only if your words are. After all, your words take the place of the references they describe. Your words should answer the questions readers ask themselves as they read:

- How big?
- How expensive?
- How much?
- What color?
- How many?
- Who?
- Where?
- When?

To write precisely, use concrete, specific words rather than vague, general ones. Choose words that appeal to the reader's five senses—words that help a reader to see, hear, smell, taste, and touch. For example, "piece of office equipment" is vague. "An IBM microcomputer with a 14-inch green phosphor screen" is precise.

Words such as *aspect, condition, creature, factor, nice, thing,* and *ways* raise more questions than they answer. Is a "nice" house made of brick or covered with aluminum siding? Does it have gas or electric heat? Will you find it in the city, suburbs, or the country? Here is another example of the advantage of using exact words:

General: With adequate storage fish keeps for some time.

Specific: If refrigerated at 32°F (0°C) and covered with crushed ice, fresh fish may be stored up to three days.

Unlike the first sentence, the second sentence provides helpful, practical information.

There is a wide range between "general" and "specific." In Table 4.1 note that the general terms in the far left column gradually become more precise as you proceed to the right.

How can you be sure that your words are precise, that they are specific and not vague? Follow three simple procedures after you have written a rough draft and before you submit the final copy:

1. *Circle all your nouns.* Do they point to a specific person, place, or object? Could your reader see and separate that person, place, or object from all others like it? If so, you have a specific word. If readers or listeners cannot quickly identify an object, person, or place from your description, you have used a general word.

2. *Underline all your adjectives.* Do they tell readers the exact color, size, texture, quantity, or quality you want to convey? Adjectives like *bad, fantastic, good, great, interesting, numerous, serious,* or *small* will not help your audience see vividly or measure accurately. Next, see if you need every adjective you have underlined. A noun or verb may render some adjectives unnecessary; the adjective or adverb could repeat what the noun or verb has already said—for example, "shout loudly" (shouts are loud), "a big Saint Bernard" (such dogs are big), "a small 3″ × 5″ card" (is there a large 3″ × 5″ card?).

Table 4.1 The range between general and specific terms

General ◄		► *Specific*	
vehicle	truck	pickup	Dodge wide cab
medication	injection	barbiturate	Seconal 100 mg.
food	protein	poultry	Chicken Kiev
residence	house	cottage	Tudor cottage
official	federal agent	USDA inspector	Mary Whitton
reasonable	inexpensive	bargain	20 percent off $500 sale price
circumstance	disaster	storm	Hurricane Frederic

3. *Star all your verbs.* Do they show lively movement or have they fallen limp on the page? Check your verbs for their activity level; they should be full of information for readers about how and why something happened. Give readers something specific and concrete to watch. Vague verbs such as *appear, concern, consider, evidence, exist, relate, seem,* or any of the forms of *to be (is, are, was, were)* lack information about specific action. These verbs are especially sluggish when combined with "there are" and "it is" constructions such as the following: "It appears that there are some troubles with the company truck." This sentence would move an employer to scream "What happened?" Note the increased action level in the revised sentence: "The company truck ran over a roofing nail, which punctured the right front tire." Choose graphic verbs such as *accelerate, complete, carry out, direct, duplicate, increase, force, juggle, mount, program, push, scatter, squeeze, support, streamline, test.* If your starred verbs vibrate with action, you help readers to grasp your meaning precisely. You will also make reading your work easier and more lively.

☞ Cutting Out Unnecessary Words

Too many people in business and industry think the more words, the better. Nothing could be more self-defeating. Your readers are busy and unnecessary words slow them down. Make every word go to work; when a word takes up space and gives no meaning, cut it. Cut out any words you can from your sentences; if the sentence still makes sense and reads correctly, you have eliminated wordiness.

The phrases on the left should be replaced with the precise words on the right:

Wordy	*Concise*
at a slow rate	slowly
at an early date	early
at the point where	where
at this point in time	now
be in agreement with	agree
bring to a conclusion	conclude; end
brings together	combines; joins
by means of	with
come to terms with	agree; accept
due to the fact that	because
expresses an opinion that	believes
feels quite certain about	believes
for the length of time that	while
for the period of	interval
for the purpose of	to
in an effort to	to
in such a manner that	so

in the area / case / field of	in
in the event that	if
in the neighborhood of	approximately
looks something like	resembles
serves the function of	functions as
shows a tendency to	tends
take into consideration	consider
take under advisement	consider
takes place in such a manner	occurs
with reference to	regarding; about
with the result that	so

The following tips will help you eliminate other kinds of wordiness just as easily.

1. Replace a wordy phrase or clause with a one- or two-word synonym.

   Wordy: The college has parking zones for different areas for people living on campus as well as for those who do not live on campus and who commute to school.

   Revision: The college has different parking zones for resident and commuter students. (Twenty words of the original sentence—everything after "areas for"—have been reduced to four words: "resident and commuter students.")

   Wordy: Many banks use a system of tubes to move small items by means of air pressure from one place to another.

   Revision: Many banks use pneumatic tubes to send small items from one place to another. (Using the phrase "pneumatic tubes" will save many words and identify the system more precisely—provided, of course, that your reader knows what pneumatic tubes are.)

2. Combine sentences beginning with the same subject or ending with an object that becomes the subject of the next sentence.

   Wordy: I asked the inspector if she were going to visit the plant this afternoon. I also asked her if she would come alone.

   Revision: I asked the inspector if she were going to visit the plant alone this afternoon.

   Wordy: Homeowners want to buy low-maintenance plants. These low-maintenance plants include the ever-popular holly and boxwood varieties. These plants are also inexpensive.

   Revision: Homeowners want to buy such low-maintenance and inexpensive plants as holly and boxwood. (This revision combines three sentences into one, condenses twenty-four words into fourteen, and joins three related thoughts.)

Another kind of wordiness comes from using redundant expressions. Being redundant means that you say the same thing a second time, in different words. "Fellow colleague," "component parts," and "corrosive acid" are phrases that contain this kind of double speech; a fellow *is* a colleague, a component *is* a part, and acid *is* corrosive. Redundant expressions are uneconomical and are often clichés. The suggested revisions on the right are preferable to the redundant phrases on the left.

Redundant	*Concise*
absolutely essential	essential
advance reservations	reservations
basic necessities	needs
cease and desist	stop
close proximity	close
each and every	all
end result	result
eradicate completely	eradicate
exposed opening	opening
fair and just	fair
final conclusions / final outcome	conclusions / outcome
first and foremost	first
full and complete	full
grand total	total
integral part	part
null and void	void
passing fad	fad (a fad always passes)
personal opinion	opinion
prerecorded	recorded
over and done with	over
tried and true	honest
unexpected surprise	surprise

Watch for repetitious words, phrases, or clauses within a sentence. Sometimes one part of a sentence needlessly duplicates another part, or a second sentence may repeat the first.

Redundant: The post office hires part-time help, especially around the holidays, to handle the large amounts of mail at Christmas time. ("Especially around the holidays" means the same thing as "at Christmas time.")

Revision: The post office often hires part-time help to handle the large amounts of mail at Christmas time.

Redundant: The fermenting activity of yeast is due to an enzyme called zymase. This enzyme produces chemical changes in yeast. (The second sentence says vaguely what the first sentence says precisely; delete it.)

Revision: The fermenting activity of yeast is due to an enzyme called zymase.

Redundant: To provide more room for employees' cars, the security department is studying ways to expand the employees' parking lot. (Since the first phrase says nothing that the reader does not know from the independent clause, cut it.)

Revision: The security department is studying ways to expand the employees' parking lot.

Adding a prepositional phrase can sometimes contribute to redundancy. The italicized words below are redundant because of the unnecessary qualification they impose on the adverb or adjective. Delete the italicized phrases:

audible *to the ear*	hard *to the touch*
bitter *in taste*	honest *in character*
fly *in the air*	light *in weight*
orange *in color*	soft *in texture*
quickly *with haste*	tall *in height*
rectangular *in shape*	twenty *in quantity*
second *in sequence*	visible *to the eye*
short *in duration*	wise *in intelligence*

Certain combinations of verbs and adverbs are also redundant. Again, the italicized words should be deleted.

advance *forward*	lift *up*
burn *up*	merge *together*
cancel *out*	open *up*
circle *around*	plan *ahead*
close *off*	probed *into*
commute *back and forth*	prove *conclusively*
combine *together*	refer *back*
connect *together*	repeat *again*
continue *on*	reply *back*
drop *down*	revert *back*
funnel *through*	written *down*

☞ Eliminating Sexist Language

Sexist language unfairly assigns responsibilities, jobs, or titles to individuals on the basis of sex. Such language discriminates in favor of one sex at the expense of the other, usually women. Sexist language is often based on sexist stereotypes that show men as superior to women. For example, calling politicians "city fathers" or "favorite sons" follows the stereotypical picture of politicians as male; such phrases discriminate against women who do or could hold public office. Sexist phrases assume engineers, physicians, or pilots are male (he, his, him) and social workers, nurses, and secretaries are female (she, her) although members of both sexes belong to these professions. Sexist language offers a distorted view of our society and deprives women of their equal rights. Sexist phrases such as *gal Friday, little woman, lady of the house, the best man for the job* are insulting and unjust.

One way to eliminate sexist language from your writing is to replace sexist words with neutral ones. Neutral words do not refer to a specific sex; they are genderless. Note how the sexist words on the left can be replaced by neutral, nonsexist ones on the right.

Sexist	*Neutral*
authoress	writer, author
businessman	business executive, manager, business person
chairman	chair, chairperson
fireman	firefighter
foreman	supervisor
janitress	cleaning person
landlord, landlady	owner
mailman	mail carrier
mankind	humanity
man-made	synthetic, natural
manpower	strength, effort, power
men	human beings
policeman	police officer
salesman	salesperson, clerk
stewardess	flight attendant

Using the masculine pronouns (*he, his, him*) when referring to a group that includes both men and women is also sexist.

Every worker must submit his travel expenses by Monday.

Workers may include women as well as men, and to assume all workers are men is misleading and unfair to women. You can avoid such sexist language by doing one of the following:

1. Make the subject of your sentence plural and thus neutral.

   Workers must submit their travel expenses by Monday.

2. Use *his or her* instead of *his*.

   Every worker must submit his or her travel expenses by Monday.

3. Reword the sentences.

   All travel expenses must be submitted by Monday.

☞ Avoiding Jargon and Slang

Jargon

Jargon is shop talk, the specialized vocabulary of a particular occupation. Jargon includes, for example, an *IPPB* (Intermittent Positive Pressure Breathing) *machine* in respiratory therapy, *hard water* (water containing more than 85.5 parts per million of calcium carbonate) in geology, or *mouse* (hand-held cursor) in computer science. Such technical terms are necessary, but should be used only when the following three conditions are met:

1. The audience understands jargon and expects the writer to use it.
2. A technical term or phrase conveys a precise idea that could not be adequately described with a common word or phrase—flange pan instead of cake pan.
3. The kind of form or report you are completing requires jargon—for example, a patient's hospital record, a specification sheet, or a legal description.

The word *jargon* has another meaning besides the legitimate technical language of a profession. More often, it refers to phony, inflated, and uselessly complex language. Jargon is a label attached to pompous words (pseudoscientific jawbreakers) some writers use instead of the much more simple, natural, and direct vocabulary their readers could better understand and value. Jargon is language that puts on airs; it reeks of the stuffiness found in some business letters (see pages 121–122). People who favor jargon dislike pleasantly clear and direct verbs. For the unassuming verb *get*, they substitute *procure;* for *simplify* or *ease,* they choose (or *elect,* in jargon) *facilitate;* rather than *join* or *connect,* they prefer to *interface.* Here are three characteristics of jargon, together with suggestions for doing away with it.

1. Pompous words. Use short, serviceable words instead of pompous expressions ("verbiage" in jargon). Your readers will appreciate your clarity and your honesty. Cut a three-word smoke screen (*scholastic achievement profile*) to one word (*transcript*). *Aquatic support system* could be written *life jacket.*

Note how the original, clear first sentences of Herman Melville's *Moby-Dick* lose their clarity and directness in the jargon translation that follows.

The Original:

Call me Ishmael. Some years ago—never mind how long precisely—having little or no money in my purse and nothing in particular to interest me on shore, I thought I would sail about a little and see the watery part of the world.

The Translation:

You may identify me by the nomenclature of Ishmael. At a point in time several years previous to the current temporal zone—the precise number of which is extraneous information—devoid of sufficient monetary resources and lacking physical and / or psychical stimuli within the confines of my sphere of activity on land, I initiated several thought processes and concluded that I would commandeer a vessel of navigation with which to explore the aquatic component of this planet.

—Vicki Hunter '81[1]

---

[1] (The examples originally appeared in the *Brown Alumni Monthly,* February 1981; by the permission of Debra Shore.)

2. Use of -ize and -ation words. Avoid words such as: finalize (for conclude); hypothesize, energize, personalize, conceptualize (for think); mortuize (for bury); prioritize (for rank); visualize (for see); utilize (for use); verbalization (for statement); conflagration (for fire); democratization (for democracy); socialization (for acceptance); precipitation (for rain, sleet, or snow); illumination (for light); institutionalization (for company policy).

3. Excessive or unclear abbreviations. Do not use abbreviations that, while they may be understood by professionals in your field, will confuse readers unfamiliar with such shorthand. For example, if a nurse told patients that they would have to be NPO (initials indicating that patients are to have nothing by mouth) for a GB vis. (X-ray of the gallbladder), the patients would certainly be baffled and perhaps terrified. The writer of the following letter to Ann Landers sums up the situation well.

Dear Ann Landers: The growing tendency to call everything by initials is extremely irritating. I've discussed this with others and find that I am not alone.

It wasn't so bad when there were just a few, such as the CIO, the AFL and the CIA. Now we have the IRS, the ERA, the IUD, the NAACP, HEW, MIT, ORT and DNA.

Where I work, quarterly meetings are mandatory. We must sit and listen for an hour and a half to talk like this: "The IAM met with the TQA and discussed the YTD. We must now check back with the IRA and do something about the LTC." I become thoroughly confused trying to sort out the meaning of the initials.

What's more, I feel like a fool because I don't know what's going on. Will you please tell those double-dome intellectuals to call things by their names and not assume that because THEY know what all the initials mean, everybody else does?—Abbreviated into Oblivion in Kalamazoo

Dear Kal.: IOU warm thanks for writing such an OK letter. I am printing it PDQ.[2]

For those readers who might be unfamiliar with an abbreviation, the writer should give the full name once, followed by the abbreviation in parentheses: political action committee (PAC). From that point on, the writer should use the abbreviation.

Slang

All of us use slang when we talk to our friends. It is a sign that we are comfortable with the people we know best. Slang, however, is out of place in

---

[2] *Hattiesburg American*, May 18, 1980. Reprinted by permission of Ann Landers and Field Newspaper Syndicate.

professional communication, written or oral. Slang is playful, irreverent, and sometimes vulgar—qualities not appreciated in business communication. You need not be a stuffed shirt, but don't be too casual, either. Here are examples of slang terms to avoid in your professional writing; a more formal equivalent is given in parentheses.

bread (money)
bull (nonsense; exaggeration)
cool it (relax)
dude (man)
far out, way out (exceptional)
get on your case (check up on someone)
pad (house; apartment)
rip off (steal)

uptight (uncomfortable; tense)
goofed off (slackened off; was lazy)
peeled out (drove off recklessly)
ticked someone off (angered someone)
it was a trip (an enjoyable experience)
bad (meaning good)
hacked off (was angered)

The following poem laments, with numerous examples, the invasion of slang into our language.

Remember when hippie meant big in the hips,
And a trip involved travel in cars, planes, and ships?
When pot was a vessel for cooking things in,
And hooked was what grandmother's rugs may have been
When fix was a verb that meant mend or repair,
And be-in meant merely existing somewhere?
When neat meant well-organized, tidy, and clean,
And grass was a ground cover, normally green?
When groovy meant furrowed with channels and hollows,
And birds were winged creatures, like robins and swallows
When fuzz was a substance, really fluffy, like lint,
And bread came from bakeries and not from the mint?
When roll meant a bun, and rock was a stone,
And hang-up was something you did with the phone?
It's groovy, man, groovy, but English it's not.
Methinks that our language is going to pot.

Anonymous

☞ A Final Word on Using Words Effectively

Words are the essential building blocks of any piece of writing. This chapter has given you some practical advice on how to become an effective wordsmith as you compose and revise your work. If you choose words skillfully to say exactly what you want, your writing will be more effective. Choose words that are lean and clean—precise and concise. Precise words provide readers with the information they need to grasp your message; concise words avoid wordiness that wastes a reader's time. Spell words correctly and be careful not to confuse one homonym with another. Finally, eliminate any sexist or discriminatory language from your work as well as unnecessary jargon or slang. By following these guidelines, you will write more readable and professional correspondence, instructions, proposals, and reports—the subjects of later chapters.

☞ Exercises

1. The following sentences contain misspelled words. Find these words and correct them.
   (a) The superviser did not find our performance acceptible on the new equiptment.
   (b) Unusual occurance reports help safety commitees make thier decesions.
   (c) If the carburator is not adjusted proparly, the timing will be alwrong.
   (d) Students must recieve twenty-five hours of instruction to become familar with trafic control problems.
   (e) Only the patients family is admited to the intensive care unit.
   (f) To describe the suspect's physical apparance, aquaint your self with the correct descripters.
   (g) Eat high nutriant foods containing protiens, carbohidrates, and sufficeint ruffage.
   (h) Unflammable liquids could be dangerus.
   (i) Some freindly newly weds occupyed the bridel suit.
   (j) These archectectural designs are unexpensive.
   (k) According to City Ordnance 67, combustables cannot be storred on open shelfs.
   (l) I will have a zerox copy of the order preparred for you.
   (m) We have printed new calandars with pictures of wild turkies and deers on them.
   (n) Gasaline prices will reach a cieling before autum.
   (o) We were ordered to precede with our work, all though the storm threatened to close the black top road leding toward home.
   (p) The class profitted from Professor Morello's lectures.

2. The following sentences contain mistakes in using apostrophes. Find and correct these mistakes.
   (a) We tried to survey everybodies opinion but couldnt include all the member's who work the night shift. Well try tomorrow to find them.
   (b) The mens' locker room was painted last March, was'nt it?
   (c) Freud and Einstein's theories changed the way we'ved looked at the world.
   (d) The Smiths new house is much larger than the Sanders.
   (e) He's report had too many words's and contained too many Is.

(f) Its not just a matter of cost; it's also a question of time and service.

(g) When the mayors conference was held in Detroit last year, the keynote speakers notes embarrassingly fell to the floor. He was startled.

(h) Marion and Beatrice's daughters both attended the accelerated math student's seminar in Kalamazoo, which wasnt too far away.

(i) The bolt came off it's shaft during the first cycle. Its' too bad we didnt doublecheck the system.

(j) Because the print was so light, all the 3s looked like 8s on everyones's copy. The vendors repair crew wasnt able to fix the word processor today.

(k) Adkins's and Kaplan's new restaurant on Broadway Street is a big success.

(l) Margaret Bridges'-Bowers new office is on the second floor. It's walls still need to be painted.

(m) Joes shirt needs a button but he doesnt own a needle. Hes planning to buy both.

3. Select the appropriate word in the following sentences and briefly explain your choice.

(a) My new listings book is larger (then / than) last year's.

(b) All new (personnel / personal) reported to pick up (there / their) identification cards.

(c) Regardless of (it's / its) price, buy the property so the firm does not (lose / loose) it. We must (attain / obtain) it.

(d) She kept her (stationary / stationery) on the desk where she could easily reach it (beside / besides) her printer.

(e) The fabric was (course / coarse) and cheap, and the buyer refused to (choose / chose) it.

(f) Please (except / accept) this (complementary / complimentary) offer with our best wishes.

(g) The (principle / principal) reason given was that our test scores were (to / too) low and the superintendent was afraid none of us would (pass / past) the test.

(h) Corn grows well on the flat (plains / planes) of Illinois.

(i) Smoking (affects / effects) blood pressure.

(j) Our squad had to (sight / cite) every violation so that it could be reported in the district commander's log.

(k) The doctor (proscribed / prescribed) no more smoking for the overweight patient.

(l) Unusually hot days in March often cause a lot of bad (weather / whether).

(m) (Its / it's) possible to find a (peace / piece) of material in the shop.

(n) The applicant (who's / whose) credentials were so suitable for our position took another job working for a (pare / pair) of attorneys.

(o) She was very (adept / adapt) at (adapting / adopting) the new guide-lines to suit our agency.

(p) Our office manager purchased a stereo with (dual / duel) speakers.

(q) The customer made the (rite / right) choice in selecting our firm; we have the (capitol / capital) to develop the project correctly.

(r) The new floor manager was on her feet (continually / continuously) during the month of August to assist customers.

(s) Each applicant was asked to fill out his or her (respectful / respective) questionnaire.

4. The following sentences contain vague and abstract words. Replace them with concrete ones. The first sentence has been done for you.

(a) The individual saw the occurrence.

The police officer from the second district saw the young boy steal Ms. Saliba's purse.

(b) Three factors disturbed the crew when it had to deliberate.

(c) The case she outlined sounded interesting.

(d) Circumstances dictated that we follow another course of action in handling this matter.

(e) The nature of the area is such that alternative measures must be sought.

(f) It happened this week.

(g) The materials were incomplete; we found defects, too.

(h) The causes of the action seemed to be good.

(i) The phenomenon she discussed happened occasionally in our area.

(j) The individual sought an immediate solution to the problem.

5. The following sentences contain limp, sluggish verbs. Rewrite these sentences replacing vague verbs with active, precise ones. The first one has been done for you.

(a) Tourists are on the beach each August.

Tourists fill the beach each August.

(b) The writer seemed concerned.

(c) All the points in the proposal relate to our expansion plans.

(d) There exist three possible solutions that appear attractive.

(e) Obtaining appraisals is important.

(f) There are many problems that appear to be significant.

(g) Computers are tools that exist in each business office.

(h) It is apparent that the new equipment has its purpose.

(i) A computer timesharing program will get our work accomplished.

(j) The new law is harmful to our district.

6. The following sentences contain wordy expressions. Rewrite them to cut these expressions out.

(a) Due to the fact that the bus was late, we did not get home until after midnight.
(b) In an effort to correct some health violations, we fixed the refrigerator in such a way that it would not cause us any more trouble.
(c) You will have to connect together the terminals with the assistance of a Phillips screwdriver.
(d) In terms of our ability to meet the demands of those individuals living in the Thames district, all that we can articulate adequately at this date on the calendar is that every effort will be made to find appropriate work crews to find, gather, and remove the refuse left by the storm.
(e) Our manager is very supportive of our efforts to expand our line of coats, hats, shirts, pants, blouses, dresses, and socks for young children between the ages of two weeks and one year.
(f) For the length of time that the powder is left around the edges of the room, you might want to check the walls and doors.
(g) The patient's arm was soaked in warm water with the result that she felt much better and in such a way that the doctor discharged her.
(h) I am in agreement with the terms in your letter of July 25 and I feel quite certain the manager will respond favorably in an effort to secure the contract.

7. The following sentences contain redundancies. Rewrite these sentences to remove unnecessary repetition.
   (a) It was a foreign import.
   (b) The owner's car was light azure blue in color and a convertible in the model.
   (c) The president told them to terminate the plan and end it.
   (d) A student delivered an oral talk to fellow classmates.
   (e) The crew was traveling and in transit; therefore, it could not be reached.
   (f) The troops advanced forward even when they were confronted face-to-face with hazardous dangers staring them in the eyes.
   (g) The chemistry major had to reread the chapter on bonding again.
   (h) The chief canceled our leaves when the mayor requested additional, further officers.
   (i) The clamp was connected together with the hose.
   (j) After explaining the new policy, the office manager centered her discussion around the ways of implementing and carrying out that policy in our routine, daily activities.
   (k) When the technician walked into the room, the patient was really bleeding profusely.
   (l) She came to her final conclusion after referring back to the occurrence report.
   (m) Although the diamond was oval in shape, it still would satisfy the buyer.

(n) First and foremost, the guests received a complimentary bottle of wine, which did not cost them a cent.

(o) He received personalized and individual care.

(p) A knife, tent, and food supplies are basic necessities on an outdoor camping trip in the woods.

(q) The report will specifically and exclusively deal with urban problems affecting the city.

(r) The local, neighborhood commission gave sufficient and adequate reasons for letting the carpenter work independently and use her own resources.

(s) They have legal recourse as promised by the law.

(t) The end result of the study was that all future changes in policy should be written down and spelled out in detail.

(u) Our firm merged together with one in Minneapolis and promises to eradicate completely any errors in the future.

(v) Commuting back and forth over 30 miles a day, the personnel director thought it was absolutely essential to keep a fair and just record of her mileage.

8. The following sentences contain sexist language. Rewrite them to eliminate all sexist words and phrases.

(a) The Constitution of the United States promises each man freedom of speech.

(b) The city will hire more firemen and policemen at the beginning of the fiscal year.

(c) In the last five years, our company has been a leader in developing man-made fibers.

(d) Taylor Community College enrolled more than 2000 co-eds last term.

(e) Our office advertised for a couple of girls to work part-time as receptionists in a 20-man department.

(f) Each pilot is required to have his physical examination this month.

(g) All attorneys and their wives are invited to attend the reception.

(h) Job applicants should always spell the employer's name correctly. Otherwise, he may not respond favorably to their letter.

(i) On the medical-surgical floors, every nurse is required to rotate her work shift.

(j) Every shopper should realize the importance of her coupons.

(k) The businessman's lunch offers a variety of specials.

(l) The new financial program is designed to help the common man.

9. The following paragraph contains jargon. Rewrite the paragraph and replace the jargon with clear and appropriate words.

It has been verified conclusively by this writer that our institution must of necessity install more bicycle holding racks for the convenience of students, faculty, and staff. These parking modules should be fastened securely to walls outside strategic locations on the campus. They could be positioned there by work crews or even by the security forces who vigilantly patrol the campus grounds. There are many students in particular who would value the installation of these racks. Their bicycles could be stationed there by them, and they would know that safety measures have been taken to ensure that none of their bicycles would be apprehended or confiscated illegally. Besides the precaution factor, these racks would afford users maximized convenience in utilizing their means of transportation when they have academic business to conduct, whether at the learning resource center or in the instructional facilities.

Section II

Correspondence

5

Letter Writing: Some Basics

Letters are probably the most frequent kind of writing you will do on your job. Because letters are so important, Chapters 5, 6, and 7 are devoted exclusively to ways of writing letters effectively. Chapter 5 introduces the entire process and provides some guidelines, definitions, and strategies common to all letter writing.

☞ The Importance of Letters

A letter can be defined as a formal or informal written message carefully planned and prepared, addressed to a specific audience, and having a clearly announced function. Letters are not telegrams, lists, or computer printouts. They are more formal than the memos that are written to people who work in your office. Letters are both a personal and professional means of communication. Effective letters clearly announce their purpose and are written in complete sentences in a style that (1) follows an appropriate format, (2) courteously addresses the reader, and (3) selects the most precise and useful language.

Companies annually spend millions of dollars writing letters. The average business letter now costs between eight and twelve dollars to compose, dictate, type, proofread, mail, store, and retrieve. Not surprisingly, many companies own computerized typewriters that allow them to send a letter across the country in a few minutes. Such electronic mail also uses sophisticated scanning and facsimile-reproduction equipment. But even with such machines, firms need people to write and proofread the letters. Numerous firms offer their employees seminars on how to write clear and appropriate letters. The skill of good letter writing can be learned and can lead the writer to advancement and rewards.

Why are letters so important to the employer and the employee? Letters represent the public image of the company and the professional competence of the writer. They can influence people favorably or unfavorably. Basically, letters serve the following five functions:

1. *Letters provide information.* They can inform readers about a new policy, a change in time for deliveries, an alteration in procedures, a new product, or a new service. They can also give instructions and present in a clear, unemotional way the facts that the company thinks are important.
2. *Letters prompt action.* They can help the writer collect money from overdue accounts, alter a city ordinance, speed the shipment of new parts, initiate a policy, call a meeting, or waive a requirement.
3. *Letters establish goodwill.* They can thank someone, convey congratulations, answer a complaint, settle an account satisfactorily, or provide a recommendation.
4. *Letters sell.* They can sell a product, a service, or the writer's own skills.
5. *Letters follow up on telephone calls and other types of conversation.* They can also provide documentation and clarification of oral agreements.

Letters accomplish all these goals by following certain conventions. These conventions are the ways in which businesses and their readers expect letters to look and to be written. This chapter will show you how to write an effective letter and will provide examples for you to study.

☞ Typing and Proofreading Letters

The first thing a reader notices about a letter is how the words and paragraphs are arranged on the page. A letter should look neat, clean, and professional to tell the reader that the work, service, or skill the writer promises to deliver will be done in the same way. Strikeovers (crossing out one letter by typing another letter on top of it), messy erasures that leave the paper bare in one spot, blotches of liquid corrector smeared across the page, handwritten changes inserted to correct errors—all look unprofessional and interfere with the reader's attempt to get the message quickly and accurately.

The way in which a letter is typed on the page significantly affects the visual impression it makes. You can avoid crowded or lopsided letters if you take a few minutes to estimate the length of the message before you type it. You do not want to start a brief letter at the top of the page and leave three-fourths of the page blank. Plan to start near the center of the page. Also avoid cramming everything onto one page; sometimes you will have to use a second sheet. A letter that is squeezed onto one page will deprive the reader of necessary and pleasant white space.

Specific typing instructions are included later in the chapter. Here are a few general hints. Leave generous margins of approximately 1½ inches all around your letter. Have more white space at the top than at the bottom, and watch right-hand margins in particular, since it is easy to exceed their limits.

Shorter letters may require wider margins than longer letters, but don't exceed a margin of 1½ inches on the right-hand side.

Be especially careful about the typewriter you use. Make sure that all the keys work and that none of them produces a broken or half letter. Clean your keys and buy a new ribbon so that your typed letter will not be fuzzy or messy.

Proofread everything that has your name on it, even if you did not type it. You cannot blame a typist for work for which you are responsible. Don't forget that when a letter goes out with your signature you are responsible for everything in it. Typographical errors can be costly and embarrassing. If you want to tell a steady customer that "the order will be hard to fill" and you type instead that "the order will be hard to bill," confusions will result. Poor typing and proofreading can also lead to omissions (the "ill arrived" for "the bill arrived"), transpositions ("hte" for "the," "nad" for "and," "fra" for "far," "sti" for "its"), or omitted words ("the market value of the was high").

Proofreading is reading in slow motion. Here are eight ways to proofread effectively. You may want to combine all of them to ensure accuracy.

1. Read the letter once backwards, bottom to top.
2. Read the letter from the start to the finish aloud. Pronounce each word carefully to make yourself more aware of typographical errors or omitted words. Look at every letter of every word. Don't skim.
3. Place your finger under each word as you read the letter silently.
4. Double-check the spelling of all names and the accuracy of dates, costs, addresses, and other factual details. Errors here are sure to cause problems. Watch for inconsistencies (Phillip in one place; Philip in another).
5. Have a friend read the letter. Four eyes are better than two.
6. Have your friend read the original copy of the letter aloud while you follow the typed copy.
7. If you have the time, proofread the letter the following day.
8. Never proofread when you are tired and avoid reading large amounts of material in one sitting.

☞ Letter Formats

Letter format refers to the way in which you type a letter—where you indent and where you place certain kinds of information. A number of letter formats exist. Two of the most popular in the business world are the full block format (Figure 5.1) and the semiblock format (Figure 5.2). Either form is acceptable, but to be safe, try to find out if your employer has a preference.

The full block style is the easiest to use because all information in the letter is typed flush against the left-hand margin. You will not have to worry about indenting paragraphs or aligning dates with signatures. For these reasons the full block form is preferred by many business. Figure 5.1 shows a full block letter typed on letterhead stationery (specially printed stationery giving a com-

Fig. 5.1 Full block format.

April 2, 1985

Ms. Molly Georgopolous, C.P.A.
Business Manager
Diversified Industries
3400 South Madison
Akron, OH 44324

All typing   Dear Ms. Georgopolous:
lined up
against   As I promised in our telephone conversation this afternoon,
left-hand   I am enclosing a study of the Ohio financial responsibility
margin   law. I hope that it will help you in your survey.

I wish to emphasize again that probably 95 percent of all
individuals who are involved in an accident do obtain
reimbursement for hospital and doctor bills and for damages
to their automobiles. If individuals have insurance, they
can receive reimbursement from their own carrier. If they do
not have insurance and the other driver is uninsured and
judged to be at fault, the State Bureau of Motor Vehicles
will revoke that party's driver's license and license plates
until all costs for injuries and damages are paid.

Please call upon me again if I may be of help to you.

Sincerely yours,

John C. Winchell

John C. Winchell, President

JCW/pck

Encl.

Letterhead reproduced by permission.

104

Fig. 5.2 Semiblock format.

Writer's address and date are indented

7239 East Daphne Parkway
Mobile, AL 36608
January 31, 1985

Mr. Travis Boykin, Manager
Scandia Gifts
703 Hardy Street
Hattiesburg, MS 39401

Dear Mr. Boykin:

I would appreciate knowing if you currently stock the Crescent pattern of model 5678 and how much you charge per model number. I would also like to know if you have special prices per box order.

The name of your store is listed in the Annual Catalog as the closest distributor of Copenhagen products in my area. Would you please give me directions to your shop from Mobile and the hours you are open.

I look forward to hearing from you.

Complimentary close and writer's name are indented

Sincerely yours,

Arthur T McCormack

Arthur T. McCormack

pany's name, address, telephone number, and sometimes the names of its chief executives or the company symbol or design). The use of letterhead stationery eliminates the need to type a writer's address. On plain stationery, the writer's address is typed flush with the left-hand margin, directly above the date.

The semiblock style, by contrast, has the writer's address (if it is not imprinted on a letterhead), date, complimentary close, and the signature at the right-hand side of the letter. The typist must make a number of adjustments to align the date with the complimentary close and must remember to go back to the left side to note any enclosures with the letter. Paragraphs in the semiblock style can be flush against the left-hand margin or indented.

If your letter runs to a second page (and it may not do this often), use a sheet of plain white bond paper rather than company letterhead. About six lines, or 1½ inches from the top of the page, type the reader's name on the left-hand side, a simple arabic 2 in the center, and the date of the letter on the right-hand side. Do it like this:

Patricia Riordan—Sanchez   2   April 30, 1985

Alternatively, put "Page 2" and the date directly under the recipient's name on the left-hand side. However, never number the first page of a letter—even if your letter is just one page long.

☞ Parts of a Letter

A letter can contain many parts to communicate its message. Those parts marked with an asterisk are found in every letter you will write. Figure 5.3 contains a sample letter displaying all the parts discussed below. Note where each part is placed in the letter.

*Date Line

Where you place the month, day, and year depends on the format you are using. If you are using the full block style, the date line is flush with the left-hand margin. If you are using the semiblock style, the date can be placed at the

Fig. 5.3   A sample letter, full block format, with all parts labeled.

Letterhead	**MADISON AND MOORE, INC.** **Professional Architects** **7900 South Manheim Road** **Crystal Springs, NE 71003**
Date line	December 10, 1985
Inside address	Ms. Paula Jordan Systems Consultant Broadacres Development Corp. 12 East River Street Detroit, MI 48001
Salutation	Dear Ms. Jordan:
Subject line	SUBJECT: Request for alternate duplex plans, No. 32134
Body of letter	Thank you for your letter of December 2, 1985. I have discussed your request with the officials in our Planning Department and have learned that the forms we used are no longer available. In searching through my files, however, I have come across the enclosed catalog from a Nevada firm that might be helpful to you. This firm, Nevada Designers, offers plans very similar to the ones you are interested in, as you can tell from the design I checked on page 23 of their catalog. I hope this will help your project and I wish you success in your venture.
Complimentary close	Sincerely yours,
Company name	MADISON AND MOORE, INC.
Signature	*William Newhouse*
Writer's name and title	William Newhouse Office Manager
Stenographic identification	WN/kpl
Enclosure	Encl. Catalog
Copy to	cc. Planning Department

center point, centered under a company letterhead, or flush with the right-hand margin.

Spell out the name of the month in full; type out "September" and "March" rather than abbreviating to "Sept." or "Mar." Most frequently the date line is typed this way: November 14, 1986. The military and other governmental agencies, however, may ask you to date correspondence with the day followed by month and year (14 November 1986), with no commas separating the day, month, and year.

*Inside Address

The inside address, which is the same address that goes on the envelope, is placed against the left-hand margin in both full block and semiblock formats. It contains the name, title (if any), company, street address, city, state, and zip code of the person or company to which you are writing. If possible, try to write to a specific individual. You will get off to a bad start if you do not spell that person's name right; don't put Anderson for Andersen, Kean for Keen, or MacDermott for McDermott.

Single-space the inside address, but do not use any punctuation at the end of the lines. The name of the individual, together with a courtesy title such as Mr., Ms., Dr., Professor, goes on the first line. When writing to a woman, use Ms. unless she expressly asked to be called Mrs. or Miss. A woman's marital status should not be an issue. The initials M.D., Ph.D., or D.P.H. should not be added after you use Dr. Use either Janice Howell, M.D. or Dr. Janice Howell, not Dr. Janice Howell, M.D. Some common initials indicating a person's position or occupation are R.N. (registered nurse), M.T. (medical technologist), P.A. (professional architect), and C.P.A. (certified public accountant). Place these initials after the individual's name, followed by a comma: Charles Barton, R.N. Any military titles (captain, corporal), academic ranks (professor, assistant professor), or religious designations (reverend, father, sister) should be written out in full and the first letter capitalized.

If the individual to whom you are writing holds an office or has a title within the company, put a comma after the person's name, followed by the title: Ms. Kathy Buel, President. Use the courtesy title Ms. and capitalize the "P" in President. If the title contains more than one word, put the title on the next line: Mr. Henry Gerald / Director of Computer Services. If you do not know the individual's name or if you are writing to an entire corporation or section of a company, put the department or company name on one line and the street address on the next line: Public Relations Department / The Doulet Brace Company / 1343 Jackson Street / Chicago, IL 60624.

The last line of the inside address contains the city, state, and zip code. Table 5.1 lists the official U.S. Postal Service abbreviations—two capital letters without a period—for the states and territories of the United States. Acceptable abbreviations for the provinces of Canada are listed below the table. Pay special attention to those abbreviations beginning with the same letter. For

Table 5.1 U.S. Postal Service Abbreviations

U.S. state / territory	Abbreviation	U.S. state / territory	Abbreviation
Alabama	AL	Montana	MT
Alaska	AK	Nebraska	NE
Arizona	AZ	Nevada	NV
Arkansas	AR	New Hampshire	NH
American Samoa	AS	New Jersey	NJ
California	CA	New Mexico	NM
Colorado	CO	New York	NY
Connecticut	CT	North Carolina	NC
Delaware	DE	North Dakota	ND
District of Columbia	DC	Ohio	OH
Florida	FL	Oklahoma	OK
Georgia	GA	Oregon	OR
Guam	GU	Pennsylvania	PA
Hawaii	HI	Puerto Rico	PR
Idaho	ID	Rhode Island	RI
Illinois	IL	South Carolina	SC
Indiana	IN	South Dakota	SD
Iowa	IA	Tennessee	TN
Kansas	KS	Trust Territories	TT
Kentucky	KY	Texas	TX
Louisiana	LA	Utah	UT
Maine	ME	Vermont	VT
Maryland	MD	Virginia	VA
Massachusetts	MA	Virgin Islands	VI
Michigan	MI	Washington	WA
Minnesota	MN	West Virginia	WV
Mississippi	MS	Wisconsin	WI
Missouri	MO	Wyoming	WY

Canadian province	Abbreviation	Canadian province	Abbreviation
Alberta	AB	Nova Scotia	NS
British Columbia	BC	Ontario	ON
Labrador	LB	Prince Edward Island	PE
Manitoba	MB	Quebec	PQ
New Brunswick	NB	Saskatchewan	SK
Newfoundland	NF	Yukon Territory	YT
Northwest Territories	NT		

example, mail going to Jackson, Mississippi (MS), could go astray if a letter without a zip code used the same abbreviation for Michigan (MI). Also note the difference between AR (Arkansas) and AK (Alaska).

*Salutation

The greeting part of your letter, or the salutation, is typed flush against the left-hand margin in both the full block and semiblock formats. Begin with *Dear,* a convention showing respect for your reader, and then follow with a courtesy title, the reader's last name, and a colon (Dear Mr. Brown:). A comma is reserved for an informal letter. The salutation is determined by the first line of the inside address. If you are not sure of the sex of the reader, type "Dear Terry Banks," using the reader's full name.

If there is no way to find the reader's name, or if you are writing to a large group of readers, use an individual's job title or other relevant designation: Dear Purchasing Agent, Dear Pilot, Dear Homeowners. When writing to a company, use the company name—Dear Macy's, Dear Saperstein Textiles—not the sexist Dear Gentlemen. (For a discussion of sexist language and how to avoid it, see pages 88–89). If you are writing to a group that includes both men and women, use Dear Ladies and Gentlemen, but not the sexist "Dear Sirs."

And finally, if you are on a first-name basis with your reader, using his or her last name would be awkward; simply write "Dear Bill" or "Dear Sue."

Subject Line

The subject line provides a concise summary of the letter (something like a title), or it lists account numbers, order notations, policy identifications, or referral numbers so that the reader can at once check the files and see what the status of your account or policy is. Your most recent letter can then be placed accurately in your file. The subject line, preceded by the word "subject" in capital letters, can be placed two spaces below the salutation, flush with the left-hand margin:

```
Dear Ms. Hogan:

SUBJECT: Repair of model 7342
```

Or it can be moved to the right-hand side of the letter, on the same line with the salutation:

```
Dear Ms. Hogan:                    SUBJECT: Repair of model 7342
```

*Body of the Letter

The body of a letter contains the message. In the full block format paragraphs are not indented; in the semiblock format, as we have seen, paragraphs may or may not be indented five spaces. Whichever style you choose, single-space within the paragraph, but double-space between paragraphs.

While some of your letters will be only a few lines long, many of them will extend to three or more paragraphs. Always begin your letter with your purpose. Tell readers in the first paragraph why you are writing to them and why your letter is important to them. In a second (or subsequent) paragraph, develop your message with factual support. But don't bury important points within the middle or end of your paragraph. Follow the techniques of paragraph writing discussed in Chapter 2. In your last paragraph bring readers to a true sense of conclusion. Tell them what you have done for them, what they should do for you, what will happen next, when they will hear from you again, or any combination of these messages. Don't leave readers hanging.

Consider the appearance of your paragraphs, too. Excessively long paragraphs can make the reader work too hard finding ideas buried in them. On the other hand, one-sentence paragraphs that follow one on top of the other give an impression of spotty, incomplete coverage. Most paragraphs in a letter usually run from three to eight typed lines (forty to sixty words, or three to six sentences).

*Complimentary Close

The complimentary close appears two spaces below the body of the letter, flush with left-hand margin in the full block format and at the center point, aligned with the date, for the semiblock format. As the term suggests, the complimentary close ends the letter politely. Your close should be appropriate for the reader. For most business correspondence, the standard close is *Sincerely yours, Sincerely, Yours sincerely,* or *Respectfully.* Avoid flowery closes such as *Faithfully yours* or *Forever yours.* Capitalize only the first letter of the complimentary close, and follow the entire close with a comma.

*Signature

The typed signature appears four spaces below the complimentary close, either on the left side (full block format) or at the center point (semiblock format). You need four spaces between the typed name and the close so that your name, when you write it out, will not look squeezed in. Never forget to sign your name in ink, just as it is typed. Your name not only indicates who you are, but also verifies that the contents of your letter have your approval. An unsigned letter indicates carelessness or, worse, indifference.

Some firms like to have the company name as well as the employee's name in the signature section. If so, type the company name in capital letters two spaces below the complimentary close, and then sign your name as was just explained. Add your title underneath your typed name. Here is an example:

```
Sincerely yours,

THE FINELLI COMPANY
```

Robert Jones

```
Robert Jones
Cover Coordinator
```

Stenographic Identification

When a letter is typed for you, the typist's initials are placed two spaces below your typed signature. The typist's (stenographer's) initials are typed in lower-case letters and follow your initials, which are typed in capital letters. The notation WBT/vgh, for example, means that Winnie B. Thompson's letter was typed by Victor G. Higgins. The company thus has a record in its files of who dictated the letter and who typed it. Do not list any initials if you typed your own letter.

Enclosure(s) Line

The enclosure line is typed two spaces beneath the stenographic initials or your typed signature if you typed your own letter. This line informs the reader that additional materials (brochures, diagrams, forms, job descriptions, architectural plans, a proposal) are being sent with your letter. You can type the word "Enclosure" in full or abbreviate it to "Encl." Most writers indicate briefly what is being enclosed (Encl. Incident report; Encl. Résumé) or at least give the number of enclosures (Encl. 3). Sometimes the title of an enclosure is given, for example, Encl. "The 1985 Sales Report to the Management of Powers Industries."

Copy or Copies Distributed

The initials "cc." (typed with no space between them and a period after) indicate that a letter has been duplicated. Type the initials two spaces below the enclosure line.

Letters are copied and sent to a third party for a variety of reasons. An individual may want to know what has happened:

```
cc. John Bandy
```

or another department in your firm may be interested in your letter:

```
cc. Service Dept.
```

When you are sending a copy of your letter to more than one individual, list these individuals in alphabetical order or by corporate rank:

```
cc. Janice Algood          cc. Plant Superintendent Swarr
    Peter Lemon                Comptroller Algood
    Robbie Swarr               Shift 1 Supervisor Lemon
```

Often letters are copied for other readers without the knowledge of the person to whom the letter is addressed. Such copies are called "blind copies." But professional courtesy dictates that you tell the reader that a copy of your letter is being sent to someone else.

☞ Addressing an Envelope

When addressing an envelope, use a standard 9½″ × 4⅛″ white envelope or, as most firms use when they mail statements, an envelope measuring 6½″ × 3⅝″, with a window (a transparent cellophane opening) showing the customer's address. Because mail is sorted now by optical scanning machines, the United States Postal Service has established regulations concerning envelope size. In particular, avoid small, invitation-sized envelopes and odd-shaped ones. Review the regulations listed on page 12 for proper envelope sizes. The Postal Service now recommends using all capitals and no punctuation on the envelope.

Outside Address

An envelope has two parts—the outside address and the return address, as in Figure 5.4. The outside address, the same as the reader's inside address on your letter, should be typed and centered on the envelope. Leave at least one-half inch of white space between the last line of address and the bottom of the envelope. Do not run your address to the very end of the envelope. Never exceed five lines for an address, and make sure that all lines of the address are lined up. If an individual's address contains both a street address and an apartment, room, or suite number, put all this information on the same line: 809 TROUP STREET APT 7B. If individuals do not live at an address permanently, you will have to send the letter in care of (C/O) the permanent resident:

```
MS MARY JANE TRUAX
C/O MS FAYE JELINICK
33 WEST 91ST STREET
NEW YORK NY 10072
```

Always use a zip code, even if a letter is going to someone in your city, because a letter with a zip code will arrive at its destination sooner.

Some companies or individuals that you write to will have a nine-digit zip code. The first five digits direct mail to a particular geographic location (New York City, Milwaukee) while the last four digits provide a further geographic breakdown (a unit within a company, a floor of a large office building, a college post office box).

Return Address and Special Instructions

The return address is your address. It should appear at the upper left-hand side of the envelope (not on the flap), single spaced, and without any courtesy title. Sometimes special mailing directions are required. In such cases one of the following designations is added to the envelope.

- **Hold for Arrival:** Individuals may be away on business or on vacation, and you want the letter to reach them on their return. Perhaps, too, you are writing to someone who will arrive at a hotel or firm after your letter does. The notation "hold for arrival" ensures that your letter is not returned or thrown away.
- **Personal** or **Confidential:** This designation indicates that only the individual to whom you are writing should open and read your letter. Otherwise, the letter will be considered routine business correspondence, and perhaps be opened by a secretary or supervisor.
- **Attention:** This word on the envelope is followed by the name of the individual you are writing to. The attention line is particularly helpful when you have been dealing regularly with one section, department, or

Fig. 5.4   The envelope.

```
THOMAS ADDINGTON  ⎫
45 SIMMONS APT 2B  ⎬   Return address
MEDVALE VT 05402   ⎭




                          ⎫ MS PATRICIA BARNES
                          ⎪ OFFICE MANAGER
        Outside address   ⎬ COURTESY MOTORS
                          ⎪ 1700 LAKEWOOD STREET
                          ⎭ BOSTON MA 02127-3160
```

individual in a large company—credit department, parts warehouse, or statistics office. An attention line also helps a company sort and route its mail faster.

- **Please Forward:** This designation asks that your letter be sent on to a new address after an individual has moved.

All such special instructions, except the attention line, are placed at the top left, two spaces below the return address. The attention line is typed on the second line of the reader's address. Figure 5.5 shows the proper format.

Figure 5.5   Envelopes with special notations.

```
KATHY KOOPERMAN
769 EAST 45TH STREET
BALTIMORE MD 21224




                    THE PLACEMENT OFFICE
                    ATTENTION MS FAYE GLADSTONE
                    EAST CENTRAL COMMUNITY COLLEGE
                    BALTIMORE MD 21228-0710
```

```
GARY ALLEN
WILCOX LABS
73 DUNWITTY LANE
ST PAUL MN 55476

PLEASE HOLD FOR ARRIVAL


                    MS NANCY PARKER
                    THE HANRAHAN COMPANY
                    C/O THE WILTSHIRE HOTEL
                    510 MAIN STREET
                    SPRINGFIELD MO 65803
```

☞ Making a Good Impression on Your Reader

You have just learned about the mechanical requirements your letter must fulfill. Now we will discuss the content of your letter—what you say and how you say it. Writing letters means communicating to influence your readers—not to alienate or antagonize them. Keep in mind that writers of effective letters are like successful diplomats in that they represent both their company and themselves.

To write an effective letter, first put yourself in the reader's position. What kinds of letters do you like to receive? You would at once rule out letters that are vague, sarcastic, pushy, or condescending. You want letters addressed to you to be polite, businesslike, and considerate of your needs and requests. If you have questions, you want them answered honestly and courteously. And you do not want someone to waste your time with a long, puffy letter when a few well-chosen sentences would have done the job much better.

What do you as a writer have to do to send such effective letters? Adopt the "you attitude"; in other words, signal to readers that they and their needs are the most important ingredients in your letter. Incorporating this "you attitude" means that you should be able to answer "yes" to these two questions: (1) Will my readers receive a positive image of me? (2) Have I chosen words that convey both my respect for the readers and my concern for their questions and comments? The first question deals with your overall view of readers. Do your letters paint them as clever or stupid, practical managers or spendthrifts? The second question deals with specific language and tone conveying your view of the reader. Words can burn or soothe. Choose them carefully.

The following four guidelines will help you make a good impression on your readers.

1. Never forget that your reader is a real person. Avoid writing cold, impersonal letters that sound as if they were punched out by a computer or tape-recorded on a telephone. Let the readers know that you are writing to them as individuals. Neglecting this rule, a large clinic sent its customers this statement: "Your bill is overdue. If you pay it by the 15th of this month, no one except the computer will know that it is late." Similarly, abandoning the personal approach, a general during the Korean War once sent this order to his soldiers: "All troops will have a Merry Christmas."

The letter below violates every rule of personal and personable communications:

```
It has come to our attention that policy number 342q765r has
been delinquent in payment and is in arrears for the sum of
$302.35. To keep the policy in force for the duration of its
life, a minimum payment of $50.00 must reach this office by the
last day of the month. Failure to submit payment will result in
the cancellation of the aforementioned policy.
```

There is no sense in the previous example of one individual writing to another, of a customer with a name, personal history, or specific needs. The letter uses cold and stilted language ("delinquent in payment," "in arrears for," "aforementioned policy"). Revised, this letter contains the necessary personal (and human) touch.

```
We have not yet received your payment for your insurance policy
(#342q765r). By sending us your check for $50.00 within the
next three weeks, you will keep your policy in force and can
continue to enjoy the financial benefits and emotional security
it offers you.
```

The benefits to the particular reader are stressed, and the reader is addressed directly as a valued customer.

Don't be afraid of using "you" in your letters. Readers will feel more friendly toward you and your message. In fact, you might even use the reader's name or the name of his or her company within your letter to create goodwill and to show your interest.

2. Keep the reader in the forefront of your letter. Make sure that the reader's needs control the letter. This is the essence of the "you attitude." No one likes people who talk about themselves all the time. What is true about conversation is equally true of letters. Stress the "you," not the "I." Again, try to find out about your readers. Here is a paragraph from a letter that forgets about the reader:

```
I think that our rug shampooer is the best on the market. Our
firm has invested a lot of time and money to ensure that it is
the most economical and efficient shampooer available today.
We have found that our customers are very satisfied with the
results of our machine. We have sold thousands of these
shampooers, and we are proud of our accomplishment. We hope
that we can sell you one of these fantastic machines.
```

The example above talks the reader into boredom by spending all its time on the machine, the company, and the sales success. Readers are interested in how they can profit from the machine, not in how much profit the company makes from selling it. To win the readers' confidence, the writer needs to show how they will find the product useful, economical, and worthwhile at home or at work. Here is a reader-centered alternative:

```
Our rug shampooer would make cleaning your Happy Rest Motel
rooms easier for you. It is equipped with a heavy-duty motor
that will handle your 200 rooms with ease. Moreover, that motor
will give frequently used areas, such as the lobby or hallways,
a fresh and clean look you can be proud of.
```

3. Be courteous and tactful. However serious the problem or the degree of your anger at the time, refrain from turning your letter into a punch through the mails. Capture the reader's goodwill, and the rewards will be greater for you. The following words can create a bad taste in the reader's mouth:

it's defective	you have failed
it's against company policy	you contend
I demand	you allege
I insist	you must have lied
we reject	you should have known
that's no excuse for	you forgot to consider
totally unacceptable	you have mishandled
unprofessional (job, attitude, etc.)	

Use words that emphasize the "you attitude," and avoid offensive language. Compare the discourteous sentences on the left with the courteous alternatives on the right:

Discourteous	*Courteous*
We must discontinue your service unless payment is received by the date shown.	Please send us your payment so that your service will not be interrupted.
You completely misunderstood my letter.	Evidently my letter did not make clear. . . .
Your claim that our product was defective on delivery is outlandish.	We are sorry to learn that you were dissatisfied with the way our product arrived.
The rotten coil you installed caused all my trouble.	The trouble may be caused by a malfunctioning coil.
You are sadly mistaken about the warranty.	We are sorry to learn about the difficulty you experienced over the service terms in our warranty.
The new printer you sold me is third-rate and you charged first-rate prices.	Since the printer is still under warranty, I hope that you can make the repairs easily and quickly.
Obviously your company is wrong. I wonder if all the people of Acme are as inept as you.	I would appreciate receiving a more detailed explanation from your home office about this matter.

4. Be neither boastful nor meek. These two strategies—one based on pride and the other on humility—often lead inexperienced letter writers into trouble. On the one hand, they believe that a forceful statement will make a good impression on the reader. Or perhaps they think that a cautious and humble approach will be the least offensive way to earn the reader's respect. Both paths are wrong.

Aggressive letters, filled with boasts, rarely appeal to readers. Letters should radiate confidence without sounding as if the writer had written a letter of self-recommendation. Letters should let the facts speak directly and pleasantly for themselves. The sentences on the left boast; those on the right capture confidence with grace.

Boastful	*Graceful*
You will find me the most diplomatic employee you ever hired.	Much of my previous work has been in answering and adjusting customer complaints.
The Sun and Sea unqualifyingly promises the nicest rooms on the Coast.	Each room at the Sun and Sea has its own private bath and bar refrigerator.
I have performed that procedure so many times I can do it in my sleep.	I have performed all kinds of IV therapy as part of standard procedure.
The Check-Pack offers you incomparable customer convenience.	The Check-Pack gives you a free safe-deposit box.

At the other extreme, some writers stress only their own inadequacy. Their attitude as projected in their letters is "I am the most unworthy person who ever lived, and I would be eternally grateful if you even let my letter sit on your desk, let alone open it." Readers will dismiss such writers as pitiful, unqualified weaklings. Note how the meek sentences on the left are rewritten more positively on the right.

Meek	*Positive*
I know that you have a busy schedule and do not always have time to respond, but I would be appreciative if you could send me your brochure on how to apply Brakelite.	Please send me your brochure on how to apply Brakelite.
The season is almost over I know, but could you possibly let me know something about rates for the rest of the summer	I am interested in renting a cabin in late August (24–30) and would like to know about your rates for that week.
I will be grateful for whatever employment opportunities you could kindly give me.	I will welcome the opportunity to discuss my qualifications with you.

☞ Using the Most Effective Language in Your Letters

For many people, the hardest problem about writing letters is putting their ideas into the right language. Three simple suggestions can help. Your letters should be (1) clear, (2) concise, and (3) contemporary. Regard these principles of letter writing as the three C's.

1. Be clear. Clarity obviously is the most important quality of a business letter. If your message cannot be understood easily, you have wasted your time. Confusion costs time and money. Plan what you are going to say—what your objective is—by taking a few minutes to jot down some questions you want answered or some answers to questions asked of you. Doing this will actually save you time.

Choose precise details appropriate for your audience. In choosing exact words, answer the reader's five fundamental questions—who? what? why? where? and how? Supply concrete words, facts, details, numbers. On the left are some examples of vague sentences that will puzzle a reader because necessary details are missing. These sentences have been rewritten on the right, with exact words replacing unclear ones.

Vague	*Clear*
Please send me some copies of your recent brochure I can use at work.	Please send me 4 copies of your brochure on the new salt substitute to share with my fellow dietitians.
You can expect an appraisal in the next few weeks.	You will receive an estimate on the installation of a new 50,000 BTU air-conditioning unit no later than July 12.
One of our New York stores carries that product.	Our store at 856 East Fifth Avenue sells the entire line of Texworld gloves.
I would like some information about your scheduling policies to Rio de Janeiro.	Please let me know if Pan Am has a morning flight to Rio de Janeiro and how far in advance reservations would have to be made for that flight.
The fee for that service is nominal.	The fee for caulking the five windows on the first floor will be $25.

2. Be concise. "Get to the point" is one of the most frequent commands in the business world. A concise letter does not ramble; instead, it is easy to read and to act on. Ask yourself these two questions: (1) What is the main message I want to tell my reader? (2) Does every sentence and paragraph stick to the main point? The secret to efficient correspondence is to get to the main point at once, as in the following examples.

```
Your order will be delivered by July 26, as you requested.

I am happy to confirm the figures we discussed in our telephone
conversation last Wednesday.
```

```
I request an extension of two weeks in paying my note.

Please accept our apologies for the damaged Movak shipped to
you last week.

Here is the report you asked our accountant to prepare. It does
contain the new figures on the Manchester store you wanted.
```

Many letter writers get off to a deadly slow start by repeating, often word for word, the contents of the letter to which they are responding:

Poor:
```
I have your letter of March 23 before me in which you ask if our
office knows of any all-electric duplexes for rent less than
five years old and that would be appropriate for senior
citizens. You also ask if these duplexes are close to shopping
and medical facilities.
```

Better:
```
Thank you for your letter of March 23. Our office does rent
all-electric duplexes suitable for senior citizens. We have
two units, each renting for $275 a month, that are four blocks
from the Mendez Clinic and two blocks from the Edgewater Mall.
```

Another way to write a concise letter is to include only material that is absolutely relevant. In a letter complaining about inadequate or faulty telephone service, mentioning color preferences for extension telephones would be inappropriate. In a request for information on transferring credits from one college to another, do not ask about intramural sports.

Finally, make sure that your letter is not wordy (review the pertinent sections of Chapters 3 and 4, pages 69–72; 85–88). By taking a few minutes to revise your letters before they are typed, you can write shorter, more useful letters.

3. Be contemporary. Being contemporary does not mean you should use slang expressions ("I had a tire ripped off"; "That rejection was a bummer") or informal language that is inappropriate ("Doing business with Bindex is a hassle"). Nor should you go to the other extreme and become too stiff and formal. Sound friendly and natural. Write to your reader as if you were carrying on a professional conversation with him or her. Business letters today are upbeat, simple, and direct. A business letter is readable and believable; it should not be old-fashioned and flowery.

Often individuals are afraid to write naturally because they fear that they will not sound important. They resort to using phrases that remind them (and the reader) of "legalese"—language that smells of contracts, deeds, and starched collars. The following list of words and phrases on the left contains musty expressions that have crept into letters for years; the list on the right contains modern equivalents.

Musty Expression	*Modern Equivalent*
aforementioned	previous
ascertain	find out
at this present writing	now
I am in receipt of	I have
attached herewith	enclosed
at your earliest possible date	soon
I beg to differ	I disagree
we beg to advise	we believe, think
I am cognizant of	I know
contents duly noted	we realize
forthwith	at once
hereafter, heretofore, hereby	(drop these three "*h*'s" entirely)
humbly request	I ask
immediate future	soon
in lieu of	instead of
in reference to yours of the 10th	your letter of the 10th
kindly advise	let us know
pursuant	concerning
please be advised that	you should know that
please find enclosed	I'm enclosing
pending your reply	until I hear from you
per our conversation	when we spoke
prior to	before
we regret to inform you that	we are sorry that
remittance	payment
remuneration	cost, salary, pay
rest assured that	you can be sure that
same (as in "your letter arrived and I have same")	I have your letter
thanking you in advance	thank you
the undersigned / the writer	I
under separate cover	I'm also sending you
the wherewithal	the way
yours of recent date	your recent letter
your communication	your phone call, your memo, your order, your conversation in my office, etc.

Figure 5.6 contains a flowery letter from Roger Hayes to his English teacher. Note how many old-fashioned, pompous expressions he uses. Figure 5.7 contains a modern translation of the same letter.

If you can be clear, concise, and contemporary, your letters will be well written and well received. These three C's will establish your reputation as a competent writer whose letters are easy to understand and easy to answer courteously and promptly.

Fig. 5.6 A letter with stilted, old-fashioned language.

23 Babson Court
Chicago, IL 60648
May 1, 1985

Professor Bernard Jackson
Department of English
Harrison College
Chicago, IL 60649

Dear Professor Jackson:

Please accept my humblest apologies for being absent on the 25th when the examination you were giving was in progress. As you requested at the commencement of the term, I am cognizant of my responsibility to advise you about the cause of my absence. Herewith is an explanation to that effect.

I am sorry to inform you that my automobile was impaired due to the fact that one of the tires was punctured when I was on my way to your classroom. Please be advised that I took every precaution to avoid this puncture but the burden of travel made such attention on my part ineffective. Lest you doubt my excuse, I herewith enclose a copy of my indebtedness to a local repair shop for road service. My situation was such that I was forced to accompany the mechanic to the repair facility. Accordingly, I thereby failed to attend your class.

The aforementioned disruption in my schedule will not occur again this term. But I beg permission to take the examination in question at your earliest possible convenience. Pending your reply, this writer will diligently prepare for said examination.

At this present point in time, I wish to express my sincerest gratitude to you and eagerly anticipate our future meeting.

Your dedicated student,

Roger Hayes

Roger Hayes

Encl.

Fig. 5.7   A clear and concise translation of Roger's letter.

23 Babson Court
Chicago, IL 60648
May 1, 1985

Professor Bernard Jackson
Department of English
Harrison College
Chicago, IL 60649

Dear Professor Jackson:

I am sorry that I missed the examination you gave on <u>Moby-Dick</u> last
Tuesday (April 25), but I do have a valid excuse. On my way to
class, I had a flat tire, and I had to go with the mechanic when he
repaired it. A copy of his bill is enclosed.

May I take a make-up examination? I will come to your office during
your office hour on Monday to discuss this possibility with you.

Sincerely yours,

Roger Hayes

Roger Hayes

Encl.

☞ Twenty Questions Letter Writers Should Ask Themselves

Here is a checklist of twenty questions you need to ask yourself as a letter writer. They deal with the format, style, and content of your letter. If you can answer each one satisfactorily, you are off to a good start at communicating with your reader.

1. Does my letter look neat and professional?
2. Have I followed one letter format (either the full block or semiblock) consistently?
3. Are my margins wide enough—1½ inches all the way around?
4. Did I spell every word, including the reader's name, correctly?
5. Have I corrected every typographical error?
6. Did I tell the reader exactly why I am writing?
7. Have I begun each sentence with "I," or does my letter adopt the "you attitude"?
8. Are my words clear and precise?
9. Is my letter free from flowery and stuffy language?
10. Do I get my message across politely?
11. Have I answered the reader's questions without including irrelevant material?
12. Have I eliminated unnecessary repetition?
13. Are all my facts—costs, policy numbers, model types, dates, addresses—correct?
14. Have I included all necessary information—dates, quantities, locations, names, costs, references to previous orders or letters?
15. Does my last paragraph sum up my letter appropriately?
16. Have I chosen an appropriate complimentary close?
17. Did I sign the letter in ink?
18. Have I indicated an enclosure line if I am sending something with the letter?
19. Is my return address on the upper left front of the envelope?
20. Does the reader's name and address on the envelope match the inside address?

☞ Exercises

1. What kinds of letters do you receive addressed to you at home? At your work? Write a paragraph about one of these kinds of letters, indicating why it was sent to you and what it wanted you to do.

2. Find two business letters and bring them to class. Be prepared to identify the various parts of a letter discussed in this chapter.

3. Bring to class a letter following the full block format and one written in the semiblock format.

4. Find a letter that is addressed to "Dear Customer," "Postal Patron," or "Dear Resident" and rewrite this form letter to make it more personal.

5. Correct the following inside addresses:

(a) Dr. Ann Clarke, M.D.
    1730 East Jefferson
    Jackson, MI. 46759

(b) To: Tommy Jones
    Secretary to Mrs. Franks
    Donlevey Labs
    Cleveland, O. 45362

(c) Debbie Hinkle
    432 Parkway
    N.Y.C. 10054

(d) Mr. Charles Howe, Acme Pro.
    P.O. Box 675
    1234 S.e. Boulevard
    Gainesville, Flor. 32601

(e) Alex Goings, man.
    Pittfield Industries
    Longview, TEXAS 76450

(f) ATTENTION: G. Yancy
    Police Academy
    1329 Tucker
    N.O., La. 3410-70122

(g) David and Mahenny
    Lawyers
    Dobbs Build.
    L.A. 94756

(h) CONFIDENTIAL
    Jordan Foods, INC.
    Miller Str.
    Lincoln, Neb. 2103

6. Write appropriate inside addresses and salutations to (a) a woman who has not specified her marital status; (b) an officer in the armed forces; (c) a professor at your school; (d) an assistant manager at your local bank; (e) a member of the clergy; (f) your postmaster.

7. Which of the following complimentary closes is suitable for a business letter to someone you have never written to before and do not know?

Yours,	Cordially,	Very truly yours,
Gratefully yours,	Blissfully,	Happily yours,
Sincerely,	Thankfully yours,	Patiently yours,
Faithfully,	Yours truly,	Truly,

8. Find and correct the typographical errors in the following letter:

Dear MR. Jones;

I am very much enterested in finding a copy of your most recent brochure on nutrition. I am najoring in in foodscience at Westgatte Community Colledge and would appreicate obtainning some infornation about your polcies and procedurs in the disrtibution of hot lucnchs in teh elemantery grades. Your extenaive operatiom in this area has been priased for its thoroghness nad flexibilty.

If you have any copies of this borchure, or other instructons I mihgt see, I would like to use them in my class repotrs. With

yoor permision, I would like to shafe these materials with my
homeeconomics calss.

Sincerly yours,

J. P. Allen

J. P. Allen

9. Rewrite the following sentences to make them more personal.
    (a) It becomes incumbent upon this office to cancel order #2394.
    (b) Management has suggested the curtailment of parking privileges.
    (c) ALL USERS OF HYDROPLEX: Desist from ordering replacement
        valves during the period of Dec. 19–29.
    (d) The request for a new catalog has been honored; it will be shipped to
        same address soon.
    (e) Unless circumstances prevent operation, repair crews will report on
        schedule for thoroughfare maintenance.
    (f) Perseverance and attention to detail have made this writer important
        to company in-house work.
    (g) The Director of Nurses hereby notifies staff that a general meeting will
        be held Monday afternoon at 3:00 P.M. sharp. Attendance is mandatory.
    (h) Reports will be filed by appropriate personnel no later than the sched-
        uled plans allow.
    (i) Company guidelines prevent awarding benefits to policy holder
        #2838y0.

10. The following sentences are discourteous, boastful, excessively humble,
    vague, or do not reflect the "you attitude." Rewrite them to correct these
    mistakes.
    (a) Something is obviously wrong in your head office. They have once
        more sent me the wrong model number. Can they ever get things
        straight?
    (b) My instructor wants me to do a term paper on safety regulations at a
        small factory. Since you are the manager of a small factory, send me all
        the information I need at once. My grade depends heavily on all this.
    (c) It is apparent that you are in business to rip off the public.
    (d) I was wondering if you could possibly see your way into sending me the
        local chapter president's name and address, if you have the time, that
        is.
    (e) I have waited for my confirmation for two weeks now. Do you expect
        me to wait forever or can I get some action?
    (f) Although I have never attempted to catalog books before, and really
        do not know my way around the library, I would very much like to be
        considered at some later date convenient to you for a part-time after-
        noon position.

(g) May I take just a moment of your valuable time to point out that our hours for the next three weeks will change and we trust and pray that no one in your agency will be terribly inconvenienced by this.

(h) Your application has been received and will be kept on file for six months. If we are interested in you, we will notify you. If you do not hear from us, please do not write us again. The soaring costs of correspondence and the large number of applicants make the burden of answering pointless letters extremely heavy.

(i) My past performance as a medical technologist has left nothing to be desired.

(j) Credit means a lot to some people. But obviously you do not care about yours. If you did, you would have sent us the $49.95 you rightfully owe us three months ago. What's wrong with you?

(k) The Sunnyside Police Force alerts all residents of the Parkway Heights section that parking violations have been noticed and cautions vehicle owners that these violations will be strictly prosecuted. If a vehicle is ticketed twice in a month period, said vehicle will be towed away. Vehicle owners will then have to reclaim their property at the police garage.

11. Rewrite the following letter to eliminate old-fashioned and stilted language.

Dear Mr. Wellington:

I am in receipt of yours of the 25th and thank you for same. Regarding your solicitation for information on our rocking chairs, model 542a, please be advised that under separate cover we are forwarding to you a brochure with pertinent details for your perusal. For your information as well, I shall herewith quote the exact remittance necessary for each unit: $79.95. Shipping and handling payments should be remitted as well.

I eagerly await your reply and beg to advise you that quantities are indeed limited.

Thanking you in advance for your patronage.

Humbly yours,

J. Alfred Stone

J. Alfred Stone

12. The following letter, wordy and awkward, is filled with musty expressions. It buries key ideas and does not consider the reader's needs. Rewrite this letter to make it shorter, clearer, and more reader-centered.

Dear Ms. Granedi:

This is in response to your firm's letter of recent date inquiring about the types of additional services that may be available to business customers of the First National Bank of Bentonville. The question of a possible time frame for the implementation of said services was also raised in the aforementioned letter. Pursuant to these queries, the following answers, this office trusts, will prove helpful.

Please be advised that the Board of Directors at First National Bank has a continuing reputation for servicing the needs of the Bentonville community, especially the business community. For the last half of a century—fifty years—First National Bank has provided the funds necessary for the growth, success, and expansion of many local firms, yours included. This financial support has bestowed many opportunities on a multitude of business owners, residents of Bentonville, and even residents of surrounding local communities.

The Board is at this present writing currently deliberating, with its characteristic caution, over a variety of options suggested to us by our patrons, including your firm. These options, if the Board decides to act upon them, would enhance the business opportunities for financial transactions at First National Bank. Among the two options receiving attention by the Board at this point in time are the creation of a branch office in the rapidly growing north side of Bentonville. This area has many customers who rely on the services of First National Bank. The Board may also place a business loan department in the new branch.

If this office of the First National Bank of Bentonville might be of further helpful assistance, please advise. Remember banking with First National Bank is a community privilege.

Soundly yours,

M. T. Watkins

M. T. Watkins
Public Relations Director

13. Write a business letter to one of the following individuals and submit an appropriate envelope with your letter:
    (a) Your mayor, asking for an appointment and explaining why you need one
    (b) Your college president, stressing the need for more parking spaces
    (c) The local water department, asking for information about fluoride

(d) An editor of a weekly magazine, asking permission to reprint an article in a school newspaper

(e) The author of an article you have read recently, telling why you like or dislike the views presented

(f) A disc jockey at a local radio station, asking for more songs by a certain group.

6

How to Get a Job: Résumés, Letters, Applications, Interviews, and Evaluations

Obtaining a job today involves a lot of hard work. Before your name is added to the payroll, you will have to do more than simply walk into a personnel office and fill out an application form. Furthermore, finding the *right* job takes time. And finding the right person to fill that job also takes time for the employer. From the employer's viewpoint, the stages in the search for a valuable employee include the following:

1. Deciding on what duties and responsibilities go with the job and determining the qualifications the future employee should possess
2. Advertising the job
3. Reading and evaluating résumés and letters of application
4. Having candidates complete application forms
5. Requesting further proof of the candidates' skills—letters of recommendation, transcripts
6. Interviewing selected candidates
7. Offering the job to the best-qualified individual.

Sometimes these steps are interchangeable, especially steps 4 and 5, but generally speaking, employers go through a long and detailed process to select employees. Step 3, for example, is among the most important for employers (and the most crucial for job candidates). At this stage employers often classify job seekers into one of three groups: those they definitely want to interview; those they may want to interview; and those they have no interest in.

The job seeker will have to know how and when to give the employer all the kinds of information the seven steps require. As a job seeker you will also have to follow a certain schedule in your search for a job. The following procedures will be required of you:

1. Analyzing your strengths and restricting your job search
2. Preparing a dossier (placement file)
3. Looking in the right places for a job
4. Constructing a résumé
5. Writing a letter of application
6. Filling out a job application
7. Going to an interview
8. Accepting or declining a job.

Your timetable should match that of your prospective employer.

Chapter 6 shows you how to begin your job search and how to prepare appropriate letters that are a part of the job-search process. You will need to write a letter of application, letters requesting others to write recommendations for you, letters thanking employers for interviews, and letters accepting or declining a position. In addition to discussing each of these kinds of letters, this chapter shows you how to assemble the supporting data—dossiers, résumés— that employers request. You will also find some practical advice on how to handle yourself at an interview. The chapter concludes with the kinds of evaluations—of self and others—that you can expect to write once you have worked on your job.

The eight steps of your job search are arranged in this chapter in the order in which you are most likely to proceed when you start looking for a job. By reading about these stages in sequence, you will have the benefit of going through a dry run of the employment process itself.

☞ Analyzing Your Strengths and Restricting Your Job Search

Individuals who advise students about how to get a job have isolated two "fatal assumptions" that many job seekers hold. If you assume the following two points, chances are that you will not be very successful in your job search. These two assumptions are stated well by Lewis E. Patterson and Ernest M. Schuttenberg.[1]

1. I should remain loose (vague) about what I want so I'm free to respond to any opportunity.
2. The employer has the upper hand in the whole process.

The first "fatal assumption" will disqualify you for any position for which your major has prepared you. Your first responsibility is to identify your profes-

---

[1] *College Board Review* (Fall 1979): 15.

sional qualifications. Employers want to hire individuals with highly developed technical skills and training. Your education and experience should help you to identify and emphasize your marketable skills. Make an inventory of your accomplishments in your major or job and then decide which specialty within your chosen career appeals to you most. If you are enrolled in a criminal justice program, do you want a position as a corrections officer, a security official, or a member of the local police force? If you are in a nursing program, do you want to work in a large hospital, a nursing home, a state health agency; what kinds of patients do you want to care for—geriatric, pediatric, psychiatric? If your major is food science, do you want to be a caterer or a restaurant owner, or would you rather work for an industrial or hospitality employer? If you already hold a position and want to advance yourself professionally, ask yourself where you would like to relocate and what type of additional responsibilities you are to assume. In short, ask yourself, Where do I want to work and why?

Avoid applying for positions for which you are either overqualified or underqualified. If a position requires ten years of on-the-job experience and you are just starting out, you will only waste the employer's time by applying. On the other hand, if you have two or three years of experience in the food industry, for example, you would not apply for a position that calls for someone who has no training.

The second "fatal assumption"—assuming that the employer controls the entire job-search process—is equally misleading. To a large extent, you can determine whether you are a serious contender for a job by the letters and résumés you write and the self-image you present. Even in today's highly competitive job market, you can secure a suitable job if you keep in mind that the basic purpose of all job correspondence is to sell yourself. Letters and résumés are sales tools to earn you an interview and eventually the job. Be confident and convincing. Employers almost always have a shortage of good, qualified employees.

☞ Preparing a Dossier

The job placement office (sometimes called the career center) at your school will assist you by providing counseling; notifying you of available, relevant jobs; and arranging on-campus interviews. The job placement office will also help you establish your dossier, sometimes referred to as your placement file.

The *dossier*, a French word for a bundle of documents, is your own personal file that is stored at the placement office. This file contains information about you that substantiates and supplements the facts you will list in your résumé and letter of application. Your dossier should contain your letters of recommendation; copies of these letters are made and sent out to prospective employers, thus relieving those who have recommended you of writing an original letter each time you apply for a job. You may also want to include unsolicited letters—those awarding you a scholarship, praising you as the employee of the month (or year), or honoring you for some community service. Be very selective about these kinds of letters; you do not want to crowd your dossier with less important items that will compete for attention with your academic recommendations. The dossier also contains biographical information, a listing of your job experiences, and your transcript(s). You may ask that your dossier be sent to an employer; or employers may request it themselves if you have listed the placement office address on your résumé.

The most important part of your dossier is the letter-of-recommendation section. Whom should you ask to recommend you? Your present or previous employer (even for a summer job) is a logical choice, but be cautious here. If your current employer knows that your education is preparing you for another profession, or if you are working at a part-time job while you are in school, you should obtain a letter of recommendation to be included in your dossier. If you are happily and successfully employed and are looking for a new position only for professional advancement or better salary, you may not want to tell your present employer you are searching for a new job. If another employer is interested in you, you have the right to request the prospective employer to respect your confidence until you become an active (and also a leading) candidate. At that point you should be happy to have your current employer consulted for a reference. On the other hand, if you are at loggerheads with your current employer and want very much to find a new, more suitable position, you need to prepare the prospective employer as honestly and professionally as you can with the least damage to yourself. No sure solution exists.

Be sure to ask two or three of your professors to be references. Choose teachers who know your work, have graded your papers, and have supervised you in fieldwork or laboratory activities. Superiors who knew your work in the military are also likely candidates. Recommendations from these individuals will be regarded as more objective than a letter from a member of the clergy or from a neighbor. Of course, if you are asked for a character reference, by all means ask a member of the clergy.

Make sure that you ask permission of these individuals before you list them as references. This is a courtesy, and it will also give them time to write an appropriate letter for you. Imagine how damaging it would be for you if a prospective employer called one of your teachers whom you had not yet asked to serve as a reference. What if the teacher responded that he or she did not even know you were looking for a job or, worse yet, said you had not had the courtesy to ask to use his or her name as a reference? When you ask for permission in a letter or in person, stress how much a strong letter of support means to you and find out if the individual is willing to write such a letter. It is important to emphasize that you need a strong letter of recommendation; a general or weak one will hurt your chances in your job search. As a help to your references, tell them what kind of jobs you are applying for and keep them up to date about your educational and occupational achievements. Figure 6.1 shows a sample letter requesting an individual to serve as a reference.

Fig. 6.1   Request for a letter of recommendation.

5432 South Kenneth Avenue
Chicago, IL 60651
March 30, 1985

Mr. Sunny Butler, Manager
A&P Supermarket
4000 West 79th Street
Chicago, IL 60652

Dear Mr. Butler:

As you may recall, I was employed at your store from September 1983
through August 1984. During the school year, I worked part-time as
a stock clerk and relief cashier, while in the summer months I was a
full-time employee in the produce department, helping to fill in
while Bill Dirksen and Vivian Rogers were away on their vacations.

I enjoyed my work at A&P, and I learned a great deal about ordering
stock, arranging merchandise, and assisting customers.

This May I expect to receive my A.A. degree from Moraine Valley
Community College in retail merchandising. I have already begun
preparing for my job search for a position in retail sales. Would
you be kind enough to write a letter of recommendation for me in
which you mention what you regard as my greatest strengths as one of
your employees? If you agree, I will send you a letter of
recommendation form from the Placement Office at Moraine Valley.
Your letter will then become a part of my permanent placement file.

I look forward to hearing from you. I thought you might like to see
the enclosed résumé, which shows what I have been doing since I left
A&P.

Sincerely yours,

Robert B. Jackson

Robert B. Jackson

Encl. Résumé

You have a legal right to determine whether you want to see your letters or not. If you have read your recommendations, that fact is noted on the dossier. Some employers feel that if the candidates see what is written about them, the writers of the letters of recommendation will be less frank and unwilling to volunteer critical information. If you waive your right to see the letters written about you, you must sign an appropriate form, a copy of which is then given to the individual recommending you. Keep in mind, too, that some individuals may refuse to write a letter that they know you will see; they may prefer absolute confidentiality. Figure 6.2 shows a confidential evaluation form. Before you make any decision about seeing your letters, get the advice of your instructors and your placement counselor.

Do not wait to establish your dossier until you begin applying for jobs. Most placement offices recommend that candidates set up their dossiers at least three to six months before they begin looking for jobs. Thus you will ensure that your letters of recommendation are on file and that you have benefited from the placement office's services. In counseling you, the placement office will ask that you complete a confidential questionnaire about your geographic preferences, salary expectations, and the types of positions for which you are qualified. With this information on hand, the placement office will be better prepared to advise you and to notify you of appropriate openings.

Some placement offices will charge a small fee for their services, while others provide their services free of charge.

☞ Looking in the Right Places for a Job

One way to search for a job is simply to send out a batch of letters to companies you want to work for. But how do you know what jobs, if any, these companies have available, what qualifications they are looking for, and what application procedures and deadlines they want you to follow? You can avoid these uncertainties by knowing where to look for a job and knowing what a specific job requires. Such information will make your search easier and, in all likelihood, more successful. Here are a number of sources to consult:

1. Do not overlook the obvious—the newspaper. Look at local newspapers as well as papers with a wide circulation: The *New York Times*, the *Chicago Tribune*, the *Los Angeles Times*, the *New Orleans Times–Picayune*, the *Cleveland Plain Dealer*. The Sunday editions advertise positions available all over the country. The ads you find may list the name, address, and phone number of the company seeking employees or may be blind, that is, listing only a post office box to conceal the employer's identity.
2. Investigate openings listed in professional journals in your major. The *American Journal of Nursing*, for example, carries notices of openings arranged by geographic location in each of its monthly issues; and *Food Technology* prints in each issue a section called "Professional Placement," which lists jobs from all over the country.

Fig. 6.2 A confidential evaluation form.

TO THE CANDIDATE: (type in)

Candidate's
Full Name _____   Name of
       first   middle   last   Reference _____

Courses under this instructor (title, quarter, year) or Period of employment _____

_____

Today's date _____Your (anticipated) date of graduation _____Degree program _____

TO THE TEACHER OR EMPLOYER:

Please note that this is a confidential evaluation. The candidate has waived his or her right of access to this evaluation. We shall appreciate both a rating and a statement regarding the candidate's suitability for employment. Your evaluation will become a permanent part of his or her placement record which is made available to employers and graduate schools. *Do not show it to the candidate.* Also, *please type* this form if possible. Blue ink does not duplicate clearly. Once this form is on file you may refer future requests concerning this candidate to the Career Development & Placement Office for a reply.

Indicate degree of acquaintance with candidate:

Length of acquaintance: _____

☐ Know personally

☐ Know as a student

☐ Know only as a member of a large class

☐ Know as an employee

	Unable to Observe	Excellent	Above Average	Average	Below Average	Poor
Appearance						
Academic Performance (within subject (s) under your supervision)						
Promptness in assignments; regularity of attendance						
Ability to communicate: Orally						
In Writing						
Initiative						
Leadership						
Social qualities (congeniality, interest in others)						
Promise in _____ (specify field)						
Suitability for graduate school						

STATEMENT: (Please elaborate on the above and comment on any other appropriate points. This statement is considered an important part of the total evaluation.)

Signature _____

Title & Dept. _____

Institution or Organization _____

Date: _____   Address _____

Reprinted by permission of Office of Career Development and Placement, Valdosta State College.

3. Visit your college's placement office. Counselors keep an up-to-date file of available positions and can also tell you when a firm's recruiter will be on campus to conduct interviews. They can also help you locate summer and part-time work, both on and off campus.
4. Check with your state and local employment offices. They also have a current file of positions and offer some counseling (free of charge). Some educational television stations even broadcast information (qualifications, salary) about positions on file at a state employment office. If you are interested in working for the U.S. government, visit a Civil Service Commission Office, a Federal Job Information Center, or any government agency. Get the addresses from the white pages of your phone book.
5. Visit the personnel department of a company or agency to see if there are any current openings or if any vacancies are anticipated. Often you will be given an application to fill out, or your name will be placed on a list.
6. Let your relatives, friends, neighbors, and professors know that you are looking for a job. They may hear of something and can notify you. Better yet, they may recommend you for the position—with a phone call, a trip to the personnel department (if they work for the company), or a letter. A respected employee can open the door for you. John D. Erdlen and Donald H. Sweet, experts on the job search, cite the following as a primary rule of job hunting: "Don't do anything yourself you can get someone with influence to do for you."
7. Write your local Chamber of Commerce. Though not a placement center, the Chamber of Commerce can give you the names and addresses of employers likely to hire individuals with your qualifications, as well as information about these companies to use in a letter of application or at an interview.
8. Register with a professional employment agency. Some agencies list two kinds of jobs—those that are found for the applicant free of charge (because the employer pays the fee) and those for which the applicant pays a fee. Sometimes that fee can be stiff—for example, a percentage of your annual salary. Employment agencies often find out about jobs through channels already available to you. Before turning your search over to a professional employment agency, however, make sure that you have exhausted all the previously mentioned services.

☞ Preparing a Résumé

The résumé, sometimes called a data sheet or vita, is a factual and concise summary of your qualifications for the job. It is not your life's history or an emotional autobiography; nor is it a transcript of your college work. The résumé is a one-page (no more than two-page) outline accompanying your letter of application for a job. Résumés are never sent alone. You may, however, bring one with you to an interview. The main function of the résumé is to present information about your education, experience, and other achievements accurately and quickly so that a busy personnel manager or department head will want to interview you. The résumé should make a good first impression.

What You Exclude from a Résumé

Preparing a résumé involves skills highly valued in any job—neatness; the ability to organize, summarize, and persuade; and most important, a sense of proportion. Knowing what to exclude from a résumé is as important as what to include. Here is information to exclude from your résumé:

1. Salary demands or expectations
2. Preferences for work schedules, days off, or overtime
3. Comments about fringe benefits
4. Travel restrictions
5. Your photograph
6. Comments about your family, spouse, or children

Save any questions or preferences you have for the interview. The résumé should be written appropriately to get you that interview.

What You Include in a Résumé

What should you include on your résumé? Both experienced candidates and recent graduates with limited experience ask this question. The dangers involve including too much or putting in too little. If you have years of experience and have recently returned to school, you may risk flooding your prospective employer with too many details. You cannot possibly include every detail of your job(s) for the last ten or twenty years. Therefore, you must be selective and emphasize those skills and positions most likely to earn you the job. Figure 6.3 shows a résumé from an individual who had years of job experience before she returned to school.

Many job candidates who have spent most of their lives in school are faced with the other extreme—not having much job experience to put down. The worst thing to do is to write "none" for experience. Any part-time or summer job, as well as work done at school for a library or science laboratory, shows a prospective employer you are responsible and knowledgeable about the obligations of being an employee. Figure 6.4 shows a résumé from a student with very little job experience; Figure 6.5 shows one from a student with a few years of experience.

Parts of a Résumé

Name, Address, Phone

Center this information at the top of the résumé under the word *résumé*. (Capitalize the word *résumé* and be sure to add the two accent marks by hand if

Fig. 6.3   Résumé from an individual with ten years' job experience.

RÉSUMÉ

ANNA C. CASSETTI

6457 South Blackstone Avenue

Ft. Worth, Texas 76119

(817) 234-5657 (Home)
(817) 432-7211 (Office)

CAREER OBJECTIVE: Full-time sales position with large real estate office in the Phoenix or Tucson area with specific opportunities in real estate appraisals and tax counseling.

EXPERIENCE:

1985-present   Real estate agent, MacMurray Real Estate, Haltom City, Texas; working in small office (two salespersons plus broker) with limited listings; sold individually $550,000 in residential property and appraised both residential and commercial listings.

1979-1984   Teller, Dallman Federal Savings and Loan, Inc., Ft. Worth. Responsible for supervising, training, and coordinating activities of six full-time and two part-time tellers. Promoted to Chief Teller, March 1982.

1979   Tax consultant, H&R Block, Westover Hills, Texas,
(Jan.-May)   office.

1976-1978   Salesperson, Cruckshank's Hardware Store, 7542 Montrose Drive, Ft. Worth.

1972-1976   U.S. Navy, honorably discharged with rank of Petty Officer, Third Class. Served as stores manager.

EDUCATION:

1978-1984   Awarded B.S. degree in real estate management from Texas Christian University, Ft. Worth. Completed thirty-three hours in business and real estate courses with a concentration in real estate finance, appraising, and property management. Also completed nine hours in computer science and data processing. Wrote a report on appraisal procedures as part of supervised training program in my last term.

1977   Diploma in Basic Income Tax Preparation earned after
(Sept.-Dec.)   completing intensive ten-week course offered through H&R Block's Ft. Worth office (Westover Hills, Texas).

Fig. 6.3 (Continued.)

Anna C. Cassetti, page 2

1973–1974	Attended U.S. Navy's Supply Management School, U.S. Naval Base, San Diego, California. Applied principles of stores management at Newport Naval Base.
PERSONAL:	Social Security Number: 329–35–9465 Texas Realtor's License: 756a2737
HOBBIES AND INTERESTS:	Chair, Financial Committee, Grace Presbyterian Church, Ft. Worth. Have also worked with Junior Achievement advising teenagers in business management. Enjoy golfing and hiking.

REFERENCES:

My complete dossier is available from the Texas Christian University College Placement Office, Ft. Worth, Texas 76119. In it are letters from the following individuals:

Dr. Peter Tolivar
Department of Business
Texas Christian University
Ft. Worth, TX 76119
(817) 266-1003

Ms. Patricia Albertson
Controller
Dallman Federal Savings and Loan
7858 South Broadway
Ft. Worth, TX 76109
(817) 266-7301

Mrs. Gladys Mates
Vice-President
Dallman Federal Savings and Loan
7858 South Broadway
Ft. Worth, TX 76109
(817) 266-7301

Mr. Pat MacMurray
Broker, MacMurray Real Estate
1732 Main Street
Haltom City, TX 77832
(817) 993-4201

your typewriter cannot.) Capitalize all the letters of your name to make it stand out. But do not capitalize every letter of your address. Include a zip code and telephone number with a proper area code so a prospective employer can call you for an interview. If you have two addresses (home and school) it is wise to list them both. It is also perfectly acceptable to list two phone numbers if one of them is where you receive messages during the day and the other in the evening.

Career Objective Statement

The first step in the job process is to prepare a career objective statement. Such a statement involves self-evaluation and will influence everything else you list. You should ask yourself four basic questions: (1) What kind of job do I want? (2) What kind of job am I qualified for? (3) What kinds of skills do I possess? and (4) What kinds of skills do I want to learn? Do not apply for a position that requires years of experience you lack or demands skills you do not possess. On the other hand, do not give the impression that you will take anything. Define your job goal precisely so that prospective employers can measure your experience and education against their needs. Do not simply say "sales work" or "law enforcement." Instead, concentrate on specific immediate and long-range goals within your chosen career, for example: "Full-time position with urban police force eventually allowing me to gain experience in correctional counseling"; "Management trainee in personnel department providing opportunity for professional growth and advancement in insurance counseling"; "Full-time position as staff nurse on medical-surgical unit with opportunity for primary care nursing." Demonstrate to your prospective employer your current level of competence and show, through a statement of objective, your willingness to advance in the organization.

The order of the next two categories—education and experience—can vary. If experience is your best selling point, list it before education, as in Figure 6.3. List education first if you are short on job experience, as in Figure 6.4.

Education

In listing your educational experiences, begin with your most recent education, and list everything significant since high school. Indicate when you received your latest degree, diploma, or certificate or when you expect to receive it. You need not list every school if you have transferred frequently. Do indicate your major and minor in college work; and pay special attention to communications (written and oral) courses you have completed. Employers are impressed by students who can write and speak well. But remember, a résumé is not a transcript. Do not simply list a series of courses. Your goal is to convince your prospective employer that you have special abilities. Simply listing standard courses will not set you apart from hundreds of other applicants taking similar courses across the country. Mention the number of credit hours you have

Fig. 6.4   Résumé from a student with little job experience.

RÉSUMÉ

ANTHONY H. JONES
73 Allenwood Boulevard
Santa Rosa, California 95401
(707) 464-6390

CAREER OBJECTIVE: Full-time position as a layout/paste-up artist with commercial publishing house.

EDUCATION:

1984-1986   Will receive A.S. degree in June from Santa Rosa Junior College, majoring in industrial graphics illustration with a specialty in layout design. Completed more than forty hours in design principles, layout and lettering, graphic communications, and photography. Am very familiar with both layout techniques and electromechanical illustration. Major projects included assisting layout editors at McAdam Publishers during an apprenticeship program completed in May 1986 and writing a detailed report on the kinds of designs, photographs, and artwork used in two local magazines—Living in Sonoma County and Real Estate in Sonoma County. Made Dean's List in 1985 with a GPA of 3.4.

1980-1984   Attended Santa Rosa High School. Took electives in drawing, photography, and industrial arts. Provided major artwork for student magazine, Thunder.

EXPERIENCE:

1984-1986   Part-time salesperson at Buchman's Department Store while attending Santa Rosa Junior College full-time. Duties included assisting customers in sporting goods and appliance departments. Also assisted sport shop manager with displaying merchandise.

PERSONAL: Height 5'8"   Weight 147 lbs.
Birth date: Jan. 23, 1965

REFERENCES:

Mr. Albert Kim
Art Department
Santa Rosa Junior College
Santa Rosa, CA 95401
(707) 464-6300

Ms. Margaret Feinstein
Layout Editor
McAdam Publishers
Santa Rosa, CA 95401
(707) 453-8699

Dr. Gloria Cernek
Art Department
Santa Rosa Junior College
Santa Rosa, CA 95401
(707) 464-6300

Fig. 6.5   Résumé from a student with some job experience.

RÉSUMÉ

MARIA H. LOPEZ

1725 Brooke Street

Miami, Florida 32701

(305) 372-3429

CAREER OBJECTIVE: Full-time position assisting dentist in providing dental health care and counseling and performing preventive dental treatments; especially interested in learning more about pedodontics.

EDUCATION:

August 1984–
May 1986

Will receive A.S. degree in dental hygiene from Miami-Dade Community College in May. Have completed nine courses in oral pathology, dental materials and specialties, periodontics, and community dental health. Currently enrolled in clinical dental hygiene program. Am familiar with procedures and instruments used with oral prophylaxis techniques. Subject of major project was proper nutrition for preschoolers. Minor area of interest is psychology (twelve hours completed). Received excellent evaluations in business writing course. GPA is 3.2. Expect to take the American Dental Assistants' Examination on June 2.

1977–1981

Miami North High School. Took electives in electronics and secretarial science.

EXPERIENCE:

April 1982–
July 1984

Full-time ward clerk on the pediatric unit at St. Francis Hospital (Miami Beach). Duties included ordering supplies, maintaining records, transcribing orders, and greeting and assisting visitors.

June 1981–
April 1982

Secretary-receptionist, Murphy Construction Company, Miami; did light typing, filing, and mailing in small office (three secretaries).

Summers
1979–1980

Water Meter Reader, City of Hialeah, Florida.

PERSONAL: Health: Excellent; Bilingual: Spanish/English

HOBBIES
  AND
INTERESTS:

Swimming, reading (especially applied psychology), and tennis. Have done volunteer work for church day-care center.

144

Fig. 6.5 (Continued.)

Maria H. Lopez, page 2

REFERENCES:

The following individuals have written letters of recommendation for my placement file, available from the Placement Center, Miami—Dade Community College, Medical Center Campus, Miami, FL 33127.

Sister Mary James
Head Nurse, Pediatric Unit
St. Francis Hospital
10003 Collins Avenue
Miami Beach, FL 33141
(305) 432-5113

Professor Mitchell Pellborne
Department of Dental Hygiene
Miami—Dade Community College
Medical Center
Miami, FL 33127
(305) 421-3872

Mildred Pecos, D.D.S.
9800 Exchange Avenue
Miami, FL 33167
(305) 421-1039

Mr. Jack Murphy
Owner, Murphy Construction
1203 Francis Street
Miami, FL 33157
(305) 421-6767

How to Get a Job: Résumés, Letters, Applications, Interviews, and Evaluations

completed and then indicate by subject area the courses in your major most relevant for the position for which you are applying.

Try to avoid vague titles such as Science I or Nursing IV. Instead, concentrate on the kinds of skills you learned. For example, "30 hours in planning and development courses specializing in transportation, land use, and community facilities and 10 hours in field methods of gathering, interpreting, and writing a description of survey data were required." Or state that "24 hours in my major included courses in business marketing, management, and materials in addition to 12 hours in computer science." In fact, the computer skills you have are especially important to employers because of the increasing use of computers in business and industry. Also note any laboratory work, fieldwork, internship, or cooperative educational work. It is important to an employer looking for someone with previous practical experience. List your GPA (grade point average) only if it is 3.0 or above and your rank in class only if you are in the top 35 percent. Otherwise, indicate your GPA in just your major or during your last term, if it is above 3.0.

Also list any academic honors you have won (dean's list, department awards, school honors, scholarships, grants, or honorable mentions). Indicate membership in any honor societies in your major, because such participation will show that you are professionally active. You also should mention military schools, training programs (E.M.T., secretarial), institutes or special workshops, company-sponsored seminars you have attended, or any apprenticeships you have completed. If you have attended many of these learning programs, do not list your high school. Applicants with limited educational experience may include their high school, the date of graduation, and, if helpful, any special training related to their current work (shops, labs, trips) and any honors. As a rule, though, high school activities should be deemphasized.

Experience

This is the most important category for many employers. It shows them that you have held jobs before and that you are responsible. Beginning with your most recent position, include both full- and part-time work, and list the dates, company name, titles you held, and major responsibilities. Do not mention why you left a job. Give the most attention to your latest, most relevant position. If it happens to be your second most recent position, keep the correct order, but spend more time on it. Discuss jobs that you held eight or nine years ago only if your experiences then are relevant to the position you are looking for now. If these jobs were not relevant, just list the places of employment or do not mention them at all.

In describing your position, emphasize any responsibility you had that involved handling money, other employees, customer accounts, services, or programs, or writing letters and reports. Prospective employers are interested in your leadership abilities, financial shrewdness, tact in dealing with the public, and communication skills. They are also favorably impressed by promotions you may have earned. Use strong, active language to pinpoint your duties (*managed, supervised, organized, directed, trained, arranged, budgeted, handled, maintained, calculated, operated, prepared, wrote, performed*). Don't just say you "worked for a newspaper"—your prospective employer will not know if you wrote editorials, took ads, or delivered papers. Perhaps you were an assistant to the ads editor and were responsible for arranging and verifying copy. Say so. That is impressive and informative. Rather than saying that you were a secretary, indicate that you wrote business letters, organized files, prepared schedules for part-time help in a large office (twenty-five people), or assisted the manager in preparing accounts. Of course, do not inflate your role to the point of calling a receptionist a "communications consultant" or a waiter a "food service manager."

If you have held many jobs, which ones should you list, and which ones should you omit? As a general rule, indicate whatever positions are most relevant for the job you are seeking. Your summer job as a lifeguard who knew life-saving techniques may help you in getting a position as a respiratory therapist. Waiting on tables is good experience for candidates who want to obtain a position with a hospitality chain or a food-service organization. Do not forget jobs you may have had at school—stacking books in the library, typing for a teacher, cleaning buildings, tutoring. Employers are not impressed by baby-sitting or lawn-mowing jobs, however, unless you can relate those duties to the position you are seeking.

If you have had several jobs in the last ten or twenty years, list only those in which your responsibilities were significant and relevant to your present search for a job. Avoid stringing out five or six temporary jobs (each under three months). Combine all of them into one brief statement or omit them. Remember, space is at a premium on your résumé. If you have been a housewife for ten years and raised three children before you returned to school or the job market, list this information and note why you are reentering the business world. Indicate the management skills you developed in running a household.

Personal (Optional)

According to federal employment laws, you are not obligated to give information about your sex, race, national origin, religion, or marital status. The laws prohibit discrimination on these bases. You may, however, want to supply information about personal matters. You will have to determine whether listing such personal details can be used to your advantage in securing a job. The trick is to know your would-be employer and to profit from that employer's preferences. For example, if you are applying for a sales position requiring extensive travel, your putting down that you are single would inform the employer that you do not have family obligations to worry about. Moreover, if you are applying for a position in a child day-care center or one as a teacher's aide, the fact that you have children may be important to your employer. Other pertinent personal details include any foreign languages you speak or any special licenses and certificates you hold. For example, if you are bilingual in Spanish, Vietnamese, or French and are applying for a position in customer relations work in a bank or hospital, list that fact. It will be a drawing card to your employer. If you have already passed nursing state boards or earned a pilot's license, state that by indicating your appropriate license numbers. Ultimately, common sense dictates that you reveal only personal information that is required or that underscores your qualifications for the job.

Hobbies or Interests (Optional)

This category is of least value to a prospective employer, *if there is no connection between it and the rest of your résumé*. Of course, if a pastime, sport, or hobby has a direct bearing on the kind of job you are applying for or the kinds of subjects you studied in school, then by all means list and briefly describe it. For example, the following activities may be appropriate for careers listed after them: weight lifting for construction work; photography for advertising; volunteer work for nursing or social work; travel for the hospitality industry; gardening for a horticultural position; civic work for law enforcement. Include extracurricular activities or community service especially if you held some office (treasurer of the local Lions Club, manager of a college basketball team).

References

You can inform readers of your résumé that you will provide references on request or that they can obtain a copy of your dossier from your placement center; or you can list the names, titles, addresses, and telephone numbers of three or four individuals directly on your résumé. Prospective employers can then write to you, ask for your dossier, or directly write or call the individuals whose names have been given. Listing the names of your references is useful only when they are well known in a community or belong to the same profession in which you are seeking employment. In these cases you profit from the magic a recognizable name or title gives you.

The Appearance of Your Résumé

The appearance of your résumé is as important as its content. It should be inviting and pleasing to the eye. Make it professional looking with wide margins, clear, dark type, and clearly divided sections to help readers locate information quickly. Employers will also look for correctness and consistency. If a résumé is carefully prepared, employers will predict that the work you do for them will be done the same way. A résumé can make that first good impression for you; a poorly prepared résumé assures you that you will not get a second chance.

Your résumé should be typed on good quality 8½″ × 11″ white bond paper. Avoid exotic colors. In fact, recruiters in a recent study preferred white to colored paper (John Penrose, "A Discrepancy Analysis of the Job-Getting

Process and a Study of Résumé Techniques," *Journal of Business Communication* [Summer 1984]: 3–15).

Avoid the twin dangers of crowding information all over the page or of leaving huge, highly conspicuous chunks of white space at the bottom and sides. A crowded résumé suggests that you cannot summarize; a résumé with too many blank spaces points to a lack of achievements. You should have white space between categories to emphasize certain points and to make reading your résumé easier. Study Figures 6.3, 6.4, and 6.5 again. Type a number of rough drafts to experiment with spacing. Better yet, hire a professional typist and explain how you want your résumé to look. The one-time cost of a professionally typed résumé is small; and the value of a well-typed résumé makes it worthwhile.

Unlike your letter of application, the résumé is not retyped for each job you apply for. Your prospective employers will not expect an original copy, but they do expect a professional-looking copy. Never send a carbon, mimeographed, or other poor-quality copy. Rather than photocopying your résumé, use the services of a professional printer, who for a relatively modest fee will phototypeset your résumé, giving it a highly professional look.

Because you are supplying a copy of your résumé, a single error in it would appear each time you sent it out. Therefore, proofread your résumé to make sure it is letter-perfect. Spell every word correctly and avoid strikeovers or crossed-out letters. Figure 6.6 contains a poorly prepared résumé and the reasons why it is bad. Figure 6.7 shows a résumé evaluation form used by six experts from business, industry, and education who judged student résumés prepared for a workshop at the University of Colorado, Boulder. After you complete the draft of your résumé, evaluate it according to the ten criteria on the form. Then revise it until it satisfies the ten criteria and is ready for final typing.

☞ Writing a Letter of Application

Together with your résumé, you send your prospective employer a letter of application, one of the most important pieces of correspondence you may ever write. Its goal is to get you an interview and ultimately the job. Letters you write in applying for jobs should be personable, professional, and persuasive— the three P's, something to remember. Knowing how the letter of application and résumé work together and how they differ can give you a better idea of how to begin your letter.

How the Letter and Résumé Differ

The résumé is a compilation of facts—a record of dates, important courses, names, places, addresses, and jobs. You will have your résumé duplicated, and you will send a copy to each prospective employer. Your letter of application,

Fig. 6.6 A poor résumé.

RÉSUMÉ

JAMES L. McPHERSON
33 North Platte Road *Poor alignment*
Noland, New Mexico *No zip code*
No telephone number

Spelling
PERSONNEL:

Not needed { Age: 22yrs. 6 mos. *Spelling* Wieght: 156 lbs
Marital Status: Engaged Height: (5'10") *Abbreviation*
Religion: Presbyterian Health: O.K. *Slang*

CAREER OBJECTIVE: I like to work outdoors and
want to get (any) suitable job *Too broad*
Poor Typing in the forrestry industry.

Spelling

EDUCATION:
1981-1985 Attended Noland Junior College,
Noland, N.M. 84546. I took courses
Listing courses at random in English, Outdoor Recreation,
says nothing about specific Forrest Surveying, Forrest *Spelling*
skills Management, Forest Economics,
Park Administration, Human
Spelling Rolations, Recreation
Margin Maintenance, Communication, and
Mathematics, and Science. I did
better my (secondyear) than my *Typing*
first. In my English and
Communications courses I wrote papers and
delivered sppeeches about
Spelling the forrest. Also, I went on *Margin*
two or three lengthy field trips in
the north. *What skills did he learn?*

Wrong 1881 I attended Noland Junior College
century part time. *Why a separate entry?*

1980 I graduated from Noland High *Hyphen*
School where I played basket——*missing*
ball my third year and fourth year.
I also was the team co-captain.
Vague phrase Helped out with The Torch.
——*What is it?*

150

Fig. 6.6   (Continued.)

Underscore   EXPERIENCE:

        1980–1981   ***Doing what?*** Worked for Walgreen's. Address:
                                       754 South Loma Blvd. Also I joined
                    Abbreviation the (N. Mexico) National Guard. We
                                       were sent to Ft. Carson for our
                                       basic training.   ***Why mention***
                                       Ft. Carson? What does he do in the
                                       Guard?

Capitalize   Hobbies: I like swimming, jogging, and water
                                     polo.   ***So what?***

        REFERENCES:

Mr. Henry R. Pepeer	Dr. John Lyons	Alice McPherson
P.O. Box 768	Noland Junior College	33 N. Platte
Noland, N.M.	Noland, N.M.	Noland, N.M.
What relationship to	***What department?***	***Relative is not an***
McPherson?		***impartial reference***

No telephone numbers

151

Fig. 6.7   A résumé evaluation form.

1. Clarity of job objective	not on résumé ☐	very unclear			extremely clear
		1 2 3 4 5			

1. Clarity of job objective — not on résumé ☐ — very unclear ___ extremely clear — 1 2 3 4 5

2. Essence of educational information — not on résumé ☐ — too much or too little information ___ extremely concise and informative — 1 2 3 4 5

3. Description of job experience with skills emphasis — not on résumé ☐ — poor description of skills ___ excellent description of skills — 1 2 3 4 5

4. Additional positive information that supports job objective — not on résumé ☐ — irrelevant additional information ___ very supportive additional information — 1 2 3 4 5

5. Correctness of typing, spelling, and grammar — poorly written and typed ___ well written and typed — 1 2 3 4 5

6. Organization — poorly organized ___ extremely well organized — 1 2 3 4 5

7. Ease of reading (layout) — very difficult to read ___ very easy to read — 1 2 3 4 5

8. Quality of reproduction (paper, print) — poor quality ___ excellent quality — 1 2 3 4 5

9. Attractiveness — not attractive ___ very attractive — 1 2 3 4 5

10. Overall rating — poor résumé ___ excellent résumé — 1 2 3 4 5

Journal of Employment Counseling 16 (September 1979):156. Copyright 1979 American Personnel and Guidance Association. Reprinted with permission.

however, is much more personal. You must write a new, original letter to each prospective employer. Photocopied letters of application say that you did not care enough, that you did not want to spend the time and energy to answer the employer's ad personally. Whereas your résumé is intended for all readers, each letter of application should be tailored to a specific job. It should respond precisely to the kinds of qualifications the employer seeks. The letter of application is a sales letter emphasizing and applying the most relevant details (of education, experience, and talents) on your résumé. In short, the résumé contains the raw material that the letter of application transforms into a finished and highly marketable product—you!

Résumé Facts You Exclude from a Letter of Application

The letter of application should not simply repeat the details listed in your résumé. In fact, the following details belong only on your résumé and should not be restated in the letter: (1) personal data including license or certificate numbers, (2) the specific names of courses in your major, (3) your hobbies, and (4) the names and addresses of your references. Duplicating these details in your letter gives no new information to help persuade prospective employers that you are the individual they are seeking.

Finding Information About Your Prospective Employer

One of the best ways to sell yourself to future employers is to demonstrate that you have some knowledge of their company. A number of years ago, a college was looking for an instructor and was pleased with one candidate who referred to the college's specific courses by their numbers in her letter of application. This individual went to the profitable trouble of reading the college's catalog before applying. Do a little similar homework; investigate the job and the company. Consult such reference works as *Industry Surveys, Directory of Corporation Affiliations,* or *Standard and Poor's Corporation Records* for information on company activities. Figure 6.8 reprints part of a page from *Standard and Poor's Corporation Records,* which supplies useful details on the history, financial status, and officers of a company. You can also obtain information from the company itself by writing for brochures, descriptions, and schedules a number of months before you actually apply. Check with the Chamber of Commerce. Ask people who work in the company.

Except in response to a blind ad, write directly to the individual responsible for hiring—the personnel officer, the supervisor, the director of nurses, the district manager. You can call the company and ask the switchboard operator to give you the name of this individual. Ask for the correct spelling of the name, too, so there is no mistake when you write to this individual.

Fig. 6.8   A company description from *Standard and Poor's Corporation Records.*

Lilly Industrial Coatings, Inc.

CAPITALIZATION (Nov. 30 '83)
LONG TERM DEBT - $1,190,000, excl. $140,000 due currently.

STOCK-	Auth. Shs.	Outstg. Shs.
Capital no par:		
Cl. A	*24,250,000	16,815,264
Cl. B	750,000	a 190,586

*Incl. 190,586 for exchange of Cl. B, and 357,118 optioned to employees, with 337,458 for future grants- all adjtd. for 2-for-1 split Apr. 12, 1984.

†Adjtd. for 2-for-1 split Apr. 12, 1984; excl. 362,754 in treas.

aAdjtd. for 2-for-1 split Apr. 12, 1984; excl. 49,414 in treas.

CORPORATE BACKGROUND

Company and subsidiaries formulate and make industrial coatings, including enamels, varnishes, lacquers, and similar coatings for decorative and protective uses. Co.'s coatings are sold directly to manufacturers of such products as aluminum siding for homes, major appliances, bottle caps, beer and soft drink cans, office machines, computer housings, metal furniture and electronic cabinetry. Others are used in finishing wood products (mainly furniture and wood panels) and products made from hardboard, plastic, and glass.

PROPERTY - Plants are owned in Ind., N.C., Cal., Mass., Tenn., N.J. (2), Ore. and Ala. A warehouse is owned in Ill.

PRINCIPAL SUBSIDIARIES- Lilly Co. (62% owned); LIC Sales Corp.; Lilly Coatings (Far East) Ltd.

CAPITAL EXPENDITURES, Yrs. End. Nov. 30: Thou. $
1983 2,377   1982 3,303   1981 2,859

EMPLOYEES- Nov. 30, 1983, 904.

INCORPORATED in Ind. Nov. 17, 1888, as Lilly Varnish Co.; present title adopted May 15, 1965.

CHAIRMAN & PRES, J.R. Pickering; V-Ps, R.S. Bailey, A.F. Mundt, J.R. Pickering, M.E. Evans, T.P. Kelly, Jr., W.I. Longsworth, Jr., J.V. Borland, Jr., V-P & SECY, P.J. Stokes; TREAS & ASST SECY, K.L. Mills.

DIRECTORS-

J. V. Borland, Jr.	R. S. Bailey
A. F. Mundt	J. R. Pickering
M. E. Evans	T. P. Kelly, Jr.
W. I. Longsworth, Jr.	P. J. Stokes
H. A. Chioupek	John D. Peterson
J. Dwight Peterson	W. M. Corrigan
R. A. Steele	T. E. Reilly, Jr.

OFFICE - 546 Abbott St., P.O. Box 946, Indianapolis, IN 46206 (Tel.: 317-634-8512). ANNUAL MEETING- in Apr.

STOCK DATA

CL. A AND B no par are identical except that the limited voting rights of Cl. A are equal to voting rights of Cl. B only with regard to voting for merger, consolidation, or dissolution of Co.; and voting for one director if the number of directors is eleven or less, or 2 if the number exceeds 11. Cl. B shall be exchanged for Cl. A, share-for-share, when the holder ceases to be an employee or decides to dispose of the shares.

STOCKHOLDERS- Nov. 30, 1983 (of record): Cl. A, 1,000; Cl. B, 90.

TRANSFER AGENT & REGISTRAR- (Cl. A) American Fletcher National Bank & Trust Co., Indianapolis.

Standard Corporation Descriptions, 45, No. 10 (May 24, 1984). Reprinted with permission.

Drafting the Application Letter

The letter of application should follow the standard conventions discussed in Chapter 5. It should be typed neatly on a plain white sheet of good bond paper, 8½″ × 11″. Make sure that your typewriter works perfectly and that the type does not appear faded. Proofread meticulously; a spelling error here will harm your chances. Avoid abbreviations ("thru" for "through," "nite" for "night") and slang expressions. Don't forget the "you attitude." Employers are not impressed by boastful proclamations ("I am the most efficient and effective safety engineer," "I am a natural-born nurse"). One student wrote that he needed the job to pay tuition and repay a car loan. The employer was not impressed. Another applicant spent so much time on advantages to her that she forgot the employer entirely: "I have worked with this kind of equipment before, and this experience will give me the edge in running it. Moreover, I can adjust more quickly to my working environment."

The best letters of application are to the point and are readable. Keep in mind that employers will receive many letters and that yours will have to compete for their time. You want your letter to be placed in the "definitely interview" category discussed on page 131. A letter of application should not exceed one page; it is to your advantage to make it shorter. On the other hand, you should not write a telegraphic message—two or three sentences. Strive for brevity and clarity. Emphasize your qualifications with specific evidence; don't let them get lost in a sea of words. A three-paragraph letter will be sufficient for most candidates. Figure 6.9 contains a model letter—Maria Lopez's application for a job. Compare her letter with her résumé (Figure 6.5). Then compare her letter with the letter in Figure 6.10, written by Anthony Jones, who has little relevant job experience; see his résumé, Figure 6.4. He must rely mainly on his educational training.

The First Paragraph

The first paragraph of your application letter is your introduction. It should answer three questions: (1) why you are writing, (2) where or how you learned of the job, (3) and what your most important qualification is for the job. Begin your letter by stating directly that you are writing to apply for a job. Do not say that you "want to apply for the job," for such an opening raises the question "Why don't you then?" And do not start off in an unconventional or annoying way: "Are you looking for a dynamic, young, and talented photographer?" Do not begin with a question; be more positive and professional. If you learned of the job through a newspaper or journal, make sure that you underscore its title.

```
I am applying for the food-service manager position you
advertised in the May 10 edition of the Los Angeles Times.
```

Do not waste the employer's time and your space on the page by repeating verbatim the words of the advertisement. If you learned of the job from a

Fig. 6.9   Letter of application from a student with some job experience.

1725 Brooke Street
Miami, FL 32701
May 14, 1986

Dr. Marvin Hendrady
Suite 34
Medical/Dental Plaza
839 Causeway Drive
Miami, FL 32701

Dear Dr. Hendrady:

Mr. Mitchell Pellborne, my clinical instructor at Miami—Dade Community
College, informs me that you are looking for a dental hygienist to work in
your northside office. I am writing to apply for that position. This
month, I will graduate with an A.S. degree in the dental hygienist program
at Miami—Dade Community College, and I will take the American Dental
Assistants' Examination in early June.

I have successfully completed all course work and clinical programs in oral
hygiene, anatomy, and prophylaxis techniques. During my clinical training,
I received intensive practical instruction from a number of local dentists,
including Dr. Mildred Pecos. Since your northside office specializes in
pedodental care, you might find the subject of my major project—proper
nutrition for preschoolers—especially relevant. I have also had some
related job experience in working with children in a health care setting.
For a year and a half, I was employed as a ward clerk on the pediatric unit
at St. Francis Hospital, and my experience in greeting patients, filling
out forms, and assisting the nursing staff would be valuable to you in
running your office. You will find more detailed information about me and
my experience in the enclosed résumé.

I would welcome the opportunity to talk with you about the position and my
interest in pedodontics. I am available for an interview any time after
2:30 until June 13. After that date, I could come to your office any time
at your convenience.

Sincerely yours,

Maria H. Lopez

Maria H. Lopez

Encl. Résumé

Fig. 6.10   Letter of application from a student with little job experience.

73 Allenwood Boulevard
Santa Rosa, CA 95401
May 25, 1986

Ms. Jocelyn Nogasaki
Personnel Manager
Megalith Publishing Company
1001 Heathcliff Row
San Francisco, CA 94123

Dear Ms. Nogasaki:

I am applying for the layout editor position advertised on May 25 in the
San Francisco Chronicle. Early next month, I will receive an A.S. degree
in industrial graphics illustration from Santa Rosa Junior College.

With a special interest in the publishing industry, I have successfully
completed more than forty credit hours in courses directly related to
layout design where I acquired skills in drafting, reproduction processes,
and production techniques. You might like to know that many of the design
patterns of Megalith publications were used as models in my graphic
communications and photographic technology classes. My studies have also
led to practical experience at McAdam Publishers, as part of my Santa Rosa
apprenticeship program. Working at McAdam's, I was responsible for
assisting the design department in photo research and in the preparation
of mockups. Other related experience I have had includes artwork and
proofreading for the student magazine, Thunder. As you will note on the
enclosed résumé, I have also had experience in displaying merchandise at
Buchman's Department Store.

I would appreciate the opportunity to discuss with you my qualifications in
industrial graphics. After June 12 I will be available for an interview at
any time that suits your convenience.

Sincerely yours,

Anthony H. Jones

Anthony H. Jones

Encl. Résumé

professor, friend, or employee at the firm, state that fact also. Next, indicate your chief qualification—you will soon graduate with an A.A. in food service, you have worked in the large restaurant of a major hotel chain, or you have ten years experience managing a cafeteria. Select one fact that justifies your suitability for the job.

The Second Paragraph

The second paragraph of your application letter emphasizes your education and work background. Recent graduates with little work experience will, of course, spend more time on their education, but even if you have much experience, do not forget your education. Stress your most important educational accomplishments. Employers want to know what skills and expertise your education has given you and how those skills apply to their particular job. Simply saying that you will graduate with a degree in criminal justice does not explain how you, unlike all the other graduates of a criminal justice program, are best qualified for the job. Indicate that in thirty-six hours of course work you have specialized in industrial security and that you have twelve hours in business and communications. That says something specific. Rather than boasting that you are qualified, give the facts to prove it. If your GPA is relatively high or if you have won an award, mention that. Do not worry about stating an important fact in both your letter and résumé.

After you discuss your educational qualifications, turn to your job experience. The best letters show how the two are related. Employers like to see a continuity between a candidate's school and job experience. Provide that link by showing how the jobs you have held have something in common with your major—in terms of responsibility, research, customer relations, community service. Say that your course work in data processing helped you to be a better programmer for your previous employer, that your summer jobs for the local park district allowed you to reinforce your studies in human services. However, do not dwell on being a nurse's aide three years ago when you have nearly completed a degree program to be an R.N. Busing tables in a restaurant is good experience, but do not let that job overshadow your current work as a management trainee for a large hotel chain.

Above all, the second paragraph of your application letter must relate your education and experience directly to the employer's job. Tell exactly how your school work and job experience qualify you to function and advance in the job advertised. Here, your homework on what the company is like should pay off. Note in Figure 6.9 how Maria Lopez uses her knowledge of Dr. Hendrady's specialty to her advantage; in Figure 6.10 Anthony Jones profitably emphasizes how he gained his knowledge of and respect for Megalith publications.

The second paragraph may run to six or seven sentences. You might want to spend three sentences on your educational qualifications and three on your job experience; or perhaps your work experiences are so rich that you will spend four sentences on them. At any rate, do not neglect education for experience or vice versa. Refer to your résumé, and do not forget to say that you are including it with your letter.

The Third Paragraph

The third paragraph has three functions: (1) to emphasize once again your major qualification, (2) to ask for an interview, and (3) to indicate when you are available for that interview. Paragraph three is short—about two or three sentences. End gracefully and professionally. Don't leave the reader with just one weak sentence: "I would like to have an interview at your convenience." Such a sentence does nothing to sell you. Say that you would appreciate talking with the employer further to discuss your qualifications. Then mention your chief talent. Indicate your interest in the job and give the times you are available for an interview. If you are going to a professional meeting where the employer might be present, or if you are visiting the employer's city, say so. Following are some poor ways to close the letter and reasons to avoid them:

Pushy:	I would like to set up an interview with you. Please phone me to arrange a convenient time. (That's the employer's prerogative, not yours.)
Too Informal:	I do not live too far from your office. Could we meet for coffee sometime next week. (Turn this around. Say that since you live nearby, you will be available for an interview.)
Too Humble:	I know that you are busy, but I would really like to have an interview. (Say you would like to discuss your qualifications further.)
Introduces New Subject:	I would like to discuss other qualifications you have in mind for the job. (How do you know what they might be?)

Note how the professional closing paragraphs in Figures 6.9 and 6.10 avoid these errors.

☞ Filling Out a Job Application

At some point in your job search, you will be asked to complete a prospective employer's application form. A recruiter may hand you a job application form at a campus interview, or you may be mailed a form in response to your letter of application. Most often, though, you will be given an application to complete when you are at the employer's office.

Application forms can vary tremendously. But they all ask you to give information about your education, any military service, present and previous employment, references, general state of health, and reasons for wanting to work for the company or agency. Since these topics overlap those on your résumé, bring the résumé with you to the employer's office to make sure you omit nothing important. Some forms even require you to attach your résumé.

But *under no circumstances* attach a résumé to a blank form instead of filling the form out. Employers want their own forms completed by job seekers.

The following general guidelines can help you to complete an application form:

1. Read the instructions before you begin.
2. Answer all the questions. Some forms instruct you to put N/A (not applicable) rather than leave a space blank.
3. Print neatly, using a dark, preferably black, ball-point pen. Do not use a felt-tip pen; what you write will smear. And do not write with a pencil.
4. Double-check numbers—social security, driver's license, area and zip codes, registration numbers, union certificates.
5. Do not write in spaces marked "For Office Use Only."
6. Check spelling and punctuation.
7. Be as neat as you can. Do not write over the lines or in the margins or insert asterisks indicating further clarification. If you need more room to answer a question, attach a separate sheet of paper. Make sure that your name and the specific question number appear on the attached sheet.
8. Be truthful. Don't say you can type seventy words a minute when you have trouble with forty.
9. Be as precise as possible. For "previous experience," do not just say "construction worker"; indicate "building inspector," "mason," "carpenter."
10. When asked about salary expectations, avoid extremes. If you have done your homework, you will have a sense of the established range. Do not put "minimum wage"; an employer has to give you that anyway.
11. Many applications ask you to comment on your training and education, giving you one or two inches of space for your answer. Fill the blank space with facts, not padding. Giving just one or two small details will not sell your talents and only points to your lack of self-expression and confidence. Many employers, including the federal government, rank prospective employees on the basis of their answers to such a question. So, as a rule of thumb, provide as much relevant information as space allows, and make sure that you are positive, not negative, about your previous position and employer.
12. Sign the application, verifying that what you have written is true and complete. Your signature is essential if you must have a security clearance or if the company has to release any of the information you have provided or obtain your permission to find out more about you.

Individuals desiring to work for one of the many branches of the United States government complete a "Personal Qualifications Statement." That form contains many of the kinds of questions you can expect future employers to ask you. The government, like so many employers, expects job candidates to have done their homework. The first question asks the applicant to identify the desired job by title and number—information readily available from a civil service or governmental agency. Since the federal government is the largest employer in the nation, many users of this book will complete this form. You can obtain a copy of the form from a Federal Job Information Center.

Figure 6.11 contains an application form similar to ones used by private companies. This form asks applicants to give reasons for leaving previous jobs and also requires them to write a "personal essay" stating why the company should hire them. Both of these questions will require tact and thought. If you were fired from a past job, it is not to your advantage to simply state the fact. Indicate further relevant information, such as that the industry suffered a recession. More frequently, though, your reasons for leaving a job will be financial, educational, or geographic. You may have received a better offer, decided to return to school, or planned to move to another town.

Writing the personal essay will require that you convince the employer of your sincerity and qualifications. In doing so, do not dwell on what the company can do for you. Concentrate on how your previous experience and education will help your employer; emphasize, too, your willingness to learn new techniques and skills on the job. Do not be afraid to cite specific accomplishments; your success will depend on it.

☞ Going to an Interview

An interview can be challenging, threatening, friendly, or chatty; sometimes it is all of these. By the time you arrive at the interview stage, you are far along in your job search. Basically, there are two kinds of interviews. One is a *screening interview*, to which numerous applicants have been invited so that a company can narrow down the candidates; campus interviews are screening interviews. The other kind of interview is known as a *line interview;* the employer invites only a few select applicants to the company's office for a tour and detailed conversation.

Preparing for an Interview

An interview gives the employer a chance to see how you look, act, and *react.* Once in a while interviewers intentionally create stressful situations for you, such as inviting you to smoke and not providing an ashtray. But most employers do not want to trick you. They want to see how well you can talk about yourself and your work; they also want to see how well you listen and respond to their answers. At some interviews job candidates are shown a film about the company and are then given a quiz about that film. Interviewers expect applicants to be nervous, but you can free yourself of some anxiety if you know what to expect.

Interviews can last half an hour or extend to two or three days. Most often, though, an interview will last about one hour. It has been estimated that the

Fig. 6.11   Job application form.

APPLICATION FOR EMPLOYMENT

Date _____

PERSONAL INFORMATION

SS# _____

Name _____
         Last   First   Middle

Present address _____

Phone no. _____

Height _____ Weight _____

If related to anyone in our company,
state name, relationship, and position _____

EMPLOYMENT DESIRED

Position applying for _____ or _____

Health Status   Good _____ Fair _____ Poor _____

EDUCATIONAL BACKGROUND

Name and location of school	Years attended	Date graduated	Subjects studied
High school			
College			
Other			

Military service _____ Duties _____

Dates _____

In case of emergency, notify:

Name _____

Address _____

Phone number _____

Fig. 6.11 **(Continued.)**

EMPLOYMENT RECORD

Former employer	Address	Salary & position	Reason for leaving	Dates employed

REFERENCES

Give the names of three persons not related to you whom you have known for at least one year:

Name	Address	Business	Years acquainted

Why did you leave your last job? Explain your answer in detail.

_____

_____

_____

PERSONAL ESSAY

Please state why you feel we should hire you for the position desired, including any qualifications not mentioned above. Attach another sheet if necessary.

_____

_____

_____

_____

_____

_____

_____

DO NOT WRITE BELOW THIS LINE—FOR OFFICE USE ONLY

Date interviewed _____ By _____

General appearance _____

Attitude _____

Date hired (if any) _____

Salary _____

Position _____

applicant will do about 80 to 90 percent of the talking. Since you will be asked to speak at length, make the following preparations before your interview:

1. Do your homework about the employer—types of services provided, location of offices, contributions to industry or the community.
2. Review the technical skills most relevant for the job. You might want to reread sections of a textbook, study some recent journal articles, or talk to a professor or an employee you know from the company.
3. Prepare a brief (one- or two-minute) review of your qualifications to deliver orally should you be asked about yourself.
4. Bring your résumé with you. Your interviewer will have a copy on the desk, so you can be sure that its contents will be the subject of many questions. Be able to elaborate and supplement what is on your résumé. Any extra details or information that bring your résumé up to date ("I received my degree last week"; "I'll get the results of my state board examinations in one week") will be appreciated.

Questions to Expect at an Interview

You can expect questions about your education, job experience, and ambitions. An interviewer will ask you questions about courses, schools, technical skills, and job goals. Through these questions an interviewer attempts to discover your good points as well as your bad ones. A common strategy is to postpone questions about your bad points until near the end of the interview. Once a relaxed atmosphere has been established, the interviewer thinks that you may be less reluctant to talk about your weaknesses. The following fifteen questions are typical of those you can expect from interviewers:

1. Tell us something about yourself. (Here, your one-minute oral presentation of yourself comes in handy.)
2. Why do you want to work for us? (Recall any job goals you have and apply them specifically to the job under discussion.)
3. What qualifications do you have for the job? (Mention educational achievements in addition to any relevant work experience.)
4. What could you possibly offer us that other candidates do not have? (Say "enthusiasm" and problem-solving abilities in addition to educational achievements.)
5. Why did you attend this school? (Be honest—location, costs, programs.)
6. Why did you major in "X"? (Do not simply say financial benefits; concentrate on both practical and professional benefits. Be able to state career objectives.)
7. Why did you get a grade of "C" in a course? (Do not hurt your chances of being hired by saying you could have done better if you tried; that response shows a lack of motivation most employers find unacceptable. Explain what the trouble was and mention that you corrected it in a course in which you made a B or an A.)

8. What extracurricular activities did you participate in while in high school or college? (Indicate any duties or responsibilities you had—handling money, writing memos, coordinating events; if you were not able to participate in such activities, tell the interviewer that a part-time job, community or church activities, or commuting a long way to school each day prevented your participating. Such answers sound better than saying that you did not like sports or fraternities or clubs in school.)

9. Did you learn as much as you wanted from your course work? (This is a loaded question. Indicate that you learned a great deal but now look forward to the opportunity to gain more practical skill, to put into practice the principles you have learned; say that you will never be through learning about your major.)

10. Why was your summer job important? (Highlight skills you learned, people you helped, employers you pleased.)

11. What is your greatest strength? (Being a team player, cooperation, willingness to learn, ability to grasp difficult concepts easily, managing time or money, taking criticism easily, and profiting from criticism are all appropriate answers.)

12. What is your greatest shortcoming? (Be honest here and mention it, but then turn to ways in which you are improving. Do not dwell on your weaknesses, but do not keep silent about them. Saying "none" to this kind of question is as inadvisable as rattling off a list of wrongdoings.)

13. How much did you earn at your last job and what salary do you expect in working for us? (Some job counselors advise interviewees to lie about their past salaries in order to get a larger one from the future employer. But if the prospective employer checks your last salary and finds that you have lied, you lose. It is better to round off your last salary to the nearest thousand. As far as present salary is concerned, if you did your homework, you should have a sense of the salary range.)

14. Why did you leave your last job? (Usually you will have educational reasons—"I returned to school full-time." Or you will have received a better offer. *Never attack your previous employer. This only makes you look bad.*)

15. Is there anything else you want to discuss? (Here is your opportunity to end the interview with more information about yourself. You might take time to reiterate a strength of yours, to correct an earlier answer, or to indicate your desire to work for the company.)

Of course, you will have a chance throughout the interview to ask questions, too. Do not forget important points about the job—responsibilities, security, and chances for promotion. You will also want to ask about salary (but do not dwell on it), fringe benefits, schedules, vacations, and bonuses. If you spend time on these subjects, especially during the first part of the interview, you tell the interviewer that you are more interested in the rewards of the job than in the duties and challenges it offers. Do not go to the interview with dollar signs flashing in your eyes.

Some questions an interviewer cannot legally ask you. Questions about your age, marital status, ethnic background, race, or any physical handicaps violate equal opportunity employment laws. Even so, some employers may disguise their interest in these subjects by asking you indirect questions about them. A question such as "Will your husband care if you have to work overtime?" or "How many children do you have?" could probe into your marital life. Confronted with such questions, it is best to answer them positively ("My home life will not interfere with my job," "My family understands that overtime may be required") rather than bristling defensively, "It's none of your business if I have a husband."

Keep in mind some other interview "dos" and "don'ts." Go to the interview alone. Dress appropriately for the occasion. Speak slowly and distinctly; do not nervously hurry to finish your sentences, and never interrupt or finish an interviewer's sentences. Refrain from chewing gum, smoking, rolling a pencil, or tapping your foot against the floor or a chair. Maintain eye contact with the interviewer; do not sheepishly stare at the floor or the desk. Body language is equally important. Do not fold your arms—that's a signal indicating you are closed to the interviewer's suggestions and comments. And one last point: *Be on time.* If you are unavoidably delayed, telephone to apologize and set up another interview.

The Follow-up Letter

After the interview, it is good strategy to send a follow-up letter within a week thanking the interviewer for his or her time and interest in you. The letter will keep your name fresh in the interviewer's mind. Do not forget that this individual interviewed other candidates, too, some of them probably on the same day as you. In your follow-up letter, you can reemphasize your qualifications for the job by showing how they apply to conditions described by the interviewer; you might also ask for some further information to show your interest in the job and the employer. You could even refer to a detail, such as a tour or film that was part of the interview. A sample follow-up letter appears in Figure 6.12.

☞ Accepting or Declining a Job

Even if you have verbally agreed to take a job, you still have to respond formally in writing. Your letter will make your acceptance official and may even be included in your permanent personnel file. Accepting a job is easy. Make this communication with your new employer a model of clarity and diplomacy. Respond to the offer as soon as possible (certainly within two weeks). Often a time limit is specified. A sample acceptance letter appears in Figure 6.13. In the first sentence tell the employer that you are accepting the job, and refer to the date of the letter offering you the position. Indicate when

Fig. 6.12   A follow-up letter.

2739 East Street
Latrobe, PA 17042
September 12, 1985

Mr. Jack Wong
Personnel Manager
Transatlantic Steel Company
1334 Ridge Road N.E.
Pittsburgh, PA 17122-3107

Dear Mr. Wong:

I enjoyed talking with you last Wednesday and learning more about
the security officer position available at Transatlantic Steel. It
was especially helpful to take a tour of the plant's north gate
section to see the problems it presents for the security officer
stationed there.

As you noted at my interview, my training in surveillance
electronics has prepared me to operate the sophisticated equipment
Transatlantic has installed at the north gate. I was happy that Ms.
Turner took time to show me this equipment.

I am looking forward to receiving the brochure about Transatlantic's
employees' services. Would it also be possible for you to include
a copy of the newsletter introducing the new security equipment to
the employees?

Thank you for considering me for the position. I look forward
to hearing from you. After my visit last week, I know that
Transatlantic Steel would be an excellent place to work.

Sincerely yours,

Mary LeBorde

Mary LeBorde

Fig. 6.13   Letter accepting a job.

73 Park Street
Evansville, WI 53536
June 30, 1985

Ms. Melinda A. Haas, Manager
Weise's Department Store
Janesville Mall
Janesville, WI 53545

Dear Ms. Haas:

I am pleased to accept the position of assistant controller that
you offered me in your letter of June 23. Starting on July 15 will
be no problem for me. I look forward to helping Ms. Meyers in the
business office. In the next few months I know that I will learn a
great deal about Weise's.

I will make an appointment for early next week with the Personnel
Department to discuss travel policies, salary payment schedules,
and insurance coverage.

I am eager to start working for Weise's.

Sincerely yours,

John Dubinski

John Dubinski

you can begin the job. Then mention any pleasant associations from your interview or any specific challenges you are anticipating. That should take no more than a paragraph. Do not douse your letter with praise for the employer or the job.

In a second paragraph express your plans to fulfill any further requirements for the job—going to the personnel office, taking a physical examination, having a copy of a certificate or license forwarded, sending a final transcript of your college work. A final one-sentence paragraph might state that you are looking forward to starting your new job.

Refusing a job requires tact. You are obligated to inform an employer why you are not taking the job. Since the employer has spent time interviewing you, respond with courtesy and candor. For an example of a refusal letter, see Figure 6.14.

Do not bluntly begin with the refusal. Instead, prepare the reader for bad news by starting with a complimentary remark about the job, the interview, or the company. Then move to your refusal and supply an honest but not elaborate explanation of why you are not taking the job. Many students cite educational opportunities, work schedules, geographic preference, health reasons, or better, more relevant professional opportunities. End on a friendly note; you may be interested in working for the company in the future.

Employment Evaluations

Even after you have been hired and have been working at your job for a while, you may be expected to write convincingly about your qualifications for that job. Many companies and agencies annually require their employees to fill out self-evaluation forms as part of a routine review used in deciding promotions and salary increases. In the past, employee evaluations were handled by supervisors and administrative personnel. Today, many companies ask employees to grade themselves in addition to having supervisors do an assessment. The two evaluations are then compared, and employees are given the opportunity to see and respond to what their supervisors have written about them. Employees may also be asked to evaluate their supervisors. The days of accountability are here, making it important for employees to know how to evaluate themselves and others effectively.

What kinds of questions can you expect your employer to ask? Here are a few of the most common:

1. What are your current duties?
2. How well do you perform them?
3. What improvements can you make?
4. What would you like to accomplish in the next year?
5. Where would you rank yourself in comparison with others in your department or on your floor?

Fig. 6.14   Letter refusing a job.

345 Melba Lane
Bellingham, WA 98225
March 8, 1985

Ms. Gail Buckholtz
Assistant Editor
The Everett News
Everett, WA 98421

Dear Ms. Buckholtz:

I enjoyed meeting you and the staff photographers at my recent
interview for the photography position at the News. Your plans for
the special weekend supplements are exciting, and I know that I
would have enjoyed my assignments greatly. But because I have
decided to continue my education part—time at Western Washington
University in Bellingham, I have accepted a position with the
Bellingham American. Not having to commute to Everett every day
will give me more time for my studies and also my free—lance work.

Thank you for your generous offer and for the time you and the staff
spent explaining your plans to me. I wish you success with the
supplements.

Sincerely yours,

George Alexander

George Alexander

6. What special contributions have you made to the company (or agency) in the last year?
7. Why do you deserve a raise or a promotion?

Before you answer such questions, keep in mind that your readers know you are automatically prejudiced in your behalf; objectivity, therefore, will be deemed a virtue. Rather than only saying that you are invaluable or that you are a hard worker, tell your employer why you hold this view of your work. Give relevant facts—cite how many customers you visited and sold products to, mention any exceptional services you performed for clients, or any ways you saved the company money or improved communication. Indicate how your work benefited the company and your fellow employees. Did you make any suggestions that improved services or schedules? If your supervisor praised your work, cite his or her comments and give dates.

Keep your assessment short and to the point. Also make sure that your comments about your accomplishments directly pertain to your assigned duties. At the other extreme, do not sell yourself short by saying that you did what was expected of you or that you accomplished what you were told. Tell your reader how you performed routine tasks with skill and to the benefit of the company. A credible answer to question 3 would indicate that you have made a mistake, but would also indicate what you have done to correct it and to ensure that it will not occur again.

When asked to evaluate your supervisor, be objective. Avoid cheap shots or any attempts to get even for grievances. Questions of leadership, honesty, respect, and clarity in explaining job goals are usually found on evaluations of one's supervisors. Respond according to these criteria with facts and with honesty.

Your employer may supply you with a form (or checklist) for your evaluation of yourself, your supervisor, or for both. Or you may be instructed to write a formal letter of assessment. In either case, proofread what you write carefully for spelling and punctuation. You should also make a copy for your own records.

☞ Exercises

1. Make a list of your marketable job skills. To do this, first concentrate on the specialized kinds of skills you learned in your major or on your job (for example, giving injections, fingerprinting, preparing specialized menus, keeping a ledger book, operating a computer, learning a computer language). List as many of these skills as you can think of; then organize them into three or four separate categories that reflect your major abilities.

2. Compile a list of local employers for whom you would like to work. Get their names, addresses, phone numbers, and the names of the managers or personnel officers. Select one company and write a profile about it—

location, services, kinds of products or services offered, number of employees working for it, clients served, types of schedules used.

3. Tell your college placement office when you will begin your job search. The office will almost certainly give you some forms to complete. Bring these forms to class and discuss the kinds of questions they contain and the most effective ways to answer them.

4. Obtain some personal evaluation forms from your placement office. Write a sample letter to a former or current teacher and employer, asking for a recommendation. Tell these individuals what kinds of jobs you will be looking for and politely mention how a strong letter would help you in your job search. Make sure that you bring them up to date about your educational progress and any employment you have had since you worked for them.

5. Request an application form for employment from a local store, hospital, government agency, or contractor. Bring the form to class and be prepared to discuss the best ways of completing it.

6. Which of the following would belong on your résumé? Why?
   (a) student I.D. number
   (b) Social Security number
   (c) the zip codes of your references' addresses
   (d) a list of all your English courses in college
   (e) section numbers of the courses in your major
   (f) statement that you are divorced
   (g) subscriptions to journals in your field
   (h) the titles of any stories or poems you published in a high school literary magazine or newspaper
   (i) your GPA
   (j) foreign languages you studied
   (k) years you attended college
   (l) the date you were discharged from the service
   (m) names of the neighbors you are using as references
   (n) your religion
   (o) job titles you held
   (p) your summer job waiting on tables
   (q) your telephone number
   (r) the reason you changed schools
   (s) your current status with the National Guard
   (t) the name of your favorite professor in college
   (u) your work for the Red Cross
   (v) hours a week you spend reading science fiction
   (w) the title of your last term paper in your major
   (x) the name of the agency or business where you worked last

7. Indicate what is wrong with the following career objective statements and rewrite them to make them more precise and professional.
   (a) Job in a dentist's office.
   (b) Position with a safety emphasis.
   (c) Desire growth position in large department store.
   (d) Am looking for entry position in health sciences with an emphasis on caring for older people.
   (e) Position in sales with fast promotion rate.
   (f) Want a job working with semiconductor circuits.
   (g) Job in agriculture.
   (h) I would like a position in fashion, especially one working with modern fashion.
   (i) Desire a good-paying job, hours: 8–4:30, with double pay for extra time. Would like to stay in the Omaha area.
   (j) Insurance work.
   (k) Computer operator in large office.
   (l) Personal secretary.
   (m) Job with preschoolers.
   (n) Full-time position with hospitality chain.
   (o) Cashier with financial institution; interested in position that promises growth and advancement within company.
   (p) I want a career in nursing.
   (q) Police work, particularly in suburb of large city.
   (r) A job that lets me be me.
   (s) Desire fun job selling cosmetics.
   (t) Any position for qualified dietitian.
   (u) Although I have not made up my mind about which area of forestry I shall go into, I am looking for a job that offers me training and rewards based upon my potential.

8. Rewrite the following bad résumé to make it more precise and persuasive. Include additional details where necessary and exclude any details that you think would hurt the job seeker's chances. Also correct any inconsistencies.

RÉSUMÉ OF

Powell T. Harrison
8604 So. Kirkpatrick St.
Ardville, Ohio
345 37 8760
614 234 4587

PERSONAL   Confidential

CAREER   Seeks good paying position with progressive Sunbelt
OBECTIVE   company.

Education

1983–1986   Will receive degree from Central Tech. Institute in Arch. St. Earned high average last semester. Took necessary courses for major; interested in systems, plans, and design development.

1979–1983   Attended Ardville High School, Ardville, OH; took all courses required. Served on committee that governed student activities.

Experience None, except for numerous part–time jobs and student apprenticeship in the Ardville area. As part of student app. worked with local firm for two months.

Hobbies.   Listening to music, playing electronic games (e.g., PACMAN, MS. Pacman). Member of Junior Achievement.

REFERENCES   Please write for names and addresses.

---

9. Determine what is wrong with the following sentences in a letter of application. Rewrite them to eliminate any mistakes, to focus on the "you attitude," or to make them more precise.
   (a) Even though I have very little actual job experience, I can make up for it in enthusiasm.
   (b) My qualifications will prove that I am the best person for your job.
   (c) I would enjoy working with your other employees.
   (d) This letter is my application for any job you now have open or expect to fill in the near future.
   (e) Next month, my family and I will be moving to Detroit, and I must get a job in the area. Will you have anything open?
   (f) If you are interested in me, then I hope that we make some type of arrangements to interview each other soon.
   (g) Your ad specified that you wanted someone who was familiar with food sanitation techniques, worked for at least one year in industry, and had at least thirty hours in course work at a community college in food science. I am the very person you are looking for.
   (h) I have not included a résumé since all pertinent information about me is in this letter.
   (i) My GPA is only 2.5, but I did make two B's in my last term.
   (j) I hope to take state boards soon.
   (k) Your company, or so I have heard through the grapevine, has excellent fringe benefits. That is right up my alley, so I am applying for a position which you may advertise.

(l) I am writing to ask you to kindly consider whether I would be a qualified person for the position you announced in the newspaper.

(m) I have made plans to further my education.

(n) My résumé speaks for itself.

(o) I could not possibly accept a position which required weekend work, and night work is out, too.

(p) In my own estimation, I am a go-getter, an eager beaver, so to speak.

(q) My last employer was dead wrong when he let me go. I think he regrets it now.

(r) When you arrange an interview time, give me a call. I am home every afternoon after four.

10. Why is the following letter of application ineffective? Rewrite it to make it more precise and appropriate.

```
Apartment 32
Jeggler Drive
Talcott, Arizona


Monday


Bob Rand
Production Supervisor
Jellco
Capital City, Arizona

Dear Sir:


I am writing to ask you if your company will consider me for the
position you announced in the newspaper yesterday. I believe
that with my education (I have an associate degree) and
experience (I have worked four years as a freight supervisor),
I could fill your job.


My school work was done at two junior colleges, and I took more
than enough courses in business management and modern
packaging. In fact, here is a list of some of my courses:
Supervision, Materials Management, Work Experience in
Management, Business Machines, Loading and Landing Tactics,
Introduction to Packaging, Art Design, Modern Business
Principles, and Small Business Management. In addition, I have
worked as a loading dock supervisor for the last two years, and
before that I worked in the military in the Quartermaster
Corps.
```

Please let me know if you are interested in me. I would like to
have an interview with you at the earliest possible date, since
there are some other firms also interested in me, too.

Sincerely yours,

George D. Milhous

George D. Milhous

---

11. From the Sunday edition of your local newspaper, clip ads for two or three
    jobs you are qualified to fill and then write a letter of application for one of
    them.

12. Write a résumé to go along with the letter you wrote for exercise 11 above.

13. Write an appropriate job application letter to accompany Anna Cassetti's
    résumé in Figure 6.3.

14. Write a letter to a local business inquiring about summer employment.
    Indicate that you can work only for one summer and that you will be going
    back to school by September 1.

15. Rewrite this follow-up letter to make it more professional.

Dear Mr. Gage:

It was good talking to you yesterday. The job is even more
attractive than I thought. I had no idea that the salary was in
the $15,000 to $16,000 range. That is excellent money for
someone starting out.

I am sorry that I did not know the answers to your questions on
the use of the new telex machines. After checking with my
instructor, Dr. Patricia Holmes, I can give you a full and
complete answer now. If you would like me to put it in writing,
please let me know, and I shall be happy to oblige you. I do not
want you to think that I am not properly trained.

I am really excited about working for your company. And I am
staying glued to the phone in the hopes that you will give me
that call that will start me on a great career.

Sincerely yours,

C. K. Randolph

C. K. Randolph

7

Types of Business Correspondence

Receiving and answering business correspondence—memos and letters—are vital to the success of a company and its employees. The way you prepare your correspondence will reflect on your professional abilities and your company's reputation. When memos and letters are written clearly, effectively, and promptly, you and your employer profit. When they are done poorly, everyone suffers. For this reason, being an effective writer of memos and letters is a necessary and prized skill. In fact, the higher up the corporate ladder you climb, the more you will be expected to write—and write well.

Chapter 7 discusses six of the most common types of business correspondence that you will be expected to write on the job:

1. Memos
2. Order letters
3. Letters of inquiry
4. Special request letters
5. Sales letters
6. Customer relations letters

These six kinds of correspondence will introduce you to a variety of formats and a number of writing techniques. Generally speaking, memos, the least formal type of correspondence, convey brief notes or instructions; order, inquiry, and special request letters give and request information in differing formats; sales letters require a description of your product or service and a convincing argument for your reader; and customer relations letters are vital to company image and customer satisfaction.

☞ Memos

Memorandum, from which the noun "memo" comes, is a Latin word signifying that something is to be remembered. The Latin meaning points to the memo's chief function—to record information of immediate importance and interest in the busy world of work. Memos are in-house correspondence. Memos are sent up and down the corporate ladder—from managers to employees and from employees to managers; they are also sent to and from coworkers. Memos allow a business or agency to communicate with itself in its day-to-day operations.

Function of Memos

Memos have a variety of functions. They are written to ask or to respond to questions affecting daily work. They can notify employees about the date of a meeting or the main points raised at that meeting. They can inform readers about appointments, policies, or new procedures. They can alert the staff to a forthcoming order and any special problems in handling it. Or they can provide some last-minute figures necessary to honor a customer's request, confirm what has been decided in telephone or in face-to-face conversations, and offer suggestions or recommendations. Memos are also used for short reports; see Chapter 15 for examples of field, trip, or progress reports in memo format. Many internal proposals (Chapter 14) are written as memos, too.

Memo Format

Memos can vary in format. Some companies use standard, printed forms (Figure 7.1) while others have their names (letterhead) printed on their memos as in Figure 7.2. Memos can be written on 8½″ × 11″ sheets of paper or on half sheets. The smaller size paper is useful for shorter communications and encourages the writer to be concise. You can make your own memos by including the necessary parts discussed below.

As you can see from looking at Figures 7.1 through 7.4, memos look different from letters. They are more streamlined and less formal. Because they are sent to individuals within your company, memos do not need the formalities necessary in business letters. Memos, therefore, do not contain an inside address, salutation, complimentary close, or signature line.

Basically, the memo consists of two parts: the identifying information at the top and the message following this information. The identifying information includes these easily recognized parts—the *To, From, Date,* and *Subject* lines as illustrated:

```
TO: Aileen Kelly              DATE: January 31, 1986
    Data Processing Manager

FROM: Stacy Jones  S. J.      SUBJECT: Progress report
      Operator, Level II                on preparing
                                         fall schedule
```

Fig. 7.1   Standard memo form without any letterhead.

TO: All RN's

FROM: Margaret Wojak, Director of Nurses   *M W*

DATE: August 12, 1985

SUBJECT: RN identity patches

Effective September 1, 1985, all RN's will have the choice of wearing their caps or an identity patch. Patches should be sewn on the upper right arm of lab coats or uniforms so that staff and patients can easily identify you as an RN. Those RN's wishing to wear identity patches may obtain them for one dollar apiece at the Health Uniforms Shop directly across from the hospital on Ames Street. Please call me at Extension 732 if you have any questions.

On the *To* line write the name and job title of the individual(s) who will receive your memo or a copy of it. If you are on a first name basis with the reader, use his or her first name. Otherwise, include the reader's first and last names. In some companies memos are sent to everyone whose name is on a distribution list. If your name is on the list for receiving information on a given project or from one or more departments, you will get every memo from these sources. Your name may appear on a number of lists. Don't send copies of your memos to individuals who don't need them. You will only increase the paper inflation in an office.

On the *From* line write your name (first name only if your reader refers to you by it) and your job title (unless it is unnecessary for your reader). Some writers put their handwritten initials after their typed name to verify that the message comes from them.

On the *Subject* line write the title and the purpose of your memo. Be precise so that readers can file your memo correctly. Vague subject lines such as "New Policy," "Operating Difficulties," or "Shared Computer Time" do not identify your message accurately and may suggest that your message is not carefully restricted or developed. "Shared Computer Time," for example, does not tell readers if your memo will discuss new equipment, corporate arrangements, or vendors, offer additional or fewer hours, or warn employees about abusing the system.

On the *Date* line do not simply list the day of the week. Give the calendar date and year—June 5, 1986. Some companies have adopted the military

Fig. 7.2   Memo on letterhead stationery.

BILL'S CATERING SERVICE
56 North Jones
Canton, Ohio 45307

TO: Marge Adcox   DATE: November 23, 1985

FROM: Roger Blackmore   *R. B.*   SUBJECT: Management Training
                                               Seminar Review

I attended the Management Training Seminar (November 19–20), as you
requested, and here is a review of the major points made by the director,
Jack Lowery.

(1) The individual conducting the training sessions should always talk in a
    loud voice so that the trainees can hear him or her.

(2) The main purpose of the training session should always be announced so
    that the trainees can focus on a specific set of topics.

(3) Instructors should allow at least a ten-minute break for each two-hour
    session. This will increase the trainee's attention span and allow for
    better learning.

(4) The easiest tasks should be assigned first, and more complicated ones
    should follow.

(5) The instructor should provide feedback to the trainees at the end of
    each major section.

I will be happy to meet with you to discuss these points in detail. These
training techniques could be used in our orientation program. Let me know
when it would be convenient for you to discuss these points.

practice of indicating the precise time of day—for example, 1400 hours instead of 2:00 P.M.

Just because a memo is an in-house communication, do not think that the quality of your writing is unimportant. Your employer and coworkers deserve the same clear and concise writing customers do. In fact, your job may depend upon preparing correct and readable memos. Keep in mind that memos require the same care and follow the same rules of effective writing as letters do.

Strategies for Organizing a Memo

Your memos need to be organized so that readers can find information quickly and act on it promptly. For longer, more complex communications, such as the memos in Figures 7.2–7.4, the message of your memo might be divided into three parts: (1) introduction, (2) discussion, (3) conclusion.

In the introductory section of your memo, tell readers clearly about the problem, procedure, question, or policy that prompted your writing to them. Link the first sentence of your memo to the subject line. Explain briefly any background information the reader needs to know. Be specific about what you are going to accomplish in your memo. Note, for example, how the writer in Figure 7.2 tells the reader why he is providing a list of items or why recommendations are included in the memo in Figure 7.4. Do not be afraid to come right out and say "This memo explains new parking procedures" or "This memo summarizes the action taken at the industrial site near Evansville to reduce soil pollution."

In the discussion section of your memo explain, with relevant detail, the procedures, issues, policies, or problems you are calling to the readers' attention. Tell them why a problem or procedure is important, who will be affected by it and why, what caused it and why changes are necessary, and what those changes are. Give precise dates, times, and locations. Note how carefully, for example, the writer of the memo in Figure 7.3 explains the problem and procedure in cleaning the brake machine.

Provide a conclusion that states specifically how you want the reader to respond to your memo. To get readers to act appropriately, you can do one or more of the following in your conclusion:

1. Ask the reader to call you if he or she has any questions.
2. Request a reply—in writing or over the telephone or in person—by a specific date.
3. Provide a list of recommendations that the reader is to accept, revise, or reject.

Throughout your memo use organizational markers to make information easy for readers to follow. When you have a large number of related points, as the writer of the memo in Figure 7.2 does, number them so that the reader can comprehend them more easily. Lists in a memo point out comparisons and contrasts easily. Underlining key sentences will also help readers by emphasiz-

Fig. 7.3   Memo with a clear introduction, discussion, and conclusion.

MEMORANDUM

Dearborne Equipment Company
204 South Mill St.
South Orange, NJ 02341

TO: Machine Shop Employees   DATE: September 25, 1985

FROM: Janet Hempstead   *J. H.*   SUBJECT: Importance of Keeping
       Shop Supervisor   Brake Machines Clean

During the past two weeks I have received a number of reports that the brake machines are not being cleaned properly after each use. This memo emphasizes and explains the importance of keeping these machines clean for the safety of all employees.

When the brake machines are used, the cutter chops off small particles of metal from the brake drums. These particles settle on the machines and create a potentially hazardous situation for anyone working on or near the machines. If the machines are not cleaned before another use, these metal particles could fly into an individual's face when the brake drum is spinning.

To prevent accidents like this from happening, all you have to do is vacuum the brake machines after each use. You will find two vacuum cleaners for this purpose in the shop—one of them is located in work area 1-A and the other, a reserve model, is in the storage area. Vacuuming brake machines is quick and easy; it should take no more than a few seconds. I am sure you will agree that this is a small amount of time to make the shop safer for all of us.

I appreciate your cooperation in this matter. If you have any questions, please call me at Extension 123 or visit my office.

Fig. 7.4 A memo that uses headings.

RAMCO INDUSTRIES

"Where Technology Shapes Tomorrow"

TO: Harrison Mohler   SUBJECT: Ways to Increase
     Vice-President, Corp. Affairs   Ramco's Community
                                            Involvement

FROM: Trudy Snowden   *T. S.*   DATE: March 3, 1986
       Public Relations Chief

At our planning session in early February, our division managers stressed
the need to generate favorable publicity for our new Ramco plant in
Mayfield. Such publicity would help to highlight Ramco's anticipated
community involvement. You asked me to investigate ways in which Ramco's
visibility in the Mayfield community might be enhanced. This memo suggests
three plans we might pursue.

Create a Scholarship Fund

Ramco would receive favorable publicity by creating a scholarship at
Mayfield Junior College for any student interested in a career in
industrial technology. A tuition scholarship for one year at Mayfield
Junior College would cost Ramco $1400. The scholarship could be awarded by
a committee composed of Ramco's executives and administrators at Mayfield
Junior College. Such a scholarship would emphasize Ramco's support for
industrial education and our interest in a local college.

Offer Factory Tours

Short, guided tours of the Mayfield factory would introduce the Mayfield
community to Ramco's products and innovative technology. The tours might
be organized for community and civic groups——the members of the Y, senior
citizens clubs, schools. On these tours, individuals might see the care we
take in our production process, our equipment, and the speed with which we
ship our products. Of special interest to visitors would be Ramco's use of
industrial robots. These tours must be scheduled well in advance so they do
not conflict with our production schedules. A short question-and-answer
period should follow each tour.

Provide Guest Speakers

A number of our employees would be excellent guest speakers at social and
educational meetings in Mayfield. Possible topics would include the
technological advances Ramco has made in manufacturing and engineering
and how these advances help consumers. It would be relatively easy to
compile a list of interested speakers from our engineering, safety, and
transportation departments.

Please give me your comments on these suggestions as soon as possible. If
we are going to put one or more of them into practice before the plant
opens, we'll need to take action by the end of this month.

ing important points. But do not abuse this technique by underlining too much. Only underline points that contain summaries or draw conclusions. Memo reports, such as in Figure 7.4, use headings to separate information for readers so that they can find it more quickly. Headings will also help you organize information as you write.

☞ Order Letters

Order letters are straightforward notices informing a seller that you want to purchase a product or service—perhaps some articles of clothing, replacement parts for an intricate machine, or large quantities of various foods. To make sure that you receive exactly what you want, your letter must be clear, precise, and accurate. Double-check the seller's brochure, catalog sales list, or agency manual before you write your order letter.

Order letters address the following five points:

1. *Description of the product or service.* Specify the name, model or stock number, quantity, color, weight, height, width, size, or any special features that separate one model from another, e.g., chrome as opposed to copper handles. Make your order letter easy to read by itemizing when you order more than one product. Typing the products or materials in tabular form will set them apart and allow the seller an opportunity to check off each item as it is being prepared for shipment.
2. *Price of the product or service.* Indicate precisely the price per unit, per carload, per carton, and then multiply that price by the number you are ordering. For example, ask for "twelve units @ $5 a unit." Do not put down the cost of one item ($5) for the dozen you are requesting. You will receive only one.
3. *Shipping instructions.* Do you want the product sent by first-class or fourth-class mail, Federal Express, by overnight carrier? Specify any special handling instructions—Do not fold; Use hand stamp; Refrigerate or Pack in Dry Ice; Ship to the Production Department.
4. *Date needed.* Is there a rush date?
5. *Method of payment.* Businesses with good credit standing are sent a bill. Individuals, however, may be required to pay beforehand. If so, are you enclosing a check or money order? Is the product to arrive COD (cash on delivery), or are you using a charge card? In the latter case, specify which card, and include your charge account number. Will you be paying in installments? State how much you are including and when and how the balance is to be paid.

Orders can be considered external or internal. An external order is sent to an individual or company you do not work for or with. You will refer to the five points just discussed and use a letter or sometimes a form provided by the company from which you are ordering the product. Figure 7.5 shows a sample order letter.

Fig. 7.5   An order letter.

DAVIS CONSTRUCTION COMPANY
1200 South Devon
Millersville, Pennsylvania 17321

August 1, 1985

E. F. Wonderlic and Associates
820 Frontage Road
P.O. Box 7
Northfield, IL 60093

Dear E. F. Wonderlic:

Please send us by first—class mail the following materials as listed in your 1985 catalog entitled <u>Personnel Forms for Testing, Selection, Administration, and Evaluation</u>:

Catalog Number	Title	Number of Copies	Total Cost
P—4	Personnel Interviewer's Guide	25	$10.00
P—5	Health Questionnaire	100	24.00
EA—4	Personnel Application Forms	25	12.00
ATS—6	Health History	1	1.50
			$47.50

When you mail these forms, send them to the Personnel Department in care of my attention. Please send these forms within the next ten days and telephone me collect if there will be any delay.

A check for one half the amount ($23.75) is enclosed and the balance will be paid upon receipt of the materials.

Sincerely yours,

THE DAVIS CONSTRUCTION COMPANY

Roberta Youngblood

Roberta Youngblood
Personnel Department

Encl. Check 3467 for $23.75

An internal order, often called a *requisition,* asks one individual or department or section of your company to supply another with necessary materials, equipment, service, or publications. A letter is not necessary for an internal order; instead, use a memo or a specially provided form such as the one illustrated in Figure 7.6, showing how a unit secretary in a hospital orders supplies for the floor.

☞ Letters of Inquiry

A letter of inquiry asks for information about a product, service, publication, or procedure. Businesses frequently exchange such letters. As a customer, you too have occasion to ask for catalogs, names of stores in your town selling a special line of products, and the price, size, and color of a particular object. Businesses are eager to receive such inquiries and will answer them swiftly because they promise a future sale.

Figure 7.7 (page 188) illustrates a letter of inquiry. Addressed to a real estate office managing a large number of apartment complexes, Jackson Brown's letter follows the three basic rules for an effective inquiry letter. It

1. States exactly what information the writer wants.
2. Indicates clearly why the writer must have this information.
3. Specifies when the writer must have the information.

Whenever you request information, be sure to supply appropriate stock and model numbers, pertinent page numbers, or exact descriptions. You might even clip and mail the advertisement describing the product you want. Vague or general letters delay a response to you. Had Jackson Brown written the following letter to Acme, he would not have helped his family move: "Please send me some information on housing in Roanoke. My family and I plan to move there soon." Such a letter does not indicate whether he wants to rent or buy, whether he is interested in a large or small apartment, furnished or unfurnished, where he would like it to be located, or the price he is willing to pay. Similarly, a letter asking a firm to "Send me all the information you have on microwave ovens" might bring back a detailed service manual when the writer wanted only prices of the top-selling models.

☞ Special Request Letters

Special request letters are not routine letters of inquiry. Making a special demand, these letters can ask, among other things, (1) a company for information that you as a student will use in a paper, (2) an individual for a copy of an article or a speech, or (3) an agency for facts that your company needs to prepare a proposal or sell a product. The person or company being asked for help stands to gain no financial reward for supplying this information; the only reward is the goodwill such a response creates.

Fig. 7.6   An internal order form or requisition.

COUNTY GENERAL HOSPITAL
DEPARTMENTAL PURCHASE REQUISITION

Department *Nursing 7E*

Date *1/16/86*

*Completed by
Receiving Dept.*

Quantity	Unit	Cat. number	Item description	Price unit	Extension
1 box	10	758A329	*Spiral notebook*		
1	1	916D572	*Downy Fabric Softener*		
1	1	389A183	*Ivory Snow*		
2 boxes	10	523E617	*Hall markers with room numbers*		

Fm. No. CGH 1222

Requested by: *J. Jones, Unit Secretary*

Make your request clear and easy to answer. One department store manager made it very easy for customers to indicate how courteously they were treated when they wanted to exchange some merchandise. In her letter to these customers, she included the following request: "Perhaps you would take a moment and list on the back of this page any remarks or suggestions you might have regarding our service and/or merchandise. (You will note that an addressed, postage-paid envelope is enclosed for your convenience.)" Supply readers with addressed, postage-paid envelopes and a telephone number for any questions.

Saying "please" and "thank you" will help you get the information you want. Also, do not expect your reader to write the paper or proposal for you. Asking for information is quite different from asking readers to organize and write it for you. Follow these seven points when asking for information in a special request letter:

1. State who you are and why you are writing.
2. Indicate clearly your reason for requesting the information.

Fig. 7.7   A letter of inquiry.

403 South Main Street
Kingsport, TN 37721
March 2, 1985

Mr. Fred Stonehill
Property Manager
Acme Property Corporation
Main and Broadway
Roanoke, VA 24015

Dear Mr. Stonehill:

Please let me know if you will have any two-bedroom furnished
apartments available for rent during the months of June, July, and
August. I am willing to pay up to $350 a month plus utilities. My
wife, one-year-old son, and I will be moving to Roanoke for the
summer so that I can attend a course at Virginia Western Community
College. If possible, we would like to have an apartment within two
or three miles of the college. We do not have any pets.

I would appreciate hearing from you within the next two weeks. My
phone number is (606) 273-8957. The best time to reach me is between
6:00 p.m. and 9:00 p.m.

If you have any vacancies, we can drive to Roanoke to look at them
and, if they are satisfactory, give you a deposit to hold an
apartment for us.

Sincerely yours,

Jackson Brown

Jackson Brown

3. Give the reader precisely and succinctly the questions you want answered. List, number, and separate the questions.
4. Specify exactly when you need the information. Allow sufficient time—at least three weeks.
5. Offer to forward a copy of your report, paper, or survey in gratitude for the help you were given.
6. If you want to reprint or publish the materials you ask for, indicate that you will secure whatever permissions are necessary. State that you will keep the information confidential if that is appropriate.
7. Thank the reader for helping.

Figure 7.8 gives an example of a letter that follows these guidelines.

Sales Letters

A sales letter is written to persuade the reader to buy a product, try a service, support some cause, or participate in some activity. A sales letter can also serve as a method of introducing yourself to potential customers. You have already received numerous sales letters from military recruiters, local banks and merchants, charitable organizations, and campus groups. Sales letters face a lot of competition that you will have to overcome.

To write an effective sales letter, you have to do three things.

1. Identify and limit your audience.
2. Find out exactly what the needs of this group are.
3. Determine precisely what you want your readers to do after reading your sales letter.

These three points require that you do adequate homework about both your audience and the product or service you are selling.

In deciding whom you want to reach, you will also be investigating the needs of your audience. Do you want to write a letter to all the nurses in your state district nurses' association or only the pediatric nurses at a particular hospital? Are you writing to all homeowners who purchased aluminum siding from your company in the last three years or in the last three months? Sometimes a sales letter will be duplicated and sent to hundreds of readers as in Figure 7.9; sometimes you may write to only one reader as in Figure 7.10. Some helpful considerations in audience analysis are occupation, age, consumer needs or habits, geographic location, and memberships. Your employer may have a mailing list that you should consult. Once you have selected those who should receive your letter, you have made a great deal of headway in knowing what you will say to that audience.

The "you attitude" is crucial. A sales letter is not written to provide a detailed set of instructions or elaborate explanations about a product. That kind of information comes after the sale. Nor is a sales letter written to pro-

Fig. 7.8   A special request letter.

234 Springdale Street
Rochester, NY 14618
March 25, 1985

Ms. Victoria Stanton
Research Director
Creative Marketing Association
198 Madison Avenue
New York, NY 10016

Dear Ms. Stanton:

I am a second-year student at Monroe College in Rochester and I am
preparing a term paper on the topic "Current Marketing Practices."
As part of my research for this paper, I am writing an overview of
marketing practices for the past twenty-five years. Could you please
send me the following pamphlets:

1. <u>A History of Marketing in the United States</u> (CMA 15)
2. <u>Creative Marketing Comes of Age</u> (CMA 27)

I would appreciate receiving these materials by April 17 and will
be pleased to send you a copy of my paper in late May. Creative
Marketing Association will, of course, be fully cited in the
bibliography.

Thank you for your assistance. I look forward to hearing from you.

Sincerely yours,

Julie Lester

Julie Lester

Fig. 7.9   A sales letter sent to a group of readers.

THE C. V. MOSBY COMPANY · 11830 WESTLINE INDUSTRIAL DRIVE, ST. LOUIS, MISSOURI 63141
314-872-8370 · CABLE ADDRESS "MOSBYCO"

Dear Doctor:

After you look it up, do you really know which drug is best for YOUR patient . . . and WHY?

It all depends on where you look. If you consult standard "cookbook" guides to current drug therapy, you'll have only the personal opinions of one or two physicians on which drug they prefer to treat a specific disease.

However, if you consult the new DRUGS OF CHOICE, you'll have an authoritative, critical, unbiased appraisal of all drugs in current use, written specifically to support and verify your selection of the optimum drug for a specific patient in a particular clinical situation.

DRUGS OF CHOICE is the only drug therapy book that recognizes that you alone can fit drug and patient together, and thus gives you all the facts necessary to assist you in that "fitting." Dr. Modell and his 45 eminent contributors discuss all drugs available for a particular condition, based on their specialized knowledge and experience, substantiated by selected references. You will note updating in every chapter, particularly those on diuretics and drugs for cardiac arrhythmias.

You'll find a more complete description of the new DRUGS OF CHOICE on the specially prepared brochure enclosed, including table of contents, distinguished contributors, and 54 timesaving tables. Take a moment now to examine it; then examine the book itself for 30 days at our expense. Just complete the examination certificate and return it to us in the postage-paid envelope provided.

Each time you sign a prescription, you, and you alone, endorse the safety and quality of the drug prescribed. If you're going to look it up, you want the whole story. And only one book offers you that . . . DRUGS OF CHOICE. Can you afford to be without it?

Sincerely,

William J. DeRoze

William J. DeRoze
for The C. V. Mosby Company

WJD:ne

Letter adapted courtesy The C.V. Mosby Company.

Fig. 7.10   A sales letter sent to an individual.

Faithful Answering Service

4300 South Wabash
Lincoln, Oregon 97407

September 27, 1985

Ms. Katherine Eubanks
Eubanks Pest Control
18 West Gannon Drive
Lincoln, OR 97411

Dear Ms. Eubanks:

How much business do you lose when your telephone rings and you are not there to answer it? A prospective client or steady customer might call one of the other twenty-two exterminators listed in the Lincoln Yellow Pages.

You will never miss a call if you use the Faithful Answering Service. Our courteous and experienced operators are on duty twenty-four hours a day, every day of the year. They are prompt, too. Your telephone will be answered before the caller hears the third ring.

You tell us when we are needed by simply calling us and giving us your identifying code number. We will be there to take messages or to transfer calls to any number you give us. When you are out of the office, a quick call to us can save you extra trips, time, and gas. Your customers will also be happier, knowing that you can be reached whenever they need you to solve their pest problems.

All this convenience and peace of mind can be yours, Ms. Eubanks, for less than $.80 a day. And if you act by October 4, you can have the Faithful service installed free of charge and save the $25.00 installation fee. We promise to have your phone connected within three days after we hear from you.

I urge you to call us at 657-3434 by October 4. You can call us at any time, day or night. Don't forget we are here twenty-four hours a day.

Sincerely yours,

Samuel Heywood

Samuel Heywood, Owner

claim the merits of your company. Here is a safe rule to follow: Don't boast or be a bore. The sales letter is written to persuade readers to buy, support, or join. Everything in the letter should be directed toward that goal. Appeal to readers' emotions, pocketbooks, or self-images. Entertain, amuse, coax, inform, or flatter the reader. The central question is, What are we trying to do for you, our customer? Ask yourself that question before you begin writing.

Sales letters follow a time-honored and workable plan; that is, each sales letter follows what can be called the "four A's":

1. Gets the reader's *attention*
2. Highlights the product's *appeal*
3. Shows the customer the product's *application*
4. Ends with a specific request for *action.*

These four parts may be handled in less than four paragraphs. Holding a sales letter down to one page or less will keep the reader's attention. Television commercials and ads in magazines provide useful models of this fourfold approach to the customer. The next time you see one of these ads, try to identify the "four A's."

Getting the Reader's Attention

Your opening sentence is crucial. If you lose readers here, you will have lost them forever. A typical television commercial has thirty to sixty seconds to sell viewers; your first sentence has about two to five seconds to catch the readers' attention and prompt them to read on. That first sentence is bait on a hook. It must show readers how their problems could be solved, their profits increased, or their pleasures enriched. The reader's attitude will be "What's in this for me?"

Avoid an opening that is flat, vague, or lengthy. Beginning with a statement such as "I have great news for you" tells the readers nothing. They are more likely to toss your letter away if it does not contain something personally relevant in the first sentence. Tell them what the news is by selecting something that will appeal to their wallets, their emotions, or their chances to look better in the eyes of others. A letter for a pesticide that begins: "The cockroach could become the next endangered species if a California manufacturer has his way" offers some interesting, specific news. Keep your opening short, one or two sentences at most. Do not lose readers before you have had an opportunity to convince them.

The following five techniques are a few of the many ways to begin a sales letter. Each technique requires you to adapt it to your product or service.

1. Asking a question. Mention something that readers are vitally concerned about that is also relevant to your product or service. Look, for example, at the opening question in Figure 7.9 (page 191). Avoid such general questions as "Are you happy?" or "Would you like to make money?" Use more specific questions. For example, an ad for a home-study training course in crime investigation and identification asked readers "Are you promotable? Are you ready to step into a bigger job?" And an ad for Air Force Reserve Nursing asked nurses if they were "looking for something 30,000 feet out of the ordinary?" These are precise questions relevant to the offers they introduce. Similarly, sales letters beginning with "Could you use $100?" or "Will you be wearing the latest jewelry at this year's Christmas party?" zero in on one particular desire of the reader. Since your main goal is to persuade readers to continue reading your letter, choose a question that they will want to see answered.

2. Employing a "how to" statement. This is one of the most frequently used openers in a sales letter. The reason for its success is simple—the letter promises to tell readers something practical and profitable. Here are some effective "how to" statements: "We can show you how to increase all your plant growth up to 91%." "Here is how to save $75.00 on your next vacation." "This is how to provide nourishing lunches on less than fifty cents a person." These "how to" statements attract the readers' attention by introducing a subject that promises rewards and then shows how to gain those rewards.

3. Using flattery. Appeal to the reader's ego. But remember that readers are not naive; they will be suspicious of false praise. Select some compliment that affects the reader professionally or that praises the reader for some specific actions. A sales letter for a school supply shop was sent to every new member of a campus sorority announcing, "You've made the right choice in joining Delta Zeta. Now, let us make the right choice in helping you select your supplies this term."

4. Offering a free gift. Everyone likes to receive something for nothing or to boast about a bargain. Often you can lure readers further into your letter by telling them that there is a sale going on and that they can save a lot of money or that they can get the second product free, or at cost, or at half price if they purchase the first one at full price. One garden club promises prospective customers, "We'll give you three books for $1.00 and a free Tote Bag to put them in . . . with membership." An automobile dealer promises $50.00 to every customer who test drives a new car. A local realtor tempts customers to see lots for sale with, "Enclosed please find a coupon worth $25.00 in gas for seeing Deer Run Trails Estates."

5. Using a comparison. Compare your product or service with conventional or standard products or procedures. Scriptomatic Addressing Systems persuasively begins with: "Address mail five times faster than typing with Scriptomatic's new Model 5, a complete addressing system designed for home or office use." A jacket firm told police officers that if they purchased a coat, they were really getting three jackets in one, since their product had a lining for winter and another lining used for greater visibility at night.

Calling Attention to the Product's Appeal

Once you have aroused the reader's attention, introduce the product or service. Make it so attractive, so necessary, and so profitable that the reader will want to buy or use the product or service. Persuade readers to want to see it, touch it, and ultimately own or use it. Don't lose the momentum you have gained with your introduction by boring the reader with petty details, flat descriptions, elaborate inventories, or trivial boasts. Appeal to the reader's intellect, emotions, or both, while introducing the product. In Figure 7.9 Mosby Company's mass-mailing letter appeals to the physician's professional requirements for an up-to-date book. Here is an emotional appeal by the Gulf Stream Fruit Company:

> Can you, when you bite into an orange, tell where it was grown? If it tastes better than any you have ever eaten . . . full of rich, golden flavor, brimming with juice, sparkling with sunshine . . . then you know it was grown here in our famous Indian River Valley where we have handpicked it, at the very peak of its flavor, just for your order.[1]

From a leading question, the sales letter moves to a vivid description of the product, name of the supplier, and the customer's ability to recognize how special both the product and he or she is to the Gulf Stream Fruit Company. Using another kind of appeal, the manufacturers of Tree Saw show how their product can decrease customers' fears and increase their safety.

> The greatest invention since the ladder, and a lot safer. With the Tree Saw, you can cut branches thirty feet above the ground. No need to call in a tree surgeon. And you don't have to risk your life on a shaky ladder. Just toss the beanbag weight of the flexible Tree Saw over a branch. Pull on each end of the control rope to make a clean cut. Spring pruning is quick and safe with this perfect tool.[2]

Showing the Customer the Product's Application

The third part of your sales letter lets the readers know how and why the product is worthwhile for them. Here is the place where you give evidence of the value of what you are selling. You have to be careful, though, that you do not overwhelm readers with facts, statistics, detailed mechanical descriptions, or elaborate arguments. The emphasis is still on the use of the product and not on the company that manufactures or sells it. The shift from your company to your prospective customer is essential to any sale. The sales letter in Figure 7.9 emphasizes the importance of the physician's role in prescribing drugs: "You alone can fit drug and patient together." The following Fisher-Price Toys sales message is addressed to parents who are worried about children damaging a

---

[1] "Gifts from Gulf Stream" Oct. 1980, Gulf Stream Fruit Company, Ft. Lauderdale, Florida. Reprinted by permission.
[2] Reprinted courtesy Green Mountain Products, Inc., Norwalk, Conn.

phonograph. Note how the details about the phonograph are all related to that reader-centered issue.

> Fisher-Price knows that children begin to appreciate music at a very early age. Usually, a little before they fully appreciate how to handle delicate things like tone arms and fragile records. That's why we designed our new phonograph with lots of features other record players don't offer. To assure that this phonograph can take the toughest treatment young music lovers can hand out and keep playing in fine tune year after year

> 1. There's a real, replaceable diamond needle that lasts five times longer than a sapphire needle.
> 2. The needle cartridge actually retracts when the tone arm is forced down, to prevent deep scratches.
> 3. The tone arm is solidly constructed so it can be pulled and tugged and still work smoothly.
> 4. The detachable case cover is specially designed to gently guide the tone arm back in place even if the cover is slammed shut.
> 5. The phonograph's 4″ speaker provides a nice clear sound. And there are just two simple controls for volume and record speed (33 and 45 rpm) plus a built-in storage space for the electrical cord.

> So you can see, the Fisher-Price Phonograph is not a toy. It's a really dependable piece of audio equipment that's made especially for children. So you, and they, can relax and enjoy its wonderful sound for years to come. And that should be music to your ears.[3]

What evidence should you use to convince the reader? Concentrate on descriptions of the product or service that emphasize convenience, usefulness, and economy. Any special features or changes in the product or service that make it more attractive for the customer should be mentioned. For example, an ad for a greenhouse manufacturer stressed that in addition to using its structure just for a place to grow plants, customers would also find it a "perfect sun room enclosure for year 'round 'outdoor' activities, gardening or leisure health spa."

Testimonials—endorsements from previous customers as well as from specialists—may also convince readers to respond favorably to your letter. Rather than saying that hundreds of customers are satisfied with your product, get two or three of those happy customers to allow you to quote them in your letter. A large nursing home published residents' compliments about the food and care to show that it was a good place to live. A private boarding school printed a brief biography (with now and then pictures) of a successful graduate to prove that the school inspires students to leadership. A roach powder firm tells

---

[3] Reprinted courtesy Waring & LaRosa, Inc., and Fisher-Price Toys, Inc.

customers that its product is used at the White House. You might also cite awards, honors, accreditations, or citations that your product or service has won.

Worth mentioning also are warranties, guarantees, services, or special considerations that will make the customer's life easier or happier. One store advises readers: "As usual, there is no charge for local deliveries when purchases are over $100." Tell the reader that labor and parts are good for a year, two years, or however long they last. Emphasize that you will refund the price if the customer is not completely satisfied. Tell customers that they do not have to wait for parts or that you will loan them a replacement if they do.

You may be obligated to mention costs in your letter. Postpone discussion of them until the reader has been shown how appealing and valuable the product is. Of course, if price is a key selling point, mention it early in the letter. Readers will react more favorably to costs after they have seen the reasons why the product or service is useful. Do not bluntly state the cost. Relate prices, charges, or fees to the benefits provided by the services or products to which they apply. After giving the price per can of its insecticide, the manufacturer tells readers that "one can covers up to a nine-room residence, plus one can for basement or garage." Customers then see how much they are getting for their money. An electric-blanket ad tells customers that it costs only four cents a night for electricity to be warm and comfortable. That sounds more inviting than just listing the cost of the blanket as $30. A dealer who installs steel shutters does not tell readers the exact price of the product, but does indicate that they will save money by buying it: "Virtually maintenance free, your Reel Shutters also offer substantial savings in energy costs by reducing your loss through radiation by as much as 65% . . . and that lowers your utility bills by 35%." Keep costs tied to the reader's profit.

Ending with a Specific Request for Action

This last section of your letter is vital. If the reader ignores your request for action, your letter has been written in vain. Tell readers exactly what you want them to do and make it easy and pleasurable to do it. Do you want them to fill out a postcard ordering your product, send for a brochure, come into your store, take a test drive, participate in a meeting? Indicate clearly the actions you want readers to take. Tell them if they have to sign an order blank or merely initial it. Is there an enclosed stamped envelope for their convenience? When do they have to notify you? Is there a deadline for taking advantage of a sale price or bonus? "Come to our store tomorrow between 10 A.M. and 10 P.M. to get your free lounge chair with the purchase of any bedroom suite." As with price, link the benefits the customers will receive to their responses. "Respond and be rewarded" is the basic message of the last section of your letter. Note that in Figure 7.9 the call to action is made in the next-to-last paragraph, but is followed by a brief reminder of the significance of the action. Figure 7.10 shows a call-to-action statement in the last paragraph. The letter urges the reader to act immediately in order to receive the free installation.

☞ Customer Relations Letters

Much business correspondence deals explicitly with promoting and maintaining friendly working relations. Such correspondence, known as customer relations letters, includes thank-you letters, congratulation letters, follow-up letters, complaint letters, adjustment letters, and collection letters. All such letters show how you and your company regard the people with whom you do business. Customer relations letters must reveal a sensitivity to customers' needs, whether you are communicating about something pleasant (a promotion, an award, a business favor) or something unpleasant (a defective piece of machinery, spoiled goods, or unpaid bills). The words you choose and the order in which you present information will determine the success or failure of a customer relations letter. As you read this section, keep in mind the two basic principles captured in the words "the customers always write":

1. Customers will write about how they would like to be or have been treated—to thank, to complain, to request an explanation.
2. Customers have certain rights that you must respect in your correspondence with them. They deserve a prompt and courteous reply, whether they are correct or not. If you refuse their request, they deserve to know why; if they owe you money, you should give them an opportunity to explain and a chance, up to a point, to set up a payment schedule.

Thank-You Letters

A thank-you letter tells someone how much that person's acts or words have meant to you. In the business world thank-you letters show that the writer is a responsible individual who values human relations. Even if you have already expressed your gratitude in person or over the telephone, a letter further emphasizes your thoughtfulness and courtesy.

Obviously, you will not write a thank-you letter for every kindness shown you or your firm. Reserve a letter for the special occasions when an individual or company does something extra—something that did not have to be done or that was especially helpful. Thank-you letters also figure significantly in a job search. The individuals who write your letters of recommendation, as well as the prospective employers who interview you, deserve thank-you letters. Figure 7.11 contains a thank-you letter to Mr. Butler, to whom Robert Jackson wrote (in Figure 6.1) for a reference. Also review the letter in Figure 6.12 to a prospective employer after the candidate has been interviewed.

Thank-you letters should be a joy to write. Your main concerns are (1) being specific about what you liked and (2) explaining why you are grateful. Begin with a simple, direct statement of gratitude identifying what has pleased you. Indicate how and when this service was provided. Mention the names of individuals responsible for the work and why their work was so helpful. Also indicate why this service deserves special thanks—that is, how the action helped you or how it applies to your company.

Fig. 7.11   A thank-you letter.

```
5432 South Kenneth Avenue
Chicago, IL 60651
April 30, 1985


Mr. Sunny Butler, Manager
A&P Supermarket
4000 West 79th Street
Chicago, IL 60652

Dear Mr. Butler:

Thank you very much for writing a letter of recommendation to be included
in my dossier at the Placement Office at Moraine Valley Community College.
I appreciate your taking the time to do this, and I am especially grateful
for the many kind things you said you had included in your letter. Your
high praise of my work for A&P will certainly help me in finding a job in
retail sales.

Once again, thank you for your recommendation. I will let you know how my
job search goes.

Sincerely yours,

Robert B. Jackson

Robert B. Jackson
```

The letter in Figure 7.12 illustrates an apt thank-you letter. A local merchant thanks a glass company for the exceptional service she received. When the Dole Glass Company has any need of hardware parts, it will certainly be favorably disposed to order from Granger Hardware because of Ms. Stovall-Granger's kind and welcome thank-you letter.

Congratulation Letters

When you put your praise into a letter, you show considerable thoughtfulness. You could call the individual on the telephone or speak to him or her in person to extend your congratulations. But a letter shows that you have made extra

Fig. 7.12   A thank-you letter.

Serving Fair View Since 1945

Granger Hardware Store

20 N.E. Hasse Road
Fair View, New Jersey 02386

February 26, 1985

Mr. Rudolph Della Sinta, Manager
Dole Glass Company
Manners Highway
Kensington, NJ 02384

Dear Mr. Della Sinta:

I am grateful to the Dole Glass Company for giving me outstanding
service last Sunday night, February 24. My store's front plate-glass
window (21 feet by 12 feet) was smashed by flying debris. Your crew,
Paula Romero and Tim Tulley, were at my store thirty minutes after I
phoned them late Sunday night. They quickly cleared away the glass
and measured my window. Realizing that the plates they had on their
truck would not fit my window, they drove all the way back to your
Devonshire warehouse to locate a suitable piece. They could have
waited until the next day to do this, but they returned and installed
the new glass window in record time.

Their service was exceptional. It allowed me to open my store on
Monday morning for business as usual. If your crew had not worked so
quickly and made that extra trip, I would have been forced to board
up my store and close on Monday to have the repairs made.

I have the highest opinion of Dole Glass and your two employees who
came to my store two days ago.

Sincerely yours,

Barbara Stovall-Granger

Barbara Stovall-Granger
Owner

effort. This personal touch also says far more than a greeting card with a printed message.

The occasions for such letters, in both your business and personal life, are many. In the business world you might congratulate someone for (1) being promoted, (2) opening a new business or expanding an existing one, or (3) being honored for an accomplishment (for example, having the highest sales record of the month or year, or becoming a broker). When you honor someone for a distinction, you also honor the company the individual represents. In your own community you create goodwill by congratulating someone for being elected to public office, serving on a civic committee, or receiving an award or medal. In addition to complimenting people for professional or civic achievements, you may congratulate them for engagements, marriages, births, graduations, and anniversaries.

Congratulatory letters must arrive at the right time. Write as soon after the accomplishment as you can. Good news travels fast; acknowledging the individual's honor quickly shows that you are keeping track of events and are eager to express your congratulations. A late letter will say that you did not have the time to write, that the news was not very important to you, or that you belatedly joined everyone else in sending your good wishes.

Keep your letters short and sincere. But a one-sentence letter—"Please accept my congratulations on being promoted"—is inappropriate. A letter this short looks as if you sent it not because you were sincerely interested in the individual, but because you thought that you must write something.

You need not write four or five long paragraphs. A long congratulatory letter with flowery language and backslapping smacks of insincerity. Excessive praise is doubtful praise.

A sincere yet brief letter of congratulations praises one or two significant points of the individual's accomplishment. The following two paragraphs provide a suitable congratulatory letter.

Dear Ms. Bozanich:

   Please accept my congratulations on being promoted to branch manager of the Powersville store. Your work in the field for the Jordan Company will profit you and us in your new position.

   I wish you great success as branch manager. Please call me if I can help you in any way.

Sincerely,

Robert Meyer

Robert Meyer

This next congratulatory letter selects a few details, including the place where the writer learned of the reader's achievement, to show the writer's sincere interest:

Dear Mr. Goshin:

   Congratulations on your new title of Certified Insurance Counselor just announced in the <u>Midtown Financial Record</u>. It certainly is an honor to be among only three thousand agents in the country who can sign C.I.C. after their name.

   You have our best wishes for continuing success in your insurance business.

                                        Sincerely yours,

                                        Jennifer Rodriguez

                                        Jennifer Rodriguez

One last point about congratulatory letters: Do not use them to sell a product or service. By calling attention to your company's services, you reveal your congratulations are only a gimmick, not a sincere expression of goodwill.

Follow-up Letters

A follow-up letter is sent by a company after a sale to thank the customer for buying a product or using a service and to ask the customer to buy more products and use more services in the future. A follow-up letter is, therefore, a combination thank-you note and sales letter. The letter in Figure 7.13 is sent to customers soon after they have purchased an appliance and offers them the option of a continued maintenance policy. The letter in Figure 7.14 shows how an income tax preparation service attempts to obtain repeat business. Both of these letters follow helpful guidelines:

1. They begin with a brief and sincere expression of gratitude for having served the customer.
2. They discuss the benefits (advantages) already known to the customer. Then, they transfer the company's dedication to the customer from the product or service already sold to a new or continuing sales area.
3. They end with a specific request for future business.

   Occasionally a follow-up letter is sent to a good customer who, for some reason, has stopped doing business with the company. Perhaps the customer has closed an account of long standing, no longer comes to the store, discontinues a subscription, or fails to send in an order for a product or service. Such a follow-up letter should try to find out why the customer has stopped doing

Fig. 7.13   A follow-up letter to sell a maintenance agreement.

DYNAMIC APPLIANCE COMPANY
100 Walden Parkway
Denver, Colorado 80203

February 9, 1985

Mr. John H. Abbott
3715 Mayview Drive
Cottage Grove, MN 53261

Dear Mr. Abbott:

We are delighted that you have purchased a Dynamic appliance. To help ensure your satisfaction, this appliance is backed by a Dynamic warranty. At the same time, we realize that you bought the appliance to serve you not just for the period covered by the warranty, but for many, many years. That's why the purchase of a Dynamic Maintenance Agreement at this time is one of the wisest investments you can make.

A Dynamic Maintenance Agreement provides savings benefits many cost-conscious customers want and look for today. It helps extend the life of the appliance by means of an annual, on-request preventive maintenance check-up. And if you need service, it provides for as many service calls as necessary for repairs due to normal use—at no extra charge to you.

All this coverage is now available to you at a special introductory price. This price takes into consideration the warranty coverage you have remaining. Act now, by filling out and returning the enclosed form.

Sincerely,

Carole Brown

Carole Brown
Sales Representative
588-9681
Extension 285

Fig. 7.14   A follow-up letter to encourage repeat business.

TAYLOR TAX SERVICE

HIGHWAY 10 NORTH
JENNINGS, TX 78326

December 1, 1985

Ms. Laurie Pavlovich
345 Jefferson St.
Jennings, TX 78326

Dear Ms. Pavlovich:

Thank you for using our services in February of this year. We were
pleased to help you prepare your 1984 federal and state income tax
returns. Our goal is to save you every tax dollar to which you are
entitled. If you ever have any questions about your return, we are
open all year long to help you.

We are looking forward to seeing you again next year. The new federal
tax laws, which go into effect January 1, will change the kind of
deductions you can declare. These changes might appreciably increase
the size of your return. Our consultants have studied these new laws
and are ready to explain them to you and apply them to your return.

Another important tax matter influencing your 1985 returns will be
any losses you may have suffered because of the hail storms and
tornadoes which hit our area three months ago. Our consultants are
specially trained to assist you in filing proper damage claims with
your federal and state returns.

To make using our services even easier next year, we have started an
appointment policy for your convenience. Please call us at 884-3457
or 885-7853 as soon as you have received all your forms in order to
set up your own appointment. We are waiting to serve you any day of
the week from 9:00 A.M. to 9:00 P.M.

Sincerely yours,

TAYLOR TAX SERVICE

J. P. Sanders

J. P. Sanders
Manager

business and to persuade that customer to resume business dealings. Study the letter in Figure 7.15, in which Jim Margolis first politely inquires whether Mr. Janeck has experienced a problem and then urges him to come back to the store.

Complaint Letters

Each of us at some time has been frustrated by a defective product, inadequate service, or incorrect billing. Usually our first response is to write a letter dripping with juicy insults. But a hate letter rarely gets results and can in fact hurt the writer and create an unfavorable image of the company being represented. A letter of complaint is a delicate one to write.

A letter of complaint is written for more reasons than just blowing off steam. You want some specific action taken. By adopting the right tone, you increase your chances of getting what you want. Do not call the reader names, hurl insults, refuse to do business with the company again. Register your complaint courteously and tolerantly. Companies want to be fair to you in order to keep you as a satisfied customer and correct defective products so that other customers will not be inconvenienced. The "you attitude" is especially important here to maintain the reader's goodwill.

An effective letter of complaint can be written by an individual consumer or by a company. Figure 7.16 shows Michael Trigg's complaint about a defective fishing reel; Figure 7.17 expresses a restaurant's dissatisfaction with an industrial dishwasher. Present your case logically, and provide enough detail to obtain a speedy settlement. To accomplish this objective, follow these five steps.

1. Begin with a detailed description of the product or service. Give the appropriate model numbers, size(s), quantity, color. Indicate when and where (specific address) you purchased it, and also how much warranty time remains. If you are complaining about a service, give the name of the company, the frequency of the service, the personnel providing it, and their exact duties. Indicate if you are returning the product to the company and how you are sending it—U.S. mail, U.P.S., or the like.

2. State exactly what is wrong with the product or service. Precise information will enable the reader to understand and act on your complaint. How many times did the machine work before it stopped, what parts were malfunctioning, what parts of a job were not done or were done poorly, and when did all this happen? Stating that "the brake shoes were defective" tells very little about how long they were on your car, how effectively they may have been installed, or what condition they were in when they ceased functioning safely. Reach some conclusion, even if you qualify your remarks with words like "apparently," "possibly," or "seemingly" when you describe the difficulty.

Fig. 7.15   A follow-up letter to maintain customer goodwill.

BROADWAY CLEANERS

Broadway at Davis Drive
Baltimore, Maryland 21228

April 3, 1985

Mr. Edward Janeck
34 Brompton Lane
Apartment 143
Baltimore, MD 21227

Dear Mr. Janeck:

You have given us the privilege of taking care of your cleaning needs
for more than three years now. It has been our pleasure to see you in
the store each week and to clean your shirts, slacks, and coats to
your satisfaction. Since you have not come in during the last month,
we are concerned that we may have in some way disappointed you. We
hope not, because you are a valuable customer whose goodwill we do
not want to lose.

If there is something wrong, please tell us about it. We welcome any
suggestions on how we can serve you better. Our goal is to have a
spotless reputation in the eyes of our customers.

The next time you need some garments cleaned, won't you please bring
them to us, along with the enclosed coupon worth $10.00 on your next
cleaning bill. We look forward to seeing you again—soon.

Sincerely yours,

Jim Margolis

Jim Margolis, Manager

Fig. 7.16   A complaint letter from a consumer.

17 Westwood
Magnolia, MA 02171
September 15, 1985

Mr. Ralph Montoya, Manager
Customer Relations Department
Smith Sports Equipment Company
P.O. Box 287
Tulsa, OK 74109

Dear Mr. Montoya:

On August 31, 1985, I purchased a Smith reel, model 191, at the
Uni—Mart Store on Marsh Avenue in Magnolia. The reel sold for $24.95
plus tax. Since the reel is not working effectively, I am returning
it to you under separate cover by first—class mail.

I had made no more than five casts with the reel when it began to
malfunction. The button that releases the spool and allows the line
to cast will not spring back into position after casting. In
addition, the gears make a grinding noise when I try to retrieve the
line. Because of these problems, I was unable to continue my
participation in the Gloucester Fishing Tournament.

I want a new reel to be sent to me free of charge in place of the
defective one I returned. I would also like to know what was wrong
with this defective reel.

I would appreciate your handling my claim within the next two weeks,
if at all possible.

Sincerely yours,

Michael Trigg

Michael Trigg

Fig. 7.17   A complaint letter from a business.

The Loft
Cameron and Dale
Sunnyside, California 91793

June 17, 1985

Customer Relations Department
Superflex Products
San Diego, CA 93141

Dear Customer Relations Department:

On September 15, 1984, we purchased a Superflex industrial
dishwasher, model 3203876, at the Hillcrest Store at 3400 Broadway
Drive in Sunnyside, for $2,000. In the last three weeks, our
restaurant has had repeated problems with this machine. Three more
months of warranty remain on this dishwasher.

The machine does not complete a full cycle; it stops before the final
rinsing and thus leaves the dishes still dirty. It appears that the
cycle regulators are not working properly because they refuse to
shift into the next necessary gear. Attempts to repair the machine
by the Hillcrest crew on June 3, 12, and 16 have been unsuccessful.

Our restaurant has been greatly inconvenienced. The kitchen team has
been forced to sort, clean, and sanitize utensils, dishes, pans, and
pots by hand. Moreover, our expenses for proper detergents have
increased.

We want your main office to send another repair crew at once to fix
this machine. If your crew is unable to do this, we want a discount
worth the amount of warranty life on this model to be applied to the
purchase of a new Superflex dishwasher. This amount would come to
$400.00, or 20 percent of the original purchase price.

So that our business is not further disrupted, we would appreciate
your resolving this problem within the next week.

Sincerely yours,

Emily Rashon

Emily Rashon
Manager

3. Briefly describe the inconvenience you have experienced. Your comments in this section of the letter of complaint show that your problems were directly caused by the defective product or service. To build your case, give precise details about the time and money you lost. Don't just say you had "numerous difficulties." If you purchased a calculator and it broke down during a mathematics examination, say so (but do not blame the calculator company if you failed the course). Were you forced to postpone a luncheon because the caterer was late, did you have to pay a mechanic to fix your car when it was stalled on the road, did you have to take time away from your other chores to clean up a mess made by a leaky new dishwasher, did you have to buy a new fishing reel?

4. Indicate precisely what you want done. Do not simply write that you "want something done," "that adequate measures must be taken," or that "the situation should be corrected." State that you want your purchase price refunded, your model repaired or replaced, or a completely new repair crew provided. Maybe you want only an apology from the company for some discourteous treatment. If you are asking for damages, state your request in dollars and cents, and include a copy of any bills resulting from the problem. Perhaps you had to rent a car, were forced to pay a janitorial service to clean up, or had to rent equipment at a higher rate because the company did not make its deliveries as promised.

5. Ask for prompt handling of your claim. Ask that an answer be provided to any question you may have (such as finding out where calls came from that you were billed for but did not make). And ask that your claim be handled as quickly as possible. You might even specify a reasonable time by which you want to hear from the writer or need the problem fixed.

Adjustment Letters

Adjustment letters tell customers dissatisfied with a product or service how their claim will be settled. Adjustment letters should reconcile the differences that exist between a customer and a firm and restore the customer's confidence in that firm.

Rather than ignoring or quarreling with complaint letters, most companies view answering them as good for business. Many large firms maintain separate claims and adjustment departments just to handle disappointed customers. By writing to complain about a product or service, the customer alerts your company to a problem that can be remedied to avoid similar complaints in the future. Customers who have taken the time to put complaints in writing obviously want and deserve a reply. If you do not answer the customer's letter politely, you may lose a lot of business—not just the customer's business, but also that of his or her friends, family, and associates, who will all have been told about your unreliable and discourteous company.

An effective adjustment letter requires diplomacy; be prompt, courteous, and decisive. Do not brush the complaint aside in hopes that it will be forgotten. Investigate the complaint quickly and determine its validity by checking previous correspondence, warranty statements, guarantees, and your firm's policies on merchandise and service. In some cases you may even have to send returned damaged merchandise to your firm's laboratory to determine who is at fault.

A noncommittal letter signals the customer that you have failed to investigate the claim or are stalling for time. Do not resort to vague statements like the following:

- We will do what we can to solve your problems.
- A company policy prohibits our returning your purchase price in full.
- Your request, while legitimate, will take time to process.
- We will act on your request with your best interest in mind.
- While we cannot now determine the extent of an adjustment, we will be back in touch with you.

Customers want to be told that they are right; or if they cannot get what they request, they will demand to know why, in the most explicit terms. At the other extreme, do not overdo an apology by saying that the company is "completely at fault," that "such shoddy merchandise is inexcusable," or that "it was a careless mistake on our part." An expression of regret need not jeopardize all future business dealings. If you make your company look too bad, you risk losing the customer permanently. When you comply with a request, a begrudging tone will destroy the goodwill created by your refund or replacement.

Adjustment Letters That Tell the Customer "Yes"

If investigation reveals the customer's claim to be valid, you must write a letter saying "Yes, you are right; we will give you what you asked for." Such a letter is easy to write if you remember a few useful suggestions. You want customers to realize that you sincerely agree with them—not to feel as if you are reluctantly granting their request. The two examples of adjustment letters saying "yes" show you how to write this kind of correspondence. The first example, Figure 7.18, says "yes" to Michael Trigg's letter in Figure 7.16. You might want to reread the Trigg complaint letter to see what problems Ralph Montoya faced when he had to write to Mr. Trigg. The second example of an adjustment letter that says "yes" is in Figure 7.19. It responds to a customer who has complained about an incorrect billing. The following four steps will help you write a "yes" adjustment letter.

1. Admit immediately that the customer's complaint is justified and apologize. Briefly state that you are sorry and thank the customer for writing to inform you.

Fig. 7.18 An adjustment letter saying "yes."

Smith Sports Equipment
P.O. Box 287
Tulsa, Oklahoma 74109

September 21, 1985

Mr. Michael Trigg
17 Westwood
Magnolia, MA 02171

Dear Mr. Trigg:

Thank you for alerting us in your letter of September 15 to the problems you had with one of our model 191 spincast reels. I am sorry for the inconvenience the reel has caused you. A new Smith reel is on its way to you.

We have examined your reel and found the problem. It seems that a retaining pin on the button spring was improperly installed by one of our new soldering machines on the assembly line. We have thoroughly inspected, repaired, and cleaned this soldering machine to eliminate the problem. Our company has been making quality reels since 1935. We hope that your new Smith reel brings you years of pleasure and many good catches, especially next year at the Gloucester Fishing Tournament.

We appreciate your business and look forward to serving you again.

Sincerely yours,

SMITH SPORTS EQUIPMENT COMPANY

Ralph Montoya

Ralph Montoya, Manager
Customer Relations Department

Fig. 7.19   An adjustment letter saying "yes."

Brunelli Motors

Route 3A
Giddings, Kansas 62034

October 6, 1986

Ms. Kathryn Brumfield
34 East Main
Giddings, KS 62034

Dear Ms. Brumfield:

We appreciate your notifying us, in your letter of September 30,
about the problem you have experienced regarding warranty coverage
on your new Phantom Hawk GT. The bills sent to you were incorrect,
and I have already canceled them. Please accept my apologies. You
should not have been charged for a new shroud or for repairs to the
damaged fan and hose, since all these parts, and labor on them, are
covered by warranty.

The problem was the result of an error in the way charges were
listed. Our firm has just begun using a new system of billing to give
customers better service, and the mechanic apparently punched the
wrong code number on your account. I have instructed the mechanics
to double-check their code numbers before submitting them to the
Billing Department. We hope that this policy will help us to serve
you and our other customers more efficiently.

We value you as a customer of Brunelli Motors. When you are ready for
another Phantom, I hope that you will once again come to visit our
dealership.

Sincerely yours,

A. Y. O'Donnel

A. Y. O'Donnel
Service Manager

2. State precisely what you are going to do to correct the problem. Are you going to cancel a bill, return a damaged camera in good working order, repaint a room, enclose a free pass, provide a complimentary dinner, or give the customer credit toward another purchase? Do not postpone the good news the customer wants to hear. The rest of your letter will be much more appreciated and convincing. In Figure 7.18 Michael Trigg is told that he will receive a new reel; in Figure 7.19 Kathryn Brumfield is informed that she will not be charged for parts or service.

3. Tell customers exactly what happened. They deserve an explanation for the inconvenience they suffered. Note how the explanations in Figures 7.18 and 7.19 give only the essential details; they do not bother the reader with side issues or petty remarks about who was to blame. Don't threaten to fire one of your employees because of a customer's problem. Assure customers that the mishap is not typical of your company's operations. While your comments should not shift the blame, they should center on the unusual reason or circumstance for the difficulty. Avoid promising, however, that the problem will never recur. Such an admission is not only unnecessary but may also be beyond your control.

4. End on a friendly, and positive, note. Do not remind customers of the trouble they have gone through. Leave them with a good feeling about your company. Say that you are looking forward to seeing them again, that you will gladly work with them on any future orders, or that you can always be reached for questions.

Adjustment Letters That Tell the Customer "No"

Writing to tell customers "no" is obviously more difficult than agreeing with them. You are faced with the sensitive task of conveying bad news, while at the same time convincing the reader that your position is fair, logical, and consistent. You should not accuse or argue. Avoid remarks such as the following that blame, scold, or remind customers of a wrongdoing and hence may cost you their business:

- You obviously did not read the instruction manual.
- Our records show that you purchased the set after the policy went into effect.
- The company policy plainly states that such refunds are unallowable.
- You were negligent in running the machine.
- You claim that our word processor was poorly constructed.
- You were careless in applying the proper measures.
- Your error, not our merchandise, is to blame.
- You must be mistaken about the merchandise.
- As any intelligent person could tell, the switch had to be on "off."
- Your complaint is unjustified.

The following five suggestions will help you say "no" diplomatically. Practical applications of these suggestions can be found in Figures 7.20 and 7.21. Contrast the rejection of Michael Trigg's complaint in Figure 7.20 with the favorable response to it in Figure 7.18.

1. Thank customers for writing. Make a friendly start by putting them in a good frame of mind. The letter writers in Figures 7.20 and 7.21 say that they are thankful that the customers brought the matter to their attention. Never begin with a refusal. You need time to calm and convince customers. Telling them "no" ("We regret to inform you") in the first sentence or two will negatively color their reactions to the rest of the letter. Also, never begin letters with "I was surprised to learn that you found our product defective (*or our service inefficient*)" or "We cannot understand how such a problem occurred. We have been in business for years, and nothing like this has ever happened." Such openings put customers on the defensive.

2. State the problem so that customers realize that you understand their complaint. You thereby prove that you are not trying to misrepresent what they have told you.

3. Explain what happened with the product or service before you give customers a decision. Provide a factual explanation to show customers that they are being treated fairly. Convince them of the logic and consistency of your point of view. Rather than focusing on the customer's mishandling of merchandise or failure to observe details of a service contract, state the proper ways of handling a piece of equipment or the terms outlined in an agreement. Instead of writing "By reading the instructions on the side of the paint can, you would have avoided the streaking condition that you claim resulted," tell the customer that "Hi-Gloss Paint requires two applications, four hours apart, for a clear and smooth finish." In this way you remind customers of the right way of applying the paint without pointing an accusing finger at them. Note how the explanations in Figures 7.20 and 7.21 emphasize the right way of using the product.

4. Give your decision without hedging. Do not say that perhaps some type of restitution could be made later or that further proof would have been helpful. Indecision will infuriate customers who believe that they have already presented a sound, convincing case. Never apologize for your decision. Avoid using the words *reject, claim,* or *grant. Reject* is too harsh and impersonal. *Claim* implies your distrust of the customers' complaint and suggests that questionable differences of opinion remain. *Grant* signals that you have it in your power to respond favorably but decline to do so; a grant is the kind of favor a ruler might give a subject. Instead, use words that reconcile.

5. Leave the door open for better and continued business. Wherever possible, help customers solve their problem by offering to send them a new

Fig. 7.20   An adjustment letter saying "no."

Smith Sports Equipment

P.O. Box 287
Tulsa, Oklahoma 74109

September 21, 1985

Mr. Michael Trigg
17 Westwood
Magnolia, MA 02171

Dear Mr. Trigg:

Thank you for writing to us on September 15 about the trouble you experienced with our model 191 spincast reel. We were sorry to hear about the difficulties you had with the release button and gears.

We have examined your reel and have found the trouble. It seems that a retaining pin on the button spring was pushed into the side of the reel casing, thereby making the gears inoperable. The retaining pin is a vital yet delicate part of your reel. In order to function properly, it has to be pushed gently. Since the pin was not used in this way, we are not able to refund your purchase price.

We will be pleased, however, to repair your reel for $5.98 and return it to you for hours of fishing pleasure. Please let us know your decision.

I shall look forward to hearing from you.

Sincerely yours,

SMITH SPORTS EQUIPMENT COMPANY

Ralph Montoya

Ralph Montoya, Manager
Customer Relations Department

Fig. 7.21   An adjustment letter saying "no."

HEALTH AIR, INC.

4300 Marshall Drive
Salt Lake City, Utah 84113

August 20, 1985

Ms. Denise Southby, Director
Bradley General Hospital
Bradley, IL 60610

Dear Ms. Southby:

Thank you for your letter of August 10 explaining the problems you have
encountered with our Puritan Bennett MAII type ventilator. We were sorry to
learn that you could not get the high-volume PAO_2 alarm circuit to work.

Our ventilator is a high-volume, low-frequency machine that is capable of
delivering up to 40 ml. of water pressure. The ventilator runs with a
center of gravity attachment that is on the right side of the diode. The
trouble you are having with the high oxygen alarm system is due to an
overload of your piped-in oxygen. Our laboratory inspection of the
ventilator you returned indicates that the high pressure system had blown a
vital adaptor in the machine. Our company cannot be responsible for any
type of overload caused by an oxygen system of which we are unaware. We
cannot, therefore, send you a replacement ventilator free of charge. Your
ventilator is being returned to you.

We would, however, be very glad to send you another model of the adaptor,
which would be more compatible with your system, as soon as we receive your
order. The price of the adaptor is $600, and our factory representative
will be happy to install it for you at no charge. Please let me know your
decision.

We welcome the opportunity to assist you in providing quality health care
at Bradley General.

Sincerely yours,

R. P. Gilford

R. P. Gilford
Customer Service Department

product or part, and quote the full sales price. Note how the second-to-last paragraphs of the letters in Figures 7.20 and 7.21 do this diplomatically.

Collection Letters

Collection letters are, unfortunately, a part of every business's concern. They require the same tact and fairness as do complaint and adjustment letters. While the majority of your customers will pay their bills promptly, some will not pay on time, and a few others may not pay until they are threatened with legal action or harassment from a collection agency.

Each nonpayment case should be evaluated separately. A nasty collection letter sent after only one month's nonpayment to a customer who is a good credit risk can damage your relationship and send that customer elsewhere. On the other hand, three very cordial, easygoing letters sent over three or four months to a customer who is a poor credit risk may encourage that individual to postpone payment, perhaps indefinitely.

Many businesses send four letters to customers before turning matters over to an attorney or a collection agency. These letters are mailed to poor credit risks at shorter intervals than to good ones. Each letter in the series employs a different technique, ranging from giving compliments and offering flexible credit terms to issuing demands for immediate payment or threats of legal consequences. One small hospital uses the four collection letters illustrated in Figures 7.22 through 7.25 to encourage ex-patients to pay their bills.

The letter in Figure 7.22 typifies the function of a first collection letter. It is a friendly reminder that an account is due. The tone of the letter is cordial and sincere—now is not the time to say "pay up or else." A first collection letter should stress how valuable the customer is, as does the first paragraph in Figure 7.22. Note also that the first paragraph underscores how pleased the hospital is to have provided the care the patient needed. The last sentence of that paragraph unobtrusively introduces the word "finances" in the context of service. The second paragraph, after allowing for possible questions concerning the bill, makes a request for payment. Inducements to make that payment are offered: (1) a flexible payment schedule and (2) an escape from the inconvenience (or embarrassment) of receiving past-due notices. The bottom of the letter conveniently lists payment-schedule options available to the patient.

If after a month to six weeks, a customer still does not make a payment, send a second letter, such as the one illustrated in Figure 7.23. This letter begins with a gentle reminder that the balance due has not yet been paid. The second paragraph politely inquires if something is wrong, thus admitting the hospital's recognition that not all nonpayments stem from a patient's willful neglect. While this second collection letter understands that there might be some "difficulty," it firmly reminds the patient to pay if there is no financial trouble. The last sentence makes another strong appeal to the patient's community obligation. Note that unlike the first letter, no payment schedule appears at the bottom of the letter, thus giving the patient a chance to explain any delay.

Fig. 7.22   A first collection letter.

Baldwin County Hospital

P.O. Box 222
Notown, MA 02138

May 15, 1986

Re: Inpatient Services
Date of Hospitalization: April 1-5, 1986
Balance Due: $3725.48

Dear Mr. Peterson:

We are grateful that we were able to serve your health needs during
your recent stay at the Baldwin County Hospital. It is our
continuing goal to provide the best possible hospital care for
residents of Baldwin County and its vicinity. You will readily
understand that to do so we must keep our finances up to date.

Our records show that the above balance remains due on your account.
Unless you have a question concerning the figure, we would appreciate
receiving your prompt payment. If you are unable to pay the full
amount at this time, we will be happy to set up a schedule of partial
payments. Just fill in the appropriate blanks below, and return this
letter to us. That will enable us to avoid billing you on a "Past
Due" basis. Thank you for your cooperation.

Sincerely,

Morris T. Jukes

Morris T. Jukes
Accounts Receivable Department

( ) I will pay $_____ ( ) weekly; ( ) monthly, on my account.

( ) Enclosed is a check for full payment in the amount of $_____

_____
Signature

Fig. 7.23   A second collection letter.

Baldwin County Hospital
P.O. Box 222
Notown, MA 02138

June 19, 1986

Re: Inpatient Services
Date of Hospitalization: April 1-5, 1986
Balance Due: $3725.48

Dear Mr. Peterson:

Since we have not received a reply to our letter of May 15, we want to remind you of the balance that remains on your account.

If there is some difficulty, drop by and see us today; we will do our best to help. Otherwise, we would appreciate receiving your payment in full by return mail.

Our ability to provide health services to others depends to a great extent upon your cooperation. Please do not let us down.

Sincerely,

Morris T. Jukes

Morris T. Jukes
Accounts Receivable Department

When still more time elapses and no payment is made, creditors send a third letter, an example of which appears in Figure 7.24. The creditor's tone and tactics have changed. From the cooperative tone of "What's wrong, can we help?" in the second collection letter, the third letter switches to the much more direct "We have waited a long time. Pay, or at least begin to pay, your bill now." The third collection letter, which must be more forceful than the second, announces that serious consequences will result if the creditor does not receive a payment from the customer. The vague threat, "further action," wisely does not commit the hospital to take legal action or to speak to a collection agency, its last resort. The third letter should still give the delinquent

Fig. 7.24   A third collection letter.

Baldwin County Hospital
P.O. Box 222
Notown, MA 02138

July 24, 1986

Re: Inpatient Services
Date of Hospitalization: April 1-5, 1986
Balance Due: $3725.48

Dear Mr. Peterson:

We regret that we have received no response from you to our letters
of May 15 and June 19 concerning your outstanding balance.

Because so much time has elapsed, we must now require full payment
(or your signed agreement to make regular installment payments)
within the next ten days.

If we have not heard from you by August 23, it will become necessary
for us to take further action.

Sincerely,

Morris T. Jukes

Morris T. Jukes
Accounts Receivable Department

( ) I will pay $_____ ( ) weekly; ( ) monthly, on my account.

( ) Enclosed is a check for full payment in the amount of $_____.

_____
Signature

Fig. 7.25   A fourth and final collection letter.

Baldwin County Hospital
P.O. Box 222
Notown, MA 02138

August 27, 1986

Re: Inpatient Services
Date of Hospitalization: April 1-5, 1986
Balance Due: $3725.48

Dear Mr. Peterson:

During the past few months we have written you several times concerning your outstanding balance.

As you may recall, we offered to arrange for installment payments or to help you in any way that we could. Since you have not responded, we must demand your payment in full at this time.

If we do not hear from you within ten days, we will have no alternative but to turn your account over to our collection agency.

Sincerely,

Morris T. Jukes

Morris T. Jukes
Accounts Receivable Department

customer a way out, and so this one contains some useful, face-saving options listed at the bottom of the letter.

If after receiving these three letters, a customer still does not respond, the creditor sends a fourth letter containing a specific threat that will be carried out. Note, though, how the letter in Figure 7.25 does not begin with that bad news. Instead, it reminds the patient of all the efforts the hospital has expended to collect its bills. The letter clearly points out that the time for concessions is over. Then it announces what consequences will result if the patient still does not pay. The letter gives proper legal notification that the patient has ten days to respond. The fourth collection letter attempts to frighten the customer into payment and does not have to seek or give any explanations. If the hospital, or any company, failed to carry out its threat to turn delinquent accounts over to a collection agency or attorney, it would quickly get a reputation for having all bark but no bite—a reputation that would make it difficult to collect its debts in the future.

☞ Business Correspondence: Some Closing Remarks for Success

This chapter has shown you how to prepare some of the most common types of business correspondence. Regardless of the kind of letter or memo you have to write, you will increase your chances for success if you adhere to the following four guidelines:

1. Plan what you are going to say. Take a few minutes to plan your message before you draft it. Think before you write. If you are responding to a letter or memo, have a copy of it before you so you don't forget to include information the reader needs to see.

2. Organize information in the most effective way for the reader. Letters and memos should follow reader-effective strategies. Always begin your correspondence by explaining why you are writing; don't make readers wade through several paragraphs to find out. When you have good news to report, tell them right away; when you have bad news to convey, prepare your readers for it.

3. Emphasize the "you attitude" with every reader—employer, customer, or coworker. Make the reader feel that you are interested in him or her. A personable, courteous approach will increase your chances of getting the reader to do what you suggest.

4. Be timely and accurate. Answer all correspondence promptly. A late letter might jeopardize a sale, irritate a customer or an employer, or reflect poorly on your own performance on the job. Send all correspondence to the right person or department. And also give readers reasonable time to receive and answer your correspondence.

☞ Exercises

1. Write a memo to your employer saying that you will be out of town two days next week and three the following week for one of the following reasons: (a) to inspect some land your firm is thinking of buying, (b) to investigate some claims, (c) to look at some new office space for a branch

your firm is thinking of opening in a city five hundred miles away, (d) to attend a conference sponsored by a professional society, or (e) to pay calls on customers. In your memo, be very specific about dates, places, times, and reasons.

2. Send a memo to your public relations department informing it that you are completing a degree or work for a certificate, and indicate how the information could be useful for its publicity campaign.

3. Write a memo to the payroll department notifying it that there is a mistake in your last paycheck. Explain exactly what the error is and give precise figures.

4. You are a manager of a local art museum. Write a memo to the Chamber of Commerce in which you put the following information into proper memo format:

Old hours: Mon.—Fri. 9–5; closed Sat. except during July and August when you are open 9–12

New hours: Mon.—Th. 8:30–4:30; Fri.—Sat. 9–9

Old rates: $1.00 children over 12; adults $1.50; children under 12 free

New rates: $1.50 children over 12; adults $2.50; children under 12 free accompanied by an adult

Added features: Paintings by Thora Horne, local artist; sculpture from West Indies and pottery from Central America in display area all summer; guided tours available with a party of six or more; lounge areas will offer patrons sandwiches and soft drinks, during the months of May, June, July, and August

5. Select some change (in policy, schedule, or personnel assignment) you encountered in a job you held in the last two or three years and write an appropriate memo describing that change. Assume you are your former employer explaining the change to employees.

6. Rewrite the following memo subject lines, making them more precise and helpful:

Schedules	Deliveries
Vacations	Refrigerators
New Equipment	Doors
Benefits	IV's
Safety	Radios
Insurance	Policy Changes

7. Order merchandise from a company. Specify the quantity, size, stock number, cost, and also include delivery instructions, the date by which you must receive the merchandise, and the way in which you will pay for it.

8. Write a letter of inquiry to a utility company, a safety or health care agency, or a company in your town, asking for a brochure describing its services to the community. Be specific about your reasons for requesting this information.

9. In which course(s) are you or will you be writing a paper or report? Write to an agency or company that could supply you with helpful information for the paper and request its aid. Indicate why you are writing, indicating precisely what information you need, why you need it, and offer to share your paper or report with the company.

10. Examine an ad in a magazine or a TV commercial and then write a one-page assessment in which you identify the four parts of a sales message.

11. Write a sales letter addressed to an appropriate audience on one of the following topics:
    (a) why they should major in the same subject you did
    (b) why they should live in your neighborhood
    (c) why they would be happy taking a vacation where you did last year
    (d) why they should dine at a particular restaurant
    (e) why they should shop at a store you have worked for or will work for
    (f) why they should have their cars repaired at a specific shop
    (g) why they should give their real estate business to a particular agency
    (h) why they would enjoy doing their cooking on a particular stove

12. Find at least two sales letters you or your family have received and evaluate them according to how well they follow the four parts of a sales letter discussed in this chapter. Attach these sales letters to your evaluation.

13. Write a sales letter about the effectiveness of sales letters to an individual who has told you that almost everyone throws them away as soon as he or she gets them.

14. Rewrite the following sales letter to make it more effective. Add any details you think are relevant.

Dear Pizza Lovers:

Allow me to introduce myself. My name is Ruddy Moore and I am the new manager of Tasty Pizza Parlor in town. The Parlor is located at the intersection of North Miller Parkway and 95th Street. We are open from 10 a.m. to 11 p.m., except on the weekends, when we are open later.

I think you will be as happy as I am to learn that Tasty's will now offer free delivery. As a result, you can get your Tasty Pizza hot when you want it.

Please see your weekly newspapers for our ad. We also are offering customers a coupon. It is a real deal for you.

I know you will enjoy Tasty's and I hope to see you. I am always
interested in hearing from you about our service and our fine
product. We want to take your order soon. Please come in.

15. Write a thank-you letter in response to one of the following:
    (a) a gift you have received
    (b) a letter of congratulation sent to you
    (c) a letter of recommendation someone wrote for you
    (d) some business that was directed to you or your employer
    (e) a dinner or other social occasion to which you were invited by a customer or your employer or agency

16. Write a congratulation letter to someone for one of the following:
    (a) being promoted
    (b) winning an award at school
    (c) being named salesperson of the month
    (d) completing a special course or degree
    (e) being elected to public office
    (f) concluding a business deal (selling a product, renegotiating a contract)
    (g) opening a new store or branch
    (h) joining your firm or agency

17. Send a follow-up letter to one of the following individuals:
    (a) a customer who informs you that he will no longer do business with your firm because your prices are too high
    (b) a family of four who stayed at your motel for two weeks last summer
    (c) a church group that used your catering services last month
    (d) a customer who exchanged a dress or coat for the purchase price
    (e) a customer who bought a new car from you one year ago
    (f) a company that bought a year's supply of pens from you nine months ago

18. Write a complaint letter about one of the following:
    (a) an error in your utility or telephone bill
    (b) discourteous service you received on an airplane or bus
    (c) a frozen food product of poor quality
    (d) a shipment that arrives late and damaged
    (e) an insurance payment to you that is fifty dollars less than it should be
    (f) a public service TV station's policy of not showing a particular series
    (g) junk mail that you are receiving

19. Write the complaint letter to which the adjustment letter in Figure 7.19 (page 212) responds.

20. Write the complaint letter to which the adjustment letter in Figure 7.21 (page 216) responds.

21. Rewrite the following complaint letters to make them more precise and less emotional:

(a) Dear Sir:

We recently purchased a machine from your New York store and paid a great deal of money for it. This machine, supposedly the best model in your line, has caused us nothing but trouble each time we used it. Really, can't you do any better with your technology?

We expect you to stand by your products. The warranty you give with them should make you accountable for shoddy workmanship. Let us know at once what you intend to do about our problem. If you cannot or are unwilling to correct the situation, we will take our business elsewhere, and then you will be sorry.

Sincerely yours,

(b) Dear Medical Supply Company:

We are writing to complain in the strongest possible terms about the infusion pumps that you sold us some time ago. As you must be well aware, a hospital like ours must have perfectly functioning equipment to handle any life-threatening situation. Your infusion pumps do not live up to that standard.

In the past few weeks we have been seriously inconvenienced because of the quality of your pumps. Our daily routine has more than once been disrupted by your unqualified repair teams, who have not yet found or fixed the trouble. In addition, the quality of health care we are giving is below standard because we have been forced to place patients on pumps that we know do not work properly.

To save our reputation in the community, we demand immediate assistance from your office.

Sincerely yours,

22. Write an adjustment letter saying "yes" to the manager of The Loft whose letter is in Figure 7.17 on page 208.
23. Write an adjustment letter saying "no" to the customer who received the "yes" adjustment letter in Figure 7.19, page 212.
24. Rewrite the following ineffective adjustment letter saying "yes":

Dear Mr. Smith:

We are extremely sorry to learn that you found the suit you purchased from us unsatisfactory. The problem obviously stems from the fact that you selected it from the rack marked "Factory Seconds." In all honesty, we have had a lot of problems because of this rack. I guess we should know better

than to try to feature inferior merchandise along with the
name-brand clothing that we sell. But we originally thought
that our customers would accept poorer quality merchandise if
it saved them some money. That was our mistake.

Please accept our apologies. If you will bring your "Factory
Second" suit to us, we will see what we can do about honoring
your request.

Sincerely yours,

25. Rewrite the following ineffective adjustment letters saying "no":

(a) Dear Customer:

Our company is unwilling to give you a new toaster or to refund your
purchase price. After examining the toaster you sent to us, we
found that the fault was not ours, as you insist, but yours.

Let me explain. The motor in our toaster is made to take a lot of
punishment. But being dropped on the floor or poked inside with a
knife, as you probably did, exceeds all decent treatment. You must
be careful if you expect your appliances to last. Your negligence
in this case is so bad that the toaster could not be repaired.

In the future, consider using your appliances according to the
guidelines set down in warranty books. That's why they are written.

Since you are now in the market for a new toaster, let me suggest
that you purchase our new heavy-duty model, number 67342, called
the Counter-Whiz. I am taking the liberty of sending you some information about this model. I do hope you at least go to see one at
your local appliance center.

Sincerely,

(b) Dear Gentlemen:

We are in receipt of your letter complaining to us about our
not delivering a shipment of goods to you when you wanted them.
You stated that you placed the order with us in February but
now, at the end of March, you still do not have it. Since we have
several customers with similar problems, we simply were not able to
answer your complaint as quickly as you would have liked.

We will ship the goods to you when we receive payment in full from
you. Your last check to us was returned by the Pittsfield Bank because of insufficient funds in your account. How can we trust you

with a new shipment of materials when your previous check was bad.
Perhaps another check you wrote to us would have the same
difficulty. Quite frankly, we do not like to do business with a
company that does not honor its business commitments.

But because you are among our largest customers, we will encourage
you to continue to do business with us. The bottom line, though, is
that we must receive your money before you receive our goods.

Please advise.

Sincerely,

26. Assume that you work in a student services department at a local college
and that you have been asked to write collection letters to those graduates
who are not paying off their student loans on time. Write a series of four
collection letters to be sent at appropriate times. The first letter is sent
after the student misses only one payment, the second letter after two
nonpayments, the third letter after three nonpayments, and the fourth
letter after four nonpayments.

27. Rewrite the following collection letter twice, the first time making it appropriate for a first notice and the second time making it suitable for a second
notice.

Dear Customer:

You may recall that you owe us the slight sum of $64.56 for the
plumbing work we did for you in January. To you such bills may
appear trivial, but in order to stay in business we have to
collect from everyone, from the little guy like you to the big
companies we help.

Do not be a problem for us. Pay what you owe. If you do not send
us a check for the above amount in the next few days, we will
somehow get the money out of you. Whether you pay the easy way
by sending us a check now or whether we put a hard-nosed
collection agency on your case is entirely up to you.

Sincerely yours,

Section III

Gathering and Summarizing
Information

8

Finding and Using Library Materials

A personnel director asked an applicant during a job interview to name the titles of two or three major journals in the applicant's field. When the applicant could not come up with any titles, chances for employment at the company seemed slim. The question was typical, fair, and relevant. The interviewer knew that an applicant's success in the job depends on the quality of information supplied to the employer. Employers expect carefully researched answers; they will not be satisfied with guesses.

Research, or the careful investigation of material found in books, magazines, pamphlets, films, or any other sources (including resource people), is a vital part of every occupation. You might conduct research by telephoning someone in the next department for information or thumbing through a company catalog. Or you might engage in research by studying reference works in a library or by preparing statistical or analytical surveys. You must be informed about the latest developments in your field, and you must be able to communicate your findings accurately and concisely. Doing research is a practical skill like swimming, running, or typing. Once learned, it is easy to perform. Knowing how to do research in your field offers lifelong benefits.

The information in Chapter 8 can save you from suffering the embarrassment experienced by the job applicant above. Specifically, Chapter 8 discusses major reference works—where to find them and how to use them. The appendix to this chapter (pages 262–268) contains information about specific reference works (indexes, encyclopedias, dictionaries, and abstracts) that will be extremely valuable to you in your research.

☞ The Library and Its Sections

You may think of your library as a single building, but that building is divided into many sections. When you walk into a library, probably the first section you see is the circulation desk—in many ways, the business center of the library. You go to the circulation desk to borrow or return books, to pick up materials you may have ordered from another library, or to find out if a book has been checked out. From the circulation desk you can move to any one of the following parts of the library to use materials. (The page numbers after each area refer to the page numbers of this chapter where you will find a description of the particular unit and the materials in it.)

- The card catalog (pages 232–236)
- The stacks (pages 236–239)
- Periodical holdings and indexes (pages 239–247)
- Reference books (pages 247–249)
- Government documents (pages 249–250)
- The popular press (pages 250–254)
- Audiovisual materials (pages 254–256)

The Card Catalog

The card catalog, your guide to the library, will be located in a prominent place, usually near the entrance. Housed in cabinets with numerous drawers, the card catalog contains three-by-five-inch index cards for each book, filmstrip, tape recording, or microfilm your library owns. The card catalog does not contain information about articles in magazines or journals. For information on the contents of individual magazines or journals, you will have to consult your library's periodical holdings list and the periodical indexes discussed later in this chapter.

Recently at some large firms and research libraries, the cabinets of the card catalog have been replaced by a computer terminal. The computer links the user to the on-line catalog, or data base, containing information about the books and other materials in the library. With access to this data base, the user can find information about titles, authors, subject areas, and location of materials as well as learn whether a book has been checked out, is placed on reserve, or is available to be checked out. Although computer-based catalogs will be used increasingly in the future, you may safely assume that the conventional card catalog will be around for many years to come.

How Material in the Card Catalog Is Alphabetized

You can use three ways to find a book in the card catalog. You can look for it under the author's name, under the title, or under the subject it discusses. Some libraries may have separate cabinets for each of these three designations (author, title, subject), while at other libraries, especially small ones, all three designations are included in one cabinet. Information in all three categories is listed alphabetically, either letter by letter or word by word. These two ways of alphabetizing entries can make a big difference, as the following examples show:

Letter by letter

fire	firefly
firearm	firetrap
fire drill	firewall
fire escape	

Word by word

fire	firearm
fire drill	firefly
fire escape	firetrap
fire wall	

The letter-by-letter method is based on the sequence of individual letters regardless of whether an entry contains one word or two. Hence, *firearm* comes before *fire drill*. Under the word-by-word method, each entry is alphabetized according to the letters in the first word, whether that entry is made up of one word or two. *Fire wall* comes ahead of *firearm* and *firefly* because the word *fire* is a part of both of these words and alphabetically precedes them. Find out which method your library uses so you can look up entries more quickly and more accurately. The following alphabetical rules apply to both methods and will help you search for an entry in the card catalog.

1. An author's last name beginning *Mc* is listed as if the *Mc* were spelled *Mac;* so *Mc*Donald will be listed in the card catalog as if it were *Mac*Donald. Hyphenated last names are found at the end of the alphabetical letter beginning the first of two hyphenated names. A book by Alan Jones-Davies, for example, would be listed at the end of the J's, not under the D's.
2. Disregard definite and indefinite articles—*the, a,* or *an*—at the beginning of a title. A book with the title *A New Fashion Guide* will be found in the N's.
3. Abbreviations, acronyms (NATO, VISTA, and other words formed from the first letters of several words), and numbers are alphabetized as if they were spelled out in full. A book entitled *Mr. and Mrs. Average American* will be found in the title section of the card catalog under *Mister; 22 Ways to Better Health* is listed under *Twenty-Two*. A book written by IBM would be listed under *International Business Machines*. And a study put out by the ANA could be found in the author section under *American Nurses Association*.

Author Card

One way to find a book is to locate the author card in a card catalog. Spell the author's name correctly and record first names or initials accurately. If you know only the last name, and if it is a common one, your search may take a great deal of extra time. An *author card* for a book by Martin Meyerson can be seen in Figure 8.1. To find Meyerson's book, you would look under the M's until you come to Meyerson and then find Martin. The author card(s) tells you what titles by that author are in your library. Each card will tell you where to find the book, when it was written, who published it, and where. Figure 8.1 is coded to show you what each number, abbreviation, and symbol means.

Title Card

Figure 8.2 shows a *title card*. It is identical to an author card except that the title of the book is listed twice—once as a heading on top of the card and again as part of the entry itself. It is easy to find this card when you know the first word of the title. Keep in mind that the articles *a, an,* or *the* at the beginning of the title are omitted in alphabetizing. With the Meyerson book you do not have an article for the first word of the title; just search for the book under the H's in the title section of the card catalog.

Subject Card

Figure 8.3 shows the *subject card* for the Meyerson book. Again, the subject card is identical to the author card except that a subject heading—marked with distinctive red or black ink—is located at the top of the card. Many times students start with the subject section of the card catalog since they do not have titles or authors in mind early in their search. The subject catalog also lists reference works (abstracts, bibliographies, dictionaries, handbooks, and indexes) that will guide you to specific titles.

The subject section divides a topic into subheadings or groups and alerts readers to other, related topics. Looking under the subject section for "construction," you would first find a cross-reference, or "see also," card, illustrated in Figure 8.4. This card alerts you to other subject categories (references) you should check for information in addition to the cards gathered under the "construction" heading. Next, you would find the following breakdown of the topic with appropriate books listed for each:

- construction dictionary
- construction equipment
- construction handbook
- construction, housing
- construction, industry

Stopping at the last subheading, "construction, industry," you could find even more subclassifications:

- accounting
- automation
- contracts

Fig. 8.1   An author card in the card catalog.

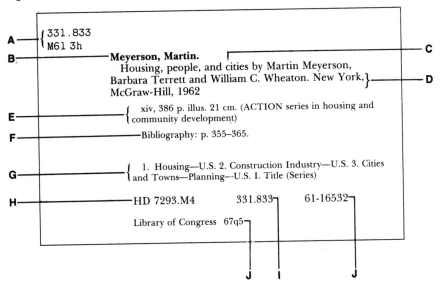

A The *call number* locates the book in the library. In this case the library has filed the book according to the Dewey decimal system.

B The *author's name* is always listed with the last name (surname) first. Sometimes a card also gives the author's date of birth and, if the author is deceased, the date of death. If a book has more than one author or editor, only the author whose name appears first in the book is listed in the upper-left-hand corner of the card.

C The *title* of the book.

D The names of any *coauthors or coeditors and pertinent publication information*—city, publisher, and date of publication.

E A *physical description of the book*—number of pages from the preface (usually numbered in lower-case roman numerals) through the index, whether the book is illustrated (illus.) and the height (in centimeters) of the book. Also noted is whether the book is part of a special series or is issued under a special imprint (or publishing arrangement).

F This book contains a *bibliography* on pages 355 to 365.

G List of the *other headings in the subject catalog under which the book is listed*.

H The *Library of Congress designation* for this book would be in the A position if the library followed the Library of Congress system of classification rather than the Dewey decimal one. "Library of Congress" means that a copy of the book is in the national library.

I The *Dewey decimal number*.

J *Identification numbers used by librarians.* You need not be concerned with this designation.

Fig. 8.2   A title card in the card catalog.

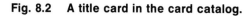

```
331.833
M613h                    Housing, people and cities.

            Meyerson, Martin.
                Housing, people, and cities by Martin Meyerson,
            Barbara Terrett and William C. Wheaton. New York,
            McGraw-Hill, 1962.

                xiv, 386 p. illus. 21 cm. (ACTION series in housing and
            community development)

                Bibliography: p. 355–365.
                1. Housing—U.S. 2. Construction Industry—U.S. 3. Cities
            and Towns—Planning—U.S. I. Title (Series)

            HD 7293.M4        331.833        61-16532

            Library of Congress   67q5
```

- costs
- data processing
- law and legislation
- management
- personnel
- subcontracting
- United States

Meyerson's book would be found under this last subheading, "United States."

Subject cards break down topics into subcategories and list appropriate titles under each subcategory or helpfully refer readers to other parts of the subject catalog. They also list on the entry card beneath the title of the book other relevant topics to consult directly. Examine the Meyerson card in Figure 8.3. Following the bibliographic information, the card lists three other subject areas that will help readers find additional information: (1) housing, (2) construction, and (3) cities and towns.

The Stacks

The majority of space in a library is taken up by the stacks—rows of shelves where the books are stored. Your library may have open or closed stacks. If the stacks are open, you are free to walk along the rows to find the books you need. If they are closed, a member of the library staff will find a book for you after you present a call slip identifying—by author, title, and number—the book you want.

Fig. 8.3   A subject card in the card catalog.

```
331.833
M613h    CONSTRUCTION INDUSTRY—UNITED STATES
```

Meyerson, Martin.
　　Housing, people, and cities by Martin Meyerson,
Barbara Terrett and William C. Wheaton. New York,
McGraw-Hill, 1962.

　　xiv, 386 p. illus. 21 cm. (ACTION series in housing and
community development

　　Bibliography: p. 355–365.

　　1. Housing—U.S. 2. Construction Industry—U.S. 3. Cities
and Towns—Planning—U.S. I. Title (Series)

　　HD 7293.M4　　　331.833　　　61-16532

　　Library of Congress　67q5

Fig. 8.4   A "see also" card in the card catalog.

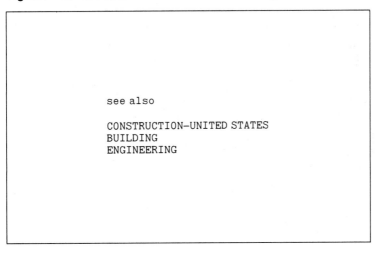

```
see also

CONSTRUCTION—UNITED STATES
BUILDING
ENGINEERING
```

Call Numbers

Regardless of which system your library uses, you will have to know the call
number of the book you want. Call numbers or letters are found in the upper
left-hand side of the card in the catalog. Your library may use either the
Library of Congress (abbreviated LC) or the Dewey decimal system. Table 8.1
shows a section of the LC system and some of the divisions in the Dewey
decimal system. The LC system divides all knowledge into twenty-one catego-

Table 8.1 Headings from call-number sections

Library of Congress		*Dewey Decimal*	
Q	Science	500	Pure sciences
	Q Science (General)	510	Mathematics
	QA Mathematics	520	Astronomy and allied
	QB Astronomy		sciences
	QC Physics	530	Physics
	QD Chemistry	540	Chemistry and allied sciences
	QE Geology	550	Sciences of earth and other
	QH Natural history		worlds
	QK Botany	560	Paleontology
	QL Zoology	570	Life sciences
	QM Human anatomy	580	Botanical sciences
	QP Physiology	590	Zoological sciences
	QR Microbiology	600	Technology (Applied
R	Medicine		sciences)
	R Medicine (General)	610	Medical sciences
	RB Pathology	620	Engineering and allied
	RK Dentistry		operations
	RT Nursing	630	Agriculture
		640	Domestic arts and sciences
S	Agriculture	650	Managerial services
	S Agriculture (General)	660	Chemical and related
	SB Plant culture		technologies
	SD Forestry	670	Manufactures
	SF Animal culture	680	Miscellaneous manufactures
	SK Hunting	690	Buildings
T	Technology		
	T Technology (General)		
	TA Engineering (General). Civil engineering (General)		
	TJ Mechanical engineering and machinery		
	TK Electrical engineering. Electronics. Nuclear engineering		
	TP Chemical technology		
	TS Manufactures		
	TX Home economics		

Library of Congress, Subject Cataloging Division, *LC Classification Outline,* 3rd ed. (Washington, D.C.: U.S. Government Printing Office, 1975); Melvil Dewey, *Decimal Classification and Relative Index: The Second Summary* (1971), p. 450.

ries that are differentiated by capital letters of the alphabet. Subdivisions are labeled with a combination of letters and numbers. As its name implies, the Dewey decimal system divides knowledge into ten large categories indicated by numerical groups ranging from 000 to the 900s. Each large division is divided into groups of ten subdivisions. The first number in a Dewey classification indicates the large category of knowledge in which a book is found, and the second and third numbers specify exact areas of that large group.

Meyerson's book, *Housing, People, and Cities,* in the LC system is classified by the letters HD. The letter H indicates that the book falls into the large category marked "Social Sciences," and D signifies that the book belongs in the subcategory "Economics," as opposed to "Statistics" (HA) or "Sociology" (HM–HX). The Dewey number for Meyerson's book is 331.833—that is, it falls into the 300s, "Social Sciences"; the 30s of the 300s is the subdivision "Economics."

Shelves

Once you know the call number, you should check where the book is shelved if your library has open stacks. Your library may post maps that show the location of books by their call numbers. When you know the approximate location of a book, go to that section of the library and look at the markers posted at the end of each row of stacks. Then walk down the appropriate row to find your book. Each book will have its call number on its spine, or where the book is bound, as illustrated in Figure 8.5. If the book you are looking for is not on the shelf, go to the circulation desk to see if it has been checked out. If so, you can ask the librarian to reserve it for you when it comes back. Perhaps the book can be used only in the library (then it is said to be "on reserve"), in which case, you will have to sign it out from the circulation desk. If the librarian discovers that the book has not been checked out or is not on reserve, it may be misshelved. Check with the library in the next few days to see if it has been found.

☞ Periodical Holdings and Indexes

Your research will not be confined exclusively to books. Some of it will lead you to the wealth of information contained in periodicals. A *periodical* is a magazine or journal that is published at established, frequent intervals— weekly, bimonthly (or once every two months), quarterly. The word *magazine* refers to periodicals—*Gentleman's Quarterly, Redbook,* or *Time*—that appeal to a diverse audience and that treat popular themes. The word *journal* characterizes technical or scholarly periodicals, such as the *American Journal of Nursing* or the *American Waterworks Journal,* whose audiences read them for professional or scientific information.

Periodicals have certain advantages over books when it comes to research. Because they take less time to produce than books, periodicals can give you more recent information on a topic. Further, periodicals are not as restricted

Fig. 8.5   Spine of a book with call number.

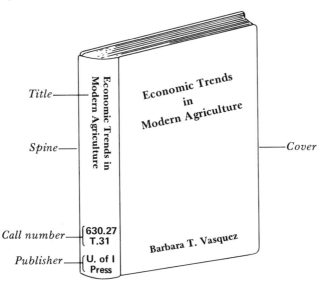

Title

Spine

Cover

Economic Trends in Modern Agriculture

Economic Trends in Modern Agriculture

Call number

630.27
T.31

Publisher

U. of I
Press

Barbara T. Vasquez

as books. A book usually discusses one subject from one point of view, but a periodical can contain ten different articles, each covering a separate topic and each offering a different perspective. This is not to imply that you should ignore books and focus solely on magazines or journals. Use both, but be aware of the differences.

To find appropriate articles in magazines and journals, you need to use indexes. An *index* is a listing by subject, and sometimes also by author, of articles that have appeared within a specified period of time. An index tells you what articles have appeared on your subject, where they were published, who wrote them, and whether they contain any special information, such as bibliographies, illustrations, diagrams and maps, or portraits. You would be lost without indexes. You could never successfully thumb through all the periodicals in the library to determine which ones contain an article you could use. Furthermore, your library might not subscribe to all the journals and magazines that contain articles related to your subject. The indexes let you know what is available beyond your own library's holdings.

The Readers' Guide to Periodical Literature

One of the most basic indexes is the *Readers' Guide to Periodical Literature*, which has been listing information on periodicals since 1900. The *Readers' Guide* indexes information from more than 200 periodicals, mostly popular magazines together with a few scientific journals. The *Guide*'s main purpose is to list periodicals of interest to the general, not technical, reader. Therefore, you will find articles from *Good Housekeeping, Parents' Magazine,* and *Reader's Digest* indexed, but not articles from *Hospitals, Journal of Petroleum Technology,* or *Professional Safety.* For journal articles, you will have to consult the more specialized indexes discussed later in this chapter.

The *Readers' Guide* is published twice a month, except during July and August when only one issue a month is published. Every three months the *Guide* combines issues to form a cumulative index for that period. Every year these three-month indexes are collected and bound into one large yearly index that can weigh as much as a large dictionary. You will find both the single issues of the *Guide* and the large bound ones on tables or shelves in or very close to the reference room.

The *Readers' Guide* allows you to search for an article by topic, subtopic, author's name, and, whenever appropriate, title. At the beginning of every issue you will find two important keys. One key tells you which periodicals were surveyed for that particular issue of the *Readers' Guide.* Along with this information is a list of abbreviations that will be used for those periodicals throughout the issue. For example, *Saturday Review* will be listed as *Sat R, Working Woman* will be found as *Work Wom.,* and *Business Weekly* is abbreviated as *Bus W.* Some periodicals will not be abbreviated in the listings (*Encore, Forbes,* or *People*). The other key lists abbreviations for months, bibliographic facts, and titles. Refer to both these keys as you "decode" the entries in an issue.

Figure 8.6 contains an excerpt from the *Readers' Guide* three-month issue for February–April 1979. This excerpt, which indexes articles on the eye, will show you how the *Readers' Guide* is organized and how abbreviations are used. Like the subject designations in the card catalog, the *Readers' Guide* refers users to other, related topics in the issue. In this excerpt, the reader is told to "see also" entries under "vision." The articles on the eye for the three-month period covered by this issue are then divided into appropriate categories—care and hygiene, diseases and defects, and so forth. Note that the entry under "care and hygiene" is translated as follows: C. Ettlinger wrote an article entitled "Eyes right!" that appeared with illustrations (il) in *House and Garden,* vol. 151; the article starts on page 26 and is continued later in the magazine (signified by the + after a page number), and the date of the issue is March 1979. The first article under "diseases and defects" contains a bibliography (bibl) as well as illustrations (il). Moving down to the entry under "eyebrows," note that no author's name is given, only the title, date, and page numbers of the article appearing in *McCalls.* The article was written by a staff member of the magazine and does not carry a by-line.

In addition to listing articles under the subjects they discuss, the *Readers' Guide* indexes articles according to author. Some authors also have articles written about them. In this case the *Readers' Guide* first lists the works by the author and immediately following those articles lists works about the author. Look at Figure 8.7. The two Jane Fonda interviews (regarded as works by an author) come first, and then come three articles about her. Note that portraits and/or photographs (pors) accompany the article about her.

Fig. 8.6   An excerpt from the *Readers' Guide*.

EXTRASENSORY perception
Psychic or psychotic? study by Bruce Greyson.
Hum Behav 8:46 F '79
Seeing the future; study by John Bisaha. il Hum
Behav 8:46 F '79
EXTRASENSORY perception in animals
Do animals have ESP? T. McGinnis. Fam Health
11:12+ F '79
EXTRATERRESTRIAL life. See Life on other
planets
EXXON Corporation
Edict from the sovereign state of Exxon. J.
O'Hara and I. Urquhart. Macleans 92:25 F 26
'79
EYE
See also
Vision
Care and hygiene
Eyes right! C. Ettlinger. il House & Gard 151:
26+ Mr '79
Diseases and defects
Cone inputs to ganglion cells in hereditary
retinal degeneration. C. M. Cicerone and oth-
ers. bibl il Science 203:1113-15 Mr 16 '79
Microsurgery for strokes and visual disorders.
il Sci News 115:69 F 3 '79
Wandering eyes; amblyopia study by Merton
Flom and David Kirchen. il Hum Behav 8:26
F '79
See also
Cataracts (eye defects)
Movements
Smooth pursuit eye movements: is perceived
motion necessary? A. Mack and others. bibl il
Science 203:1361-3 Mr 30 '79
Protection
Eclipse: don't let the sun catch you spying.
P. Carlyle-Gordge. il Macleans 92:10 Ja 29 '79
Surgery
Cataracts: technologic explosion creates debate
on surgery need. N. S. Jaffe. Sci Digest 85:
46-8+ F '79
That dreaded cataract operation can go smoothly
these days. B. Hitchings. Bus W p 101-2 F 19
'79
EYE (animals)
See also
Vision (animals)
EYE (crustaceans)
Both photons and fluoride ions excite limulus
ventral photoreceptors. A. Fein and D. W.
Corson. bibl il Science 204:77-9 Ap 6 '79
EYE make-up. See Make-up
EYE malformations (animals) See Abnormalities
(animals)
EYE movements. See Eye—Movements
EYEBROWS
Shapely brows. il McCalls 106:43-4 F '79
EYEGLASSES
What's new in eyeglasses. il Glamour 77:180-1 F
'79
See also
Contact lenses
EYES. See Eye
EYESIGHT. See Vision
EYEWITNESSES. See Witnesses

Fig. 8.7   Entries from the *Readers' Guide* for articles by and about one person.

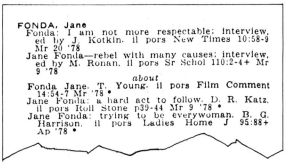

Readers' Guide to Periodical Literature, copyright © 1979, 1980 by the H. W. Wilson Company. Material reproduced by permission of the publisher.

Specialized Indexes

While the *Readers' Guide* is a good source to consult, remember that the *Guide* is limited to "periodicals of general interest published in the United States." Your research will require you to read professional journals in your field—journals that the *Readers' Guide* does not index. To find information published in professional journals, you will need to consult a specialized index. These indexes are guides to the literature in particular subject areas—business, farming, food service, nursing, public safety, respiratory therapy, and many others. Some indexes cover sixty or more years of work (*Applied Science & Technology Index* or *Index Medicus*); other indexes were established within the past five to ten years (*Criminal Justice Periodical Index* or *Environmental Index*). You will find a list of some important specialized indexes in the appendix to this chapter. But perhaps the two most important specialized indexes are the *Applied Science & Technology Index* and the *Business Periodicals Index*.

Applied Science & Technology Index

If you need to locate information about a technical subject, you would be wise to start with the *Applied Science & Technology Index*. The *Index* was first published in 1958, although from 1913–1957 it was part of the *Industrial Arts Index*. It is published each month except July and issues are cumulated quarterly and bound yearly.

The *Index* is a guide to more than 300 specialized journals in a wide range of scientific and technical fields. The prefatory note to each issue of the *Index* reminds readers of this breadth of coverage.

> Subject fields indexed include aeronautics and space science, atmospheric sciences, chemistry, computer technology and applications, construction industry, energy resources and research, engineering, fire and fire prevention, food and food industry, geology, machinery, mathematics, metallurgy, mineralogy, oceanog-

raphy, petroleum and gas, physics, plastics, textile industry and fabrics, transportation and other industrial and mechanical arts.

Like the *Readers' Guide,* the *Index* is organized alphabetically by subject. Many of these subjects are subdivided to assist users further. Take a look at Figure 8.8, which reprints a section of the *Index,* to see how useful these subclassifications can be. Information published about helicopters is categorized according to blades, design, electronic equipment, military use, noise, and so forth. The subclassifications in the *Applied Science & Technology Index* might give you an idea for a research paper and then assist you in gathering relevant and thorough information on that topic.

Business Periodicals Index

Published since 1958, the *Business Periodicals Index* is invaluable when you are researching a topic in or about business and industry. It appears each month except August and offers quarterly cumulations, which are combined into bound yearly ones. The *Business Periodicals Index* surveys more than 300 business publications published in English. Subjects that are indexed include accounting, advertising, communications, computer technology and applications, finance, industrial relations, management, occupational health and safety, office automation, personnel, real estate, telecommunications, and transportation. Like the *Applied Science & Technology Index,* the *Business Periodicals Index* is organized alphabetically by subject and offers many useful subheadings. To help readers further, the *Index* lists articles about a company or executive under the name of that company or executive. Note how the excerpt from the *Business Periodicals Index* contained in Figure 8.9 arranges and classifies information about word processors and how it helps users to find information about companies and individuals.

Computerized Searches

Bibliographic information is also available through computers that store (in online data bases) the information contained in indexes, abstracts, and other bibliographic sources. In a few seconds, a computer can search through millions of these entries. More than 350 data bases of bibliographic information exist. In fact, almost every professional discipline has its own data base—criminal justice, chemistry, economics, engineering, business, law, marketing, medicine, nursing, psychology, and so forth. An especially helpful data base is the Educational Resources Information Center (ERIC), which will give you access to journal articles in education and to numerous government-sponsored publications.

Computer searches are efficient and quick. In a matter of minutes, they will give you a print-out of articles, reports, books, and even patents covering a specific topic for a particular period of time. But if you want to have a computer search run, a librarian will have to do it for you. Be prepared to assist the

Fig. 8.8   An excerpt from *Applied Science & Technology Index.*

Heisenberg uncertainty principle *See* Uncertainty principle
Helical springs *See* Springs (Mechanism)
Helicopter pilots
   Training
   Computer enhances simulator realism. E. H. Kolcum.
      il *Aviat Week Space Technol* 119:205+ N 14 '83
Helicopters
   See also
   Heliports
   Canada picks Bell to build joint helicopter facility. E.
      J. Bulban. il *Aviat Week Space Technol* 119:24-5 O
      17 '83
   Helicopter sales tied to energy market. E. J. Bulban.
      il *Aviat Week Space Technol* 119:63+ O 3 '83
      Blades
   An aeroacoustic model for high-speed, unsteady blade-
      vortex interaction. R. Martinez and S. E. Widnall.
      bibl diags *AIAA J* 21:1225-31 S '83
   Enhancing ground safety. D. Manningham. il *Bus Commer
      Aviat* 53:124+ O '83
      Design
   Some mathematical tools for a modeler's workbench.
      E. Cohen. bibl il *IEEE Comput Graph Appl* 3:63-6
      O '83
      Electronic equipment
   Bendix building advanced unit for Vertol research helicop-
      ter. K. J. Stein. *Aviat Week Space Technol* 119:81+
      O 31 '83
   Sperry unit updates helicopter cockpit. W. B. Scott. diags
      Aviat Week Space Technol 119:79-80 S 5 '83
      History
   Flight of the Froebe. G. C. Larson. il *Bus Commer
      Aviat* 53:34-5 S '83
      Manufacture
   Hughes boosts AH-64 production rate. B. A. Smith. il
      Aviat Week Space Technol 119:70-1 O 24 '83
      Military use
   Agusta testing low-cost A129 antitank helicopter. M.
      Feazel. il diag *Aviat Week Space Technol* 119:69-70
      O 10 '83
   Competition mounts over LHX contract. il *Aviat Week
      Space Technol* 119:61-4 O 10 '83
   Hughes boosts AH-64 production rate. B. A. Smith. il
      Aviat Week Space Technol 119:70-1 O 24 '83
   LAMPS Mk III system: a step closer to 'operational'
      [Sikorsky SH-60B Seahawk helicopter] D. M. Graham.
      il *Sea Technol* 24:27 N '83
   Westland upgrading Lynx 3 naval roles. D. A. Brown.
      diags *Aviat Week Space Technol* 119:51-2 O 31 '83
      Noise
   An aeroacoustic model for high-speed, unsteady blade-
      vortex interaction. R. Martinez and S. E. Widnall.
      bibl diags *AIAA J* 21:1225-31 S '83
      Police use
   Air bears; getting airborne with the California Highway
      Patrol. M. Patiky. il *Air Prog* 45:4-6+ O '83
      Rotors
   See Helicopters—Blades
Heliostats
   Theoretical concentration of solar radiation by central
      receiver systems. T. Sakurai and Y. Shibata. bibl diags
      Sol Energy 31 no3:261-70 '83
Heliports
   FAA selects sites of new heliports. *Aviat Week Space
      Technol* 119:121 N 14 '83
Helium
   Auger vs resonance neutralization in low energy He$^+$
      ion scattering. D. P. Woodruff. bibl diags *Vacuum*
      33:651-3 O-D '83
   Sellmeier fits with linear regression; multiple data sets;
      dispersion formulas for helium. E. R. Peck. bibl *Appl
      Opt* 22:2906-13 S 15 '83
   Simple sensitive techniques for absolute and differential
      helium pycnometry. J. H. Petropoulos and others. bibl
      diags *J Phys E* 16:1112-15 N '83
   Theoretical aspects of helium scattering from metal sur-
      faces. J. Harris and A. Liebsch. bibl diags *Vacuum*
      33:655-63 O-D '83
Helium, Liquid
   A cryostat for investigating inelastic scattering of neutrons
      on liquid He^4 between 4.2 and 0.5 K. I. V. Bogoyav-
      lenskii and others. bibl diag *Cryogenics* 23:498-500
      S '83
   Measurement of the transient heat transfer to liquid
      helium from a thin metal film. B. A. Danil'chenko
      and V. N. Poroshin. bibl diags *Cryogenics* 23:546-8
      O '83
   Spontaneous magnetization in He^3-B. *Phys Today* 36:23
      N '83
   Ultrasonic excitations in He^3-B. bibl diag *Phys Today*
      36:21-3 O '83

   Storage
   Automatic liquid helium transfer system. E. B. Flint
      and others. diag *Cryogenics* 23:561-2 O '83
Helmets, Football
   Computer helping in football-helmet design. *Mach Des*
      55:4 S 8 '83
Helmets, Safety *See* Hats, Safety
Helmholtz equation
   Nearfield of a large acoustic transducer [continued from
      72:1056-61 S '82] G. S. Garrett and others. bibl il
      diags *J Acoust Soc Am* 74:1013-20 S '83
Helmholtz resonators *See* Resonators
Hematins
   Heme-heme orientation and electron transfer kinetic
      behavior of multisite oxidation-reduction enzymes. M.
      W. Makinen and others. bibl *Science* 222:929-31 N
      25 '83
   Proton NMR study of the mechanism of the heme-
      apoprotein reaction for myoglobin. T. Jue and others.
      bibl diag *J Am Chem Soc* 105:5701-3 Ag 24 '83
Hematology *See* Blood
Heme *See* Hematins
Heparin
   Human endothelial cells: use of heparin in cloning and
      long-term serial cultivation. S. C. Thornton and others.
      bibl *Science* 222:623-5 N 11 '83
Hepatitis, Infectious
   High-frequency transfection and cytopathology of the
      hepatitis B virus core antigen gene in human cells.
      G. H. Yoakum and others. bibl il diag *Science* 222:385-9
      O 28 '83
   New hepatitis vaccine developed. *New Sci* 99:409 Ag
      11 '83
Heptane
   Excess volumes of binary mixtures of *n*-heptane with
      hexane isomers. F. Kimura and G. C. Benson. bibl
      J Chem Eng Data 28:387-90 O '83
Herbicides
   See also
   Dioxin
   Weeds—Control
      Laws and regulations
   Dow ends fight over 2,4,5-T, silvex safety. *Chem Eng
      News* 61:5 O 24 '83
      Physiological effect
   Chlorinated dioxins as herbicide contaminants. A. L.
      Young and others. bibl il *Environ Sci Technol*
      17:530A-40A N '83
   A new method for determining the heart beat rate of
      daphnia magna. M. Présing and M. Véró. bibl diags
      Water Res 17 no10:1245-8 '83
Herbs and spices *See* Spices and herbs
Heredity
   See also
   Genes
   Genetics
   Hybridization
Heredity (Botany)
   See also
   Genetics (Botany)
Herpesviruses
   Carbocyclic arabinofuranosyladenine (cyclaradine): efficacy
      against genital herpes in guinea pigs. R. Vince and
      others. bibl diags *Science* 221:1405-6 S 30 '83
   Detection of antibodies to herpes simplex virus with
      a continuous cell line expressing cloned glycoprotein
      D. P. W. Berman and others. bibl il diags *Science*
      222:524-7 N 4 '83
Heterocyclic compounds
   See also
   Azetidine
   Thiophene
   Anti-Bredt bridgehead nitrogen compounds in ring-opening
      polymerization. H. K. Hall, Jr. and A. El-Shekeil. bibl
      diags *Chem Rev* 83:549-55 O '83
   Oxirenes. E. G. Lewars. bibl(p532-4) diags *Chem Rev*
      83:519-34 O '83
   Synthesis of 2,6-disubstituted piperidines, oxanes, and
      thianes. V. Baliah and others. bibl(p415-23) diags *Chem
      Rev* 83:379-423 Ag '83
Heterotrophic bacteria *See* Bacteria, Heterotrophic
Heuristic algorithms *See* Algorithms—Non-numerical al-
      gorithms
Hewlett-Packard Co.
   HP to merge PC lines. E. K. Yasaki. il *Datamation*
      29:100+ O '83
Hexandioic acid *See* Adipic acid
Hexane
   Excess volumes of binary mixtures of *n*-heptane with
      hexane isomers. F. Kimura and G. C. Benson. bibl
      J Chem Eng Data 28:387-90 O '83

Fig. 8.9   An excerpt from the *Business Periodicals Index.*

Word processing equipment
> *See also*
> Dictating machines
> Typewriters, Automatic
> Word stations (Office automation)

Document reader eases law firm's work load [Oppenheimer Wolff Foster Shepard & Donnelly] il *Office* 97:78 + Je '83

New word processors to get token-passing local network [Harris Corporation's new 9000 series] il *Data Commun* 12:163–4 + Jl '83

Paper processors speed work of automated office systems [Institute of Nuclear Power Operations] il *Office* 97:102–3 Je '83

Turning typewriters into input stations with OCR [Wharton Econometric Forecasting Associates] G. J. Marquez. *Office* 97:68 + Je '83

Add-ons
> *See* Word processing equipment—Plug compatible equipment

Plug compatible equipment

ACS moves in on Wang peripherals [Applied Computer Sciences Inc.] J. Levine. *Venture* 5:94 S '83

Prices

IBM cuts tags up to 30% on Displaywriter. I. Sager. *Electron News* 29:26 + Je 13 '83

Printers
> *See* Printers (Data processing systems)

Programs

Climbing to the top of the charts [top 10 in business software] A. Solomon. *Inc* 5:141 + S '83

Does your printer work with Wordstar? C. Stevenson. *Byte* 8:411–12 + S '83

IBM cuts tags up to 30% on Displaywriter. I. Sager. *Electron News* 29:26 + Je 13 '83

Innovative office automation training [program for word processing operators] *Train Dev J* 37:10 S '83

Word processing: it's never been easier [tables] D. R. Roman. il *Comput Decis* 15:152–4 + Je '83

Selection

Word-processing systems: the matter of selection [Arrow Electronics] *Office* 97:110 Je '83

Word processing equipment industry
> *See also*
> Compucorp
> Data General Corp.
> Harris Corp.
> Lanier Business Products, Inc.
> NBI Inc.
> NCR Corp.
> Wang Laboratories Inc.

Acquisitions and mergers

Harris to buy Lanier for $415M in stock. L. Antelman. *Electron News* 29:1 + Jl 25 '83

Office automation's new marriage [proposed Harris-Lanier merger] M. Price. *Ind Week* 218:20–1 Ag 8 '83

Competition

ACS moves in on Wang peripherals [Applied Computer Sciences Inc.] J. Levine. *Venture* 5:94 S '83

Exhibitions

Syntopican bounces back with a record turnout [San Francisco] J. B. Dykeman. *Mod Off Proced* 28:34 Ag '83

Marketing

Product switch saves company [Systel Computers Inc.] A. Heller. *Venture* 5:17 + S '83 librarian by supplying three or four descriptive phrases or key words that will pinpoint the topic you want to know about. A computer search is helpful but not free. It will cost you a set fee, which varies from one institution to another, for each minute the librarian uses the computer to search through one or more data bases to locate appropriate information for you.

Finding a Periodical in Your Library

Once you find an article in an index or through a computer search, your next job is to locate and read it. First, consult your library's periodical holdings list. A card catalog for periodicals, the holdings list will most likely be a computer print-out or a file (series of folders). The holdings list will tell you to which journals and magazines your library subscribes and how far back the subscription goes. Perhaps your library has a complete backlist of the journal you are looking for or maybe it has issues for only the last three years. If the journal you are looking for is not on your library's periodical holdings list, you will have to go to another library or seek assistance through interlibrary loan.

If the library has the periodical you are looking for, it may be in a number of places, depending on the date of the issue. Recent periodicals are usually shelved alphabetically in a periodicals reading room. If the article you need was written more than a year ago, it may be bound with other issues for that year and gathered together in a hard, permanent cover and shelved like a book. Many libraries shelve bound periodicals alphabetically by title in an area of the library separate from the stacks. Another method of storing back issues is to put them on microfilm, a process of storing information concisely and economically. (Microfilm and microfiche are discussed on pages 254–256.)

☞ Reference Books

The works discussed in this section are kept in the reference room in the library, usually located across from the card catalog. Reference books may not be checked out of the library. More detailed information on specific reference works is given in the appendix to this chapter.

Encyclopedias

The word *encyclopedia* comes from a Greek phrase meaning "general education." Some encyclopedias provide information on an incredibly broad range of subjects. These comprehensive encyclopedias take years to produce and are written by a staff of experts from every major field of knowledge. These experts sign their initials after their work, and you can find out who they are by checking the encyclopedia's preface, where their names are listed after their initials.

The information in an encyclopedia is arranged alphabetically, with some subjects receiving as much as twenty pages of coverage. A general encyclopedia can get you started in your research by explaining some key terms, offering a quick summary, and supplying you with a list of further readings. Another advantage of encyclopedias is the colorful and varied illustrations they offer. Three useful general encyclopedias are *Collier's Encyclopedia*, *Encyclopedia Americana*, and *Encyclopaedia Britannica*.

Do not attempt to do all your research using only encyclopedias, however. They have their limitations. For one thing, the information in them is designed for the general reader, not the specialist. For another reason, general encyclopedias, however good, do not contain the most current information on a subject, especially on technical matters. For that kind of up-to-date material, you must consult periodicals and specialized reference books. Finally, relying on encyclopedias alone reveals your lack of ability to find and use more specialized and restricted sources.

Certain encyclopedias are limited to special areas of knowledge and will be much more helpful than general encyclopedias. These works include more background information, technical details and terminology, and references in their bibliographies. Almost every occupation has its own encyclopedia.

Dictionaries

Dictionaries are perhaps the most important reference tool, since they help you to understand the information gathered from other works (books, periodicals, pamphlets) that comprise the bulk of your research. If you do not know the meaning of a term, you will have trouble understanding a discussion in which that term is used. In addition to giving the meaning of words, dictionaries indicate spelling, pronunciation, *etymology* (word history), and usage. Generally speaking, dictionaries fall into two categories—general English-language dictionaries and more specialized dictionaries used by a specific profession.

English-language dictionaries are either unabridged or abridged. An unabridged dictionary is a large, comprehensive guide to the words of the language. Found in libraries and classrooms, these dictionaries are usually placed on a stand and are extremely heavy. The following unabridged dictionaries are excellent references: *Funk & Wagnalls New Standard Dictionary of the English Language*, the *Oxford English Dictionary*, the *Random House Dictionary of the English Language*, and *Webster's Third New International Dictionary of the English Language*. The *Oxford English Dictionary* is a historical dictionary—that is, it lists the dates when a word was first used and how it was used and supplies illustrative quotations. Regarded as the greatest dictionary in the language, the *OED* is invaluable.

Abridged dictionaries are much smaller. They can range from a vest or pocket dictionary to a large compilation with photographs and other illustrations. The following abridged dictionaries are useful: the *American Heritage Dictionary*, the *Random House College Dictionary*, *Webster's New Collegiate Dictionary*, and *Webster's New World Dictionary*.

You will frequently use dictionaries, such as those described in the appendix, that contain the specialized vocabulary of your profession. These specialized, or field, dictionaries not only define the words used in the literature of a profession but also help to characterize that profession's scope and importance.

Abstracts

An abstract is a short summary. In addition to listing the author's name, title, and publication data, an abstract will give a brief (usually a few sentences) summary of the content and scope of the book, article, or pamphlet. By condensing this information, an abstract can save users hours of time by letting them know if the work is relevant to their topic.

Use abstracts with caution, however, for they are not a substitute for the article or book they summarize. A few sentences highlighting the content of a book or article obviously omit much. When in doubt about what is omitted, read the original work to uncover the details, the rationale, and the dimensions of the whole problem. Never quote from an abstract; always cite material from the original work.

Not every field has an abstracting service, nor is every article or book always abstracted. The titles of abstracts found in the appendix to this chapter will give you a clear idea of the range of fields that do offer this valuable service.

Handbooks, Manuals, and Almanacs

Handbooks, manuals, and almanacs supply you with definitions of terms in your field, statistical facts, explanations of procedures, and authoritative reviews of the kinds of practical and professional problems and solutions you will encounter on the job. In the card catalog these works will be marked *Ref.,* indicating that they are shelved in the reference section of your library.

Numerous reference books are available for each profession. When you look for the reference books in your field, make sure that you use the most up-to-date ones. Information changes rapidly, and works not listing the most recent and improved techniques will not help. Also, consult more than one manual or handbook in your field. Compare their discussions of the same topic; different approaches or emphases will help you to research a given procedure more accurately.

☞ Government Documents

The U.S. government, through its diverse agencies and departments, engages vigorously in conducting research and in publishing its findings. This published material, collectively referred to as government documents, can be in the form of journal articles, pamphlets, research reports, transcripts of government hearings, speeches, or books. These materials have immense practical value for the research you do in your field. Government reports, for example, will discuss care of the aged, flood insurance, farming techniques, fire precautions, housing costs, outdoor recreation, and urban development.

Three indexes to government documents are especially helpful in guiding you through this vast store of information. While other indexes and guides to government publications do exist, these three are the most useful for the kind of research you will be doing.

1. The *Monthly Catalog of U.S. Government Publications.* Published since 1895 by the GPO (Government Printing Office), this index lists government documents published during that month. The catalog is arranged by agencies that publish or sponsor works (for example, the departments of Agriculture, Commerce, Interior, State, and so forth). At the back of each issue there is also an index to subjects, authors, titles, key words in titles, reports, and contract numbers. Each entry provides the author or agency's name, the title, the date, a brief description of the contents of the document (including whether it contains a bibliography, maps, or index), when and where the research was conducted, who sponsored it (including a contract number), the price, and how to order a copy. Figure 8.10 shows you how to interpret a sample entry.

2. The *Index to Government Periodicals.* Published since 1970, this subject and author guide to 170 periodicals published by the federal government is issued quarterly and cumulated annually. The titles of some of these periodicals suggest their research value: *American Rehabilitation, Fire Management Notes, Highway and Urban Mass Transportation, Marine Fisheries Review, Occupational Outlook Quarterly, Pesticides Monitoring Journal,* and *Tree Planters' Notes.* Figure 8.11 shows some entries from this index.

3. The *Index to Publications of the United States Congress.* Published monthly since 1970 by the Congressional Information Service (CIS), this reference work indexes and abstracts House and Senate documents, reports, hearings, investigations, and other publications. It is a particularly valuable guide to legislative investigations and decisions.

States and counties also engage in research and publish their findings. The Library of Congress publishes the *Monthly Checklist of State Publications,* which lists, according to the individual states, such materials as pamphlets, statistical studies, yearbooks, and histories. At the county level, practical advice and publications are available on a wide range of topics in agriculture, education, food science, housing, and water resources.

☞ The Popular Press

The "popular press" includes reading material written in nontechnical language for the general public. Pamphlets, brochures, consumer manuals,

Fig. 8.10   Sample entry with explanation of codes from the _Monthly Catalog of U.S. Government Publications._

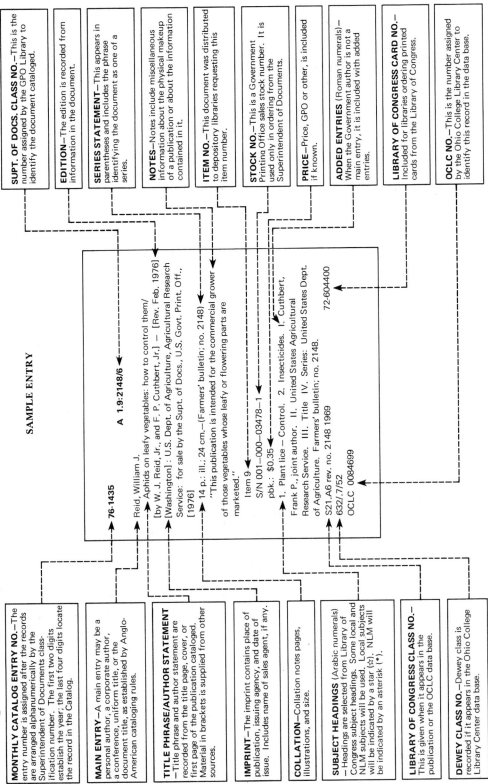

SAMPLE ENTRY

SUPT. OF DOCS. CLASS NO.—This is the number assigned by the GPO Library to identify the document cataloged.

EDITION—The edition is recorded from information in the document.

SERIES STATEMENT—This appears in parentheses and includes the phrase identifying the document as one of a series.

NOTES—Notes include miscellaneous information about the physical makeup of a publication or about the information contained in it.

ITEM NO.—This document was distributed to depository libraries requesting this item number.

STOCK NO.—This is a Government Printing Office sales stock number. It is used only in ordering from the Superintendent of Documents.

PRICE—Price, GPO or other, is included if known.

ADDED ENTRIES (Roman numerals)—When the Government author is not a main entry, it is included with added entries.

LIBRARY OF CONGRESS CARD NO.—Included for libraries ordering printed cards from the Library of Congress.

OCLC NO.—This is the number assigned by the Ohio College Library Center to identify this record in the data base.

MONTHLY CATALOG ENTRY NO.—The entry number is assigned after the records are arranged alphanumerically by the Superintendent of Documents classification number. The first two digits establish the year; the last four digits locate the record in the Catalog.

MAIN ENTRY—A main entry may be a personal author, a corporate author, a conference, uniform title, or the document title, as established by Anglo-American cataloging rules.

TITLE PHRASE/AUTHOR STATEMENT—Title phrase and author statement are recorded from the title page, cover, or first page of the publication cataloged. Material in brackets is supplied from other sources.

IMPRINT—The imprint contains place of publication, issuing agency, and date of issue. Includes name of sales agent, if any.

COLLATION—Collation notes pages, illustrations, and size.

SUBJECT HEADINGS (Arabic numerals)—Headings are selected from Library of Congress subject headings. Some local and NLM subjects will be used. Local subjects will be indicated by a star (✰). NLM will be indicated by an asterisk (✱).

LIBRARY OF CONGRESS CLASS NO.—This is given when it appears in the publication or the OCLC data base.

DEWEY CLASS NO.—Dewey class is recorded if it appears in the Ohio College Library Center data base.

76-1435   A 1.9:2148/6

Reid, William J.
   Aphids on leafy vegetables: how to control them/
[by W. J. Reid, Jr., and F. P. Cuthbert, Jr.] — [Rev. Feb. 1976]
[Washington]: U.S. Dept. of Agriculture, Agricultural Research
Service: for sale by the Supt. of Docs., U.S. Govt. Print. Off.,
[1976]
   14 p.: ill.; 24 cm.—(Farmers' bulletin; no. 2148)
   "This publication is intended for the commercial grower
of those vegetables whose leafy or flowering parts are
marketed."
   Item 9
   S/N 001—000—03478—1
   pbk.: $0.35
   1. Plant lice — Control. 2. Insecticides. I. Cuthbert,
Frank P., joint author. II. United States Agricultural
Research Service. III. Title IV. Series: United States Dept.
of Agriculture. Farmers' bulletin; no. 2148.
S21.A6 rev. no. 2148 1969   72-604400
632/.7/52
OCLC 0084699

Fig. 8.11 Some entries from *Index to Government Periodicals*.

FINLAND (cont)

Trade

Finland: continuing revival in economic activity fosters burgeoning demand for U.S. products. Albert Caya, Jr., il Bus Amer 2 9 22-23 Ap 23 79-216

Finland: U.S. sales prospects improve as demand gains strength. Philip Combs, rep, gr Overseas Bus Rep 79-04 13 Mr 79-085

Packaging abroad: packaging and labeling regulations. Cont & Packag 31 24 19-20 Sum-Fall-Wint 78-79-154

FINN, J. J.

1978 annual report. Secretariat. Fed Home Loan Bk Bd J 12 4 70 Mr 79-046

FINN, Joseph T.

Materials requirements for sewer works construction. tab Const Rev 25 1 4-13 Ja 79-152

FINNEY, Lynne D.

1978 annual report. Office of Industry Development. il, tab, gr Fed Home Loan Bk Bd J 12 4 42-49 Mr 79-046

FIR trees

Diseases

Branch mortality of true firs in west-central Oregon associated with dwarf mistletoe and canker fungi. Gregory M. Filip and others, ref, tab, gr Plant Dis Rep 63 3 189-193 Mr 79-087

Pests

Developing a long-range fuel program. John Maupin, il, gr Fire Man Notes 40 1 3-5 Wint 78-79-184

FIRE

Saga of mining's darkest days—the Comstock lode tragedy. il Mine Safe & H 4 1 10-15 F-Mr 79-207

Management

Determining arrival times of fire resources by computer. il, ref, tab Fire Man Notes 39 4 12-13 Fall 78-184

Forest Service and fire administration team up on rural fire problem analysis. R. Michael Bowman, Fire Man Notes 40 1 7 Wint 78-79-184

Han~~~~~for fire d~~~~be~~~~or.

From *Index to U.S. Government Periodicals* Apr.– June 1979: 96. Reprinted by permission.

and newspapers comprise the popular press. This section will show you where to find them indexed.

Vertical File Materials

Every library receives, as part of its collection of "popular press," materials that are best classified as "temporary, or ephemeral, documents." These materials—pamphlets, catalogs, promotional materials, posters, charts, and maps—are stored in the library's vertical files, often one or a series of file cabinets. Although these materials are not listed in the card catalog, the titles (and sources) may suggest the kinds of topics they cover: "A Guide to the New Jelico

Drill" (from a manufacturer), "High Blood Pressure" (from the American Heart Association), "Highway Safety" (from a state highway department), "So You Want to Be a Geologist" (from a professional society), "A Map of the Olympic Sites" (from an Olympic committee). In addition, you will find clippings from newspapers and magazines on topics that the librarian believes are of interest to patrons.

You may also want to consult the *Vertical File Index* (1936–), which lists pamphlets, posters, maps, charts, brochures, and so forth under subject headings. A title index is also included. Another especially helpful feature of the *Vertical File Index* is that it lists the addresses of the companies and associations from whom you may obtain a copy of the publication, sometimes free of charge.

Indexes to Newspapers

In many ways newspapers provide a valuable source of information relevant to the research you do in school or on the job. News of local events can translate into business for you. Newspapers supply details about forthcoming construction, thus alerting building suppliers, construction workers, realtors, and community service employees of a market for their skills. Newspapers provide information about community projects, financial changes, or recreational facilities that might be equally useful. And newspapers can help you to locate new markets or sites or expand those your company or agency already has.

A thorough guide to the newspapers published in the United States and Canada is the *Ayer Directory of Periodicals*. This work, issued annually, lists the date a paper began publication; its current address, rates, and circulation; and its religious or political preference. The directory also includes a capsule history of the community served by the paper. Unfortunately, it will not refer you to specific stories. For that information you need to consult an index. The best one is the *New York Times Index*, which indexes by subject and author stories that have appeared in its paper since 1851. This index also summarizes stories and reprints the photographs, maps, and other illustrations that accompanied some of the stories. Still another advantage this comprehensive index offers is that you can find the date of an event in it and then use that date to see how a local newspaper covered the story. Many libraries have the back issues of the *New York Times* on microfilm.

Another index to consult is the *Newspaper Index*, published since 1972. Although it covers far fewer years than the *New York Times Index*, this work lists the stories published in four newspapers representing four main areas of the country—the East Coast (*Washington Post*), the Midwest (*Chicago Tribune*), the South (*New Orleans Times-Picayune*), and the West Coast (*Los Angeles Times*). You might also consult the very valuable *Wall Street Journal*, which publishes its own index.

Every newspaper is indexed. You can find the index to your local newspaper in that section of a newspaper office called "the morgue," where all the back issues of a paper are stored. All you need to use the index is the date of the story you are interested in. Newspapers gladly allow readers access to back issues, often helping by conducting computerized searches of topics, and may even help you photocopy a story.

☞ Audiovisual Materials

Audiovisual materials include sound, still or moving pictures, or both together. Some types of audiovisuals are records, cassettes, tape recordings, photographs, films, and microforms. These materials may be shelved in a separate part of the library that contains the room and proper equipment to use them conveniently and properly. Audiovisual titles are listed in the card catalog and perhaps also in a separate audiovisual catalog. One particular type of audiovisual material, microforms, deserves special attention.

The name *microforms* refers to a number of research tools—microfilm, microfiche, microcards—that all make use of microphotography. Each of these library tools presents a great deal of information reduced from its original size and stored compactly on film or tape. The microform process saves the library space, increases the durability of the documents, and offers libraries a wider range of titles for far less money. Microforms are used frequently in business and industry as well. Hospitals can store patients' records much more economically; banks put canceled checks on microforms for safe storage and easy reference; and the government can condense miles of documents for easy and accurate retrieval.

Microfilm

A microfilm is a strip of black-and-white film on which reduced images are found and which is stored on reels, cartridges, or cassettes, such as in Figure 8.12. These reduced images are microscopic pictures of the pages of books, articles, newspapers, court proceedings, and so forth. The size of these pages has been reduced by microphotography to a fraction of their original size. Believe it or not, "a 1,245-page Bible can be reproduced on a one-inch square piece of microfilm. If the Library of Congress chose, it could store its 270 miles of books and other reference material in six standard filing cabinets" (*Nation's Business* Mar. 1971:20). A library could save 95 percent of its space if it converted all its holdings to microfilm.

The advantages microfilm offers are many. No library could possibly save all the back issues of a local newspaper, let alone a large, nationally famous paper such as the *New York Times*. Moreover, newspapers tear, fade, and crumble after being used by readers for a few weeks. Using microfilm, a library can store a newspaper's daily issues from one month on one reel, such as any of the reels seen in Figure 8.12. A special machine called a microfilm reader, similar to the one in Figure 8.13, enlarges the images for reading. Your library has at

Fig. 8.12 **Examples of microfilm stored on (a) reels, (b) cartridges, and (c) cassettes.**

(a)   (b)   (c)

Fig. 8.13 **A microfilm reader.**

least one or two of these machines and possibly more. Your librarian will be pleased to show you how to operate one.

Microfiche

Microfiche (pronounced micro feesh) is a close cousin to microfilm. The microfiche process puts the film of the reduced pages of books, periodicals, catalogs, or any other printed materials on flat, transparent four-by-six-inch cards. Each fiche (or film strip) may hold as many as 90 to 100 pages. Superfiche, an even more compact method of reproduction, can put 300 to 400 pages on a single four-by-six-inch card. A common reduction rate is 24:1. Figure 8.14 shows a sample microfiche. More than fifty-five pages of a periodical are placed on this single card. As with microfilm, you need a special machine to see the material condensed onto microfiche. Using a microfiche reader, you slide the four-by-six-inch card onto a tray, push the tray underneath a magnifying lens, and see the material projected and enlarged on a lighted screen. To find the page you want, you simply slide the tray up or down or from right to left.

A *microcard* is identical to a microfiche except that the film is printed on an opaque, not transparent, card.

☞ Note Taking

Once you have consulted the appropriate sources, you need some systematic way to record relevant information from them in preparing your paper or report. Before you can begin to make a rough draft, you must be able to organize and classify data from your research efficiently. (Even after you start to draft your report, you might find you need to continue your research and take additional notes.)

Note taking is the crucial link between finding sources and writing a report. Never trust your memory to keep all your research facts straight. Taking notes is time well spent. Do not be too quick in getting it done or too eager to begin writing your paper. Careless note taking may cause you to forget page numbers, publishers, dates, or even titles; you might need this information at 2:00 a.m. when the library is closed and your paper is due at 9:00 a.m. Not copying accurately from a source could lead you to omit key words in a quotation or, even worse, misrepresent or contradict what the author has said. Carelessness could result in crediting one author with another's work.

Basically, you will be preparing two kinds of notes. One type will be on the sources you read, as in Figure 8.15. These cards will become your working bibliography. The other type will be reserved for the specific information you take from these sources in the form of direct quotations, paraphrases, or summaries. Figures 8.16 and 8.17 show the kinds of information that can be taken from sources.

Fig. 8.14   A sample microfiche.

E. Stevens Rice, *Fiche and Reel* (Ann Arbor, MI.: Xerox, n.d.), p. 13. Used by permission.

How to Prepare Bibliography Cards

To record accurate and meaningful information, follow these practical guidelines:

1. Use three-by-five-inch index cards, and use the same size consistently. Do not be tempted to use slips of paper, looseleaf notebook paper, or notebooks; cards are less likely to get lost, and they will help you to organize, alphabetize, and label material.
2. Write on only one side of the card. It is easier to copy and check information when you list it all on one side.
3. Use a ballpoint pen to write your notes. Felt-tip pens or pencils may smudge. Write legibly; print if necessary.
4. Put only one title (article or book or film) on each card. These cards will later have to be arranged in alphabetical order for your Works Cited page (see pages 273–280); if you place two titles on one card, you could end up retyping your entire Works Cited page (to put these "missing" entries in), or you could run the risk of omitting one of the titles.
5. Include full bibliographic information for each source. For books, list author, title, chapter titles, edition, date, city of publication, publisher, and

Fig. 8.15   Note card containing bibliographic information on a source.

> *Jenkes*   *Food and Nutrition*
>
> *Jenkes, Thomas H. "Predicament of*
>   *Food and Nutrition"*
> *Food Technology 44*
> *Oct. 1979 : 45-46.*

Fig. 8.16   Note card containing a direct quotation.

> *Jenkes 46*   *DISCOVERY OF VITAMINS*
>
>   *"The discovery, isolation, and synthesis of*
> *vitamins was one of the great scientific and*
> *public health achievements of the 20th century.*
> *They [nutritionists] made it scientifically*
> *possible to eliminate the nutritional deficiency*
> *diseases that had plagued human beings for*
> *centuries. This was an immediate and*
> *complete victory, unlike the incessant and*
> *on-going war against malaria, diabetes,*
> *cancer, and heart disease."*

page numbers; for articles, supply author, title, journal, volume number, date, and page numbers.

6. Decode and spell out any periodical index or journal abbreviations. Record periodical entries with their full and accurate bibliographic information. (See Chapter 9 on documentation.) The abbreviated entries in indexes such as the *Readers' Guide* or the *Applied Science & Technology Index*

Fig. 8.17   Note card containing a paraphrase.

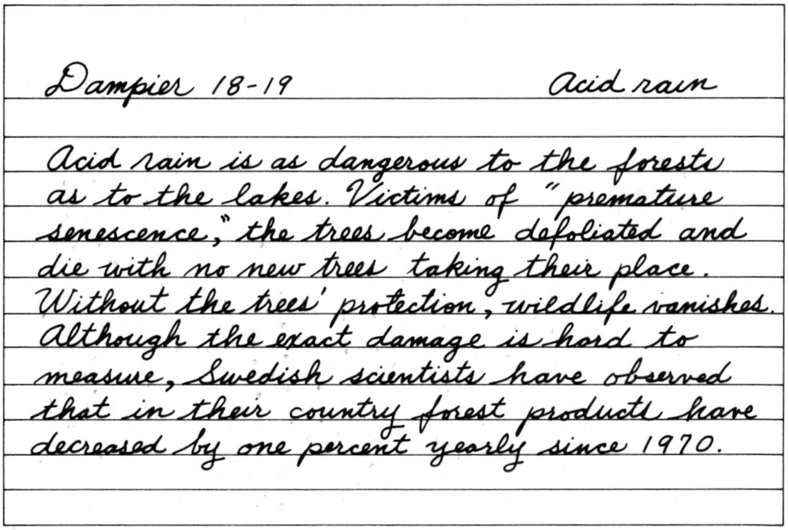

Dampier 18-19   Acid rain

Acid rain is as dangerous to the forests
as to the lakes. Victims of "premature
senescence," the trees become defoliated and
die with no new trees taking their place.
Without the trees' protection, wildlife vanishes.
Although the exact damage is hard to
measure, Swedish scientists have observed
that in their country forest products have
decreased by one percent yearly since 1970.

are not in acceptable format for parenthetical documentation or bibliographic entries in your paper or report.

7. Write down the call numbers of the book or periodical in the upper left-hand corner of the card so you will know where to find the source again if you need it. If you are using more than one library, also indicate at which library you found the source.

How to Prepare Note Cards

While your bibliography cards will give you important facts about authors, titles, and publication data, your note cards will give you the specific information from these sources that you need to write your paper. Your note cards will contain direct quotations from, or paraphrases of, your sources. Quotations and paraphrases are discussed on pages 260–262. Here are some guidelines to follow when preparing note cards:

1. Use four-by-six-inch cards to keep them separate from the three-by-five bibliography cards.
2. Write on only one side of the card. It will be easier for you to arrange the cards in the order you may need them for your paper.
3. Don't include notes from two different sources on one card. Keep notes from each source separate.
4. Copy names, facts, dates, statistics accurately from the source. Be sure, too, that you record the author's words correctly; you may want to quote these words verbatim in your paper. Always compare what you have written with the original.

5. Make sure that you distinguish quotations from your own paraphrase. Be sure to place quotation marks around any words you record directly from a source.

6. Write a code word or phrase in the upper-right-hand corner of the card to identify the topic treated by the source or the information written on the card from that source. Using code words such as "characteristics," "function of," "history of," or "location of" on your cards will help you to organize when you write your paper. See Figure 8.16.

7. Write a short title of the book or journal article in the upper-left-hand corner or include the author's last name so that the note card is coded to your bibliography card.

To Quote or Not to Quote

Before recording information from sources, ask yourself these three questions: (1) How much should I take down? (2) How often should I copy the author's words verbatim to use direct quotations? (3) When should I paraphrase or summarize? A safe rule to follow is: Do not be a human copying machine. If you write down too many of the author's own words, you will simply be transferring the author's words from the book or article to your paper. That will show that you have read the work but have not evaluated its findings. Do not use direct quotations simply as a filler.

Direct quotations should be used sparingly and saved for when they count most. When an author has summarized a great deal of significant information concisely into a few well-chosen sentences, you may want to quote this summary verbatim. Or if a writer has clarified a difficult concept exceedingly well, you may want to include this clarification exactly as it is listed. And certainly the author's chief statement or thesis may deserve to be quoted directly. Figure 8.16 contains such an important statement. Just be careful that you do not quote verbatim all of the evidence leading to that conclusion. The conclusion may be pointedly expressed in two or three sentences; the evidence could cover many pages. If you are worried about exactly how much to quote verbatim, keep in mind that no more than 10 or 15 percent of your paper should be made up of direct quotations. Remember that when you quote someone directly, you are telling your readers that these words are the most important part of the author's work as far as you are concerned. Be a selective filter, not a large funnel.

There will be times when a sentence or passage is particularly useful, but you may not want to quote it in its entirety. You may want to delete some words that are not really necessary for your purpose. These omissions are indicated by using ellipsis dots, three spaced dots within the sentence to indicate where the words are omitted (four spaced dots if the omitted words end the sentence). Here are some examples.

Omitted words within a sentence

Full Quotation: "Diet and nutrition, which have been studied by researchers, significantly affect oral health."

Quotation with Ellipsis: "Diet and nutrition . . . significantly affect oral health."

Omitted words at the end of a sentence

Full Quotation: "Decisions on how to operate the company should be based on the most accurate and relevant information available from both within the company and from the specific community that establishment serves."

Quotation with Ellipsis: "Decisions on how to operate the company should be based on the most accurate and relevant information available. . . ."

At times you may have to insert your own information within a quotation. This addition, called an *interpolation,* is made by enclosing your clarifying identification or remark within brackets inside the quotation. For example, "It [the new transportation network] has been thoroughly tested and approved." In other words, anything within brackets is not part of the quotation.

Most of your note taking will not be devoted to writing down direct quotations. It will be concerned with writing paraphrases. A paraphrase is a restatement of the author's ideas point by point in your own words. Even though you are using your own words to translate or restate, you still must document the paraphrase because you are using the author's facts and interpretations. You do not use quotation marks, though. When you include a paraphrase in your paper, you should be careful to do four things.

1. Be faithful to the author's meaning. Do not alter facts or introduce new ideas.
2. Follow the order in which the author presents the information.
3. Include in your paraphrase only what is relevant for your paper. Delete any details not essential for your work.
4. Use paraphrases in your report selectively. You do not want your work to be merely a restatement of someone else's.

Figure 8.17 shows a note card containing a paraphrase of the following quotation:

While the effects of acid rain are felt first in lakes, which act as natural collection points, some scientists fear there may be extensive damage to forests as well. In the process described by one researcher as "premature senescence," trees exposed to acid sprays lose their leaves, wilt and finally die. New trees may not grow to replace them. Deprived of natural cover, wildlife may flee or die. The extent of the damage to forest lands is extremely difficult to determine, but scientists find the trend worrisome. In Sweden, for example, one estimate calculates that the yield in forest products decreased by about one percent each year during the 1970s.[1]

---

[1] Bill Dampier, "Now Even the Rain Is Dangerous," *International Wildlife* 10 (March–April 1980): 18–19.

Paraphrased material can be introduced in your paper with an appropriate identifying phrase, such as "According to Dampier's study," "To paraphrase Dampier," or "As Dampier observes."

☞ Appendix: Some Helpful Reference Works

After the title of each of the following reference works is a brief annotation indicating, sometimes with a direct quotation taken from the particular work, its audience, organization, and coverage. The dates in parentheses after indexes and abstracts refer to the year in which they began publication.

Indexes

Biological and Agricultural Index (1945). This index is published monthly with quarterly and yearly cumulative issues. Formerly called *Agricultural Index,* this work indexes about 200 periodicals in such fields as agricultural economics, animal husbandry, ecology, food science, forestry, horticulture, marine biology, nutrition, soil science, and veterinary medicine. Its organization is by subject headings; it contains a separate section on book reviews.

Criminal Justice Periodical Index (1975). Published yearly, this index contains both an author and subject list. It is a guide to articles in more than 100 journals in the fields of law enforcement, corrections, paralegal, security, and traffic enforcement.

Cumulative Index to Nursing & Allied Health Literature (1955). Published bimonthly, this index surveys over 250 journals and magazines in the nursing and allied health fields. Nurses, respiratory and physical therapists, social workers, radiological and medical technicians will find a convenient guide to literature in their fields. A two-part index— one a subject guide to periodicals and the other an alphabetical index of these subjects— makes it convenient to use.

Education Index (1929). This index is published every month except July and August. It lists periodicals that deal with all aspects of education from driver training to adult and continuing education.

Environmental Index (1971). Published annually, this index "offers *keyword direct access* to more than 55,000 citations appearing in 2,000 of the world's most significant environmental publications. To provide a comprehensive and accurate environmental perspective, the index compiles and cross-references environmental material from major scientific, technical, professional, trade, and general periodicals, government documents, proceedings, research reports, newspapers, books and speeches."

Hospital Literature Index (1945). Published quarterly, this "is a subject-author index of literature about the administration, planning, financing of medical care facilities and about administrative aspects of medical, paramedical, and prepayment fields." It is arranged by subject headings. While it does not survey nursing literature, it does cover administrative and educational issues in allied health fields (dietetics, dental hygiene, x-ray technology, medical technology, physical and respiratory therapy).

Index to Legal Periodicals (1926). This index is published monthly, except September, and contains a subject and author index to more than 350 law journals published worldwide. "Case notes or discussions of recent cases are listed by the name of the case discussed at the end of the subheading 'Cases.' " It also includes a book review index.

Index Medicus (1879). Published monthly by the National Library of Medicine in Washington, D.C., this index surveys 2,500 journals published worldwide in medicine and ancillary fields (for example, medical technology, medical records, respiratory therapy, etc.). It contains subject and author sections and translates titles of articles not written in English. This index is invaluable for students in the health sciences.

Index of Supermarket Articles (1935). Published by the Supermarket Institute in Chicago, this index surveys articles on supermarkets and food suppliers published in such journals as *Chain Store Age, Grocery Editions, Progressive Grocer, Supermarket Merchandising,* and *Supermarket Manager.*

Social Sciences Index and *Humanities Index* (1907). Known as the *International Index* from 1907 to 1965 and the *Social Sciences and Humanities Index* from 1965 to 1974, these two works now list articles in many of the social sciences (for example, sociology, political science) and the humanities.

Encyclopedias

The Arnold Encyclopedia of Real Estate, edited by Alvin Arnold and Jack Kusnet. Boston: Warren, Gorham & Lamont, 1978. 1 vol. A topical "Entry Finder" at the back "classifies selected entries into twelve major subjects."

Encyclopedia of Accounting Forms and Reports. Englewood Cliffs, New Jersey: Prentice-Hall, 1964. 3 vols. This work provides a survey of reports used in accounting practice (vol. 1), accounting systems (vol. 2), and specific industries (vol. 3).

Encyclopedia of Animal Care, edited by Geoffrey P. West. 12th ed. Baltimore: Williams and Wilkins, 1977. 1 vol.; 265 illustrations. This work gives information on "the diseases, breeding, and health of domesticated animals and is intended for farmers, public health officials, and breeders who do not need a veterinary reference work or who need more detail than a popular magazine provides."

Encyclopedia of Architectural Technology, edited by Pedro Guedes. New York: McGraw-Hill, 1979. 1 vol. "Architect, art historian, and engineer" as well as the "concerned" layperson should "profit" from this book. It is divided into six sections: stylistic periods, building forms and building types, structures, structural, mechanical and environmental systems, building materials, and tools, techniques, and fixings. The encyclopedia offers 800 illustrations.

Encyclopedia of Computer Science and Engineering, edited by Anthony Ralston. 2nd ed. New York: Van Nostrand Reinhold, 1983. 1 vol. This work has a helpful list of titles on related subjects at the beginning of each section. It also has appendixes on abbreviations, acronyms, mathematical notations, numerical tables, and key high-level languages.

Encyclopedia of Food Technology and Food Service Series. Westport, Connecticut: Avi Publishing. Vol. 1 *The Encyclopedia of Food Engineering,* edited by C. W. Hall, A. W. Farrall, and A. L. Rippen, 1971. Vol. 2 *The Encyclopedia of Food Technology,* edited by Arnold H. Johnson and Martin S. Peterson, 1974. Vol. 3 *The Encyclopedia of Food Science,* edited by Arnold H. Johnson and Martin S. Peterson.

Encyclopedia of Marine Resources, edited by Frank E. Firth. New York: Van Nostrand Reinhold, 1969. 1 vol. Information on the "most significant aspects of the ocean's resources" will be of interest to biologists, food technologists, fishery management specialists, and others.

Encyclopedia of Materials Handling, edited by Douglas Woodley. New York: Pergamon, 1964. 2 vols. It contains valuable chapters on machines (conveyors, elevators, cranes, hoists, trucks, etc.), unitization, and loading and transportation.

Encyclopedia of Practical Photography, edited by Eastman Kodak Company. Garden City, N.Y.: Amphoto, 1979. 14 vols. In this work the "emphasis . . . is on practical advice and instruction in using light, film, and chemicals to get the most of your equipment. Here you will find the how-to information necessary for actual production of photographic images."

Encyclopedia of Textiles, edited by the editors of *American Fabrics Magazine*. 3rd ed. Englewood Cliffs, New Jersey: Prentice-Hall, 1980. 1 vol. This is a "reference guide for every person concerned with the producing and marketing of fibers and fabrics, and for the professions of designing and advertising which service the textile industry." A lavishly illustrated work, this encyclopedia contains information on the history, production, and manufacturing of natural and synthetic fibers, colors and dyes, and textile printing.

Encyclopedia of Urban Planning, edited by Arnold Whittick. New York: McGraw-Hill, 1974. 1 vol. A preface describes and defines urban planning. Numerous pictures, maps, and drawings and a bibliography at the end of each section are included in this encyclopedia, which provides information on international projects, urban renewal, legislation, and other topics.

Food & Nutrition Encyclopedia, edited by A. H. Ensminger et al. Clovis, CA: Pegus Press, 1983. 2 vols; 1600 illustrations. The goal of this work is "to produce the most complete and in-depth foods and nutrition source ever." Containing over 2,800 entries, it "covers all aspects of food-nutrition-health with adequate historical and interpretive context. Each article includes all relevant aspects of the topic."

Goodheart-Wilcox Automotive Encyclopedia, edited by W. K. Toboldt and Larry Johnson. South Holland, Illinois: Goodheart-Wilcox, 1981. 1 vol. Detailed guide to auto repair and maintenance.

McGraw-Hill Encyclopedia of Energy, edited by Daniel N. Lapedes. New York: McGraw-Hill, 1981. 1 vol. This encyclopedia is divided into two sections—"Energy Perspectives" and "Energy Technology." The *Encyclopedia* "with its more than 300 articles written by specialists is designed to aid the student, librarian, scientist, engineer, teacher, and lay reader with any information on any aspect of energy from the economic and political to the environmental and technological."

McGraw-Hill Encyclopedia of Environmental Science, edited by Daniel N. Lapedes. New York: McGraw-Hill, 1974. 1 vol. This work contains 300 alphabetically arranged articles, most of which include a bibliography. There is also an analytical index.

McGraw-Hill Encyclopedia of Food, Agriculture & Nutrition, edited by Daniel N. Lapedes. New York: McGraw-Hill, 1977. 1 vol. Following five feature articles are 400 alphabetically arranged articles on subjects dealing with "the cultivation, harvesting, and processing of food crops; food manufacturing; and health and nutrition—from the economic and political to the technological."

McGraw-Hill Encyclopedia of Science and Technology, Sybil P. Parker, Editor in Chief. New York: McGraw-Hill, 1982. 15 vols; vol. 15 is an index. Extremely wide-ranging, this is the most comprehensive encyclopedia you can consult for scientific and technological subjects.

The New Encyclopedia of Furniture, edited by Joseph Aronson. New York: Crown, 1967. 1 vol. This work contains numerous drawings and designs of period pieces. A bibliography and a glossary of designers and craftsmen is found at the end of the work.

The New York Botanical Garden Illustrated Encyclopedia of Horticulture, edited by Thomas H. Everett. New York: Garland Publishing, 1980. 14 vols. This work provides a "comprehensive description and evaluation of horticulture as it is known and practiced in the United States and Canada by amateurs and by professionals, including those responsible for botanical gardens, public parks, and industrial landscapes." "Emphasis throughout is placed on the appropriate employment of plants both outdoors and indoors, and particular attention is given to explaining in considerable detail the how-and-when-to-do-it aspects of plant growing."

Dictionaries

Dictionary of Architecture and Construction, edited by Cyril M. Harris. New York: McGraw-Hill, 1975. This dictionary provides definitions of terms "encountered in the everyday practice of architecture and construction and in their associated fields." It emphasizes terms from the building trades and includes information on "building products and materials, and related terms dealing with their design, appearance, performance, installation, and testing"; it also covers construction equipment.

Dictionary of Computers, Data Processing, and Telecommunications, edited by Jerry M. Rosenberg. New York: Wiley, 1983. Offering more than 10,000 entries, "this work contains terms that relate directly or indirectly to usage of hardware and software, including the broad categories of computers, data processing, distributed data processing, home computers, information transmission, microprocessors, minicomputers, personal computers, programming languages, telecommunications, and word processing." The aim of the work is to give multiple definitions of words based on their use in various technological fields. "Commonly used symbols, acronyms, and abbreviations" are also given.

Dictionary of Nutrition and Food Technology, edited by Arnold E. Bender. New York: Chemical Publishing Company, 1976. This dictionary is for students in agriculture, commerce, food science, dietetics, home economics, sociology, and medicine. "The purpose of this dictionary is to assist the specialist from one field to understand the technical terms used by the variety of specialists in the food fields."

Dictionary of Practical Law, edited by Charles F. Hemphill, Jr., and Phyllis D. Hemphill. Englewood Cliffs, New Jersey: Prentice-Hall, 1979. "This dictionary was prepared for the needs of law students, paralegal courses, legal secretaries, and students in the administration of justice, corrections, and rehabilitation. It was also written for the needs of working police officers, and for those who simply want a definition of legal terms in everyday language."

Fairchild's Dictionary of Textiles, edited by Isabel B. Wingate. 5th ed. New York: Fairchild, 1979. It includes "terms, often of several words used or once used in the textile industry, to identify the thousands of fiber-based products employed for either the consumer or industrial purposes, along with the fibers and production processes and major equipment." It is useful to "people in all branches of the industry: manufacturing, sales, producers, designers."

Stedman's Medical Dictionary. Illustrated. 24th ed. Baltimore, Maryland: Williams and Wilkins, 1982. This is a highly technical work that contains terms from all medical specialties. Heavily illustrated, it provides information on pronunciations, etymologies, spellings, and word groups.

McGraw-Hill Dictionary of Scientific and Technical Terms, edited by Daniel N. Lapedes. 2nd ed. New York: McGraw-Hill, 1978. It includes terms used by professionals in agriculture, ecology, data processing, food engineering, graphic arts, medicine, microbiology, navigation, oceanography, petrology, and veterinary medicine; it supplies "also known as" terms and emphasizes definitions rather than pronunciation.

Mosby's Medical & Nursing Dictionary, Laurence Urdang, general editor. St. Louis: C. V. Mosby Company, 1983. According to the preface, this is "a reference book of consummate usefulness to nurses and other health professionals." Contains full-sentence definitions, includes information about etymology and pronunciation, and provides extensive cross references and illustrations.

Office Automation: A Glossary and Guide, edited by Nancy MacLellan Edwards. White Plains, New York: Knowledge Industry Publishers, Inc., 1982. Intended for office service managers, operations managers, purchasing agents, or "anyone who is not a professional in any of the technical areas, but who must understand their applications, their abbreviations, their symbols, and their jargon when undertaking needs analyses, evaluating equipment, talking with vendors, implementing systems, and training personnel." This work contains definitions and descriptions of data processing hardware components, software packages, peripherals, new and unusual interfaces, and general processing methodology. Information "on word processing and its relationship to data processing" is also included.

Prentice-Hall Dictionary of Business, Finance, and Law, edited by Michael Downey Rice. Englewood Cliffs, New Jersey: Prentice-Hall, 1983. Intended "for business people who deal with the law, and for lawyers who deal with business," this work is also useful for students of business and law, engineering, economics, and public administration. It includes a wide range of business subjects, for example, corporate and environmental law, personnel profit-sharing plans, insurance, and taxation.

Private Secretary's Encyclopedic Dictionary, edited by the Prentice-Hall Editorial Staff, revised by Mary A. DeVries. 2nd ed. Englewood Cliffs, New Jersey: Prentice-Hall, 1978. This work contains information on all aspects of secretarial practice, covering everything from "color coding" to "records management." "Entries have been grouped into six major subject areas [Office Procedures, Written Communication, Business Law, Accounting and Finance, Real Estate and Insurance, and Reference] and further arranged within these sections into eighteen categories representing the principal fields of business."

Abstracts

Abstracts for Social Workers (1965–). Published quarterly by the National Association of Social Workers, this abstract contains a subject and author index. Topics are divided into six categories, of which "Fields of Service" is the largest.

Abstracts on Criminology and Penology (formerly *Excerpts Criminologica*) (1961–   ). This is "an international abstracting service covering the etiology of crime and juvenile delinquency, and control and treatment of offenders, criminal procedure, and the administration of justice."

Air Pollution Abstracts (1970–1976). Compiled by the Air Pollution Technical Information Center of the Environmental Protection Agency, this work contains a subject and author index and surveys periodicals, books, hearings, investigations, and other legislative actions.

Applied Ecology Abstracts (1974–   ). Compiled monthly by Information Retrieval Limited, this abstract reviews 5,000 journals for appropriate articles. Subject categories include terrestrial and aquatic resources, control, agrochemicals, grasslands, wetlands, and pollution and pollutants.

Biological Abstracts (1926–   ). This work surveys more than 5,000 journals in every biological field; it also lists new books.

Communication Abstracts (1977–   ). Published four times a year, this work provides a "comprehensive source of information about communication-related publications worldwide," including articles, reports, and books. Subject categories include advertising, broadcasting, communication theory and practice, journalism, public relations, and radio and television (for example, audiences, effects, programming). It excludes "general film-related topics."

Computer & Control Abstracts (1966–   ). Published monthly, this work "forms the world's major, English-language abstracting service covering the fields of computer and control engineering." It includes more than 35,000 items per year and contains subject, author, and subsidiary indexes.

Criminal Justice Abstracts (1968–   ). Issued quarterly by the National Council on Crime and Delinquency, this volume contains an author and subject index.

Metals Abstracts (1968–   ). Previously known as *Metallurgical Abstracts* (1934–1967), this abstract covers more than 1,000 journals.

Nursing Research. Beginning with the 1960 volume, each issue of this journal has carried "Abstracts of Reports of Studies in Nursing"; the Spring 1959 issue contained "Abstracts of Studies in Public Health Nursing, 1924–1957."

Oceanic Abstracts (1964–   ). This work surveys information on oceans (pollution, food source, oil exploration, geology) found in periodicals, books, and reports from government and private agencies. It was known as *Oceanic Journal* (1964–1967) and *Oceanic Citation Journal* (1968–1971).

Psychological Abstracts (1927–   ). This abstract appears in two, bound volumes a year and offers "nonevaluative summaries of the world's literature in psychology and related disciplines"; it includes a subject and author index. Some of the topics are nervous disorders, motor performance, sex differences, and sleep disorders.

Sociological Abstracts (1952–   ). Issued five times a year, this work divides sociological literature into 31 categories (for example, poverty, violence, women's studies). Issues are bound every three months; it contains a subject and author index.

Solar Energy Update (1978–   ). Published monthly by the Technical Information Center of the Department of Energy (Oak Ridge, Tennessee), these abstracts cover current scientific and technical reports, journal articles, conference papers and proceedings, books, patents, theses, and monographs.

☞ Exercises

1. Find out if your library gives patrons a map or description of its holdings. If it does, bring a copy of the map or description to class. If the library does not offer such a map or description, draw one of your own indicating the location of the circulation desk, the card catalog, the reference room, the stacks, the periodicals room or section, vertical files, government documents, and audiovisuals.

2. Find any book in the library and write a brief description of the steps you took to locate that book—from your search in the card catalog to your actually checking the book out of the library. Refer to your map you used in exercise 1.

3. Using the materials discussed in this chapter, locate the following works in your major. If your library does not have them, select titles that are most closely related your major and explain how they would be useful to you. Prepare a separate bibliography card for each title.
   (a) an index to periodicals
   (b) titles of three important journals or magazines
   (c) an abstract of an article appearing in one of these journals
   (d) a term in a specialized dictionary
   (e) a description or illustration in a specialized encyclopedia
   (f) a film or tape recording
   (g) two government documents
   (h) a story in *The New York Times* or one of the newspapers covered by the *Newspaper Index* which, in the last year, discussed a topic of interest to students in your major.

4. In the subject section of the card catalog find a topic that is subdivided in the way this chapter showed you books on construction are listed. After you do this, divide these subdivisions even further until you have a restricted topic for a research report. Bring your topic to class.

5. Using the subject, author, and title catalogs, find four or five books on the topic you selected for exercise 4. Write a bibliography card for each book.

6. Prepare a list (providing full bibliographic information) of 15 articles for the restricted topic you selected for exercise 4. At least five of these articles should come from periodicals not listed in the *Readers' Guide*.

7. Choose a term that is frequently used in your profession—a technical, scientific, or occupational word or phrase. Then look up its meaning in a (a) specialized dictionary or encyclopedia and (b) general dictionary or ency-

clopedia. You might also check the *Oxford English Dictionary*. Write a brief report (one or two paragraphs) on how these definitions are alike and how they differ—that is, what's left out in the general dictionary and why?

8. Using appropriate reference works discussed in this chapter, answer any five of the following questions. After your answer, list the specific works you used. Supply complete bibliographic information. For books, indicate author or editor, title, edition, place of publication and publisher, date, and volume and page number. For journals and magazines, include volume and page number; for newspapers, precise date and page number.

   1. Who invented the digital computer?
   2. What is biomass?
   3. How many calories are there in an orange?
   4. List three interviews that Henry Kissinger granted between 1968 and 1975.
   5. Whom did *Time* magazine select as "Man of the Year" for 1980?
   6. What is the boiling point of coal tar?
   7. What was the headline in the *New York Times* the day you were born?
   8. List three pamphlets published by the U.S. Department of the Interior from 1983 to 1985 on outdoor recreation.
   9. What was the population of Spokane, Washington, in 1970?
   10. List three articles published between 1984 and 1985 on the advantages of teleconferencing.
   11. Who discovered the neutrino?
   12. What is the first recorded (printed) use of the word *ozone*?
   13. List three articles giving job applicants information on the effective use of body language during an interview.
   14. Who wrote *The Advance of American Nursing* in 1978?
   15. Give the title, date, and page number and author (if listed) of a story in your local newspaper that focused on child abuse.
   16. When was Sandra Day O'Connor appointed to the Supreme Court? Give the exact day and year.
   17. List the titles of three articles on the abuse of credit cards that have appeared in professional journals within the last year.
   18. What is a high key photograph?
   19. Name five plants that have the word *fly* as part of their common name?

9. Write a paraphrase of two of the following paragraphs:
   (a) Deep-fat frying is a mainstay of any successful fast-food operation and is one of the most commonly used procedures for the preparation and production of foods in the world. During the deep-frying process, oxidation and hydrolysis take place in the shortening and eventually change its functional, sensory, and nutritional quality. Current fat tests available to food operation managers for determining when used shortening should be discarded typically require identification of a change in some physical attribute of the shortening, such as color, smoke, foam development, etc. However, by the time these changes

become evident, a considerable amount of degradation has usually already taken place.[2]

(b) Ponds excavated in areas of flat terrain usually require prepared spillways. If surface runoff must enter an excavated pond through a channel or ditch, rather than through a broad shallow drainageway, the overfall from the ditch bottom to the bottom of the pond can create a serious erosion problem unless the ditch is protected. Scouring can take place in the side slope of the pond and for a considerable distance upstream in the ditch. The resulting sediment tends to reduce the depth and capacity of the pond. Protect by placing one or more lengths of rigid pipe in the ditch and extend them over the side slope of the excavation. The extended portion of the pipe or pipes may be either cantilevered or supported with timbers. The diameter of the pipe or pipes depends on the peak rate of runoff that can be expected from a 10-year frequency storm. If you need more than one pipe inlet, the combined capacity should equal or exceed the estimated peak rate of runoff.[3]

(c) The transient nature of the foster child, whether he is in his natural family or after coming into care, is a problem for the nurse who tries to provide adequate health care. Large segments of the child's past may not be known to her. A medical history may be entirely absent or extremely spotty. There may be no record of early childhood shots, serious accidents, illnesses, hospitalizations, allergies, or food dislikes. The child himself is often a very poor source of information. For example, when he talks about his parents, one is unsure whether he means his natural parents, some past foster parents, or the fantasized parents he wished he had.[4]

(d) Police administrators have long recognized the value of computers for records management, crime analysis, manpower deployment, and other vital areas. The ability to manage information over short and long terms is directly proportional to the success of an individual or an agency. Until recently, however, computers have not been financially feasible for most police agencies. The National Crime Information Center (NCIC), established by the FBI in 1967, provided the only computerized resource for many departments. Other police agencies were able to use their state government's computer, but they were required to share it with other agencies. Consequently, only a few programs for law enforcement could be developed.[5]

---

[2] Vincent J. Graziano, "Portable Instrument Rapidly Measures Quality of Frying Fat in Food Service Operations," *Food Technology* 33 (September 1979): 50. Copyright © by Institute of Food Technologists. Reprinted by permission.

[3] U.S. Department of Agriculture, Soil Conservation Service. *Ponds for Water Supply and Recreation* (Washington, D.C.: U.S. Department of Agriculture Handbook No. 387, 1971) 48.

[4] Robert L. Geiser and Sister M. Norberta Malinowski, "Realities of Foster Child Care," *American Journal of Nursing* 78 (March 1978): 431. Copyright by the American Journal of Nursing Company. Reprinted by permission.

[5] Lee McGhee and Glenn Whiteacre, "Microcomputers for Law Enforcement," *FBI Law Enforcement Bulletin* (March 1983): 24.

9

Documenting Sources

To document means to furnish readers with information about the materials (books, articles, pamphlets, films, interviews, questionnaires) you have used for the factual support of your statements. When you document, you acknowledge that you consulted (and profited from) someone else's work and that you are giving readers necessary information about that source. You must provide all the essential facts, such as author's name, title of the work, where and when it was published (or produced), and the precise page numbers where you took the information.

☞ Documentation of Sources

When you document, you transfer the information listed on your note and bibliography cards (see pages 256–260) to the text of your paper and to the list of references at the end of that paper. Documentation, therefore, is a vital step in the process of writing a research paper.

In this chapter we will give you practical and precise directions on what to document and how to do it efficiently and consistently. Of the various systems (or formats) of documentation, perhaps footnoting is the one most familiar to you. In this chapter you will learn about other methods of documenting your sources. The major emphasis, however, will be on the *parenthetical documentation* system advocated by the Modern Language Association. You will find a sample research paper using parenthetical documentation at the end of this chapter.

What Functions Documentation Serves

1. Documentation informs your readers that you consulted experts on the subject and that you relied on the most current and authoritative sources to build your case.
2. Documentation gives proper credit to these sources. Citing works by name is not a simple act of courtesy; it is an ethical requirement and, because so

much of this material is protected by copyright, a point of law. By documenting your sources, you will avoid *plagiarism*—that is, stealing someone else's ideas and listing them as your own. If you are found guilty of plagiarism, you could be expelled from school or fired from your job.

3. Documentation informs readers about a specific book or article you used if they want to read it themselves for additional information or to verify the facts you have listed from that source.

What Must Be Documented?

This question often puzzles writers. If you document the following materials, you will be sure to avoid plagiarism and to assist the reader of your research paper or report:

1. Any direct quotations, even if it is a single phrase or key word. Quotations from the Bible, from Shakespeare, or any literary text should be identified according to the specific work (*Exodus, Merchant of Venice*) and the place in that work (for example, act 3, scene 4, line 23, listed as 3.4.23).
2. Any paraphrase or summary of another individual's written work.
3. Any opinions—expressed verbally or in writing—that are not your own.
4. Any statistical data that you have not compiled yourself.
5. Any visuals that you have not constructed yourself—photographs, tables, charts.

Of course, do not document obvious facts, such as normal body temperature, well-known dates (the first moon landing in 1969; Harry Truman was the thirty-third president of the U.S.), formulas (H_2O; the quadratic formula), or proverbs from folklore ("The hand is quicker than the eye").

☞ Parenthetical and Footnote Documentation

Numerous formats exist for documenting sources. Two of these formats are parenthetical documentation and footnote documentation. The following section will introduce you to parenthetical documentation by contrasting it with the footnote method.

A widely used system of parenthetical documentation is found in the *MLA Handbook for Writers of Research Papers*, Second Edition, edited by Joseph Gibaldi and Walter S. Achtert (New York: Modern Language Association, 1984). Although used primarily by individuals in the humanities, the MLA system is in many ways very similar to the methods of documenting sources in the sciences, technological fields, and business. For that reason this method will be emphasized in this chapter. The MLA system does not recommend footnotes—footnote numbers, footnote pages—to document sources, nor does it contain a bibliography of works the writer may have consulted but has not cited directly in the paper.

Instead, the MLA method uses parenthetical, or in-text, documentation. According to this method, the writer tells readers directly in the text of the paper, at the moment the acknowledgment is necessary, what reference is being cited—by including the author's last name in parentheses together with the appropriate page number(s) from which the information is borrowed. Seeing (Morgan 205), for example, the reader knows that the writer has borrowed information from Morgan, specifically from page 205 of Morgan's work. Such sources (authors' names with page numbers) refer to an alphabetical list of works that the writer has cited in the text of the paper. This list—called "Works Cited" or "References Cited"—is placed at the end of the paper.

As you may recall from other writing courses, when you document using footnotes you insert a slightly raised arabic numeral in the place in the text to which the source refers, like this.[1] The order in which the footnotes are cited in your paper must correspond exactly to the order in which they are listed at the end of the paper on a footnote page, which gives details about author's name, title of the work, and date and place of publication. When readers see a footnote [7], for example, they expect to find information about the particular source for this footnote under [7] on the notes page.

Figure 9.1 shows a paragraph that uses footnote documentation and a section of the footnote page containing information about the footnoted sources. Figure 9.2, on the other hand, shows how the same paragraph is prepared using parenthetical documentation and reprints the relevant section of the Works Cited page.

To provide accurate parenthetical documentation for your readers, you must first prepare a careful Works or References Cited page and then include the documentation in the right form and place in your text. Preparing the Works Cited page and documenting within the text of a paper are discussed in the next two sections.

☞ Preparing the Works Cited Page

Before you can document your sources parenthetically within your paper you must first establish what those sources are. Even though the list of references cited comes at the end of your paper, it is important that you prepare this list before you start to document. By preparing the list first you will know what sources you must cite and what page numbers you must list.

When you prepare your list of references, you must include the information in the following order:

Books	*Articles*
author(s)	author(s)
editor(s)	title of article (put in quotation
title (underscored)	marks)
edition (if second or subsequent)	name of journal (underscored)

place of publication
publisher's name
date of publication

volume number (in arabic numerals)
date of publication
page number(s)

The examples below will show you how to list different types of books and articles.

- *Book with one author*

  Enockson, Paul G. <u>A Guide for Selecting Computers and Software for Small Businesses</u>. Reston, VA: Reston Books, 1983.

Note that no page numbers are listed in this citation because the appropriate page numbers to Enockson's book would be included parenthetically in the paper.

- *Two or more books by the same author*

  Flesch, Rudolf. <u>Art of Readable Writing</u>. New York: Harper, 1974.

  ---. <u>Say What You Mean</u>. New York: Harper, 1972.

When you cite two or more works by the same author, do not repeat the author's name in the second or subsequent reference. Type three hyphens in place of the name and then a period. (List the works in alphabetical order.)

- *Book with two authors.*

  Muggins, Carolyn, and Keith Applebauer. <u>The Art of Interviewing</u>. Chicago: General Books, 1986.

Both authors' names are listed in the order they appear on the title page; do not worry about alphabetical order. But make sure that the first author's name is listed in reverse order.

- *Book with three or more authors*

  Andreoli, Kathryn G., and others. <u>Comprehensive Cardiac Care: A Text for Nurses, Physicians, and Other Health Care Practitioners</u>. St. Louis: Mosby, 1978.

When there are three or more authors, list only the first author's name in reverse order and add et al. or "and others" after the comma following

Fig. 9.1   A paragraph using footnotes to document sources.

Technical writing has expanded rapidly since World War II. The newest market seeking technical writers is in data processing. In fact, it is "one of the fastest growing fields for technical writers."[1] Technical writers are especially in demand to prepare the documentation necessary for computer software systems manufactured by many different companies.[2] In preparing this documentation the technical writer often has to explain complex information to audiences totally unfamiliar with computers. This obstacle is increasingly difficult to overcome because of the growing complexity of computers. To solve this problem, "the technical writer must function like a computer specialist while thinking like a layperson."[3]

Footnotes

[1]Julie Teunissen, "Opportunities for Technical Writers," Computer Outlook 10 (1985): 98.

[2]George Tullos, "Technical Writers and the Needs of the Computer Industry," Journal of Computer Operations 17 (1985): 13.

[3]Mary Bronstein, The New Generation of Technical Writers (San Francisco: Harbor House, 1982) 45.

Fig. 9.2   A paragraph using parenthetical documentation of sources.

Technical writing has expanded rapidly since World War II. The newest market seeking technical writers is in data processing. In fact, it is "one of the fastest growing fields for technical writers" (Teunissen 98). Technical writers are especially in demand to prepare the documentation necessary for computer software systems manufactured by many different companies (Tullos 13). In preparing this documentation, the technical writer often has to explain complex information to audiences totally unfamiliar with computers. This obstacle is increasingly difficult to overcome because of the growing complexity of computers. To solve this problem, "the technical writer must function like a computer specialist while thinking like a layperson" (Bronstein 45).

Works Cited

Bronstein, Mary. The New Generation of Technical Writers. San Francisco: Harbor House, 1982.

Teunissen, Julie. "Opportunities for Technical Writers." Computer Outlook 10 (1985): 98–99.

Tullos, George. "Technical Writers and the Needs of the Computer Industry," Journal of Computer Operations 17 (1985): 13.

the first author's name. When a book has a subtitle, include it. The title and subtitle are separated by a colon as in the example on page 274.

- *Corporate author*

```
National Institute for the Foodservices Industry. Applied
    Foodservice Sanitation. Lexington, MA: Heath,
    1978.
```

A corporate author refers to an organization, society, association, institution, or government agency that publishes a work under its own name, for example, Federal Aviation Administration. In the example above, the institute (often cited as NIFI) wrote the book. Notice how the state is given after the city. This further identification tells readers that the book was published in Lexington, Massachusetts, as opposed to Lexington, Kentucky, or Lexington, Virginia. The name of the state is not used after well-known cities such as Boston, Chicago, or San Francisco. For this reason the writer using the Enockson book—the example under *Book with one author*—cites the state, Virginia.

- *An edited collection of essays*

```
Tyson-Jones, Sandra, ed. The Ten Best Ways to Invest in
    Stocks and Bonds. New York: Merrimack, 1985.
```

The abbreviation "ed." for *editor* follows the editor's name listed in reverse order.

- *An essay included within a collection*

```
Holcomb, Barry T. "Municipal Bonds: A Good Investment
    Opportunity." The Ten Best Ways to Invest in Stocks and
    Bonds. Ed. Sandra Tyson-Jones. New York: Merrimack,
    1985. 321-329.
```

The name of the author of the article in this collection comes first—in reverse order—then the title of the article in quotation marks. Next comes the title of the collection underscored. The editor's name is listed after the title, with "Ed." before her name to indicate that she is the editor. The editor's name is *not* listed in reverse order.

- *An article in a professional journal*

```
Mahlin, Stuart J. "Peak-Time Pay: A Way to Attract and
    Keep Better Part-Time Employees." Bank Administration
    55 (Mar. 1984): 85-88.
```

Note how a reference to a journal article differs from one to a book. The title of the article is in quotation marks, not underscored; no place of publication is listed for a journal. The volume number immediately follows the title of the journal with no intervening punctuation. And the page numbers on which the article is found follow the colon placed after the publication information within parentheses.

- A *signed magazine article*

```
Marcial, Gene G. "Bulls Who Snort at IBM Bears."
    Business Week 2 July 1984: 78.
```

Unlike the more scholarly journal articles, popular and frequently issued magazines (such as *Business Week, Time, U.S. News & World Report*) are listed by date and not volume number. Note again, the page number(s) following the date. No "p." or "pp." should be used with them.

- *An unsigned magazine article*

```
"When Dream Homes Turn into Nightmares." U.S. News &
    World Report 11 Dec. 1978: 43.
```

Many magazine articles do not carry an author's name (or by-line) because they are written by one of the staff members of the magazine. If this is the case, begin with the title of the article. Unsigned works are always listed according to the first word of their title (excluding *a, an,* or *the*).

- *An article in a newspaper*

```
Wittington, Delores. "The Dollar Buys More Vacation
    Overseas This Year." Springfield Herald 30 July 1984,
    late ed.: A10.
```

Give the title of the newspaper as it appears at the top of the first page of the newspaper, including the name of the city if it is part of that title. List the article by day, month, and year, not according to the cumbersome volume and issue numbers. Identify section, page, and edition information for readers. In the example above, readers know that the story appeared in the late edition on page 10 in section A. Sometimes the story you cite will not require these details as the example below on page 2 of a paper that issues one edition per day:

```
Bulkeley, William M. "Data General Corporation Is Ready
    to Introduce Portable Computers with 25-Line Display."
    Wall Street Journal 4 Sept. 1984: 2.
```

- *An article in an encyclopedia*

Truxal, John. "Telemetering." <u>McGraw-Hill
    Encyclopedia of Science and Technology</u>. 5th ed.

Because it is a multivolume, alphabetical work, only the particular edition or year of an encyclopedia has to be listed on the Works Cited page. If you cite the name of the author of an article in an encyclopedia, begin your reference with his or her last name. Some encyclopedia articles are not signed or are signed only with the author's initials (see page 247).

- *A pamphlet*

Boone, Roberta T. <u>Ghetto Children and Their Diets.</u>
    Washington, DC: U.S. Children's Bureau, 1968.

Document a pamphlet the same way you would a book.

- *A film*

<u>Understanding Emphysema</u>. Sound filmstrip. New York: Eye
    Gate Media, 1978. Order number TP835. 37 min.

Underscore the title of a film and include the distributor and order number. If you indicate the length of the film—45 min., 1 hr., 10 min., include this information last.

- *Radio or television program*

<u>Sixty Minutes</u>. CBS News. 7 Oct. 1984.

"The Dilemma." <u>Rich Man, Poor Man</u>. PBS. WTQA,
    Springfield. 21 Apr. 1985.

Underscore the title of a program but put an individual episode in a series within quotation marks, as in the title from *Rich Man, Poor Man* above. (In your Works Cited page, *Sixty Minutes* would be listed under S.)

- *Computer program*

Smith, Judith. <u>Learner's Guide to Computer Graphics.</u>
    Computer software. Tulsa: General Computers, Inc.,
    1985.

- *A published interview*

```
Zeluto, Thomas. "Interview with Former Budget Director."
    Findlay Magazine, Feb. 1985: 2-4.
```

Begin with the name of the individual being interviewed. Then indicate the title of the interview.

- *An unpublished interview*

```
Jensen, Barbara. Professor of Physics, Berry College.
    Telephone interview. 15 May 1985.
```

Begin with the name of the individual—in reverse order—and then indicate how and when the interview was conducted.

- *A questionnaire*

```
Questionnaire for Secretaries. Distributed between
    5-10 Oct. 1985 by Seager Construction Company.
```

How to Alphabetize the Works in Your Reference List

Your list of references must be in alphabetical order to enable readers to find them quickly. Here are some guidelines to follow when you alphabetize your list.

1. Make sure that each author's name is in correct alphabetical sequence with the author's (or the first of multiple authors) names in reverse order. Jones, Sally T., not Sally T. Jones.

2. Hyphenated last names should be alphabetized according to the first of the hyphenated names.

   Grundy, Alex H.
   Mendez-Greene, A. Y.
   Mundt, Jill.

3. List corporate authors as you would names of individuals, but do not invert the corporate name.

   Marine Fisheries Association.
   Nally, Mark.
   National Bureau of Standards.
   Nuttal, Marion.

4. List names beginning with the same letters according to the number of letters in each name—the shorter names precede the longer ones.

Lund, Michael.
Lundford, Sarah.
Lundforth, Jeffrey.

5. Disregard the article (*a, an, the*) when you list an unsigned article or a film.

The Cable Television Guidebook. (an unsigned pamphlet, listed under C on the Works Cited page)
The Godfather, Part II. (film)
Harris, Timothy. "Rebates." *The Economist* 25 (1986): 21–30.
"An Improved Means of Detecting Computer Crime." (unsigned article)

☞ Documenting Within the Text

The list of Works Cited does not of course tell readers what you actually borrowed from your sources or where that information is located within a source. To give readers that information you must include documentation within the text of your paper or report. As you write your rough draft(s), make sure that you insert the author's name and appropriate page number(s) for each one of the sources that you use. Be sure also that the information you include parenthetically within the text—names, page numbers, short titles—precisely matches the information you supplied under Works Cited for the end of your paper or report. Double-check the spelling of names, page numbers, and publication data against the titles on your Works Cited page. If you fail to document within your text, you are guilty of plagiarism; and if your documentation is incorrect or incomplete, readers will doubt the reliability of your work.

In-text documentation is a relatively simple and straightforward matter. Keep your documentation brief and to the point so you do not interrupt the reader trying to get through your work. In most cases, all you will need to include is the author's last name and appropriate page number(s) in parentheses that usually come at the end of the sentence. For unsigned articles or radio and television programs, you would use a shortened title in place of an author's name. Note in the following example that no mark of punctuation appears before the parentheses and that a period follows them. Also, no "page" or "p." or comma comes between the author's name and the page number within the parentheses.

```
About 5 percent of the world's population has diabetes
mellitus, and 25 percent of the world's population act as
carriers of the disease (Walton 56).
```

Seeing this parenthetical documentation, the reader will expect to find the title and publication information about Walton's study correctly listed after Walton's name on your Works Cited page.

```
Walton, J. H. Common Diseases of the World. New York: Medical
    Books, 1985.
```

The number after Walton's name in the parenthetical documentation refers to the page number where the information you cite can be found.

You may refer to the same work more than once in your paper or report. For second or subsequent references you will use the same method of documentation. As in the Walton example above, you will place Walton's name and the appropriate page number—even if it is the same as in the previous reference(s)—within parentheses following the borrowed information. Of course, if you include Walton's name within the sentence, there is no need to repeat it in the parentheses; all you need do is give the page number. The exact placement of the author's name within the sentence will be discussed later.

If you are using a work that has two authors, list both their last names parenthetically:

```
Tourism has increased by 21 percent this last quarter thanks to
individuals passing through our state on their way to the
World's Fair (Muscovi and Klein 2-3).
```

If one of the works you use has three or more authors, list just the first author's last name in parentheses followed by et al. or "and others" and the page number(s).

```
An understanding of ergonomics has revolutionized the design of
office furniture (Brodsky et al. 345-47).
```

If the work you are borrowing from has a corporate author, use a shortened version of the name within the parentheses as in the following example where "Commission" replaces "Commission on Wage and Price Control":

```
Salaries for local electricians were at or above the national
average (Commission 145).
```

In all of the preceding examples, the names of the authors have appeared in parentheses. However, you may cite the author's name within your text. If so, there is no need to repeat it parenthetically. Within parentheses include the appropriate page number(s) only. The following examples show three different ways of citing an author's name in the text and indicate how writers can document page references.

> Clausen sees the renovation of downtown areas as one of the most challenging issues facing city governments today (29).

> As Clausen notes, the renovation of downtown areas is one of the most challenging issues facing city governments today (29).

> The renovation of downtown areas, according to Clausen, is one of the most challenging issues facing city governments today (29).

Similarly, if you list the title of a reference or anonymous work within the text of your paper, you need not repeat it for your parenthetical documentation.

> According to the <u>Encyclopaedia Britannica</u>, Cecil B. deMille's <u>King of Kings</u> was seen by nearly 800,000,000 individuals (3: 458).

The first number refers to the volume number of the *Encyclopaedia Britannica;* the second points to the page number of that volume. In this case, the writer wisely gives both volume and page numbers to indicate that the information is listed under deMille and not the title of the film.

If you are citing information from two or more works by the same author, you will have to inform readers clearly from which work a particular fact or opinion comes. Let's say that you used information from the following works:

> Howe, Grace. <u>The Management of an Office</u>. New York: Smith, 1984.
>
> ———. "Systems Control for Small Businesses." <u>The Modern Office</u> 15 (1985): 67–81.

You have a number of ways to tell readers from which specific work by Grace Howe you are borrowing material.

1. Cite the author's name, short title, and page number parenthetically:

> Communication stations are important in an office to provide a maximum flow of information (Howe, <u>Management</u> 132).

Note that a comma follows the author's name when you also cite a title within parentheses.

2. Mention the author's name in your sentence and a short title and page number within parentheses:

```
Howe thinks communication stations are important in an office
to provide a maximum flow of information (Management 132).
```

3. Give the author's name and a shortened title in the text with only the page number included parenthetically:

```
According to Howe's article "Systems Control," productivity
increases by at least 20 percent after each training session
involving data processing techniques (71).
```

Occasionally you will have to cite two sources at the same time to document a point. Include the names of the authors of both sources just as if you were listing them individually but separate each source with a semicolon.

```
The use of salt domes to store radioactive wastes has come
under severe attack (Jelinek 56-67; McPherson and Wong 23-29).
```

Be careful, though, that you do not overload readers by including a long string of references in your parenthetical documentation as the following example does:

```
Wind energy has been successfully used in both rural and urban
settings (Bailey 34; Henderson 9; Kreuse 78; Mankowitz 98-99;
Olsen 456-58; Vincenti 23; Walker and Smith 43).
```

Rather than interrupting the reader and bunching references together, consider revising your sentence to make the subject more precise and the references more restricted:

```
Wind energy has long benefited the farm community (Kreuse 78;
Walker and Smith 43). But recent experiments in New York City
have shown the effectiveness of this form of energy for
apartment dwellers, too (Bailey 34; Henderson 9). Similar
experiments in San Francisco also show how wind power helps
urban residents (Mankowitz 98-99; Olsen 456-58; Vincenti 23).
```

If you include a quotation, place the parenthetical documentation at the end of the sentence containing the quotation:

```
Pilmer has observed that coffee "is only mildly addicting in
the sense that withdrawal will not harm you or produce violent
symptoms" (16).
```

Note that the period follows the parentheses, not the quotation marks. Even if the quotation is short and appears in the middle of the sentence, place the documentation at the end of the sentence.

Alvin Toffler uses the phrase "third wave" to characterize the
new scientific and computer revolution (34).

If the material you quote runs to more than four typed lines, set the quotation apart from the text by indenting it and by eliminating the quotation marks. Place the parenthetical documentation after the quotation as in the following example:

L. J. Ronsivalli offers this interesting analogy of how
radiation can penetrate solid objects:

One might wonder how an X-ray, a gamma ray or a cosmic ray
can penetrate something as solid as a brick or a piece of
wood. We can't see that within the atomic structures of the
brick and the wood are spaces for the radiation to enter. If
we look at a cloud, we can see its shape, but because
distance has made them too small, we can't see the droplets
of moisture of which the cloud is made. Much too small for
the eyes to see, even with the help of a microscope, the
atomic structure of solid materials is made of very small
particles with a lot of space between them. In fact, solids
are <u>mostly</u> empty spaces. (20–21)

If you omit anything from a quotation, follow the rules governing ellipses on pages 260–261.

If you take a quotation from any place but the original source (if, for example, the quotation you want to use is included in the book you are citing but originally came from another book or article), you should document that fact by including "qtd. in" in your parenthetical documentation.

The monthly business meeting serves a number of valuable
functions. In fact, perhaps the most important one is that
"chain-of-command meetings provide the opportunity to pass
information up as well as down the administrative ladder" (qtd.
in Munroe 87).

This documentation lets readers know that you found the quotation in Munroe, not in the original work from which these words come.

☞ Documentation in Scientific and Technical Writing

Numerous other formats exist for documenting sources. Many professions publish their own style sheet or book to provide such instruction (for example, the *Publication Manual of the American Psychological Association,* the Council of Biology Editors' *CBE Style Manual,* the *American Institute of Physics Handbook*) or recommend that writers follow the format used in a specific journal. Every professional group, however, would advise writers *against* using the formats and abbreviations found in periodical indexes such as the *Readers' Guide* or the *Applied Science & Technology Index.* The way information is listed in these sources is not offered as a model in documentation. Before you write a paper or submit a report, ask instructors or employers about the format they prefer.

Many professions use the author-date method of documentation or the ordered references method. Like the MLA style just discussed, both methods rely on parenthetical documentation; that is, rather than using footnotes with raised arabic numerals, the particular information about the source is placed directly in the text within parentheses. A brief overview of these two methods will show how this is done.

The Author-Date Method

With this method the writer does not use footnotes or note numbers at all. Instead, information about a reference or quotation is placed in the text of the paper or report. For example:

```
The theory that new housing becomes increasingly expensive as
buyers move farther north has been recently advanced (Jones,
1984, p. 13).
```

The reader sees that Jones advanced this theory in 1984 and specifically on p. 13. If Jones's name were mentioned in the text, "Jones advances the theory that new housing . . . ," only (1984, p. 13) would be listed. To find Jones's work, readers turn to an alphabetical list of references at the end of the paper, report, or article where, under *Jones,* they find a bibliographic entry for the work. As in the MLA system, only works actually cited in a paper are listed in the reference list. If two works by Jones were cited, the references for both of them are given. If they were done in the same year, they are differentiated in the text *and* in the list of references by a lower-case letter *a* and *b.* For example:

```
Housing is increasingly more expensive on the north side than
on the south (Jones, 1984a, p. 22).
```

```
A recent study has established a demographic pattern for small
cities in the Midwest (Jones, 1984b, p. 73).
```

In the accompanying list of references, the two works by Jones might be listed as follows:

> Jones, T. 1984a. The cost of housing on Lincoln's northside. Urban Studies, <u>72</u>:10–24.
>
> Jones, T. 1984b. Demographic density in three Midwestern small cities. Columbia: University of Missouri Press.

According to this method of documentation in the reference list, only the first word of the title (even if it is *a, an,* or *the*) and proper nouns are capitalized. Titles are neither underscored (books, journals) nor put into quotation marks (articles). The volume number of a journal is often underscored or italicized and followed by a colon to separate it from the page numbers that are listed immediately thereafter.

The Ordered References Method

Like the author-date method, the ordered references method uses parenthetical documentation, but uses numbers rather than authors' names to identify a source. The references in a paper are numbered in the order in which they appear. For example,

> Three new products help reduce bacterial infection in restaurant kitchens (7:47).

The 7 indicates that this is the seventh source found in the reference list; *47* refers to the page number of that source. Sources, therefore, are not listed in alphabetical order, as they are in the author-date method. Each time a source is mentioned, the same number is used. If your first cited source is listed again near the middle or end of your paper, or if it is cited three times in a row, it is still listed parenthetically as (1:   ). The page numbers after the colon may or may not change.

☞ Sample Research Paper Using MLA In-Text Documentation

Study the following sample research paper on stress and computer programmers to see how the student author has successfully used the MLA documentation. Compare the references mentioned in the text with the Works Cited page to see how one writer has handled documentation appropriately.

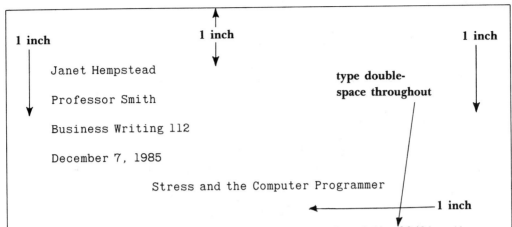

1 inch   1 inch   1 inch

Janet Hempstead

Professor Smith

Business Writing 112

December 7, 1985

type double-space throughout

Stress and the Computer Programmer

1 inch

Since computers were born in the middle of the 1940's, they have gradually become a part of everyone's life. Once computers were used "primarily to construct and control our nation's missiles and spaceships" (Fisher, Origins 6). But now they have made their way into corporations, classrooms, and homes. It is a rare business that does not own at least one microcomputer.

The computer's enormous capacity for information processing offers us more control over our lives, greater freedom of choice, and the opportunity for richer interactions with one another and the world around us (Fisher, "Freedom" 11). In fact, computers could not perform the numerous tasks they do without human management. Without being programmed to do a specific job, the computer would be worthless. In the world of business and industry, the importance of such programming functions makes a computer programmer essential. According to the Bureau of Labor Statistics, there were more than 266,000 jobs for computer programmers in the early 1980's, and the opportunities for future positions are excellent (179).

The computer programmer's job, however, is neither easy nor calm. It is misleading to view the programmer as a cold, robot-like creature who acts more like a machine than a human being. The programmer is often wrongly seen as an individual unthreatened by emotions or untouched by the conflicts and demands that affect other workers. On the contrary, programmers are under considerable stress on their highly technical jobs. This paper will study the problems of job-related stress of computer programmers by discussing (1) the symptoms of stress that can result from programming a computer, (2) the causes of that stress, (3) the effects of that stress for programmers and their employers, and (4) the ways programmers can reduce or control stress on the job.

Symptoms of Stress Related to Computer Programming   2

Stress is any disturbance or reaction that alters the body's normal functions. Katherine Lodjac, a noted researcher on stress management, has said that "Everyone needs some stress to function, but the major question is how we handle that stress" (qtd. in Holden 182). Some people are naturally stress prone; others are not. Recent research has shown that individuals' reactions to potentially stressful situations vary greatly, depending on their personalities (Rice 84–85) What is true for the general population is equally true for programmers. Those who bury themselves in programs, instructions, and codes will be more likely to exhibit the symptoms of stress than those who do not. Programmers who allow separate time for work and relaxation will be freer of stress than their colleagues who do not. Yet regardless of how it is handled, stress is an inescapable part of every computer programmer's life.

Because of their particular work, programmers are especially susceptible to symptoms linked to stress. Programmers have to spend long hours at their terminals, often straining their eyes to focus images on a moving CRT screen. This eye movement can trigger tension around the eyes, headaches, blurred vision, nausea, and fatigue, many of the symptoms identified in a study by Wong and Johnson (108–10). Programmers often complain of severe lower backaches from having to sit for hours in poorly designed chairs and having to slouch into uncomfortable positions to read CRT screens clearly. Perhaps in the future ergonomically designed office furniture will relieve some of this stress for the programmer (Overton 89–90).

If the programmer does not identify and treat stress–related symptoms, even more serious ones may develop. Many symptoms of prolonged or severe stress include spastic colitis, gastritis, migraines, urinary problems, and rashes (Danner and Dworkin 66). For the programmer under constant stress, the risk of high blood pressure, or hypertension, is great (Danner and Dworkin 68). If the programmer has a family history of blood pressure problems, of course the danger is higher. But even if the computer programmer does not have such a history, a few years immersed in the pressures of the job may cause a dangerously elevated blood pressure (Wong and Johnson 109). Besides these physical problems, the programmer under prolonged stress can develop emotional problems that affect job performance, lifestyle, and family life (Rice 81).

Causes of Stress on Computer Programmers

Computer programmers are under almost constant stress.
As we have seen, part of that stress may come from the kinds
of hardware programmers use. But the full cause of the
programmer's stress goes far beyond hardware. Stress is built
into the programmer's very occupation. According to a recent
computer science graduate from Northeast Community College,
now a computer programmer at Denver Industries, "The stress
starts from the day you accept the position" (Ricks's
interview).

Companies have high expectations for their programmers.
They demand perfect work and may not always allow the
programmer sufficient time to debug a program. The importance a
company assigns to programming is, of course, justified. A
company depends on the programmer to develop and test programs
and to prepare instruction sheets for computer operators. The
following job description for a computer programmer from the
Bureau of Labor Statistics points to the stress-producing
responsibilities placed on the individual choosing programming
as a career.

> In hiring programmers, employers look for people who can
> think logically and are capable of exacting analytical
> work. The ability to work with abstract concepts and do
> technical analysis is especially important for systems
> programmers because they work with the software that
> controls the computer's operation. The job calls for
> patience, persistence, and the ability to work with extreme
> accuracy even under pressure. Ingenuity and imagination are
> particularly important when programmers must find new ways
> to solve a problem. (179)

One of the most significant causes of stress for programmers
is working under a deadline to produce a highly technical
document, often on very short notice. The programmer knows that
a delay can seriously affect his or her work—creating a
terrifying backlog—or the work of another individual or
department in the company. As Bob Turnbull, the chief
programmer at Data Processing Corporation, observed, "I once
had an hour to write a program for an important set of
instructions my employer needed when I could have used at least
three hours to get the job finished" (Interview).

The way in which programmers work with others can also
elevate their stress level. In some companies, programmers
work in groups or teams for large, highly technical projects.

This arrangement may be easy and pleasant for the programmer   4
who enjoys interacting with others, thus lessening an
individual programmer's tension and stress. But not every
programmer prefers to work as part of a team. As Lee A. Norris
has observed, the team approach may be more terrifying for the
programmer than the deadline (32). For the highly sensitive
programmer, this situation--loaded with criticism from
peers--may be intolerable. Disagreements and potential delays
may result from team interaction. And when two or more
programmers disagree, because of either egos or errors,
deadlines may be missed and levels of stress may increase. "The
Group Stress Syndrome is . . . a frequent and disturbing
occurrence at many large plants" (Norris 33).

Effects of Stress for Programmers and Their Employers

Stress on the job can have many serious side effects for
both programmer and employer. On-the-job stress can lead
employees to adopt potentially unhealthy ways of handling
stress. In a survey published in Industrial Psychology Review,
the most frequently reported harmful methods for coping with
stress were overeating, overdrinking, smoking, drug use, and
"perpetual anger to thwart what the individual perceives
as a growing number of personal attacks" (Danner 73). These
unhealthy reactions to stress can seriously hurt programmers
and their work.

When stress attacks the programmer, the employer also
suffers. A weakened or harried programmer is more likely to
make mistakes. Brown and Rosenbaum argue that repeated
exposure to highly stressful situations--like programming--
can temporarily lower an individual's IQ (112). This may be the
reason why more mistakes are made by employees under stress.
Even a slight error by a programmer can cost the company time
and money: "Last year a single programming error resulted in
our having to redo the payroll for the first week of March--a
six-hour job" (Ricks's interview). If only 1 percent of the
more than 266,000 computer programmers--266--made one error
each week, companies could stand to lose millions of dollars
each year.

Illnesses caused by stress can also significantly increase
absenteeism. The physical ravages of stress--ulcers, fatigue,
hypertension--are responsible for many lost work days. An
employee suffering from stress-induced illnesses may lose as
many as ten to thirty working days each year ("High Costs of
Stress" 29). This lost time spells trouble for the employer

worried about decreased productivity. When the programmer is   5
ill, work in a number of departments may fall behind or an
additional burden is placed on other employees.

How the Computer Programmer Can Control Stress

Stress has been correctly called a disease (Danner 73; Rice
78; Wong and Johnson 106). As we have seen, it is a disease to
which programmers may be particularly vulnerable. In order to
control this disease successfully, programmers must
acknowledge that their symptoms are stress related and then
take steps to control these symptoms. To do this, programmers
must be prepared to make changes in their work habits and in
their attitudes toward work.

On the job, the programmer should in Fisher's words be aware
of "working for long periods of time without a single restful
break" ("Freedom" 12). A few rest periods throughout the day
will help to relieve the programmer's tension and reduce the
level of stress. These rest periods do not have to be long or
costly for the company. Some might be taken right where the
programmer works—"minute vacations" as Ricks calls them
(Interview). Relaxation or breathing exercises, such as those
advocated by Jablonski (8-10), take only a few minutes and can
quickly refresh and relax the programmer. A brief change of
scenery—a short walk to the water cooler, a few steps around a
desk—will relieve eye strain. "Escape from the computer or the
desk even for a few seconds heightens the worker's spirits"
(Jablonski 9).

Vigorous physical activity in the middle of the day can
reduce stress, which, without release, can build up to
monstrous proportions by the end of the day. During lunch
breaks many executives are beginning to jog, play a quick game
of handball, or do calisthenics. Programmers, too, need to
follow this approach.

Many companies now have stress-reduction programs or
psychological counseling services for employees (Rice 84). If
these sessions are available, the programmer should take
advantage of them. These services benefit both the employee and
the company by defusing the worker's tension and thereby
increasing productivity. As Fisher points out in his
influential study The Origins and Development of the Computer
in the Modern World, "Sophisticated hardware can solve many of
our technological problems but the ultimate success of this
hardware depends upon the mental health of human beings who use
it" (169).

The programmer also needs to have a healthy attitude about 6 work. Perhaps one of the greatest causes of stress in technologists' lives is "their desire for perfection" (Danner and Dworkin 65). Some programmers believe that they will be regarded as failures if they write just one bad program. This "Win-or-Lose-Everything Syndrome," as Danner calls it (75), can be devastating. Programmers should not view their future careers on the outcome of a single program. If a program fails, the programmer should adopt an optimistic attitude that the next one will be better (Norris 34).

Conclusion

Because of their highly technical and demanding positions, computer programmers are frequent victims of stress. The symptoms of stress may be eye strain, fatigue, backaches, ulcers, or even more serious, hypertension. Stress may be caused by computer hardware, by unrealistic expectations of employers, and by the programmers' own desire for job perfection. The effects of stress in the workplace are serious for programmers and employers. Confronted with stress, the programmer may develop unhealthy coping mechanisms. Moreover, stress-related diseases can lead to employee absenteeism, costing an employer time and money. While programmers cannot eliminate stress from their lives, they can alleviate it by taking "minute vacations" devoted to relaxation and exercise techniques. Perhaps, though, the most effective antidote for the problems of stress on the job is for programmers to put a healthy distance between their job and their home life.

Works Cited

7

Bureau of Labor Statistics. "Computer Programmers."
    Occupational Outlook Handbook. 1984–85 ed.

Brown, Bernard, and Lilian Rosenbaum. "How Stress Lowers IQ
    Scores." Science Digest 91 (Oct. 1983): 112–14.

Danner, G. T. "Wrong Ways of Coping with Stress: A Survey."
    Industrial Psychology Review 32 (Mar. 1984): 73–89.

––– and Martin Dworkin. "A Correlation of Physical Diseases
    with Stress Factors." Journal of Health and Society 11
    (Jan. 1982): 63–70.

Fisher, Harold. "Computers and Personal Freedom." Computer
    World 31 Jan. 1985: 11–12.

–––. The Origins and Development of the Computer in the Modern
    World. San Francisco: Data-Master, 1984.

"The High Costs of Stress." U.S. News & World Report 10 May
    1983: 29.

Holden, W. A. "When Stress Can Hurt Your Health." McCalls
    Apr. 1981: 182–84.

Jablonski, Margaret. "Exercise Your Stress Away." Healthy
    Executive May 1984: 8–10.

Norris, Lee A. "Together or Apart?: Group Dynamics and
    Deficiencies in the Computer Center." Computer Science 7
    (Oct. 1984): 31–35.

Overton, James P., Jr. "Ergonomics, Office Design, and
    Stress." Today's Office 27 (Feb. 1983): 89–92;
    101–02.

Rice, Berkeley. "Can Companies Kill?" Psychology Today 15
    (June 1981): 78–85.

Ricks, Larrisa. Personal interview. 2 Nov. 1984.

Turnbull, Bob. Personal interview. 8 Nov. 1984.

Wong, Carl, and Janis Johnson. "Stress and Health in Silicon
    Valley." Industrial Management 14 (July 1984): 106–11.

☞ Exercises

1. Ask a professor in your major what he or she regards as the most widely respected periodical in your field. Find a copy of this periodical and explain with examples its method of documentation. How does it differ from the MLA method?

2. Put the following pieces of bibliographic information in proper form according to the MLA method of documentation for Works Cited.
   (a) New York, Hawthorn Publishing Company, John Anderson, 1986, pages 95–97, second edition, *A New Way to Process Film.*
   (b) *American Journal of Nursing,* Karen E. Forbes and Shirlee A. Stokes, July 1984, pages 884–88, "Saving the Diabetic Foot." vol. 84.
   (c) *The FCC Procedures and Manual Book,* the Federal Communication Commission, the Government Printing Office, price $8.50, available after June 1976, page 32, Washington, D.C.
   (d) *Southern Living,* Margaret Holmes Franklin, page 45, May 1985, "News and Reactions from Baltimore County."
   (e) an interview with your local police chief that took place in the college auditorium after he delivered a talk on crime prevention on Wednesday, April 2, 1986.
   (f) today's editorial in your local newspaper.
   (g) Pyramid Films, Inc., *Pulse of Life,* 1986, Santa Monica, California, order number 342br.
   (h) *Essays on Food Sanitation,* John Smith, editor, Framingham, Massachusetts, 3rd edition, pages 345–356, Mary Grossart (author), Albion Publishing Company, "Selection of Effective Chemical Agents," 1986.
   (i) *Time,* "Inflation Eats Up the Pie," page 34, December 1984.

3. Put the bibliographic references you listed in MLA format in exercise 2 into the format that one of the periodicals in your major uses.

4. Convert the bibliographic information given for one article in exercise 1 to the MLA parenthetical style.

10

Summarizing Material

A summary is a brief restatement of the main points in a book, report, article, meeting, or convention. A summary saves readers hours of time, because they do not have to study the original or attend a conference. A summary can reduce a report or article by 85 to 95 percent or capture the essential points of a three-day convention in a one-page memo. Moreover, a summary can tell readers if they should even be concerned about the original; it may be irrelevant for their purposes. Finally, since only the most important points of a work are included in a summary, readers will know they are given the crucial information they need.

☞ The Importance of Summaries

Summaries can be found all around you. Television and radio stations regularly air two-minute news broadcasts—sometimes called "newsbreaks"—to summarize in a few sentences the major stories covered in more detail on the evening news. Popular news magazines such as *Time, Newsweek,* or *U.S. News & World Report* have a large readership because of their ability to condense seven days of news into short, readable articles highlighting key personalities, events, and issues.

Newspapers also employ summaries for their readers' convenience. Daily newspapers such as the *Wall Street Journal* or weekly papers such as *Barron's: A Business and Financial Weekly* or the *National Law Journal* print on the first page brief summaries of news stories that are discussed in detail later in the paper. Some newspapers simply print a column entitled "News Summary" on the first or second page of an issue to condense major news stories. *Facts on File's News Digest* comprehensively summarizes world news every week. Figure 10.1 illustrates a summary that appeared in *Facts on File* about a bill to regulate water

Fig. 10.1   A summary of water safety regulations.

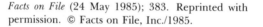

> **Drinking Water Rules Tightened.** The Senate approved by voice vote May 16 a bill that would require the Environmental Protection Agency to set safety limits for concentrations of 64 chemicals in drinking water. [See 1984, p. 793G1]
>
> The agency had been studying the chemicals for three years to determine whether to regulate them. The agency currently had regulations on 22 chemicals in drinking water.
>
> The bill also required distributors of tap water to monitor it for hazardous compounds even if federal standards on some 200 potential contaminants had not been set.
>
> The legislation in addition would provide funding for states to plan ways to prevent pollution of aquifers that were sources of community drinking water supplies.
>
> Similar legislation was being considered in the House, having been approved by the House Energy and Commerce Committee May 15. The House had passed an almost identical measure by a 366–27 vote in 1984.   □

Facts on File (24 May 1985); 383. Reprinted with permission. © Facts on File, Inc./1985.

safety rules. Note how a few paragraphs capture and emphasize the most significant data that may have taken weeks and numerous reports or stories to record. The *Reader's Digest,* one of the most widely read publications in America, is devoted largely to condensing articles, stories, and even books while still preserving the essential message, flavor, and wording of the original.

On the job, writing summaries is a regular and important responsibility. Each profession has its own special needs for summaries. Chapter 15 discusses a variety of reports—progress, sales, periodic, trip, test, and incident—whose effectiveness depends on a faithful summary of events. You may be asked to summarize a business trip lasting one week in one or two pages for your company or agency. A busy manager may ask you to read and condense a ninety-page report so that she will have a knowledgeable overview of its contents. Or your job may require you to keep supervisors informed of congressional action. To do this, you may want to consult a handy reference work such as the *Congressional Quarterly Almanac* that succinctly summarizes Congress's deliberations and decisions and supplies readers with just enough facts to understand what has happened and why. To cite another example of using summaries on the job, acute-care nurses must write a one- or two-page discharge summary for patients who are being referred to another agency (home health, nursing home, rehabilitation center). These nurses must read the patient's record carefully and summarize what has happened to the patient since admission to the hospital. They must note any surgeries, treatments, diagnoses, and prognoses and indicate necessary follow-up treatments (medication, office visits, out-patient care, radiotherapy).

☞ Contents of a Summary

The chief problem in writing a summary is deciding what to include and what to omit. As you have just seen, a summary, after all, is a much abbreviated version of the original; it is a streamlined review of *only* the most significant points. You will not help your readers save time by simply rephrasing large sections of the original and calling the new version a summary. All you will have succeeded in doing is to supply readers with another report, not a summary. You need to make your summary lean and useful by briefly telling readers about the main points—the purpose, scope, conclusions, and recommendations. A summary should concisely answer the readers' two most important questions: (1) What findings does the report or meeting offer? and (2) How do these findings apply to my business, research, or job?

How long should a summary be? While it is hard to set down precise limits about length, effective summaries are generally 5 to 15 percent of the length of the original. The complexity of the material being summarized and your audience's exact needs can help you to determine an appropriate length. To help you know what is most important for your summary, the following suggestions outline what to include and what to omit.

What to Include in a Summary

1. *Purpose.* A summary should indicate why the article or report was written or a convention held or a meeting convened. (Often a report is written or a meeting is called to solve a problem or to explore new areas of interest.) Your summary should give the reader a brief introduction (even one sentence will do) indicating the main purpose of the report or conference.
2. *Essential specifics.* Include only the names, costs, codes, places, or dates essential to understanding the original. To summarize a public law, for example, you need to include the law number, the date it was signed into law, and the name(s) of litigants.
3. *Conclusions or results.* Emphasize what was the final vote, the result of the tests, the proposed solution to the problem.
4. *Recommendations or implications.* Readers will be concerned especially with important recommendations—what they are, when they can be carried out, why they are necessary.

What to Omit in a Summary

1. *Opinion.* Avoid injecting opinions—your own, the author's, or speaker's. You do not help readers grasp main points by saying that the report was too long or that it missed the main point, or that a salesperson from Detroit monopolized the meetings, or that the author in a digression took the Land Commission to task for failing to act properly. A later section of this chapter will deal with evaluative summaries (pages 308--314).
2. *New data.* Stick to the original article, report, book, or meeting. Avoid introducing comparisons with other works or conferences, because readers will expect a digest of only the material being summarized.
3. *Irrelevant specifics.* Do not include any biographical details about the author of an article. Although many journals contain a section entitled "notes on contributors," this information plays no role in the reader's understanding of your summary.
4. *Examples.* Examples, illustrations, explanations, and descriptions are unnecessary in a summary. Readers must know outcomes, results, recommendations—not the specific details leading up to those results.
5. *Background.* Material in introductions to articles, reports, and conferences can often be excluded from a summary. These "lead-ins" prepare a reader of the report for a discussion of the subject by presenting background information, anecdotes, and details that will be of little interest to readers who want a summary to give them the big picture.
6. *Reference data.* Exclude information found in footnotes, bibliographies, appendixes, tables, or graphs. All such information supports rather than expresses conclusions and recommendations.
7. *Jargon.* Technical definitions or jargon in the original may confuse rather than clarify the essential information the general reader is seeking.

☞ Preparing a Summary

To write an effective summary, you will have to read the material very carefully, making sure that you understand it thoroughly. Then you will have to identify the major points and exclude everything else. Finally, you will have to put the essence of the material into your own words. This process demands an organized plan. Use the following steps in preparing your summary.

1. Read the material once in its entirety to get an overall impression of what it is about. Become familiar with large issues, such as the purpose and organization of the work, and the audience for whom it was written. Look at visual cues—headings, subheadings, words in italics or boldface type, notes in the margin—that will later help you to classify main ideas and summarize the work. Also see if the author has included any mini-summaries within the article or report or if there is a concluding summary after an article or a chapter of a book.

2. Reread the material. Read it twice or more often if necessary. To locate all and only the main points, underline them in the work; or, if the work is a book or an article in a journal that belongs to the library, take notes on a separate sheet of paper. (You may find it easier to photocopy articles so that you can underline.) To spot the main points, pay attention to the key transitional words (see page 37 in Chapter 2). Such words often fall into the following categories.

(a) *Words that enumerate:* first, second, third; initially, subsequently, finally; next; another
(b) *Words that express causation:* accordingly, as a result, because, consequently, therefore, thus
(c) *Words that express contrasts and comparisons:* although, by the same token, despite, different from, faster, furthermore, however, in contrast, in comparison, in addition, less than, likewise, more than, more readily, not only . . . but also, on the other hand, the same is true for . . . , similar, unlike
(d) *Words that signal essentials:* basically, best, central, crucial, foremost, fundamental, indispensable, in general, important, leading, major, obviously, principal, significant

Also pay special attention to the first and last sentences of each paragraph. Often the first sentence of a paragraph contains the topic sentence, and the last sentence summarizes the paragraph or provides some type of transition to the next paragraph.

You also have to be alert for words signaling information you do not want to include in your summary, such as the following:

(a) *Words announcing opinion or inconclusive findings:* from my personal experience, I feel, I admit, in my opinion, might possibly show, perhaps, personally, may sometimes result in, has little idea about, questionable, presumably, subject to change, open to interpretation
(b) *Words pointing out examples or explanations:* as noted in, as shown by, circumstances include, explained by, for example, for instance, illustrated by, in terms of, learned through, represented by, such as, specifically in, stated in

3. Collect your underlined material or notes and organize the information into a rough-draft summary. At this stage do not be concerned about how your sentences read. Use the language of the original, together with any necessary connective words or phrases of your own. You will more than likely have more material here than will appear in the final version. Do not worry; you are engaged in a process of elimination. Your purpose at this stage is to extract the principal ideas from the examples, explanations, and opinions surrounding them.

4. Read through your rough draft and delete whatever information you can. See how many of your underlined points can be condensed, combined, or eliminated. You may find that you have repeated a point. Check your draft against the original for accuracy and importance. Make sure that you are faithful to the original by preserving its emphases and sequence.

5. Now put the edited version into your own words. Again, make sure that your reworded summary has eliminated nonessential words. Connect your sentences with conjunctive adverbs (*also, although, because, consequently, however, nevertheless, since*) to show relationships between ideas in the original. Compare this final version of your summary with the original material to double-check your facts.

6. Do not include remarks that repeatedly call attention to the fact that you are writing a summary. You may want to indicate initially you are providing a summary, but avoid such remarks as: "The author of this article states that water pollution is a major problem in Baytown"; "On page 13 of the article three examples, not discussed here, are found."

7. Identify the source you have just summarized. Do this by including pertinent bibliographic information in the title of your summary or in a footnote.

Figure 10.2, a 1,500-word article entitled "Counting on the Census," appeared in the *Journal of American Insurance* and hence would be of primary interest to insurers. Assume that you are asked to write a summary of this article for your boss, a busy insurance executive. By following the steps outlined previously, you would first read the article carefully two or three times and then underscore the most important points, signaled by key words. Note what has been underscored in the article. Also study the comments in the margins; these explain why certain information is to be included or excluded from the summary.

After you have identified the main points, extract them from the article and, still using the language of the article, join them into a coherent rough-draft summary as in Figure 10.3. The necessary connective words added to the language of the original article are underscored. This rough draft then has to be shortened and rewritten in your own words to produce the compact final version of your summary as in Figure 10.4. Only 153 words long, this summary is 12 percent of the length of the original article and records only major conclusions relevant to the audience for the article.

To further understand the effectiveness of the summary in Figure 10.4, review the wordy and misleading summary of the same article in Figure 10.5. The latter not only is too long but also dwells on minor details at the expense of major points. It includes unnecessary examples, statistics, and names; it even adds new information while ignoring crucial points about the function of the census to insurers. But even more serious, this summary distorts the meaning and the intention of the original article. The reader concludes that the article

Fig. 10.2   An original article with important points underscored for use in a summary.

Counting on the Census

Delete introductory material, here used to provide a background

Probably no other people but Americans have such an obsession with constantly counting and cataloguing themselves. With help from computers, we've now got more information about ourselves than ever before: an awe-inspiring amount of information, highly sophisticated and often very specific in nature.

With so much data-mania around, it's no wonder that the most well-known survey, that just-completed, once-a-decade population count conducted by the Census Bureau, is generating more interest than ever. Aside from the controversies—questions about its accuracy and debate over the problem of illegal aliens— <u>Americans are paying attention to the 1980 Census because</u> not only will it confirm our own notions of what we as a nation have become, but also because <u>there's a lot of cold hard cash riding on the results.</u>

Delete details of lesser importance

Important conclusion

Include significant point

This massive <u>survey will document</u>, on both a large and local scale, the <u>far-reaching social changes</u> of the 1970s. It will chronicle what has happened to each of us over the past ten years: if, like other Americans, we've moved often, and ever south and westward; if we've had smaller families, and bought larger homes. The population count will lend a certain sense of continuity or historical perspective to these changes measuring them against nearly 200 years of American demographic history. The fact that <u>the twentieth census will find a majority of one- and two-person households</u> (they numbered nearly half in 1970 and have been on the rise ever since) <u>is all the more remarkable in light of the 1790 count</u>, in which half of all those fledgling American households consisted of six or more people, and only a tenth had one or two persons living alone.

Delete explanations and examples

Important finding

Delete explanation and following quotation

Results from the head count will add depth and specificity to what we already know, filling in the outlines of our broadbrush figures. "Sur-

Journal of American Insurance (Winter 1979/80). Reprinted by permission.

Include "important" information

Delete statistics

Significant conclusion

Key words signaling important application

Delete facts indicating former use

Include financial use

Combine types of programs

Delete examples

Key words "also much" introducing important idea

Include reason why census is so important to insurers

veys may tell you what's happened," says Roger Herriot of the Census Bureau, "the census tells you to whom and where."

The <u>final tally</u> will <u>reveal</u> both small group and small area data—<u>important, useful information</u> that is <u>available nowhere else</u>. A <u>housewife's</u> decision to <u>return to work</u> is <u>significant</u> as part of a <u>national trend</u> (since 1978, half of all American women age 16 and older—42 million of them—were in the labor force); yet it's even <u>more meaningful</u> when also placed <u>in</u> the <u>context</u> of how many other women of the same age, living in the same state, town, or even neighborhood, are also working.

<u>On the more pragmatic side</u>, the census appeals to our more avid interests, as we are urged to stand up and be counted to get our fair share—of political representation, and federal money. The constitutionally mandated count is no longer just a means of changing the boundaries of congressional districts to reflect population shifts; since 1970, it <u>also</u> has been used to <u>determine</u> where and how more than <u>$50 billion in public welfare and federal revenue-sharing money will be spent.</u> <u>Of special interest</u> to insurers are <u>federal programs</u> on <u>vocational rehabilitation, highway safety, law enforcement assistance, energy research and development, and alcohol and drug abuse,</u> which are among the more than 100 programs using census statistics to guide the allocation of funds to states and local communities. Funding for the Cooperative Extension Service, for example, hinges upon a state's rural and farm population; while spending for the Headstart program relies on the number of children of poverty-level families in a particular community.

There is <u>also much</u> that the insurance industry, the <u>property/casualty side of the business</u> included, can <u>cull</u> from the reams of data generated by <u>the census</u>. The count will be industry's first opportunity for a look at the demographic trends of the next decade, trends which will play a <u>major role in shaping business</u> in the years just ahead. This glimpse into the future will allow insurers, known for their sophisticated application of data, to <u>evaluate</u>—and <u>antici-</u>

Include relevant change affecting insurers; delete statistics

Include these "two areas" significantly highlighted by key words "vital role"

Another important point, but delete the statistics

Emphasize insurance needs

Include main point here

"Although" points to subordinate idea; delete it and examples

Major observation

Delete examples of types of questions

Restatement of main point

Delete explanation

pate—these changes on a local level, where business is actually conducted.

One change in store for this country is that, in the 1980s, the elderly as a group will be getting larger. Between 1950 and 1978, that part of our population age 65 and older doubled in size, and it is expected to increase even further in the coming years. This means a growing need for more resources to meet the financial and medical requirements of the elderly—two areas where the insurance industry will play a vital role.

Also getting its first few gray hairs will be the "baby boom" generation, whose members now fall into the 25 to 34 age group. The fastest-growing segment of the population, its ranks swelled by 35 percent between 1970 and 1978, according to census figures. Members of this group, who have dominated the social changes of the past 20 years, will again set the pace in the next decade. They'll enter their prime years in terms of earning and buying power, pumping up demand for both durable goods and housing, as well as property insurance to cover their investments.

Indeed, property/casualty insurers will be able to glean some valuable information from the questions asked on this year's census. Although only two relate directly to property insurance (one asks homeowners the annual premium for fire and hazard insurance on their property; another inquires whether the regular monthly mortgage payment includes these payments or not), more than half of all the questions are concerned with housing. Some are general, requesting information on owning or renting, the number of rooms in living quarters, and the type of building; while others are quite specific, asking how you heat your home, which fuel you use for cooking, house and water heating, and how much you pay each month for electricity, water, gas, oil or coal (interestingly, census tests have shown that people tend to overestimate their utility costs).

Compiling housing data has been a census assignment since 1850, yet the emphasis placed on the topic on this year's questionnaire is unprecedented. This is due, in part, to the growing number of requests the Census Bureau has received about housing in general, and shelter costs in particular, according to Census housing expert Bill Downs, who says that federal agencies, as well as state and local governments, are among the big users of this type of information.

Delete example

A 1976 bureau survey found, for example, that the average owner of a mortgaged home was paying 18 percent of his annual income in that year for the mortgage, real estate taxes, property insurance, utilities, fuel, and trash collection. How much that figure will change in 1980, in light of soaring fuel costs, and other factors such as the 45 percent jump in the average price of a new, one-family home, should be

Include main point relevant to insurers

Of less significance, but still include

of wide interest to property insurers, among others.

Also of interest but of somewhat more limited use, will be both the number and size of America's homes. Analysts predict that the 1980 count will find that the number of housing units in this country has increased 20 percent since the last census was taken in 1970: twice the rate of the population growth. Along with an increase in the number of households (at a rate three times as fast as that of the rise in population between the years 1970 and 1978 alone), these figures reflect a continuing decline in the average size of households.

Delete statistics

Include main points

At the same time people are choosing to live with fewer other people, they are also living in larger houses. Between 1970 and 1976, the number of five-room housing units (homes, mobile homes and trailers, apartments, and condominiums) rose from 16.9 to 19.2 million; while homes with seven or more rooms grew in number from 11.9 to 15.9 million.

Delete statistics following this point

Unless a change is imminent, this trend, which reflects to a degree the self-indulgent and free-spending lifestyle cultivated by many during the 1970s, has dire implications for our energy needs, in the future. Fewer people in bigger living areas means energy inefficiency, wasting the energy and resources needed to construct and heat these homes—a loss that increased conservation can only partly remedy.

Delete opinion and qualification

Parallel point

Equally ominous in view of the energy

Key phrase for audience Include essential point	crunch, <u>and of interest to automobile insurers,</u> is the fact that <u>the 1980 census should show no let-up in America's dependence on the car as a means of transportation.</u> In 1975, of the 73 million households in the U.S., nearly 63 million had at least one automobile, according to cen-	
Delete statistics	sus bureau figures. <u>Further, owning a home seems to go hand in hand with owning a car:</u> nearly all homeowners have at least one car,	
Key word indicating another conclusion	while <u>renters are</u> considerably <u>less likely to purchase a vehicle.</u> Moreover, the number of two-car households more than doubled between 1960 and 1975, and is expected to have	
Delete clarifying statistics	jumped even higher in the years since.	
Key word emphasizing results	The <u>final report, however, may shed light on one transportation alternative.</u> <u>Questions on the number of one-ton trucks and vans, and on whether people</u> who use cars, trucks, or vans to	
Key reference to audience's use of information	get to work <u>ride with other people</u> (and if so, how many) <u>will give transportation planners as well as auto insurers some insight into the extent of car and van pooling.</u> This <u>information</u> is the <u>first step in learning how to encourage</u> more people to try <u>this energy-efficient way for commuting.</u>	
Not an essential point	Of course, insurance companies use many sources of information other than the once-a-decade census to keep themselves abreast of	
Brief restatement of article thesis	important demographic changes. <u>Yet insurers,</u> like many other businesses, <u>still count on the census</u> and the more than 300,000 pages of resulting statistics to tell them where we've been and where we as a nation are going.	

	1970	1980	% Change
Population of the U.S.	207,976,452	222,000,000 (est.)	9%
No. of Housing Units in the U.S.	69,000,000	86,000,000 (est.)	23%
No. of Households in the U.S.	64,000,000	79,000,000 (est.)	26%

Delete information in tables—used only for support

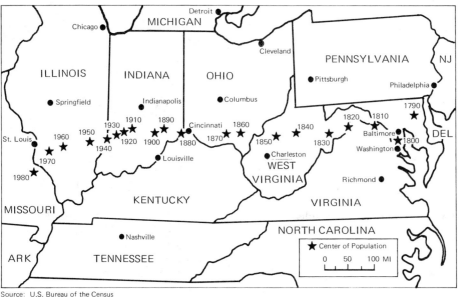

Source: U.S. Bureau of the Census

Delete this caption explaining map—not essential to article.

Westward Ho!

If the United States were a gigantic table, and everybody stood up right now where they lived, where would the table balance? This may seem like a question of demographic trivia, but in 1980 it will take on historical importance as the nation's center of population moves, for the first time, west of the Mississippi River.

After the first census in 1790, the center of population was just east of Baltimore. It has moved slowly westward ever since, reflecting the general migration of the population. After the 1970 census, it was just south of Mascoutah, Illinois, about 30 miles east of the Mississippi. After the 1980 head count, the center of population will move across the river and slightly to the south, reflecting the recent population shift to sunbelt states.

Fig. 10.3   A rough-draft summary of Fig. 10.2.

Aside from the controversies about its accuracy, Americans are paying
attention to the 1980 Census because there's a lot of cold, hard cash
riding on the results. This massive survey will document far-reaching
social changes. The twentieth census will find a majority of one- and
two-person households, all the more remarkable in light of the 1790 count.
The final tally will reveal important useful information available nowhere
else. A housewife's decision to return to work is significant as part of a
national trend, <u>and</u> even more meaningful in context. On the more pragmatic
side, the census count is no longer just a means of changing boundaries
<u>but</u> it also affects where $50 billion in public welfare and federal
revenue-sharing will be spent. Of special interest to insurers are federal
programs on vocational rehabilitation, highway safety, law enforcement
assistance, and energy research. There is also much the property/
casualty side of the business can gain from the census, <u>which will</u> play a
major role in business—evaluating and anticipating changes. One change is
that the elderly population will be increasing. This means more
resources—financial and medical—in two areas where the insurance
industry will play a vital role. Also, the 25 to 34 age group, which is the
fastest-growing part of the population, will demand property insurance.
Indeed, property/casualty insurers will glean valuable information from
the questions asked on the census, more than half of all the questions are
concerned with housing. <u>This</u> is an emphasis on the topic of this year's
questionnaire <u>that</u> is unprecedented. How much <u>costs for houses</u> will change
should be of wide interest to property insurers among others. Also of
interest but of somewhat more limited use, the number and size of American
houses <u>have</u> increased. Along with an increase in the number of households,
<u>there is</u> a continuing decline in the average size of households. At the
same time people are choosing to live with fewer other people, they are
also living in larger houses. This trend has dire implications for our
energy needs in the future. Fewer people in bigger living areas mean energy
inefficiency. Equally ominous and of interest to automobile insurers, the
1980 census should show no let-up in America's dependence on the car as a
means of transportation. Further, owning a home seems to go hand in hand
with owning a car; renters are less likely to purchase a vehicle. The final
report, however, may shed light on one transportation alternative.
Questions on the number of trucks and vans and on whether people who use
cars, trucks, or vans to go to work will ride with other people will give
transportation planners as well as auto insurers some insights into the
extent of car and van pooling. This information will be the first step in
learning how to encourage this energy-efficient way for commuting.
Insurance companies use many sources of information, yet insurers still
count on the census.

Fig. 10.4 A final, effective summary of Fig. 10.2.

"Counting on the Census," *Journal of American Insurance* (1979/80): 13–15.

A lot of money rides on the results of the 1980 Census. Information on
where we live, our household size, and women in the work force affects the
funding of federal programs. Because many of these programs concern public
safety, health, and energy, they are of crucial importance to insurers.
Census figures will also help insurers evaluate the needs of future policy
holders. A larger elderly population will require more medical and
financial assistance; the fast-growing adult population (ages 25–34) will
need more property insurance. Since a majority of census questions deal
with housing, property/casualty insurers will learn more about
increasingly expensive home ownership. The census will also tell insurers
that Americans will waste energy by occupying larger homes with fewer
people per household. Moreover, homeowners (as opposed to renters) will
buy more cars for transportation. However, information on vehicle pooling
may give auto insurers encouraging news about energy conservation.

---

says the census is not very valuable for insurers—just the opposite of the point
the article makes. You can avoid such mistakes by not overemphasizing minor
points, by making sure that all parts of your summary agree with the original,
and by not letting your own opinions cloud issues that the author of the article
stresses.

☞ Evaluative Summaries

To write an evaluative summary, follow all the guidelines previously discussed in this chapter except one. The one major exception is that an evaluative summary includes your *opinion*, or view, of the material.

Your instructors and employers may often ask you to summarize and assess
what you have read. In school you may have to write a book report or compile
a critical, annotated bibliography commenting on the usefulness of the material
you found in those sources. On the job your employer may ask you to condense a report and in your summary judge the merits of that report, paying
special attention to whether the report's recommendations should be followed,
modified, or ignored. Your company or agency may also ask you to write short
evaluative summaries of job applications (see pages 138–161) or sales proposals
(see pages 447–455) it has received or perhaps of conferences you might have
attended.

An evaluative summary is usually short—not more than 5 to 10 percent of
the length of the original. Your evaluation should blend in with your summary
of the material. Rather than save all your assessments until the end of your
summary, place them directly next to the summary of the points to which they
apply so that your reader sees them in context. Keep in mind that your evalua-

Fig. 10.5   A poor summary of Fig. 10.2.

Nonessential introductory material	Americans like to keep track of themselves with very advanced computers.
Possible flaw in census not important to article's thesis	People wonder, though, about the accuracy of the census as a counting tool since it sometimes includes information about illegal aliens.
Delete historical background and official's name	But the census, a part of America's demographic history since 1790, does serve many important functions, says Roger Herriot of the Census Bureau in Washington, D.C. The census tells us that half of all American women over the
Minor point in article given major attention; new information and opinion also added	age of 16 work full time. Also, the census establishes our congressional districts, and this is very important for our representatives, especially if they find themselves in a new district because of changes in the population.
Examples not necessary; do not call attention to summary	The census also helps allocate federal funds for such programs as the Cooperative Extension Service and Headstart, which are important programs to list in this summary. Furthermore, the census
Omit opinion	helps predict future insurance business, always a laudable goal. Old
Ambiguous statement; misses main point that elderly group is increasing	people and the young, too, will increase our population. But as far as property insurance is concerned, only two
Distorts article, which deals with value of census for insurers	questions appear on this topic on the census which is almost exclusively concerned with what home fuels, mortgages, and building materials we have.
Statistics not related to insurers	Bill Downs says the government needs this kind of information. It is no wonder since 1976 people paid 18 percent of their income for housing and will
How is all this relevant to insurers?	pay 45 percent in 1980. Extravagant Americans want big houses, big cars, and will waste energy using them. Americans
Distorts article, which emphasizes usefulness of census for insurers; this statement makes census sound unimportant for insurers and overemphasizes a minor point in conclusion of article	should use car pools. But the insurance companies, as the last crucial paragraph of the article states, will not be at too bad a disadvantage since they can rely on other sources of information than what is provided in the census.

tions will be considered recommendations. You may also want to include an especially helpful quotation from the original to emphasize the kind of recommendation you are making. In evaluating the material, include information on both the content and style of the original. Here are some questions on content and style that you should answer for readers of your evaluative summary.

Evaluating the Content

1. *How carefully is the subject researched?* Is the material accurate and up to date? Are important details missing? Exactly what has the author left out? Where could the reader find the missing information? If the material is inaccurate, will the whole work be affected or just a part of it?
2. *Is the writer or speaker objective?* Are conclusions supported by evidence? Is the writer or speaker following a particular theory, program, or school of thought? Is this fact made clear in the source? Has the author or speaker emphasized one point at the expense of others?
3. *Does the work achieve the goal?* Is the topic too large to be adequately discussed in a single talk, article, or book? Is the work sketchy? Are there digressions, tangents, or irrelevant materials? Do the recommendations make sense?
4. *Is the material relevant to the audience for whom you are writing your evaluative summary?* How would that audience use it? Is the entire work relevant or just part of it? Why? Would this work be useful for all members of your agency or only those working in certain areas? Why? What answers offered by the work would help to solve a specific problem you or others have encountered on the job?

Evaluating the Style

1. *Is the material readable?* Is it well written and easy to follow? Does it contain helpful headings, careful summaries, and appropriate examples?
2. *What kind of vocabulary does the writer or speaker use?* Are there many technical terms or jargon? Is the language precise or vague? Would your audience have to skip certain sections that are too complicated?
3. *What visuals are included?* Charts? Graphs? Photographs? Are they used effectively? Are there too many or too few of these visuals?

Figures 10.6, 10.7, and 10.8 contain evaluative summaries. Note how the writer's assessments are woven into the condensed version of the original. Figure 10.6 contains a student's opinions of an article summarized for a class in office management procedures. Figure 10.7 shows an evaluative summary in memo format written by an employee who has just returned from an out-of-town seminar. Another kind of evaluative summary—a book review—is shown in Figure 10.8. Many journals print book reviews to inform their professional audiences about the most recent studies in their field. Reviews condense and

Fig. 10.6   An evaluative summary of an article.

R. Alec Mackenzie and Billie Sorensen, "It's About Time . . ." The
Secretary 40 (January 1980): 12–13.

According to this practical article, secretaries can find ways to decrease
interruptions that rob them and their bosses of time. Instead of practicing
an open-door policy, managers could save time by observing a "quiet hour"
to curtail drop-in visitors and calls. Secretaries could help their bosses
during this time by restricting drop-in visitors and handling minor
details. Many valuable suggestions are given on how secretaries can
further save their bosses' time by arranging and limiting meetings.
Because secretaries' desks are located in busy areas, partitions could
control some of their interruptions. But the authors wisely point out that
managers forced to use the same arrangement lose privacy and flexibility.
Partitions are unsuitable for conferences, encourage socializing, and are
uneconomical. This readable and profitable article suggests techniques
that will help all office personnel to save one of the manager's most
valuable assets—his or her time.

assess books, reports, government studies, tape cassettes, films, and other materials. The short review in Figure 10.8 comments briefly on style, provides clarifying information, and explains how the book is developed.

Minutes

Minutes of a meeting are a special type of summary. If you are appointed secretary at an office meeting or for a committee or organization to which you belong, you will be required to submit to members of that group an official record of the actions taken. That record, known as the minutes of a meeting, is distributed usually within twenty-four or forty-eight hours after the meeting has adjourned. Copies of the minutes will be on file as a matter of record. Minutes help individuals recall what happened at a previous meeting and assist them to prepare for a forthcoming one.

The way in which a meeting is conducted may be governed by highly formal parliamentary procedures known as *Robert's Rules of Order*. Usually, though, business and community meetings are less formal. Still, certain matters of protocol generally are observed at meetings. For example, a chairperson (or convener) usually brings a list of topics to be discussed; this list is known as the *agenda*. Participants then make *motions* (proposals) about these and other topics and then approve, modify, or vote against them. "I move that we accept the Acme Corporation's bid on the two new heating units"; "I would like to change the wording of the original motion to read 'All employees on the night shift will receive a $0.75 per hour differential.'" Each motion is then *seconded* (endorsed) by another member of the group. A member who cannot attend may send a *proxy* (substitute) to vote. A motion may be *carried* (passed), defeated, withdrawn, or *tabled* (postponed).

Fig. 10.7 An evaluative summary of a seminar.

SABINE COUNTY HOSPITAL
Sabine, TX 77231

TO: Marge Geberheart, R.N.   SUBJECT: Evaluation of Physical
      Director of Nurses   Assessment Seminar
FROM: Paul Danders, R.N. *P. D.*   DATE: September 15, 1985

On September 7, Doris Gandy, R.N., and Rick Vargas, R.N., both on the staff of Houston Presbyterian Hospital, conducted a practical and worthwhile seminar on physical assessment. The one-day seminar was divided into three units: (1) Techniques of Health Assessment, (2) Assessment of the Chest Cavity, and (3) Assessment of the Abdomen.

Techniques of Health Assessment

Four procedures used in physical assessment--inspection, percussion, palpation, auscultation--were carefully defined and demonstrated. The instructors also stressed the proper use of the stethoscope and the ways of taking a patient's medical history. We were asked to take the medical history of the person next to us. Such return demonstrations, which were used throughout the seminar, meant we did not have to wait until we returned to work to practice our skills.

Assessment of the Chest Cavity

After we inspected the chest externally, we discussed the proper placement of hands for percussion and palpation and the significance of various breath sounds. Using stethoscopes, our instructors helped us identify areas of the lung. We also listened to and identified heart sounds. The film we saw on examining the heart and lungs was ineffective, since it included too much detailed information for the seminar participants.

Assessment of the Abdomen

The instructors warned that the order of examination of the abdomen differs from that of the chest cavity. Auscultation, not percussion, follows inspection so that bowel sounds are not activated. The instructors then clearly identified how to locate the organs in the abdominal quadrants, how to palpate these organs, and how to detect bowel sounds.

Conclusion

I would strongly recommend this kind of seminar for all nurses whose role in the health care system will include more physical assessments. Although the seminar covered a wealth of information, the instructors admitted that they discussed only basics. In the future, however, it would be better to offer a separate seminar on the chest cavity and another on the abdomen instead of combining the two topics because of the amount of information involved and the time required for demonstrations.

Fig. 10.8   A book review.

Forty Years of Murder: An Autobiography. *By Keith Simpson. Charles Scribner's Sons, 597 Fifth Ave., New York, NY 10017. 1979. 319pp. Cloth/$12.95.*

This is a fascinating, readable narrative of cases handled by one of the world's leading pathologists during his forty years as a medico-legal examiner for the British Home Office. In language largely devoid of technical terminology, the author presents a series of murder cases investigated throughout his career and relates how, working backward by piecing together scant bits of evidence, he reaches a logical conclusion on how a victim met a grim death and identifies the perpetrator. The clues he works with for the most part are bits of flesh, tissue, and bone; soiled or tattered pieces of clothing; or, as in one case, gallstones which were not destroyed by sulphuric acid in which the victim's body was immersed. The cases range from young women whose battered bodies were found in desolate places to a prince of Siam who was assassinated in bed. The author includes some interesting bouts in court with defense attorneys who attempted to discredit his forensic testimony and how he successfully refuted such challenges.

Reproduced from *The Police Chief* magazine, March 1980, with permission of the International Association of Chiefs of Police.

To be effective, minutes should be short. Obviously, you cannot repeat what everyone has said. Readers will be more interested in what participants did than in what they said or how they felt about it. Emphasize the decisions made or the conclusions reached. For example, do not mention any motions (or discussions of them) that have been withdrawn. Nor should you spend a great deal of time on discussions of other motions. Save your readers' time by condensing, in your own words, lengthy discussions and debates (pro and con) as well as reports presented at meetings. Concentrate on the major facts surrounding motions that are voted on. List each motion exactly as it is worded in its *final* form and spell accurately and consistently the names of those proposing and seconding the motion (not T. Richey in one place and Terry Richey or Office Manager Richey in others). Finally, record precisely the vote for each motion (carried 11 to 2).

Be careful not to inject your opinions into the minutes. Avoid any words that interpret (positively or negatively) rather than impartially record. "The motion was offered just in time"; "Each motion was relevant to the topic"; and "The motion was poorly stated" violate the rules of impartiality. When you cite individuals by name, do not qualify their actions, saying that "Mr. Sanders pushed the point for the third time" or that "Mrs. Hicks customarily offered the right solutions." And resist any urge to summarize the usefulness of a discussion or the meeting itself: "The proceedings cleared up a lot of doubts the subcommittee had expressed"; "The meeting was productively short and simple"; or "Little was accomplished today."

What to Include in Minutes

1. The name of the company, agency, group, committee, or organization holding the meeting.
2. The subject of the meeting—regular monthly meeting, special sales meeting, rules committee meeting.
3. The date, time, and place of the meeting.
4. The names of those present and those absent (if your list does not exceed twenty or twenty-five individuals).
5. The time the meeting actually begins once a *quorum* (sufficient number of members present) arrives.
6. The approval or amendment of the minutes of the previous meeting, or that their reading is waived by a majority of those present.
7. Any old business—further discussion and votes on motions tabled at previous meetings.
8. Any reports (merely submitted or read) from *standing* committees (permanent) or *ad hoc* committees (created for a special purpose).
9. The new business of the meeting—motions proposed, seconded, and voted on. Indicate briefly the discussion preceding the motion and then the names of those making and seconding the motion. Indicate how the vote is taken—by secret ballot, a show of hands, by voice—and its results, including the number of abstentions (decisions not to vote on a motion), if any.
10. The business to be continued at the next meeting—reports to be made, motions to be voted on. If studies or other tasks are to be performed in the meantime, specify who is to do them, how, and why.
11. The time the next meeting is to be held—date and hour—and where it is to be held.
12. The time the meeting is officially concluded.
13. Your signature as the recording secretary verifying the accuracy of the minutes.
14. The signature of the chairperson, president, or convener.

Figure 10.9 shows the minutes of a meeting incorporating each of these fourteen parts. Not every meeting, of course, will require all of them. Observe the use of subheadings and the numbering of business issues for the readers' convenience.

☞ Abstracts

The Differences Between a Summary and an Abstract

The terms *summary* and *abstract* are often used interchangeably, resulting in some confusion. This problem arises because there are two distinct types of abstracts—*descriptive abstracts* and *informative abstracts*. The informative abstract is another name for a summary; the descriptive abstract is not. Why? An

Fig. 10.9   Minutes of a meeting.

The City of Hampton

Minutes of the Hampton City Council Open Meeting
February 2, 1986

PRESENT: Thomas Baldanza, Grace Corlee (President), Virginia Downey,
          Victor Johnson, Roberta Koos, Kent Leviche (Secretary), Ralph
          Nowicki, Barbara Poe, Willard Ralston, Daniel Sullivan, Morgan
          Tachiashi, Ruth Vanessa, Wanda Wagner, and Carlos Zandrillia

ABSENT: Millard Holmes, Wendy O'Gorman

The meeting was held in Room 102 of City Hall and began at 7:04 P.M. with
Grace Corlee presiding. The minutes of the previous meeting (January 4,
1986) were approved as read.

OLD BUSINESS

The Council returned to a discussion of a motion tabled at the last meeting
concerning holding open meetings twice a month rather than once a month.
The motion, which was made by Barbara Poe and seconded by Willard Ralston,
was voted on and defeated 9 to 5.

REPORTS

Two reports were given.

Victor Johnson noted that the Downtown Beautification Committee had
conferred with both the State Office of Historical Landmarks and the U.S.
Department of Housing and Urban Development about helping (financial and
architectural planning) Hampton to restore the Brandon Building. Johnson
said he expected to hear from both departments before next month's meeting.

Giving a report on the Zoning Committee, Wanda Wagner observed that
fourteen requests for changes had been submitted in January. The Zoning
Board has already approved ten of them including rezoning South Evans
Street from residential to medical.

NEW BUSINESS

1. The problems with the downtown parking meters were discussed. Besides
   the city's difficulties with maintaining them, local merchants have
   complained that the meters are bad for business. Roberta Koos supplied
   documentation that removing them would decrease city revenue and
   increase parking violations. But Morgan Tachiashi identified greater
   losses to the city from decreased business in the downtown section
   because of the meters. He therefore moved, and Virginia Downey
   seconded, that the parking meters should be removed from the downtown

Fig. 10.9 (Continued.)

section of the city. The motion carried 10 to 4 by secret ballot. Grace Corlee said she would forward an official order to Police Chief Dunn for the removal of the meters effective March 15, 1986.

2. Mary Ricks, President of the Park Ridge Citizens Group, appeared before the Council requesting that automatic traffic lights be installed at the intersection of Brown and Crawford Avenues. After listening to her comments about the dangers to pupils at the Epstein School from speeding cars and the increased flow of traffic from the Granger Furniture Plant, the Council voted unanimously to install automatic signals at the intersection of Brown and Crawford Avenues. A directive was sent to J. T. Adams, Head of the Traffic Department.

3. Congratulations were extended to Carlos Zandrillia for being honored as an Outstanding Citizen by the Hampton Chamber of Commerce.

4. A committee to study ways to increase tourism to Hampton was formed. The committee members appointed were Ruth Vanessa (chairperson), Ralph Nowicki, and Victor Johnson. President Corlee speaking for the Council requested that the committee pay special attention to the use of Lake Hughes in tourism advertisements and asked for a preliminary report in two months.

5. Thomas Baldanza moved, and Virginia Downey seconded, a motion to set aside $3700.00 from the Recreation Department budget for the improvement of equipment at Alice V. Davis Park. The motion carried by a vote of 12 to 1, with 1 abstention.

There being no further business, the meeting was adjourned at 9:37. The next open meeting of the Hampton City Council was set for March 6 at 7:00 P.M. in Room 102 of City Hall.

Respectfully submitted,

Kent Leviche

Kent Leviche, Secretary

Minutes Approved

Grace Corlee

Grace Corlee, President

informative abstract (or summary) gives readers conclusions and indicates the results or causes. Look at the summary in Figure 10.4. It explains why the census is important for insurers—the census helps insurers provide better coverage to specific groups. Informative abstracts are found before long reports, such as the report on robots in industry found on page 514.

A descriptive abstract is short, usually only two or three sentences; it does not go into detail or give conclusions. Hence it is not a summary. A descriptive abstract provides table-of-contents information—what topics a work discusses, but not how or why they are discussed. Here is a descriptive abstract of the article summarized in Figure 10.4 (page 308).

> The census will provide information about changes in America's housing preferences, transportation, and energy needs. This data will be valuable to insurers.

Figure 10.10 contains a group of descriptive abstracts about books of interest to professionals in public welfare. In a few words each abstract tells what kinds of information the books contain, but does not reveal the solutions, plans, views, or recommendations that the authors of these books advance.

Fig. 10.10 Descriptive abstracts of books.

Adult Illiteracy in the United States: A Report to the Ford Foundation
By Carman St. John Hunter and David Harman. New York: McGraw Hill, 1979. 206 pp. $10.95.
  Defines the scope of illiteracy in the U.S.—a problem of major proportions that prevents many disadvantaged poor from being able to deal positively with the demands made by society—and calls for a long-range national strategy to eradicate the problem.

The Adoption of Black Children: Counteracting Institutional Discrimination
By Dawn Day. Lexington, Mass.: D.C. Heath, 1979. 156 pp. $15.95.
  Looks at how the adoption system works and suggests realistic ways of raising the adoption rate of black children.

Community Mental Health in the Social Work Curriculum
By Allen Rubin. New York: Council on Social Work Education, 1979. 84 pp. $4.
  Describes the place of community mental health in our nationwide service delivery system, evaluates suitability of the MSW level curriculum in the U.S., and offers examples of curriculum innovations.

Public Welfare 32 (Spring 1980): 49. Reprinted with permission of the American Public Welfare Association.

Where Abstracts Are Found

1. At the beginning of an article, report, or conference proceedings; on a separate page; or on the title page of the report.
2. On the table-of-contents page of a magazine, briefly highlighting the features of the individual articles in that issue, or at the beginning of the chapter in a book or in advertisements.
3. In reference works devoted exclusively to publishing collections of abstracts of recent and relevant works in a particular field (e.g., *Abstracts of Hospital Management Studies, Science Abstracts, Sociological Abstracts*). See Chapter 8 (page 249) for a discussion of the usefulness and limitations of abstracts.

☞ Conclusion

By following the process of writing a summary presented in this chapter you will acquire an invaluable skill. If done concisely and accurately, your summary will save readers a great deal of time and demonstrate your ability to provide the big picture. This skill will help you in preparing the types of documents stressed in subsequent chapters—questionnaire reports, proposals, and short, long, and oral reports.

☞ Exercises

1. Summarize a chapter of a textbook you are now using for a course in your major field. Provide an accurate bibliographic reference for this chapter (author of the textbook, title of the book, title of the chapter, place of publication, publisher's name, date of publication, and page numbers of the chapter).

2. Summarize a lecture you heard recently. Limit your summary to one page. Identify in a bibliographic citation the speaker's name, date, and place of delivery.

3. Listen to a television network evening newscast and also to a later news update on the same station. Select one major story covered on the evening news and indicate which details from it were omitted in the news update.

4. Bring an article from the *Reader's Digest* to class and the original material it condensed, usually an article in a journal or magazine published six months to a year earlier. In a paragraph or two indicate what the *Digest* article omits from the original. Also point out how the condensed version is written so that the omitted material is not missed and does not interfere with the reader's understanding of the main points of the article.

5. Assume that you are applying for a job and that the personnel manager asks you to summarize your qualifications for the job in two or three paragraphs. Write those paragraphs and indicate how your background and interests are suited for the specific job. Mention the job by title at the outset of your first paragraph.

6. Evaluate the following summary of a speech given at an energy congress. List the writer's use of key words and phrases—those that signal the speaker's main points.

Today's lamps produce 100 times as much light and operate for thousands of hours longer than Edison's original carbon filament lamp did in 1879, General Electric executive Robert T. Dorsey told government, commerce and industry leaders at a meeting of the World Energy Engineering Congress in Atlanta.

Two new areas of technology are being used to increase the light output produced by incandescent filaments, said Mr. Dorsey, manager of lighting technology development at GE's Lighting Business Group, Cleveland.

One deals with the optical design of the bulb, such as the 75-watt elliptical reflector lamp which delivers as much light as a standard 150-watt reflector bulb in a variety of downlight fixtures.

A second area of technological improvement for incandescent lamps is the development of coatings for spherical bulbs which transmit light but reflect infrared back to the filament, Mr. Dorsey said. This allows the filament to be operated at a more efficient temperature and with fewer watts. Laboratory models have been designed which increase the filament efficiency by as much as 20%, the GE executive said.

The most significant development in the fluorescent lamp field, Mr. Dorsey reported, is the combining of a high efficiency 35-watt fluorescent lamp with a new ballast, which incorporates several technological advances. Among these are a formed coil wire that conducts heat away from the inner part of the core and improved circuitry that provides a better wave shape to the lamp. This new ballast/lamp combination cuts energy use 15 to 20%.

In the area of lighting technology, Mr. Dorsey cited the advances made in task and ambient lighting but cautioned about potential drawbacks. One obstacle, he warned, is the problem of acoustical privacy. Another is that most of the direct lighting built into furniture today has the wrong light distribution and creates serious ceiling reflections. Daylight and indirect illumination are being evaluated for ambient lighting, said Mr. Dorsey, but both have glare, efficiency and maintenance problems. Ceiling-mounted fixtures, he maintained, are preferable both in terms of economics and energy.

Great strides are also being made in computer technology and lighting design with the advent of personal computers, Mr. Dorsey noted. Computers are being widely used to design nonuniform lighting layouts, calculate equivalent sphere illumination and predict visual comfort probability for a space. Numerous computer programs also are available for lighting cost analysis to determine payback and return on investment for one lighting system compared with another, and for maintenance programs to calculate the point at which lamps should be replaced and fixtures cleaned, he said.

Control technology was still another area cited by Mr. Dorsey that can mean significant energy and cost savings for management. Most of today's control systems, he believes, need to operate large numbers of lighting fixtures if they are to be economical. The next generation in light control technology, however, will be "smart" fixtures which will know their address and how to obey commands from a central computer or microprocessor, Mr. Dorsey predicted. This means building intelligence into the fixtures in the form of a signal decoder or as a component.

Concluding, the internationally known lighting engineer outlined the important role thermal technology plays in bringing lighting heat under control.

"One should never recommend additional light to provide additional heat for a building since this represents neither a cost-effective nor an energy-efficient option," Mr. Dorsey said. "However, when brought under control, it can have a significant positive impact on a building's heating cycle and a relatively small impact on the cooling cycle."[1]

7. Write a summary of one of the following articles:
   (a) "Microwaves," in Chapter 1, pages 23–25.
   (b) "Intensive Care for Your Typewriter," below.
   (c) "Word Processing for Library Patrons," pages 322–324.

8. Write a descriptive abstract of one of the articles you selected in exercise 7.

Intensive care for your typewriter

By W. Tim Meiers

Are you guilty of carelessness with your typewriter? Carelessness can result in a typewriter that doesn't operate properly and in needless repair calls.

Although typewriters with mistake-correcting capability are becoming increasingly widespread, most secretaries must still cope with hand corrections by (1) erasing, (2) using strike-over correction paper, or (3) using paint-over correction fluid. Surprisingly, these methods for correcting errors can lead to service calls.

How many times, for example, have you been told to move the carriage to one side or the other when erasing and to brush the erasings away from the machine? How often do you follow that suggestion? There's actually a practical, valid reason for such advice. Erasings that fall into the segment can cause slow-striking type bars. The slow-striking type bars will usually be those bars located near the center of the segment where most of the erasings will fall.

Strike-over paper also presents a similar debris problem but less can be done about it; the carriage has to be positioned wherever the strike-over is to be made. When you insert and withdraw strike-over paper, however, patience is indeed a virtue. The coating on the correction paper scrapes off on the cardholders, the type bar guide, and the ribbon vibrator. Like erasings, the scraped off coating can fall into the segment, causing slow-striking type bars.

---

[1] *The Office* Mar. 1980: 211–12. Reprinted with permission.

W. Tim Meiers, "Intensive Care for Your Typewriter," *Today's Secretary* (November 1980): 31. Reprinted with permission of Today's Secretary, Gregg Division, McGraw-Hill Book Company, copyright November 1980.

If patience is advisable when you use correction paper, it's definitely a necessity when you use correction fluid. When mistakes on a page you are typing are "painted over" and the paper is rolled back into typing position *before* the correction fluid has dried, some of the fluid probably will come off onto the feed rolls. Over a period of time, as the feed rolls become coated with correction fluid, they become slick and paper slippage begins to occur. Such slippage is especially noticeable when you are typing near the bottom of a page because the paper is being held by only the front feed rolls.

How frequently do you wave various liquids above your typewriter? As you might guess, liquids spilled into a typewriter can result in expensive service calls. Simply put, soft drinks and sweetened coffee, when spilled, are absolute demons. They act like glue all over your typewriter. Some of the troubles that spilled liquids can cause include slow-striking bars (segment glued), sluggish keys (keyboard glued), and utter mechanical chaos (internal mechanical components glued).

You can also avoid service calls by not using your typewriter as a work bench. While seated at a typewriter, it is not unusual to clip, un-paper clip, hand staple, or unstaple stacks of papers. A common tendency is to perform these tasks near or above the typewriter. A paper clip or staple dropped into a machine can dislocate the springs, lodge under the keyboard, and bind moving parts.

When dealing with paper clips and staples, make an effort to work away from your typewriter. Certainly it takes only a second to use a paper clip or remove a staple, but equally true, it takes only a second to drop one.

Inevitably, certain office situations will require that your typewriter be unplugged and moved. It also seems inevitable that after a typewriter has been moved, it won't operate correctly. But if you are aware of a few simple trouble areas when moving a typewriter (or supervising one being moved), you can prevent more needless service calls.

Most typists know that typewriter keys cannot be depressed when the machine switch is off. This is because connected with the on-off switch of most typewriters is a device called a line lock, which "locks" the keyboard when the switch is off but "unlocks" the keyboard when the switch is on.

What frequently happens when a typewriter is unplugged and moved is that the on-off switch accidentally gets turned on. Remember that on many typewriters the keys *can* be depressed when the typewriter is turned on *even if* the machine is unplugged. The keys that get depressed when a typewriter is being moved are usually the ones near the edge of the keyboard, such as the carriage return, tabulator, shift, and space. Thus when the machine is plugged in again, it jams.

When moving a typewriter, be conscientious of the on-off switch and make certain that it stays off. When carrying a typewriter, keep your thumbs away from the keyboard.

Although this may seem ludicrous, another cause of service calls is a typewriter that is not plugged in. Believe me, it happens. It happens mostly when a typewriter has been unplugged but not moved. Custodians, construction workers, or even fellow office workers might unplug your typewriter for whatever reason and forget to plug it back in. Sure enough, it can be a perplexing situation when your typewriter won't even turn on.

A service call that necessitates merely plugging in a machine can be both embarrassing to you and expensive to a business. Depending on service contracts, a business can be billed—and probably will be billed—for such a service call. Check the plug if your typewriter won't turn on. One final hint is to try a different outlet if your typewriter is plugged in but still won't turn on. Electric outlets can go bad.

Despite all of your efforts to avoid service calls, repairs will occasionally be needed. But even then, you can help if you will learn the names of the different parts of your typewriter as explained in the owner's manual. That way you can be more specific when describing a typewriter malfunction to a repair person. You'll make this person's work easier and have your typewriter back into use sooner.

Word processing for library patrons

By Victor Rosenberg

The microcomputer revolution will have a great impact on all scholars, particularly those in the humanities and social sciences. This will occur because many of the functions that are being altered by the computer, and which will affect all scholarship, are outside the realm of pure and applied science. The processes of information compilation and writing are the essence of much scholarly activity and it is here that automation is making the greatest strides.

Word processing is not merely the automation of the typing process. It is a widely held misconception that word processors are merely fancy typewriters and that they are only of use to clerical processes and workers. The word processor is a tool that will enhance productivity in scholarship as the assembly line expanded productivity in manufacturing. Word processors will not make pedestrian scholars brilliant, but automation will make the brilliant scholar many times more productive by removing the drudgery always present in research and writing.

Imagine the doctoral student who has just completed the first draft of a dissertation (after the usual six years of effort) and submits it to his / her advisor. The advisor sees that all the important material is covered and that it is essentially a solid piece of scholarship, but the presentation is hopeless. The material in chapter 1 should be in chapter 4, the conclusions should come after the analysis of the data . . . . Under conventional conditions, a complete rewrite would require several months of work and a complete retyping of the manuscript. Armed with a word processor, however, the student returns with a completely revised draft the next week. The process of scholarship has been expedited because it is possible to make frequent major revisions and produce a better result. The word processor, with its capacity to copy and relocate blocks of text and to insert new text by command becomes a tool for organizing ideas. It allows the writer to take more chances and removes writer's block since everything that is written can easily be revised.

Even before writing begins, the scholar can make effective use of a microcomputer. It is now possible to take notes directly on a computer. A number of manufacturers are producing portable computers with remarkable power. This author has spent the past three years developing a program to link the user to the on-line library catalog. The resulting software product, the Personal Bibliographic System and its companion program the Data Transfer System, allows the user of the library to look up a work in the

Reprinted by permission from *Library Hi Tech* 6(1984): 25–26.

automated catalog, download the catalog record to his or her microcomputer, and convert the catalog record to a correctly punctuated citation for a bibliography. The automatically generated citation can be merged with manually entered citations and with citations from other catalog systems. The user can add abstracts, index terms, or analytic author or title entries. Citations can be modified as needed. Abstract fields can be used for taking notes and the printing of these notes is under user control. The scholar can even print the citations and accompanying notes on index cards. (So much for the paperless society.)

It is ironic that an automated library will provide a CRT terminal in a prominent location so that a patron can "look up" a bibliographic entry only to copy that information on a slip of paper (thoughtfully provided in a neat little stack next to the terminal). It is equally ironic that where libraries provide a printing terminal, patrons leave with small scrolls of paper on which is recorded valuable information along with much useless data. No editing capability is provided on most such systems, a void that should be overcome for the benefit of scholarship. Patrons should be able to plug their own portable computers into the libraries' terminals and download selective and edited copy to the portable.

As more works are electronically published, it will become possible for another author to copy parts of a work to a microcomputer, presumably with permission and without plagiarism. Such excerpting will be especially useful in studies requiring extensive note taking and the gathering of textual material from many sources. Footnoting can be accomplished automatically. A particularly interesting example of the automation of idea compilation is the project "Xanadu." This is a long-running research project, originally conceived by Ted Nelson, where a work is stored in a computer along with all the works it cites, and the works cited by the cited works, etc. This forms what researchers call "hypertext." It has the unique property of allowing the reader of the main work to refer directly to the cited works in a virtually endless chain. Although the concept of hypertext has not yet proved to be practical, the continuing growth of on-line data base services combined with electronic publishing and electronic mail will eventually provide a network of automated textual resources that will bring hypertext closer to reality. The scholar will have to (and will want to) learn to deal with electronic information as primary research material.

New developments on the technological horizon will soon make the current generation of word processors look ancient. Today a manuscript produced on a word processor still looks like a typed manuscript. The output of the new generation of word processors will be indistinguishable from the product of a printing press. A manuscript can be made to look like a finished typeset document with various fonts of type in various sizes and with sophisticated graphics. This technology will remove control over the appearance of a finished book or article from the publisher and will return it to the author.

This new technology has been under development for almost 15 years. Originally developed by Xerox Corporation, the technology is now widely available with the Apple Lisa and Macintosh computers. Dot matrix and letter-quality impact printers will soon be replaced by this technology—sophisticated laser-driven copy machines that produce output identical to typeset copy.

Librarians cannot afford to be bypassed by the technological revolution in word processing. Libraries have always had a close relationship to scholarship and to the production of that scholarship. It is fitting that libraries be among the first to adopt technology that will support that scholarship. In this context, libraries will have to provide more than typewriters for patron use, and librarians will have to possess skills to teach patrons the use of the new "productivity" devices. As automation moves from technical services to public services, the responsibility for technology will increasingly shift from the "systems librarian" to all reference and circulation librarians. Every professional in a library will need familiarity with "new technology" and will employ that technology if effective service is to be provided the public in its quest of scholarship.

11

Preparing a Questionnaire and Reporting the Results

A questionnaire asks carefully selected respondents to supply answers to a list of questions. Properly designed, questionnaires can be valuable reference tools that measure the changing winds of opinion, help forecast trends, and record a wide range of statistical data. Opinion sampling can be a very elaborate operation requiring expertise in psychology, statistics, and computer science. Some questionnaires, therefore, are costly, sophisticated measuring devices prepared by firms that specialize in gathering information. Other questionnaires, including the ones described in this chapter, are shorter, less formal ones for use on the job or in school. Chapter 11 shows you how to design this type of questionnaire, distribute it, and summarize the results.

☞ The Usefulness of Questionnaires

Questionnaires play a particularly practical role in schools, business and industry, and government. As a student, you may have completed a questionnaire recently asking you to evaluate a course or a program. You can find questionnaires on campus about extracurricular activities, the hours a pool or tennis court is open, the quality of food at a cafeteria. These questionnaires seek to measure student opinion to improve campus life—academic and social. In addition to answering a questionnaire, you may at some point in your college career have to design one to gather information for a report or paper.

Questionnaires in business can increase a company's or agency's sales and profits by determining the consumer's needs. A customer's likes and dislikes readily translate into buying power. To determine what consumers say they want, a store can distribute a questionnaire asking for specific comments on store hours, a particular line or brand of merchandise, credit policies, effec-

Fig. 11.1   A short questionnaire.

We hope that you enjoyed your stay at the Happiness Hotel. In order to make your return visit even more pleasurable, would you please take a few minutes to fill out this question-naire. Thank you. We hope to see you again—soon.

1. How did you find out about the Happiness Hotel?
   ☐ friends   ☐ travel agent   ☐ magazine ads   ☐ billboard

2. What condition was your room in when you checked in?
   ☐ spotless   ☐ satisfactory   ☐ unsatisfactory

3. How would you describe your maid service?
   ☐ excellent   ☐ good   ☐ fair   ☐ poor

4. How was the food in our dining room?
   ☐ superior   ☐ good   ☐ satisfactory   ☐ needs improvement (please specify)

5. Please rank in order of preference the recreational facilities you used often at Happiness Hotel.
   ☐ pool   ☐ tennis courts   ☐ golf course   ☐ horseback riding

Name_____ Room number_____
(optional)

tiveness of salesclerks, services after the sale, and the like. A brief question-naire left in hotel guest rooms is found in Figure 11.1. By analyzing the answers to the short questions, the hotel will know better where to advertise, what to stress in those advertisements, and what to correct or expand in its dining room and recreational facilities.

The government is actively engaged in gathering facts and opinions from its citizens. Every ten years a long questionnaire from the Bureau of the Census asks detailed questions about occupation, income, health, language, and household size. The answers to this lengthy questionnaire help determine how many representatives are sent to Congress and how much of the tax dollar returns to the communities. At the local level, elected officials may distribute questionnaires asking whether a street should be converted into a four-lane highway, a residential area rezoned for shopping facilities, or a new water treatment plant constructed.

Mail Questionnaires Versus Personal Interview Questionnaires

There are some important practical differences between gathering information by mailing a questionnaire or by conducting an interview. Mail questionnaires have the following advantages over interviews:

1. A mail questionnaire can save time and money; it will reach individuals whether they live in your town or across the country. Contrast this method of collecting information with interviews, which require appointments, travel, and time.
2. Mail questionnaires can be completed in the privacy of the home or office by respondents who will not be embarrassed by an interviewer's eye-to-eye questions about age, income, grievances, or preferences. A questionnaire can assure respondents of anonymity and give them more time to answer. Interviews require immediate responses.
3. Properly worded, mail questionnaires can elicit honest, unthreatened responses. An interviewer, on the other hand, might unintentionally sway a respondent by gesture, tone of voice, or facial expression.

Mail questionnaires do have drawbacks. The response rate can be very low, because people may think that filling out the questionnaire is a waste of time. Even if they do fill it out, you never know when respondents plan to return the questionnaire. Generally, though, a mail questionnaire is a much more efficient method of gathering information than is the interview. You can reach more people in less time with less expense. Reserve interviews for times when you have a very small number of people to reach (not more than ten or fifteen) and when those individuals are authorities in the field rather than a cross-section of a population.

Another "personal" type of interview is that conducted over the telephone. Telephone interviews are used when an individual or a company wants to sample a large segment of an audience. Polls about preferences for a candidate or a product are examples. Telephone interviews can be expensive and have drawbacks similar to face-to-face interviews. They also require the interviewer to have skills in asking questions especially suited to the ear rather than the eye.

A Questionnaire's Two Audiences

You have two primary audiences to keep in mind when you prepare a questionnaire: (1) the respondents who will fill out your questionnaire and (2) the individuals who will read your report based on responses to the questionnaire. You may later share the results (or, occasionally, even the report itself) with respondents, but they are not the primary audience for whom you write your report. The primary audience is the person or people who will read your report and make decisions based on it. Respondents usually do not make decisions on how to translate opinions into action. The questionnaire links both groups. For example, students, employees, patients, or customers complete a questionnaire to give facts, express opinions, or emphasize the need for change. Using their responses, you write a report for an employer or elected official who can decide what changes, if any, need to be made.

How carefully you poll your questionnaire audience will determine how successful you are with your report audience. You will not meet the needs of either group if your questionnaire contains gaps. Questionnaires that are vague or confusing will produce a report containing these same weaknesses. When questions are clear, concise, and relevant, respondents have a better opportunity to voice their opinions. Your report readers will not have the time or the inclination to read every questionnaire; they will depend on you to summarize the results accurately, arrange them into neat categories, and provide pertinent recommendations.

Chapter 11 emphasizes the needs of both audiences. It first discusses choosing a restricted topic, writing effective questions, and preparing a successful, attractive questionnaire. It then outlines how to select respondents, distribute the questionnaire, and tabulate the results. How to meet report readers' specific expectations comprises a second part of the chapter and includes guidelines on how to condense information, record numbers properly, incorporate direct quotations, and make recommendations.

☞ Choosing a Restricted Topic

Before constructing your questionnaire, settle on a restricted topic. The key to finding such a topic is remembering that successful questionnaires solicit answers to help solve a particular problem or initiate a specific change. Responses to precise questionnaires can help you to formulate a knowledgeable recommendation to your employer or teacher. The more precise your topic, the more accurate your recommendation will be. A school, business, or agency would soon go bankrupt if it were concerned only with the vague or the general. The topic of your questionnaire should lead to specific action.

If you decided to write a questionnaire on working conditions in your place of employment, you might have found a practical subject but not a precise one. What, specifically, are you interested in learning? You certainly could not write a report on every aspect of your working conditions. Too much is involved. You would spread yourself, your recommendations, and your respondents' answers too thin if you tried to tackle this vast subject. Using the brainstorming technique discussed in Chapter 1 (page 20), you might want to begin by asking yourself what is included in the topic. What smaller, more precise topics can you find in the large issue "working conditions"? Here are some:

supervisors	eating facilities
coworkers' responsibilities	lighting
schedules	safety measures
grievance committees	temperatures
union involvement	profit sharing
fringe benefits	machinery
salaries	coffee/rest breaks
parking	promotions

You would then choose a restricted topic from these subjects and build your questionnaire around it. You will more easily determine respondents' opinions when you ask them about fringe benefits or safety measures than when you ask a series of general questions. The results from your questionnaire, consequently, will be more precise, easier to organize, and more understandable and useful to readers.

Another example might be helpful. Perhaps you want to question respondents about television. That is a roomy topic, so you will have to narrow the range. For example, are you interested in the following different kinds of television stations?

Public Broadcasting System
the three major networks, ABC, CBS, NBC
local television stations
Christian Broadcasting Network
independent stations, English language
independent stations, foreign language
cable television networks

Each of these station types is also a broad subject. You will have to ask yourself exactly what you want the respondents to say about one aspect of television. Again, make a list of suitable topics. Brainstorm to narrow your focus and restrict your topic.

editorials	personalities
children's programs	news broadcasts
schedules	community service messages
advertising rates	sporting events
reception in your area	contemporary issues programs

By developing a questionnaire on one of these much more limited subjects, you will achieve useful results.

☞ Writing the Questions

Relevant Questions

Once you have a topic, ask this question: "Exactly what kinds of information about this topic am I looking for?" Determine the types of information you need and then include only relevant questions. Since many of the questionnaires you will have to write are brief (ten to twenty questions), make every question count. However interesting a side issue may be, keep it off your questionnaire. Why ask respondents to write more than is necessary? And why risk distracting them with irrelevant issues?

To illustrate the process of selecting only relevant questions, let's assume that you work for Speedee Tax Consultants and that your manager wants you to write a questionnaire to determine whether first-time customers approve of what Speedee is doing. You are to ask them questions about your service, the time and money they invested, and their suggestions for improving your service. Anything else is unnecessary. The questions on the left side below would be relevant for your questionnaire; those on the right would not.

Relevant questions	*Irrelevant questions*
Did anyone help you fill out your return last year?	Were you good in high school mathematics?
Did you earn any income outside this state?	Do you consider yourself a blue- or white-collar worker?
Did you have to file a state form this year?	Do you find the state or federal form more confusing?
How did you hear about Speedee?	Have you ever been audited by the IRS?
Did you make an appointment to speak to a Speedee consultant?	Should the IRS extend the filing deadline to June 1?
Was there ample parking room?	What make of car do you drive?
How long did you have to wait if you did not have an appointment?	Did you think the Speedee office was tastefully decorated?
Was the Speedee consultant courteous?	Do you know how much training our employees receive?
Were the consultant's explanations clear or were they given in terms you did not understand?	What kind of calculator did the Speedee consultant use?
On the federal return, were you told whether the short or long form was better for you?	Are there too many tax loopholes for the rich to escape paying their fair share?
Which form (long or short) did you file?	Are you currently employed?
Did the consultant show you how you could lawfully reduce the amount you owed? Increase your refund?	What will you do with your refund, if you receive one?
Were the costs for Speedee's services clearly explained?	Will you have to live on a tighter budget next year?
Did you find those costs fair?	Do you know the name of the owner of Speedee's or how many people we helped last year?
Would you come to Speedee next year?	Would you write your representative in Congress if you had to pay back more than five hundred dollars?

The relevant questions stick to the issue of most concern to the Speedee Tax Consultants—transforming first-time customers into repeat business. The irrelevant questions stray from the issues of service and costs.

Two Basic Types of Questions

In preparing a questionnaire you can write two kinds of questions: open-ended (or essay) questions and closed questions. The following sections define each type of question, provide examples, and point out their benefits and drawbacks.

Open-Ended Questions

An open-ended, or essay, question asks respondents to formulate their answers without being given certain answers to choose among, thus allowing considerable freedom of expression. Open-ended questions use verbs that elicit amplified responses—*appraise, comment on, compare, describe, discuss, estimate, evaluate, explain, judge.* Here are some sample open-ended questions:

> Describe the changes you would make in the registration process at Mesa College.

> Explain which part of your job is the hardest to perform and why.

> Discuss your reasons for attending Monmouth College.

> Judge the effectiveness of a family health practice in which a registered nurse screens patients and decides which ones will see a doctor.

> Comment on how you would correct abuses in the food stamp program in Taylorsville.

Open-ended questions are useful for a variety of purposes. They provide a practical means of soliciting information on subjects that would otherwise require options too numerous (or impossible) to list one by one. For example, the question on why students attend a particular college might bring back ten or twelve different and valid answers, some of which might never have occurred to you. Open-ended questions may also be helpful in gathering information on sensitive professional issues. Furthermore, respondents will reveal how knowledgeable they are, thus allowing you to gauge the value of their opinions.

Open-ended questions can be useful to you even before you write the final version of your questionnaire. You can send a few open-ended questions to a small sample of your respondents who, in their answers, can suggest the topics and options to include on the final questionnaire. And on the final copy of your questionnaire the last question can be an open-ended one asking respondents to comment in detail on any topic covered in the questionnaire or on any topic you may have overlooked.

Finally, open-ended questions are valuable for lengthy studies searching for in-depth responses. If you have much time and relatively few (under fifteen or twenty) respondents, a questionnaire composed mainly of open-ended questions can be rewarding.

But open-ended questions can also pose problems for you and your respondents. This type of question requires a great deal of effort from respondents, who will have to organize, compose, and write their answers. If your question is not direct and sufficiently focused, you could easily get many irrelevant answers from respondents. Moreover, valuable answers might be mixed with these irrelevant comments. Finally, responses to open-ended questions are challenging to summarize, especially when large groups are surveyed, and these responses must be properly coded. (A later section of this chapter, pages 346–349, discusses one way to code, record, and tabulate responses).

Closed Questions

Closed questions offer respondents a limited number of choices to mark or write in. Because closed questions are easier to code and tabulate, they are used more often than open-ended questions. Closed questions fall into the five categories shown on the next pages.

1. Questions that offer only two choices. These are sometimes called dichotomous questions because they present the respondent with a dichotomy, a division of the subject into two mutually exclusive parts. The respondent's choice is limited to one of these two parts. Use this type of question only when the topic can be reasonably understood and explained in either/or terms.

(a) Yes/no questions

Should women be drafted?   yes_____   no_____

Is there a history of breast cancer in your
family?   yes_____   no_____

Have you already taken Banking 117—Princi-
ples of Banking Operations?   yes_____   no_____

(b) True/false questions

People who smoke in public places should be
fined.   true_____   false_____

Licensed Practical Nurses should, after special
training, be allowed to start IV's.   true_____   false_____

Lanse Street must be changed into a one-way
street.   true_____   false_____

(c) Two specific objects or types identified

Which kind of radio station do you prefer?   AM_____   FM_____

Where would you rather shop?   downtown____ the mall____

What kind of stove does your apartment have?   gas_____   electric____

2. Multiple-choice questions. These questions usually offer respondents three to five answers from which to choose. One of those answers can include a category marked "other," asking respondents to list "option not given," "do not know," or "undecided."

What type of domesticated animal would you choose for a pet?
dog_____   cat_____   bird_____   fish_____   other (please specify) _____

Which kind of music do you like to listen to most often?
rock 'n' roll_____ country/western_____ jazz_____ classical_____ blues_____

Which agent called on you last month?
Ms. Kelly_____ Mr. Tumbrel_____ Ms. Baldwin_____ Mr. Lopez_____
No one called_____

How many times a day do you use the Fast Copier?
1_____ 2_____ 3_____ 4_____ more than 4 (please specify)_____

3. Rating-scale questions. These questions ask readers to rate (or evaluate) an individual, program, policy, or option according to a carefully graduated scale. The respondent indicates the degree or extent of his or her opinion by marking an appropriate number on the scale. Always make sure that you specify precisely what the numbers on a scale mean, as the following examples do:

What is your overall view of Mayor Smith's administration?

Excellent   Poor
  1   2   3   4   5

Central College should move from a semester to a quarter calendar.

Strongly   Strongly
 agree   disagree
  1   2   3   4   5

Figure 11.2 includes a questionnaire that uses rating-scale questions exclusively.

4. Ranking questions. With these questions a respondent is asked to assess the relative significance of a series of options and to assign each a value, often by labeling them 1, 2, 3, 4.

Indicate your order of preference for the kind of nursing you would like to do after graduation:
acute care_____ industrial_____ home health_____ school_____

Please rank the following reasons in order of importance as to why you decided to do your banking at First National.
Superteller_____ Saturday hours_____ Totalpak checking_____ Location_____
Investment accounts_____

Rank the following types of cuisine in terms of their appeal to you.
Chinese_____ Mexican_____ Italian_____ French_____ German_____

5. Short-answer questions. These questions require respondents to fill in the blank or write a brief answer.

Give your date of birth (day, month, year): _____

How long have you lived at your current address? _____

Give the names of any community groups to which you belong: _____

What was your chief reason for accepting a job at Peterson's? _____

_____

Which types of power tools do you use most often in your job? _____

_____

What magazine do you read most? _____

Reliable and Valid Questions

Writing questions that work requires much thought and testing. Questions must be reliable *and* valid. A reliable question has the same meaning each time it is asked. It stands the test of time and is precisely and objectively worded so that respondents do not answer it one way on Monday and another way on Wednesday, depending on their mood. Reliable questions are not tricky or filled with loaded words; they are firm and constant. Valid questions do the job the writer intended—that is, they elicit the desired information. An invalid question contains ambiguous, vague words, thus calling into doubt any response made to it. Valid questions are worded so that respondents can understand exactly what the questioner wants to find out. To write reliable and valid questions, follow these suggestions:

1. Phrase your questions precisely. Specify exact quantities, times, or money. The following questions are vague:

Is there enough free swim time at the pool?	yes____ no____
If you were offered a good salary, would you work inside a nuclear power plant?	yes____ no____
Is industry responsible for pollution?	all____ some____ none____

Words like *enough, good, industry,* and *pollution* are vague. Someone trying out for the swim team will interpret "enough" to mean far more hours than does the respondent who goes to the pool two times a week for relaxation. A "good" salary is equally imprecise. The final question does not identify the industry (plastics, textile, oil refinery, paint, rubber), the type of responsibility (through dumping waste into water, into the air, burying contaminants), and the kind of pollution (air, water, food, soil) involved. To correct vague questions, use exact words, as the following revised examples show:

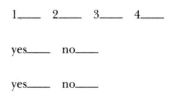

How many hours of free swim time should there be at the pool each day?	1____ 2____ 3____ 4____
Would you work inside a nuclear power plant for $25,000 a year?	yes____ no____
Has All-Fix, Inc., dumped any oil in the marsh near your home within the last six weeks?	yes____ no____

2. Ask manageable questions. Broad questions, such as the following, ask respondents to write ten pages just to begin answering them.

What do you think of our government?

What is your view of the economy?

What insurance will a homeowner need?

Like a vague question, a broad question offers the respondent no direction. The words *government, the economy,* and *insurance* cover a multitude of issues. Wide open, general questions like these really list the whole subject of the questionnaire rather than having each question cover one restricted part of the topic. That one large question needs to be cut into many smaller, more manageable queries. For example, by "government" does the writer mean federal, state, county, or local? And which governmental function, agency, or service (or lack of service) is involved? "The economy" also covers a lot of territory— should the respondent comment on the rate of inflation last month, current interest rates for new home loans, the percentage of unemployment in one city or in one profession, the national trade deficit, or what? When you ask about insurance for a homebuyer, do you expect your respondents to discuss all kinds of insurance—life (term and whole life), medical, personal property, and even burial? A request for such an extensive amount of information in a single essay answer would overwhelm even an actuary (an expert in computing statistics on insurance risks and premiums). Replace a broad question with a more manageable one, such as the following examples show:

Do you agree with a congressional plan to replace our current income tax with a flat-rate tax?	agree_____ disagree_____
Should the United States government store nuclear wastes in salt domes in Blanton County?	yes_____ no_____
What percentage of your monthly house payment goes for mortgage insurance?	_____%

3. Write questions that let respondents decide for themselves. Avoid using loaded words, such as those in the following questions:

Should we continue to waste taxpayers' money on the construction of the George Street Bridge?

Do you believe we have elected too many weirdos to city council?

Isn't it useless to keep making agriculture majors submit daily reports?

Should the government start the draft again to make sure we have quality and quantity in America's armed services?

You reveal an emotional bias and thereby prejudice respondents with words like *waste, weirdos, useless,* or *quality and quantity.* The last example is particularly unfair because it suggests that those who answer "no" are against a strong

America. Keep the language of your questions impartial, as in these revised examples:

Would you vote for continuing work on the George Street Bridge?	yes___	no___
Do you believe your neighborhood is adequately represented on the city council?	yes___	no___
Do you want agriculture majors to submit daily reports?	yes___	no___
Do you believe that there should be a draft?	yes___	no___

A question like the following one demands a "yes" response:

Residents of Lake Mills need better sewerage facilities, don't they?

Rephrase the question to eliminate bias:

Do Lake Mills residents need more sewerage facilities?	yes___	no___

4. Your questions should not insult or indict the respondent. No matter how a question such as "Have you stopped beating your spouse?" is answered, it accuses the respondent of the deed. The following two questions are worded improperly:

Are you still getting speeding tickets?

Have you missed many payments lately?

Do not assume that respondents have ever received speeding tickets or missed payments. Instead, ask if they ever did get a ticket or miss a payment.

Did you ever receive a ticket for speeding?	yes___	no___
Have you ever missed a payment?	yes___	no___

If the answer is yes, you can ask the number of tickets or missed payments in a following question.

5. Do not write a question that requires the respondent to do your research. Courtesy requires that you not ask them to go to any more trouble than it takes to fill out the questionnaire. Avoid questions such as the following:

Ask your immediate superior to supply you with the number of models sold last month and please list that number.

After checking your files and last year's order book, indicate the differences between this year's engine specifications and last year's.

You are imposing on respondents when you require them to speak to other people or when you make them search their records to answer your question.

If you want information from a supervisor, send the supervisor a questionnaire also. If you want to know about last year's records, consult them yourself.

6. Limit your questions to recent events. Do not ask respondents to search their memories to recall opinions they held years ago or to discuss details of an event they may not now clearly remember. The following questions are inappropriate:

Was your apartment building constructed with energy conservation in mind?

What was your exact gas mileage for city driving when you purchased your brand-new Cougar in 1984?

What kinds of meals did you eat on your vacation two years ago?

7. Write questions in language appropriate for your audience. A questionnaire directed to specialists may well include a few technical terms. If respondents are not familiar with your jargon, avoid it. Patients asked about hospital service would have difficulty understanding this question:

Did you receive p.r.n. meds stat?   yes____   no____

Reworded as follows, the question is easier to answer:

Were you given medication when you
needed it?   yes____   no____

Avoid pretentious vocabulary as well:

Did the policy of merit raises exacerbate the crew's feelings?

Translated into understandable terms, this question reads:

Did the policy of merit raises anger the
crew?   yes____   no____

8. Each question should cover only one item. Do not confront respondents with a question that may demand an unnecessary, misleading, or contradictory choice. For example, "Do you prefer the Beatles or the Rolling Stones?" asks respondents to choose between the two. But respondents may like both groups and could not register their preference as the question is worded. Make two separate questions to be sure of obtaining a reliable response. The following question is also poor, because it assumes that respondents will automatically agree with both adjectives:

Are the new models more streamlined
and economical than last year's?   yes____   no____

Some may think that the new models are more streamlined but less economical than last year's, while others think just the reverse. Again, ask two separate questions, and do not use more than one adjective per question.

Overloading a question with a series of short interrogative words (*why? how? where? when? what?*) at its close should also be avoided. For example:

> Approximately how many times have you visted Baltimore in the last year? Why? When? For how long? How did you travel?

If you need the additional information, ask a series of related questions.

9. Do not ask the same question twice. A question writer may think that there is a fine, subtle difference between two questions, but respondents may be unable to detect any difference. Check one question against another. Make sure, for example, that a question 2 does not duplicate a question 7.

> (2) What is your favorite television program?
> (7) Which program do you like to watch most on television?
>
> (2) State your opinion about when placebos should be used.
> (7) What are the values of placebos?

The writer of the first set of redundant questions failed to see that a favorite program means the one you like to watch. In the second pair the writer wrongly saw a difference between the use of placebos and their value. If they are prescribed for specific patients or used in different kinds of tests, these uses automatically characterize the placebo's value.

10. In multiple-choice questions supply respondents with clearly differentiated options. The following question confusingly presents overlapping choices:

> What kind of car do you think gets the best mileage in the city?
> (a) a compact
> (b) a subcompact
> (c) a foreign-made car
> (d) an American car
> (e) a diesel

These choices are not distinct. A compact or subcompact may also be either a foreign or an American car. The same is true of the diesel. Confronted with these options, respondents are asked two or three questions at the same time. Any answer they would give will be invalid and incomplete. Turn such a question into three separate questions:

> (1) Do you think that a compact or a subcompact gets better mileage in the city?   compact_____   subcompact_____
>
> (2) Name any American-made car that equals or surpasses the best import in city mileage. _____
>
> (3) Would a diesel or a gasoline engine be more economical in city driving? diesel_____   gasoline_____

Be especially careful that questions containing an age category do not overlap as the following example does:

Into which age group do you belong:

18–25 _____
25–37 _____
37–45 _____
45–59 _____
59 and over _____

Revised, the question will elicit clear and distinct responses:

Into which age group do you belong:

18–25 _____
26–37 _____
38–45 _____
46–59 _____
over 59 _____

Figure 11.3 contains an effective example of nonoverlapping categories for age.

11. Include all necessary options in multiple-choice questions and those that ask respondents to rank items. Omissions are especially dangerous when respondents are forced to choose between two extremes and are not given enough options for qualified agreement or disagreement. Give respondents the option of saying that they have no opinion or that they see no change. Here are some ineffective questions because they have limited (omitted) options:

Do you believe in the death penalty for all cases?	yes____ no____
How do you feel about the new uniforms we are required to wear?	I like them____ I do not like them____
When is the busiest time at your factory?	morning____ afternoon____

Respondents might believe in or oppose the death penalty, but only in certain circumstances; they may approve of one part of a uniform code and not another; and workers may find a night shift the busiest or want to say that the workload varies from one week to another. As these questions are worded, valid responses are impossible. Make the first question, for example, valid by including differentiated options, as follows:

never ____ murder of a police officer ____ any murder ____ other ____
undecided ____

☞ Writing Effective Instructions

A clear and brief set of instructions should appear at the top of the first page of your questionnaire. To emphasize instructions, you might want to use boldface type or capital letters for certain points. In addition to showing respondents how to fill in their answers, instructions can summarize the topic the questionnaire surveys. A clear set of instructions will emphasize how easy a questionnaire is to answer and will increase your chances of having respondents complete the questionnaire.

Specifically, what should you tell respondents in your instructions? Indicate the kinds of questions they will be answering—multiple-choice, ranking, fill-in-the-blank, essay. Clearly specify how respondents are to indicate their choices—are they to put a check (√) or an X, circle a response, or underscore their answers? Look at the questionnaire in Figure 11.2 for an example of helpful instructions. Also, be consistent in the kinds of questions you use and the method respondents are to employ to answer them. For example, do not force respondents to jump from a group of multiple-choice questions to a set of ranking ones and then back to multiple-choice. Do not have respondents circle some answers and check others. As was noted earlier, many questionnaires composed of one type of closed question conclude with an open-ended question. However, this shift in question type is commonly used and therefore is not disturbing to respondents.

Indicate whether respondents are to sign their names or remain anonymous. If their signatures are optional, say so. Tell respondents the date by which you would like them to return the questionnaire and include a postage-paid envelope. Give your name, address, and telephone number and offer any assistance. Even though this information may duplicate what you have written in a cover letter (discussed on page 346 of this chapter), give it anyway. It is safer to repeat the information than to risk having the respondent not know when and where to return the questionnaire.

Make your instructions as clear as possible. Respondents will be annoyed if they are frequently interrupted by new instructions. If you use a term or concept that must be defined or explained, do it in the question itself. For example:

Is there any encumbrance (lien, mortgage, judgment, or
easement) on your property?   yes____ no____

A question may require some kind of clarification for a respondent to answer it properly:

Which three-hour session is best for you to attend: (*To clarify, add:*
10:00 A.M.____   2:00 P.M.____   8:00 P.M.____)

Fig. 11.2 A portion of a questionnaire with explicit instructions.

National Restaurant Association
1976 Travel Study

Name _____   Code _____

City _____

Directions: Listed below are a number of statements, some of which deal with eating out and restaurants and some of which deal with general life-style factors. For each statement listed, we would like to know whether you personally agree or disagree with the statement.

After each statement, there are five numbers from one to five. The higher the number, the more you tend to disagree with the statement. The lower the number, the more you tend to agree with the statement. The numbers 1–5 can be described as follows:

1. I strongly agree with the statement.
2. I generally agree with the statement.
3. I neither agree nor disagree.
4. I generally disagree with the statement.
5. I strongly disagree with the statement.

For each statement, please circle the number that best describes your feelings about that statement.

(After you complete the questionnaire, please place this form into the attached stamped, self-addressed envelope and mail.)

	Statement	Strongly Agree				Strongly Disagree
1	I prefer to order a la carte rather than order a dinner.	1	2	3	4	5
2	I prefer a service charge be automatically added to my bill rather than having to tip.	1	2	3	4	5
3	I like to try new and different menu items.	1	2	3	4	5
4	I prefer a self-service salad bar to being served a salad at the table.	1	2	3	4	5
5	I usually tip a fixed percentage of the bill regardless of the service I get.	1	2	3	4	5
6	Atmosphere is just as important as the quality of the food in selecting a restaurant.	1	2	3	4	5
7	I love to eat.	1	2	3	4	5
8	I usually look for the lowest possible prices when I shop.	1	2	3	4	5
9	Information I get about a product from a friend is usually better than what I get from advertising.	1	2	3	4	5
10	I have annual physical check-ups.	1	2	3	4	5
11	If a new restaurant opened in town, I would probably be among the first to try it out.	1	2	3	4	5
12	My days tend to follow a definite routine, such as eating meals at a regular time, etc.	1	2	3	4	5
13	I exercise regularly.	1	2	3	4	5
14	I enjoy most of my business trips.	1	2	3	4	5
15	Sometimes I like to do things on the "spur of the moment."	1	2	3	4	5
16	I would like to take a trip around the world.	1	2	3	4	5
17	Most people are in too much of a rush.	1	2	3	4	5
18	I like fast-food restaurants.	1	2	3	4	5
19	When I must choose between the two, I usually dress for fashion, not for comfort.	1	2	3	4	5
20	I often wish for the good old days.	1	2	3	4	5
21	I like to be considered a leader.	1	2	3	4	5
22	A party wouldn't be a party without liquor.	1	2	3	4	5
23	I would rather spend a quiet evening at home than go to a party.	1	2	3	4	5
24	I like to pay cash for everything I buy.	1	2	3	4	5
25	I love the fresh air and out-of-doors.	1	2	3	4	5
26	I follow at least one sport very closely.	1	2	3	4	5
27	I enjoy a cocktail before dinner.	1	2	3	4	5
28	I often check prices, even for small items.	1	2	3	4	5
29	I eat more than I should.	1	2	3	4	5
30	No matter how fast our income goes up, we never seem to have enough.	1	2	3	4	5
31	I often seek out the advice of my friends regarding which brands to buy.	1	2	3	4	5
32	I like to try new and different things.	1	2	3	4	5
33	I feel uneasy when things aren't neat and organized.	1	2	3	4	5
34	I just can't relax when eating out.	1	2	3	4	5
35	I prefer to use a credit card rather than cash when eating out.	1	2	3	4	5
36	Business takes me away from home more often than I'd like.	1	2	3	4	5
37	I am an impulsive individual.	1	2	3	4	5
38	I'd like to spend a year in some foreign country.	1	2	3	4	5

The Restaurant Habits of the Business Traveler, prepared by Edward J. Mayo for National Restaurant Association Consumer Attitudes Survey Series, June 1976. Reprinted with permission of the National Restaurant Association.

☞ Presenting an Attractive Questionnaire

The visual impression your questionnaire makes may determine whether or not respondents complete it. If your questionnaire looks sloppy and is difficult to read and follow, respondents will not bother with it. Therefore, strive to make your questionnaire neat, clear, and easy to read and answer. A questionnaire printed on a faded mimeo sheet or on a copying machine that leaves smudges will not invite quick replies, if any. Avoid reducing the size of your questionnaire on a copying machine in an attempt to save space; the small print will be hard to read and also intimidating. Use plenty of white space, which will be pleasing to the respondents' eyes. Consider having the questionnaire copied on attractive paper by a printer. Proofread meticulously. Also make sure that your questionnaire contains a title, a place for the respondent's name, if desired, and instructions. To review the material discussed so far in this chapter, examine Figure 11.3, a questionnaire distributed by Auburn University. It is a fine example of a carefully worded, clearly arranged questionnaire. Note that because travelers complete this questionnaire while resting at an Alabama hospitality center, the questionnaire does not contain instructions on where and when it should be returned.

☞ Selecting Respondents

Once you have restricted your topic and have determined who will read the results of your questionnaire and why, you will have a better idea about the kinds of individuals you need to question. To receive useful answers, you have to exercise great care in selecting your respondents; you cannot do it haphazardly. Finding appropriate respondents for extremely technical questionnaires involves sophisticated sampling strategies far beyond the scope of this book. Texts on statistics and audience surveys will contain detailed instructions explaining the specialized methods used by pollsters like George Gallup or Lou Harris; such pollsters can survey small sections of the population and predict outcomes with less than a 2 percent margin of error. Although not offering this kind of statistical information on sampling techniques, the following discussion does suggest guidelines you can follow when selecting respondents.

To how many people must you send a questionnaire in order to have reliable results? The answer depends on your statistics. If you are interested in finding out how radiological technicians in a particular hospital feel about rotating shifts, then your respondents would be all the radiological technicians in that one hospital. Similarly, if you want to determine whether your sorority chapter should have a barbeque or dance at the end of the spring term, you would question every member of your chapter. But your respondents may not always belong to such a limited and easily accessible group. Many times you will have to consider a larger audience, whose members could not all be reached and questioned individually. You might want to find out how customers at a

Fig. 11.3   A carefully worded, clearly arranged questionnaire.

AUBURN UNIVERSITY TRAVEL SURVEY
In Cooperation With
Alabama Bureau of Publicity and Information

Dear Traveler: Thank you for traveling in Alabama. We would like to make Alabama a more enjoyable travel destination or vacation state.   Please help us by completing this form **if you have not already done so on this trip.** There is no need to sign your name.

1 Season of travel: 1 ☐ Dec.-Feb.   2 ☐ Mar-May   3 ☐ June-Aug   4 ☐ Sep.-Nov.

2 Home: City _____ State/Country _____

4 Major point *away from home* you are now traveling to/returning from:

6 City/Place _____ State _____

8 Principal mode of travel: 1 ☐ Highway   2 ☐ Air   3 ☐ Bus   4 ☐ Rail

Number and age of persons in party:

Males		Females	
9 ____	Under 14	15 ____	Under 14
10 ____	14-17	16 ____	14-17
11 ____	18-29	17 ____	18-29
12 ____	30-49	18 ____	30-49
13 ____	50-64	19 ____	50-64
14 ____	65 or over	20 ____	65 or over

Activities engaged in while in **Alabama only**—check as many as apply:

21 ☐ Passing thru only
22 ☐ Passing thru, but engaging in the
       following activities checked
23 ☐ Visiting friends/relatives
24 ☐ Visiting historical sites/places
25 ☐ Beaches/swimming
26 ☐ Commercial attractions (gardens,
       amusement parks/centers, etc.)

27 ☐ Business
28 ☐ Golfing
29 ☐ Camping
30 ☐ Boating/fishing
31 ☐ Watching sports
32 ☐ Personal affairs
33 ☐ Attending show or event
34 ☐ Attending convention/meeting

35 ____ How many days spent in Alabama on this trip?

37 ____ How many nights spent in Alabama on this trip?

39 ____ How many days spent on entire trip?

Nights in **Alabama** were (or will be) at:
41 ☐ Home of friend or relative
42 ☐ Motel
43 ☐ Hotel
44 ☐ Rented house/apartment

45 ☐ Cabin/cottage
46 ☐ Tent
47 ☐ Recreational Vehicle
48 ☐ Travel Trailer

While in **Alabama only,** how much will your party spend on this trip for:

49 _____ Lodging

52 _____ Food and beverages

55 _____ Auto expenses (gas, oil, etc.)

58 _____ Entertainment/sightseeing

61 _____ Recreation/sports

64 _____ Other purchases

67 Annual family income (for statistical purposes only):
1 ☐   Under $5,000   4 ☐ $15,000-20,000   7 ☐ $30,000-40,000
2 ☐ $5,000-10,000   5 ☐ $20,000-25,000   8 ☐ $40,000-50,000
3 ☐ $10,000-15,000   6 ☐ $25,000-30,000   9 ☐ $50,000 or over

We welcome your comments. Please write them on the back side.

THANK YOU FOR YOUR HELP

James W. Adams, "Travel in Alabama, 1980," December 31, 1980, p. 56. Reprinted by permission from Dr. James W. Adams, Associate Professor of Transportation, Department of Marketing and Transportation, Auburn University.

certain store feel about a warehouse branch that would sell merchandise at a reduced rate. Certainly you could not question everyone who shops at this store. Or you might be interested in surveying how a certain profession (dairy farmers, dietitians, medical secretaries) would react to a piece of impending legislation. Being unable to question everyone in a particular profession, you would use some form of sampling.

Systematic Random Sampling

The most respected, and valid, way of finding respondents is to follow a *systematic random sampling* technique. Much marketing research is done this way. According to this technique, you choose your target audience or population (all the nurses in your hometown, all students attending your college, all holders of credit cards from a department store), and from this large target population you obtain a cross section by selecting names at random from the group. A random sampling is not like picking names out of a hat. It is far more systematic and fair. For example, from a college directory listing the names of all students enrolled at your school you can choose by random selection every tenth name or, for a smaller margin of error, every fifth name. Thus all respondents (all students listed in the school directory) have an equal chance of being selected for your sample. This equal chance is the heart of the random sampling technique. Figure 11.6 (to be discussed in detail later in this chapter) contains a report on student opinions of a campus newspaper. Because the editors of the paper could not question the entire student body, they sent a questionnaire to every sixth name in the directory and had a 66.66 percent response rate.

Citing another example, let's say that you wanted to find out the customers' preferences for shopping hours at your store. You could stand outside the store and ask everyone who happens to walk by. However, you might talk to people who are visitors to your town and who never have or never will shop at the store, or you could select residents of the town who just stopped to avoid the rain and who never have shopped at the store. To obtain a cross section of those who in fact are customers of the store, you must select as your target population those who are on record as having purchased goods from the store. Perhaps their names are on record as credit card holders. You could then go through the store's list of credit card holders and by random selection pick out names of individuals to whom you will send your questionnaire.

Another way to get a statistically valid sample is to pick names randomly out of the residential listings of your town's telephone book. This selection technique would be a good one if you wanted to find out how a relatively small town or suburb (under 30,000 people) felt about a bond proposal or welfare services.

Stratified Random Sampling

Another valid sampling technique is known as *stratified random sampling*. This approach is used when you have a number of different groups or subgroups to question; it means that you survey each group proportionately. For example, you want to determine opinion about college facilities at a school that was formerly all female but a few years ago became coed. Now the student body is composed of 70 percent women and 30 percent men. In order to obtain a fair cross section of these two groups, you need to question each group according to the same percentage it occupies in the college population. Accordingly, if you sent questionnaires to 100 students, you would make sure that 70 questionnaires went to women and 30 to men to reflect the enrollment percentages at the college.

Quota Sampling

Still another type of sampling technique is known as *quota sampling*. Use this technique with great care. Here you choose an audience almost as one would select a quota. You might question the first twenty-five males and first twenty-five females you meet. Such a sampling might be helpful if, for example, it consisted of customers in a store who all saw a dishwasher and you wanted to get their opinions of that dishwasher. The population is chosen arbitrarily and not selected as carefully as it would be with random sampling, but such a group can help answer your questions, since everyone has seen the product. The problem with quota sampling is that it can lead to a distorted sample in many circumstances. If you wanted to poll student opinion about a campus radio station and all you did was ask for the opinion of ten of your friends who you knew did not like the station, your sample would be biased. These ten friends are a homogeneous (presorted) group that may not truly represent the view of the student body. To get a valid sample, you would have to obtain a larger sample to ensure coverage of a variety of ideas and opinions.

Distributing a Questionnaire

Before submitting your questionnaire to respondents, have someone evaluate it. Ask a student in your major, a teacher, or a coworker to read your questionnaire and tell you whether any of your questions are vague, misleading, or irrelevant. Or you might pretest your questionnaire on a small representative sample of the larger group you want to survey. Have these individuals pay particular attention to the options you list for multiple-choice questions; make sure that the options are reasonable and sufficient. Such screening may take a few days, but in the long run you will save time and energy. If you send out a questionnaire flawed by poorly worded or irrelevant questions, the answers you receive will be of dubious value. You will have to redo the questionnaire, or you may find yourself busy explaining the questions verbally to respondents who call you for help.

Once you are sure that the questionnaire is right, deliver or mail it to your respondents. Decide which approach is more feasible. Delivering the questionnaire in person may create goodwill and may increase your chances of receiving a completed questionnaire back from these individuals. However, when you think a personal visit might influence the content of a reader's response, mail your questionnaire. In any case, make sure your questionnaire reaches respondents at times convenient for them, not just for you. Do not give questionnaires to respondents when other commitments prevent their answering you. For example, students preparing for final or state board examinations will not postpone their studies to fill out your questionnaire. Some large companies close for two weeks in the summer and give all employees and supervisors a vacation. Sending a questionnaire to anyone just before or during shutdown would be pointless. Asking for completed questionnaires around the Christmas holidays is equally ill advised. If you are aware that respondents will be on vacation, busy, or out of town on business, send your questionnaire at another time.

If you mail your questionnaire, send it by first-class mail and include a stamped, self-addressed envelope. Respondents are far more likely to answer when you make it as easy as possible for them. Make certain that the respondents' names and addresses are correct. People will not be inclined to respond if you spell their names incorrectly or if you address someone with a Mr. when that person is a Ms., or vice versa. Some given names (Pat, Leslie, Terry) apply to both men and women. If you are uncertain, omit the courtesy title and write "Dear Pat Hayes" or "Dear Terry Bronti."

When you mail the questionnaire, enclose a cover letter and follow these procedures:

1. Introduce yourself and tell why you are writing.
2. Explain why you are sending the questionnaire.
3. Emphasize how important the respondent's answers are.
4. Tell what benefits the respondent can gain by answering—the most important function of the letter.
5. Discuss the kind of questionnaire you have devised.
6. Ask that the questionnaire be returned by a specified time.
7. Perhaps promise a gift for returning the questionnaire or even send a gift along with the questionnaire.
8. Thank the respondent and promise, if practical to do, to inform him or her of the outcome.

Depending on your topic and the questionnaire you have constructed, you may also want to assure respondents that their answers will remain confidential. Or you might want to promise them anonymity. Not being required to sign their names, respondents will not worry that anyone, including you, knows what they have answered. Figure 11.4 illustrates a sample cover letter sent with a questionnaire.

☞ Tabulating Responses

A new phase of your research begins with the return of your questionnaire. You will have to count the completed questionnaires and keep a record

Fig. 11.4   A cover letter sent with a questionnaire.

CASSON'S DEPARTMENT STORES
1800 South Paulina
Topeka, KS 66620

June 3, 1985

Mr. Howard Anderson
73 Crestway Park Drive
Topeka, KS 66621

Dear Mr. Anderson:

Thank you for purchasing your new Clearvision television set from
Casson's. Your opinions about our store and its service policies are
important to us.

For this reason, I hope you will complete the enclosed questionnaire. It
should not take more than ten minutes of your time, and your answers will
help us provide you with even better service for your set. You will find
twelve multiple-choice questions; but elaborate on any of your answers, if
you wish, on the back of the questionnaire.

The questionnaire is easy to return. Just put it in the enclosed
postage-paid envelope and drop it in the mail. Please return the
questionnaire by June 27, if at all possible. If you have any questions,
please give me a call at 783-3423, extension 41.

Once again, thanks for shopping at Casson's. We will let you know how the
results of the questionnaire will improve our service to you.

Sincerely yours,

Susan Shapiro

Susan Shapiro
Customer Services

Encl. Questionnaire

of specific responses. Tallying is an important link between the questionnaire
and the report; a mistake here can distort (or defeat) all your other efforts.

Responses can be tallied in numerous ways. If the number of your respondents is large and your employer has a computer to tabulate the answers,
consult someone in the computer department during the design stage of a
questionnaire and before you start to count or categorize responses. A com-

puter consultant can suggest different ways of coding options to your questionnaire to make sure the computer will assess them properly. Responses may be translated into numerical (or alphabetical) symbols to represent various responses.

If you are using a small number of respondents for a school or a civic project, or if you lack access to a computer, you will have to tabulate by hand. Your record keeping will be relatively easy if you follow a consistent and orderly system for listing and categorizing information. One good method is to buy a yellow legal-size note pad and use a separate tally sheet for each question on your questionnaire. Write the question and its number at the top of the sheet; directly beneath the question, list the options horizontally (the range of choices) that the question offers. For dichotomous questions you will have two columns; for multiple-choice, as many columns as there are choices. For closed questions, be sure to include the category "no response" in a separate column. If respondents give two contradictory answers to one question, indicate "no response" in your tally since you do not know which answer was intended.

With a separate tally sheet for each question, you will be ready to tabulate responses. When a questionnaire comes in, assign it a code number. The first questionnaire to be returned could be labeled 01, the second 02, the third 03, and so forth. List the identifying numbers (and the names of respondents, if requested, after the numbers) vertically on the left-hand side of each tally sheet. Then, as you check each questionnaire in, you can record a respondent's answer to an individual question in the correct column on the appropriate tally sheet. Figure 11.5 (page 349) illustrates a sample master tally sheet for the first question.

The use of separate tally sheets for each question offers these advantages:

1. You are better able to tabulate, organize, and summarize responses for each question, since all answers to that question are on one sheet.
2. You can more easily check responses against individual questionnaires, since each response is coded by identification and question number.
3. You have the flexibility of comparing responses to various questions by simply pulling tally sheets for these questions and laying the sheets side by side.
4. You have a record of the number of questionnaires returned by any specific date.
5. You can conveniently keep a running tally and will not have to wait until all questionnaires are in to begin counting.

Coding and tabulating open-ended questions may present problems. You will have to make option columns as you go along, but still impose some type of manageable limits on these options. When you read essay answers, use a highlighter pen to mark the exact comments that most relevantly answer the question. Those comments may be buried in useless remarks; the highlighter pen will make the most relevant remarks stand out. A different color highlighter pen can be used to identify statements you foresee quoting directly in your report, thus making them easier to find later.

Fig. 11.5   A tally sheet.

		YES	NO	
	Question 1: Have you ever served in the Armed Forces ?			
01	John Malone		X	
02	Bill Brownly	X		
03	Kathy Rivers	X		
04	Ruth Tapes		X	
05	Henry Stuart		X	
06	Tim Gordon	X		
07	Shirley McManus		X	
08	Debbie Buzak	X		
09	Donald Shatz		X	
10	Willa Jackson		X	
11	Bruce Page	X		
12	Mary Holka		X	
13	Frances Watts		X	
14	Richard Saperstein	X		
15	Terry Myers		X	
16	Roberta Zimmerman		X	
17	Paula Huppard		X	
18	Chris Sholds	X		
19	John Tzarki	X		
20	Billy Lamar	X		
21	Lucy Bennini		X	
22	Marge Appleby	X		
TOTALS		10	12	

☞ Writing Effective Questionnaire Reports

After tabulating the responses, you will have to write a report on your findings. The report should accomplish three functions: (1) summarize the range of responses, (2) draw conclusions, and (3) make recommendations. The report may be brief; a one-page memo or a two-page letter will suffice. At first you may wonder if such a memo or letter is long enough, considering the time and effort you have devoted to the project. But the chief function of the report is to consolidate responses and comment on them. The report should give readers the big picture, of which individual questionnaires are only a part. Providing generalizations based on individual responses, the report does not duplicate every response you have obtained or identify every individual who made a response. If you repeated every scrap of information you obtained, it would be like giving readers the complete set of questionnaires without any necessary summary or commentary.

Writing a report means being selective. Selectivity is not a problem with responses to closed questions. Unless a respondent provides two choices for a dichotomous or multiple-choice question, you will simply tabulate his or her response with all the others you receive. Open-ended questions are more challenging to summarize. Some respondents will include more than you can use; while some of their information may be extremely interesting, it may also be irrelevant. Remember, the report is not a catchall for every comment written in response to an open-ended question. It should reflect only those answers that will help readers reach a decision. Figure 11.6 contains a sample questionnaire survey report and the questionnaire on which it is based. Study this report to see how information is selected and condensed. You might want to refer to this report throughout the following discussion.

Rules for Writing Numbers

Your report will rely heavily on numbers, especially percentages. Spell out the word *percent* in a report; do not use a symbol (%). When listing responses in terms of percentages, express the specific percentage in numbers, not words:

Incorrect: Because of inflation, fifty-eight percent of the workers will not buy a new car this year.

Correct: Because of inflation, 58 percent of the workers will not buy a new car this year.

Remember one exception to listing percentages as figures. If a percentage begins a sentence, write the percentage *as a word:*

Incorrect: 55 percent of the sales force thought that the new lights were easy on their eyes.

Correct: Fifty-five percent of the sales force thought that the new lights were easy on their eyes.

Fig. 11.6   A report and the questionnaire on which it is based.

TO: Professor Marion Andretti
           Faculty Adviser, the Campus Informer
FROM: Debrah H. Hinkel, Bob Banks, Joe Moore, Alice Frantione
SUBJECT: Student Opinion of the Campus Informer
DATE: September 24, 1985

PURPOSE AND SCOPE OF THIS SURVEY

Since a number of us have recently joined the staff of the Informer, we
wanted to assess student opinion of the campus newspaper in order to guide
our future editorial decisions. To obtain a clearer sense of students'
needs, we distributed the enclosed questionnaire to a random sample of 300
students out of 1,800 students at Detroit Community College (DCC) during
the week of September 1—7.

Two hundred students replied, giving us a fair cross section. Respondents
came from every major in occupational education, with a slight majority
(42 percent) representing three areas—nursing, automotive mechanics, and
retail merchandising. Since many of our respondents (53 percent) have
spent at least two semesters at DCC, they are familiar with the campus.

RESULTS OF SURVEY

For the most part, these respondents are loyal readers of the Informer.
Fifty—four percent read each issue of the paper, while 31 percent noted
they look at the paper at least once a week. Only 7 percent said that they
rarely read the Informer. Of most interest to our readers are articles on
campus events and sporting activities, the two areas ranked first and
second by 76 percent of the students. Sixty—nine percent of the students
noted that the ads were the third most significant reason for reading the
paper. News of academic programs and school clubs ranked fourth and fifth
in student interest, according to 71 percent of the respondents.

Most students (68 percent) think the Informer should continue to be
published twice a week, although a small percentage of these students
(21 percent, or 27 students) want to see the Informer come out on Monday and
Friday rather than on Tuesday and Friday. Little support exists for a daily
paper (20 percent) and even less for a weekly or bimonthly one (12
percent). (Students probably think there is not enough news for a daily
paper, and that news would be too old if it appeared a week or two weeks
late.)

The Informer did not receive high marks on its appearance. Forty—six
percent of the students thought the layout was only average, while 23
percent of the students believed that the size of our type is too small,
that the blue color of our paper is too dark, and the placement of articles
is inconsistent. Gladys Potter, a sophomore welding major, offered this
representative comment: "It's hard to follow a story when it is continued
on one or two other pages, because the subsequent headlines aren't always
clear." A related complaint deals with our photographs. Although 27
percent of the students thought we use enough pictures, 42 percent would

Fig. 11.6   (Continued.)

like to see us use more. "Stories are more enjoyable when an accompanying picture clarifies or highlights the action," stated a business student who has been at DCC for three semesters. Students were much more satisfied with the way articles are written. Seventy-two percent thought that the language was easy to understand.

Students reached a consensus about retaining our "Faculty Profile" feature. Eighty-two percent of them like to know about the faculty. As one graphic arts major put it: "I find it interesting to learn about a teacher's hobbies, family, and professional accomplishments."

RECOMMENDATIONS

Based upon the responses to our questionnaire, and especially to the last question on proposed major changes in the paper, we offer the following recommendations:

1. Increase the point size of type and change the color of our paper from blue to white or cream for easier reading.

2. Use more photographs, especially in our coverage of sports events.

3. Expand our ads section and group together different types of ads--jobs, items for sale, housing, entertainment--and supply a heading for each group.

4. Run our "Faculty Profile" in each issue, rather than printing it only once or twice a month.

Thank you for considering these recommendations. We would like to have a meeting with you early next week to get your opinion about these changes. If you approve them, we can incorporate these changes in the Informer next semester.

QUESTIONNAIRE

Please take a few minutes to fill out the following questionnaire about the Campus Informer, our student newspaper. We on the newspaper staff are eager to know what you think about the paper so that we can make sure that it serves your needs. Please return your questionnaire to Debrah H. Hinkel, the editor, at Scott Hall 107 by Tuesday, September 14. If you have any questions, drop by the newspaper office in Scott Hall or call 264-3450 between noon and 6:00 p.m. Your viewpoints are important to us and will count. Thanks. Please feel free to sign or not sign your name.

Name _____

Fig. 11.6   (Continued.)

1. How many semesters have you attended Detroit Community College?
   ___ 1
   ___ 2
   ___ 3
   ___ 4
   ___ more than 4

2. What is your major? _____

3. How often do you read the <u>Informer</u>?
   ___ twice a week, or every time it comes out
   ___ once a week
   ___ once every two weeks
   ___ I rarely look at it

4. Rank your reason for reading the <u>Informer</u> (first = 1, second = 2, etc.)
   ___ find out about sports events
   ___ learn more about academic programs
   ___ look at the ads
   ___ follow campus events
   ___ learn more about campus clubs

5. How often would you like to see the <u>Informer</u> published?
   ___ daily
   ___ twice a week (as it is now)
   ___ once a week
   ___ once every two weeks

6. How would you evaluate the <u>Informer</u>'s layout (its physical appearance)?
   ___ outstanding
   ___ very good
   ___ average
   ___ poor

7. Is the <u>Informer</u> written in clearly understood language?
   ___ yes
   ___ no

8. What do you think of the number of pictures used in the <u>Informer</u>?
   ___ not enough
   ___ just right
   ___ too many

9. Should the <u>Informer</u> continue to run its "Faculty Profile" feature?
   ___ run as is (once or twice a month)
   ___ run more often (every issue)
   ___ run less often (once every two months)
   ___ delete it

10. What one major change would you like to make in the <u>Informer</u>? Why?

You can also list a percentage parenthetically:

Correct: A majority of students (75 percent) prefer the quarter to the semester system.

The word *percentage* should not be used for *percent*. *Percentage* is used without numbers to indicate a range or a size:

Incorrect: A large percent of the residents favored the new health care policies.

Incorrect: A thirty-five percentage of the residents favored the new health care policies.

Correct: A large percentage of the residents favored the new health care policies.

Explaining What the Numbers Mean

Numbers in your report will make it effective and impressive. However, beware of letting figures speak for themselves. Your report is not a statistical table. Organize and assess the numbers you include by telling readers what those numbers mean, why they are significant, and how they characterize various opinions. Numbers are most meaningful when they are placed in a context readers will understand and welcome. Avoid writing a wooden opening that provides no background information:

Poor: A fifteen-question questionnaire was distributed to forty students at Coe Community College between the dates of February 15 and February 28, 1985.

Provide a brief explanation of the reasons why you constructed and distributed the questionnaire. Supply information that will help readers connect your topic to the need you saw to question people about it. The lifeless opening just cited could be transformed for the reader's benefit into this kind of introduction:

Effective: For the last two semesters, students at Coe Community College have complained about the textbook rental service. In order to determine what types of changes students wanted, I constructed a questionnaire and sent it to forty students from seven different majors.

In discussing responses to specific questions, use numbers selectively. Prepare readers for the numbers you cite. Do not overwhelm readers with a series of unorganized and uninterpreted figures. If you simply list every response to every question, you will confuse readers. It is your job to impose some order by briefly and simply summarizing the responses.

> ***Poor:*** Question 2 asked respondents: "How long have you lived in the Hillcrest subdivision?" Twenty-seven percent said they lived in Hillcrest for more than five years; 17 percent indicated they were residents there for at least three years; 34 percent said they lived in Hillcrest for more than one year; and 22 percent said they lived in Hillcrest for less than one year.

> ***Effective:*** A clear majority of the respondents (78 percent) have lived in the Hillcrest subdivision for more than one year.

Here is another example in which unorganized responses are thrown at the reader:

> ***Poor:*** For question 3 ("How would you evaluate the service you received after the sale?"), respondents answered as follows: 35 percent said it was all right but a little slow; 25 percent thought it was not adequate; and 40 percent said they had no complaints.

To eliminate confusion, divide the responses into two manageable groups. Readers will profit from a conclusion such as the following:

> ***Effective:*** Customers were generally satisfied with the service after the sale; only 25 percent answered that it was inadequate.

The revision above shows the writer's desire to present only essential facts. For example, in reporting responses to yes/no questions, there is no need to give percentages for both the yes answers and the no answers: 75 percent liked the new office hours; 25 percent did not. When you write that 75 percent liked the new office hours, you do not have to tell the reader that 25 percent did not. Of course, if a number of respondents left the question blank, you will have to state that fact.

Using Direct Quotations

In addition to recording percentages, you may want to include a few direct quotations for emphasis. A direct quotation, if it is carefully worded, can serve three useful functions: (1) it can precisely capture the views of an entire group, (2) it might contain a colorful expression that can enliven your report, and (3) it can lend support to your recommendation, especially if it comes from a recognized authority. Because of their summary power, direct quotations will make your report more compact, relevant, and credible.

Choose direct quotations carefully and use them sparingly. Figure 11.6, for example, contains only three quotations. To avoid bias, try not to use the same person for each quotation you include; your report will appear prejudiced if you do not give equal time to both sides. If you are distributing a questionnaire on grading procedures at your college, you might ask whether students prefer one comprehensive final examination to a number of tests. By recording only the following quotation, you would present an unfair picture of students as lazy:

> Students in favor of a single comprehensive final examination liked the freedom from daily preparation and weekly quizzes. As a sophomore majoring in environmental resources noted, "You're playing Russian roulette, but it's worth it for the extra time you have during the semester."

By adding the following observation, you will be giving a more balanced view:

> Those opposed to a single, comprehensive examination, however, worried that they could have a bad day or not know what the instructor was looking for. A junior plant science major summarized much of this group's thinking when she wrote, "I want to have more than one chance to make a good grade."

Before using a direct quotation, always obtain permission. If given, put the exact words of the person you are quoting in double quotation marks. And, whenever possible, identify the respondent by name, status, position, or major.

Writing a Recommendation

A recommendation should show readers how to transform respondents' answers into action. You can recommend that readers perform certain actions (often by a set time), refrain from performing actions, or choose between alternatives.

Make your recommendations specific and clear-cut. Readers will not benefit from general or indecisive comments. Since profits, customer satisfaction, and improved service may depend on your recommendations, be precise. If you hedge, you betray both respondents and readers. To say that you are not sure what should be done reveals shortcomings. The following recommendations leave no doubt concerning a definite course of action:

> Based on the respondents' answers, I recommend that we do three things:
>
> - Expand the employee parking lot to include space for one hundred more cars by August 1, 1986
> - Install gates around the parking lot
> - Station a security guard on Norris Street between shifts to direct traffic

Keep your recommendation section short. A single concluding paragraph should be enough. You might want to list recommendations as separate items, each preceded by a raised period, or bullet, as the example above shows, or by numbers, as in Figure 11.6. Or you may want to give your recommendations without itemizing them, as in Figure 11.7. Do not repeat unnecessary percentages and comments you have already listed in your report. Focus instead on the way readers can accomplish what respondents do or do not want. Usually your recommendation will be easy to formulate. It will entail implementing what the majority of respondents want done. Your hardest job will be finding a practical solution to the problem as the respondents define it. It would be foolish to express the opposite of what respondents want without hard facts to back up your opposition. By so doing, you invalidate your questionnaire and discredit yourself. Your recommendation should help readers who are looking for facts to support the right decision.

In some instances, however, you will find that opinions on a crucial issue are almost equally divided. With no majority opinion to guide you (and your readers), your recommendation will take on added significance. Make a recommendation, but admit that opinion is divided. Mary Snyder in Figure 11.7 endorses the city of Madison as the convention site but includes a necessary warning. There may be times, too, when a majority opinion still calls for qualification. In recommending that a chartered bus be ordered, Ms. Snyder at once acknowledges the majority's wishes, but still allows for the most flexible interpretation of the responses. No one loses by the recommendation that she submits.

At the end of your report, tell readers exactly what you would like them to do next—approve your recommendations, meet with you (specify a date) to discuss the recommendations, and the like. See page 181 of Chapter 7 for some ways to conclude your report.

Fig. 11.7   A report, the questionnaire on which it is based, and a cover letter.

TO: Gerald Morgan, President, Northern Chapter WREA
FROM: Mary Snyder
SUBJECT: Report on Convention Preference Questionnaire
DATE: 6 February 1986

PURPOSE OF CONVENTION QUESTIONNAIRE

    Four weeks ago, when the state office asked us to poll our chapter members about their preferences for this year's Wisconsin Real Estate Association convention, I volunteered to prepare, distribute, and summarize the results of a questionnaire. Judging from the responses to that questionnaire (a copy of which is attached), distributed over the last three weeks, next year's convention will be well attended and productive. One hundred of our 136 members returned the questionnaire: 22 secretaries/receptionists, 57 salespersons, 12 brokers, and 9 builders. Eighty-five percent of these individuals attended last year's convention in Green Bay.

RESULTS OF QUESTIONNAIRE

    Opinion is sharply divided between Madison (38 percent) and Milwaukee (35 percent) for the site of the convention. Respondents were more in agreement when it came to the length of the convention; 69 percent want it to last 2½ days during the week, not the weekend. Pat Laskey, a salesperson

Fig. 11.7 (Continued.)

from Door County, added later in his questionnaire that "if the convention were any shorter, we could not get our business completed; if it were any longer we would be away from the office too long." Many members want to get back home the third day.

To get to the convention, 64 percent of our members will come by car. Actually, the number of cars will be less, since twenty respondents expressed an interest in forming a carpool when asked for further suggestions in question 13. Sixty-one percent of our members will bring spouses with them. This preference plus the fact that some of our members will be sharing rooms accounts for the large request for single rooms with double beds (41 percent) and twin beds (33 percent).

An impressive majority (88 percent) wants the annual presidential address scheduled for the banquet. This may be one of the few times our chapter members see each other at meals. Sixty-seven percent disliked the idea of having meals included in the price of the convention. A representative comment comes from Marsha Jabolowicz, a receptionist from Rhinelander, "I want to be able to go to different places suited to my schedule; I do not want to be tied to a rigid itinerary." If they miss each other at meals, members may likely see each other at night spots. Forty percent prefer going to a nightclub for convention entertainment; and 32 percent voted for dancing ("a swinging disco") to be included.

Our members will represent our chapter in force on state committees. Eighty-two percent have agreed to serve on a committee; the committee on marketing captured the attention of 59 members.

RECOMMENDATIONS

On the basis of these responses, I think we should tell the state office that our members prefer a 2½-day convention in Madison, although Milwaukee is a strong alternate location. We will need a large block of double occupancy rooms; and meals should not be part of the convention package, but dancing or a nightclub should. Further, our members want the presidential address delivered at the banquet.

Our members' preferences are clear in most instances. In forwarding their responses to the state office, I would recommend that we try to charter a bus for those individuals (36 percent) who did want group transportation provided.

Please let me have your comments on these recommendations by 21 February so that we can start making plans for this year's convention.

A Questionnaire on
Preferences for the 1986 Convention of
the Wisconsin Real Estate Association

Dear Members of the Northern Chapter of the WREA:

Please complete the following questionnaire so that our state office
will be better able to plan for this year's convention. Your comments will
help make this year's gathering even more productive than last year's.

Thank you for returning your questionnaire to me by 30 January. A
stamped, addressed envelope is included. If you have any questions, please
write or call me.

Sincerely yours,

Mary Snyder

Mary Snyder
Mary's Realty
742 Kane Avenue
Superior, WI 54880-2607
882-5030

Name _____

Business address _____

Business telephone _____

Home address _____

Home telephone _____

1. What kind of membership do you hold in the WREA?
   ___ secretary/receptionist
   ___ salesperson
   ___ broker
   ___ builder

2. Did you attend last year's WREA convention in Green Bay?
   ___ yes
   ___ no

3. Where would you like the 1986 WREA convention to be held?
   ___ Milwaukee
   ___ Madison
   ___ Eau Claire
   ___ La Crosse
   ___ other (please specify) _____

4. How long would you like the convention to last?
   ___ 1 day
   ___ 1½ days
   ___ 2 days
   ___ 2½ days
   ___ 3 days

5. When would you like the convention to be held?
   ___ during the week
   ___ on the weekend

6. How would you like to travel to the convention?
   ___ by car
   ___ by bus
   ___ fly
   ___ have group transportation provided

7. Will your spouse accompany you?
   ___ yes
   ___ no

8. What kinds of accommodations will you need?
   ___ single room (one bed)
   ___ single room (two twin beds)
   ___ single room (two double beds)
   ___ two rooms

9. When should the presidential address be given?
   ___ at a breakfast meeting
   ___ at a luncheon meeting
   ___ at a banquet
   ___ alone, at a separate meeting

10. Would you prefer to see meals included in the cost of the convention
    fees?
    ___ yes
    ___ no

11. What type of entertainment do you think the WREA should provide at the
    convention?
    ___ dancing
    ___ theater
    ___ nightclub
    ___ other (please specify)

12. Which state committees would you be willing to serve on?
    ___ finance
    ___ marketing
    ___ appraisal
    ___ planning
    ___ I do not want to serve on a committee

13. Please add any further comments about any of the previous questions or any other relevant topic you think the WREA should consider. _____

_____

☞ Conclusion

Questionnaires are an invaluable tool that can help you in school and on the job. You need to follow a careful process to prepare an effective questionnaire and summarize the results. Most important, revise and pretest your questions to make sure they are reliable. In selecting your respondents, follow a systematic plan to sample a significant number of people who have the appropriate background to answer your questionnaire knowledgeably. After tabulating the results of the questionnaire, you are ready to write your survey report. The report should concisely summarize respondents' major opinions without burdening readers with unnecessary details. Any recommendations your report offers must be precise to help readers make the most effective use of your respondents' opinions.

☞ Exercises

1. Write a memo (see pages 178–184 for format and organization) to an employer—previous or current—about a specific problem that needs investigation. Indicate why a questionnaire would be the best means of gathering information and stress how the results would lead to increased sales, better service, or greater productivity. In your memo specify whom you will question, how you will get their names and addresses, and the timetable you will follow in constructing the questionnaire, distributing it, making a tally, and writing the report.

2. Select some area of interest to a civic organization, club, fraternity or sorority, union, or church group to which you belong. In a letter to the president of this organization, explain how a questionnaire on this specific area would help the group—in membership, long-range planning, meetings, dues, etc. Volunteer to construct a questionnaire and to distribute it to members of the organization.

3. Write an appropriate closed question (dichotomous, multiple-choice, rating-scale, ranking, or fill-in-the-blank) for each one of the following topics. Where necessary, supply appropriate options.

(a) marital status
(b) health
(c) income
(d) religion
(e) credit rating
(f) expectation for promotion
(g) vacation preferences
(h) a household product
(i) college tuition
(j) local liquor laws
(k) medical costs
(l) security on campus
(m) airplanes vs. buses for travel
(n) writing a résumé
(o) senior citizen discounts
(p) garbage pickup
(q) a local television station
(r) telephone service

4. The following closed questions (and some of their options) are incorrectly worded. Rewrite the questions and the options to eliminate vague terms, loaded words, jargon, overlapping responses, double adjectives, an insufficient range of responses, and the other kinds of errors discussed in this chapter (pages 334–339).

(a) Should our city risk legalizing gambling?   yes___   no___

(b) Are people upset with the new leash laws? yes___   no___   maybe___

(c) I find everything I need at one store.   agree___ disagree___

(d) What kind of classes do you like?
    ___ morning
    ___ afternoon
    ___ evening
    ___ fifty-minute
    ___ seventy-minute

(e) Do you regularly read a newspaper or current events magazine?   yes___
    no___

(f) Would you characterize yourself as being carpophagous?   yes___   no___

(g) Do you agree that teaching sex education in our schools has led to more teenage pregnancies and abortions and to looser morals in our already too permissive society?   agree___   disagree___

(h) Are you married or divorced?   yes___   no___

(i) What kind of beverage do you like?
    ___ coffee
    ___ tea
    ___ milk
    ___ soft drinks
    ___ carbonated drinks

(j) Do you vote in all elections as a patriotic citizen?   yes___   no___

(k) Have you purchased any articles of clothing recently?   yes___ no___

(l) Into which group would you place yourself?
___ full-time employee
___ part-time employee
___ work weekends only
___ work nights

(m) Don't you think our government has spent too much money on relocating refugees? yes___ no___

(n) Did you see the recession coming four years ago? yes___ no___

(o) Give the name of the person who, in your opinion, cheats most on the time card: _____

(p) How often do you ride your bicycle?
___ not very often
___ a few times
___ several times
___ as much as I can

(q) Rank the following in their order of importance to you:
___ fringe benefits
___ health insurance policy
___ two-weeks paid vacation
___ company car

(r) Is your education meaningful to you now? yes___ no___

(s) Where do you live?
___ with my parents
___ in a trailer court
___ in a duplex
___ by myself
___ in an apartment building

(t) All housing loans should be guaranteed by the federal government, shouldn't they? yes___ no___

(u) Do you like to swim and to fish? yes___ no___

(v) Did the RPT come in the morning or the afternoon? A.M.___ P.M.___

(w) Do you understand enough mathematics to be able to complete this simple form by yourself? yes___ no___

5. Rewrite the following open-ended questions to make them more precise and answerable.

(a) What kinds of experiences have you had in the hospital?
(b) What improvements in city services are necessary in the future?
(c) Describe your philosophy of life.
(d) What kinds of entertainment do you like?
(e) Compare and contrast the kinds of housing opportunities in your town.
(f) What appeals to you about your career?
(g) Comment on any changes you have seen in the last year.

(h) Describe in detail all the lectures you have attended this term.

(i) What kinds of investments should a family make today?

(j) Comment on the state of the environment.

(k) Tell me all you know about horse husbandry.

(l) Should transportation be increased?

(m) Does the government impose too many regulations on citizens?

(n) What are some problems in higher education today?

(o) What agencies are most successful today?

6. The following questionnaire contains unclear instructions, an inconsistent format, poorly worded and irrelevant questions, and inappropriate options. Rewrite the instructions and the questionnaire.

> Hi, how are you today? We think that it would be a good idea for everyone to participate in a coffee fund soon. Complete the enclosed questionnaire soon and return it to me. You will have to circle some of the responses, check others, and write in still some other answers. Answer all the questions you feel confident about. If you check "I do not drink coffee" for any of the responses, use a pen or pencil; this will help flag your answer. If you do not check this as a response, use a blue or black pen. When you see questions asking for opinions you would rather not give, answer them anyway.

(1) Do you like working here?　yes＿　it's all right＿　no＿

(2) How long have you worked in this office?　0–1 month＿　3–12 months＿　1–3 years＿　3–8 years＿　more than 8 years but less than 12 years＿　more than 12 years＿

(3) What is your current salary?＿＿＿＿＿　Is it fair?＿＿＿

(4) Do you have a cup of coffee before work?　yes＿　I do not drink coffee＿　sometimes＿　no＿　it varies＿

(5) When do you drink most of your coffee?　A.M.＿　P.M.＿　nights＿

(6) Where do you get your coffee while at work?
　＿ I bring a thermos bottle from home.
　＿ I purchase it before coming to work.
　＿ I stop off at a restaurant and have it.
　＿ I borrow some.
　＿ I do not drink coffee.

(7) How much coffee do you drink at work?
　＿0–2 cups a day　＿1–2 cups　＿3–5 cups　＿more than 5 cups a day　＿I do not drink coffee　＿I seldom drink coffee at work

(8) How do you like your coffee? Circle one of the following:
　(a) black　　　　　　　(g) milk
　(b) black with sugar　　(h) dry roasted
　(c) freshly perked　　　(i) freeze-dried
　(d) decaffeinated　　　(j) decaffeinated freeze-dried
　(e) cream　　　　　　(k) mellow roast blend
　(f) instant's o.k.

(9) Would you like to have a coffee fund in our office?
  (a) Yes, right now.
  (b) Yes, not right now.

  If you circled (b), answer one of the following:
    __ within the next month
    __ within the next six months
    __ within the next year
  (c) No, but I would not oppose a coffee fund.
  (d) No, I think it is a bad idea.

(10) Do you think a coffee fund would be a good idea?   yes__ no__

(11) Would a coffee fund bring people together?   yes__ no__ I do not know right now__

(12) Should we let people buy coffee by the single cup? If so, how much should we charge per cup?
    __ we should charge .05¢ a cup
    __ twenty cents a cup
    __ thirty-five cents
    __ whatever they want to contribute

(13) Should we allow people outside our office to participate in the coffee fund? yes__ no__ on a limited basis__

(14) How much should we charge people outside the office for a cup of coffee?
    __ ten cents   __ thirty cents
    __ fifteen cents   __ thirty-five cents
    __ twenty cents   __ the same as we pay
    __ twenty-five cents   __ twenty to thirty cents a cup
    __ I do not want them to buy our coffee

(15) Who should prepare the coffee and collect for it?
    __ Let's hire a caterer.
    __ Everyone in the coffee fund should take a turn.
    __ We should appoint two people.
    __ We should draw lots.
    __ Each of us should share the responsibility by drawing lots.

(16) Please add any other comments. You might want to state again whether you are in favor of the fund, how much coffee you drink, and whether the office manager should provide the funds or the time to prepare the coffee.

7. Construct a questionnaire for the topic you selected in either exercise 1 or exercise 2 above. Distribute it, and then, after tabulating the responses, prepare a report about your findings for your employer or the president of the organization to which you belong. Also supply your employer or president with a blank copy of the questionnaire and a sample cover letter you have sent out with your questionnaire.

12

Designing Visuals

Experts estimate that as much as 80 percent of our learning comes through the visual sense. Words, of course, form a large part of our visual information. In conjunction with words, visual aids (hereafter shortened to "visuals") convey a giant share of the facts we receive. Visuals are especially useful on the job because they help readers to see what you are discussing. Chapter 12 surveys the kinds of visuals you will encounter most frequently and shows you how to read, construct, and use them. Visuals, however, are not confined to just this chapter. They are important in preparing successful instructions, proposals, and written and oral reports.

The kinds of visuals we will deal with can be divided into two categories—tables and figures. A table lists information in parallel columns or rows for easy comparison of data. Anything that is not a table is considered a figure, including graphs, circle charts, bar charts, pictographs, organizational charts, flow charts, maps, photographs, and drawings. Before looking at the various kinds of visuals, you may find it helpful to know more about the benefits they offer and the caution you must exercise in using them.

☞ The Usefulness of Visuals

What can visuals do to improve your written work? Here are four reasons why you should use them. Each of the four points is graphically reinforced in Figure 12.1.

1. Visuals arouse immediate interest. Their size, shape, color, and arrangement are dramatic. They also offer readers relief from looking at sentences and paragraphs. Note how eye-catching (in both number and shape) the symbols are for the world's ten most populous countries represented in Figure

Fig. 12.1   A visual showing the ten most populous countries.

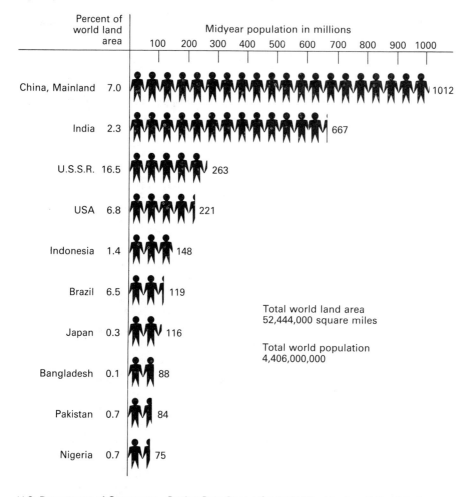

U.S. Department of Commerce. *Pocket Data Book USA 1979* (Washington, D.C.: U.S. Government Printing Office, 1979) iv.

12.1. A visual captures readers' attention by setting important information apart.

2. Visuals simplify concepts. Because many readers are visually oriented, graphics unlock doors of meaning. A visual shows ideas in action when a verbal description may be less forceful or more difficult to understand. A visual can make technical information easier to comprehend. Moreover, visuals can simplify densely packed statistical data. The vastness of a country's population and how that population compares with other nations' is much easier to grasp and to remember because of the picture symbols in Figure 12.1.

Saying that China has more people than India or the Soviet Union and naming the differences is more complicated in words than it is in pictures. Other kinds of visuals also make learning easier. For example, a visual could show the interior parts of a machine or enlarge one element of a piece of equipment to clarify its function or relationship to another part. Readers would therefore feel more confident about operating the machine or performing a procedure.

3. Visuals condense a large quantity of information into a relatively small space. Figure 12.1 collects twenty different pieces of information about ten countries—their populations and the amount of land they occupy—and records the data in far less space than it would take to describe these facts in words. How many times would a writer have to repeat the words *population, land area, percent, more, less, greater, lower, in comparison,* or *in contrast?* A visual expresses a fact once without having to repeat it. And even if the writer transcribed all the facts in Figure 12.1 into words, readers would not be able to understand the percentages as easily as they can the rows of symbols.

4. Visuals emphasize relationships. Through the use of arrangement and form, visuals quickly show contrasts, similarities, growth rates, downward and upward movements, spirals, fluctuations in price and time, and the influence of one item on another. Figure 12.1 shows not only how countries compare in population, but also how population compares with land area. India, for example, has about two and one-half times more people than the Soviet Union does, but occupies about one-eighth the space. Other kinds of visuals (pie and bar charts are discussed on pages 380–387) show the relationship of parts to the whole. And the curve of a graph can indicate the time sequence of various events, such as average annual snowfall.

☞ Choosing Effective Visuals

You will have to select visuals very carefully. The following suggestions may help you to answer two important questions: (1) When should I use a visual? and (2) How many of them will I need?

1. Use visuals only when they are strictly relevant for your purpose and audience. Visuals should not be included simply as decoration for impressing readers. A short report on fire drills does not need a picture of a fire station to enhance it; a list of instructions on how to prepare a company report does not require a picture of an individual writing at a table.
2. Use visuals in conjunction with, not as a substitute for, written work. Visuals do not always take the place of words. You may need to explain information contained in a visual. A set of illustrations or a group of tables alone will not satisfy readers looking for summaries or evaluations of the details those visuals present.

3. Make sure that visuals do not interfere with your message. Too many visuals (some of them duplicating information in your text) will distract readers. If something is self-explanatory, do not include a visual. Avoid visuals that include many more details than you discuss or, worse yet, that present information that contradicts your work.

4. Consider carefully how a specific visual will help your readers. Elaborate computer-generated graphs are unnecessarily complex for a community group interested in a clear representation of the rise in food prices over a three-month period. If you have to include a detailed, complex visual to make an important point, be prepared to explain it to your readers, especially if they are not familiar with your work or the technical discipline you are writing about. Generally, the less technical your audience, the more helpful a visual is.

5. Never include a visual of poor quality; each should be clear and easy to read. Do not assume that readers will have magnifying glasses on their desks or that they will tolerate a messy drawing or a faded blueprint. If you photocopy a visual, make sure the copy is readable and that it does not cut off important parts of the original.

6. When you construct your own visual, do a model or sample first; it is hard to make a perfect visual on the first try.

7. Consider how your visuals will look on the page layout. Visuals should add to the overall appearance of your work, not detract from it. Observe generous margins. Don't cram visuals onto a page. If you type your paper and intend to add visuals later, make sure you leave enough room for them.

☞ The Graphic Artist's Desk

To prepare your own effective visuals you need the right tools. That does not mean that you must purchase elaborate equipment to produce clear and professional-looking visuals to accompany your assignments. The materials to do the job can easily be obtained at your college bookstore or your local office equipment or supply store. You would be wise to have the tools and materials discussed in this section on your desk. For you will use them not only in your writing courses but also on any job where visuals will make your work more understandable and useful to readers.

The basic tools of the illustrator's trade include a straightedge (or twelve-inch ruler), a plastic triangle to measure and make angles, a protractor, and a compass to make arcs. Also it is a good idea to have scissors, some glue, and transparent tape.

You will certainly need some high-quality writing instruments. You might want to invest in an artist's pen set containing various points for lettering, sketching, and making elegant designs. A pen set provides pens that use water-soluble ink in a variety of colors including black. (If you do not anticipate using the pen set often, then buy a fine felt-tipped pen, or perhaps a few of them in different colors.) Use the artist's pens for your final copy, but for rough sketches have a supply of pencils in hard and soft leads. If you make a mistake, soft lead erases easily.

Not only must visuals be designed effectively, they should appear on suitable paper. Depending on your needs, you might want to purchase a drawing pad, some graph paper, maybe a pasteboard, and even some tracing paper.

One of the most serviceable materials you can buy for any graphic work will be templates. These are clear plastic sheets that contain a variety of cutout designs that can be traced onto a sheet of paper. Templates offer such basic shapes as circles, triangles, rectangles, trapezoids, dollar signs, and crosses. Other templates offer chemical and mathematical symbols. Depending on your technical needs and interests, you can find a template to suit any purpose. Templates offer designs of air-conditioning and heating ducts, structural steel shapes, house plans and plumbing systems, traffic patterns, home furnishings, and especially important today, computer flow-chart symbols. Figure 12.2 contains some designs drawn from sample templates.

Fig. 12.2   Templates for office planning, for traffic control, and for chemistry.

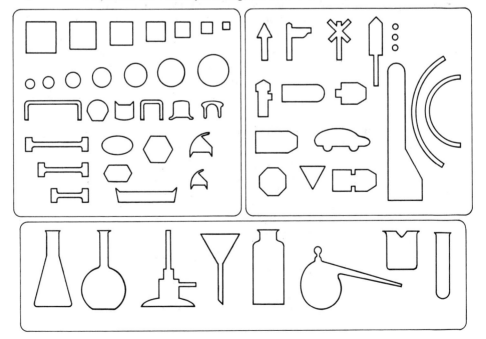

☞ Writing About Visuals

Never include a visual without mentioning it in your paper or report. Readers should be told where the visual is located and why it is there. The following guidelines on identifying, inserting, introducing, and interpreting visuals will help you use them more efficiently.

1. Identifying visuals. Each visual must have a number, title, or both, that indicate the subject and the way in which it is discussed. An unidentified visual is meaningless. Tables and figures should be numbered separately throughout the text.

Table 1: Paul Jordan's Work Schedule, January 15–23.
Figure 2: The Proper Way of Applying for a Small Business Loan.
Figure 5: Income Estimation Figures for Weekdale Shopping Center.

If you use a visual that is not your own work, you must identify your source (a specific newspaper, magazine, textbook, federal agency, or individual). If your paper or report is intended for publication, you are required by law to obtain permission to reproduce copyrighted material from the copyright holder.

2. Inserting visuals in the text. Place visuals as close as possible to the discussion of them. Never introduce a visual before a discussion of it (for readers will wonder why it is there). Place a visual about the topic at the beginning of your discussion; do not force readers to go through an elaborate discussion and then present a visual that would have simplified that discussion. Be sure to tell readers where the visual is found—"directly below," "on the opposite page," "to the right," "at the bottom of the next page." If the visual is small enough, insert it directly in the text (rather than on a separate page). If your visual occupies an entire page, place that page containing your visual immediately after the page that makes the first reference to it.

3. Introducing visuals. Refer to the visual by its number and, if necessary, mention the title as well. In introducing the visual, though, do not just insert a reference to it; relate the visual to the context of your discussion. Here are three ways of writing a lead-in sentence for visuals.

> ***Poor:*** Our store saw a dramatic rise in the shipment of electric ranges over the five-year period as opposed to the less impressive increase in washing machines. (See Figure 3.)

This sentence does not tie the visual (Figure 3) into the sentence where it belongs. The visual just trails insignificantly behind.

> ***Improved:*** As Figure 3 shows, our store saw a dramatic rise in the shipment of electric ranges over the five-year period as opposed to the less impressive increase in washing machines.

Mentioning the visual in Figure 3 at the beginning is distracting. Readers will want to stop and look at the visual immediately before they know what it is or how you are using it.

> ***Best:*** Over the last five-year period, our store realized a dramatic rise in the shipment of electric ranges as opposed to the less impressive increase in the shipment of washing machines, as shown in Figure 3.

This sentence is the best of the three because the figure reference and the explanation are in the same sentence, but the reference is not a distraction.

4. Interpreting visuals. In addition to mentioning a visual by number and title, it may also be necessary to tell readers why it is there and what specifically to look for. Of course, you should not spend time repeating information that is obvious from looking at the visual. But occasionally you will want to interpret the visual for an audience. A director of an alumni association, eager to sell alumni life insurance, used the following table and then supplied a "sales" conclusion for it.

> Consider this table based upon the U.S. Department of Labor Consumer Price Index for the past ten years. The value of insurance-benefit dollars decreases right along with dollars used in everyday expenses.

Average annual inflation rates

Year	Inflation rate	Relative dollar value
1969	5.4	$1.00
1970	5.9	.95
1971	4.3	.89
1972	3.3	.85
1973	6.2	.82
1974	10.9	.77
1975	9.1	.69
1976	5.8	.63
1977	6.5	.60
1978	7.7	.55
1979	11.3	.51
1980	12.2	.45

> If you haven't looked at your life insurance coverage recently, you may be surprised. Benefit levels thought sufficient just a few years ago may be inadequate for current and future needs. For example, a $10,000 benefit from 1969 would have to be increased to $22,222 in 1980 to provide the same level of protection.[1]

---

[1] Example used courtesy Department of Alumni Relations, Northwestern University, Evanston, Illinois.

Sometimes the figures in a visual tell an incomplete or misleading story and you will need to interpret them in context. In a study on the benefits of vanpooling, one writer supplied the following visual:

Travel time (in minutes): automobile versus vanpool

Private automobile	Vanpool
25	32.5
30	39.0
35	45.5
40	52.0
45	58.5
50	65.0
55	71.5
60	78.0

Source: U.S. Department of Transportation, *Increased Transportation Efficiency Through Ridesharing: The Brokerage Approach* (Washington, D.C., January, 1977, DOT-OS-40096): 45.

The writer then called attention to what the visual did not say:

> Although it is estimated that the travel time in a vanpool may be as much as 30% longer than in a private automobile (to allow for pickups), the total trip time for the vanpool user can be about the same as with a private automobile because vanpools eliminate the need to search for parking spaces and to walk to the employment site entrance.[2]

☞ Tables

Tables, or parallel columns or rows of information, often present statistical data that have been compiled over several weeks or months. The figures are then organized and arranged into categories to show changes in time, distance, cost, employment, or some other quantifiable variable. The visuals on pages 375 and 377 are tables.

But the tabular form can present more than numerical information. Lists of words can also be put into tables. Tables in textbooks summarize material for easy recall—causes of wars, symptoms of diseases, provisions of a law. Various forms of business organizations are compared in Table 12.1, opposite. Observe how the table easily summarizes much information and arranges it in quickly identifiable categories.

To construct a table properly, you must know how to type and label it. Refer to Table 12.2 (page 377) as you read the following instructions.

---

[2] James A. Devine, "Vanpooling: A New Economic Tool," *AIDC Journal* 15 (Oct. 1980): 13. Reprinted by permission.

Table 12.1 Comparison of forms of business organization.

	Single proprietorship	*Partnership*	*Corporation*
Ease of organization	Easiest	Moderately difficult	Most difficult
Capital generally available for operation	Least	Intermediate	Most (best able to raise capital)
Responsibility	Centered in one person	Spread among partners	Policy set by directors; president supervises day-to-day operation
Incentive to succeed	Centered in one person	Spread among partners	Spread among many people
Flexibility	Greatest	Intermediate	Least
Ability to perform varied functions (production or purchasing, accounting, selling, etc.)	Dependent on one individual's versatility	Dependent on capabilities of two or more individuals	Best able to employ individuals with different capabilities
Possibility of conflict among those in control	None	Most prone to conflict, especially if partners have equal interest in business	Chain of command reduces internal conflict; wide ownership minimizes disagreement
Taxation	No corporate income tax	No corporate income tax	Corporate income tax
Distribution of profits or losses	All to proprietor	Distributed to partners in accordance with terms of partnership agreement	Profits retained or given to stockholders as dividends; losses reduce price of stock
Liability for debts in event of failure	Unlimited	Unlimited, but spread among partners	Limited to each stockholder's investment
Length of life	Limited by one individual's life span (or until he goes out of business)	Limited (partnership is reorganized upon death or withdrawal of any partner)	Unlimited (with ownership of shares readily transferable)

Source: Reprinted by permission of the publisher from *Introductory Economics*, 4th ed., by Sanford D. Gordon and George G. Dawson (Lexington, Mass.: D. C. Heath and Company, 1980): 75.

Typing a Table

First determine the size of the table. If it is small (two or three columns) and you include it within the text, center the table on the page. Leave at least one inch of white space above and below the table. If the table has a title, place it at the top (figure titles go above or below the visual), and triple space before and after the table. You might first want to draw a border and then very neatly with a straightedge (ruler) put in the columns. Then you will have the right spaces and slots in which to insert your numbers or words. Leave adequate space between columns so that the table will not look crowded or be difficult to decipher.

If the table is large (running to five or six columns), use a separate sheet of paper. Again, depending on the size of the table, type the rows at the top of the page or turn the piece of paper broadside and then type the table that way. If possible, use the same margins as with the text of your paper. Make sure that the reader can easily understand the numbers and letters of your table.

Labeling a Table

Provide headings for both the column and subcolumns; in Table 12.2 the column is entitled "Years attending," and the subcolumns are the years (1970, 1975, 1980, 1985) about which the table gives data. Also provide a title for the *stub*—the first vertical column on the left-hand side. The stub heading is "Period of service" in Table 12.2. The stub lists the items (the wars and conflicts in which the Lincoln-area veterans participated) that are broken down under the subheadings. To separate the stub title and column/subcolumn headings from the body of the table, draw a rule (a line) across the table as in Table 12.2.

Label the categories appropriately and consistently. If some form of measurement is consistently involved, include the unit of measurement as part of the column heading—weight (in pounds), distance (in miles), time (per hour), quantity (per dozen). The unit of measurement should not be repeated for each entry in a column. Also, units should be consistent; do not jump from miles to meters, pounds to ounces.

Wrong:	*Weight*	*Height*
	120 lbs	165 cm
	132 lbs	5′ 9″
	122 lbs	5′ 7″
	58.5 kg	172 cm

Correct:	*Weight* *(in kilograms)*	*Height* *(in centimeters)*
	54.0	165
	55.2	176
	54.9	166
	58.5	172

Table number   Subcolumn heading

Column heading

Table 12.2 Veterans attending Lincoln-area VFW Posts[a]

Period of service	*Years attending*			
	1970	*1975*	*1980*	*1985*
World War I	59	55	22	12
World War II	1330	1309	1100	963
Korean Conflict	240	230	205	186
Vietnam[b]	389	423	461	485

Source: Lincoln VFW Association ◄——— Origin of data
[a]Does not include Bayside, Morton, or Westover. ⎫ Footnotes
[b]August 1964–May 1975 ⎭

Stub

If something in the table needs to be explained or qualified, put in a footnote (often signaled by a small raised letter: [a] or [b]) in the table where the information is to be further identified or qualified. The letter will then refer readers to an explanation directly below the table. In Table 12.2 the [a] after the title points to the qualification that three communities are not considered in the Lincoln area when data for the table were gathered. The [b] after the Vietnam entry in the stub clarifies the official dates for that conflict.

☞ Figures

As mentioned at the beginning of this chapter, any visual that is not a table is classified as a figure. We will now look at nine types of useful figures starting with graphs.

Graphs

Graphs transform numbers into pictures. They take statistical data presented in tables and put them into rising and falling lines, steep or gentle curves. Graphs vividly portray changes, fluctuations, trends, increases and decreases in profits, building permits, employment, energy, temperatures, or any other numbers that change frequently. The way the lines rise and fall in the graph depicts the kinds of changes and sometimes helps readers forecast trends. The resulting pictures are more dramatic than tables and are easier to read and interpret. Many issues of the *Wall Street Journal*, for example, contain a graph on the first page for the benefit of busy readers who want a great deal of financial information summarized quickly.

Basically, a graph consists of two lines—a vertical axis and a horizontal axis—that intersect to form a right angle as in Figure 12.3. The space between the two lines contains the picture made by the graph (in Figure 12.3 the amount of snowfall in Springfield between November 1985 and April 1986). The vertical line represents the dependent variable; the horizontal line, the independent variable. The dependent variable is influenced most directly by the independent variable, which is almost always expressed in terms of time or distance. Hence, in Figure 12.3 the given month affects the amount of snow Springfield received. The vertical axis is read from bottom to top; the horizontal axis is read from left to right. When the dependent variable occurs at a particular time on the independent variable (horizontal line), the place where the two points intersect is marked, or plotted, on the graph. After the points are plotted, a line is drawn to connect them; the resulting curve gives a picture of which months had the greatest snow and which the least and what the overall pattern of snowfall was in Springfield.

The way in which scales are set up is crucial to the success of a graph. Many graphs may not have ranges indicated by equally spaced lines (tick marks):

But on most of the graphs you construct, use tick lines as a scale to show values, distances, or time as in Figure 12.3. The topic will dictate the intervals to use. The time scale (independent variable) can be calculated in minutes, hours, days, or years.

A temperature-pulse-respiration graph is illustrated in Figure 12.4. The day is divided into six four-hour periods, and seven days are represented on one sheet. The temperature axis is divided into degrees (with .2° differences), and a heavy black line shows the normal line, making it easier to spot dangerous elevations. The pulse measurements are registered in two-beat differences (each dot represents two beats within the larger grouping of tens). And the respirations are also measured in twos, each dot there representing every time a patient takes two breaths. Note that the temperature and pulse scales have *a suppressed zero line*; they begin with 95° and thirty beats, not with zero. It would be impossible to have lower numbers for pulse and temperature and expect a patient to live. But the respiration scale begins with zero because it has a lower range (0–60). If these recordings were expressed in tabular form, they would be hard to follow because they would deprive the reader of a curve depicting much information quickly and impressively.

The graphs in Figures 12.3 and 12.4 contain only one line per category. But a graph can have multiple lines to show how a number of dependent variables (conditions, products) compare with each other. The relative productivity of corn, wheat, and soybeans in American agriculture can be seen in the graph in Figure 12.5. The graph contains a separate line for each of these three crop groups. At a glance readers can see how the three crop groups

Fig. 12.3 A graph is made by plotting data on the vertical and horizontal axes.

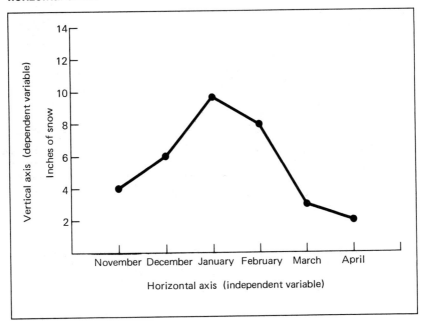

compare and also how many billions of bushels of each group were produced annually. Note how every group is clearly differentiated from the others by means of dots, dashes, or an unbroken line. Color, if available, can also help distinguish lines. Also, note how each line is clearly labeled so that the label does not cover up other lines or their points of intersection. If the lines do run close together, a *legend*, or explanatory note, underneath or above the graph identifies individual lines. Never put the legend within the graph; readers may confuse legend information with the data depicted in the graph. Although some graphs may contain as many as five or six lines, it is better to limit multiple-line graphs to two or three lines (or dependent variables) so that readers can interpret the graph more easily.

Keep in mind the following guidelines when you construct a graph:

1. Inform readers what your scale is: how many dots, boxes, or spaces equal what amounts or times. You may want to use graph paper that has hatch marks or carefully divided lines.

2. Keep the scale consistent and realistic. If you start with hours, do not switch to days or vice versa. If you are recording annual rates or accounts, do not skip a year or two in the hope that you will save time or be more concise. Do not jump from 1979, 1980, 1981–1983, 1984, 1985. Put in all the years you are surveying.

Fig. 12.4   A temperature-pulse-respiration graph showing the breakdown within ranges.

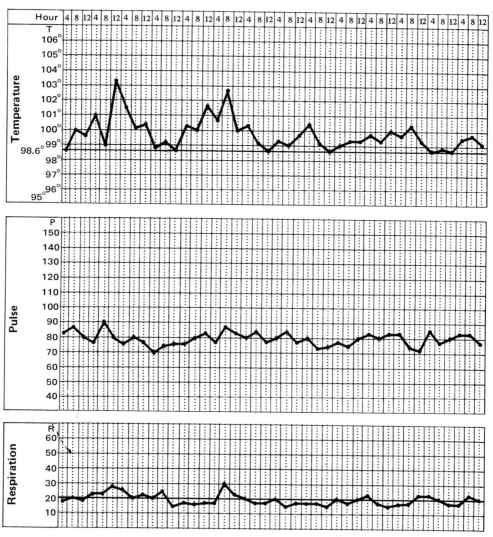

3. For some graphs there is no need to begin with a zero, as was seen in Figure 12.4. For others, you may not have to include numbers beyond seven or eight.
4. Do not draw a line or plot a curve that goes outside the limits of the graph and extends beyond the margin of the page.

Circle Charts

Circle charts are also known as pie charts, a name that descriptively points to their construction and interpretation. Figure 12.6 shows an example of a circle

Fig. 12.5   A multiple-line graph showing how three dependent variables compare.

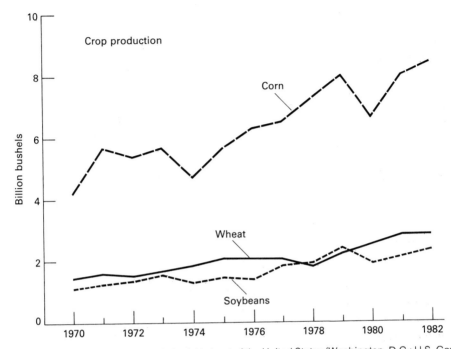

U.S. Bureau of the Census, *Statistical Abstract of the United States* (Washington, D.C.: U.S. Government Printing Office, 1984) xxviii.

chart. The full circle, or pie, represents the whole amount (100 percent)—an entire industry, profession, or population group. The full circle can stand for the entire budget of a company or family, or it can represent just a single dollar of that budget and show how it is broken down for various expenses. Each slice of the pie, then, stands for a part of the whole. A circle chart effectively allows readers to see two things at once—the relationship of the parts to one another and the relationship of the parts to the whole.

The circle chart is one of the most easily understood illustrations. For that reason, it is popular in government documents (the Bureau of the Census relies heavily on it), financial reports, and advertising messages. Although many circle charts are based on tables, tables can be very complex and dry and also more detailed than circle charts. The circle gives percentage totals; the table shows how those percentage groups are broken down.

To construct a successful pie chart, you will need a compass to make your circle and a protractor to measure sections of it. The mathematical principle underlying the construction of the circle chart is simple. A circle contains 360°. Translated into percentages, 100% = 360°, 10% = 36°, and 1% = 3.6°. To determine how much space you need for each of your slices, or wedges, figure

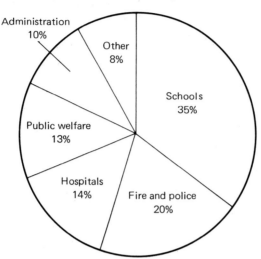

Fig. 12.6 A circle chart showing the proposed Midtown city budget for 1986.

out the percentage of the whole it expresses and then multiply that number by 3.6. For example, if you are drawing a circle chart to represent a family's budget, the percentage/degree breakdown might be as follows:

Housing	25%	90.0°
Food	22%	79.2°
Energy	20%	72.0°
Clothes	13%	46.8°
Health care	12%	43.2°
Miscellaneous	8%	28.8°

Follow these five rules to construct a circle chart:

1. Do not divide a circle, or pie, into too few or too many slices. If you have only three wedges, consider using another type of visual to display them (a bar chart, for example, which will be discussed later). If you have more than seven or eight wedges, you will divide the pie too narrowly, and the overcrowding will destroy the dramatic effect of the illustration. All the individual slices of the pie must total 100 percent.

2. Put the largest slice of the pie first, at the 12:00 o'clock position, and then move clockwise with proportionately smaller slices. Beginning with the biggest slice, you call attention to its importance. (The one exception is that the "other" category [see rule 3 below] is often placed last, as in Figure 12.6.) The "other" category should be placed last even when it is largest.

3. Avoid listing a number of small slices separately. Rather than individually listing slices of small percentages (2 percent, 3 percent, 4 percent), combine

these small pieces into one slice labeled "Other," "Miscellaneous," or "Related Items."

4. Label each slice of the pie. If the slice is large enough, write the identifying term or quantity inside, but make sure that it is easy to read. Do not put in a label upside down or slide it in vertically. All labels should be horizontal for easy reading. If the individual slice of the pie is small, do not try to squeeze in a label. Draw a line to the outside of the pie nearest the slice and write the appropriate label there, as in Figure 12.6.

5. You can shade or color each slice of the pie to further separate the parts. If you do, be careful not to obscure labels and percentages; also make certain that adjacent slices can be distinguished readily from each other.

Bar Charts

A bar chart shows a series of vertical or horizontal bars to indicate comparisons of statistical data. Vertical bars are used to show increases in quantities (students using a library) in Figure 12.7. Horizontal bars depict increases in distance (the number of feet the shotput is thrown by a women's track and field team) in Figure 12.8. Bar charts make a dramatic visual impression on the audience. They are valuable tools in sales meetings to demonstrate how well (or poorly) a product, a service, the company, or a salesperson has done. You often see bar charts at an office recording the financial goals for the United Way or other charitable drives.

Bar charts are less exact than tables, as Figures 12.7 and 12.8 show. Note that the number of students using the library or the number of feet the shotput is thrown are not expressed in precise figures, as they would be in a table, but are approximated by the length of the bar. Do not assume, however, that the bar chart is inaccurate; many bar charts are based on tables. What you lose in precision with a bar chart, you gain in visual flair. Another advantage of a bar chart is that it is easier to construct than a line graph. Finally, a bar chart is much more fluid and dynamic than a circle. The circle is static; the bar chart (like the graph) presents a moving view.

When should you use a bar chart rather than a table or graph? Your audience will help you decide. If you are asked to present statistics on costs for the company accountant, use a table. There the reader demands a precise listing; an accountant does not judge a visual by its eye appeal. However, if you are presenting the same information to a group of stockholders or to a diverse group of employees, a bar chart may be more relevant; such readers are interested in seeing the statistics in action. They are more concerned with the effects of change than with underlying causes and precise statistical details. Since it is limited to a few columns, however, a bar chart cannot convey as much information as a table or graph.

Types of Bar Charts

One of the most common types of bar charts is the type shown in Figure 12.7. Each undivided bar represents one day of the week, and the height of the bar

Fig. 12.7   A vertical bar chart showing the number of students using the Adams Memorial Library.

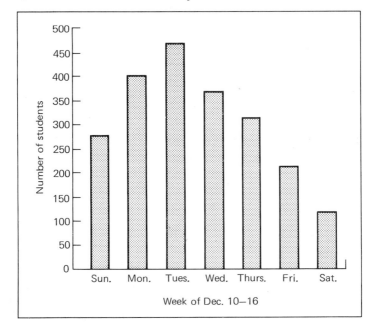

Fig. 12.8   A horizontal bar chart showing length of shotput throws by a women's track and field team.

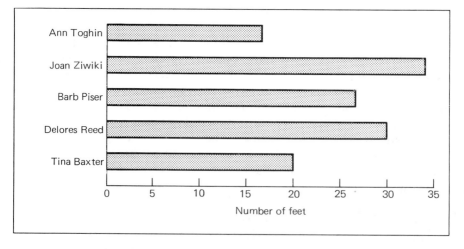

Fig. 12.9 A multiple-bar chart showing advertising expenditures by selected media: 1970 to 1985.

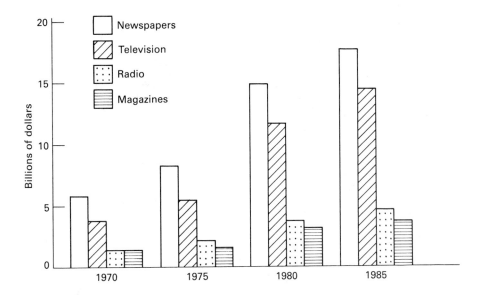

corresponds to the number of students using the library on that day. To read the chart effectively, you simply note where the top of the bar is in relation to the vertical scale on the left. The chart compares one type of data (the number of students using the library) over a period of time (one week in the school year).

Another type of chart—a multiple-bar chart—is represented in Figure 12.9. Four differently shaded bars are used for each year to represent the amount of money spent on different types of advertising in America. A legend at the top of the chart explains what each bar stands for. This chart measures the amount of money spent over a period of time (fifteen years) on different media. Consider how wasteful it would be to provide four separate charts for each of the four media. It would also be more difficult for readers to compare the expenditures among the media, since the data would have to be collected separately and then brought together for comparison of the results. A word of caution is in order about multiple-bar charts: never use more than four bars in a group for any one year. Otherwise, your chart will become crowded and difficult to read.

Still another kind of bar chart is the segmented, or cross-hatched (divided), bar, used to show differences within a given category for each comparison. The differences are the components, percentages, or subgroups that make up the whole. A single segmented bar representing the per capita cost for hospital care is seen in Figure 12.10. The entire bar totals $297, the payment for which came from four sources (direct payments, private health insurance, philan-

Fig. 12.10 A segmented-bar chart showing per capita hospital care spending by funding source.

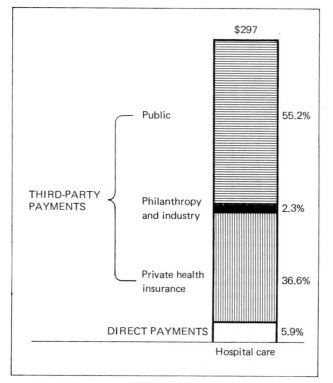

Robert M. Gibson and Charles R. Fisher, "National Health Expenditures 1977," *Social Security Bulletin* 41 (July 1978): 10.

thropy and industry, and the public). Each of these sources is represented by a different type of shading on the one column. Combined, the multiple sources account for all hospitalization payments. A group of segmented bars can be used to show multiple comparisons among many categories as in Figure 12.11, which depicts energy consumption levels and types in five states.

Making a Bar Chart

To construct an accurate bar chart, follow these instructions:

1. Make all the bars the same width; vary only the height (or length) to show differences.
2. Select an appropriate scale, and inform the readers about proportions. Be realistic. Do not construct a bar chart in which columns go off the page or are so small that readers cannot easily note differences. Look at the scale in Figure 12.7, where each division of the vertical column represents fifty students. Keep such divisions consistent; do not make one ten students and another twenty. Also, begin with zero so that the reader can correctly

Fig. 12.11   A multiple-bar, segmented-bar chart showing energy consumption by sector in five states that consumed the most energy, 1982.

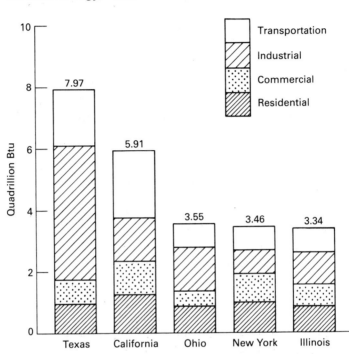

U.S. Energy Information Administration, *Monthly Energy Review,* Mar. 1984.

chart fluctuations. Use appropriate proportions on the horizontal scale as well.
3. Identify and use distinctive markings and shading on divided bars. Supply a clarifying legend for readers or otherwise indicate the meaning of different portions of a single cross-hatched bar, as in Figure 12.10. But do not introduce unnecessary marks or decorations.

Pictographs

Similar to a bar chart, a pictograph uses pictures instead of bars to represent differences in statistical data, as in Figure 12.1. The pictures or symbols appropriately represent the item(s) being compared. Sometimes the number of pictures indicates change, as in Figure 12.12, where the cartoon figures show Social Security recipients and workers. A pictograph can also show quantities by increasing the size of the picture or symbol for each year, as in Figure 12.13, rather than increasing the number of symbols.

If you use a pictograph, it is usually better to increase the number of symbols rather than their size. (Sizes are often difficult to construct accurately

Fig. 12.12 A pictograph indicating change in the relationship between Social Security recipients and workers.

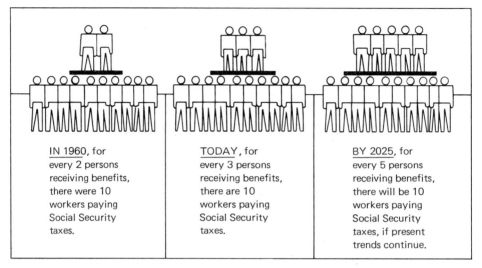

IN 1960, for every 2 persons receiving benefits, there were 10 workers paying Social Security taxes.

TODAY, for every 3 persons receiving benefits, there are 10 workers paying Social Security taxes.

BY 2025, for every 5 persons receiving benefits, there will be 10 workers paying Social Security taxes, if present trends continue.

Reprinted from *U.S. News & World Report,* issue of Jan. 12, 1981, p. 65. Copyright, 1981 U.S. News & World Report, Inc. Reprinted by permission.

and hard for the reader to interpret.) Whatever type of pictograph you use, though, always indicate the precise quantities involved by placing numbers after the pictures so that the reader knows exactly how much the pictures represent.

Organizational Charts

Unlike the charts discussed so far, the organizational chart does not contain statistical data; nor does it record movements in space or time. Rather, it pictures the chain of command in a company or agency, with the lines of authority stretching down from the chief executive, manager, or administrator to assistant manager, department heads, or supervisors to the work force of employees. The organizational chart also shows the various offices, departments, and units out of which the company or agency is constituted and through which orders and information flow. Organizational charts help to inform employees and customers about the composition of the company and also help to coordinate employee efforts in routing information to appropriate departments.

An organizational chart shows relationships by connecting rectangles (boxes), circles, or lines to each other, starting at the top with the chief executive and moving down to lower-level employees. (Sometimes the name of the individual holding the office is listed in addition to the title of the office.) Examine the organizational charts in Figures 12.14 and 12.15. Positions of

Fig. 12.13   A pictograph indicating increases in U.S. peanut production.

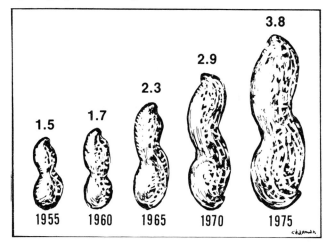

Congressional Quarterly Weekly Report, 34 (Sept. 11, 1976): 2483. Reprinted by permission.

equal authority are on parallel lines, and all jobs under the supervision of one individual are joined by bracketing lines. See, for example, the three services directly under the supervision of the Director of Agriculture Economics in Figure 12.14. Individuals who serve in advisory capacities or who are directly responsible to a higher administrator are listed with broken or dotted lines, as depicted in the unit clerk positions in Figure 12.15.

When you draw an organizational chart, first determine how much of the company or agency you want to depict. All the major offices that comprise the U.S. Department of Agriculture (USDA) are depicted in Figure 12.14. Note that the organizational chart does not list specific staff and line positions, but instead concentrates on the various offices that comprise the USDA. On the other hand, just one branch of nursing services at a large metropolitan hospital—the division of critical care nursing—is presented in Figure 12.15. Note that the intensive and cardiac care units work two shifts a day (8 A.M. to 8 P.M.; 8 P.M. to 8 A.M.), while the cardiac rehabilitation unit works three shifts in a twenty-four-hour period.

Select the extent to which you want to visualize the organization. Then draw appropriate circles or boxes to represent units. The shapes should be large enough to contain the titles of the offices they represent. Make sure you label each shape; otherwise, the reader will not know which unit is being depicted. If you represent just a portion of your organization, say so in your text.

Flow Charts

Like the organizational chart, a flow chart does not present statistical information. But as its name implies, a flow chart does show movement. It displays the

Fig. 12.14 An organizational chart showing the major offices that comprise the U.S. Department of Agriculture.

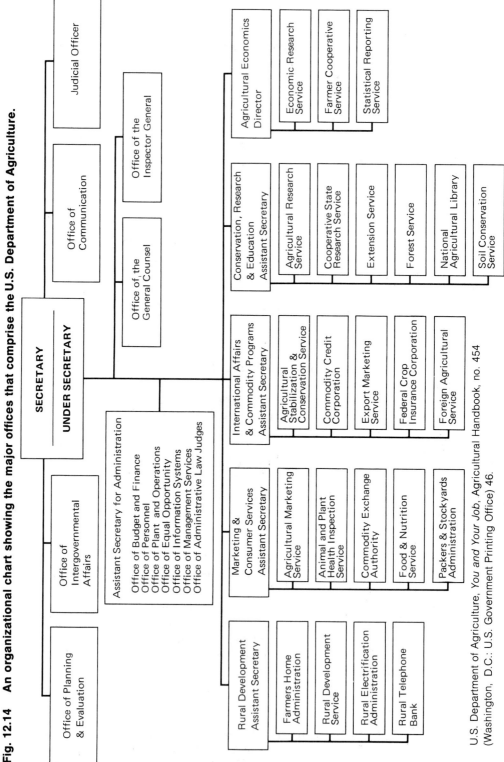

U.S. Department of Agriculture, *You and Your Job*, Agricultural Handbook, no. 454 (Washington, D.C.: U.S. Government Printing Office) 46.

Fig. 12.5   An organizational chart showing critical care nursing services at Union General Hospital.

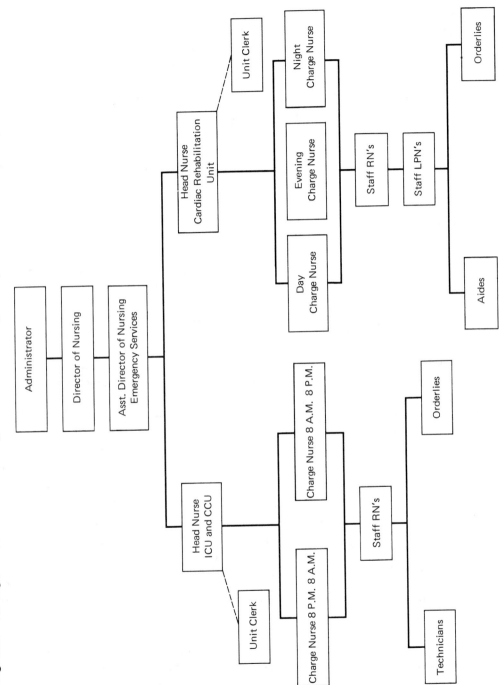

Fig. 12.16   A flow chart showing steps to be taken before graduation.

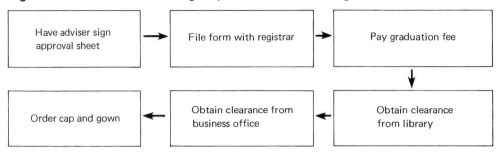

stages in which something is manufactured, accomplished, or produced from beginning to end. Flow charts can also be used to plan the day's or week's activities or, for accounting purposes, to show how income data go into a balance sheet.

A flow chart tells a story with arrows, boxes, and sometimes pictures. Boxes are connected by arrows to visualize the stages of a process. The presence and direction of the arrows tell the reader the order and movement of events involved in the process. Flow charts often proceed from left to right and back again, as in Figure 12.16. Or, they can also be constructed to read from top to bottom, as in Figure 12.17. Computer programming instructions frequently are written in this way. See, for example, Figure 12.18, which uses a computer programming flow chart to show the steps a student must follow in writing a research paper. The flow chart in Figure 12.19 depicts a more complex procedure—the stages in the operation of a nuclear power plant; readers are asked to follow arrows in several directions. The jagged lines show the contents of the cooling coil and reactor. The cooling water enters from and returns to sources (a pond, a pool, the ocean) not shown at the right-hand side of the chart.

A flow chart should clarify, not complicate, a process. Do not omit any important stages, but at the same time do not introduce unnecessary or unduly detailed information. Do show at least three or four stages, however. As with the organizational chart, use shapes that are large enough so that labels can be read quickly and easily. Mark every step with words or numbers. Arrows should be straight, and the various stages should appear in the correct sequence.

Maps

The maps you use on the job may range from highly sophisticated and detailed geographic tools to simple, hand-drawn sketches. You may use a small-scale map that shows large areas (a continent, a state, a county) in rough outline without great detail, such as the map in Figure 12.20. Or you may need a large-scale map that displays a good deal of social, economic, or physical data (such as

Fig. 12.17 A flow chart showing the 1978 Corporation Return, Form 1120, Simplified, Internal Revenue Service.

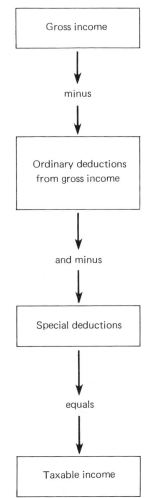

population density, location of retail businesses, hills, expressways, or rivers). That kind of detail is given in the map used by the Smithville Water Department in Figure 12.21. Look at the campus map included in your college catalog. How much detail does it supply and of what kind?

Your job requirements will dictate how detailed your map should be. Architects and builders need extremely detailed maps showing the location of pipes, telephone cables, and easement lines. An urban planner involved in developing a new community or an employee submitting site plans for a company's new location will use less detailed maps. Between these two extremes, the individual working for a government agency investigating fire or flood

Fig. 12.18   A computer programming flow chart showing steps in writing a research paper.

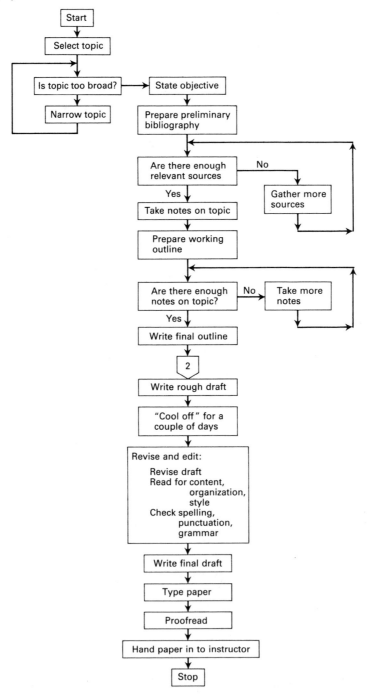

Fig. 12.19   A complex flow chart showing the operation of a nuclear power plant.

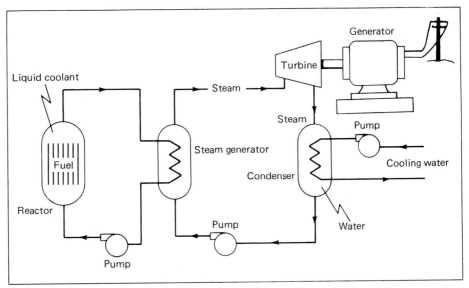

Reprinted by permission of the publisher from *An Environmental Approach to Physical Science*, by Jerry D. Wilson (Lexington, Mass.: D. C. Heath and Company, 1974) 363.

damage to a neighborhood may require a map that indicates individual houses without presenting detailed features of those dwellings.

You may have to construct your own map or find one in a published source (a government document, an atlas, or a publication of an auto club). If you photocopy the map from your source, remember that you will not be able to reproduce colors or fine shading. When preparing a map to include in a report, follow these steps:

1. Put your map on paper of the same size as the rest of the report. You may be able to purchase a blank map that contains only the shape of the area so that you can fill in the details. Or you may want to trace from a copy of a map the boundaries of the area onto a sheet of paper.
2. Provide a distance scale that identifies the proportion of inches to miles or inches to feet (1″ = 10 miles).
3. Use dots, lines, colors, symbols (Δ, ×, ○, □) or shading to indicate features. Markings should be clear and distinct.
4. If necessary, include a legend providing a key to dotted lines, colors, shadings, or symbols. A legend is the key to your map. Note the legend for water filter plants and pumping stations in Figure 12.21.
5. Eliminate any features (rivers, elevations, county seats) that do not directly depict the subject you are discussing. For example, a map showing the crops grown in two adjacent counties need not show all the roads and highways in those counties. But if you are recording the location of a

Fig. 12.20 A small-scale map showing location of world's record water depth for petroleum exploration.

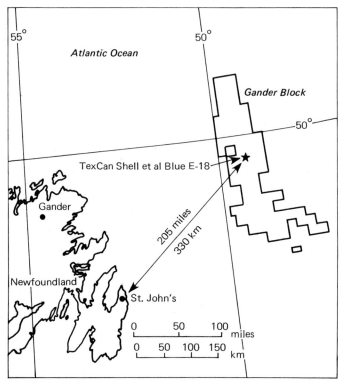

World Oil Dec. 1979: 87. Reprinted by permission.

restaurant in a small city, major access roads must be listed. A map show-ing the presence of strip mining needs to indicate elevation, but a map depicting population or religious affiliation need not include topographical (physical) detail. Reservoirs, lakes, and highways are essential in a map locating fire-damaged zones, details easily omitted in a map depicting strip mines.

6. Indicate direction by including an arrow and then citing the direction to which it points, for example N ↑ .

Photographs

Correctly prepared, photographs are an extremely helpful addition to job-related writing. The photograph's chief virtues are realism and clarity. To a reader unfamiliar with an object or a landscape, a photograph may provide a much more convincing view than a simple drawing. Photographs of "before and after" scenes are especially effective.

Fig. 12.21 A large-scale map showing location of Smithville Water Department's filter plants and pumping stations.

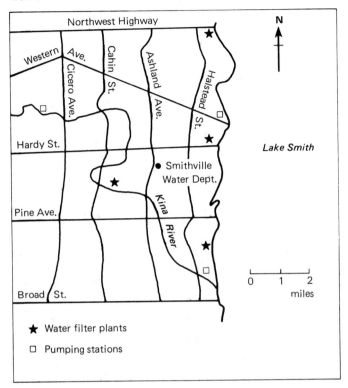

The company you work for may have a photography or art department to assist you with your picture taking and preparation. A photograph can be touched up by enlarging crucial sections, deleting unnecessary parts (called *cropping*), or inserting white arrows on a black-and-white glossy to draw a reader's attention to relevant details.

If photographic cosmetics are unavailable, however, you will have to use special care when you take a picture. The most important point to remember is that what you see and what the camera records might be two different sights. Before you take a picture, decide how much foreground and background information you need. Include only the details that are *necessary and relevant* for your purpose. Inexperienced photographers need to remember the following four points:

1. Keep the camera in *focus*, and make sure that the lighting is proper.
2. Select the *correct angle*. Choose a vantage point that will enable you to record essential information as graphically as possible.
3. Give the *right amount of detail*. Pictures that include too much clutter compete for the reader's attention and detract from the subject. A realtor

Fig. 12.22 An effective photograph—truck in foreground, enough background information, and a worker to show size and function of truck.

Fig. 12.23 A poor photograph—taken from the wrong angle so that everything merges and becomes confusing.

Photograph by David Longmire.

Photograph by David Longmire.

wanting to show that a house has an attractive front does not need to include sidewalks or streets. At the other extreme, do not cut out a necessary part of a landscape or object. Avoid putting people in a photograph when their presence is not required to show the relative size or operation of an object.

4. Take the picture from the *right distance*. The farther back you stand, the wider your angle will be, and the more the camera will capture with less detail. If you need a shot of a three-story office building, your picture may show only one or two stories if you are standing too close to the building when you photograph it. Standing too far away from an object, however, means that the photograph will reduce the object's importance and record unnecessary details.

To get a graphic sense of the effects of taking a picture the right and the wrong way, study the photographs in Figures 12.22, 12.23, 12.24, 12.25. A clear and useful picture of a hydraulic truck (often called a "cherry picker") used to cut branches can be seen in Figure 12.22. The photographer rightly

Fig. 12.24 A poor photograph—focus is on worker, but there is nothing else to identify person or work going on.

Fig. 12.25 A poor photograph—focus is on work going on, but there is nothing to indicate that worker is operating from a hydraulic truck.

Photograph by David Longmire.

Photograph by David Longmire.

placed the truck in the foreground, but included enough background information to indicate the truck's function. The worker in the gondola helps to show the size of the parts of the truck and also enables the reader to visualize the truck in operation.

In Figure 12.23 everything merges because the shot was taken from the wrong angle. The reader has no sense of the parts of the truck, their size, or their function. Another kind of error can be seen in Figure 12.24. Here the photographer was more interested in the person than in a piece of equipment. But looking at this picture, the reader has no idea where the worker came from or what he is doing up there. Finally, the reader looking at Figure 12.25 has a view of work going on, but no idea of the truck from which the worker is performing the job.

Drawings

A drawing serves many functions. For example, it can show where an object is located, how a tool or machine is put together, or what signals are given or steps taken in a particular situation. A drawing can explain the appearance of an object to individuals who may never have seen it. A drawing is also helpful to individuals who may have seen the object but do not have it in front of them as they read your work. By studying your drawing and following your discussion, readers will be better able to operate, adjust, repair, or order parts for equipment. As you will see, drawings are essential in giving instructions (pages 420; 430).

Unless you can call on the services of an expert professional photographer, you will find that drawings have two advantages over the ordinary photograph:

1. The artist can include as much or as little detail as necessary in a drawing. A pen or pencil will put down only as much as the user wants it to. The eye of the camera is not usually so selective; it tends to record everything in its path, including details that may be irrelevant for your purpose.
2. A drawing can show interior as well as exterior views, a feature that is particularly useful when the reader must understand what is going on under the case, housing, or hood.

You do not have to be a Rembrandt to create drawings. A steady hand and a careful eye are the only skills necessary. Often the only tools you will need are a straightedge (a ruler), a compass, a protractor, and crayons or colored pens. A drawing can be simple, such as the one in Figure 12.26 showing readers exactly where to place smoke detectors in a house. A photograph could not give such an uncluttered picture. Stick figures may also be a useful part of a drawing, as in Figure 12.27, which shows correct landing and take-off signals for pilots.

A more detailed drawing can reveal the interior of an object. Such sketches are called *cutaway drawings* because they show internal parts concealed from view. The underground pipes and service lines in a sanitary sewer are shown in Figure 12.28. The earth banking left in the foreground of the sketch shows where these pipes are buried.

Another kind of sketch is known as an *exploded drawing*. The drawing blows the entire object up and apart to show how the individual parts, each kept in order, are arranged. An exploded drawing of a chair is seen in Figure 12.29. The owner can better see how the chair is assembled and can more easily determine how to repair it. Fig. 12.29 also uses *callouts*, or labels identifying the components of whatever is being depicted. These labels are often attached to the parts with arrows or lines. As the name suggests, the labels "call out" the parts so readers can identify them quickly.

When you construct your own drawings, follow these rules:

1. Whenever necessary, indicate which view of the object you are presenting (for example, aerial, frontal, lateral, reverse, exterior, or interior).
2. Keep the parts of the drawing proportionate unless you are purposely enlarging one section. Then provide readers with a scale.
3. Do not include any extra details. Even the addition of a line or two might distort the reader's view. A sketch serves a practical purpose, not an esthetic one. Do not add decorations to make a drawing look fancy.

Fig. 12.26   A drawing showing where to place smoke detectors in a house.

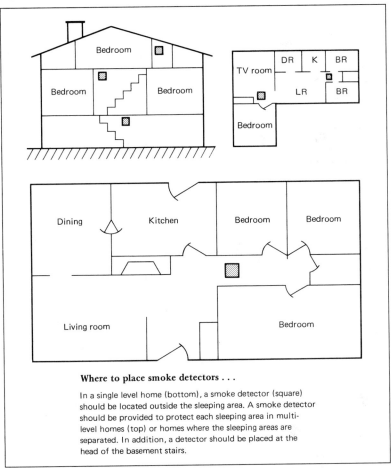

Where to place smoke detectors . . .

In a single level home (bottom), a smoke detector (square) should be located outside the sleeping area. A smoke detector should be provided to protect each sleeping area in multi-level homes (top) or homes where the sleeping areas are separated. In addition, a detector should be placed at the head of the basement stairs.

Southern Building (Dec. 1978–Jan. 1979): 10. Reprinted by permission.

☞ Computer Graphics

Computers are rapidly changing the way businesses and industries communicate internally and with customers. For a number of years computers have been used for a variety of data and word processing functions. Today, however, companies are showing an additional interest in computers to produce visuals of all kinds. In fact, numerous large firms rely on computer-generated graphics instead of on the hand-drawn varieties. Some examples of visuals created by a computer are included in Figure 12.30.

A variety of computer software packages offers graphics capabilities. Soft-

Fig. 12.27   A drawing using stick figures to show correct landing and take-off signals.

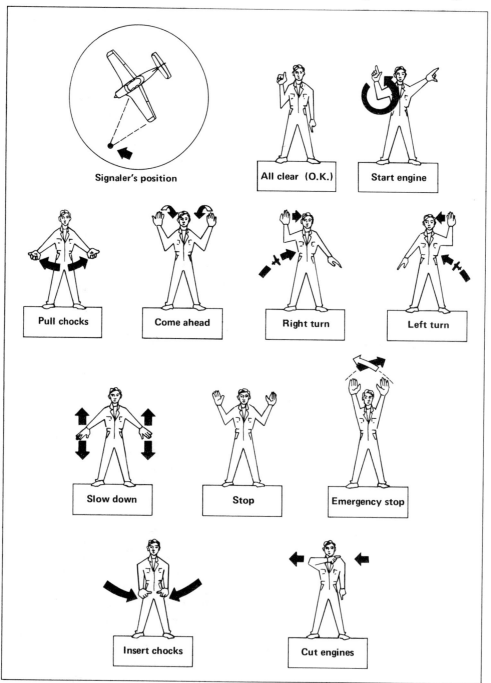

U.S. Department of Transportation, *Flight Training Handbook*, AC 61-21A, p. 54.

Fig. 12.28   A cutaway drawing showing construction of sanitary sewers with a steel trenching box.

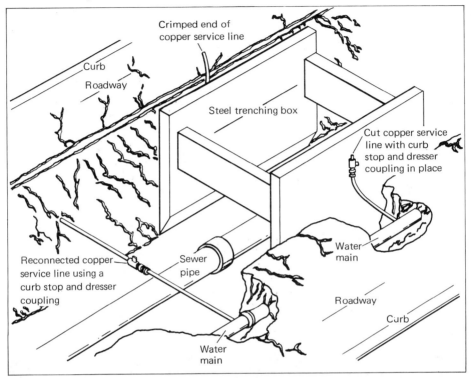

August A. Guerrera, "Grounding of Electric Circuits to Water Services: One Utility's Experience." Reprinted from *Journal of the American Water Works Association* 72 (Feb. 1980): 86 by permission. Copyright 1980, the American Water Works Association.

ware refers to the computer program or plan that changes statistical data into visuals. These software packages enable computer users to draw lines, circles, rectangles, columns, arcs, graphs, maps, and many other types of visuals. But computer users cannot just sit down and begin creating visuals. First they must enter the statistical data into the computer's data base. Then they have to instruct the computer to plot points or draw lines based upon the statistical data.

Graphics first appear on the computer's CRT screen; then, with the assistance of a printer they can be produced on hard copy (on paper) in black and white. If you have a special and expensive attachment—a two- or six-pen plotter—your computer can draw visuals that come in high resolution colors. And you can even make colored transparencies that can be used with an overhead projector.

Computer graphics have many applications in marketing, sales, and all types of scientific and technological projects. For example, an office manager

Fig. 12.29   An exploded drawing of a chair.

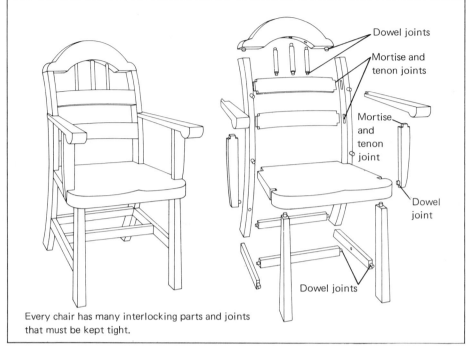

Dowel joints

Mortise and tenon joints

Mortise and tenon joint

Dowel joint

Dowel joints

Every chair has many interlocking parts and joints that must be kept tight.

From Reader's Digest *Fix-It Yourself Manual*, p. 67. Courtesy of Reader's Digest Association, Inc.

Fig. 12.30   Examples of computer graphics.

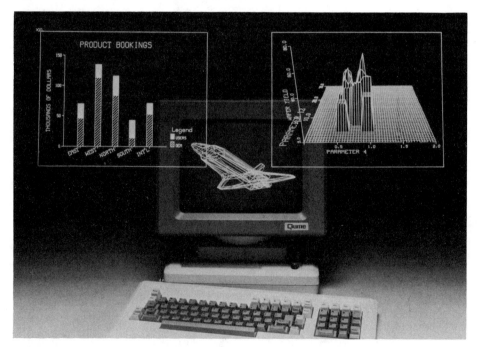

Printed by permission of the Qume Corporation, a subsidiary of ITT.

can show relative achievements of different salespersons through colored columns or colored slices of a pie chart using computer graphics.

While many firms may purchase the sophisticated hardware and software to produce computer graphics, you will always use the basic information discussed in this chapter.

☞ Glossary

By way of review, the following is a glossary of terms used in this chapter:

Bar chart: a visual using vertical or horizontal bars to measure different data in space and time; bars can also be segmented to show multiple percentages within one bar. Bar charts are used to show a variety of facts for easy comparison.

Callouts: labels that identify the parts of an object in a visual.

Captions: titles or headings for visuals.

Circle chart: a visual shaped in a circle, or pie, whose slices represent the parts of the whole. Circle charts portray budgets, expenditures, shares, and time allotments.

Computer graphics: a variety of visuals generated by a computer; software (plans) and hardware (computer screens, plotters) create these visuals.

Cropping: the process of eliminating unnecessary, unwanted details of a photograph by reproducing only the desired portion.

Cross-hatching: the process of marking parts of a visual with parallel lines that cross each other obliquely; used to differentiate one bar or slice of a circle chart from another.

Cutaway drawing: a sketch in which the exterior covering of an object has been removed to show an interior view.

Dependent variable: the element (cost, employment, energy) plotted along the vertical axis of a line graph and most directly influenced by the independent variable.

Exploded drawing: a sketch of an entire object that has been blown up and apart to show the relationship of parts to one another.

Figures: any visuals that are not tables—charts, drawings, graphs, pictographs, photographs, maps.

Flow chart: a sketch revealing the stages in an activity or process.

Graph: a picture that represents the relationship of an independent variable to one or more dependent variables; produces a line or curve to show their movement in time or space. Graphs are used to depict figures that change often—temperatures, rainfall, prices, employment, productions, and so forth.

Independent variable: the element, plotted along the horizontal axis of a graph, which most directly and importantly affects the dependent variable; most often, the independent variable is time or distance.

Large-scale map: a map that shows a great deal of detail, whether physical (elevations, rivers), economic (income levels), or social (population, religious affiliation).

Legend: the explanation, or key, indicating what different colors, shadings, or symbols represent in a visual.

Organizational chart: a visual showing the structure of an organization from the chief executive to the work force of employees. An organizational chart reveals the chain of command with areas of authority and responsibility.

Pictograph: a visual showing differences in statistical data by means of pictures varying in size, number, or color.

Pie chart: see **Circle chart.**

Small-scale map: a map that depicts large areas without detail (a town with no streets or subdivisions represented or a state with no cities shown).

Stub: the first column on the left-hand side of a table; contains line captions, listing those units to be discussed in the columns.

Suppressed zero: a graph beginning with a larger number, when it would be impossible or impractical to start plotting at zero.

Table: a visual in which statistical data or verbal descriptions are arranged in rows or columns.

Templates: clear plastic sheets containing a variety of symbols, shapes, and designs which can be traced on paper.

Tick marks: equally spaced marks drawn on the vertical or horizontal scale of a graph to show units of measurement; see **Cross-hatching.**

☞ Exercises

1. Record the highest temperature reached in your town for the next five days. Then collect data on the highest temperature reached in three of the following cities—Boston, Chicago, Dallas, Denver, Los Angeles, Miami, New Orleans, New York, Philadelphia, Phoenix, Salt Lake City, San Francisco, Seattle—over the same five days. (You can get this information from a newspaper.) Prepare a table showing the differences for the five-day period.

2. Go to a supermarket and get the prices of four different brands of the same product (hair spray, aspirin, a soft drink, a box of cereal). Put your findings in the form of a table.

3. The Foreign Agricultural Service of the USDA supplied the following statistics on the world production of oranges (including tangerines) in thousands of metric tons for the following countries during the years 1969–1972: Brazil, 2,005, 2,132, 2,760, and 2,872; Israel, 909, 1,076,

1,148, 1,221; Italy, 1,669, 1,599, 1,766, 1,604; Japan, 2,424, 2,994, 2,885, 4,070; Mexico, 937, 1,405, 1,114, 1,270; Spain, 2,135, 2,005, 2,179, 2,642; and the United States, 7,658, 7,875, 7,889, 9,245. Prepare a table with this information and then write a paragraph in which you introduce the table and draw conclusions from it.

4. Keep a record for one week of the number of miles you drive each day. Then prepare a line graph depicting this information.

5. The price of gasoline in one city was as follows:

	1980	*1984*
January	59.9	99.9
February	62.9	109.9
March	67.9	119.9
April	68.9	123.9
May	73.9	128.9

Make a multiple-line graph showing a comparison of gasoline prices for the two years. Distinguish the two different lines.

6. Prepare a table to show the following statistical data. According to the 1970 Census, the town of Ardmore had a population of 34,567. By the 1980 Census the town had decreased its population by 4,500. In the 1970 Census the town of Morrison had a population of 23,809, but by the 1980 Census the population had increased by 3,689. The 1980 Census figure for the town of Berkesville was 25,675, which was an increase of 2,768 from the 1970 Census.

7. Prepare a line graph for the information in exercise 6.

8. Prepare a bar graph for the information in exercise 6.

9. Write a paragraph introducing and interpreting the table printed below.

Year	*Brewing companies*	Plants	*Per capita consumption* (gallons)*
1935	750	750	10.3
1940	578	611	12.5
1945	457	466	18.6
1950	380	407	17.2
1955	231	292	15.9
1960	171	229	15.4
1965	118	197	16.0
1970	92	154	18.7
1975	54	102	21.1
1980	43	88	23.1
1985	45	82	25.3

*Domestic beer only

10. Prepare a circle chart showing the breakdown of your budget for one week or one month.

11. According to a municipal study in 1984 the distribution of all companies classified in each enterprise industry in that city was as follows: minerals, 0.4%; selected services, 33.3%; retail trade, 36.7%; wholesale trade, 6.5%; manufacturing, 5.3%; and construction, 17.8%. Make a circle chart to represent this distribution.

12. Construct a segmented bar chart to represent the kinds and numbers of courses you took in a two-semester period or during your last year in high school.

13. Prepare a bar chart for the different brands of one of the products in exercise 2. Write a paragraph introducing this illustration.

14. Find a pictograph in a textbook or magazine and make a bar graph from the information contained in it. Then write a paragraph introducing the bar graph and drawing conclusions from it.

15. Make an organizational chart for a business or agency you worked for recently. Include part-time and full-time employees, but indicate employees' status with different kinds of shapes or lines. Then write a brief letter to your employer, explaining why such an organizational chart should be distributed to all employees.

16. Prepare a flow chart for one of the following activities:
    (a) setting a table in a restaurant
    (b) jumping a "dead" battery
    (c) giving an injection
    (d) crocheting an afghan
    (e) painting a set of louvered doors
    (f) making an arrest
    (g) training a dog
    (h) making homemade wine
    (i) putting out an electrical fire
    (j) calling up a computer program
    (k) any job you do

17. Make a map representing at least two blocks of your neighborhood. Include with appropriate symbols any stores, police or fire stations, churches, parks, or schools. Supply a legend for your readers.

18. Draw a map for a visitor who wants to know how to get from your college library to the downtown area of your city. Supply a distance scale.

19. Draw an interior view of a piece of equipment you use in your major; then identify the relevant parts using callouts.

20. Prepare a drawing of one of the following simple tools and include appropriate callouts with your visual.

    (a) golf club
    (b) hammer
    (c) pliers
    (d) stethoscope
    (e) swivel chair

    (f) scissors
    (g) ballpoint pen
    (h) soldering iron
    (i) table lamp
    (j) pair of eyeglasses

21. Prepare appropriate visuals to illustrate the data listed in any two of the following lettered items. In a paragraph immediately after each visual explain why the type of visual you selected is appropriate for the information.

    (a) Life expectancy is increasing in America. This growth can be dramatically measured by comparing the number of teenagers with the number of older adults (over age 65) in America during the last few years and then by projecting these figures. In 1970 there were approximately 28 million teenagers and 20 million older adults. By 1980 the number of teenagers climbed to 30 million and the number of older adults increased to 25 million. In 1990 it is expected that there will be 27 million teenagers and 31 million older adults. By the year 2000 the number of teenagers will level off to 23 million, but the number of older adults will soar to more than 36 million.

    (b) The percentage of women in the work force is steadily increasing. According to the U.S. Department of Labor of all women sixteen years and older 37.7 percent of them were employed in the work force in 1960. In 1965 there were 38.9 percent; by 1970 43.3 percent; by 1975 46.3 percent; by 1980 51.5 percent; and by 1985 the percentage had reached almost 55.

    (c) Researchers estimate that for every adult in America 3,985 cigarettes were purchased in 1970; 4,100 in 1975; 3,875 in 1980; and 3,490 in 1985.

22. Find a photograph that contains some irrelevant clutter. Write a letter to the photography department of a company for which you presumably work that wants to use the photograph. Tell the department what to delete and why.

23. Make a simple line drawing of only the relevant portions of the photograph in exercise 22. Explain in two paragraphs why the drawing is better than the photograph.

Section IV

Instructions, Proposals, and Reports

13

Writing Clear Instructions

Clear instructions are essential if work is to get done in business and industry. This chapter contains suggestions on how to prepare, organize, write, and arrange instructions.

☞ The Importance of Instructions

Instructions tell, and frequently show, how to do something. They indicate how to perform a procedure (draw blood); operate a machine (run a forklift); assemble, maintain, or repair a piece of equipment (a photocopier; a carburetor); or locate an object (coils in a circuit). Readers use instructions for reasons of safety, efficiency, convenience, and economy. Product labels in a medicine chest, for example, inform users when and why to take the medications and how much to take. Owners' manuals instruct buyers on how to avoid the inconvenience of a product breakdown by keeping the product in good working order. Magazines such as *Popular Mechanics, Popular Photography,* and how-to books offer consumers money-saving instructions on topics ranging from repairing their homes to training guard dogs. You might want to read some of these how-to publications to see how they identify and meet the needs of their audiences.

As part of your job, you may be asked to write instructions for your co-workers as well as for the customers who use your company's services or products. Your employer stands to gain or lose much from the kinds of instructions you write. Imagine how costly it would be if employees had to stop their work each time they could not understand a set of instructions. Also, your employer may lose money if the instructions to customers are unclear. Clearly written instructions can save your company costly service calls. Even more important, careful instructions can help to prevent damage claims or even lawsuits. Poorly written instructions may result in injury to the person trying to follow them.

☞ The Variety of Instructions

Instructions vary in length, complexity, and format. Some instructions are one word long—*stop, lift, insert, push, erase.* Others are a few sentences long: "Use a warm, damp cloth before glue dries." "Be sure to close after using." "Store in an upright position." Short instructions are appropriate for the numerous, relatively nontechnical chores performed every day. For more elaborate procedures, however, detailed instructions may be as long as a page or a book. When your firm purchases a new computer or a piece of earth-moving equipment, it will receive an instruction pamphlet or book containing many steps, cautionary statements, and diagrams. Many businesses prepare their own training manuals containing instructions for 200 or 300 different procedures.

Instructions can be given in paragraphs or in lists, and you will have to determine which format is most appropriate for the kinds of instructions you write. Figures 13.1 and 13.2 show two sets of brief instructions written in paragraph format. In Figure 13.1 hospital employees are told how to prepare and administer a sitz bath; in Figure 13.2 park rangers are given instructions on how to repair a halyard, or tackle, used to raise a flag or move a pulley.

The instructions shown in Figures 13.3 and 13.4 are printed in list form. In Figure 13.3 typists will find directions on how to change a ribbon on an IBM Selectric typewriter; the directions in Figure 13.4 give details on how to assemble an outdoor grill.

Either a straight narrative account or a list can be used if your employer asks you to put instructions in a memo or letter. The following example shows an instructional memo that uses a list:

```
                              MEMO

    TO:    All Laundry Room Staff    DATE:    January 30, 1986

    FROM:  Candy Dwyer               SUBJECT:  Fire evacuation
           Safety Engineer                     procedures


    In the event of a fire in the laundry, follow these instructions:

    1. Turn in an alarm. Dial extension 311.
    2. Shut off all machinery.
    3. Turn off all exhaust fans.
    4. Close interior doors.
    5. Vacate area.
```

Fig. 13.1   Instructions on how to prepare and administer a sitz bath.

First, adjust water temperature dial to 105–110°F. Then turn on the faucet and fill sitz tub with enough water to cover the patient's hips. Before assisting patient into the tub, place bath towel in the bottom of the tub. Allow the patient to sit in the tub for 15–20 minutes. At the end of this time, help patient out of the tub. Then dry the patient thoroughly.

Fig. 13.2   Instructions on how to repair a halyard.

Easy Temporary Join for Synthetic Ropes

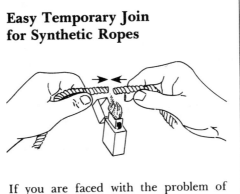

If you are faced with the problem of reeving a new halyard on a flagpole or mast, or through a block or pulley in an inaccessible location, the solution can be easy if both old and new lines are made of nylon or polyester (Dacron, Terylene, etc.). Simply join the ends of the old and new lines temporarily by melting end fibers together in a small flame (a little heat goes a long way). Rotate the two lines slowly as the fibers melt. Withdraw them from the flame before a ball of molten material forms, and if the stuff ignites, blow out the flame at once. Hold the joint together until it is cool and firm.

R. I. Standish, *Parks* 51 (Apr.–June 1980): 21.

Fig. 13.3   Instructions on how to change the ribbon on an IBM Selectric typewriter.

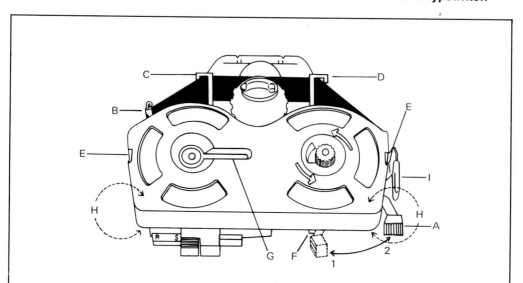

To Remove a Ribbon

- Center the Carrier and turn the motor OFF.
- Lift the cover.
- Keep the Paper Bail against the Platen.
- Move the Ribbon Load Lever A* to the load position 1 until it snaps against the Stop F.
- Using both hands, hold the Ribbon Cartridge at the front corners H and lift straight up.

* The Ribbon Load Lever on the IBM Correcting "Selectric" Typewriter cannot be moved if the Tape Load Lever I is in the load position.

To Install a New Ribbon

- Be sure the Ribbon Load Lever A is in the load position 1.
- Put the ribbon leader (uninked portion) over the *outside* of the Guidepost B and Ribbon Guides C and D. *Failure to do so will cause ribbon breakage.*
- Position the Ribbon Cartridge so that it fits between the Spring Clips E. Firmly push down both ends of the Cartridge.
- Thread the leader through Ribbon Guides C and D.
- Turn the Knob on the Cartridge in the direction of the arrow until the leader disappears inside the cartridge.
- Move the Ribbon Load Lever A to the type position 2.
- Close the cover.

Note: The name and reorder number of each ribbon appear on the underside of the Ribbon Cartridge.

Fig. 13.4   Instructions on how to assemble an outdoor grill.

ASSEMBLY INSTRUCTIONS

The instructions shown below are for the basic grill with tubular legs. If you have a pedestal grill, or a grill with accessories, check the separate instruction sheet for details not shown here.

NOTE: Make sure you locate all the parts before discarding any of the packaging material.

TOOLS REQUIRED ... A standard straight blade screwdriver is the only tool you need to assemble your new Meco grill. If you have a pedestal grill, you will need a 7-16 wrench or a small adjustable wrench.

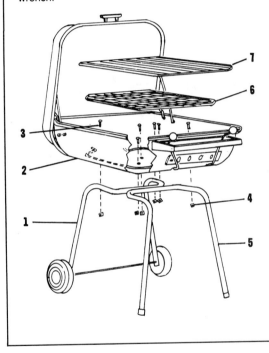

1. Before you start, take time to read through this manual. Inside you will find many helpful hints that will help you get the full potential of enjoyment and service from your new Meco grill.

2. Lay out all the parts.

3. Assemble roller leg (1) to bottom rear of bowl (2) with 1¼″ long bolts (3) and nuts (4).

4. Assemble fixed leg (5) to bottom front of bowl (2) with 1¼″ long bolts (3) and nuts (4).

5. Place fire grate—ash dump (6) in bottom of bowl (2) between adjusting levers.

6. Place cooking grid (7) on top of adjusting levers. Make sure top grid wires run from front to back of grill.

Meco Assembly Instructions and Owners Manual, Metals Engineering Corp., P.O. Box 3005, Greenville, TN 37743. Reprinted by permission.

☞ Before Writing Instructions

Regardless of their format (paragraphs or lists), instructions have to be clear, complete, and easy to follow. In most instances you will not be available for readers to ask you questions when they don't understand something. Consequently, they will have to rely on your written instructions. Your goal in writing those instructions is to get readers to perform the same steps you followed and, most important, to obtain the same results you did. Writing instructions is like teaching. You have to understand the material yourself and know the best way of presenting it.

To make sure that your instructions are clear and accurate, plan them carefully. You must first completely understand the job or procedure that you are asking someone else to perform. Make sure you know the reason for doing something, the parts or tools required, the steps to be followed to get the job done, and the results of that job. If you are not completely sure about the procedure, watch someone who is an expert perform it.

Next, actually perform the procedure (assembling, repairing, maintaining, ordering, dissecting) yourself. If possible, go through a number of trial runs. Take notes as you go along and be sure to divide the procedure into simple steps for readers to follow. You should not give the reader too much to do in one step. Transfer your notes to a rough draft of the instructions you want readers to follow.

To test your rough draft, ask someone from the intended audience (consumers, technicians) who may never have performed the procedure before to follow it to complete the task. Ask this individual to identify any places in your instructions that are vague, hard to follow, inconsistent (steps bunched up or out of order), or incomplete. Then revise your rough draft for the final copy of the instructions that you will give to readers.

Pay special attention to the technical language and the amount of detail you include. Try to determine your reader's level of experience and education. A set of instructions accompanying a chemistry set would be much different in terminology, abbreviations, and detail from a set of instructions a professor gives a class in organic chemistry:

General
Audience: Place 8 drops of vinegar in a test tube and add a piece of limestone about the size of a pea.

Specialized
Audience: Place 8 gtts of $CH_3\,COOH$ in a test tube and add 1 mg of CO_3.

Do not assume that your readers have done the procedure or have operated the equipment as many times as you have. (If they had, there would be no need for your instructions.) The readers may never have seen the particular machine or have performed the specific procedure. No writer of instructions ever disappointed readers by making directions too clear or too easy to follow. Use language and symbols that will be readily understood. If someone is puzzled by your directions, you defeat the reasons for writing them.

☞ Selecting the Right Words and Visuals

To write instructions that readers can understand and turn into effective action, follow these guidelines:

1. Use verbs in the imperative mood. Imperatives are commands that have deleted the pronoun "you." Almost all the sentences in Figures 13.1, 13.2, and 13.3 contain imperatives: "adjust water temperature" for "you adjust water temperature"; "fill the sitz tub with enough water" for "you fill the sitz tub with enough water"; "lift the cover" for "you lift the cover." Deleting the "you" is not discourteous, as it certainly would be in a letter or a report. Instructions are best expressed as commands to show that the writer speaks with authority. Instructions say "These steps work, so do it exactly this way." Imperatives also get the reader to do something specific without hesitation. Do not water down your directions with statements such as "Please see if you can remove the outside panel"; "Try to allow the mixture to cool for five minutes"; or "If at all possible, adjust the thermostat to 78°." Wishy-washy statements may lead the reader to believe that there are some choices involved, when in fact there are none. For this reason, avoid *might, could, should:* "you might want to ignite the fire next" does not have the force of "ignite the fire next." Instead, choose action verbs (*apply, close, cut, dissect, drain, drop, insert, push, rotate, rub, shut off, turn, wipe*).

2. Write clear, short sentences. Since readability is especially important in instructions, keep sentences short and uncomplicated. Keep them under twenty words and preferably under fifteen. Note that the sentences in Figures 13.1, 13.2, 13.3, and 13.4 are, for the most part, under fourteen words. Avoid the passive voice. In place of "The air blower is to be used last," write "Use the air blower last." Also avoid addressing the reader as "one" or "the user": "The user should apply the air blower last" or "One must use the air blower last" are, again, best listed as "Use the air blower last."

You can keep your sentences clear by avoiding ambiguity. Do not write a sentence that sends the reader a message opposite from what you intend. A direction such as "Before using the soldering iron on metal, clean it with Freon" may mislead the inexperienced welder to put Freon on the iron rather than on the metal that is to be cleaned. Similarly, "Perform venipuncture with the arm in a downward position" does not clearly specify whose arm is to be in that position; appropriately revised, the instruction reads "Put the patient's arm in a downward position."

3. Use precise terms for measurements, distances, and times. Indefinite, vague directions leave users wondering if they are doing the right thing. (Review pages 83–85 in Chapter 4.) The following imprecise directions are better expressed through the revisions listed in parentheses: "Turn the distributor cap a little." (How much is "a little?" "Turn the distributor cap three-quarters of an inch."); "Pack the contents in a bag." (What bag? "Pack the contents in a one-eighth-inch barrel bag."); "Let the contents stand for a while." (How long? "Let the contents stand for ten minutes."). Precise timing is essential to the success of many kinds of instructions ranging from baking a cake to completing an experiment in a chemistry laboratory.

4. Use connective words as signposts to specify the exact order in which something is to be done (especially when your instructions are written in paragraphs). Words such as *first, then, before* in Figure 13.1 help readers stay on course, telling them how and why the various procedures are connected to produce the desired results.

5. Label each step with a bullet (Figure 13.3) or **a number** (Figure 13.4) (when you present your instructions in a list). Plenty of white space between each step also distinctly separates steps for the reader. If circumstances permit the use of color, employ it sparingly to set off important elements of your instructions. Color is especially effective for safety notices (see page 430).

6. Whenever feasible, use visuals to make your instructions easier to understand and follow. Visuals are graphic and direct, showing readers precisely what they must do. Visuals, therefore, can simplify a process for readers, save you words, and help your readers to get the job done faster and with more confidence. For example, the illustration in Figure 13.2 reinforces the process of joining the two parts of the halyard by fire; the diagram in Figure 13.3 labels the typewriter parts that users must understand if they are to insert a new ribbon. Another frequently used visual in instructions is the exploded drawing, such as that in Figure 13.4, to help consumers see how the various components of the grill fit together for easy assembly. The types of visuals you can use will, of course, depend on the procedure or equipment you are describing. A simple line drawing such as that illustrated in Figure 13.5 not only makes the order of the steps clear, but also helps to eliminate any confusion readers may have about the two kinds of postage to use when returning their product with a complaint letter. Note in Figure 13.6 how line drawings and symbols (triangle, square, circle) graphically portray the proper use of fire extinguishers. Place visuals next to the steps to which they refer, not on another page or at the bottom of the page. To gain the most from visuals, readers must be able to see the illustrations or diagrams immediately before and after reading the directions that they clarify. Whenever possible, place the visual next to the step the reader is to perform. Assign each visual a number (Figure 1, Figure 2), and in your directions tell readers where those visuals can be found ("to the left of these instructions"; "see the sketch at the right"). Wherever necessary, label parts of the visual material. Make sure the visual looks like the object the user is trying to assemble, maintain, or repair. Furthermore, inform readers if a part of an object is missing or reduced in size in your visual.

☞ The Four Parts of Instructions

Except for very short instructions, such as those illustrated in Figures 13.1–13.4, a set of instructions generally contains four main parts: (1) an introduction, (2) a list of equipment and materials, (3) the actual steps to perform the process, and (4) a conclusion, when necessary.

Fig. 13.5   Instructions on how to mail an appliance.

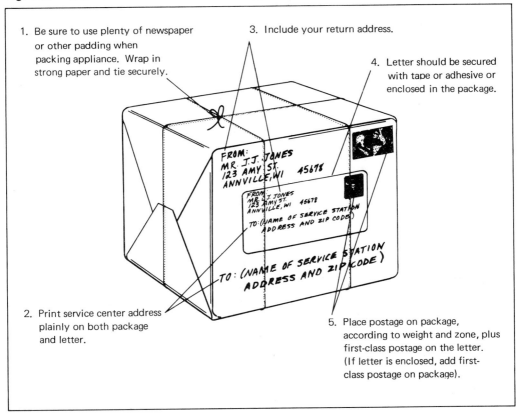

1. Be sure to use plenty of newspaper or other padding when packing appliance. Wrap in strong paper and tie securely.

2. Print service center address plainly on both package and letter.

3. Include your return address.

4. Letter should be secured with tape or adhesive or enclosed in the package.

5. Place postage on package, according to weight and zone, plus first-class postage on the letter. (If letter is enclosed, add first-class postage on package).

Reprinted by permission of The West Bend Company, West Bend, WI 53095.

The Introduction

Whether you need an introduction depends on the particular process or machine you are describing. Short instructions require no introduction or only a brief one- or two-sentence introduction such as the one in Figure 13.4. More complex instructions require lengthier introductions. For instance, a ninety-page manual may contain a two- or three-page introduction. An introduction should be proportional to the kinds of instructions to be given. Instructions on how to sand a floor will not need a one-page introduction on how friction works.

The function of an introduction is to provide readers with enough *necessary* background information to understand why and how your instructions work. An introduction must make readers feel more comfortable and better prepared. Accordingly, an introduction can do one or all of the following:

1. State why the instructions are useful for a specific audience.   Here is an introduction from a safety procedure describing the protective lockout of equipment: "The purpose of this procedure is to provide a uniform method of

Fig. 13.6   Instructions on the proper use of fire extinguishers.

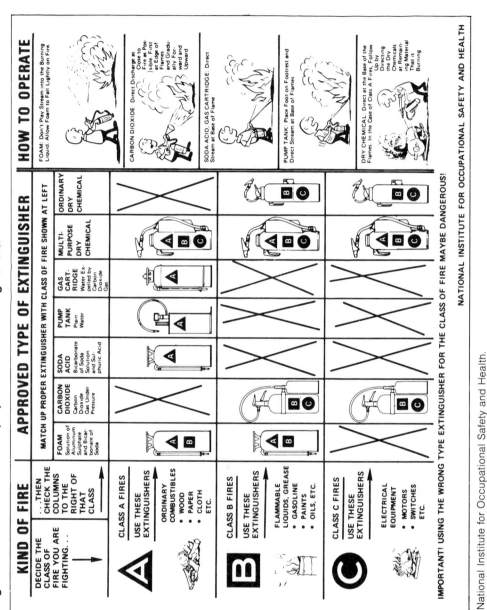

National Institute for Occupational Safety and Health.

locking out machinery or equipment. This will prevent the possibility of setting moving parts in motion, energizing electrical lines, or opening valves while repair, set-up and adjustment, or cleaning work is in progress." Instructions on how to write an appraisal of a piece of property might list these purposes: (1) to estimate the value of the property, (2) to indicate which owner's interest is being appraised if the property is jointly owned, (3) to provide a legal description of the property. Many instructions in training manuals contain introductions that stress the educational benefits to the user: "These instructions will serve as a valuable training tool for the beginning draftsperson, showing him or her the proper ways of preparing detailed drawings that will be useful in woodwork manufacturing today."

2. Indicate how a particular machine or procedure works. Explain the scientific or management principles by which a device or procedure operates. A brief discussion of the "theory of operation" will help readers understand why something works the way your instructions say it should. The introduction to instructions on how to run a machine begins by stressing the function of the machine: "These instructions will teach you how to operate an autoclave. The autoclave is used to sterilize surgical instruments through live additive-free steam." Laboratory experiments usually begin with a discussion of reasons why a particular effect will occur or how something develops under certain circumstances. Such discussion sometimes describes a scientific law or principle. For example, the following paragraph introduces an experiment on osmosis, the process by which fluids flow from one cell to another.

> The distribution of water among the various fluid compartments of the body is determined in part by the solute [dissolved substance] content of these fluids. Since most solutes penetrate cell membranes relatively slowly, water, because of its abundance and permeability, plays an important role in establishing osmotic equilibrium between cells and their environment. When placed in a solution whose water concentration is different from that in its own protoplasm, a cell either gains or loses water. The process of direct migration of solvents through membranes is called osmosis. This experiment will demonstrate the movement of water across a membrane because of differences in solute concentration across the two sides.[1]

3. Establish how long it should take the user to complete all steps of the instructions. If users know how long a procedure should take, they will be better able to judge whether they are doing it correctly—if they are waiting too long or not long enough between steps or if they are going too slowly or too quickly: "It should take about three and one-half hours from the time you start laying the floor tiles until the time they dry well enough to walk on."

4. Inform the user about any special circumstances to which the instructions apply. Some instructions precede others or are used only on special occasions. Readers must be informed about those changes or emergency situa-

---

[1] Byron A. Schottelius, John D. Thomson, and Dorothy D. Schottelius, *Physiology: Laboratory Manual*, 4th ed. (St. Louis: C. V. Mosby, 1978) 11. Reprinted by permission.

tions. A supervisor of a large chemical plant sent employees the memo contained in Figure 13.7 to describe operating procedures to be followed during energy shortages. Note the brief introduction emphasizing the special circumstances. A safety procedure introduction in Figure 13.8 informs users when they have to obtain a "hot work permit," by first defining the term and then supplying examples of the jobs requiring that permit.

Not every introduction to a set of instructions will contain facts on all the categories of information listed above. Some instructions will require less detail. You will have to judge how much background information specific instructions call for.

List of Equipment and Materials

Immediately after the introduction, inform readers of all equipment or materials they will need. This list should be complete and clear. Do not wait until the readers are actually performing one of the steps in the instructions to tell them that a certain type of drill or a specific kind of chemical is required. They may have to stop what they are doing to find this equipment or material; moreover, the procedure may fail or present hazards if users do not have the right equipment at the specified time.

Do not expect your readers to know exactly what size, model, or quantity you have in mind. Tell them precisely. For example, if a Phillips screwdriver is necessary to complete one step, specify this type of screwdriver under the heading *"Equipment and Materials";* do not just list "screwdriver." Here are some additional examples of unclear references to equipment and materials, with more helpful alternatives listed in parentheses after them: solution (0.7% NaCl solution); maps (four aerial reconnaissance maps); pencils (two engineering pencils); electrodes (four short platinum wire electrodes); file (cheese-grater file); sand (10-lb. bag of sand); needle (butterfly needle); water (10 gallons untreated sea water).

If you are concerned that readers will not understand why certain equipment or materials are used, give the explanation in parentheses after the item. For example, listing alcohol and cotton as materials needed to take a blood pressure might confuse readers not familiar with the uses of these materials. A clarifying comment after the materials such as "used to clean stethoscope headphones" would help. The following example, "Instructions for Absentee Voters," contains such helpful comments.

This absentee ballot package has been sent to you at your request. It contains the following items:

1. Sample paper ballot (for information only).
2. Official ballot (this is a punch card).
3. Punching tool.
4. Envelope with attached declaration.
5. Addressed return envelope.

Fig. 13.7   Instructions alerting readers to special circumstances.

 **HERCULES**

To: All Shift Supervisors
     All Firefighters

From: Robert A. Ferguson *Robert A Ferguson*

Subject: Operating Procedures During Energy Shortages

Date: October 10, 1982

The following policy has been formulated to aid in maintaining
required pressures during periods of low wood flow and severe natural
gas curtailment.

All boilers are equipped with lances to burn residue or no. 6 fuel oil
as auxiliary fuels. When wood is short, no. 6 oil should be burned in no. 2
and no. 3 boilers at highest possible rate consistent with smoke standards.
To do this, take these steps:

1. Put no. 6 oil on no. 3 boiler lances.

2. Shut down overfire air.

3. Shut down forced draft.

4. Turn off vibrators.

5. Keep grates covered with ashes or wood until ash cover exists.

This will result in an output of 25,000 to 35,000 lbs./hr. steam from
no. 3 boiler and will force wood on down to no. 4 boiler.

If required, the same procedure can be repeated on no. 2 boiler.

Voters will know that the punch card is their official ballot and that it does not look like the sample ballot because of the parenthetical information in number 2. The point is reinforced later in the directions by this statement:

IMPORTANT

Punch only with tool provided—never with a pencil or pen. Your vote is recorded by punching this ballot card—not by marking the paper ballot.

Do not return the sample paper ballot.

Fig. 13.8   Instructions that describe a safety procedure.

 **HERCULES**

HATTIESBURG PLANT
SAFETY PROCEDURE NO. 7
WELDING AND HOT WORK PERMIT PROCEDURE

1.0 Permits Required

    All work in hazardous areas involving the use of equipment or tools that may produce heat or sparks shall require a HOT WORK PERMIT. The following are examples of jobs requiring hot work permits: welding, burning, soldering, babbitting, sand blasting, chipping, grinding, drilling, and the use of portable pumps or tools powered by internal combustion engines or non-explosion-proof motors, Remington stud driver.

2.0 Hazardous Area Defined

    All areas of the plant are defined as hazardous areas except the following, which are defined as non-hazardous: Shop Area (including the Boiler Shop, Tractor and Auto Shop, Machine Shop, Pump Shop, Pipe Shop, Welding Shop, and Salvage Yard), Mill Room, Shredder House, Power House Boiler Room and Engine Room, Office and Office Annex, the five Smoke Houses, and smoking lounge in the Laboratory, and Area Maintenance Shops.

Used by permission of Hercules, Incorporated.

Some equipment and material sections may also warn readers about limitations and dangers in using specific materials. The makers of a small appliance give these instructions on cleaning the "No-stick finish" on their Wok:

> Always use a nylon pad such as Dobie or Scotch-Brite Cookware Scrub'n Sponge. A dishcloth may give No-stick finish a clean look, but it will not remove tiny food particles which settle into the finish. If not removed, they will burn when the Wok is reheated, causing stains and reducing the non-stick qualities of the finish. Do not use a metal pad or abrasive cleaning powder.[2]

An even more detailed list of materials used to clean and smooth wood surfaces follows.

Refinishing

Preparing the Surface

Before attempting to refinish a wood item, be sure the surface is smooth and free from dirt, dust, and grease.

Materials
The following materials are suitable for cleaning and smoothing wood surfaces:

Abrasives

- *Sandpaper.* Sandpaper is not made of sand as the name suggests. It is made of various kinds of abrasive material applied to paper or cloth backing and made in sheet, drum, belt, and other forms. Sandpaper comes in various grades ranging from No. 4/0 to No. 1. No. 4/0 is used when an extra fine finish is required; No. 2/0 for a fine finish; No. 1/2 for rubbing down undercoats of paint and varnish in preparation for final finish; and No. 1 to No. 3 for sanding down old coats of paint too badly chipped to repaint.
- *Sanding Disks.* Sanding disks are flat, circular pieces of sandpaper of various types, sizes, and coarseness for use on a power sander. These disks can also be used either on a disk or rotary hand sander.
- *Commercial Steel Wool.* Steel wool is a fluffy or wool-like mass of steel turnings. It is made in grades No. 00, 0, 1, and 3, ranging from extra fine to coarse. It is a mild abrasive for rubbing down and smoothing wood and is well suited for removal of light rust from metal prior to repainting.

Cloth, Sponges, and Waste

- *Jute Burlap.* Jute burlap is a coarse, heavy, loose-woven material, used for all general purpose cleaning.
- *Osnaburg Cotton Cloth.* Osnaburg cloth is a coarse, heavy cloth used as a substitute for jute burlap and serves the same purposes.

---

[2] Reprinted by permission of The West Bend Company.

- *Cotton Wiping Cloth.* This cloth is relatively free from lint. It is used as a substitute for cotton waste, especially when lint deposits are undesirable, and as a substitute for sponges when washing wood and metalwork. It can be used to apply strong soap, lye, soda ash, or other solutions, which destroy sponges quickly.
- *Cellulose Sponge.* This is a synthetic material. It *cannot* be used with solutions containing soda ash, trisodium phosphate, or caustic soda (lye) because they will break down the fibers and ruin the sponge.
- *Natural Sponge.* This is a natural material that has great liquid-absorption capacity. It becomes soft when wet without losing its original toughness and is used with mild cleaning solutions. Solutions of soda ash, trisodium phosphate, and caustic soda affect the natural sponge the same as the synthetic sponge.[3]

The Steps in Instructions

The heart of your directions will consist of clearly distinguished steps that readers must follow to achieve the desired results. To make sure that you help your readers understand your steps, observe the following rules.

1. Put the steps in their correct order. If a step is out of order or is missing, the entire set of instructions can be wrong or, worse yet, dangerous. Double-check your steps before you write them down. Each step should be numbered to indicate its correct place in the sequence of events you are describing. Never put an asterisk (*) before or after a step to make the reader look somewhere else for information. If the information is important, put it in your instructions; if it is not, delete it.

2. Group closely related activities into one step. Sometimes closely related actions are grouped into one step to help the reader coordinate activities and to emphasize their being done at the same time, in the same place, or with the same equipment. Study the following instructions listing the receptionist's duties of a ward clerk in a hospital.

(1) Greet patients warmly and make them feel welcome. Never fall into the trap of groaning and saying "not another one." Remember the patient probably did not want to come to the hospital in the first place.

(2) Check the identity bracelet against the summary sheet and addressograph plate. If the bracelet is not on the patient's wrist, place it there immediately. Set about correcting any errors you may find in any of this information at once.

(3) If asked, escort the patient to his room. Explain the signal light, answer any questions, and introduce the patient to his roommate, if any.

(4) Notify the head nurse and/or the nurse assigned to that room of the patient's arrival.

---

[3] U.S. Army Manual FM 43-4, *Repair of Wood Items.*

(5) Notify the admitting physician by phone of the patient's arrival and location. If the patient lacks admission orders, mention this to the physician's secretary at this time.[4]

Note how step 3 contains all the duties the ward clerk performs, once patients are taken to their rooms. It is easier to consolidate all the activities that take place in the room—explaining machinery, answering questions, making introductions—than to list each as a separate step. But be careful that you do not overwork a single step. To combine steps 4 and 5 would be wrong, and impossible, for those two distinct steps require the ward clerk to speak to someone in person and to make a phone call. These two actions are two separate stages in a process. But do not divide an action into two steps if it has to be done in one. For example, instructions showing how to light a furnace would not list as two steps actions that must be performed simultaneously.

> *Incorrect:* Step 1: Depress the lighting valve.
>   Step 2: Hold a match to the pilot light.
>
> *Correct:*   Step 1: Depress the light valve while holding a match to the pilot light.

3. Give the reader hints on how best to accomplish the procedure. Obviously, you cannot do this for every step, but if there is a chance that the reader might run into difficulties or may not anticipate a certain reaction, by all means provide assistance. For example, telling readers that a certain aroma or color is to be expected in an experiment will reassure them that they are on the right track. Particular techniques on how to operate or service equipment are also helpful: "If there is blood on the transducer diaphragm, dip the transducer in a blood solvent, such as hydrogen peroxide, Hemosol, etc." If readers have a choice of materials or procedures in a given step, you might want to list those that would give the best performance: "Several thin coats will give a better finish than one heavy one."

4. State if one step directly influences (or jeopardizes) the outcome of another. Since all steps in a set of instructions are interrelated, you could not (and should not) have to tell readers how every step affects another. But stating specific relationships is particularly helpful when dangerous or highly intricate operations are involved. You will save the reader time, and you will stress the need for care. Forewarned is forearmed. For example,

> Step 2: Tighten fan belt. Failure to tighten the fan belt will cause it to loosen and come off when the lever is turned in step 5 below.

Do not wait until step 5 to tell readers that you hope they did a good job in tightening the fan belt. That information comes after the fact.

---

[4] Myra S. Willson, *A Textbook for Ward Clerks and Unit Secretaries* (St. Louis: C. V. Mosby, 1979) 70. Reprinted by permission.

5. Insert warning, caution, and note statements only where absolutely necessary. A warning statement tells readers that a step, if not prepared for or performed properly, can endanger their safety:

 WARNING: UNPLUG AIR CONDITIONING UNIT BEFORE CLEANING.

WARNING: DO NOT TOUCH EXPOSED WIRE.

A caution statement tells readers to take certain precautions—wear protective clothing, check an instrument panel carefully, submit forms in triplicate, use special care in running a machine, measure weights or dosages exactly.

CAUTION
MAKE SURE BRAKE SHOES WON'T RUB TIRE AND THAT
SHOES MATE WELL WITH RIM WHEN BRAKES ARE APPLIED.

Because of the extremely important information they impart, warning and caution statements should be graphically set apart from the rest of the instructions. There should be no chance that readers will overlook them. Put these statements in capital letters, in boldface type, in boxes, in different colors (red is especially effective); use one or all of these devices. Distinctive symbols, such as a skull and crossbones or an exclamation point inside a triangle, often precede a warning notation. Warning and caution statements should not be used just because you want to emphasize a point. Putting too many of these statements in your instructions will decrease the dramatic impact they should have on readers. Use them sparingly—only when absolutely necessary.

A note statement simply adds a clarifying comment:

Note: All models in 3500 series have a hex nut in the upper right, not left, corner.

The following instructions on how to paint a garage floor contain steps that offer hints on how best to do the job, comment on how one step affects another, and issue warning, caution, and note statements. Not every instruction requires this amount of detail. Use such comments and signals only when the procedure you are describing calls for them and when they will help your readers.

How to Paint a Garage Floor

Cleaning the Floor

(1) Remove anything sitting on the floor.

(2) Scrape areas where there is old chipped paint with a metal scraper. For hard-to-reach places such as corners or underneath pipes, use a 3-inch wire brush. New paint will not stick to the floor if old paint is not first removed.

(3) Sweep the floor first with a broom; then to make sure that all particles of dust and dirt are removed, use a vacuum sweeper.

(4) Open all windows for proper ventilation. Fumes from cleaning solution used in step 5 should not be inhaled.

CAUTION: USE PROTECTIVE EYEWEAR AND RUBBER GLOVES FOR NEXT STEP.

WARNING: DO NOT USE DETERGENTS CONTAINING AMMONIA. AMMONIA ADDED TO THESE INGREDIENTS WILL CAUSE AN EXPLOSION.

---

(5) Mop the entire floor with a solution composed of the following ingredients:
⅓ box of Floorex
1 quart of bleach
10 quarts of water
1 cup powdered detergent
Note: Do not worry if the mixture does not appear soapy; it does not need suds to work.

(6) For any grease spots that remain, sprinkle enough dry Floorex powder to cover them entirely. Scrub these spots with a 5-inch wire brush.

(7) Rinse the entire floor thoroughly with water to remove cleanser. Allow floor to dry (30 min) before painting.

Painting the Floor

(8) Mix the paint with a stirrer ten or fifteen times until the color is even.
Note: If the paint has not already been shaken by machine before being opened, shake the can for about three minutes, open, and stir the contents for about five to ten minutes or until the paint is mixed.

(9) Pour the paint into the paint tray.

(10) With the 3-inch paint brush, paint the floor around the baseboard. Come out at least two to three inches so that roller used in the next step will not touch the baseboard.

(11) Paint the rest of the floor with a roller attached to an extension handle. A roller handles much more easily than a brush and distributes the paint more smoothly.

Move the roller in the same direction each time. Overlap each row painted by one-half inch to avoid spaces between rows of paint.

(12) Allow two hours to dry. The floor will be ready to walk on.

CAUTION: DO NOT DRIVE VEHICLES ONTO FLOOR FOR TWENTY-FOUR HOURS. TIRES WILL PICK UP NEW PAINT.

The Conclusion

Not every set of instructions requires a conclusion. For short instructions containing a few simple steps, such as those in Figures 13.1–13.4, no conclusion is necessary. These instructions usefully end with the last step the reader must perform. For longer, more involved jobs, a conclusion can help readers finish the job with confidence and accuracy. For example, a short conclusion like the following might help users who have just followed the directions on painting a garage floor.

> With proper care this procedure should have to be repeated only once every three years. To keep the floor in top shape, sweep it at least twice a month to prevent gritty materials such as sand from scaling the painted surface. If possible, wipe grease and oil up immediately to prevent them from soaking into the paint. (Dispose of rags properly to avoid chance of fire.)

When they are necessary, conclusions can help the reader in a variety of ways. They might either provide a succinct wrap-up of what the reader has done or end with a single sentence of congratulation. A conclusion might tell readers what to expect once a job is finished, describing the results of a test, explaining how a piece of equipment is supposed to operate, or emphasizing the benefits of following a certain procedure. Conclusions can also give readers practical advice on how to maintain a piece of equipment or how to follow a certain procedure. Study the conclusion in Figure 13.9 included in an instructional booklet for consumers who have purchased a Sunbeam iron. Note how this conclusion gives readers useful information on cleaning, packing, and protecting their iron after they have used it.

Instructions: Some Final Advice

Perhaps the most important piece of advice to leave you with is this: Do not take *anything* for granted when you have to write a set of instructions. It is wrong and on occasion dangerous to assume that your readers have performed the procedure before, that they will automatically supply missing or "obvious" information, or that they will easily anticipate your next step. No one ever complained that a set of instructions was too clear or too easy to follow.

Fig. 13.9   A conclusion to a set of instructions.

CARING FOR YOUR IRON

1. When you've finished ironing, turn the Temperature Selector to "OFF." Set the Steam / Dry Control to "DRY." Remove the cord from the outlet by grasping the plug rather than pulling on the cord.

2. Empty the Water Tank after each use while the iron is still hot.

3. Let the iron cool completely before putting it away.

4. Always store the iron upright on the Safety Heel Rest with the Temperature Selector in the "OFF" position and the Steam / Dry Control in the "DRY" position. DO NOT store in the carton as any small residue of moisture may cause the Soleplate to discolor.

5. Avoid ironing over snaps, zippers, rivets on jeans, etc., as they will scratch the Soleplate. Iron around them instead. If the iron should become deeply scratched so as to catch on fabric, take it to your nearest Sunbeam Appliance Service Company station.

6. If you wish to pack your iron for shippng, be sure it is thoroughly dry. Heat for a short period after emptying, then cool completely.

7. If starch or other material clings to the Soleplate of your iron, cool the iron, then clean with a non-abrasive household cleaner. Wipe clean. Set the Temperature Selector to the "A" setting and heat. Run iron over waxed paper, then over a dry cloth or paper towel.

Sunbeam *Self-Cleaning Shot Steam Iron Instructions.* Reprinted by permission.

To make sure that your instructions are clear and complete, write, edit, proofread, and test them with your reader in mind. Give the reader all the appropriate information needed for the task—and in the right order. Make sure your instructions have all the parts the reader must have—introduction, list of materials, the steps, and conclusion—to do the job safely and accurately. Use visuals to clarify a tricky step, and always insert warning, caution, or note statements where needed.

☞ Exercises

1. Bring to class two examples of short directions that require no introduction, list of materials and equipment, or conclusion. Look for these two

examples on labels, carton panels, or backs of envelopes. Evaluate the effectiveness of these instructions by commenting on how precise, direct, and useful they are.

2. Find at least one example of long instructions containing an introduction, list of materials and equipment, statements of warning, caution, or note, and a conclusion. Bring this example to class and be prepared to show how the various steps in this set of instructions follow the principles outlined on pages 428–430 in this chapter. You can find a set of full instructions in many technical manuals and in some manuals to help consumers assemble or maintain large or complex home appliances.

3. Find a set of instructions that does not contain any visuals, but which you think should have some graphic materials to make it clearer. Design those visuals yourself and indicate where they should appear in the instructions.

4. Write a set of instructions in numbered steps (or in paragraph format) on one of the following relatively simple activities.
   (a) tying a shoe
   (b) brushing your teeth
   (c) unlocking a door with a key
   (d) making a local telephone call
   (e) planting a tree or shrub
   (f) logging on to a computer
   (g) removing a stain from clothing
   (h) pumping gas into a car
   (i) building a campfire
   (j) checking a book out of the library
   (k) parallel parking a car

5. Write a set of full instructions on one of the following more complex topics. Identify your audience. Include an appropriate introduction, a list of equipment and materials, numbered steps with necessary warning, caution, and note statements, and an effective conclusion. Also include whatever visuals you think will help your readers.
   (a) outfitting a kayak for a sea expedition
   (b) changing a flat tire
   (c) designing a computer program
   (d) developing black-and-white film
   (e) shaving a patient for surgery
   (f) changing the oil and an oil filter in a car
   (g) making a blueprint
   (h) installing a wind turbine on a roof
   (i) filling out an income tax return
   (j) surveying a parcel of land
   (k) pruning hedges
   (l) jumping a dead car battery

(m) using the Heimlich maneuver to help a choking individual

(n) fingerprinting a suspect

(o) arranging a footlocker for inspection

(p) taking someone's blood pressure

(q) changing a cash register tape

(r) finding and plugging a leak in a tire

(s) taking reservations at a hotel / motel

(t) painting a car

(u) cooking a roast

(v) flossing a patient's teeth after cleaning

(w) making a shirt, skirt, or blouse

6. The following set of instructions is confusing, vague, and out of order. Rewrite these instructions to make them clear, easy to follow, and correct. Make sure that each step follows the guidelines outlined in this chapter.

Reupholstering a Piece of Furniture

(1) Although it might be difficult to match the worn material with the new material, you might as well try.

(2) If you cannot, remove the old material.

(3) Take out the padding.

(4) Take out all of the tacks before removing the old covering. You might want to save the old covering.

(5) Measure the new material with the old, if you are able to.

(6) Check the frame, springs, webbing, and padding.

(7) Put the new material over the old.

(8) Check to see if it matches.

(9) You must have the same size as before.

(10) Look at the padding inside. If it is lumpy, smooth it out.

(11) You will need to tack all the sides down. Space your tacks a good distance apart.

(12) When you spot wrinkles, remove the tacks.

(13) Caution: in step 11 directly above, do not drive your tacks all the way through. Leave some room.

(14) Work from the center to the edge in step 11 above.

(15) Put the new material over the old furniture.

P.S. Use strong cords whenever there are tacks. Put the cords under the nails so that they hold.

14

Proposals

A proposal is a detailed plan of action that a writer submits to a reader, or group of readers, for approval. These readers are usually in a position of authority—supervisors, managers, department heads, company buyers, elected officials, civic leaders—who will endorse or reject the writer's plan. Proposals are among the most important types of job-related writing. Their acceptance can lead to improved working conditions, a more efficient and economical business, additional jobs and income for a company, or a safer and more attractive environment.

☞ Writing Successful Proposals

Proposals are written for many purposes. You might write a proposal to your boss seeking authorization to purchase a new piece of equipment for the office—a copier with a reduction mode to handle the special printing needs you see on the job. Proposals also routinely go to potential customers offering to do a job for them—sell a product or a service. For instance, you might write a proposal to a manager of a high school cafeteria to convince her to stock your company's brand of potato chips or to a fire chief offering to supply special firefighting gear. Government agencies (Department of Interior; Health and Human Services) regularly request and receive proposals from individuals hoping to gain funding for research projects that might study the mating habits of a particular species or determine the mercury levels at a certain lake.

Depending on the job, proposals can vary greatly in size and in scope. A proposal to your employer could easily be conveyed through a memo of a page or two. A proposal to do a research project for a class assignment can also be successfully completed in a brief memo. For a small job for a prospective client—redecorating a waiting room in an accountant's office—a letter with information on procedures, costs, materials, and a timetable might suffice. But for an extremely large and costly job—constructing a ten-story office building, for example—the customer would require a long, detailed report with appendixes containing sections on engineering specifications, detailed budgets, and even résumés of all key personnel working on the project.

☞ Proposals Are Persuasive Plans

Proposals—large or small—have one thing in common. They must be highly persuasive to succeed. Without your audience's approval, your plan will never go into effect, however accurate and important you think it is. Through the details of your proposal you must convince readers that your plan will help them, improve their businesses or generally make their jobs easier. The tone of your proposal should be "Here is what I can do for you." Stress the precise benefits your plan has for the reader. Show readers how approving your plan will save them time and money or will improve their employees' morale or their customer relations.

Competition is fierce in the world of work, and a persuasive proposal frequently determines which company receives a contract. Demonstrate to your reader why your plan is better—more efficient, practical, economical—than a competitor's. In a sense, a proposal combines the persuasiveness of a sales letter, the documentation of a report (see Chapters 15 and 16), and the binding power of a contract, for if the reader accepts your proposal, he or she will expect you to live up to its terms.

☞ Types of Proposals

Proposals are classified according to how they originate and where they are sent after they are written. Distinctions are made between *solicited* and *unsolicited* proposals based on how they originate and between *internal* and *external* proposals based on where they are sent. Both classifications are used to describe proposals. Depending on your audience and your purpose, you may write an internal, solicited or unsolicited proposal; or you may write an external, solicited or unsolicited proposal.

Solicited and Unsolicited Proposals

When a company has a particular problem to be solved or a job to be done, it will solicit—or invite—proposals. The company will notify you and other competitors by preparing a Request for Proposals (an RFP), a set of instructions that specify the exact type of work to be done, and how and when the company wants the work completed. Figure 14.1 contains a sample RFP. RFP's are mailed to firms with track records in the area the company wants the work

Fig. 14.1   A sample RFP.

REQUEST FOR PROPOSALS

Mesa Community College solicits proposals to construct and to install fifty individual study carrels in its Holmes Memorial Library. These carrels must be highly serviceable and conform to all specification standards of the ALA. Proposals should include the precise measurements of the carrels to be installed, the specific acoustical and lighting benefits, and the types and amount of storage space offered. Work on constructing and installing the carrels must be completed no later than the start of the fall semester, August 26, 1985. Proposals should include a schedule of when different phases of work will be completed and an itemized budget for labor, materials, equipment, and necessary tests to ensure high quality acoustical performance. Contractors should state their qualifications, including a description of similar recent work and a list of references. Proposals should be submitted in triplicate no later than May 15, 1985 to

> Mrs. Barbara Feldstein
> Director of the Library
> Mesa Community College
> Mesa, NV 89203

done. RFP's are also printed in trade publications to attract the highest number of quality bidders for the job.

An RFP helps you to know what the customer wants. It is often extremely detailed and even tells you how the company wants the proposal prepared—for example, what information is to be included, where it needs to appear, and even how many copies of the proposal you have to submit. Your own proposal will be judged according to how well you fulfill the terms of the RFP. For that reason follow the directions in the RFP exactly. (Note how the solicited proposal in Figure 14.3 directly refers to the terms of the RFP.)

With an unsolicited proposal, you—not the reader—make the first move. You identify a problem for readers and prepare a proposal to solve it. Doing that is not as difficult as it sounds. See how the writers of the unsolicited proposal in Figures 14.2 and 14.4 identify a problem for readers.

Before you write an unsolicited proposal, though, you may want to speak with an appropriate manager at the company or write an inquiry letter to that individual to determine if he or she would be interested in receiving your proposal. Many times companies are eager to learn about a problem and how the writer proposes to solve it for the company. Sometimes the company will even help by giving you information through an interview or a tour. If so, acknowledge that assistance in your proposal.

Unlike a solicited proposal, when the company knows about the problem, an unsolicited proposal has to convince readers in the first place that there is a problem and in the second place that you and your firm are the individuals to solve it. Accordingly, your unsolicited proposal has to document the existence of the problem and demonstrate how solving it is in the best interest of the readers. If they accept your identification of the problem, you have greatly increased your chances of their accepting your plan to solve it. On the other hand, if you do not convince readers that a problem exists, your solution, and hence your proposal, will be rejected or ignored.

Internal and External Proposals

An *internal proposal* is written to a decision maker within your own organization. As you will see on pages 441–446, this type of proposal can deal with a variety of topics, including changing a policy or procedure or requesting additional personnel or equipment.

An *external proposal*, on the other hand, is sent to a decision maker outside of your company. It might go to a potential client you have never worked for or to a previous or current client. An external proposal can also be sent to a government funding agency such as the Department of Agriculture. External proposals tend to be more formal than internal ones.

☞ Guidelines for Writing a Successful Proposal

Regardless of the type of proposal you are called on to write, the following guidelines will help you to persuade your audience to approve your plan. Refer to these guidelines both before and while you formulate your plan.

1. Approach writing a proposal as a problem-solving activity. Your goal is to solve a problem that affects the reader. Don't lose sight of the problem as you plan and write your proposal. Everything in your proposal should relate to the problem, and the organization of your proposal should reflect your ability as a problem-solver. Psychologically, make the reader feel that you can solve the problem in a profitable way.

2. Regard your audience as skeptical readers. Even though you offer a plan that you think will benefit readers, do not be overconfident that they will automatically accept it as the best and only way to proceed. To determine the feasibility of your plan, readers will question everything you say. They will withhold their approval if your proposal contains errors, omissions, or inconsistencies. Consequently examine your proposal from the reader's point of view.

3. Research your proposal carefully. A winning proposal is not based only on a few well-meaning, general suggestions. All your good intentions and enthusiasm will not substitute for the hard facts readers will demand. Concrete examples persuade readers; unsupported generalizations do not. To make your proposal complete and accurate, you will have to do a lot of homework—for example, reading previous correspondence or research about the problem, doing comparative shopping for the best prices, verifying schedules and time-tables, interviewing customers and/or employees, making site visits.

4. Prove that your proposal is workable. Your proposal should be well thought out. It should contain no statements saying "let's see what happens if we do X or Y." By analyzing and, when possible, by testing each part of your proposal in advance, you can eliminate any quirks and revise it appropriately before readers evaluate it. What you propose should be consistent with the organization and capabilities of the company. It would be foolish to recommend, for example, that a small company (fifty employees) triple its work force to accomplish your plan.

5. Be sure that your proposal is financially realistic. This point is closely associated to and follows from guideline 4. Do not submit a proposal that would require an unnecessarily large amount of money to implement. For example, it would be unrealistic to recommend that your company spend $20,000 to solve a $2,000 problem that might not ever recur. Most short proposals, the type you will most likely be writing, offer plans that can be put into effect for under $10,000 to $15,000.

6. Package your proposal attractively. Make sure your proposal is letter-perfect, inviting, and easy to read (for example, use plenty of headings and other visual devices discussed on pages 16–17). The appearance as well as the content of your proposal can determine whether it is accepted or rejected. Remember that readers, especially those unfamiliar with your work, will evaluate your proposal as evidence of the type of work you want to do for them.

☞ Internal Proposals

The primary purpose of an internal proposal, such as the one included in Figure 14.2, is to offer a realistic and constructive plan to help your company run its business more efficiently and economically. On your job you may discover a better way of doing something or a more efficient way to correct a problem. You believe that your proposed change will save your employer time, money, or further trouble. (Angie Quinn in Figure 14.2 has discovered a more efficient way to get mail delivered in her company.) You decide to notify your boss—a department head, a manager, a supervisor. Your proposal will be an informal, in-house message, so a brief (usually one- or two-page) memo should be appropriate.

Fig. 14.2   An internal unsolicited proposal.

 MIDWEST PETROCHEMICAL CORPORATION
Des Moines, IA 50351

TO: O. L. Higgins, Office Manager   *A.Q.*
FROM: Angie Quinn, Accounting Department
DATE: June 15, 1985
SUBJECT: A proposal to change mail delivery by using a golf cart

PURPOSE

I am writing to propose a cost—effective solution to what I believe is a
growing problem at Midwest: the inefficiency of our current mail
distribution system. I recommend the purchase of a motor—driven golf cart
and the partial reassignment of a mailroom clerk for twice—daily delivery
and pick—up of mail and packages to each of the fifteen buildings within
our operation.

THE COSTLY PROBLEM WITH CURRENT MAIL SERVICE

Currently, each office dispatches an employee to the mailroom in the
Administration Building to send and pick up mail. Considering the
seven—acre size of our operation, the employees traveling the greatest
distance to the mailroom spend at least 50 minutes a day in this activity.
I estimate that for all 42 offices, an average of 20 minutes per office a
day is spent in mail delivery and pick—up.

    20 minutes/day × 42 offices = 840 minutes/day or 14 hours/day

Fourteen employee—hours per day is a costly investment of time to spend for
mail service. This activity translates into 70 hours per week just for mail
service. At an average rate of employees' pay ($5.50) per hour, this task
costs the company $385.00 (70 hrs. × $5.50) a week. The amount of money and
time per year is even more staggering—$385 × 52 weeks = $20,020.00. A
more cost—effective and efficient method of mail delivery needs to be
found.

A SOLUTION TO THE MAIL PROBLEM

By using a golf cart to deliver mail to each of our fifteen buldings twice
each day the company can realize significant savings. Mr. A. J. Pandolf of
Smith's Hobby Port informed me that a cart can be delivered within five
days of ordering it.

No special training or license is necessary to operate a golf cart. A
mailroom clerk earning entry level wages ($4.50 per hour) could easily make
the deliveries. Each delivery would require no more than 75 minutes per
trip, or a total of 2½ hours a day.

Fig. 14.2 (Continued.)

We will need to construct a mail drop in front of each of the fifteen buildings. I have already spoken to Janis Leeds, Head of our Buildings and Grounds Department, and learned that these mail drops are relatively inexpensive and can be purchased and installed within two weeks.

The reduction in walk-in traffic resulting from this new delivery system will decrease the work load in our mailroom thus allowing a clerk to be reassigned easily to this delivery work with very little loss of efficiency to the mailroom. Moreover, the efficient use of one clerk for mail drop service can significantly reduce the amount of frustration employees have experienced in waiting for mail.

COSTS

The costs of implementing my proposal follow:

1 Golf Pro golf cart, model 750, with gasoline engine and canvas canopy (from Smith's Hobby Port)	$2,900.00
Purchase and installation of mail drops in each building ($250.00 × 15 buildings)	3,750.00
Salary for mail clerk/driver ($4.50/hr × 12½ hrs/wk × 52)	2,925.00
Maintenance (Plant Motor Pool estimate for 1 year)	100.00
Gasoline/oil	75.00
Total	$9,750.00

Compared with the $20,020 the company now spends in employees' time to receive and deliver mail, this cost <u>reduces by more than half the amount of money the company will have to spend on mail service</u>.

The company will have a further financial benefit. Because employees will spend less time away from each office picking up and sending the mail, they can devote more time to their office duties and thereby increase the productivity of each office.

CONCLUSION

Using a golf cart for our mail service is both feasible and cost effective. Adoption of this proposal will save our company more than $10,000 in wasted time. I will be happy to discuss this proposal with you at any time at your convenience.

An internal proposal can be written about a variety of topics such as:

purchasing new or more advanced equipment—word processors, transducers, automobiles

hiring new employees or training current ones to handle a new technique or process

eliminating a dangerous condition or reducing an environmental risk to prevent accidents—for employees, customers, or both

revising a policy to improve customer relations (eliminating an inconvenience, speeding up a delivery) or employees' morale (offering vanpooling; adding more options for a schedule)

As this list shows, internal proposals cover almost every activity or policy that affects the day-to-day operation of a company or agency.

Your Audience and Office Politics

Writing an internal proposal requires you to be aware of and sensitive to office politics. To be successful, your internal proposal should be written with the needs and dislikes of your audience in mind. Remember that your boss will expect you to be very convincing about both the problem you say exists and the solution you propose to correct it. You cannot assume that your reader will automatically agree with you that there is a problem or that your plan is the only way to solve it.

Your reader in fact may feel threatened by your plan. After all, you are advocating a change. Some managers regard such changes as a challenge to their administration of an office or department. Or your reader may be indifferent—not even wanting to give your work serious consideration. Or your manager-reader may have certain "pet" projects or ways of doing things that you must take into account. To surmount these and other obstacles, show that the change you propose is in everyone's best interest. Do not overlook the possibility that your boss may have to take your proposal up the organizational ladder for commentary and, eventually, approval.

Before you write an internal proposal, consider the implications of your plan for your boss and for other offices or sections in your company. A change you propose for your department or office (transfers; new budgets or schedules) may have sweeping and potentially disruptive implications for another office or division within your company. It is wise to discuss your plan with your boss before you put it in writing.

Never submit an internal proposal that offers an idea you think will work but relies on someone else to supply the specific details on *how* it will work. For example, do not write an internal proposal that says payroll, industrial relations, maintenance, or advertising departments can give the reader the details and costs he or she needs about your proposal. That is pushing the responsibility onto someone else, and your proposal could be rejected for lack of concrete evidence.

The Organization of an Internal Proposal

A short, internal proposal follows a relatively straightforward plan of organization—from identifying the problem to solving it. Internal proposals usually contain four parts, as shown in Figure 14.2. Refer to this proposal as you read the following discussion.

The Introduction

Begin your proposal with a brief statement of why you are writing to your boss: "I propose that . . ." State why you think a specific change is necessary now. Then succinctly define the problem and emphasize that your plan, if approved by the reader, will solve that problem. Where necessary, stress the urgency to act.

Background of the Problem

In this section prove that a problem does exist by documenting its importance for your boss and your company. As a matter of fact, the more you show how the problem affects the boss's work (and area of supervision), the more likely you are to persuade him or her to act. And the more concrete evidence you cite, the easier it will be to convince the reader that the problem is significant and action needs to be taken now.

Avoid vague (and unsupported) generalizations such as: "we're losing money each day with this procedure (or piece of equipment)"; "costs continue to escalate"; "the trouble occurs frequently in a number of places"; "numerous complaints have come in"; "if something isn't done soon, more difficulty will result."

Instead, provide readers with quantifiable details about the number of dollars a company is actually losing per day, week, or month. Emphasize the financial trouble so that you can show how your plan (described in the next section) offers an efficient and workable solution. Indicate how many employees (or work-hours) are involved or how many customers are inconvenienced or endangered by a procedure or condition. Verify how widespread a problem is or how frequently it occurs by citing specific occasions. Rather than just saying that a new word processor would save the company "a lot of money," document how many work-hours are lost using other equipment for the routine jobs your company now has employees perform.

The Solution or Plan

In this section describe the change you want approved. Tie your solution (the change) directly to the problem you have just documented. Each part of your plan should help eliminate the problem or should help increase the productivity or efficiency you think is possible.

Your reader will again expect to find factual evidence. Do not give merely the outline of a plan or say that details can be worked out later. Supply details that answer the following questions: (1) Is the plan workable—can it be accomplished here in our office or plant? and (2) Is it cost effective—will it really save us money in the long run or will it lead to even greater expenses?

To get the boss to say yes to both questions, supply the facts that you have gathered as a result of your research. For example, if you propose that your firm buy a new piece of equipment, do the necessary homework to locate the most efficient and cost-effective model available, as Angie Quinn does in Figure 14.2. Supply the dealer's name, the costs, major conditions of service and training contracts, and warranties. Describe how your firm could use this equipment to obtain better results in the future. Cite specific tasks the new equipment can perform more efficiently at less cost than the equipment now in use.

If you are proposing that your company hire or reassign employees, indicate where these employees will come from, when they will start, what they will be paid, what skills they must have, where they will work and for how long. If you propose to assign current employees to a job, keep in mind that their salary will still have to be paid by your company. Just because they are coworkers does not mean they will work for nothing. Note how Angie Quinn in Figure 14.2 handles the reassignment of one of the employees in the mailroom.

A proposal to change a procedure must include the following details:

1. how the new (or revised) procedure will work
2. how many employees or customers will be affected by it
3. when it will go into operation
4. how much it will cost the employer to change procedures
5. what delays or losses in business might be expected while the company switches from one procedure to another
6. what employees, equipment, or locations are available to accomplish this change

As these questions indicate, your boss will be concerned about schedules, working conditions, employees, methods, locations, equipment, and the costs involved in your plan for change. The costs, in fact, will be of utmost importance. Make sure that you supply a careful and accurate budget so that your reader will know what the change is going to cost. Moreover, make those costs attractive by emphasizing how inexpensive they are as compared to the cost of not making the change, as Quinn does in her section labeled "Costs."

The Conclusion

The conclusion to your internal proposal should be short—a paragraph or two at the most. Your intention is to remind the reader that the problem is serious, that the reason for change is justified, and that you think the reader needs to take action. Select the most important benefit and emphasize it again. In Figure 14.2, Angie Quinn again emphasizes the savings that the company will see by following her plan. Also be willing to discuss your plan with the reader.

☞ Sales Proposals

A sales proposal is the most common type of external proposal. Its purpose is to sell your company's products or services for a set fee. Whether short or long, a sales proposal is a marketing tool that includes a sales pitch as well as a detailed description of the work you propose to do. Sales proposals are the life's blood of many companies; through them they generate business and keep individuals employed. Many firms depend upon proposals to win government contracts to stay in business. Figures 14.3 and 14.4 contain sample sales proposals.

The Audience and Its Needs

Your audience will usually be one or more business executives who have the power to approve or reject a proposal. Unlike readers of an internal proposal, those for a sales proposal may be even more skeptical since they may not know you or your work. Your proposal may also be evaluated by experts in other fields employed by your prospective customer. Readers of a sales proposal will evaluate your work according to (1) how well it meets their needs and (2) how well it compares with the proposals submitted by your competitors. Your proposal must convince readers that you can provide the most appropriate work or service and that your company is more reliable and efficient than any other firm.

The key to success is incorporating the "you attitude" (see pages 116–119) throughout your proposal. Relate your product, service, or personnel to the buyer's exact needs as stated in the RFP for a solicited proposal or through your own investigations for an unsolicited proposal. You cannot submit the same proposal for every job you want to win and expect to be awarded a contract. Different firms have different needs. The most important question the reader will raise, therefore, about your work is, "How does this proposal meet our company's special requirements?" Some other fairly common questions readers will have as they evaluate your work include the following:

1. Does the writer's firm understand our problem?
2. Can the writer's firm deliver what it promises?
3. Can the job be completed on time?
4. What assurances does the writer offer that the job will be done exactly as proposed?

Answer each of these questions by demonstrating how your product or service is tailored to the customer's needs.

Organizing a Sales Proposal

A sales proposal can have the following parts: introduction, description of the proposed product or service, timetable, costs, qualifications of your company, and conclusion.

Fig. 14.3   An external, solicited proposal.

REYNOLDS INTERIORS

250 Commerce Avenue, S.W.
Portland, OR 97204
763-2000

January 14, 1985

Mr. Floyd Tompkins, Manager
General Purpose Appliances
Highway 41 South
Portland, OR 97222

Dear Mr. Tompkins:

In response to your Request #7521 for bids for an appropriate floor
covering at your new showroom, Reynolds Interiors is pleased to submit the
following proposal. After carefully reviewing your specifications for a
floor covering and inspecting your new facility, we believe that the
Armstrong Classic Corlon 900 is the most suitable choice. I am enclosing a
sample of the Corlon 900 so that you can see how it looks.

CORLON'S ADVANTAGES

Guaranteed against defects for a full three years, Corlon is one of the
finest and most durable floor coverings manufactured by Armstrong. It is a
heavy-duty commercial floor 0.085 inch thick for protection. Twenty-five
percent of each tile consists of interface backing; the other 75 percent is
an inlaid wear layer that offers an exceptionally high resistance to
everyday traffic. Traffic tests conducted by the Independent Floor
Covering Institute repeatedly proved the superiority of Corlon's
construction and resistance.

Another important feature of Corlon tile is the size of its rolls. Unlike
other leading brands of similar commercial flooring—Remington or
Treadmaster—Corlon comes in 12-foot-wide rather than 6-foot-wide rolls.
This extra width will significantly reduce the number of seams in your
floor tile, thus increasing its attractiveness and reducing the danger of
tile split.

INSTALLATION PROCEDURES

The Classic Corlon requires that we use the inlaid seaming process, a
technical procedure requiring the services of a trained floor mechanic.
Herman Goshen, our floor mechanic, has over fifteen years of experience
working with the inlaid seam process. His professional work has been
consistently praised by our customers.

INSTALLATION SCHEDULE

We can install the Classic Corlon on your showroom floor during the first
week of March, which fits the timetable specified in your request. The tile

---

448

Fig. 14.3 (Continued.)

will take three and one-half days to install and will be ready to walk on immediately. We recommend, though, that you not move equipment onto the floor for twenty-four hours.

COSTS

The following costs include the Classic Corlon tile, labor, equipment, and tax:

750 sq. yards of Classic Corlon at $12.50 per yd.	$ 9,375.00
Labor (28 hrs. @ $15.00/hr.)	420.00
Sealing Fluid (10 Gallons @ $10.00/gal.)	100.00
Total	9,895.00
Tax (5 percent)	491.00
Grand Total	$10,386.00

Our costs are $250.00 under those you specified in your request.

REYNOLDS' QUALIFICATIONS

Reynolds Interiors has been in business for more than twenty-five years. In that time we have installed many commercial floors in Portland and its suburbs. In the last year, we have served more than sixty customers, including the new multipurpose Radon plant in Portland.

CONCLUSION

Thank you for the opportunity to submit this proposal. We believe you will have a great deal of success with an Armstrong tile floor. If we can provide you with any further information, please call me.

Sincerely yours,

M. T. Chin

M. T. Chin
Sales Manager

Fig. 14.4 An external unsolicited proposal.

National Business Equipment

470 Rodgers Rd.
Camden, NJ 08104

7 March 1986

Mr. Daniel Taylor
Business Manager
Madison Tool and Die Company
3400 Veterans Boulevard
Camden, NJ 08104

Dear Mr. Taylor:

While we were servicing your Wellington 1268 copier last week, it occurred
to me that you might be interested in purchasing a newer model that will
give you state-of-the-art features to make your copying work more efficient
and reliable. Since you purchased your Wellington four years ago, copier
technology has changed tremendously, giving users many advantages at
surprisingly low costs.

Knowing that you want the most reliable office equipment available, I would
appreciate your considering this proposal to supply Madison Tool and Die
with our latest Superior copier, model 4000.

PROBLEMS WITH THE WELLINGTON

Although an advanced product four years ago, Wellington technology has
caused a number of problems for users, leading to frequent and expensive
service calls. The Wellington uses special and costly (5¢ a sheet) paper,
which if not fed into the paper track carefully, can often stick and block
the copier. Even a delay of three or four minutes to unblock the paper
track slows down an important job.

The liquid toner the Wellington uses also causes problems. The operator has
to wait for it to dry or risk smudging important documents.

Finally, for sheet use the Wellington has to be fed by hand, which further
wastes time.

ADVANTAGES OF THE SUPERIOR 4000

The following description of the main features of the Superior 4000 will
show you its advantages over your current Wellington copier.

450

Fig. 14.4   (Continued.)

Printing Technology

The Superior 4000 uses a new dry toner that does not require waiting time on the part of the operator. Your copies will never be smudged again because of toner problems. The development of the dry toner also allows the Superior to copy on both sides of a sheet of paper, saving time and money.

The Superior also offers savings in using a variety of paper sizes and shapes, including heavyweight construction paper that you may use for specifications and drawings. Using standard paper—$8\frac{1}{2} \times 11$, 9×10, and 10×14 sizes—the Superior will save you a great deal of money over the paper your Wellington must use. The cost of a copy on paper made from your machine is 5¢, figuring the price of 500 sheets of paper to be $25.00. The cost per page using paper on the Superior is only $1\frac{1}{2}$¢. Being able to copy on both sides of that page will further reduce your costs.

Feeding/Sorting Capacity

An automatic feeder can accelerate a photocopying job by 50 percent. Once paper is fed into the machine, you can use the automatic sorter (or collator)—also standard equipment. Never again will you have to worry that a page may be missing or may be out of order in multiple copies of a report.

Printing Quality

The new Superior 4000 offers top-quality, high-resolution reproduction. Since seeing is believing, I am enclosing a copy of this proposal made on the 4000 as well as a copy of a blueprint to show you how both copied documents look.

Size

The Superior 4000 measures $4' \times 3' \times 4'$, which will take up one-quarter less space than your Wellington copier. Once the machine is installed you will find this extra space useful for your storage needs.

INSTALLATION, TRAINING, AND SERVICE

We will install your new Superior 4000 within one week of receiving your order. The installation takes approximately forty-five minutes.

We will give you two hours of free training to show your employees how to achieve the maximum results with the 4000. If a problem occurs, we offer customers our "hot-line" service on business days from 8:00 a.m. to 5:00 p.m. Our service technician will arrive within an hour of your call.

Fig. 14.4 **(Continued.)**

<u>COSTS</u>

Below is the price of the Superior 4000 and appropriate initial supplies:

Superior 4000	$3,495.00
Toner (2 gal.)	28.00
Paper (500 sheet box of regular 8½ × 11)	7.50
Service Contract—Optional ($30.00 per month/year)	360.00
Total	$3,890.50

The installation of your new Superior 4000 is free.

<u>NATIONAL'S REPUTATION</u>

Having been in business for over twenty-two years, National knows about the equipment needs of companies like Madison Tool and Die. We have sold copiers to more than sixty companies in the greater Camden area, including Biscayne Industries, Northeast Manufacturing, and Aronson Accounting, Inc. In addition to supplying quality products and service, we are interested in our customers long after a sale.

We appreciate your using National Business Equipment for your repair needs and hope that you will decide to purchase the new Superior 4000. Please call me if I may answer any questions you have.

If this proposal is acceptable, please sign and return a copy of this letter.

Sincerely yours,

Marion Copely

Marion Copely

I accept this proposal made by National Business Equipment.

_____

for Madison Tool and Die Company

Introduction

The introduction to your sales proposal can be a single paragraph in a short sales proposal or several pages in a more complex one. Basically, however, the introduction should prepare readers for everything that follows in your proposal. The introduction itself may contain the following sections, which sometimes may be combined.

1. Statement of purpose and subject of proposal. Tell readers why you are writing and identify the specific subject of your work. If you are responding to an RFP, use specific code numbers or cite application dates, as the proposal in Figure 14.3 does. If your proposal is unsolicited, indicate how you learned of the problem as Figure 14.4 does. Briefly define the solution you propose.

2. Background of the problem you propose to solve. Show readers that you are familiar with their problem and that you have a firm grasp of the importance and implications of the problem. Describe the problem in convincing detail in an unsolicited proposal—identifying the specific trouble areas, documenting losses through specific occurrences.

Description of the Proposed Product or Service

This section is the heart of your proposal. Before spending their money, customers will demand hard, factual evidence of what you claim can and should be done. Here are some points that you should cover.

1. Carefully show your potential customers that your product or service is right for them. Stress specific benefits of your product or service most relevant to your reader. Blend sales talk with descriptions of hardware.

2. Describe your work in suitable detail—what it looks like, what it does, and how consistently and well it will perform in the readers' office, plant, hospital, or agency. You might include a brochure, picture, or, as the writer of the proposal in Figure 14.3 does, a sample of your product for customers to study. Convince readers that your product is the most up-to-date and efficient one they could select. Note how the proposals in Figures 14.3 and 14.4 accomplish this.

3. Stress any special features, maintenance advantages, warranties or service benefits. Highlight features that show the quality, consistency, or security of your work. For a service, emphasize the procedures you use, the terms of that service, and even the kinds of tools you use, especially any "state-of-the-art" equipment. Be sure to provide a step-by-step outline of what will happen and why each step is beneficial for readers.

Timetable

A carefully planned timetable shows readers that you know your job and that you can accomplish it in the right amount of time. Your dates should match any listed in an RFP. Provide specific dates when the work will begin, how long it will continue, and when you will be finished, for example, installing equipment, testing equipment, training employees to use equipment. For proposals offering a service, specify how many times—by the hour, week, month—customers can expect to receive your help—for example, spraying three times a month for an exterminating service or making deliveries by 10:00 a.m. for a trucking company. Indicate whether follow-up visits or service calls will be provided.

Costs

Make your budget accurate, complete, and convincing. Don't underestimate costs thinking that a low bid will win you the job. You may get the job but lose money doing it, for the customer will rightfully hold you to your unrealistic figures. Similarly, don't inflate your prices; competitors will beat you in the bidding.

Give customers more than the bottom-line cost. Show exactly what readers are getting for their money so they can determine if everything they need is included. Itemize costs for specific services, equipment, labor (by the hour or by the job), transportation, travel, training you propose to supply. If something is not included or is considered optional, say so—additional hours of training, replacement of parts, and the like. If you anticipate a price increase, let the customer know how long current prices will stay in effect. That information may spur them to act favorably now.

Qualifications of Your Company

Convince readers that your company has the ability to perform the necessary tasks to solve the customer's problem. Emphasize your company's accomplishments and expertise in using relevant services and equipment. You might list previous work you have done that is identical or similar to the type of work you are proposing to do for the customer. Perhaps you have installed a heating or cooling system at another plant similar to the one you are now proposing. You may even want to mention the names of a few local firms for whom you have worked that would be pleased to recommend you. By all means cite any previous work you may have already done for this customer. You may also want to include the qualifications of key personnel who will be assigned to the potential customer's job.

Conclusion

This is the "call to action" section of your proposal. As with the conclusion in an internal proposal, encourage your reader to approve your plan. Stress the major benefits your plan has for the customer. Notice how the last paragraphs of Figures 14.3 and 14.4 do this effectively. Offer to answer any questions the reader may have. Some proposals end by asking the reader to sign and return a copy of the proposal thus indicating their acceptance of it, as the proposal in Figure 14.4 does.

☞ Proposals for Research Papers and Reports

You may have to write a proposal like the one in Figure 14.5 when your instructor asks you to submit a report or research paper, a topic for an independent study, or some other type of major term project.

Writing for Your Teacher

The principles guiding internal and sales proposals also apply to research proposals. As with internal and sales proposals, you will be writing to convince your reader—the teacher—to approve a major piece of work. But otherwise the goals of your teacher-reader will be considerably different from those of other proposal readers. A teacher will read your proposal to help you write the best possible paper or report. In examining your proposal, the teacher will want to make sure of four things:

1. that you have chosen a significant topic
2. that you have a sufficiently restricted topic
3. that you will investigate important sources of information about that topic
4. that you can accomplish your work in the specified time

Your proposal gives your teacher an opportunity to spot omissions or inconsistencies and to provide helpful suggestions.

In order to prepare an effective proposal for a research project you must do some preliminary research. You cannot pick any topic that comes to mind, or guess about procedures, sources, or conclusions. As other proposal readers do, your teacher will want convincing and specific evidence for your choice of topic and your approach to it. Be prepared to marshal key facts to show that you are familiar with the topic and that you can handle it successfully.

Organization of a Proposal for a Research Paper

Your proposal for a school research project can be a memo divided into five sections, as illustrated in Figure 14.5: introduction, scope of the problem or topic to be investigated, methods or procedures, timetable, and request for approval. However, be ready to reverse or expand these sections if your teacher wants you to follow a different organizational plan.

Fig. 14.5   A proposal for a research paper.

TO: Prof. Barbara Felton-Parks
           Business Management 200

FROM: James Salinas

DATE: February 5, 1985

SUBJECT: Proposal for a report on the advantages and disadvantages of
           electronic mail

Purpose

For my term project, I propose to research and write a report on the
advantages and disadvantages for an office in switching to an electronic
mail system.

Electronic mail has been increasingly used by many private companies and
government agencies. Even the U.S. Post Office offers E-COM (Electronic
Computer Originated) service on a limited basis. In fact, Postmaster
General William F. Bolger stated that E-COM "has proved itself to be
dependable for generating and delivering a wide range of office
communications" (The Office [Jan. 1983]: 124).

Although electronic mail has brought many companies closer to the paperless
office of the future, it also poses some major problems. An understanding
of the benefits as well as the drawbacks of electronic mail is important
for any office manager thinking of converting to it. My paper will serve as
a background report for an office manager considering electronic mail.

Problems to Be Investigated

At this stage of my research I think my report needs to answer the following
questions:

(1) How does electronic mail work as compared to conventional methods?

(2) What kinds of special applications does it offer users in preparing and
    sending routine messages (invoices, monthly sales reports) or special
    ones?

(3) Will electronic mail provide the same level of security and
    confidentiality as conventional mail?

(4) Do the costs of switching to electronic mail—terminals, modems,
    hook-ups—offset the costs of conventional preparation, forwarding,
    and storing of mail?

I propose, therefore, to divide the body of my paper according to the four
key issues of operation, application, security, and costs.

Having the right kind of equipment would save us hours and money. I suggest
that we call a few of the office equipment supply offices for their opinion
about the kinds of changes we need to make.

We should also call one of the new assistant managers in the engineering
department to find out how that office is run. I have been there a number of
times and things seem to be going very smoothly. Clearly they do not have
the organizational problems we do.

Along with these investigations, I suggest that we have someone from
accounting give us an estimate about how much we could afford to spend this
year.

As for costs, though, I don't think the investment would be bad and the
company would be getting a lot for its money, more than they are now with
our outmoded communication system in this office.

Please let me know what you think of my idea. I think it is worth pursuing.

5. Write an unsolicited sales proposal, similar to the one in Figure 14.4, on
   one of the following services or products you intend to sell, or on a topic
   your instructor approves.

   - providing exterminating service to a store or restaurant
   - supplying a hospital with rental televisions for patient rooms
   - doing typing or word processing for students
   - offering temporary office help or nursing care
   - providing landscaping and lawn care work
   - testing for noise, air, or water pollution in your community or neighbor-
     hood
   - furnishing transportation for students, employees, or members of a com-
     munity group
   - providing consultants' expertise to save a company money
   - supplying laboratory animals to your school's biology department
   - designing business forms for a local bank or hospital
   - digging a septic well for a small apartment complex
   - supplying insurance coverage to a small (five to ten employees) firm
   - cleaning the parking lot and outside walkways at a shopping center
   - selling a piece of equipment to a business
   - changing the accounting procedures at a company
   - making a work area safer
   - offering a training program for employees
   - increasing donations to a community or charitable fund

6. Write a solicited proposal for one of the topics listed in exercise 5 or on a
   topic that your instructor approves. Review Figure 14.3 (pages 448–449).

7. Write an appropriate proposal—internal or solicited or unsolicited sales—based upon the information contained in one of the following magazine articles. Assume that your or your prospective customer's company, school, or community faces a problem similar to one discussed in one of these articles. Use as much of the information in these articles as you need and add any details of your own that you think are necessary.

Turning Schoolgrounds Green[1]

"If our conservation district doesn't take the initiative to show our children and school leaders how to stop erosion on their playgrounds, then who will?" said Bobby Joe Ganey, chairperson of the Lasalle Soil and Water Conservation District in Lasalle Parish, Louisiana.

Ganey, along with other conservation district board members, was tired of seeing bare, eroded soil outside classroom doors so the district board initiated a project to put cover on the schoolgrounds.

The district board members talked with school principals in the parish about erosion problems on their school campuses. The district board determined that six school campuses were suffering from a lack of vegetative cover, and erosion was keeping their playgrounds bare. Board members asked the Soil Conservation Service to prepare a vegetative plan for the schools.

"Schoolgrounds get a lot of foot traffic from the students, so it was necessary for us to establish a species of grass that could withstand this problem," Ganey said.

The Lasalle Soil and Water Conservation District supplied the funds to buy bermudagrass seed and fertilizer.

"It was our intention from the beginning to have the students take an active part in establishing vegetative cover on the playgrounds," said Ganey. "In this way not only could they see the value of erosion control at their school but they also could learn how erosion is bad for the community and for their futures."

The district board and SCS introduced the students to erosion problems through a slide show. More than 650 students from the six elementary schools participated in the erosion control work on their campuses. They helped till, seed, and fertilize the eroding areas.

To be sure that the newly established grass would be properly maintained, the vegetative plan included cutting height and fertilizer requirements.

Self-illuminating Exit Signs[2]

The Marine Corps Development and Education Center (MCDEC), Quantico, Va., submitted a project recently, to replace incandescent illumination exit signs with self-illuminating exit signs for a cost of $97,238. The first-year savings were anticipated to

[1] *Soil and Water Conservation News* (Oct. 1984): 9.
[2] Lt. James F. McCollum, CEG, USN. "Self-illuminating Exit Signs Equal High Payback." *Navy Civil Engineer* (Summer 1983): 30–31.

be about $37,171 with an anticipated payback time of 2.6 years—an excellent prospect. The contractor bid much lower, however, and the actual payback will be about 1.5 years!

What are the benefits of these self-illuminating exit signs? . . . The primary benefit is that virtually all operation and maintenance expense is eliminated for the life of the device; normally from 10 to 12 years. Power failures or other disturbances will not cause them to go out.

In new construction, expensive electrical circuits can be totally eliminated. In retrofits, the release of a dedicated circuit for other use may be of considerable benefit. Initial total cost of installing circuits and conventional devices approximately equals the cost of the self-illuminating signs. Installation labor and expense for the self-illuminating signs is about that of hanging a picture.

The amount of electricity saved varies and depends on whether your existing fixtures are fluorescent (13 to 26 watts) or incandescent (50 to 100 watts). Multiply the number of fixtures × wattage / fixture × hours operated / day × days / year = KWH / year savings. For example assume:

400 incandescent fixtures

0.08 $ / KWH   0.05 KW / fixture

24 hours / day

365 day / year operation

400 × 0.1 × 365 = 350400 KWH / year

350400 × 0.08 = $28,032 / year for electricity

Now add in savings achieved from:

- Avoiding labor to change bulbs
- Avoiding bulb material, stocking and storage costs
- Avoiding transportation costs involved in bulb changes
- Reuse of existing bulbs

The above savings can be significant. For the MCDEC Quantico project, estimates of bulb change interval and savings were 700 hours (29 days) and $13,512 / year when all factors were considered.

The cost of a self-illuminating sign depends on whether one or two faces are illuminated primarily and varies between different suppliers. Single-face prices will likely be $100 to $150 while double-face prices may be $250 to $330. The contractor at Quantico found better prices than these ranges indicate. The labor cost should be about $10 per sign.

If you can use a high dependability, no-maintenance, zero operations cost exit-signing system in your retrofit on new construction projects, try a self-illuminating exit-sign system in your economic analysis today. "Isolite" signs, by Safety Light Corp., are listed as FSC (Fire Safety Code) Group 99, Part IV, Section A, Class 9905, signs and are available through GSA contract. Contact Gerald Harnett, Safety Light Corp., P.O. Box 266, Greenbelt, MD 20070 for more information at (301) 441-2775.

8. Write a suitable research proposal upon which the research paper on "Stress and the Computer Programmer" (pages 287–293) could have been based.

9. Write a research proposal to your instructor seeking approval for a major term project. Do the necessary preliminary research to show that you have selected a suitable topic, that you have narrowed it, and that you have identified the sources of information you have to consult. As a part of your proposal, identify at least six or seven relevant articles and books for your topic.

15

Short Reports

This chapter will show you how to write short reports, also called informal, semi-formal, or semi-technical reports. The skills necessary for writing these reports are among the most important ones you can develop because you will be expected to prepare short reports very often on your job.

☞ The Importance of Short Reports

Business and industry cannot function without written reports. A report may be defined as an organized presentation of relevant data on any topic—money, travel, time, personnel, equipment, management—that a company or agency must keep track of in its day-to-day operations. Reports tell whether schedules are being met, costs contained, sales projections met, clients and patients efficiently served. Reports also are likely to be required if unexpected problems occur.

You may write an occasional report in response to a specific question, or you may be required to write a daily or weekly report on routine activities about which your readers expect detailed information. Many organizations—clinics, mass transportation systems, schools—must submit regularly scheduled reports in order to maintain their funding by state or federal agencies.

☞ Types of Short Reports

To give you a sense of some of the topics that you may be required to write about, here is a list of various types of short reports that are found in business and industry:

appraisal report	medicine / treatment error report
audit report	operations report
construction report	periodic report
design report	production report
evaluation report	progress report
experiment report	project completion report
incident report	recommendations report
inventory report	research report
investigative report	sales report
laboratory report	status report
library report	test report
manager's report	trip report

Discussing each of these reports is too large a task for one chapter. Instead, Chapter 15 will concentrate on six of the most common types of reports you are likely to encounter in your professional work:

1. periodic reports
2. sales reports
3. progress reports
4. trip reports
5. test reports
6. incident reports

The first five reports can be called *routine reports* because they give information about planned, ongoing, or recurring events. *Incident reports,* on the other hand, describe events that writers did not foresee or plan for—accidents, breakdowns, delivery delays, or work stoppages. All six, however, may be termed "short" reports. They deal with current happenings rather than with long-range forecasts. Short reports focus on the "trees," not the "forest."

☞ How to Write Short Reports

The most important point to keep in mind is that reports are written for readers who need information so that they can get a job accomplished. Never think of the reports you write as a series of short notes jotted down for *your* convenience. Under each of the following categories you will find guidelines applicable to writing *any* short report you encounter. More specific information pertinent to particular types of reports is given within a discussion of those reports later in this chapter.

1. Audience. Short reports are written to coworkers, employers, and customers. The needs of each audience will vary. Consider how much your audience knows about your project and its reason for reading your report *before* writing it. While it is likely that coworkers in your department will be familiar with your project, readers in another department or section of your company may not be. Even employers, who will constitute your largest group of readers for your short reports, may not always know about the details of your work. These managers will use your reports to help them make decisions. Always give readers the details most relevant for their job. In a report for a business manager about equipment failure, your reader will be less concerned with the technical details about what went wrong than with the costs of parts replacement or the amount of lost work time.

2. Length. Short reports are *brief*—one paragraph to two or three pages. They get right to the point and do not waste a busy reader's time. Some test reports ask for nothing but numbers—for example, the glucose level on a blood test. A progress report, however, calls for written evaluations.

3. Format. Since so many short reports are done within a company, the memo is the most frequently used format. Review pertinent sections of Chapter 7 dealing with memos (pages 178–184). When you are writing to individuals outside your business, you will generally use a letter format. Prepared forms can also be used—or may be required—for reports. Regardless of format—letter or memo—be sure that you use headings to help readers follow your work and also help you classify information into easily understood categories. Most of the examples in this chapter employ headings to highlight and preview information for readers.

4. Content. The emphasis is on the objective reporting of the facts: costs, eyewitness accounts, observations, statistics, test measurements. Impressions, personal opinion, and guesswork are outlawed. Readers want a straightforward account of current events. Past activities may sometimes be mentioned, but only to clarify the present and to help readers follow current details. Always give dates and specify the exact period the report covers and indicate A.M. or P.M. Just listing "Thursday" is often not enough. Give the date. To record time in compact and specific terms, employers may use a twenty-four-hour clock: 1:00 A.M. is 0100 hours; 1:00 P.M. is 1300 hours. An event occurring on February 19, 1986, at 2:30 P.M. is 86 / 2 / 19 / 1430—year, month, day, time (hours / minutes). Give precise locations as well. "Highway 30" is not as helpful as "Highway 30, three miles southeast of the Morton exit." Call a machine by its precise technical name. Never use "thing," "gizmo," or "contraption" to refer to parts or tools. Refer to individuals by their proper names, not nicknames (Buddy, Lindy, Red, Sis, Shorty).

5. Organization. Organization means order. Effective organization of a short report means that you include the right amount of information in the most appropriate places for your audience. The organization of a short report will not be as elaborate as that for a long report (see pages 502–507). Many times a simple chronological or sequential organization will be acceptable for your readers' needs. Or you may follow one of the patterns of organization discussed in Chapter 2, pages 41–47.

Here is a fairly standard outline to follow when you are not required to submit a specially prepared form:

- Purpose
- Findings
- Conclusion
- Recommendations

Purpose. Always begin with a statement of purpose. Tell readers why you are writing to them and alert them to what you will discuss. When you establish the scope (or limits) of your report, you help readers zero in on the specific times, places, procedures, or problems you will discuss. You may also need to provide necessary background information (for example, a summary of an earlier report or occurrence) to assist readers.

Findings. The data that you collected goes under the section on findings. Data includes the facts you have gathered about prices, personnel, equipment, events, locations, incidents, or experiments. Many times you will find it convenient and helpful to readers to list your data in an appropriate visual, especially a table. See how visuals are used in the reports contained in Figures 15.3, 15.9, and 15.12. Some short reports even attach a computer printout with statistical data.

Conclusion. The conclusion can be a brief summary of what has happened or a review of what actions were taken. In a conclusion you might also explain the outcome or results of a test, a visit, or a program. The conclusion tells readers what your data means.

Recommendations. Some short reports (for example, those included in Figures 15.1, 15.2, 15.5, 15.8) do not require a recommendations section. But when you must supply recommendations, keep in mind that their placement in a report may vary. Some employers may prefer to see recommendations at the very beginning of a report instead of at the end. Recommendations tell readers what specific actions to take—where, when, why, and how. Recommendations must be based upon the conclusions of your investigations.

☞ Periodic Reports

Periodic reports, as their name signifies, provide readers with information at regularly scheduled intervals—daily, weekly, semi-monthly (twice a month, not every two months), monthly, quarterly. They help a company or agency keep track of the quantity and quality of the services it provides and the amount and types of work done by employees. Information in periodic reports helps managers make schedules, order materials, assign personnel, budget funds, and, generally speaking, determine corporate needs.

You may already be familiar with some kinds of periodic reports. For example, if you have ever punched a timecard and turned it in at the end of the week, you were filing a periodic report. Or, if you have ever taken inventory in a stockroom, you were preparing a periodic report.

Periodic reports are used for numerous jobs. Delivery services require drivers to keep a daily record documenting the number of packages delivered, the time, and the location. A log, another kind of periodic report, is shown in Figure 15.1. At the end of a tour of duty, for example, law enforcement officers submit a daily activity log showing hours worked and actions taken. Employees at television and radio stations may have to keep weekly reports of calls received by the station to aid management in determining the types of programming to offer.

Periodic reports follow no single format. Most often, though, employers supply routine forms on which to list information. These forms, such as the one illustrated in Figure 15.1, are relatively easy to complete. They ask for numbers, dates, codes, and expenses; occasionally a few clarifying or descriptive comments have to be added. Clearly distinguished categories on routine forms help to organize information for readers.

Other kinds of periodic reports may require more writing. You may be responsible for compiling a report based on individual periodic reports. Figure 15.2, a report submitted to a police captain, summarizes, organizes, and interprets the data collected over a three-month period from individual activity logs similar to the one in Figure 15.1. Such a report answers the reader's questions about the frequency and types of crimes committed and the work of the police force in the community. Because of this report, Captain Alice Martin will be better able to plan future protection for the community and to recommend changes in police services.

☞ Sales Reports

Sales reports provide businesses with a necessary record of accounts, purchases, and profits over a specified period of time. Sales reports might be considered a special type of periodic report, but because of their importance in the world of business they deserve a separate category here. They are important at various levels of business. Retail stores require a daily sales report in which purchases, coded by clerks on the cash register tapes, are arranged into major categories. Salespersons often submit weekly reports on the types and costs of products sold in a given district. Branch managers write monthly reports based on the figures given to them by their sales force. Higher up the business ladder, the president of a company sends stockholders an annual report assessing the financial health of the business. A report sent to someone at the same level of management as the writer is known as a *lateral report* (branch manager to branch manager). A report sent to a higher executive level than the level of the writer is known as a *vertical report* (branch manager to vice-president of marketing).

Sales reports help businesses assess past performance and plan for the future. In doing this they fulfill two functions—financial and managerial. As a financial record, sales reports list costs per unit, discounts or special reductions, and subtotals and totals. Like an accountant's ledger, sales reports show gains and losses. They may also provide statistics for comparing two quarters' sales. The method or origin of a sale, if significant, can also be recorded. In selling books, for example, a publisher keeps a careful record of where sales originate—direct orders for single copies from readers, adoptions for classroom use, purchases at bookstores, or orders from wholesale distributors handling the book.

Sales reports are also a managerial tool, since they help businesses make both short- and long-range plans. By indicating the number of sales, the report alerts buyers and managers about which items or services to increase, modify, or discontinue. The sales report illustrated in Figure 15.3 guides a restaurant owner in menu planning. Knowing which popular dishes to highlight and

Fig. 15.1 A log, a type of periodic report.

DENVER POLICE DEPARTMENT

DAILY ACTIVITY LOG

Page ____ of _____ pages

Name				Ser. No.	Name				Ser. No.
Date | Mo. | Day | Yr.	Unit No.	Unit No.	Class 1 Actions	No.	Min.	ON DUTY TIME Assgnd. & O'time:		Sgt. Approved:	Ser. No.
Detail	Mileage Off	Mileage Off	Class 2 Actions			Total Time Used: All Action Classes		Clerk Recapped:	Ser. No.
From: To	Mileage On	Mileage On	Class 3 Actions						
Dist. & Precinct /	Total	Total	Total Class Actions			Patrol Time		Captain Approved:	Ser. No.

Act. Cl.	Call Code	Time Out	Time In	Time Used	LOCATION, KIND OF ACTION AND DISPOSITION: Names, License, Citation No., etc.		
						CLASS 1 Felony Arr.	
						CLASS 1 Misc. Arrests	
						CLASS 2 Felony Arrests	
						CLASS 2 Misc. Arrests	
						CLASS 2 DUI Arrests	
						CLASS 2 Open Door	
						Recovered Units	
						Contact Cards	
						Offense Reports	
						Other Reports	
						Moving Violations	
						Parking Violations	
						Warning Violations	
						Accident Violations	
						Accident Reports	

DPD 120 (Rev. 11-74) ACTION CLASS 1-Radio Call ACTION CLASS 2-On Sight ACTION CLASS 3-Other

Reprinted courtesy of the Denver Police Department.

which unpopular ones to delete, the owner can increase profits. Note how the recommendations follow from the figures Sam Jelinek gives to Gina Smeltzer and Frank Drew.

To write a sales report, keep a careful record of order forms, invoices, and production figures. Sales information might be arranged in list form, as in Figure 15.3, or in narrative form, as in Figure 15.4. If you use the narrative format, make sure you do not overload your readers with numbers. Underlining key numbers will emphasize them for a reader, as Jessica Alonzo does in Figure 15.4.

☞ Progress Reports

A progress report informs readers about the status of an ongoing project. It lets them know how much and what type of work has been completed by a

Fig. 15.1 (Continued.)

Page ___ of ___ pages					
Act. Cl.	Call Code	Time Out	Time In	Time Used	LOCATION, KIND OF ACTION AND DISPOSITION: Names, License, Citation No., etc.

Fig. 15.2   A quarterly periodic report.

GREENFIELD POLICE DEPARTMENT
Greenfield, TX 77003

TO: Captain Alice Martin

FROM: Sergeant Daniel Huxley   *). 7⁄.*

SUBJECT: Crime rate for the first quarter of 1985

DATE: April 12, 1985

From January 1 to March 31, 1,276 crimes were committed in Greenfield, representing a 20 percent increase over the 1,021 crimes recorded during the previous quarter.

The following report discusses the specific types of crimes organized into three categories: felonies, traffic, and misdemeanors.

FELONIES

The greatest increase in crime was in robberies, 20 percent higher than last quarter's figure (126 robberies). Downtown merchants reported 75 burglaries totaling more than $450,000. The biggest theft occurred on January 21 at Weisenfarth's Jewelers when three armed robbers stole more than $50,000 in merchandise. (These suspects were apprehended three days later.) Home burglaries accounted for 43 crimes, though the thefts were not confined to any one residential area. We also had 39 car thefts reported and investigated.

The number of homicides decreased from last quarter. During the first quarter we had 8 homicides as opposed to 9 last quarter. The battery charges, however, increased to 82—15 more than we had last quarter. There were 5 charges for arson, 11 for carrying a concealed weapon, and 20 for possession of a controlled substance. The number of rapes for this quarter was 8, fewer than last quarter (9). Three of those rapes happened within one week (February 3–8) and have been attributed to the same suspect, now in custody.

TRAFFIC

Traffic violations for this period were lower than last quarter's figures. The 319 citations for moving violations for the first quarter represent a 5 percent decrease over last quarter's 335 violations. Most were issued for speeding (158) or for failing to observe signals (98). Officers issued 45 citations to motorists who were driving while under the influence. These citations point to an impressive decrease over the 78 issued last quarter. The new state penalty of withholding for six months the driver's license of anyone convicted of driving while under the influence appears to be an effective deterrent.

Fig. 15.2   (Continued.)

Captain Martin
April 12, 1985
Page 2

MISDEMEANORS

   The largest number of arrests in this category were for disturbing the
peace—53. Compared to last quarter, this is an increase of 10 percent.
There were 48 charges for vagrancy and public drunkenness, a decrease from
the 59 charges brought last quarter. We issued 32 citations for violation
of leash laws, which represents a sizeable increase over last quarter's 21
citations. Fifty citations were issued for violations of city codes and
ordinances; 37 of those 50 citations were issued for dumping trash at the
Mason reservoir.

Encl. computer printout

---

particular date and how close the entire job is to being completed. A progress
report emphasizes whether you are keeping on schedule, staying within a
budget, using the proper equipment, making the right assignments, and completing the job efficiently and correctly. Almost any kind of ongoing work can
be described in a progress report—research for a paper, construction of an
apartment complex, preparation of a fall catalog, documentation of a patient's
rehabilitation.

   A progress report is intended for people who are generally not working
alongside you, but who need a record of your activities in order to coordinate
them with other individuals' efforts and to learn about problems or changes in
plans. For example, since local management or supervisors at the home office
cannot be in the field or at the construction site, they will rely on a progress
report for much of their information. Customers, too, will expect a report on
how carefully their money is being spent. Health care professionals will consult
the progress notes from the previous shift to provide continuity of care of their
patients. Your audience will be managers who need your report to help them
in their decision making.

   The length of the report will depend on the complexity of the project. A
short memo about organizing a time management workshop, such as that in
Figure 15.5, might be all that is necessary. A report to a teacher about the
progress a student is making on a research paper could easily be handled in a
one-page memo, such as James Salinas's report in Figure 15.6 for his paper
proposed on pages 456–457. Similarly, Dale Brandt's assessment of the progress his firm is making in renovating Dr. Burke's office is given in a two-page
letter in Figure 15.7.

Fig. 15.7   (Continued.)

WORK REMAINING

The finishing work is scheduled for May. By May 10, the floors in the
reception area, laboratory, washrooms, and hallways should be tiled and the
examination rooms and your office carpeted. By May 15, the reception area
and your office should be paneled and the rest of the walls painted. If
everything stays on schedule, touch-up work is scheduled for May 18–22.
You should be able to move into your new clinic by May 23.

You will receive a third and final progress report by May 15.

Sincerely yours,

Dale Brandt

Dale Brandt

---

completed; be realistic. Do not promise to have a job done in less time than you
know it will take. Readers will not expect miracles, only informed estimates.
Any conclusion must be tentative. Note that the good news Dale Brandt gives
Dr. Burke about moving into her new clinic is qualified by the words "if everything stays on schedule." A recommendation may also find a place in the
conclusion. Such a recommendation might advise readers, for example, of a
less costly, equally durable siding than the one originally planned, suggest that
a joint meeting of two committees would expedite production of a college
yearbook, or show that hiring an additional part-time salesclerk would help
ease the busy holiday sales period.

☞ Trip Reports

Reporting on the trips you take is an important professional responsibility.
Trips can range from a brief afternoon car ride across town to a two-week
journey across the country. They inform readers about your activities outside
the office, plant, clinic, or agency. In documenting what you did and saw, these
trip reports help your readers to better understand what has happened and
even give them information they can use for later reports. Specifically, a trip
report should answer the following questions for your readers:

1. Where did you go?
2. When did you go there?
3. Why did you go there?
4. Whom did you see?
5. What did they tell you?

Fig. 15.3 A sales report in tabular form.

The Palace
Dayton, OH 43210

TO: Gina Smeltzer   DATE: June 27, 1985
      Frank Drew, Owners

FROM: Sam Jelinek   SUBJECT: Analysis of entree
      Manager   sales, June 10–24

As you requested at our monthly meeting on June 5, here is a tabulated analysis of entree sales for two weeks to assist us in our menu planning. Below is a record of entree sales for the weeks of June 10–17 and June 18–24 that I have compiled into a table for easier and more valid comparisons.

	Portion Size	June 10–17 Amount	June 10–17 Ratio	June 18–24 Amount	June 18–24 Ratio	2 weeks combined Amount	2 weeks combined Ratio
Strip Steak	12 oz	168	12%	198	11%	366	11%
Veal à la Viennoise (2)	8 oz	112	8	182	10	294	9
Shrimp Newburg	8 oz	154	11	217	12	371	12
Brook Trout	12 oz	56	4	70	4	126	4
Prime Rib (1) (2)	10 oz	343	25	413	23	756	24
Lobster Tails	2–4 oz	147	10	161	9	308	10
Delmonico Steak	10 oz	182	13	252	14	434	13
Beef Stroganoff (2)	8 oz	238	17	307	17	545	17
		1,400	100%	1,800	100%	3,200	100%

(1) 14 cuts / 22# rib.
(2) Prepared in advance.

Recommendations

Based on the figures in the table above, I recommend that we do the following:

1. order at least one hundred more pounds of prime rib each two-week period to be eligible for further quantity discounts at the Northern Meat Company

2. delete the brook trout entree because of low acceptance

3. introduce a new beef or pork entree to take the place of the brook trout item. I would suggest stuffed pork chops.

Please give me your reactions within the next week. It shouldn't take more than two weeks to implement these changes.

Table from *The Financial Ingredient in Foodservice Management* 1976. Reprinted with permission from The National Institute for the Foodservice Industry.

Fig. 15.4   A narrative sales report.

HAMILTON COIN SHOP
Erie, PA 17321

TO: Harry T. Udall   DATE: September 8, 1985
        Owner

From: Jessica Alonzo   *J A*   SUBJECT: Favorable August sales
        Manager

Our sales were brisk during August. Sales of mint sets and proof sets totaled $1,634. The sale of individual coins came to $2,340. Commemorative coin sales were $521. These sales total $4,495.

The most impressive sales came from our offer to sell pennies by the pound. We placed ads in the Erie Times–News and in Coin World Today. Our ads over WTOR AM may also have helped sales. Although it is hard to determine what portion of our walk-in business came from the radio announcements, possibly it is as much as a third. The total amount of sales for the pennies by the pound was $5,930.

Sales for the month of August come to $10,425. Detailed breakdowns of these figures will appear in the September 30 quarterly report.

Progress reports should contain information on (1) the work you have done, (2) the work you currently are doing, and (3) the work you will do.

They can be written daily, weekly, monthly, quarterly, or annually. Your specific job and your employer's needs will dictate how often you have to keep others informed of your progress. Nurses have to write progress notes for each eight- or twelve-hour shift; management trainees may have to submit a weekly report of their accomplishments. A single progress report is sufficient for Philip Javon's purpose in Figure 15.5. On the other hand, James Salinas has been asked to submit two progress reports, the first of which is in Figure 15.6. Contractor Brandt in Figure 15.7 has found that three separate reports, spaced four to six weeks apart, are needed to keep Dr. Burke posted.

How to Begin a Progress Report

In a brief introduction indicate why you are writing the report. Provide any necessary project titles or codes and specify dates. Help readers recall the job you are doing for them. If you are writing an initial progress report, supply

Fig. 15.5   A one-time progress report.

REPUBLIC INDUSTRIES
Trenton, NJ 08542

TO: Kathy Sands   DATE: September 12, 1985

FROM: Philip Javon *P. J.*   SUBJECT: Preparations for the
                                              Time Management
                                              Workshop

     As you requested last week, I called the managers of all departments on Thursday (September 5) to alert them to the time management workshop we will offer on October 2–3. I also sent follow-up notices to the managers today.

     I have reserved the cafeteria annex for both October 2 and 3 and ordered all the supplies we will need. The management kit will have the company brochures on organization policies, the time sheets used in the plant, the report forms we used last March, note pads, and ballpoint pens. I have also arranged with Ms. Suarez in the audiovisual department to set up the projector on the morning of October 2. By tomorrow I hope to have typed a list of all those who will participate in the workshop.

     Plans are going according to schedule.

---

background information. Philip Javon's first two sentences in Figure 15.5 quickly establish his purpose by reminding Kathy Sands of their discussion last week. Similarly James Salinas in Figure 15.6 reminds his teacher of the purpose and scope of his work in the first paragraph. If you are submitting a subsequent progress report, show where the previous report left off and where the current one begins. Make sure that the period covered by each report is clearly specified. See how Dale Brandt's first paragraph in Figure 15.7 calls attention to the continuity of his work.

How to Continue a Progress Report

The body of the report should provide significant details about costs, materials, personnel, and times for the major stages of the project. Emphasize completed tasks, not false starts. If you report that the carpentry work or painting is finished, readers do not need an explanation of paint viscosity or geometrical patterns. Omit routine or well-known details ("I had to use the library when I wanted to read the back issues of *Safety News*") in your progress report. De-

Fig. 15.6   A progress report from a student to a teacher.

TO: Professor Barbara Felton-Parks

FROM: James Salinas

DATE: April 8, 1985

SUBJECT: First Progress Report on Research Paper

This is the first of two progress reports that you asked me to submit about my research paper on the advantages and disadvantages of electronic mail.

From March 8 until April 7, I gathered information from library materials and from an interview. Of the ten references listed on my proposal, I found only seven. Stevenson's Telecommunications: An Introduction and the articles by Barks ("Can You Count on Electronic Mail?") and Hannan ("The Uncertain Road to Improved Communications") are not in our library. I have ordered them through interlibrary loan.

On February 25, I had an extended interview with Mr. Keith Wellbridge of General Dynamics who gave me some brochures as well as a copy of a report on electronic mail he wrote for General Dynamics, materials I hope to use in my paper.

Because of a long business trip to Denver, Ms. Alice Phillips of Dodge & Spenser could not meet with me. At her suggestion, I am trying to schedule an interview with Ms. Gloria Miller, the office manager at Mid-Atlantic Power Company. Her firm has recently switched to electronic mail.

Even if Ms. Miller cannot meet with me, I believe that Mr. Wellbridge gave me enough information about a business manager's view of electronic mail systems. However, not having the Stevenson book and the articles cited above may slow my work a little.

Starting tomorrow, I will begin organizing my paper. I will be able to submit a rough draft by April 28. You will receive my second progress report on the organization of my paper by April 21.

scribe in the body of the discussion, too, any snags you encountered. See Dale Brandt's section on electrical problems in Figure 15.7. It is better for the reader to know about trouble early in the project, so that appropriate changes or corrections can be made.

How to End a Progress Report

The conclusion should give a timetable for the completion of duties or when the next progress report can be expected. Give the date by which work will be

Fig. 15.7   The second of three progress reports.

BRANDT CONSTRUCTION COMPANY

Halsted at Roosevelt

Chicago, Illinois 60608

April 28, 1986

Dr. Pamela Burke
1439 Grand Avenue
Mount Prospect, IL 60045

Dear Dr. Burke:

Here is my second progress report about the renovation work at your new
clinic at Hacienda and Donohue. Work proceeded satisfactorily in April
according to the plans you had approved in March.

REVIEW OF WORK COMPLETED IN MARCH

As I informed you in my first progress report on March 31, we had torn down
the walls, pulled the old wiring, and removed existing plumbing work. All
the gutting work was finished in March.

WORK COMPLETED DURING APRIL

By April 9, we had laid the new pipes and connected them to the main sewer
line. We had also installed the two commodes, the four standard sinks, and
the utility basin. The heating and air-conditioning ducts were installed
by April 13. From April 16 to 20, we erected soundproof walls in the four
examination rooms, the reception area, your office, and the laboratory. We
had no problems reducing the size of the reception area by five feet to make
the first examination room larger, as you had requested.

PROBLEMS WITH ELECTRICAL SYSTEM

We had difficulty with the electrical work, however. The number of outlets
and the generator for the laboratory equipment required extraduty power
lines that had to be approved by both Con Edison and county inspectors. The
approval slowed us down three days. Also, the wholesaler, Midtown
Electric, failed to deliver the recessed lighting fixtures by April 23 as
promised. These fixtures and wiring are now being installed. Moreover, the
cost of those fixtures will increase the materials budget by $345. The cost
for labor is as we had projected--$49,450.

For a business trip you are likely to have to inform readers how much the trip cost and to supply them with a travel voucher.

Common Types of Trip Reports

Trip reports can cover a wide range of activities and are called by different names to characterize those activities. Undoubtedly, you will encounter the following three types of trip reports:

1. Field trip reports. These reports, often assigned in a course, are written after a visit to a local plant, military installation, garage, hospital, forest, detention center, or other facility. Their purpose is to show what you have learned about the operation of these places. You will be expected to describe how an institution is organized, the equipment or procedures it uses, the ecological conditions present, or the ratio of one group to another. The emphasis is on the educational values of the trip, as Mark Tourneur's report in Figure 15.8 demonstrates.

2. Site inspection reports. These trip reports are written to inform readers—managers, department heads, section chiefs—about conditions at a branch office or plant, a customer's business, or at an area directly under an employer's jurisdiction. Site inspection reports tell how machinery or production procedures are working or provide information about the physical plant, environment (soil, trees, water), and computer or financial operations. A site inspection report will be written for an employer or a customer who wants to relocate or build new facilities (a record shop, a half-way house, a branch office) to assess the suitability of a particular location. After visiting the site, you will determine whether it meets your employer's (or customer's) needs. Figure 15.9, which shows a report written to a manager interested in acquiring land for a fast-food restaurant, begins with a recommendation.

3. Home health or social work visits. Nurses, social workers, and probation officers report daily on their visits to patients and clients. Their reports describe clients' lifestyles, assess needs, and make recommendations. A report from a social worker to a county family services agency can be seen in Figure 15.10. The report begins with the information Jeff Bowman acquired from his visit with the Scanlons and concludes, not with a recommendation, but rather with a list of the actions this social worker has taken.

How to Gather Information for a Trip Report

Regardless of the kind of trip report you have to write, your assignment will be easier and your report better organized if you follow these suggestions.

Fig. 15.8   A student's field trip report.

TO: Katherine Holmes, RN, MSN   DATE: November 9, 1985
       Director, RN Program

FROM: Mark Tourneur   *M. J.*   SUBJECT: Field Trip to
       RN Student   Water Valley
                                                 Convalescent Center

On Tuesday, November 2, I visited the Water Valley Convalescent Center, 1400 Medford Boulevard, in preparation for my internship in a nursing home next semester.

Before the tour started, the Director, Marge LaFrance, explained the holistic philosophy of health care at Water Valley and emphasized the diverse kinds of nursing practiced there. She stressed that the agency is not restricted to geriatric patients but admits anyone requiring long-term care. She pointed out that Water Valley is a medium-sized center (150 beds) and contains three wings: (1) the Infirmary, (2) the General Nursing Unit, and (3) the Ambulatory Unit.

My tour began with the Infirmary, staffed by one RN and two LPN's, where I observed a number of life-support systems—IV's, oxygen setups, electrocardiograph equipment. Then I was shown the General Nursing Unit, a forty-bed unit that is staffed by three LPN's and four aides. Patients can have private or semiprivate rooms; bathrooms have wide commodes and sinks for patients using wheelchairs or walkers. The ambulatory section cares for ninety patients.

Before lunch in the main dining room, I was introduced to Doris Betz, the dietitian, who explained the different diets she coordinates. The most common are low sodium and restricted calorie. Staff members eat with the patients, reinforcing the holistic concern of the agency.

After lunch, Jack Tishner, the pharmacist, discussed the agency's procedures for ordering and delivering medications. He also stressed the teaching of patients and the inservice workshops he does. I then observed patients in both recreational and physical therapy. Water Valley has a full-time physical therapist, who works with stroke and arthritic patients and helps those with broken bones regain the use of their limbs. In addition to a weight room, Water Valley has a small sauna that most of the patients use at least twice a week. The patients' spiritual needs are not neglected, either. A small chapel is located on the Ambulatory Unit.

From my visit to Water Valley, I learned a great deal about the health care delivery system at a nursing home. I was especially pleased to have been given so much information on emergency procedures, medication orders, and physical therapy programs. My forthcoming internship will be much more useful, since I have first-hand knowledge about these available services.

Fig. 15.9   A site inspection report and accompanying map.

VAIL'S, INC.
Denver, CO 87123

TO: Dale Gandy   DATE: July 1, 1986
       District Manager

FROM: Delores Marshack *D M*   SUBJECT: New site for Vail's #8
       Development Department

RECOMMENDATION:

The best location for the new Vail's Chicken House is the vacant Dairy
World shop at the northeast corner of Smith and Fairfax Avenues--1701 South
Fairfax. I inspected this property on June 23 and 24 and also talked with
Marge Bloom, the broker at Crescent Realty representing the Dairy World
Company.

THE LOCATION:

Refer to the map below. Located at the intersection of the two busiest
streets on the southeast side, the property can take advantage of the
traffic flow to attract customers. Being only one block west of the
Cloverleaf Mall should also help business. Only two other fast-food
establishments are in a one-mile vicinity. McGonagles, 1534 South Kildare,
specializes in hamburgers; Noah's, 703 Zanwood, serves primarily fish
entrees. Their offerings will not directly compete with ours. The closest
fast-food restaurant serving chicken is Johnson's, 1.8 miles away.
Customers have easy access to our location. They can enter or exit the
Dairy World from either Smith or Fairfax, but left turns on Smith are
prohibited from 7 A.M. to 9 A.M. However, since most of our business is
done after 11 A.M., the restriction poses few problems.

PARKING FACILITIES:

The parking lot has space for 45 cars. The area at the south end of the
property (38 feet × 37 feet) can accommodate another 11 to 15 cars. The
driveways and parking lot were paved with asphalt last March and appear to
be in excellent shape. We will be able to make use of the drive-up window on
the north side of the building.

THE BUILDING:

The building has 3,993 square feet of heated and cooled space. The
air-conditioning and heating units were installed within the last fifteen
months and seem to be in good working order; nine more months of
transferable warranty remain on these units. The only major changes we
would have to make are in the kitchen. To prepare items on the Vail's menu,
we would have to add more exhaust fans (there is only one now) and expand
the grill and cooking areas. The kitchen also has three relatively new
sinks and ample storage space in the fourteen cabinets. The restaurant has

Fig. 15.9   (Continued.)

Dale Gandy
July 1, 1986
Page 2

a seating capacity of up to 54 persons; ten booths are covered with red
vinyl and are comfortably padded. A color coordinated serving counter
could seat 8 to 10 patrons. The floor does not need to be retiled, but the
walls must be painted to match Vail's color decor.

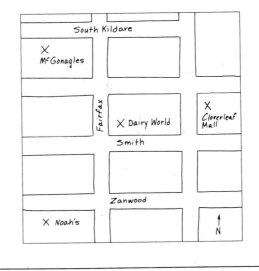

Before You Leave for the Site

1. Obtain all necessary names, addresses, and telephone numbers.
2. Check the files for previous correspondence, case studies, terms of contracts or agreements.
3. Locate a map of the area or a blueprint of the building.
4. Look for brochures, work orders, instructions, or other documents pertinent to your visit.
5. Make sure you have a notebook and a pen with you. Depending on your job, you may also need to bring a tape recorder, camera, or calculator. Use these instruments to record important data.

When You Return

1. Write your report promptly. If you put it off, you may forget important items.

Fig. 15.10   A social worker's visit report.

GREEN COUNTY FAMILY SERVICE
Randall, VA 21032

TO: Margaret S. Walker, Director
           Green County Family Services

FROM: Jeff Bowman, Social Worker   *J B.*

SUBJECT: Visit to Mr. Lee Scanlon

DATE: October 17, 1985

PURPOSE OF VISIT

   At the request of the Green County Home Health Office, I visited Mr. Lee
Scanlon at his home at 113 West Diversy Drive on Tuesday, October 15. Mr.
Scanlon and his three children (ages six, eight, and eleven) live in a
two-bedroom apartment above a garage. Last week, Mr. Scanlon was
discharged from Methodist General Hospital after leg surgery and has asked
for financial assistance.

DESCRIPTION OF VISIT

   Mr. Scanlon is a widower with no means of support except a monthly
Social Security check of $405 and unemployment compensation totaling $130 a
month. He lost his job at Baymont Manufacturing when the company went out
of business four weeks ago and wants to go back to work, but Dr.
Canning-Smith advised against it for six to seven weeks. His oldest child
is diabetic, and the six-year-old daughter must have a tonsillectomy. Mr.
Scanlon also told me the problems he was having with his refrigerator; it
"was off more than it was on," he said.

   Mrs. Alice Gordon, the owner of the garage, informed me that Mr.
Scanlon had paid last month's rent but not this month's. She also stressed
how much the Scanlons need a new refrigerator and that she had often let
them use part of hers to store their food.

   Mr. Scanlon's monthly bills and income are as follows:

Expenses	Income
$270 rent	$405 Social Security
65 utilities	130 unemployment
350 food	———
60 drugs	$535
80 transportation	
———	
$825	

Fig. 15.10   (Continued.)

```
Margaret S. Walker
October 17, 1985
Page 2


ACTION TAKEN

     To assist Mr. Scanlon, I have done the following:

1. Set up an appointment (10/21/85) for him to apply for food stamps.
2. Talked with Blanche Derringo regarding Medicaid assistance.
3. Asked the State Employment Security Commission to aid him in finding a
   job as soon as he is well enough to work.
4. Visited Robert Adkins at the office of the Council of Churches to obtain
   food and money for utilities until federal aid is available; he also
   will try to find the Scanlons another refrigerator.
5. Telephoned Sharon Munez at the Green County Health Department to have
   Mr. Scanlon's diabetic daughter receive insulin and syringes gratis.
```

2. When a trip takes you to two or more widely separated places, note in your report when you arrived at each place and how long you stayed.
3. Do not include in your report everything you saw or did on the trip. Exclude irrelevant details, such as whether the trip was enjoyable, where you stayed overnight, what you ate, or how delighted you were to meet people.

☞ Test Reports

Much physical research (the discovery of facts) is communicated through reports. These reports have various names. Depending on your profession's terminology, they may be called experiment, investigation, laboratory, operations, or research reports. They all record the results of tests, whether the tests were conducted in a forest, laboratory, parking lot, shopping center, or soybean field.

No doubt you have already written a test report (or laboratory report) after performing an experiment in a science class. To write an effective test report involves specific training in a scientific or technological field.

Objectivity and accuracy are essential ingredients in a test report. Readers want to know about your empirical research (the facts), not about your feelings (the "I"). Record your observations without bias or guesswork in a laboratory journal or log book and always include precise measurements. When you write

Fig. 15.11   A laboratory (or test) report with recommendations.

CHARLESTON CENTRAL HOSPITAL
CHARLESTON, WV 25324

TO: James Dill, Supervisor
      Housekeeping

FROM: Janeen Cufaude *J. C.*
      Infection Control Officer

DATE: December 2, 1985

SUBJECT: Routine sanitation
         inspection

As part of the monthly check of the psychiatric unit (11A), the following areas were swabbed and tested for bacterial growth. The results of the lab tests of these samples are as follows:

AREA	FINDINGS
1. cabinet in patients' kitchen	1. positive for 2 colonies of strep germs
2. rug in eating area	2. positive for food particles and yeasts and molds
3. baseboard in dayroom	3. positive for particles of dust and fungi
4. medicine counter in nurses' station	4. negative for bacteria––no growth after 48 hrs.
5. corridor by south elevator	5. positive for 4 colonies of staph germs

ACTIONS TO BE TAKEN AT ONCE

1. Clean the kitchen cabinet with K-504 liquid daily, 3:1 dilution.

2. Shampoo rug areas bimonthly with heavy-duty shampoo and clean visibly soiled areas with Guard-Pruf as often as needed.

3. Wipe all baseboards weekly with K-12 spray cleanser.

4. Mop heavily traveled corridors and access areas with K-504 cleanser daily, 1:1 dilution.

your report, tell readers why the test was made, under what circumstances (or controls) it was made, and what the outcome was. When you sign your test report, you are certifying that things happened exactly when, how, and why you say they did.

Figure 15.11 contains a relatively simple and short test report in memo format regarding sanitary conditions at a hospital psychiatric unit. This report follows a direct and useful pattern of organization:

- statement of purpose
- findings
- recommendations

Submitted by an infection control officer, the report does not provide elaborate details about the particular laboratory procedures used to determine if bacteria were present; nor does it describe the pathogenic (disease-causing) properties of the bacteria. Such descriptions are unnecessary for the audience (the housekeeping department) to do its job.

A more complex example of a short test report is found in Figure 15.12; it studies the effects of four light periods on the growth of paulownia seedlings. This report, published in a technical journal, is addressed to specialists in forestry. To meet the needs of this expert audience, the writer had to include much more detailed information than Janeen Cufaude did about the way the test was conducted and about the types of data the audience would need to confirm and use the scientific data from the author's tests. Such a test report follows a different pattern of organization than the one in Figure 15.11 and includes the following parts:

- an informative abstract
- an introduction to provide background information about the importance of the test and perhaps to review previous research on the topic
- a materials and methods section to describe the exact scientific procedures and equipment the author(s) used to conduct the test
- a results and discussion section (sometimes separated into two sections) to record the data obtained from the test and to explain the significance of the data. Many times a test report will conclude by confirming previous studies, emphasizing the need for further tests, or offering researchers new interpretation of the evidence
- a list of references cited in the study

Notice how the needs of two different audiences as well as the authors' purpose control the way each report is organized and how much and what type of information is included. Janeen Cufaude's reader is a nonspecialist, less interested in scientific theory than in the practical application of that theory; Immel, Tackett, and Carpenter's readers are experts demanding scientific documentation and commentary. As these two reports show, you should always determine (a) how much technical knowledge an audience has about your field and (b) how they will use your report to accomplish their specific job.

Fig. 15.12   A short test report in a scientific journal.

Paulownia Seedlings Respond to Increased Daylength[1]

M. J. Immel, E. M. Tackett, and S. B. Carpenter

Abstract

Paulownia seedlings grown under four photoperiods were evaluated after a growing period of 97 days. Height growth and total dry weight production were both significantly increased in the 16- and 24-hour photoperiods.

Introduction

Paulownia (*Paulownia tomentosa* [Thunb.] Steud.), a native of China, is a little-known species in the United States. Recently, however, there has been increased interest in this species for surface mine reclamation (*1*).[2] Paulownia seems to be especially well adapted to harsh micro-climates of surface mines; it grows very rapidly and appears to be drought resistant. In Kentucky and surrounding states, wood of paulownia is actively sought by Japanese buyers and has brought prices comparable to black walnut (*2*).

This increased interest in paulownia has resulted in several attempts to direct seed it on surface mines, but little success has been achieved. The high light requirements and the extremely small size of paulownia seed (approximately 6,000 per gram) may be the limiting factors. Planting paulownia seedlings is preferred; but, because of their succulent nature, seedlings are usually produced and outplanted as container stock rather than bareroot seedlings. Daylength is an important factor in the production of vigorous container plants (*5*). Our study compares the effects four photoperiods, 8, 12, 16, and 24 hours, had on the early growth of container-grown paulownia seedlings over a period of 97 days.

Materials and Methods

Seeds used in this study were stratified in a 1:1 mixture of peat moss and sand at 4°C for 2 years. Following cold storage, seeds were placed on a 1:1 potting soil–sand mix and mulched with cheesecloth. They were then placed under continuous light until germination occurred. Germination percentages were high, indicating paulownia seeds can survive long periods of storage with little loss of viability (*3*). Thirty days after germination, 3- to 4-centimeter seedlings were transplanted into 8-quart plastic pots filled with an equal mixture of potting soil, sand, and peat moss. Seventy-five seedlings were randomly assigned to each of the four treatments. Treatments were four photoperiods— 8, 12, 16, and 24 hours—replicated three times in 12 light chambers. Each chamber was 1.2- by 1.2-meters in size with an artificial light source 71 centimeters above the chamber floor.

---

[1] *Tree Planters' Notes* (Winter 1980): 3–5.
[2] All actual references have been omitted to save space.

The light source consisted of eight fluorescent lights: four 40-watt plant growth lamps alternated with four 40-watt cool white lamps. Light intensity averaged 550 foot-candles (1340μ einsteins / m^2 / sec) at the top of each pot and temperature averaged 23°C ($\pm$2°C).

Seedlings were kept watered and were fertilized after transplanting with a 6-gram 14–4–6 agriform container tablet. Beginning 1 month after transplanting, two seedlings were randomly selected and harvested from each chamber for a total of 24 trees. Height, root collar diameter, length of longest root, and oven-dry weight (at 65°C) were determined for each seedling. Harvests continued every week for 5 additional weeks.

Results and Discussion

Results indicate that early growth of paulownia is influenced by photoperiod (table 1). Increasing the photoperiod from 8 to either 16 or 24 hours increased height growth by 100 percent. Height growth in the 12-hour treatment also increased, but did not differ significantly from the 8-hour treatment. Heights under photoperiods of 8, 12, 16, and 24 hours were 13.1, 17.8, 27.3, and 29.2 centimeters, respectively.

Previous studies have also shown that photoperiod affects the growth of paulownia seedlings (*4, 6*). Sanderson (*6*) found that paulownia seedlings grown under continuous light averaged 27.2 centimeters in height after 101 days compared with 29.2 centimeters for our 24-hour seedlings. Other corresponding photoperiods were equally comparable. Downs and Borthwick (*4*) also concluded that height growth of paulownia was affected by extending the photoperiod.

The greatest treatment differences were shown in total dry weight production (table 1). The mean weight of 1.65 grams for seedlings in the 8-hour treatment was significantly less than that of any of the other photoperiods. The 16- and 24-hour treatments did not differ significantly, and more than doubled the average weight for seedlings in the 12-hour treatment.

Root-to-shoot ratio (R / S) indicates the relative proportion of growth allocated to roots versus shoots for the seedlings in each photoperiod. In this study, shoots were developing at nearly three times the rate of the roots for seedlings in the 12-, 16-, and 24-hour photoperiods. The 0.18 R / S ratio for seedlings in the 8-hour treatment was much lower. It indicates that relative growth of the shoot is approximately five times that of the root. The shorter photoperiod therefore decreased root development relative to shoot development as well as significantly reduced total dry weight production.

Although root collar diameter and root length did not significantly differ under the

Table 1. Height, diameter, root length, total dry weight, and R / S ratio for paulownia seedlings grown under four photoperiods after 97 days

Photo-period (hrs.)	Height (cm)	Diameter (cm)	Root length (cm)	Total dry weight (gm)	R / S ratio
8	13.1b	0.48	16.0	1.65c	0.18
12	17.8b	0.67	34.7	7.27b	0.32
16	27.3a	0.93	31.1	15.92a	0.39
24	29.2a	0.90	43.9	18.56a	0.33

different photoperiods after 97 days, there was a trend for greater diameter and root growth with longer photoperiods.

Conclusions

Results indicate that the growth of paulownia seedlings is affected by changes in the photoperiod. By increasing the photoperiod, height growth and total dry matter production were both significantly increased. The distribution of dry matter (R / S ratio) was altered by increasing the photoperiod; the ratio was larger in the longer photoperiods. In contrast to earlier studies (4), we found paulownia seedlings subjected to extended photoperiods to be still growing after 97 days.

☞ Incident Reports

The reports discussed thus far in this chapter have dealt with routine work. They have described events that were anticipated or supervised. But every business or agency runs into unexpected trouble that delays routine work. Employers, and on some occasions government inspectors, insurance agents, and attorneys, must be informed about those events that interfere with normal, safe operations. A special type of report known as an *incident report* is submitted when there is an accident, law enforcement offense, machine breakdown, delivery delay, cost overrun, or production slowdown.

Protecting Yourself Legally

The incident report can be used as legal evidence. It frequently concerns the two topics over which powerful legal battles are waged—health and property. The report can sway the outcome of insurance claims, civil suits, or criminal cases. To ensure that what you write is legally proper, follow these three rules:

1. Be accurate, objective, and complete. Never omit or distort facts; the information may surface later, and you could be guilty of a cover-up. Do not write "I do not know" for an answer. If you are not sure, state why. Also be careful that there are no discrepancies in your report.

2. Give facts, not opinions. Provide a factual account of what actually happened, not a biased interpretation of events. Indirect words, such as "I guess," "I wonder," "There was some apparent injury," "perhaps," or "possibly," weaken your objectivity. Stick to details you witnessed or that were seen by eyewitnesses. Indicate who saw what. Keep in mind that stating what someone else saw will be regarded as hearsay, and therefore be inadmissible in a court of law. State only what *you* saw or heard. When you describe what happened, avoid drawing uncalled-for conclusions.

Wrong: The patient seemed confused and caught himself in his IV tubing.

Right: The patient caught himself in his IV tubing.

Wrong: The equipment was defective.

Right: The bolt was loose.

Be careful, too, about blaming someone. Saying that "Baxter was incompetent" or that the "company knew of the problem but did nothing about it" are libelous remarks.

3. Do not exceed your professional responsibilities.   Answer only those questions you are qualified to answer. Do not presume to speak as a detective, inspector, physician, or supervisor. Do not represent yourself as an attorney or claims adjuster in writing the report.

Parts of an Incident Report

You will use either a memo or a specially prepared form with spaces for detailed comments. Figure 15.13 contains an incident report written in memo format; Figure 15.14 shows a typical incident report form used to report an accident. Regardless of the format, all incident reports will ask for the following information:

1. Personal details.   Record titles, department, and employment identification numbers. Indicate if you or your fellow employees were working alone. For customers and victims, record home addresses, phone numbers, and places of employment. Insurance companies will also require policy numbers. Note that the first four questions in Figure 15.14 request this kind of information.

2. Type of incident.   Briefly identify the incident: personal injury, fire, burglary, delivery delay, equipment failure. In the case of injury identify the part(s) of the body precisely. "Eye injury" is not enough; "injury to the right eye, causing bleeding" is better. "Dislocated shoulder," "punctured left forearm," and "twisted left ankle" are descriptive and exact phrases. A report on damaged equipment should list model numbers. Note how Ned Roane's report (Figure 15.13) specifies the grain car numbers. For thefts, supply colors, brand names, quantities, and serial numbers. "A stolen watch" will not help detectives locate the right object; "a seven-jewel lady's Benrus" will.

3. Time and location of the incident.   Follow the advice given at the beginning of this chapter, page 467.

4. Description of what happened.   This section is the longest part of the report. Some forms ask you to write on the back, to attach another sheet, or to add a photograph or diagram. Put yourself in the reader's position. If you were not present or did not speak directly to witnesses, would you know by reading the report what happened exactly and why, how it occurred, who and what were involved, and what led up to the incident?

The two most common errors writers make are that they do not give (1) enough information or (2) the right kinds of information. Recount what happened in the order in which it took place. What you (or eyewitnesses) saw,

Fig. 15.13   An incident report.

THE GREAT HARVESTER RAILROAD

P.O. Box 4005
Des Moines, IA 50306

TO: Marge O'Brien   DATE: March 2, 1986
       District Manager
       James Day
       Safety Inspector

FROM: Ned Roane *n. R.*   SUBJECT: Derailment of Train #28
       Engineer   on March 1, 1986

DESCRIPTION OF INCIDENT

    At 7:20 A.M. on March 1, 1986, I was driving engine #457 traveling north at a speed of fifty-two miles an hour on the single mainline track four miles east of Ridgeville, Illinois. Weather conditions and visibility were excellent. Suddenly the last two grain cars, #3022 and #3053, jumped the track. The train automatically went into emergency braking and stopped immediately. There were no injuries to the crew. But the train did not stop before both grain cars turned at a 45° angle. After checking the cars, I found that half the contents of their load had spilled. The train was not carrying any chemical shipments.

    I notified Supervisor Bill Purvis by AMAX telephone at 7:40 A.M. and within forty-five minutes he and a twelve-person section crew arrived at the scene with rerailing equipment—a bulldozer and a derrick. The section crew removed the two grain cars from the track, put in new ties, and made the mainline track passable by 9:25. At 9:45 a vacuum car arrived with engine #372 from Hazlehurst, Illinois, and its crew proceeded with the clean-up operation. By 10:25 A.M. all the spilled grain was loaded onto the cars brought by the Hazlehurst train. Bill Purvis called Barnwell Granary and notified them that their shipment would be three hours late.

CAUSES OF INCIDENT

    Supervisor Purvis and I checked the stretch of train track where the cars derailed and found it to be heavily worn. We believe that a defective fisher joint slipped when the grain cars hit it, and the track broke.

RECOMMENDATIONS

    We made the following recommendations to the switchyard in Hazlehurst to be carried out immediately:

1. Check the section of track ten miles either side of Ridgeville for defective fisher joints.

2. Repair all such defective joints at once.

3. Instruct all engineers to slow to five to ten mph over this section of the road until the rail check is completed.

Fig. 15.14   An accident report form.

DIVERSIFIED INDUSTRIES, INC.
Baltimore, Maryland

ACCIDENT REPORT

1. Name of the employee (last, first, middle) _____

2. Employee identification number _____

3. Social Security number _____

4. Home address and telephone number _____

5. Time of injury _____ A.M. P.M. Location _____

6. Type of injury (specify exact body part[s]) _____
   _____

7. What kind of treatment did injured party receive? Where was treatment given?
   _____

8. Describe what happened (give a narrative of events before, during, and after; describe materials or tools involved in accident):

9. Provide names and addresses of eyewitnesses:

10. What caused the accident?

11. What action should be taken to prevent similar accidents from occurring in the future?

12. Which company employees (e.g., supervisor, union representative) were notified?

Signature of person filling out form _____

Date form is filled out _____

Send one copy to Home Office; one copy to Safety Department; and one to Personnel Department.

heard, felt, and smelled are the essentials of your description. Describe what happened before the incident, if that is relevant—for example, environmental or weather conditions for storm damage or an automobile accident, or warning signals for a malfunctioning machine. If you are depending on an eyewitness account, use quotation marks to set off statements by the witness. But delete any emotional reactions of eyewitnesses—how much an object meant or how surprised they were to see something happen. Filter out other irrelevant details. If you are reporting a work stoppage, it is unnecessary to indicate what the employees did while waiting for machinery to be repaired. Do not duplicate information found elsewhere in the report—license numbers, times, employee identification numbers. Finally, wherever necessary, give information about expenses.

5. What was done after the incident. After describing the incident, be concerned with the action you took to correct conditions, to get things back to normal. Readers will want to know what was done to treat the injured, to make the environment safer, to speed delivery of goods, to repair damaged equipment, or to satisfy a customer's demands.

6. What caused the incident. Make sure that your explanation is consistent with your description in number 4. Pinpoint the trouble. In Figure 15.13, for example, the defective fisher joint is discussed under the heading "Causes of Incident." In the following example, two causes cited are exact and helpful in a report of an accident involving a pipe falling from a crane:

1. The crane's safety latch had been broken off and was never replaced.
2. A tag line was not used to guide the pipe onto the truckbed.

7. Recommendations. Readers will be looking for specific suggestions to prevent the incident from happening again. Recommendations may involve discussing the problem at a safety meeting, asking for further training from a manufacturer, adapting existing equipment to meet customer's needs, modifying schedules, or cutting back on expenses. In the example of the falling pipe in number 6, the writer of an incident report listed the following two recommendations:

1. Order safety latches to replace the broken latch and have additional spare latches on hand.
2. Have a pipeshop supervisor conduct a safety meeting for employees and use a representative drawing of the incident as an aid.

☞ Main Points to Remember About Short Reports

Before considering long reports, the subject of the next chapter, let's review the main points about short reports:

1. They are a few pages at most and get to the point.
2. They can be prepared in a variety of formats—memo, letter, or special form.
3. Their content will vary with the type of report—periodic, sales, progress, trip, test, or incident. In all types of short reports, however, the emphasis is on facts and objectivity.
4. They are generally organized to include information on purpose, data, conclusions, and recommendations.

☞ Exercises

1. Bring to class an example of a periodic report from your previous or present job or from any community, religious, or social organization to which you belong. In an accompanying memo to your instructor, indicate who the audience is and why such a report is necessary, stressing how it is submitted and organized and what kinds of factual data it contains.
2. Assume that you are a manager of a large apartment complex (200 units). Write a periodic report on how many units are vacant, filled, ready to become vacant, or soon to be leased as of June 1.
3. Write a periodic report to an employer on how you spent company time for any one week. Indicate the times you spent on individual assignments, special duties, or overtime work. Compute a rate of pay for regular, special, and overtime work. Give your employer an itemized account of the pay that is due to you.
4. Assume you work for a household appliance store. Prepare a second-quarter sales report based upon information contained in the following table.

| | Numbers Sold | |
Product	1st Quarter	2nd Quarter
Kitchen appliances		
Refrigerators	72	103
Dishwashers	27	14
Freezers	10	36
Electric Ranges	26	26
Gas Ranges	10	3
Microwave Ovens	31	46
Laundry appliances		
Washers	50	75
Dryers	24	36
Air treatment		
Room air-conditioners	41	69
Dehumidifiers	7	2

5. Write a progress report on the wins, losses, and ties of your favorite sports team for last year. Address the report to the Director of Publicity for the team and stress how the director might use these facts for future publicity.

6. Submit a progress report to your writing teacher on what you have learned in his or her course so far this term, which writing skills you want to develop in greater detail, and how you propose doing so. Mention specific papers you have written or will soon write.

7. Compose a site inspection report on any part of the college campus or plant, office, or store in which you work that might need remodeling, expansion, or air-conditioning or heating work.

8. You have been asked to write a short preliminary inspection report on the condition of a historic building for your state historical society. Inspecting the building, the home of a famous late nineteenth-century governor, you discover the following problems. Include all in your report:

   - eight front columns are all in need of repair; two of them in fact may have to be replaced
   - the area below the bottom window casements needs to be excavated for waterproofing
   - the slate tile on the roof has deteriorated and needs immediate replacement
   - the front stairs show signs of mortar leaching requiring attention at once
   - sections of gutter on the northwest and northeast sides of the house need changing; other gutters are in fair shape
   - wood louvers need to be repainted; four of the twelve may even need to be replaced
   - all trees around the house need pruning; an old elm in the backyard shows signs of decay
   - the siding is in desperate need of preparation and painting
   - the brick near the front entrance is dirty and moss covered

9. Assume that you are a social worker, law enforcement officer, or youth counselor. Write an appropriate trip report based on the following information. Make sure to include your reasons for the visit, a description of the visit, and some recommendations based on the visit.

   George Morrow, age 15, was put on probation last August for stealing. He has missed a number of school days this term. The principal at his high school said he also got into some trouble about library books—defacing them or not returning them. George's parents were recently divorced, and he lives with his mother. His mother has requested some help and wants to know what kinds of programs are available. George is very eager to go to technical school and become an electrician. He feels as though his misdeeds will hurt him. George has to report to the court at least once a month for the next year.

10. Write a report to an instructor in your major about a field trip you have taken recently. Indicate why you took the trip, name the individuals you

met on the trip, and stress what you learned and how that information will help you in course work or on your job.

11. Submit a test report on the purpose, procedures, results, and recommendations of an experiment you conducted on one of the following subjects:

    (a) soil   (i) computers
    (b) machinery   (j) forests
    (c) water   (k) food
    (d) automobiles   (l) housing
    (e) textiles   (m) money
    (f) animals   (n) transportation
    (g) fingerprinting   (o) blood
    (h) recreational facilities   (p) noise levels

12. Write an incident report about a problem you encountered in your work in the last year. Use the memo format or use the form reprinted in Figure 15.14 (page 493).

13. Write an incident report about one of the following problems. Assume that it has happened to you. Identify the audience for whom you are writing and the agency you are representing or trying to reach. Include all relevant details in your report.

    (a) After hydroplaning, your company car hits a tree and has a damaged front fender.
    (b) You have been the victim of an electrical shock because an electrical tool was not grounded.
    (c) You twist your back lifting a bulky package.
    (d) Your boat capsizes while you are patrolling the lake.
    (e) The crane you are operating breaks down and you lose a half day's work.
    (f) The supplier shipped the wrong replacement part and you cannot complete a job without renting an expensive tool.

14. Choose one of the following descriptions of an incident and write a report based on it. The descriptions contain unnecessary details, vague words, insufficient information, an unclear cause-and-effect relationship, or all of these errors. In writing your report, correct the errors by adding or subtracting whatever information you believe is necessary. You may also want to rearrange the order in which information is listed. Use the form in Figure 15.14 (page 493) or a memo format to write the report.

    (a) Joe Williamson is hurt. It took the ambulance about ten minutes to arrive and another five to get Joe on a stretcher headed for St. Paul's Hospital, which is about four miles away. The spot where Joe was installing the light was very close to the employee cafeteria. His right arm may be broken, and his left ankle is twisted. His shirt sleeve is ripped, and so are his trousers. Joe was installing a new high-wattage electric light, and he cut himself when the light broke in the socket.

Trying to install that light without someone holding the ladder was foolish, said Cynthia Parker, who saw the whole thing. The plant nurse was called; her name is Mary Noonan, and she told Joe not to move and tried to stop the bleeding in his hand. When Joe got a handkerchief to stop the bleeding when he was still on the ladder, he lost his balance, and that's what led to the fall. The ladder wobbled and gave way. Joe fell quite a distance. It's too bad all this happened so close to lunch. All the employees saw poor Joe, and they felt bad.

(b) After sliding across the slippery road late at night, my car ran into another vehicle, one of those imported Japanese cars. The driver of that car must have been asleep at the wheel. The paint and glass chips were all over. I was driving back from our regional meeting and wanted to report to the home office the next day. The accident will slow me down.

(c) Whoever packed the glass mugs did not know what he or she was doing. The string was not the right type; nor was it tied correctly. The carton was too flimsy as well. It could have been better packed to hold all those mugs. Moreover, since the bus had to travel across some pretty rough country, the package would have broken anyhow. The best way to ship these kinds of goods is in specially marked and packed boxes. The value of the box was listed at $350.

16

Long Reports

This chapter will introduce you to long reports—how they differ from short reports, how they are organized, and how they are written. It is appropriate to discuss long reports in one of the last chapters of *Successful Writing at Work*. The long report is often assigned last in class because writing one gives you an opportunity to use and combine many of the writing skills and strategies you have already learned. In business, a long report is the culmination of many weeks or months of hard work on an important company project.

The following skills and strategies will be most helpful to you as you prepare to study long reports; appropriate page numbers appear below where these topics have already been discussed.

1. gathering and summarizing information, especially from reference works (pages 232–268; 298–308)
2. reporting the results of your research accurately and concisely (pages 83–88)
3. writing a variety of paragraph patterns and sentence types (pages 41–47; 60–72)
4. creating and introducing visuals (pages 367–406)
5. using an appropriate method of documentation (pages 272–286)
6. preparing an informative abstract (pages 314; 317)

Having improved these skills, you should be ready to write a successful long report.

☞ How a Long Report Differs from a Short Report

Both long and short reports are invaluable tools in the world of work. They provide essential information to help a company or agency function.

They both should be written in formal, standard English and should have an objective, professional tone. Basic differences exist, though, between these two types of reports. A short report is not a watered-down version of a long report; nor is a long report simply an expanded version of a short one. These reports differ in purpose, scope, format, and, many times, audience. The following section explains some of the key differences between these two reports. By understanding these differences, you will be better able to follow the rest of Chapter 16 as it covers the process of writing a long report and the organization and parts of such a report. A model long report is included in Figure 16.3 on pages 510–525.

(1) A long report is a major study that provides an intensive and in-depth view of the problem or idea. For example, a long report written for a course assignment may be eight to twenty pages long; a report for a business or industry may be that long or longer, depending on the scope of the subject. The implications of a long report are wide-ranging for a business or industry— relocating a plant, adding a new line of equipment, changing an accounting system. While the long report examines a problem or idea in detail, the short report covers just one part of the problem. Unlike a short report, a long report may discuss not just one or two current events, but rather a continuing history of a problem or idea (and the background information necessary to understand it in perspective). For example, the short test report on paulownia in Figure 15.12 (pages 488–490) would be used together with many other test reports for a long report for a group of industrialists on the value of planting trees to prevent soil erosion at mine sites.

Titles of some typical long reports further suggest their extensive (and in some cases exhaustive) coverage—"A Master Plan for the Recreation Needs of Syracuse, New York," "The Transportation Problems in Kingsford, Oregon, and the Use of Monorails," "The Revolutionary Advances in the Manufacture and Use of the Compact Disc Player."

(2) A long, comprehensive report requires much more extensive research than a short report does. The research provides writers with the essential documentation readers need. Such research can be gathered over time from questionnaires, laboratory experiments, library research, on-site visits, interviews, and the writer's own observations. For a course report, you will have to do a great deal of library research to identify a major problem or topic, to track down the relevant background information, and to discover what experts have said about the subject and what they propose should be done.

Information gathered in many short reports can also be used to help prepare a long report. In fact, as the example of paulownia shows, a long report can use the experimental data from the short report to arrive at a conclusion. Also for a long report writers often supply one or many progress reports (one type of short report—review pages 471–479).

(3) Another significant difference between a long and short report is in format. Because a long report contains extensive documentation, it is too de-

tailed and complex to be adequately organized in a memo or letter format. The product of thorough research and analysis, the long report gives readers detailed discussions of large quantities of data. To present this information in a logical and orderly fashion, the long report contains more parts, sections, headings, subheadings, and supplements (appendixes) than would ever be included in a short report. The long report often includes many graphs, charts, and tables to provide readers with extensive background information and documentation. The long report also incorporates many summaries of data at the beginning, at the end, and at key points in between for the reader's convenience.

(4) The two types of reports also differ in the time it takes to prepare them and in the way in which they are written. Writers of the two types of reports are working under different expectations from their readers and under different kinds of deadlines. A long report is generally commissioned by a company or agency to explore in detail some subject involving personnel, locations, costs, safety, or equipment. Many times a long report is required by law—investigating the feasibility of a new missile system or a change in the ecosystem. The long report is so important that it becomes a record a company will keep on file for employees to consult. A short report is often written as a matter of routine. Sometimes a writer is given little or no advance notice. The long report may take weeks or even months to write. Over this period the researchers have to gather the extensive documentation readers will expect. When you prepare a long report for a class project, make sure that you select a topic that really interests you, for you will spend a good portion of the term working on it.

(5) The audience for a long report is generally broader—and goes higher in an organization's hierarchy—than that for a short report. Your short report may be read by your coworkers or a first-level supervisor, but a long report may be read by people in the top levels of management—presidents, vice-presidents, superintendents, directors—who make long-range financial and organizational decisions. In addition, copies of long reports may be sent to appropriate department heads for their information and commentary. A long report written about a campus issue or problem may at first be read by your teacher and then sent to an appropriate decision-maker—a dean of students, a business manager, a director of athletics.

(6) Unlike many short reports, the long report in the business world and industry is not necessarily the work of one employee. Rather, it may be the product of a committee or group whose work is reviewed by one main editor to make sure that the final draft is consistent and accurately written. Individuals in many departments within a company—art, computer programming, engineering, public relations, industrial safety—may cooperate in planning and producing a long report, which may reflect their various skills—graphics production, statistical analysis, interviewing. Your instructor may ask you to work in a group (or alone) in preparing your long report.

☞ Parts of a Long Report

A long report may include some or all of the following twelve parts, which form three categories—front matter, the text, and back matter. The entire report may be placed in a clear plastic folder or other suitable cover.

Front Matter

As the name implies, the front matter of a long report consists of everything that precedes the actual text of the report. Such elements introduce, explain, and summarize to help the reader locate various parts of the report.

1. Letter of transmittal. This three- or four-paragraph letter states the purpose, scope, and major recommendation of the report. If written to a teacher, the letter should additionally note that the report was done as a course assignment. Sometimes the letter of transmittal is bound with the report as part of it; most often it comes before the report, serving as a kind of cover letter. Figure 16.1 is a sample letter of transmittal for a business report; Figure 16.3 contains a letter of transmittal for a student's long report.

2. Title page. The title, which should be listed in all capital letters, indicates a specific subject and how or why you studied it. This page also gives the name of the company or agency preparing the report, the name(s) of the report writer(s), the date, any agency or order numbers, and the name of the firm for which the report was prepared. Figure 16.3 shows a typical title page for a long report. Note that the various elements are centered and well spaced on the page.

3. Table of contents. The major sections of the report are listed on the contents page. By looking at the table of contents in Figure 16.2, for example, the reader sees at a glance how the report, "A Study to Determine New Directions in Women's Athletics at Coastal College," is organized and can find the location of the various sections of that report. When preparing a table of contents, use lower-case roman numerals for front matter elements as in Figures 16.2 and 16.3. Never list the contents page itself and never have just one subheading under a heading. You cannot divide a single topic by one.

Incorrect:	EXPANDING THE SPORTS PROGRAM
	Basketball
	BUILDING A NEW ARENA
	The West Side Location
Correct:	EXPANDING THE SPORTS PROGRAM
	Basketball
	Track and Field
	BUILDING A NEW ARENA
	The West Side Location
	Costs

Fig. 16.1   A letter of transmittal for a long business report.

α

ALPHA CONSULTANTS

1400 Ridge
Evanston, California 97213-1005

August 1, 1985

Dr. K. G. Lawry, President
Coastal College
San Diego, California 93219

Dear Dr. Lawry:

We are enclosing the report "A Study to Determine New Directions in Women's
Athletics at Coastal College" that you asked us to prepare. The report
contains our recommendations about strengthening existing programs and
creating new ones at Coastal College.

After studying Coastal's sports facilities and the college's plans for
expansion, we interviewed the coaching staff and many of the women
athletes. We also polled the coaching staffs and 100 women athletes at
three local colleges—Baystown Community College, California State
University of Arts and Sciences, and Central Community College.

Our recommendation is that Coastal should engage in more active recruitment
to establish a competitive women's basketball team, start to offer athletic
activities in women's track and field by August 1986, and create a new
interdisciplinary program between the Athletic Department and the Women's
Studies Program.

We hope that you find our report useful in meeting students' needs at
Coastal College. If you have any questions or if you would like to discuss
any of our recommendations, please call us.

Sincerely yours,

Barbara Gilcrest

Barbara Gilcrest

Lee T. Sidell

Lee T. Sidell

Encl. Report

Fig. 16.2   A table of contents for a long report.

CONTENTS

4. List of illustrations. This list of all the figures and tables indicates where in the report they are found. Figure 16.3 shows a list of illustrations.

5. Abstract. As discussed in Chapter 10 (pages 314–317), an abstract presents a brief overview of the problem and conclusions; it summarizes the report. An informative abstract is far more helpful to readers of a report than is a descriptive one, which gives no conclusions or results.

Not every member of your audience will read your entire report. But almost everyone will read the abstract of your long report. For example, the president of the corporation or the director of an agency may use the abstract as the basis for approving the report and passing it on for distribution. Thus the abstract may be the most important part of the report.

Abstracts may be placed at various points in long reports. They may be placed on the title page, on a separate page, or on the first page of the report text.

Text of the Report

6. Introduction. The introduction may comprise as much as 10 or 15 percent of your report but should not be any longer. If it were, the introduction would be disproportionate to the rest of your work, especially the body section. The introduction is essential because it tells readers why your report was written and thus helps them to understand and interpret everything that follows. Do not regard the introduction as one undivided block of information. It includes the following related parts, which should be labeled separately in the introduction with subheadings. Keep in mind, though, that your instructor or employer may ask you to list these parts in a different order.

(a) Background. To understand why your topic is significant and hence worthy of study, readers need to know about its history. This history may include information on such topics as who was originally involved, when, and where, how someone was affected by the issue, what opinions have been expressed on the issue, what the implications of your study are. See how the report on robots (page 515) provides useful background information.

(b) The problem. Identify the problem or issue that led you to write the report. Since the problem or topic you investigated will control everything you write about in the report, your statement of it must be clear and precise. That statement may be restricted to a sentence or two.

(c) Purpose statement. The purpose statement, crucial to the success of the report, tells readers why you wrote the report and what you hope to accomplish or prove. In explaining why you gathered information about a particular problem or topic, indicate how such information might be useful to a specific audience, company, or group. Like the problem statement, the purpose statement does not have to be long or complex. A sentence or two will suffice. You might begin simply by saying, "The purpose of this report is . . . ."

(d) Scope. This section informs readers about the specific limits—

number and type of topics, times, money, locations, personnel, and so forth— you have placed on your investigation. For example, a report on waste disposal might include a scope statement such as, "This report examines the recent techniques involved in the disposal of liquid and solid wastes; gaseous wastes are not discussed in this report." In your report, you may not have studied individuals in an adjacent town or counties because of time or may not have reviewed certain types of electronic equipment because of their costs or availability. If so, indicate this in your scope section. A careful statement of the scope should tie in with the purpose of your report.

   7. The body, or discussion, section is the longest part, possibly comprising as much as 70 percent of your report. The body should supply readers with statistical information, details about the environment, physical descriptions, as well as the various interpretations and comments of the authorities whose work you consulted as part of your library research. (Follow the method of documentation discussed on pages 280–284.)

   The body of your report should be carefully organized to reveal a coherent and well-defined plan. Your goal is to impose a rational order on your material to help readers understand it easily and accurately. To do that, you have to separate the material in the body of your report into meaningful parts. Make sure that you identify the major topics as well as the subtopics in your report. These topics and subtopics must be clearly related to each other. Headings help your reader identify major topics more quickly.

   Your organization should be carefully reflected in the different headings (and maybe even subheadings) included in your report. Use them throughout your report to make it easy to follow. These organizational headings will also enable someone skimming the report to find specific information quickly. These headings, of course, will be included in the table of contents page.

   The order in which you present these topics is equally important for your readers. Divide your information based upon the categories into which it logically falls. For example, in tracing an idea or a program through various stages, you might follow a straight chronological order. If you were writing a feasibility report, one in which you study and weigh conflicting options (locations, equipment, programs) for readers, you would devote a section of the body to each one of the options being studied. If you were investigating the usefulness of a piece of equipment, you might divide your discussion according to the value of each major part of that equipment. An investigation of the public transportation of a community might be divided into the modes of transportation you had investigated—"Rail," "Buses," "Cabs," "Van and Car Pooling," and "Private Automobile." Study the way in which the body of the model report included in Figure 16.3 is organized.

   In addition to headings, use transitions to reveal the organization of the body of your report. At the beginning of each major section of the body tell readers what they will find in that section and why. Summary sentences at the end of a section will tell readers where they have been and prepare them for any subsequent discussions. The report in Figure 16.3 does an effective job of providing these internal summaries.

8. Conclusion. The conclusion should tie everything together for readers by presenting the findings of your report. These findings will explain to readers what the data you have gathered mean. Findings, of course, will vary depending on the type of research you engage in. For a library research report, the conclusion should summarize the main viewpoints of the authorities whose works you have cited. For a marketing report done for a business or industry, you must spell out the implications for your readers in terms of costs, personnel, products, location, and so forth. Regardless of the type of research you do, your conclusions should be based on the information and documentation you presented in the body of the report. To write an effective conclusion, you will have to summarize carefully a great deal of information.

9. Recommendations. A research report for a course may not require a recommendation section. But for a business or scientific report, the most important part of the report, after the abstract, is the recommendation(s) section, which tells readers what should be done about the findings recorded in the conclusion. Review the principles of writing effective recommendations in Chapter 11 (pages 356–357).

Back Matter

Included in this section of the report are all the supporting data which, if included in the text of the report, would bog the reader down in details and cloud the main points the report makes.

10. Glossary. An alphabetical list of the specialized vocabulary with its definitions appears in the glossary (see pp. 405–407). A glossary might be unnecessary if your report does not use highly technical vocabulary or if all members of your audience are familiar with the specialized terms you do use.

11. References cited. Any sources cited in your report must be listed in this section—books, articles, television programs, audiovisual materials, interviews, and reviews (see Chapter 9, pages 273–280, on preparing a Works Cited page).

12. Appendix. All the supporting materials for the report are gathered in the appendix—tables and charts too long to include in the discussion, sample questionnaires, budgets and cost estimates, correspondence about the preparation of the report, case histories, transcripts of telephone conversations. Group like items together in the appendix, as the example in Figure 16.2 shows.

☞ The Process of Writing a Long Report

Writing a long report requires a lot of time and effort. Your work will be spread over many weeks, and you need to see your report not as a series of static or isolated blocks but as an evolving and accomplishable project. Before you embark on that project, review the comments on the writing process found on pages 19–21. You may also want to study the flow chart found on page 394, illustrating the different stages in writing a research paper.

The first steps involve choosing a broad subject area to explore. You can do this by doing some preliminary research—reading generally, consulting relevant indexes, talking to experts about the subject. From this preliminary research you are better able to arrive at a restricted topic, the second major step in the process. After that, you need to assemble information (the documentation) on that topic and read and think about it carefully. From this information and your analysis of it you can prepare an outline. You may find it helpful to prepare one or several outlines. A good, well-thought-out outline can lead to a carefully thought-out report. Then start the series of rough drafts that will ultimately lead to the final copy of your report. (Some writers find it helpful to outline and draft at the same time, moving back and forth between drafting and outlining.)

In the course of each stage of writing the long report, expect to revise your work often—and sometimes extensively. You will have to reexamine and re-think your ideas. While you do this, your organization and analysis may change. You may have to consult new sources and arrive at a *new interpretation* of those sources. Not everything you need will be available to you right away. As you narrow your purpose and scope, you may find yourself deleting information. You may even substitute a better for a weaker source. At the earlier stages of outlining and preparing rough drafts, you may move material around a great deal to avoid unnecessary duplications and to ensure adequate coverage. At the later rough draft stages, you will be revising sentences and paragraphs to make them read more smoothly and logically. At this stage you should also pay increasing attention to the transitions between and among sentences and paragraphs.

Keep in mind, even as you work on your rough drafts, that a long report is not written in the order in which the parts will finally be assembled. You cannot write in "final" order—abstract to appendix. Instead you will write in "loose" order to reflect the order in which you gathered information and assembled it for the final copy of the report. Accordingly, the body section is written first, for authors must obtain material included here in order to construct the rest of the report. The abstract, which appears very early in the report, is written last—after all the facts have been recorded and the recommendations made or the conclusions drawn. Introductions are written later as well, since authors can then make sure that they have not left anything out.

To keep track of your work, prepare both a work calendar and a checklist. Keep both posted where you do your work—above your desk, typewriter, or word processor. The calendar should mark the dates by which each stage of your work must be completed. Match the dates on your calendar with the dates your instructor or employer may have given you for a copy of the outline, for progress reports, for the final copy. Your checklist should contain the major parts of your report. As you complete each section, check it off. Before assembling the final copy of your report for readers, use the checklist to make sure that you do not haphazardly leave something out.

☞ The Model Long Report in This Chapter

The long report in Figure 16.3 is a research report written by a student for a communications class. It deals with robots in American industry, a popular topic about which the student gathered relevant data primarily through library work. It contains all the parts of a long report discussed on pages 502–507 except a recommendation, glossary, and appendix. Intended for a general audience unfamiliar with robot technology, the report consequently avoids the technical terms and descriptions for which a glossary might be necessary. Because the student is surveying authorities' opinions, he does not supply a recommendation section of his own.

The student's main task is to investigate what has been said about robots in American industry and to report the results of his research in a logically organized discussion. Notice how the body section of his report is divided into four closely related areas—employment, safety in the workplace, benefits to employers, and future advances from robot technology. A number of these areas are even further subdivided, as you will see from the table of contents and the subheadings in the report.

This report will show how one writer researched, organized, and discussed a major problem (or topic) suitable for a long report.

Fig. 16.3   A long report.

345 Spruce Lane
Apt. 34-C
Gunderson, NE 68345

May 17, 1984

Professor Dorothy Ridgely
Communications Department
Fairmont Central College
Fairmont, NE 68339

Dear Professor Ridgely:

With this letter I am enclosing my research report on the robotics topic
you approved six weeks ago. My report discusses the various contributions
robots can make to American industry, both for workers and employers.

Robotization offers significant and widespread technological benefits.
Contrary to some views, robots will not take jobs away from American
workers but will instead increase employment opportunities. Robots also
make the work environment safer and offer employers many financial
benefits. Finally, robots of the future will radically improve American
industry and the lifestyle of workers.

I hope that you will find this report interesting and carefully researched.
If you should need to discuss it with me, I can be reached at 678-3400
during the day and at 456-8294 after 6:00 P.M.

Sincerely yours,

John Mark Russell

John Mark Russell

Enclosure

Fig. 16.3   (Continued.)

THE POSITIVE EFFECTS OF ROBOTS IN AMERICAN INDUSTRY

John Mark Russell

Communications 102

Professor Dorothy Ridgely

May 17, 1984

Fig. 16.3   (Continued.)

Table of Contents

Fig. 16.3   (Continued.)

List of Illustrations

iii

513

Fig. 16.3 (Continued.)

ABSTRACT

After twenty years of slow growth, the robot worker in American
industry is finally becoming an indispensable part of our
technology. This robot revolution has created fears that many
human workers will lose their jobs. Most industry experts agree,
however, that only a small displacement of human workers will occur
and that most of these workers will be transferred to other related
or upgraded jobs. Through their greater productivity, robots are
expected to create more jobs than they eliminate. They will also
make the workplace safer for human employees and improve their
effectiveness. Robots will reward employers by giving them
improved efficiency and productivity at lower costs. Moreover,
robots will bring even greater benefits to workers through better
jobs and a higher standard of living.

iv

514

Fig. 16.3   (Continued.)

INTRODUCTION

Background

For centuries people have been fascinated by amazing stories of
machines that could be programmed through remote control to do
superhuman feats. However, we have seen less enthusiasm about
robots in such places as an assembly line or chemical plant. The
name robot itself (from the Czech word meaning "compulsory labor,
drudgery") underscores the reaction many people have to mechanical
devices that perform human jobs in the workplace.

The first industrial robot was used in 1959, and shortly
thereafter in 1962 General Motors installed its first Unimation
robot (Ayres and Miller 4). But the growth of robots in American
industry was slow. In 1970 only a few hundred robots were in use in
American plants. It was not until the 1980's that industry readily
accepted them (Teresko 35). The successful introduction of robots
by several major companies, especially Detroit auto makers,
encouraged other industries to make the same investment (Aronson
22-23). In the early 1980's, more than 5,000 robots were found in
the U.S., with a growth rate projected by the firm of Bache
Investments to be 35 percent annually (Ayres and Miller 5). Robert
Lund, senior research associate at the MIT Center for Policy
Alternatives, stresses that the new robotics technology is the
only salvation for American industry if it is to match and surpass
the production levels of other countries in the world market (Dodd
691).

Problem

Robotics technology is not universally understood or accepted.
Although this new technology will certainly shape American
industry in the future, many workers and some managers fear it and
do not understand its benefits.

Fig. 16.3 (Continued.)

Purpose of Report

The purpose of this report is to discuss the benefits robots offer American industrial workers and their employers.

Scope

This report includes information on how robots can establish new jobs, make the workplace safer, improve production for employers, and create a better future for American workers through advanced technology.

DISCUSSION

Robots Will Encourage, Not Threaten, Employment

Unjustified Fears About Unemployment

A recurrent fear about the widespread use of robots is that they may put American workers out of a job. Some industrialists are predicting that by the year 2000 robots will replace 16 to 18 percent of all manufacturing workers, resulting in millions of lost jobs (Cromie 16). Each robot installed today displaces about two workers a day, but as robot capabilities increase, they may displace more than three workers a day. See the table on the following page to find a proposed breakdown of these statistics for use of robots in the auto industry.

These statistics are misleading, however. Most industry experts, including officials of the United Auto Workers, consider these projections to be excessively high (Dodd 691). These and other experts "predict that robots will never displace more than 5

Fig. 16.3   (Continued.)

Table 1. Projected Impact of Industrial Robots on Labor in the
North American Automobile Industry, 1980–1990

	1980	1983	1985	1988	1990
Number of Robots	1,065	2,600	4,700	10,800	18,500
Direct Labor Loss	2,200	5,750	12,000	31,500	60,000
Skilled Trades Gain	250	650	1,250	2,800	5,100
Net Loss	1,950	5,100	10,750	28,700	54,900

Source: Toepperwein 312.

percent of the work force" (Aronson 26). In fact, robots have
displaced only about 15,000 workers in America, most of whom were
shifted into related or more technologically advanced positions.
This occupational relocation, together with a declining birth rate
over the next few decades, should remove any fears of widespread
unemployment caused by robots (Aronson 26–27; Rice interview).

Fewer Robots Mean Fewer Jobs

When American companies do not use robots, they jeopardize the
jobs of American workers. James Albus, an expert in industrial
systems and robotics, has precisely identified the cause–and–
effect relationship between advanced technology, such as robotics,
and employment:

It is in the industries that fall behind in productivity that
job layoffs are prevalent. Inefficient industries lose
market–share to competitors, shrink, and eventually die. Thus,
the biggest threat to jobs is not in industries that adopt the
fastest robot technology but in those that do not (27).

Fig. 16.3   (Continued.)

4

To illustrate this principle on an international scale,
consider that "Britain's sagging economy employs fewer than 200
robots; Japan's booming economy employs nearly 8000 robots"
(Cromie 16). Applying this principle closer to home, R. Weisel of
Prab Robots proposed that United States auto makers will lose
400,000 jobs to foreign competitors by trailing them in the use of
robots (Teresko 39). American workers are unemployed because of
the robots in Japan, not the robots in Detroit (Albus 27). More
than one expert has predicted that by failing to use robots,
certain industries will become "obsolete" (Coates and Coates 32)
and that workers in these industries will suffer.

Increased Employment Because of Robots

Not only will the robot boom help to prevent unemployment
but it may, in all likelihood, increase employment. Thomas
Weekly of the United Auto Workers sees "new types of jobs created"
because of robots (qtd. in Cromie 16). Robotics should, like
earlier automation in industry, create more jobs than it
eliminates through increased production (Aronson 26). Greater
industrial productivity means more human involvement in the
decision making, manufacturing, and marketing processes.
Moreover, robot technology will create new opportunities for
workers in maintaining and repairing these machines (Cromie 13;
Toepperwein 308) as well as in constructing them. Additional human
supervisors will be needed if problems on the assembly or
transportation line result (Teresko 39). Thus, robots "will
complement, not compete with, humans" (Albus 27).

Fig. 16.3 (Continued.)

5

Robots Provide Efficiency and Safety in the Workplace

Some authorities believe that the robot revolution will, in the long run, provide vast improvements and benefits for Americans in their workplaces. Not only will new and better jobs result because of robots but they will enhance many existing jobs. Vary T. Coates, an expert on technology assessment, speculates that companies will purchase robots to help especially in those environments that "may be inefficient, unsafe, and inhospitable for human workers" (qtd. in Coates and Coates 32).

Robots Can Improve Workers' Efficiency

Coates's first area of concern--inefficiency--is one in which robots on the job site can be of great help. A robot can assist a human worker to accomplish specific duties much more carefully and precisely. For example, robots can be designed to reach into very small or awkward places that would be impossible or extraordinarily difficult for human workers. A robot can also precisely measure the insides of a pipeline (Coates and Coates 32) or test the interior components of a machine without disassembling the machine.

Robots Will Make the Workplace Safer

Perhaps the ultimate contribution of robots will be making the workplace safer for human beings. Thanks to robots, human beings may not have to be exposed to occupational environments that threaten their health. Robots do not have lungs, skin, ears, or eyes to protect. Nor do they have to worry about noise levels, dust or asbestos particles, or eye-strain and headaches from uninterrupted work. Robots on hazardous work sites will, therefore, help to decrease employment-related injuries and illnesses (Coates and Coates 31).

Fig. 16.3 (Continued.)

6

Robots can be invaluable in providing safety nets in potentially dangerous industries such as nuclear power plants. Countless human lives could be spared because of robots. For example, if there were a leak of lethal radioactive material, robots rather than human beings would be exposed at the power plant. Likewise, robots would reduce hazards to human workers at factories that produce toxic chemicals or explosives. Robots can also safely load and transport toxic materials (Coates and Coates 31–32; Toepperwein 207). "Robots can be important in assisting individuals who work in mines, one of the most dangerous occupational sites in America" (Rice interview).

Robots Offer Employers Benefits

Robots also offer employers numerous benefits. They improve the quality and output of the employer's plant and they reduce the cost of materials.

Robots Can Increase Output and Quality

An important benefit of robotization is the increased output and amazingly high quality that a robot can provide. While human welders can keep their torches on the job only 30 percent of the time, robot workers can keep going 90 percent of the time. Robots used for welding also have the capability of correcting errors during a job, saving time and increasing production. When General Dynamics started using a robot in 1978 to prepare and install sheet-metal parts for the F–16 fighter jet, the production of the jet quadrupled (Sugarman 54).

Fig. 16.3   (Continued.)

7

Robots on the job also improve the quality of work done for an
employer. T. E. Baker of General Electric convincingly describes
one of the robot's chief virtues:

> The robot is a maddeningly demanding and consistent
> machine. . . . If materials fed to it are not completed,
> uniform, and reasonably flawless, it will either correct the
> problem itself, summon its human supervisor with a bell or
> whistle, or just quit (qtd. in Teresko 39).

A robot can deliver high quality by also being extremely accurate.
It is capable of drilling sets of holes within .005 inches of error
and can machine 250 different parts. A human worker on the job
produces 6 parts per shift with 10 percent rejections, while a
robot in the same job makes 24 to 30 parts with zero rejections
(Dodd 691).

Every aspect of our economy benefits from the increased
production and improved quality of American-made products.
Certainly two of the most welcome advantages will be more orders
for American goods and increased employment for American workers.

Robots Can Decrease Manufacturing Costs

As the initial price of purchasing a robot falls with improved
technology, lower labor cost becomes a principal argument for the
robotization of American factories. Joseph Engleberger, president
of the largest U.S. robot manufacturer, estimates that the cost per
hour of a medium-priced hypothetical robot is $6.00. This figure
represents only a 50 percent increase since 1967, while hourly
rates for human laborers have increased by 180 percent over the
same period (Ayres and Miller 72). The following graph records the
differences in labor costs between the human and robot workers.

Fig. 16.3   (Continued.)

8

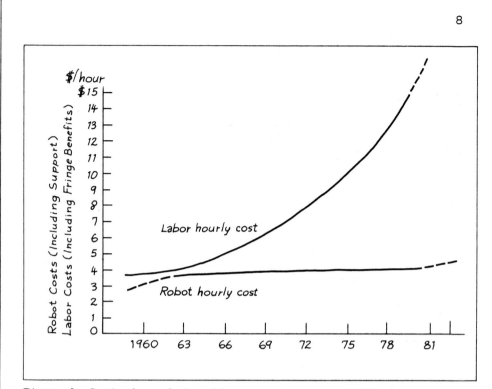

Figure 1. Costs for robot and human workers as of 1981.
Source: Ayres and Miller 72.

Moreover, as the production of robots increases, the cost per unit
will surely decrease (Sugarman 56).

Significant savings can also result from a robot's efficient
use of materials. At one General Electric factory, a robot used for
painting saved $19,000 worth of paint in one year while improving
coverage and finish (Ayres and Miller 77). Because of their
mechanical capabilities, robots waste fewer parts, materials (die,
plastic for moulding, bolts), and energy in any manufacturing
process (Toepperwein 307–308). This increased cost efficiency may
be the chief method of protecting American industry from foreign
competitors.

Fig. 16.3   (Continued.)

9

What Robots Will Do in the Future

So far this report has emphasized the current advantages robots offer industrial workers and employers. Compared to what robots will do for us in the future, these benefits are relatively small. David Nitzan, the program manager at the robotics research and development firm of SRI International, claims that despite their amazing current feats robots are in their "infantile" stage of development (qtd. in Dodd 690). Robots today have limited capabilities and applications. For the most part they are restricted to performing pick-and-place operations (Aronson 26).

Although experts say that we are many years from seeing highly skilled robots (Albus 22-23), advances are already taking place in experimental laboratories with robots that have extraordinary vision and tactile sensory systems (Dodd 690-91). The next generation of robots will have sensory capabilities unmatched by their human counterparts. Like Bionic Man, Wonder Woman, and Superman, they will be able to see, touch, smell, and hear perfectly and under extremely dangerous conditions. Within the next decade some robots will be equipped for voice recognition. Robots will be used extensively in space exploration, crime-detection work, medicine, and all types of engineering.

This growth in capabilities will be matched by the increase in the number of robots in industry. Robots will be found in almost every manufacturing process in the 1990's. Bache Investments is projecting implementation of 200,000 robots in the United States by 1990. With such large corporations as General Electric, General Motors, IBM and Texas Instruments entering the robotics field, these estimates may not be unreasonable (Ayres and Miller 8).

All of these technological advances will translate into a better life for workers. According to Thomas Weekly, robots will

Fig. 16.3 (Continued.)

10

soon give workers "shorter hours, longer vacations, and higher wages" (qtd. in Cromie 16). Looking further into the future, James Albus predicts that "If all humans could own the equivalent of one or two robots, they would be financially independent, regardless of whether they were employed or not" (27). Robots may not make everyone rich, but one thing is certain: "Combined with other emerging technologies, robotics can contribute to a transformation of society--both in the United States and throughout the world--that is as encompassing a change as the Industrial Revolution" (Coates and Coates 32).

CONCLUSION

The steadily increasing use of robots in American industry will benefit workers and employers. Although some individuals have worried about potential jobs being lost to robots, many indus-trialists and union leaders maintain that robots will create more jobs than they eliminate. Previous successes with automation confirm this assessment. Despite a temporary displacement of a small percentage of the work force, industrial robots can improve overall working conditions for employees. Robots help human workers to perform more efficiently and to escape hazardous jobs and work sites. Employers find robots desirable because they will make it possible to cut costs, to reduce errors, and to improve quality and output. As robot technology improves, it will offer numerous future benefits including a higher standard of living for the American industrial worker.

11

WORKS CITED

Albus, James. "Robots in the Workplace." The Futurist 17 (Feb. 1983): 22–27.

Aronson, Robert. "The Robot Boom Is On." Machine Design 52 (Nov. 1980): 22–24, 26–28.

Ayres, Robert, and Steven Miller. Robotics Applications and Social Implications. Cambridge, MA: Ballinger, 1983.

Coates, Vary, and J. F. Coates. "The Potential Impacts of Robotics." The Futurist 17 (Feb. 1983): 28–32.

Cromie, William. "Robots: A Growing, Maturing Population." SciQuest 54 (Mar. 1981): 12–16.

Dodd, John. "Robots: The New Steel–Collar Worker." Personnel Journal 60 (Sept. 1981): 688–95.

Rice, Barbara. Industrial Technology Professor, Fairmont Central College. Personal interview, 30 Apr. 1984.

Sugarman, Robert. "The Blue–Collar Robot." IEEE Spectrum 17 (Sept. 1980): 53–57.

Teresko, John. "Robots Come of Age." Industry Week 25 Jan. 1982: 35–36, 38–39, 42.

Toepperwein, L. L., and others. Robotics Applications for Industry: A Practical Guide. Park Ridge, IL: Noyes Data Co., 1983.

☞ Exercises

1. Write a memo to your instructor on how one of the short reports in Chapter 15 could be useful to someone who has to write a long report.

2. Using the information contained in Figures 16.1 and 16.2, write an introduction for the report "A Study to Determine New Directions in Women's Athletics at Coastal College." Add any details you think will be relevant.

3. What kinds of research did the student do to write the long report in Figure 16.3? As part of your answer, include the titles of any specific reference works you think the writer may have consulted. (You may want to review Chapter 8.)

4. Study Figure 16.3 and answer the following questions:
   (a) Why can the abstract be termed informative rather than descriptive?
   (b) How has the writer successfully limited the scope of the report?
   (c) Where does the writer use internal summaries especially well? (See pages 506–507 for a discussion of the values of such summaries.)
   (d) What visual devices does the writer employ to separate parts of the report and divisions within each part?
   (e) How does the writer introduce, summarize, and draw conclusions from the expert opinions he cites in order to substantiate the main points?
   (f) What are the ways in which the writer documents information he has gathered?
   (g) What functions does the conclusion serve for readers? Cite specific examples from the report.

5. Come to class prepared to discuss at least two major problems that would be suitable topics for a long report. Consider an important community problem—traffic, crime rate, air and water pollution—or a problem at your college. Then write a letter to a consulting firm or other appropriate agency or business, requesting a study of the problem and a report.

6. Write an outline of the report appropriate for one of the problems listed in exercise 5. Use major headings and include the kinds of information listed on pages 506–507.

7. Have your instructor look at and approve the outline you prepared for exercise 6. Then write a long report based on the outline.

17

Oral Reports

Every job requires employees to have carefully developed speaking skills. In fact, in order to get hired, you had to be a persuasive speaker at your job interview. On the job you will have oral communication responsibilities that will vary in the amount of preparation you have to do for them, the time they last, and the audience and occasion for which they are intended. This chapter offers practical advice on how to become a better, more assured communicator in informal briefings and formal speeches.

☞ Informal Briefings

If you have ever given a book report or explained laboratory results in front of a class, you have given an informal briefing. Such semiformal reports are a routine part of many jobs. Nurses and law enforcement officers, for example, give their colleagues or supervisors end-of-shift reports, summarizing major activities for the previous eight or twelve hours. During "walking rounds," the nurse leaving one shift identifies pertinent patient data for the nurse starting the next shift as the two of them go from one patient room to another. The nurse giving the report summarizes from patient care cards, while the nurse taking the report listens, asks questions, or takes notes.

Another kind of briefing involves explaining a new procedure or policy to other departments. As a personnel officer, you may have to inform plant employees of extended coverage on an insurance policy. If your company has just purchased a new piece of equipment, you may have to demonstrate it. Or you may introduce a speaker, a visitor to your agency, or a new employee or report on a convention you attended. Finally, you may give a brief report at a public hearing—before a school board, group of county supervisors, or government agency.

These informal reports are usually short (one to seven minutes, perhaps), and you always will be given advance notice that you are expected to report. Your comments should be brief and to the point. When the boss tells you to "say a few words about the new Minivac (or the new parking policy)," she does not expect a lengthy formal speech. For example, the personnel officer informing employees about extended insurance coverage should not read the fine print in the policy, but rather cover its key points, saving detailed personal questions for a private conference.

Rather than writing down all your comments in full sentences, make a few rough notes and jot them down on a three-by-five note card you can easily hold in the palm of your hand or attach to a piece of equipment as you talk. Your notes should consist of only the major points you want to mention, preferably in chronological order or from cause to effect (see pages 43–44; 47). A note card with key facts used by an employee who is introducing Ms. Rizzo, a visiting speaker, to a monthly meeting of safety directors might include the following items:

- Diana T. Rizzo, Chief Engineer of the Rhode Island State Highway Department for twelve years.
- Experience as both a civil engineer and safety expert.
- Consultant to Secretary Taft, Department of Transportation.
- Member of the National Safety Council and author of "Field Test Procedures in Highway Safety Construction."
- Designed specially constructed aluminum posts used on Rhode Island highway system.
- Advocate of standardized gradings.

Similarly, a note card used by a personnel officer to inform employees about new insurance coverage might list the following major points:

- American Democratic Insurance has changed some of the coverage on employees' policies.
- If you are hospitalized, American Democratic will pay up to $221.75 per day on your room. This is an increase of $38.35 per day from the old policy.
- Outpatient lab benefits are also increased. American Democratic will now pay $400 a year rather than the $275 under the old policy.
- Premiums will also increase by about $3.40 a week, but Tramco, the employer, will pay 90¢ of that increase, meaning employees will have $2.50 more deducted from weekly checks.
- Currently we are exploring a dental rider on the American Democratic policy.
- If any questions, call me or Ms. Blackwell at extension 3452 or drop by the Personnel Office in the Administration Building, Monday through Friday, 8:00 A.M. to 4:30 P.M.

☞ Formal Speeches

Whereas an informal briefing is likely to be short, generally conversational, and intended for limited numbers of people, a formal speech is likely to be longer, less conversational, and intended for a wider audience. Therefore, it involves more preparation and less interaction between speaker and audience; it is, in other words, more "formal."

Most of us are uncomfortable in front of an audience because we feel frightened or embarrassed. Much of this fear and anxiety can be eased, though, if you know what to expect. The two areas you should investigate thoroughly before you begin to prepare your speech are (1) who will be in the audience and (2) why they are there.

Analyzing the Audience

The more you learn about the members of your audience, the better equipped you will be to give them what they need and want to hear. Find out whether anything unites them as a group—search for a common denominator. For example, are they all members of one profession (architecture, computer programming, mechanical engineering, secretarial science), or are they a group of individuals who have similar professional interests (court reporters, paralegals, legal secretaries, police officers)? Perhaps your audience will consist of all the students at your school majoring in your field of specialization. Or your audience may be linked not by professional training, but by place of employment: all the employees—mechanics, bookkeepers, salespeople—in a car dealership. Other bonds, too, may unite an audience: ethnic background, hobbies, membership in clubs, age, sex, or religion.

Once you have defined your audience, assess how much they will know about the topic you are discussing. Everything depends on what your audience will understand and need—the terms you use, how many details you have to give, the number of explanations and definitions you supply, and the amount of background information required. Terms taken for granted in one group must be explained or never used with another group.

Your audience will also determine the approach you take toward the material. For example, the details you select about the resort hotel you work for, and the emphasis you give them, will vary.

Speaking for the Occasion

Understanding why your audience is there will help you deliver a successful speech. An audience may be present for a variety of reasons—for a social gathering, a business meeting, or an educational forum. Shape your remarks to fit the occasion.

In addition to selecting material appropriate for the occasion, consider both the time allotted for your speech and whether you are the only speaker scheduled to address the audience. It makes a big difference in your preparation if you are the first speaker at an 8:00 A.M. breakfast meeting or the last of four speakers at an evening meeting. Take into account what will happen before you speak and what will follow.

The number of people in your audience is also a significant factor. A formal presentation to a small group—five or six supervisors or buyers—seated around a conference table can nonetheless be made more intimate; you can walk around, perhaps leave more time for questions, or stop your talk a few times to ask if there are any questions. You will have much less flexibility when addressing a large group—seventy or eighty people—in an auditorium.

Ways of Presenting a Speech

Your effectiveness depends directly on the extent of your preparation. Of the four approaches we will consider, the extemporaneous is best suited to most individuals and occasions. But first we will examine three other possibilities and their advantages and disadvantages.

1. Speaking off-the-cuff. The professional speechmaker may be comfortable with an off-the-cuff approach, but for the average person, the worst way to deliver a speech is to speak without any preparation whatsoever. You may know a subject very well and think that your experience and knowledge qualify you for an on-the-spot performance. But you will only be fooling yourself if you think you have all the details and explanations in the back of your head. It is equally dangerous to believe that once you start talking, everything will fall into place smoothly. The "everything works out for the best" philosophy, unaided by a lot of hard work, does not operate in public speaking. Without preparation, you will be at the mercy of your memory. Once on stage, you are likely to forget or to confuse important points entirely or to annoy your audience by returning to an earlier point with a vital fact that has just popped into your mind. Without notes in front of you, you will be at a distinct disadvantage if someone asks you a question. Mark Twain's advice is apt here: "It takes three weeks to prepare a good impromptu speech."

2. Memorizing a speech. This type of public speaking is the exact opposite of the off-the-cuff approach. A memorized speech does have some advantages for certain individuals—tour bus drivers, guides at museums or amusement parks, or salespeople—who must deliver the same speech many times over. But for the individual who has to deliver an original speech just once, a memorized speech contains pitfalls. First, it is difficult to do. You might spend hours memorizing exact words and sentences—time that would be better spent in organizing your speech or gathering information for it. Second, if you forget a single word or sentence, you may forget the rest of the speech. It is easy to lose the whole speech when you are panic-stricken over one small part, for that one small part suddenly becomes your entire speech. Third, a memorized delivery can make you appear mechanical. Rather than adjusting, second by second, to an audience's reactions to your speech, you will be obligated to speak the exact words you wrote before you saw your audience.

3. Reading a speech. Reading a speech to an audience may be appropriate if you are presenting information on company policy or legal issues on which there can be no deviation from the printed word. Most of the speeches you have to make, however, will not require this rigid adherence to a text. Your speeches will be more personal and acceptable, socially and professionally, when you interact with the audience. In reading, you set up a barrier between yourself and the audience. With your head in your notes, you will not establish eye contact with your audience for fear of losing your place. Moreover, the tone of your voice will be too formal, even mechanical.

4. Delivering a speech extemporaneously. An extemporaneous delivery is the best way of giving a speech for the widest variety of occasions. Unlike a speaker using a memorized or written speech, you do not come before your audience with the entire speech in hand. *By no means, though, is an extemporaneous delivery an off-the-cuff performance.* It requires a great deal of preparation. But what you prepare is an outline of the major points of your speech, as discussed later in this chapter. You will rehearse using that outline, but the actual words you use in your speech will not necessarily be those you have rehearsed. Your words to the audience should flow naturally and knowledgeably. You should stand confidently in front of the audience with your outline reminding you of major points but not the precise language to express them. In this way you can establish contact with the audience rather than presenting a programmed, robotlike appearance.

The rest of this chapter will discuss various effective ways of preparing and delivering an extemporaneous speech.

Preparing the Parts of a Speech

The Introduction

The introduction is the most important part of your speech. Its goal is to capture the audience's attention. An effective introduction answers these questions for the audience: (1) Who are you? (2) What are your qualifications? (3) What restricted topic are you speaking about, and how is that topic restricted? and (4) How is that topic, and your presentation of it, relevant to the audience? An effective introduction is proportional to the length of your speech. A ten-minute speech requires no more than a sixty-second introduction; a twenty-minute speech needs no more than a two-minute introduction.

You will probably begin by introducing yourself, emphasizing your professional qualifications. "I'm Felicia Manheim, and I've been a riveter at Gibson Steel Works for six years." (This self-introduction may be unnecessary if someone else introduces you or if everyone in the room knows you.) Never apologize for wasting your audience's time or for your limitations as a professional speaker.

Thank the audience for the opportunity of addressing the group and indicate at once what your topic is and how it is divided. The most interesting speeches are the easiest to follow. By restricting your topic, you will help to ensure that it will be organized carefully. Focus on one major (and restricted) idea—home health programs for the aged in Niles, Illinois; a new word processor model; a tasty diet under 1,200 calories a day; a course in canoeing.

Give your listeners a road map at the beginning of your talk so that they will know where you are, when you are there, and what they have to look forward to or to recall. "I believe there are three reasons why gasohol is preferable to gasoline for our mass transit system: it is cheaper, it is more fuel-efficient, and it makes us less dependent on foreign suppliers." Or, "Tonight I will discuss the three problems a foodstore manager faces when deciding to stock inventory: (1) the difficulty in predicting needs, (2) the inability of the production department to record current levels of stock accurately, and (3) the uncertainty of marketplace conditions."

Moving from your announcement of the topic to your presentation of it requires skill at inducing an audience to listen. After introducing yourself and the topic, concentrate on how you will get the audience to "bite" on the "hook" you offer. You can use a variety of tactics to get the audience's attention. Perhaps the simplest way is to ask a question—"Do you know how much actual meat there is in a hot dog?" "How many of you have taken Graphics 201?" "How serious is a nosebleed?" Choose a question closely linked to your topic.

Another often used technique for beginning a speech is to cite some interesting statistics. Listeners' curiosity should be so piqued that they will stay tuned in for an explanation or description: "In 1985 two million heart attack victims in America lived to tell about it." "Seventy-five percent of those taking the sales refresher course pass their state board examination." "By 1990, more than half of America's population will be over thirty-five." Of course, you can combine techniques, as the following opening does with a question containing statistics: "Did you know that 40 percent of all house pets get lost each year?"

You might also begin with an anecdote, or brief story, that illustrates the main points of your speech. Sometimes effective speakers start with something humorous. But be careful about using jokes to get the audience in a good mood. Some may not find your joke amusing, in good taste, or relevant to your speech. You will have lost your audience before you start.

The Body of the Speech

Coming between the introduction and the conclusion, the body is the longest part of your speech just as it is in a long report. The body supplies the substance of your speech. Specifically, the body of a speech can (1) explain a process, (2) describe a condition, (3) tell a story, (4) argue a case, or (5) do all of the previous four tasks.

Fig. 17.1   How to find out if you are a boring person.

© 1980 United Features Syndicate, Inc.

To get the right perspective about the body of a speech, recall your own experiences as a member of an audience. How often did you feel bored or angry because a speaker tried to overload you with details? The Peanuts cartoon in Figure 17.1 bluntly points out the consequences of boring an audience.

When you prepare the body of your speech, consider your audience as a group of listeners, *not readers.* Readers will have more time to digest the ideas in your work. They can read as slowly or as quickly as they want, reread and double-check details, or skim wherever they want. Listeners, however, cannot absorb as much as readers can. The speaker's audience has a shorter attention span. In fact, a good rule to follow in preparing the body of your speech is to be direct and relevant. You cannot include every available detail. The body of your speech should be lean and attractive, not swollen with every fact you gathered in preparing the speech. Select only details that are relevant to your audience.

Here are a few helpful ways you can present and organize information in the body of your speech. In writing a report, you can assist readers by supplying them with headings, labels, underscorings, and bullets. In a speech, switch from purely visual devices to aural ones, as in the following:

1. Give signals (directions) to show where you are going or where you have been.   These signals will convince an audience that your speech does not ramble. Enumerate your points: "first," "second," "third." Tell the audience which way your description is moving by reminding listeners of their position in your speech. In describing a piece of property to prospective buyers, for example, say "from the inside of the house" or "looking at the northeast corner of the building." When you tell a story, follow a chronological sequence and fill your speech with signposts—*before, following, next, then.*

2. Comment on your own material. Tell the audience if some point is especially significant, memorable, or relevant. "This next fact is the most important one in my speech." "Please remember that the current law expires in June." "The best determiner of pressure is the amount of liquid present in the chamber."

3. Repeat key ideas. You can repeat a sentence or a word for emphasis and to help the audience remember it. But do this sparingly; repeating the same point over and over again bores an audience. Here is an example of the effective use of repetition. "The mayor-council form of government is our best financial investment. Yes, our best financial investment. Here's why."

4. Provide internal summaries. These are "minisummaries" supplied after you finish one point but before you move to another. Spending a few seconds to recap what you have already covered will reassure your audience and you as well. These summaries are bridges between the material and the listeners. For example, "We have already discussed the difficulties in establishing a menu repertory, or the list of items that the food-service manager wants to appear on the menu. Now we will turn to ways of determining which items should appear on a menu and why."

The Conclusion

Plan your conclusion as carefully as you do your introduction. Stopping with a screeching halt is as bad as trailing off in a fading monotone. An effective conclusion leaves the audience with a good feeling, satisfied that you have come full circle and accomplished what you promised. Your last words should echo in your listeners' ears, not fall limp to the ground. Conclusions, even for long speeches (twenty minutes), should never run more than sixty to ninety seconds. Moreover, you should clearly inform your audience when you are approaching the end of your speech: "finally," "in conclusion," "to summarize," "to wrap up."

What belongs in a conclusion? A conclusion should contain something lively and memorable. Under no circumstances should you introduce a new subject in a conclusion; nor should you simply repeat your introduction. A conclusion contains a restatement and reemphasis of your most important points (or the conclusions you reached about them). For example, "The installation of the stainless steel heating tanks has, as we have seen, saved our firm 32 percent in utility costs, since we do not now have to run the heating system twenty-four hours a day." If you are delivering a persuasive speech, issue a call for action, just as in a sales letter (see Chapter 7). Stress what you want your listeners to do and why it is beneficial for them to do it or harmful (or less desirable) if they do not follow your advice.

Think of a conclusion as not closing doors but opening avenues. If a question-and-answer period has been planned, remind your audience at the conclusion of your speech that you are available for questions.

The Speech Outline

Construct a speech outline to represent the three parts of your speech—the introduction, the body, and the conclusion. As was pointed out earlier in this chapter, in an extemporaneous speech you do not write out the entire speech you are going to deliver. But you must have some speaking notes to guide you. The speech outline has great psychological value in that it gives you enough facts to handle your speaking engagement confidently, yet it is not so detailed that it places you in a straitjacket.

The speech outline illustrated in Figure 17.2 contains the right amount of detail to represent the introduction, body, and conclusion of Tim Phalen's speech. A roman numeral designates each major point; capital letters indicate appropriate supporting facts. Be careful about crowding too much into a speech outline; in other words, you do not need an outline as highly structured as the following:

I.
   A.
      1.
         a.
            (1)

Your talk will not be taking an hour, which is what such a detailed outline suggests. Not every point will require four or five capital letters. But each point, whether indicated by a roman numeral or a capital letter, should be written as a complete sentence. Since your outline must be easy to read and follow, leave wide margins and triple space between your points. Mark, perhaps with a red pen, a red typewriter ribbon, or capital letters, where visuals appear in your speech. Thus you will not forget them in your concern with moving to the next point in your talk.

Using Visuals

You may use a number of different visuals during your talk: photographs, maps, chalkboards, models, pasteboards (a large, two-by-three-foot, stiff piece of white cardboard), diagrams, tables, or slides. Visuals are used in a speech for the same reasons as in a report—to explain quickly, condense information, and add interest and variety. But visuals used in an oral presentation must be constructed even more carefully than for a written report. Unlike a reading

Fig. 17.2   A speech outline.

SPEAKER: Tim Phalen, Assistant Vice-President, Madisonville Savings and Loan

AUDIENCE: Madisonville Optimist Club

PURPOSE: To encourage members of the Optimist Club to do business with Madisonville Savings and Loan

<u>INTRODUCTION</u>

   I.   Is there a secret to financial success?

       A.   Authors of books on "how to make a million dollars" say that readers will profit from their advice.

       B.   Fashion designers claim that the way we dress determines our success.

       C.   Psychologists maintain that the key to success rests with how well we manipulate people.

       D.   Real success is knowing how to turn your dreams into reality.

       E.   Madisonville Savings and Loan can show you how to make your dreams of financial success come true. SHOW POSTER WITH WORDS "MADISONVILLE SAVINGS AND LOAN," "DREAMS," AND "REALITY" TO EMPHASIZE RELATIONSHIP FOR AUDIENCE.

<u>BODY OF THE SPEECH</u>

  II.   Madisonville Savings and Loan will help you find the best way to save.

       A.   We pay the highest interest rates allowed by law.

       B.   Our staff of financial counselors will assist you in selecting the right savings account.

       C.   Madisonville Savings and Loan currently offers customers five types of savings accounts.

           1.   The Basic, or Standard, Account is the most flexible; it pays interest daily from the day of deposit and requires no minimum balance.

           2.   A Payroll Savings Account automatically deposits money into your account.

Fig. 17.2   (Continued.)

3. An Ambassador Account allows you to get money away from home when you need it.

4. A Certificate Account pays more interest than the Basic Account but requires a $500 minimum.

5. A Money Market Account, requiring a $10,000 balance, pays the highest interest rate.

D. Our Retirement Plan assures you of trouble-free years to travel or to do anything else you wish; you will have a steady income when you need it.

E. All savings accounts and retirement plans are insured by the Federal Savings and Loan Insurance Corporation.

F. With any account you select, you will receive a quarterly statement showing the interest earned and, where appropriate, maturity dates.

III. Madisonville Savings and Loan will help you to borrow as well as to save money.

A. Savings and loans have been in the lending business for 100 years.

B. Madisonville Savings and Loan is dedicated to strengthening the community.

C. Madisonville Savings and Loan is a leader among local financial institutions in giving home owners and businesses long-term loans. STOP. SHOW GRAPH.

D. Most of our savings are invested in mortgages.

E. In fact, 70 percent of all houses in Madisonville in the last fifty years were built or bought with mortgage money obtained from Madisonville Savings and Loan.

F. Madisonville Savings and Loan offers customers four types of mortgages.

Fig. 17.2 (Continued.)

1. VA loans give veterans interest rates fixed by the U.S. government, no closing costs, and no down payments.

2. FHA loans, another federally assisted program, also offer fixed interest rates below the conventional market, but buyers must purchase insurance to protect an FHA loan.

3. Conventional mortgages allow buyers to obtain their money in Madisonville; on a month-to-month basis they are cheaper than FHA loans.

4. Adjustable Rate Mortgages (ARM's) offer home owners flexible rates, which can help to lower monthly payments.

IV. Our new Fast Account gives you checking benefits you have not had before.

A. You can write checks and earn interest on the same account.

B. You can pay your bills by telephone--no postage to worry about.

C. You receive a monthly statement of all transactions, including the interest your money has earned.

D. If your checking account has ever been overdrawn, you will like the automatic line of credit a Fast Account gives you.

CONCLUSION

V. Let Madisonville Savings and Loan help you to find your most successful financial opportunities.

A. The three services we offer--savings, loans, and checking--are interrelated. SHOW TRIANGLE DEPICTING RELATIONSHIP.

B. Come to Madisonville Savings and Loan and allow us to show you how to take advantage of all our services.

Thank you for the opportunity to be with you today. I will be happy to answer any questions you may have.

audience, a listening audience cannot refer to a visual again; nor does this audience have the time to study the visual in detail.

The size and shape of your visuals are important. If they cannot be seen clearly from a distance and understood at once, they are not very useful. If possible, before using any visual, mount it in the front of the room and sit in the last row of chairs in the room in which you will speak to see if your audience will be able to decipher it. After this experiment, you might decide to increase the size of your visual (blow up a picture, for example), hold it up higher, or show it to different sections of your audience by walking from one side of the room to another. Or you might want to change color schemes for greater visibility.

Determining How Many Visuals to Use

Your speech may not require any visuals, such as a very brief presentation of two to four minutes. But even a very long speech may need only two or three visuals. Use visuals sparingly. Their purpose is to clarify (or supplement), not to compete with what you say. (Note Tim Phalen's limited use of visuals in Figure 17.2.) If you use too many visuals, your audience will not pay strict attention to what you are saying, but will instead be trying to watch each new visual that comes along.

Getting the Most from Your Visuals

The following practical suggestions will help you get the most from your visuals:

1. Do not set up your visuals before you begin speaking. The audience will try to determine what they mean or how you are going to use them and so will not give you full attention.
2. Make sure that any maps or illustrations are firmly anchored. Having a map roll up or a picture fall off a stand during your presentation is an embarrassment you can prevent by checking equipment ahead of time.
3. Never obstruct the audience's view by standing in front of the visuals you are explaining. Also, when you finish with a visual, do not leave it standing to block the audience's view of you or of other visuals for the rest of your talk.
4. Avoid crowding three or four visuals onto one pasteboard to save space or time. Use different pasteboards instead.
5. Do not put a lot of writing on a visual. Elaborate labels, markings, or descriptions defeat your reason for using the visual. Your audience will spend more time trying to decipher the writing on your visual than attempting to understand the visual itself.
6. Be extra cautious with a slide projector. Check beforehand to make sure that all your slides are in the order in which you are going to discuss them and that they are right side up. A slide out of sequence can ruin a large section of your speech. Test the equipment a few times before you make

your delivery. It's wise to carry an extra light bulb with you in case the bulb in a projector burns out while you are talking. Make sure, too, that you turn a projector off when you are finished with it, so the noise of the projector will not disturb the audience as you continue speaking.

Rehearsing a Speech

An efficient writer never submits a rough draft of a paper or report as final copy to an employer. Rather, the rough draft is edited and carefully checked before it is typed to produce the final copy, and that final copy is carefully proofread before it goes to the boss's desk. Similarly, an effective speaker does not write a speech and march off to deliver it. Between the time you write a speech and deliver it, rehearse it several times. You will gain self-assurance by becoming familiar with your material. Going over your ideas aloud may help you to spot poor organization and to correct insufficient or inaccurate content.

Rehearsing will also help you to acquire more natural speech rhythms, pitch, pauses, and pacing. Try speaking in front of a full-length mirror for at least one of your rehearsals to see how an audience might view you. At another time, speak into a tape recorder or in front of someone to determine if you sound friendly or frantic, poised or pressured. You can also catch and correct yourself from going too quickly or too slowly. Time yourself so that you will have a fairly accurate idea if your talk falls within the time allotted you. Practice with the visuals or equipment you intend to use in your speech, for this kind of "hands-on" experience will make you aware of how and when to use them.

In rehearsing your speech, pay special attention to your pronunciation. Mispronouncing a word is embarrassing—the audience might laugh and break the flow of your speech. Double-check your dictionary for the correct pronunciation of any word about which you are unsure. Or you might wish to consult such pronunciation guides as Abraham and Betty Lass's *Dictionary of Pronunciation* (Quadrangle, 1976) and Samuel Noory's *Dictionary of Pronunciation*, second edition (A. S. Barnes, 1971). Always check the pronunciation of proper names carefully. You will quickly offend your audience if you mispronounce their hometown. It is Reading (red + ing) not (read + ing), Pennsylvania. The *s* is silent in Illinois (Illin + oi), and someone from Arkansas is an Ark + Kansan. If you are unsure about how to pronounce an individual's name, ask long before you deliver your speech. Is Patricia's last name Le + viche or Lev + iche? Is Bob's last name pronounced Cut + tone or Cut + toni?

Delivering a Speech

A poor delivery can ruin a good talk. When you speak before an audience, you will be judged on more than what you have to say; you will be evaluated on the type of image you project—how you look, move, and talk—your body language. Do you mumble into your notes, never looking out into the audience?

Do you clutch the lectern as if to keep it in place? Do you shift nervously from one foot to another? All these actions betray your nervousness and detract from your presentation.

Physical appearance and speaking skills correspond to format and neatness in your written work. The following suggestions on how to present a speech will help you to be a well-prepared speaker.

Before You Speak

Your name is called, and within a minute or two you will have to begin addressing the audience. You will be nervous. Accept the fact and even allow a few seconds for a "panic time." But then put the nervous energy to work for you. Chances are, your audience will have no idea how fearful you are. The audience cannot see the butterflies in your stomach. If you have to go to a lectern, walk slowly so you do not trip. Watch carefully for any steps you may have to make if the lectern is on a platform. Distribute any brochures or handouts before you reach the lecturn.

Once you are before the lectern, remove any pitchers or glasses of water if you are worried about spilling them. Always have a wristwatch with you. Before speaking, lay it on the desk or lectern so that you can occasionally glance down to see how much time you have left. This unobtrusive act is far preferable to reminding the audience that you are running out of time by noticeably raising your arm to look at your watch. If you are the first to speak into a microphone, you might want to test it by beginning "Can everybody hear me?"

Giving Your Talk

Begin your speech slowly. You have to give your listeners a chance to sit back in their chairs, adjust themselves, and establish a mental connection with your topic. Rushing into your speech may be startling, causing you to lose the audience from the start. To speak effectively, pay attention to the following four points.

1. Establish eye contact with your listeners to form a special relationship with them. If you do not look into their faces, they will rightfully think that you are not interested in them. Burying your head in notes signals your lack of interest in the audience or your fear. Some timid speakers think that if they look only at some fixed place or object in the back of the room, the audience will still regard this as eye contact. But this kind of cover-up does not work. Another tactic poor (or frightened) speakers use is to look at only one member of the audience or to focus, with frequent sidewise glances, on the individual next to them on the stage, perhaps the person who has introduced the speakers. Again, this approach slights the audience.

Establish a pattern of gazing at your notes and then looking up at various individuals in the audience. If the group you are addressing is small (ten to twenty people), look at each person in the course of your talk. When you speak to a large audience (forty or fifty or more individuals), visually divide this group into four or five sections, and look at each section a number of times as you speak.

2. Make the volume, tone, and rate of your delivery a favorable part of your image. Speak in a natural, conversational voice. But avoid such "verbal tics" as "you know" or "I mean" repeated several times each minute. Such nervous habits will make your audience nervous too and make your speech less effective. Be yourself, someone your community or business knows and expects to hear. Talk slowly enough for your audience to understand you, yet quickly enough so that you don't sound as if you were emphasizing each word. By going too quickly, you will lose your audience and sound as though you are in a hurry to finish.

Your voice should be easy and pleasant to hear. Talk loudly enough for everyone to hear, but be careful if you are using a microphone. Your voice will automatically be amplified, so if you are already speaking loudly, you will boom rather than send messages pleasantly to your audience. Watch the other extreme—speaking so softly that only people in the first two rows can hear you.

3. Watch your posture. If you stand motionless, looking as if rigor mortis has set in, your speech will be judged as cold and lifeless, no matter how lively your words are. Be natural, move, and let your body react to what you are saying. Smile, frown, nod your head, move your arms, point your fingers at an object, stand back a little from the lectern. This is not to say that you should be a moving target. Never sit on a desk or lean on a lectern in front of your audience. You may want your listeners to believe that you are trying to get closer to them, but they will be waiting to see if you fall off your newly discovered perch.

4. Let your gestures be a help, not a hindrance. Be natural and consistent. If your style of delivery is calm and deliberate, you will startle, not enlighten, an audience by suddenly pounding on the lectern for emphasis. Any quick, unexpected movement will detract from what you are saying. Let your material suggest appropriate movements. If you are itemizing four or five points, hold up the appropriate number of fingers to indicate which point you are discussing. Using your hands and arms to indicate direction, size, or relationships is also a way to use body language to comment on your material. But each gesture should be well timed and meaningful.

Avoid any gesture that will distract your audience; do not provide your own sideshow. The following nervous habits, engaged in frequently during a speech, can divert the audience's attention: scratching your head, rubbing your nose, pulling your ear, twirling your hair, pushing up your glasses, fumbling with your notes, tapping your foot, or moving your finger back and forth across the top of the lectern.

When You Have Finished Your Speech

Don't just smugly sit down, walk back to your place on the dais or in the audience, or, worse yet, march out of the room, your notes grasped firmly in your hand. Thank your listeners for their attention, and stay at the lectern for them to applaud, ask questions, or perhaps give the person who introduced you a chance to thank you while you are still in front of the group. If a question-and-answer session is to follow your speech, give your audience a time limit for questions. For example, you might say, "Ladies and gentlemen, I'll be happy to answer any questions you may have now before we break for lunch in ten minutes." Or you might say, "Ladies and gentlemen, I have set aside the next ten minutes for questions." By setting limits, you reduce the chances of engaging in a lengthy debate with particular members of the audience, and you also can politely leave after your specified time elapses.

☞ Speech Evaluation Form

A large portion of Chapter 17 has given you information on how to construct and deliver a formal speech. As a way of reviewing that advice, study Figure 17.3, an evaluation form similar to those used by instructors in speech classes. Note that the form gives equal emphasis to the speaker's performance and to the organization and content of the speech.

☞ Exercises

1. In two or three paragraphs explain some of the fears you have had about delivering a briefing or speech. Be specific about anything that caused you anxiety. Then, in another two or three paragraphs, describe how what you learned in this chapter (analyzing your audience ahead of time, preparing a speech outline, using visuals) can help calm your fears.

2. Prepare a three- to five-minute talk explaining how a piece of equipment that you use on your job works. If the equipment is small enough, bring it with you to class. If it is too large, prepare an appropriate visual that you can use in your talk.

3. You have just been asked to talk about the students at your school. Narrow this topic and submit a speech outline to your instructor, showing how you have limited the topic and supplied appropriate evidence. Use two or three appropriate visuals (tables, photographs, etc.). Follow the format of the outline in Figure 17.2.

4. Prepare a ten-minute talk on a controversial topic that you would present before some civic group—a local PTA, Lions' Club, local chapter of the

Fig. 17.3   A speech evaluation form.

Name of speaker _____   Date of speech _____

Title of speech _____   Length of speech _____

PART I—THE SPEAKER   (circle the appropriate number)

1. Appearance: 1   2   3   4   5
                         sloppy   well groomed

2. Eye contact: 1   2   3   4   5
                         poor   effective

3. Voice: 1   2   3   4   5
                      monotonous   varied

4. Posture: 1   2   3   4   5
                         poor   appropriate, natural

5. Gestures: 1   2   3   4   5
                      disturbing   appropriate

6. Self-confidence: 1   2   3   4   5
                        nervous   poised

PART II—THE SPEECH   (circle the appropriate number: 1 = poor; 5 = superior)

A. Overall performance

    1. Speaker's knowledge of the subject—carefully researched; factual errors; missing details:

       1   2   3   4   5

    2. Relevance of the topic for audience—suitable for this group:

       1   2   3   4   5

    3. The speaker's language—too technical; filled with cliches or slang expressions; or crisp and descriptive:

       1   2   3   4   5

    4. Use of visuals—too many or too few; well placed; appropriate size; handled with care; interfered with speech:

       1   2   3   4   5

Fig. 17.3 **(Continued.)**

B. Parts of the speech

    1. The introduction—brief and attention getting; informative about division and presentation of topic:

        1   2   3   4   5

    2. The body—carefully organized and easy to follow; appropriate amount of information; message developed and conveyed clearly:

        1   2   3   4   5

    3. The conclusion—brief, effective summary of the main points:

        1   2   3   4   5

PART III—YOUR FINAL REACTIONS (briefly complete the following)

1. Of all the speakers on the platform today, this speaker should be ranked: _____

_____

2. The speaker's main strengths were: _____

_____

_____

_____

3. The speaker needs to improve on: _____

_____

_____

_____

American Heart Association, a post of the Veterans of Foreign Wars, a church club. Submit a speech outline similar to that in Figure 17.2 to your instructor, together with a one-page statement of your specific call to action and its relevance for your audience.

5. Using the information contained in the research paper in Chapter 9 (pages 287–293) or the long report in Chapter 16 (pages 510–525), prepare a short speech—five to seven minutes—for your class.

6. Using the evaluation form contained in Figure 17.3, evaluate a speaker; this person can be someone in a speech class, a local politician, or perhaps someone delivering a report at work. Specify the time, place, and occasion of the speech.

Index

Fig. 14.5   (Continued.)

Methods of Research

I will rely heavily on literature dealing with electronic mail. Judging from the number of entries on this topic in the Business Periodicals Index from 1982 to 1984, the subject is popular and significant. For these years I located more than 85 entries. Of course, not all of them focus on comparisons and contrasts with conventional mail systems. From a preliminary check of some articles available in our library, I think the following may be most useful to me:

Barks, J. V. "Can You Count on Electronic Mail?" Distribution 83 (Mar. 1984): 72; 78–79.

"Bidirectional Electronic Mail System Helps Account for Firm's Increased Productivity." Communication News 21 (Feb. 1984): 54.

Canning, B. "Electronic Mail Systems Can Develop Costly Problems." Office Administration Automation 44 (Apr. 1983): 98–99.

Hannan, J. "The Uncertain Road to Improved Communications." Infosystems 30 (May 1983): 42–44.

Kay, Susan S. "Electronic Mail Growth Rests on Its Acceptance." The Office 97 (Aug. 1982): 48; 52; 60.

Kelly, R. L. "Electronic Mail: Will It Work on Your System?" The Office 99 (April 1984): 42; 47.

McQuillan, J. M. "The Market for Electronic Mail: Turbulence and Change." The Office 99 (Jan. 1984): 104.

Panko, R. R. "Electronic Mail: The Alternatives." Office Administration Automation 45 (June 1984): 37–40.

Stevenson, Patricia. Telecommunications: An Introduction. Pittsburgh: Data Processing Press, 1984.

I intend to interview two office managers in Springfield whose companies have recently switched to electronic mail. My choices right now are Alice Phillips at Dodge & Spenser Hydraulic Systems and Keith Wellbridge at General Dynamics. But because of their possible schedule conflicts, I may have to interview two other individuals.

Timetable

I hope to complete my library research by April 1 and my interviews by April 8. Then I will spend the following two weeks working on a rough draft, which I will submit by April 21, the date you specified. After receiving your comments on my rough draft, I will work on the final copy of my paper and turn it in by May 14, the last day of class. I will submit two progress reports—one when I finish my research and another when I decide on the final organization of my paper.

Request for Approval

I ask that you approve my topic and approach to it. I would appreciate any suggestions on how you think I might best proceed.

The Introduction

Keep your introduction short—a paragraph, maybe two. Begin with a statement pinpointing the subject and purpose of your work.

> I propose to do research on and write a report about the "hot
> knife" laser used in treating port wine stain and other
> birthmarks.

> I intend to investigate the relationship that exists in today's
> office between office design and the employee's need for
> "psychological space."

Then briefly indicate why the topic or the problem you propose to study is significant. In other words, be prepared to explain why you have chosen that topic and why research on it is relevant or worthwhile for a specific audience or course objective. Note how James Salinas in Figure 14.5 states how and why his paper will be useful to an office manager.

Supply your teacher-reader with a few background details about your topic, for example, the importance of using a laser as opposed to conventional ways of treating birthmarks or why psychological space plays a crucial role in employee productivity or morale. Prove that you have thought carefully about a suitable topic.

The Scope of the Problem or Topic to Be Investigated

The second section, which might be entitled "Problems to Be Investigated" or "Areas to Be Studied," shows how you propose to break the topic into meaningful units. Tell your reader what specific issues, points, or areas you hope to investigate. Doing this, you show how you will limit your topic to establish an appropriate scope for your work.

Some instructors ask students to formulate a list of questions their research paper or report intends to answer. The topics included in these questions, or a list of areas or problems to be covered, might later become major sections of your paper. Make sure that the issues or questions do not overlap and that each relates directly to and supports your restricted topic. Note how the student in Figure 14.5 hopes to divide his study of electronic mail into four distinct and useful areas.

Methods or Procedures

In the third section of your proposal inform your teacher how you expect to find the answers to the questions you raised in the previous section, or how you intend to locate information about your list of subtopics. It's not enough to write, "I will gather appropriate information and analyze it." Specify what data you hope to include, where they are located, and how you intend to retrieve them. Most students gather data from literature published about their topics.

(In fact, many research papers are exclusively based on library work.) This literature can include books, encyclopedias or other reference materials, articles in professional publications, newspapers, bulletins, manuals, or audiovisual materials. Inform your teacher what indexes, abstracts, or even computer searches you intend to use (review pages 239–249) as part of your literature search. To document your preliminary library work, provide your instructor with a list of a few appropriate titles on your topic following the style of documentation used for a Works Cited page (discussed on pages 273–280).

In addition to library materials, you might collect information from (a) experiments you will perform in a laboratory or from a field test, (b) interviews with experts, (c) replies to letters of inquiry, (d) questionnaires, or (e) a combination of any of these sources.

Timetable

Your proposal should indicate when and in what order you expect to complete the different phases of your project. Your teacher needs this information to keep track of your progress and to make sure that you will turn in an assignment on time. Specify tentative dates for completing your research, rough draft(s), and final copy.

Some instructors also ask students to turn in progress reports at regular intervals. If you are asked to do this, indicate when those progress reports will be submitted, as James Salinas did in Figure 14.5.

Request for Approval

End your proposal with a request for approval of your topic. You might also indicate that you would appreciate any suggestions from your teacher on how you might restrict, research, organize, or write about your topic.

☞ Preparing Proposals—A Final Reminder

This chapter has given you some basic information about writing proposals. Keep in mind that a proposal presents a plan to a decision maker for his or her approval. To win that approval, your proposal must be *realistic, carefully researched*, and *highly persuasive*. These essential characteristics apply to internal proposals in memo format written to your employer, more formal sales proposals sent to a potential customer, and research proposals submitted to your instructor.

☞ Exercises

1. In two or three paragraphs identify and document a problem (in services, safety, communication, traffic, scheduling) you see in your office or plant

or at your school. Make sure that you give readers—a school official (chairperson; dean) or employer (section or department head; manager)—specific evidence that a problem does exist and that it needs to be corrected.

2. Write a short internal proposal, modeled after Figure 14.2 on pages 442–443, based upon the problem you identified in exercise 1.

3. Write a short internal proposal, similar to Angie Quinn's in Figure 14.2 on pages 442–443, recommending for a company or a college a specific change in procedure, equipment, training, safety, personnel, or policy. Make sure that you provide an appropriate audience (a college administrator or department manager or section chief) with specific evidence about the existence of the problem and your solution of it. Here are some possible topics:

- providing more and safer parking
- extending the bookstore or company credit union hours
- purchasing new office or laboratory equipment
- hiring more faculty, student workers, or office help
- subscribing to new journals in your major at the school or company library
- reorganizing or redesigning the school yearbook or company annual report or sales catalogue
- changing the decor in a student or company lounge
- expanding the number of weekend or night classes in your major
- adding more offerings to a school or company cafeteria menu
- altering the programming on a campus radio station
- improving access for handicapped students or employees
- decreasing waiting time at registration or in a computer lab
- advising incoming freshmen more efficiently

4. Rewrite the following vague and unconvincing internal proposal to make it more effective. Supply any details you think necessary.

```
TO: Holly Gordon              SUBJECT: Changes at Acme Corp.

FROM: K. T. Smith             DATE: April 10, 1986

For some time now I have noticed a problem with the way the office handles
information. Things are often out of place and sometimes hard to find. I
know that it took me more than 15 minutes one day to find an important
report for Mr. Swanson. Others in the office too have been complaining
about this problem. I propose that we do something about the way
information is conveyed in our department.
```